Provence
and the Côte d'Azur

THE ROUGH GUIDE

Written and researched by

Kate Baillie, Danny Aeberhard
and Rachel Kaberry

THE ROUGH GUIDES

THE ROUGH GUIDES

TRAVEL GUIDES • PHRASEBOOKS • MUSIC AND REFERENCE GUIDES

We set out to do something different when the first Rough Guide was published in 1982. Mark Ellingham, just out of university, was travelling in Greece. He brought along the popular guides of the day, but found they were all lacking in some way. They were either strong on ruins and museums but went on for pages without mentioning a beach or taverna. Or they were so conscious of the need to save money that they lost sight of Greece's cultural and historical significance. Also, none of the books told him anything about Greece's contemporary life – its politics, its culture, its people, and how they lived.

So with no job in prospect, Mark decided to write his own guidebook, one which aimed to provide practical information that was second to none, detailing the best beaches and the hottest clubs and restaurants, while also giving hard-hitting accounts of every sight, both famous and obscure, and providing up-to-the-minute information on contemporary culture. It was a guide that encouraged independent travellers to find the best of Greece, and was a great success, getting shortlisted for the Thomas Cook travel guide award,

and encouraging Mark, along with three friends, to expand the series.

The Rough Guide list grew rapidly and the letters flooded in, indicating a much broader readership than had been anticipated, but one which uniformly appreciated the Rough Guide mix of practical detail and humour, irreverence and enthusiasm. Things haven't changed. The same four friends who began the series are still the caretakers of the Rough Guide mission today: to provide the most reliable, up-to-date and entertaining information to independent-minded travellers of all ages, on all budgets.

We now publish more than 100 titles and have offices in London and New York. The travel guides are written and researched by a dedicated team of more than 100 authors, based in Britain, Europe, the USA and Australia. We have also created a unique series of phrasebooks to accompany the travel series, along with an acclaimed series of music guides, and a best-selling pocket guide to the Internet and World Wide Web. We also publish comprehensive travel information on our Web site:

www.roughguides.com

HELP US UPDATE

We've gone to a lot of effort to ensure that the fourth edition of *The Rough Guide to Provence and the Côte d'Azur* is accurate and up-to-date. However, things change – places get "discovered", opening hours are notoriously fickle, restaurants and rooms raise prices or lower standards. If you feel we've got it wrong or left something out, we'd like to know, and if you can remember the address, the price, the time, the phone number, so much the better.

We'll credit all contributions, and send a copy of the next edition (or any other Rough Guide if you prefer) for the best letters. Please mark letters: "Rough Guide Provence and the Côte d'Azur Update" and send to:
Rough Guides, 62–70 Shorts Gardens, London WC2H 9AH, or Rough Guides, 345 Hudson St, 4th floor, New York NY 10014. Or send email to: mail@roughguides.co.uk
Online updates about this book can be found on Rough Guides' Web site at www.roughguides.com

Provence
and the Côte d'Azur

THE ROUGH GUIDE

There are more than two hundred Rough Guide titles
covering destinations from Alaska to Zimbabwe
and subjects from Acoustic Guitar to Travel Health

Forthcoming travel guides include
The Algarve • The Bahamas • Cambodia • Caribbean Islands
Costa Brava • New York Restaurants • Bolivia • Zanzibar

Forthcoming Reference guides include
Elvis • Online Travel • Internet Radio • Cult TV

Rough Guides on the Internet
www.roughguides.com

ROUGH GUIDE CREDITS

Text editor: Judith Bamber
Series editor: Mark Ellingham
Editorial: Martin Dunford, Jonathan Buckley, Jo Mead, Kate Berens, Amanda Tomlin, Ann-Marie Shaw, Paul Gray, Chris Schüler, Helena Smith, Judith Bamber, Kieran Falconer, Orla Duane, Olivia Eccleshall, Ruth Blackmore, Sophie Martin, Jennifer Dempsey, Geoff Howard, Claire Saunders, Anna Sutton, Gavin Thomas, Alexander Mark Rogers (UK); Andrew Rosenberg, Andrew Taber (US)
Production: Susanne Hillen, Andy Hilliard, Link Hall, Helen Ostick, James Morris, Julia Bovis, Michelle Draycott, Cathy McElhinney

Cartography: Melissa Flack, Maxine Burke, Nichola Goodliffe, Ed Wright
Picture research: Eleanor Hill, Louise Boulton
Online editors: Alan Spicer, Kate Hands (UK); Geronimo Madrid (US)
Finance: John Fisher, Neeta Mistry, Katy Miesiaczek
Marketing & Publicity: Richard Trillo, Simon Carloss, Niki Smith, David Wearn (UK); Jean-Marie Kelly, SoRelle Braun (US)
Administration: Tania Hummel, Charlotte Marriot

ACKNOWLEDGEMENTS

Many thanks to Henry Barkmann and Loretta Chilcoat for updates to Basics, Carole Mansur for proofreading, and Lucy Head for preparing the index. Also, this edition would have been much the poorer without all the readers who sent in their comments, advice, criticisms and recommendations: the full roll of honour (barring those whose signatures defeated us) appears on p.v

PUBLISHING INFORMATION

This fourth edition published May 1999 by
  Rough Guides Ltd, 62–70 Shorts Gardens,
  London, WC2H 9AH. Reprinted April 2000, May 2001 & April 2002.
Distributed by the Penguin Group:
Penguin Books Ltd, 80 Strand, London WC2R ORL.
Penguin Putnam Inc., 375 Hudson Street, New York 10014, USA.
Penguin Books Australia Ltd, 487 Maroondah Highway, PO Box 257, Ringwood, Victoria 3134, Australia.
Penguin Books Canada Ltd, 10 Alcorn Avenue, Toronto, Ontario, Canada M4V 1E4.
Penguin Books (NZ) Ltd, 182–190 Wairau Road, Auckland 10, New Zealand.
Typeset in Linotron Univers and Century Old Style to an original design by Andrew Oliver.
Printed in England by Clays Ltd, St Ives PLC.
Illustrations in Part One and Part Three by Edward Briant.

Illustrations on p.1 and p.397 by Henry Iles.
© Rough Guides 1999
No part of this book may be reproduced in any form without permission from the publisher except for the quotation of brief passages in reviews.
448pp – Includes index.
A catalogue record for this book is available from the British Library.
ISBN 1-85828-420-1

READERS' LETTERS

We would like to thank all the readers who have taken the time and trouble to write in with comments, suggestions and helpful advice: Olivia Blanchard, Brian D. Coe, R. W. Crawshaw, John G. Davies, Carmel and Peter Dwerryhouse, Julian Fenn, Mick Greenwood, Lilias Hair, Karen Harrison, Andrew Maude, Niko and Karo Prin, Paul Quenby, Maria and Tony Rosato, T. K. Whitaker, Jori White, Heather and Roger Wilby.

CONTENTS

Introduction xi

PART THREE CONTEXTS 398

LIST OF MAPS

MAP SYMBOLS

▬▬▬	Motorway	⋏	Viewpoint
═══	Road	⌇	Cliffs
───	Minor road	⅃	Waterfall
▭▭▭	Steps	⌃⌃	Mountain range
- - - -	Path	▲	Mountain peak
▬▬─▬	Railway	ⓘ	Tourist office
— —	Ferry route	⊠	Post office
▪━▪━	National border	Ⓜ	Métro station
▬ ▬ ▬	Chapter division boundary	▮▮▮▮	Wall
───	River	◼	Building
✕	Airport	➕	Church
△	Campsite	⁺⁺⁺	Cemetery
◉	Accommodation	▨	Park
⌂	Lodge	▨	National park
◆	Point of interest	⬚	Beach

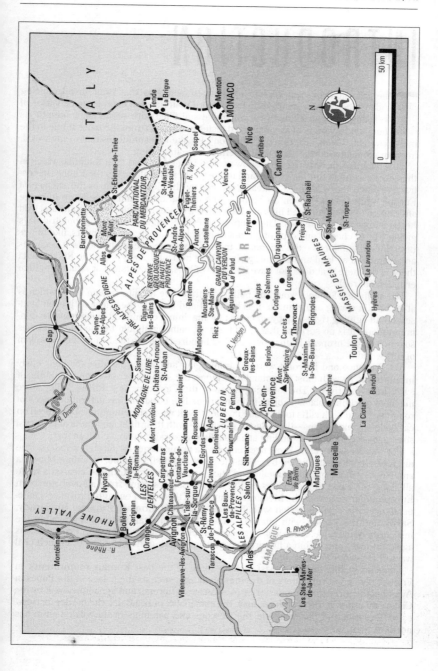

INTRODUCTION

The ancient Provençal version of Genesis maintains that prior to introducing Adam, the Creator realized he had several materials left over: large expanses of celestial blue, all kinds of rocks, arable soil filled with seeds for a sumptuous flora, and a variety of as yet unused tastes and smells from the most subtle to the most powerful. "Well," He thinks, "why don't I make a beautiful résumé of my world, my own special paradise?" And so **Provence** came into being.

This paradise encompasses the snow-peaked lower Alps and their foothills, which in the east descend to the sea's edge, and to the west extend almost to the Rhône. In central Provence the wild, high plateaux are cut by the deepest cleft in the surface of Europe – the Grand Canyon du Verdon. The coastal hinterland is made up of range after range of steep, forested hills in which the warm scent of pines, eucalyptus and wild herbs intoxicates the senses. The shore is an ever changing series of geometric bays giving way to chaotic outcrops of glimmering rock and deep, narrow inlets, like miniature Norwegian fjords – the *calanques*. In the Camargue, the shoreline itself becomes an abstraction as land and sea merge in infinite horizons. Away from the Rhône delta there is nowhere that does not have its frame of hills, or mountains, or strange sudden eruptions of rock.

But all these elements would be nothing without the Mediterranean light, which is at its best in spring and autumn. It is both soft and brightly theatrical, as if each landscape had lighting rigged up by an expert for maximum colour and definition with minimum glare. It is no surprise that of all the arts, painting should be the one that owes so much of its European history over the last hundred years to the beauty and escapism of this world.

Yet Provence and its coast were far from being an earthly paradise for their **early inhabitants**. As with most mountainous regions, the soil is poor and cultivation difficult away from the rivers. The low-lying areas of the Camargue and Rhône Valley were marshes or rubbly plains subject to inundation. The coast had no natural defences of rough seas and high cliffs to dissuade invaders. So it was that communities clustered on easily defensible hilltops – the **villages perchés** – with their tight labyrinths of medieval streets, passageways and winding stairs leading inexorably up to a château fort.

For hundreds of years, Provence remained a prime target for foreign invaders. The **ancient Greeks** established bases on the coast and on the Rhône, including Massalia and Nikea – modern-day Marseille and Nice – and, later, the **Romans** cleared a route all along the coast to their cities on the Rhône. Settlers came from all over northern Europe and from across the Mediterranean, and if this wasn't enough, Provence's independence was also contested with **France**, the **Holy Roman Empire**, **Burgundy**, **Savoy** and the **Popes**, with internal feuding between rival fiefdoms aggravating the insecurity of daily life. After just fifty years of reunification with France, Provence was again invaded, and within a hundred years was suffering the bloodiest of French civil wars, the *Guerres de Religion*.

Legacies of this turbulent past include some of the best **Roman monuments** in France, plus great reminders of the **medieval age**, such as the palace of the Popes in Avignon; the three great monasteries of Silvacane, Thoronet and Sénanque, built by the Cistercian order in the twelfth century; the ruined city of Les Baux; the border fortresses of Tarascon and Sisteron; and the frescoes and paintings in the village churches north of Nice.

By the 1800s, the character of coastal Provence was already beginning to change. Foreign aristocrats and royals, who had already turned Nice into Europe's most fashionable winter watering hole, began to spread their influence east and westwards. Tiny fishing villages such as Cannes, Villefranche, Le Lavandou and St-Tropez began to follow the course that Nice had taken, as avant-gardists in art and lifestyle and successions of celebrities gradually discovered how much simple and sophisticated pleasure this coast could provide. By the 1950s mass tourism on an upmarket scale began to take off in these parts, the Sixties brought the starlets and the hippies in their droves, and in the 1970s the French government began to realize the horror that their greatest tourist asset was threatening to become. Today, the **Côte d'Azur** is one of the most built-up, overpopulated and expensive stretches of coast anywhere in the world.

Yet between the urban conurbations and the tourist developments there still lies the remarkable scenery that drew artists here in their droves in the decades either side of 1900. Seduced by the light and relative ease of living, they bade farewell to the gloom of northern winters and set themselves up on the Côte d'Azur, making the region as much a part of the European art scene as Montmartre and Montparnasse. The great names of the Modern period who painted and sculpted on this coast include **Matisse**, **Renoir**, **Signac**, **Léger**, **Dufy**, **Miró**, **Bonnard**, **Chagall**, **Cocteau**, **Dérain**, **Modigliani**, **Soutine** and **Picasso**, all of whom came in summer and shocked the natives by swimming in the sea. Many of their works are permanently exhibited in superb **museums** from St-Tropez to Menton; reason in itself for a visit to the Côte today.

The one great artist native to Provence is **Cézanne**, who was born in Aix in 1839. Many of his canvases were inspired by the landscapes around his home town but very few remain in the region. Because of his relationship with his subjects, a pilgrimage to the **Mont Ste-Victoire** and other favourite scenes is still compelling. The man whose works on show outnumber any other artist is Hungarian-born **Vasarely**, who chose **Aix** and **Gordes** as centres for his studies into an all-embracing concept of art, science, architecture and social life. In and around **Arles** and **St-Rémy** you can follow the sad passage of **Van Gogh**, but again there are hardly any original paintings to be seen.

Food and wine are the other great inducements to bring you to Provence. This is the one French region where fruits and vegetables, fish and seafood, are on an equal footing with meat. The **foods** that grow in Provence – olives and garlic, asparagus and courgettes, white peaches, muscat grapes, melons and strawberries, *cêpe* and *morille* mushrooms, almonds and sweet chestnuts, basil and wild thyme, to name but a few – are an essential part of the hot, sensual environment. The **wines** too, from the dry, light rosés of the Côtes de Provence to the deep and delicate reds of the Côtes du Rhône and Châteauneuf-du-Pape, both complement and owe their brilliance to the intensity of sunshine. The great chefs, of which Provence has more than its fair share, buy everything they need, except for beef and butter, from local suppliers. Wandering through the food markets, you may well feel that, in this respect at least, the local version of Genesis is not far off the mark.

When to go

Beware **the coast** at the height of summer. The heat and humidity can be overpowering and the crowds, the exhaust fumes and the costs overwhelming. For **swimming** the best months are from June to mid-October, with May a little on the cool side, but only by summer standards. As for sunbathing, that can be done from **February through to October**. February is one of the best months for the Côte d'Azur – museums, hotels and restaurants are mostly open, the mimosa is in blossom, and the contrast with northern Europe's climate at its most delicious. The worst month is **November** when almost everything is shut and the weather turns cold and wet.

The same applies to **inland Provence**. Remember that the lower Alps are usually under **snow** from late **November to early April** (though recent winters have had snow in Nice followed by no falls on the lower ski-resorts). **October** can erupt in storms that quickly clear and in **May**, too, weather can be erratic. In **summer**, vegetation is at its most barren save for high up in the mountains. Wild bilberries and raspberries, purple gentians and leaves turning red to gold are the rewards of autumn walks. **Springtime** brings such a profusion of wild flowers you hardly dare to walk. In March a thousand almond orchards blossom.

The only drawback with the off-seasons is the **Mistral** wind. This is a violent, cold, northern airstream that is sucked down the valley of the Rhône whenever there's a depression over the sea. It can last for days, wrecking every fantasy of carefree Mediterranean climes. **Winter** is its worst season but it rarely blows east of Toulon, so be prepared to move that way.

AVERAGE DAYTIME TEMPERATURES

	Jan	Feb	Mar	Apr	May	Jun	Jul	Aug	Sep	Oct	Nov	Dec
Central Provence	12.2	11.9	14.2	18.5	20.8	26.6	28.1	28.4	25.2	22.1	16.8	14.1
Rhône Valley	7.4	6.7	10.8	15.8	17.3	25.6	27.6	27.6	23.5	16.5	10.4	7.8
Riviera/Côte d'Azur	12.2	11.9	14.2	18.5	20.8	26.6	28.1	28.4	25.2	22.2	16.8	14.1

AVERAGE SEA TEMPERATURES

	May	Jun	Jul	Aug	Sep	Oct
Montpellier to Toulon	15	19	19	20	20	17
Île du Levant to Menton	17	19	20	22	22	19

All temperatures are in **Centigrade**: to convert to **Fahrenheit** multiply by 9/5 and add 32. For a recorded **weather forecast** you can phone the Paris forecasting office at ☎45.55.91.09 (☎45.55.95.02 for specific inquiries).

PART ONE

THE

BASICS

GETTING THERE FROM BRITAIN AND IRELAND

Getting to the south of France by car isn't difficult, though it is a long trip, particularly if you're starting from Ireland. Using an overnight Channel ferry and the *autoroutes,* **you'd be hard pressed to make the trip in much less than 24 hours, and using the Channel Tunnel will reduce the time by only a couple of hours. If you are going to drive, far better to break your journey and arrive at your destination in daylight.**

These days, **train travel** is a surprisingly swift, though still not especially cheap, alternative to driving. Going by **bus** can be considerably cheaper, while **hitching** remains the most cost-effective means of getting there. However, if you shop around, **flying** may turn out to be the best bet, especially if your time is limited and you book early to take advantage of one of the cheap deals to Nice.

High season is June to August; **low season** from January to March and September to mid-December.

FLIGHTS

Flying to Provence or the Côte d'Azur is a real treat. For the last few hundred miles clear skies are virtually guaranteed, giving you breathtaking views of the Alps and the sea, and for most of the year there's the enveloping warmth when you get off the plane.

Nice and **Marseille** are the region's two airports, though Marseille is not a particularly cheap destination. You're more likely to find cheap deals to Nice, which has the most charter traffic; Marseille caters mainly for business travellers, with flights often booked up weeks in advance. Flight times are around two hours from London, and there are quick and frequent bus links to the city centres. Alternative points of arrival include **Montpellier** and **Lyon**, and, slightly further afield, **Perpignan** and **Toulouse**; there are direct flights from London to all these destinations, but only Montpellier is especially convenient for Provence, particularly if you're considering exploring Arles, Avignon or the Camargue.

Flying from Britain to any of these airports, you have a choice between summer **charter** flights and year-round **scheduled** flights. Charter flights have fixed dates for both outward and return travel and a maximum stay of one month. Scheduled flights are generally more expensive (though percentage reductions for children are bigger), but offer rather more flexibility.

Most travel agents can advise on both charter and scheduled flights, though it's a good idea to contact some of the **specialist operators** detailed on p.4. It's also worth checking the **classified adverts** in the Sunday newspapers and the Saturday travel sections of *The Guardian, The Independent* and *The Daily Telegraph,* and, for flights from London, the classifieds of *Time Out, The Evening Standard,* and the free travel magazine, *TNT,* found outside mainline train stations.

FLIGHTS

For scheduled flights, the best deals are with British Airways which has frequent direct flights to Nice from Heathrow (4 daily; from £140); and to Marseille (3 daily; from £160) and Montpellier (daily; from £160) from Gatwick. The cheaper tickets require you to stay at least a Saturday night, and are valid for a maximum of three months. Air France flies from Heathrow to Marseille, Nice and Montpellier with a change at Paris. They have one direct flight daily from Heathrow to Nice (from £140). British Midland also flies direct to Nice from Heathrow (2 daily; from £125). A Saturday night stay is required for the best deals. Scheduled flights from British regional airports tend to hook up with flights from Heathrow (or Paris in the case of Air France), the exception being the British Midlands service direct to Nice from East Midlands Airport.

AIRLINES

Aer Lingus Dublin ☎01/705 3333; Belfast ☎0645/737747.

Air France ☎0181/742 6600; *www.airfrance.fr*

British Airways ☎0345/222111; Dublin ☎0800/626747; Belfast ☎0345/222111; *www.british-airways.com*

British Midland ☎0345/554554; *www.iflybritishmidland.com*

Debonair ☎0541/500300; *www.debonair.co.uk*

Easy Jet ☎0870/6000 000; *www.easyjet.com*

SPECIALIST AGENCIES FOR INDEPENDENT TRAVEL

Budget Travel, 134 Lower Baggot St, Dublin 2 (☎01/661 1866).

Campus Travel, 52 Grosvenor Gardens, London SW1W 0AG (☎0171/730 3402); 39 Queen's Rd, Clifton, Bristol BS8 1QE (☎0117/929 2494); 112 George St, Glasgow G1 1RF (☎0141/553 1818); 105–106 St Aldates, Oxford OX1 1DD (☎01865/242067). Plus branches in YHA Adventure shops and university campuses nationwide.

Council Travel, 28a Poland St, London W1V 3DB (☎0171/287 3337). Plus several offices around France.

French Holiday Centre, 3 Malboro St, Cork (☎021/272 527).

STA Travel, 86 Old Brompton Rd, London SW7 3LH & 117 Euston Rd, London NW1 2SX (Europe ☎0171/361 6161; worldwide ☎0171/361 6262); 75 Deansgate, Manchester M3 2BW (☎061/834 0668); 88 Vicar Lane, Leeds LS1 7JH (☎0113/244 9212); 25 Queen's Rd, Bristol BS8 1QE (☎0117/929 4399); 38 Sidney St, Cambridge CB2 3HX (☎01223/366966); 36 George St, Oxford OX1 2OJ (☎01865/792800). Plus branches on high streets and campuses nationwide.

USIT, 19/21 Aston Quay, O'Connell Bridge, Dublin 2 (☎01/679 6833); 10–11 Market Parade, Patrick St, Cork (☎021/270900); Fountain Centre, College St, Belfast BT1 6ET (☎01232/324073).

These flights are often significantly more expensive than flying out of London, and it often pays to get to London yourself and fly on to France from there.

Charter flights to Nice are fast becoming the way most holiday-makers are getting to the south of France. Easy Jet has flights from Luton to Nice (4 daily in summer and 3 daily in winter; from £98), and booking can be done over the Internet. Debonair also flies from Luton (daily in summer), with special offers that have gone as low as £39 return; during winter they cooperate with AB Air, which has daily flights out of Gatwick (from £119). Book early to claim the cheapest deals, especially in July and August; otherwise try the Charter Flight Centre (☎0171/931 0504) or the holiday pages of Teletext, and you might strike it lucky and get a cheap last-minute deal. **Regional charters** do exist, such as Easy Jet's daily flight from Liverpool (from £98) but availability can be a problem. This market is likely to grow, however, so scan the papers and ask the charter companies.

Full-time **students** and those **under 26** can take advantage of discounted flights from specialist agents such as Campus Travel and STA see box above).

One offer which is worth considering if you are flying from outside London is **Air France's deal with SNCF**, the French state rail network, whereby you fly direct to Lille in the north of France, then take a train down to Provence. **Prices** are the same whichever airport you fly from; getting to Marseille costs around £200, with prices to Nice and St-Raphaël starting a little higher. For details contact Air France or Rail Europe (see p.6). There are special rates for children.

It's also worth considering a **package deal**, which can offer exceptionally cheap travel even if you go it alone on the actual holiday. See the box on p.5 for contacts.

FLIGHTS FROM IRELAND

There are no **direct flights** to Nice or Marseille from either Dublin or Belfast; most services go via London, with Air France routing via Paris. Aer Lingus combines with partner airlines to offer flights from Dublin through Paris/Brussels to Marseille for IR£245, or to Nice for IR£256, not including airport taxes of IR£12–14. USIT can offer student flights to Nice from IR£230 in the summer and as low as IR£110 in winter. Again, though, the best deal is likely to be Air France's combined **air-and-rail ticket** (see above).

TOUR AND ACCOMMODATION OPERATORS IN THE UK

Any travel agent will be able to provide details of package deals available in France, though some of the following are only available direct to the public. As many include ferry crossings – or, occasionally, flights – in the deal, they can be very good value especially for a family or large group. In addition to this selection, more complete lists are available from the **French Government Tourist Office** in the **French Travel Centre**, 178 Piccadilly, London W1V 0AL (Mon–Fri 10am–6pm, Sat 10am–5pm; information line ☎0891/244123 Mon–Fri 8.30am–8pm, Sat 9am–5pm, calls charged at premium rate). The same number is also good for Brittany Ferries, which now runs the old **Gîtes de France**, one of the main sources of cottage rental.

The Alternative Travel Group
(☎01865/315678, fax 315697). "Walking through History" tours in Provence, with special-interest trips on the area's artistic legacy. Also fly-drive and cycling tours.

Belle France (☎01797/223777, fax 223666). Walking and cycling tours in Haute Provence and the Camargue; emphasis on food and family hotels.

Canvas Holidays (☎01383/621000). Great camping packages and lots of sites.

CEI French Centre (☎0171/734 7224, fax 734 1357). French-language courses run year-round in Aix-en-Provence, Avignon and Nice. Tuition prices from £251 for a two-week course of general French in Nice, to £560 for a two-week intensive course in Aix; family-stay and B&B accommodation offered. Also all-inclusive junior camps in St-Raphaël (residential; £627 for 2 weeks) and Montpellier (family-stay; £572 for 2 weeks).

Club Cantabrica Holidays (☎01727/866177, fax 843766). Specializing in the upper end of the mobile home, caravan and campsite market, with sites in Antibes and Port Grimaud. Also, air, bus or self-drive packages.

Dominique's Villas (☎0171/738 8772, fax 498 6014). Upmarket agency with a diverse and tempting range of properties, mostly for large groups.

Drive France/The Individual Travellers' Company (☎0990 143681). Gîtes, cottages and farmhouses for rent along the Rhône Valley and in the Vaucluse.

Eurocamp (☎01565/626262, fax 654930). Family-holiday specialist offering camping, self-drive and mobile-home packages with a selection of sites along the coast.

France Afloat (☎ & fax 0171/704 0700). Canal holidays throughout France, including the delta land of the Camargue. Cruisers from £446 per week in April to £1100 in July & Aug.

Inntravel (☎01653/628811, fax 628741). Upmarket walking, cycling and horseback riding holidays with expert local guides in the Alpes Maritimes and around Manosque.

Keycamps (☎0181/395 4000). Camping and mobile-home holidays. A two-week tent holiday on the Côte costs £390 for two adults and two children in high season.

La France des Villages/La France des Activités (☎01449/737664). Off-the-beaten-track specialists with villas, farms and attractive chambres d'hôtes. Plus horse-riding and boating holidays.

Lagrange (☎0171/371 6111, fax 371 2990). From camping to self-catering apartments and houses at coastal resorts and at the foot of Mont Ventoux. Specializes in the Côte d'Azur. From £160 a week for a studio in low season.

Martin Randall Travel (☎0181/742 3355, fax 742 7766). Changing cultural tours led by specialists: "Art on the Côte d'Azur" (one week £945); "A Week in the South" (8 days £1150); plus the Aix Music Festival and other special-interest subjects. All prices include flights, half board at three- to five-star hotels, and admission charges.

Martin Sturge (☎01225/310623, fax 447055) A range of upmarket, historic properties in the Var, Vaucluse and Avignon for self-catering trips. High-season prices per week from £531 (sleeping 2) to £1925 (sleeping 10–11).

NSS Riviera Holidays (☎01482/342240, fax 448905). Budget chalets, mobile homes and cottages in and around Fréjus. Mainly self-drive.

Susie Madron's Cycling for Softies (☎0161/248 8282, fax 248 5140). Easy-going cycle holidays operator; starting point in St-Rémy-de-Provence. Seven-day tours with flight, half-board accommodation, bike and back-up from around £860 per person.

Vacances en Campagne (☎08700/780185, fax 780191). Self-catering specialist with a selection of apartments, cottages and large manor houses in the Rhône Valley and the Côte d'Azur. High standards; not cheap, but good value.

GETTING THERE BY TRAIN

You can buy train tickets from large travel agents to get you from any station in Britain to any station in Provence. Most routes will involve going through London and almost certainly Paris – where you may have to change from the Gare du Nord to the Gare de Lyon. For the London–Paris leg you can either take the **Eurostar** service through the Channel Tunnel, a journey of three hours, or catch a train to one of the southern ferry ports and then cross the Channel by **ferry** or **hovercraft**. From Paris there's the choice of an ordinary train or the world's fastest, the **TGV**; the fast track goes as far as Valence and is set to link up with Marseille by early 2001, with TGVs continuing at slower speeds along the coast to Nice.

Eurostar runs services from London Waterloo to Paris Gare du Nord (up to 27 daily; journey time 3hr) and Lille (6 daily; journey time 2hr). A return ticket to Lille costs from around £69 for a second-class promotional advance fare, with fares for Paris starting at around £89. There are also now direct Eurostar services from Scotland, the Midlands and the North of England. Bookings can be made through high-street travel agents, by calling Eurostar direct or through Rail Europe in London (see box below).

Combining a Eurostar deal with an onward journey on the **TGV** is a very attractive option and is only marginally more expensive than using ordinary trains. The cost of the compulsory supplement varies: from Paris to Aix-en-Provence it's an extra 38–95F. By booking seven days in advance you can get to Marseille or Nice with Eurostar and the TGV for £129 in approximately nine hours.

Special fare options include thirty percent discounted BIJ tickets, available for anyone under

---

RAIL AND BUS

Eurolines, National Express, 164 Buckingham Palace Rd, London SW1W 9JP (☎0990/808080 or 143219; *www.eurolines.co.uk*).

Eurostar, Waterloo Station, London SE1 8SE (☎0990/186186 or 0345/303030; *www.eurostar.com*).

Eurotunnel, PO Box 300, Folkestone, Kent CT19 4QW (☎0990/353535).

Rail Europe, 179 Piccadilly, London W1V 0BA (☎0990/848848).

Wasteels, Victoria Station (platform 2), London SW1V 1JZ (☎0171/834 7066).

---

26 from Eurotrain, Wasteels, or any student travel office. The over 60s who hold a British Rail Senior Card can extend the cover with a Rail Europe Senior Card – also from Wasteels or major travel agents – which covers most of Western Europe and gives thirty to fifty percent reductions on train tickets. There are also discounts available with the various rail passes, detailed below.

RAIL PASSES

If you plan to use the rail network a great deal in Provence, or to visit other parts of France, it's worth considering a Eurodomino or InterRail pass. The **Eurodomino** pass, available from Rail Europe (see box below) and some major travel agents, offers unlimited travel (including, with normal supplements, the TGV) throughout France for any three, five, or ten days during a period of one month. There are substantial reductions for those under 26, plus reductions on Eurostar and Hoverspeed Channel crossings. A three-day pass costs £105 (adult) or £85 (under 26); a five-day pass, £145/£115; and a ten-day pass, £220/£185.

If your trip is part of a wider tour of Europe, look to buying a continent-wide pass like the **InterRail** (for those based in Britain and Ireland) or the **Eurail** (for North Americans and Antipodeans; see p.11 and p.12). Neither pass is valid on trains in Great Britain and Northern Ireland, but will help you get across to France more cheaply, with substantial discounts on Eurostar and the Channel ferries. Once you get to France, you will still have to pay seat reservation supplements if you wish to use the TGV.

The **InterRail** pass is valid across eight geographical zones. For the **under 26s** any one zone costs £159 for fifteen days, any two zones £209 for one month, and an all-zones pass costs £259 for one month. The "**26 plus pass**" costs £229 for one zone and is valid for 22 days; multiple-zone tickets are valid for one month and cost from £279 for two zones to £349 for all zones.

GETTING THERE BY BUS

Travelling to Provence by bus costs around fifteen to twenty percent less than rail fares. The journey, at around 23 hours, is tolerably comfortable, broken up by the ferry crossing, a couple of meal stops, and additional short halts for coffee.

The route is a direct run from London to Dover, ferry across to Calais, then down to Nice via

1999 FERRY DETAILS

ROUTES AND PRICES

	Operator	Crossing time	Frequency	One-way fares Small car, 2 adults	Foot passenger
BRITTANY					
Portsmouth–St-Malo	Brittany Ferries	8hr 45min –11hr 30min	1–2 daily	£162–314	£36–64
Plymouth–Roscoff	Brittany Ferries	6hr–8hr 30min	1–3 daily; late Nov to early March 2–3 weekly	£148–286	£34–58
NORMANDY					
Portsmouth–Cherbourg	P&O European Ferries	5–7hr	1–4 daily	£53–110	£19–32
Poole–Cherbourg	Brittany Ferries	4hr 15min– 6hr 45min	1–2 daily	£140–270	£32–56
Portsmouth–Caen	Brittany Ferries	6–8hr	2–3 daily	£140–270	£32–56
Portsmouth–Le Havre	P&O European Ferries	6–7hr	3 daily	£70–150	£18–35
Newhaven–Dieppe	P&O Stena Line	2hr 15min	2 daily	£110–259	£48
PAS-DE-CALAIS					
Folkestone–Boulogne (Catamaran)	Hoverspeed	4hr	4 daily	£140–188	£50
Dover–Calais Dover–Calais	P&O Stena Line	50min	30 daily	£115–210	£48
Dover–Calais (Hovercraft)	Sea France	1hr 15min	10–15 daily	£147–200	£22
Dover–Calais (Catamaran)	Hoverspeed	1hr 30min	6–12 daily	£154–210	£50
Ramsgate–Dunkerque	Hoverspeed	35min	5 daily	£154–210	£50
FROM IRELAND					
Cork–Roscoff	Brittany Ferries	13hr– 15hr 30min	April to early Oct 1 weekly	IR£190–520	IR£60–120
Rosslare–Roscoff	Irish Ferries	15–16hr	mid-April to early Oct, 1 weekly	IR£238–598	IR£80–160
Rosslare–Cherbourg	Irish Ferries	17–19hr	3 weekly	IR£238–598	IR£80–160

FERRY OPERATORS IN ENGLAND AND IRELAND

Brittany Ferries
Portsmouth ☎0990/360360
Plymouth ☎0990/360360
Poole ☎0990/360360
Cork ☎0121/277801
Hoverspeed
Dover ☎0990/240241

Irish Ferries
Dublin 2 ☎016610511Cork
☎021/504333
Rosslare ☎053/33158
Cork ☎021/551995
P&O European Ferries
Portsmouth ☎0990/980555

P&O Stena Line
Central reservations
☎0990/980980
Information ☎0990/980111

Sea France
Kent ☎0990/711711

Sisteron, Grasse, Cannes, Juan-les-Pins and Antibes; and to St-Raphaël via Valence, Aix-en-Provence, Marseille, Toulon, Hyères and Fréjus.

All services are operated by **Eurolines** (see p.6) and leave London's Victoria Coach Station three times a week, with an extra express service in summer. Tickets are available from any National Express bus station in Britain, and add-on fares are sold from any British destination. Sample return fares from London are £109 to Nice and £99 to Marseille. Open-dated return tickets lasting up to six months give good long-stay flexibility, but the return journey must be booked four days in advance.

BY CAR

Eurotunnel runs frequent daily services through the Channel Tunnel, with fares that are becoming ever more competitive, making it the most convenient way to get your car to France. There are still regular **ferry** crossings from British and Irish ports, but journey times are considerably longer and companies are relying more and more on deals for day-trippers and duty-free shopping to entice customers on board.

The entrance to the **Channel Tunnel** is off the M20 at Junction 11A, just outside Folkestone. Because of the frequency of the service (24hr; every 30min 6am–midnight, then every 75min), you don't have to buy a ticket in advance. The journey to Sangatte, near Calais, takes only 35 minutes, which is just as well as there is nowhere for passengers to go during the trip – you're expected to sit inside your car. Fares are calculated per car, regardless of the number of passengers, and start at around £145 for a five-day return ticket, or £133 one way, in high season. Tickets are available through Eurotunnel's Customer Service Centre (see p.6) or from your local travel agent.

If you would prefer to continue your journey by rail once you've reached France, you can take advantage of **SNCF's Motorail** (contact Rail Europe on ☎0990/848848), putting your car on the train in Calais or Paris. Prices, however, are prohibitive; for example, the return fare in summer from Calais to Nice costs £502 for car and driver, plus £102 for an additional adult and £51 for children aged between four and eleven. Since the fourteen-hour trip is overnight, you're also looking at £24 per person, no child reductions, for an obligatory couchette – breakfast is included.

Though you can meander through Normandy, the Loire and the Massif Central to get to Provence, the most direct **driving routes** go south from Paris. If you're crossing from Britain by **ferry**, the best ports to head for are Calais, Boulogne and Dunkerque as they offer the most direct connections to Paris and the routes south into Provence. Dieppe is an hour closer to Paris, but crossings are considerably more expensive. Note that the minimum age for driving in France is 18. For more about driving in France, see p.24. From Ireland, the best port to head for is Le Havre, which has excellent road links with Paris. Cherbourg is a long way west with more than 100km before you hit the autoroute to the capital.

GETTING THERE FROM NORTH AMERICA

Getting to France from the USA or Canada is straightforward; there are direct flights from over thirty major US cities to Paris (the only transatlantic gateway in France), with **connections from all over the continent. Nearly a dozen different scheduled airlines operate flights, making Paris one of the cheapest destinations in Europe.**

It's worth knowing that several outlets in the USA and Canada can do **rail** bookings and special rail passes (see p.11). Note that Eurail passes (see p.11) are also useful if France is part of a wider European trip.

FLIGHTS

The cheapest fare on any scheduled flight is usually a non-refundable **APEX**, which normally entails booking at least 21 days in advance, travelling midweek, and staying for at least seven days (maximum stay three months). You also get penalized if you change your schedule.

AIRLINES AND TOUR OPERATORS IN THE USA AND CANADA

AIRLINES

Air Canada Canada ☎1-888/247-2262; US ☎1-800/776-3000.

Air France US ☎1-800/237-2747; Canada ☎1-800/667-2747.

American Airlines ☎817/267-1151 or 1-800/433-7300.

British Airways US ☎1-800/247-9297; Canada ☎1-800/243-6822.

Canadian Airlines Canada ☎1-800/665-1177; US ☎1-800/426-7000.

Continental Airlines ☎1-800/231-0856.

Delta Airlines US ☎1-800/241-4141; Canada ☎1-800/221-1212.

Icelandair ☎1-800/223-5500.

Northwest/KLM US ☎1-800/374-7747; Canada ☎1-800/581-6400.

Sabena ☎1-800/955-2000.

Swissair US ☎1-800/221-4750; Canada ☎1-800/267-9477.

Tower Air ☎1-800/221-2500.

TWA ☎1-800/221-7702.

United Airlines ☎1-800/538-2929.

US Air ☎1-800/622-1015.

Virgin Atlantic Airways ☎1-800/862-8621.

NORTH AMERICAN TOUR OPERATORS

Abercrombie & Kent (☎1-800/323-7308). Deluxe trekking, biking, canal, rail and skiing packages.

American Express (☎1-800/241-1700). Packages and city breaks.

AESU Travel (☎1-800/638-7640). Packages to the Riviera for the under 35s.

Backroads (☎1-800/462-2848). Trendy bike tours. Their "Taste of Provence" cycling tour costs from $2495 for five nights.

Butterfield & Robinson (☎1-800/678-1147). Trekking tours including the "Provence Classic" eight-day walking tour ($3975); "Provence Getaway" five-day biking trip ($2475); and the "Provence Classic" eight-day biking trip ($3950).

Contiki Tours (☎1-800/CONTIKI). Vacations for those aged between 18 and 35.

Cosmos Tourama/Globus (☎1-800/338-7092). Group tours and city breaks; Cosmos has the budget trips.

Daily-Thorp Travel (☎212/307-1555). Specialist tours of the music festivals.

Euro-Bike Tours (☎1-800/321-6060). Luxury trekking tours including the "Taste of Provence" seven-day biking tour ($2095); "Walking in Provence" eight-day walking tour ($2395); and the "Provence Complet" eleven-day biking tour ($2845).

Europe Train Tours (☎1-800/551-2085). Their escorted "Provence and French Riviera" bus tour costs from $1492.

The French Experience (☎1-800/28-FRANCE). Self-drive tours, apartment and cottage rental.

International Study Tours (☎1-800/833-2111). Introductory sightseeing.

Mountain Travel-Sobek (☎1-800/227-2384). Trekking specialists with a "Pleasures of Provence" nine-day summer tour starting at $2390.

Wilderness Travel (☎1-800/368-2794). Trekking packages include the "Country Provence" eight-day walking tour in April, June and September ($2345); and "Rustic Provence" eleven-day walking/hiking tour in May and September ($2795).

Many airlines offer youth or student fares to those **under 26**; a passport or driving licence is sufficient proof of age, though these tickets are subject to availability and can have eccentric booking conditions. It's worth remembering that most cheap return fares involve spending at least one Saturday night away and that many will give only a percentage refund if you need to cancel or alter your journey, so make sure you check the restrictions carefully before buying a ticket. Apart from special offers, this is likely to be the best deal you'll get direct from an airline ticket counter.

The best guarantee of a cheap flight, however, is to contact a **travel agent** specializing in **discounted fares** (see p.10) or the travel sections of the *New York Times*, *Washington Post*, and *Los Angeles Times*. Restrictions on such tickets are often not all that stringent; you need not assume that youth or student fares are the

DISCOUNT FLIGHT AGENTS AND CONSOLIDATORS IN THE USA AND CANADA

Air Brokers International (☎1-800/883-3273 or 415/397-1383). Consolidator and specialist in RTW tickets.

Air Courier Association (☎303/278-8810). Courier flight broker.

Airhitch (☎212/864-2000). Standby-seat broker. For a set price, they guarantee to get you on a flight as close to your preferred destination as possible, within a week.

Cheap Tickets (☎1-800/377-1000). Great discounted tickets for international destinations.

Council Travel (☎1-800/2-COUNCIL; in New York ☎212/822-2700). Student and youth travel organization offering discounted air fares, rail passes and travel gear. For those over 26, it acts like a regular travel agency.

Educational Travel Center (☎1-800/747-5551 or 608/256-5551). Student, youth and consolidator fares.

Interworld Travel (☎305/443-4929). Consolidator.

Nouvelles Frontières/New Frontiers (US ☎1-800/366-638; Canada ☎514/526-8444). French discount travel firm.

Now Voyager (☎212/431-1616). Courier flight broker and consolidator.

STA Travel (☎1-800/777-0112). Worldwide discount travel firm specializing in student/youth fares; also student IDs, travel insurance, car rental, rail passes, etc.

TFI Tours International (☎1-800/745-8000 or 212/736-1140). Consolidator.

Travel CUTS (☎416/979-2406). Organization specializing in student fares, IDs and other travel services.

Travelers Advantage (☎1-800/548-1116). Full-service travel club.

Travac (☎1-800/872-8800, fax 1-888/872-8327). Consolidator and charter broker.

Travel Avenue (☎1-800/333-3335). Full-service travel agent that offers discounts in the form of rebates.

UniTravel (☎1-800/325-2222 or 314/569-2501). Consolidator.

Worldtek Travel (☎1-800/243-1723 or 203/772-0470). Discount travel agency.

Worldwide Discount Travel Club (☎305/534-2082). Discount travel club dealing in packages and cruises only.

best bargain, or worry if you're not eligible for them. The independent travel specialists STA Travel and Council Travel are two of the most reliable, but not surprisingly the French group Nouvelles Frontières has some good offers. These firms, together with several of the other larger agents, act as **consolidators** for particular airlines, whereby they maintain contracts to sell seats on specific terms, invariably below the airlines' own fares, though sometimes less conveniently.

Charter flights are sold by most agents, and can be even cheaper than scheduled services. However, they tend to hedge you in with restricted dates and major financial penalties if you cancel.

High season is June to mid-September, **Low season** is January to March and mid-September to mid-December.

FLIGHTS FROM THE US

Airlines are always running special deals, particularly from January to March when prices tend to be cut considerably. As an example, a low-season special fare from New York to Paris is around $330 midweek; the standard low-season price is $560 midweek.

The most comprehensive range of flights from the US is offered by **Air France**, the French national carrier, which flies non-stop to Paris Charles de Gaulle airport from Atlanta, Boston, Chicago, Cincinnati, Houston, Los Angeles, Miami, New York, San Francisco and Washington DC – in most instances daily.

The major American competitors are not much cheaper than Air France, and offer fewer non-stop routes. **American** flies direct into Paris Orly from Boston, Chicago, Dallas Fort Worth, Miami and New York. The rest of the American airlines fly into Charles de Gaulle airport: **TWA** has direct flights from St. Louis and New York; **Continental** flies direct from its Houston and Newark hubs; **Delta** flies from Atlanta, Cincinnati and New York; **Northwest** flies from Detroit; and **United** flies direct from Chicago, Washington DC and San Francisco. Each airline offers connecting flights from other major cities via these hubs, with the exception of Northwest which routes its connecting flights via Amsterdam.

It is possible to book a connecting flight from the US **directly into Provence**: Air France flies out of New York to Paris, with a continuing service to Marseille (using Air Inter airline), for $660 in low season and $910 in high season. Other fares with major US carriers are comparable: American flights connect in Paris from New York and Los Angeles; Continental flights connect in Paris from Newark; Delta flights connect in Paris from New York; and Northwest flights connect in Amsterdam from New York and San Francisco. Montpellier is also served by various European airlines out of Paris and London.

FLIGHTS FROM CANADA

The strong links between France and Québec's Francophone community ensure regular air services from Canada to Paris. The main route is Vancouver–Toronto–Montréal–Paris Charles de Gaulle. Most departures are from Toronto, with **Air France** flying almost daily to Charles de Gaulle, either non-stop or via Montréal for about CN$600 in low season and CN$960 in high season. Again, you can fly direct to Marseille, with a stop in Paris for CN$855 in low season and CN$1100 in high season. The fares from Montréal are comparable. **Air Canada** and **Canadian Airlines** fly direct to Paris from Toronto and Montréal, again almost daily; Canadian Airlines also flies in from Vancouver twice weekly.

TRAIN PASSES

Although there are a number of train passes available for travel within France, all of which are

good value (see p.23), a **Eurail Pass** makes most sense if you're planning to travel through other European countries as well. You can purchase a Eurail pass for travel on consecutive days ($538 for 15 days, $698 for 21 days; $864 for 1 month, $1124 for 2 months, $1512 for 3 months), or for those travelling at a more leisurely pace, there's the **Flexipass**, which allows a given number of days travel in a two-month period ($634 for 10 days', $836 for 15 days). An even better option if you're under 26 is the **Eurail Youth Fare**, which gives you unlimited second-class travel (from $376 for 15 days consecutive; and $448 for a 10-day Flexipass). For the over 26s there's the **Eurail Saver Pass**, which offers a further 15 percent reduction on the standard Eurail fares, but is available only if two or more people travel together between October and March, or three or more people from April to September. Finally, there's the scaled-down version of the Flexipass, the **Europass**, which allows first-class train travel on any number of days from five to fifteen over a two-month period in France, Germany, Italy, Spain and Switzerland, with options to combine these countries with up to four additional zones (Austria and Hungary; Belgium, Luxembourg and the Netherlands; Greece; or Portugal). Prices range from $326 for the basic five-country, five-day pass; to $864 for a fifteen-day, all-zones pass. The **Europass youth pass**, which offers second-class travel, starts at $216 for a basic five-day, five-country pass; ranging to $628 for a fifteen-day, all-zones pass. You can purchase Eurail passes from one of the agents listed below.

USEFUL RAIL ADDRESSES IN NORTH AMERICA

The **Eurail Pass** is the main discount rail deal available to travellers from North America. For details contact STA Travel (see box on p.10) or one of the addresses below.

BritRail Travel International, 1500 Broadway, New York, NY 10036 (☎1-800/677-8585). UK passes, rail-drive and multi-country passes plus Channel Tunnel tickets. Also sells ferry tickets across the Channel.

Canadian Reservations Centre, 2987 Dundas East, Suite 105, Mississauga, ON L4X 1M2 (☎1-800/361-7245). Specializes in Eurail and other passes.

CIE Tours International, 108 Ridgedale Ave, Morristown, NJ 07962 (☎1-800/243-7687). Major agent for booking rail travel in Europe.

Forsyth Travel Library, 226 Westchester Ave, White Plains, NY 10604 (☎1-800/367-7984). Eurail passes.

Rail Europe, 226 Westchester Ave, White Plains, NY 10604 (☎1-800/438-7245). Official Eurail pass agent in North America; also sells the widest range of European regional and individual country passes.

GETTING THERE FROM AUSTRALIA AND NEW ZEALAND

There are no direct flights to Provence from Australia or New Zealand. All routes require either a transfer or stopover in the carrier's hub cities. Alternatively, you could pick up a cheap flight to London and then travel on to Provence by land or air. For cheap flights see "Getting There from Britain and Ireland" on p.3.

High season is from mid-May to March, June to August and December to mid-January; **low season** is from mid-January to February and October to early November.

FLIGHTS FROM AUSTRALIA

Some of the cheapest deals from Australia are with **Aeroflot** (in conjunction with Qantas and British Airways) which flies from Sydney to Marseille via Moscow once a week from A$1462 low season. **Swissair** offers good-value deals to Nice (around A$1600 low season); **KLM** flies from Sydney to Nice and Marseille via Amsterdam from A$1600 low season; while **Air France/Qantas** has weekly flights from Sydney, Melbourne, Adelaide and Brisbane via Singapore and Paris for A$1880.

Some airlines offer **fly-drive packages** and **free onward flights** to Provence; prices are about the same as the standard published fare. **Alitalia** flies from all gateway cities to Rome (3 weekly); **Singapore** flies to Paris or Rome (several weekly); **Thai** airlines flies to Rome or Paris (3 weekly) from all gateways but Adelaide; and **JAL** flies to Paris or Rome from Cairns, Brisbane and Sydney. Contact a travel agent for the latest information on special deals as they change throughout the year.

FROM NEW ZEALAND

Flights to Provence from New Zealand are limited, with usual published fares at around NZ$2400 in low season and NZ$3200 in high season. At the cheap end is **Garuda** flying to Nice twice weekly from Auckland via a stopover in Jakarta or Bali and a transfer in either Amsterdam or Paris. More expensive, but offering **fly-drive** and **free onward travel** to Provence, are: **British Airways** to London several times weekly from Auckland; **Alitalia** to Rome several weekly from Auckland; **Cathay** to Paris once weekly or Rome twice weekly from Auckland; and **Thai** to Paris or Rome three times weekly.

TRAIN PASSES

There are a number of **train passes** available for travel within France (see p.23), which can be obtained through most travel agents or from CIT, 123 Clarence St, Sydney ☎02/9267 1255), which also has branches nationwide. There is no New Zealand office, so all enquiries should go through the Australian offices.

However, the best value, if you are planning to travel through other European countries as well, is the **Eurail pass** (see p.11 for details), available through Thomas Cook and most travel agents. Eurail passes cost from A$966/NZ$1030 (15 consecutive days' travel) and **Eurail Flexipases** from A$1143/NZ$1220 (for 10 days in 2 months), while **Eurail Youth Flexipasses** for the under 26s cost from A$800/NZ$860 (10 days in 2 months).

AIRLINES IN AUSTRALIA AND NEW ZEALAND

Aeroflot Australia ☎02/9262 2233; no NZ office.

Air France Australia ☎02/9321 1000; New Zealand ☎09/303 3521.

Air New Zealand Australia ☎13/2476; New Zealand ☎09/366 2803.

Alitalia Australia ☎1300/653 757; New Zealand ☎09/379 4457.

British Airways Australia ☎02/9258 3300; New Zealand ☎09/356 8690.

Cathay Pacific Australia ☎02/931 5500; New Zealand ☎09/379 0861.

Garuda Australia ☎02/9334 9944; New Zealand ☎09/366 1855.

JAL Australia ☎02/9272 1111; New Zealand ☎09/379 9906.

KLM Australia ☎02/9231 6333 or 1-800/505 747; no NZ office.

Lauda Air Australia ☎02/9251 6155 or 1-800/642 438; New Zealand ☎09/303 1529.

Lufthansa Australia ☎02/9367 3888; New Zealand ☎09/303 1529.

Malaysian Airlines Australia ☎02/364 3500 or 13/2627; New Zealand ☎09/373 2741.

Qantas Australia ☎02/957 0111 or 13/1313; New Zealand ☎09/357 8900.

Royal Brunei Airlines Australia ☎07/3221 7757; no NZ office.

Singapore Airlines Australia ☎02/9236 0144 or 13/1011; New Zealand ☎09/379 3209.

Thai Airways Australia ☎1300/651 960; New Zealand ☎09/377 3886.

United Airlines Australia ☎13/1777; New Zealand ☎09/307 9500.

TRAVEL AGENTS IN AUSTRALIA AND NEW ZEALAND

AUSTRALIA

Accent on Travel ☎07/3832 1777.

Anywhere Travel ☎02/663 0411.

Brisbane Discount Travel ☎07/3229 9211.

European Travel Office ☎03/9329 8844.

Flight Centres ☎02/9460 0555 or 13/1600.

France and Travel ☎03/9670 7253.

France Unlimited ☎03/9531 8787.

French and International Travel ☎02/9956 5699

French Bike Tours ☎03/9531 8787.

French Cottages and Travel ☎03/9859 4944.

French Travel Connection ☎02/9966 8600.

Passport Travel ☎03/9824 7183.

STA Travel ☎02/9212 1255, 03/9654 7266 or 1300/360 960.

Topdeck Travel ☎08/8232 7222.

Tymtro Travel ☎02/9223 2211.

NEW ZEALAND

Budget Travel ☎09/306 0061 or 0800/808 040.

European Travel Office ☎09/525 3074.

Flight Centres ☎09/309 6171 or 04/472 8101.

STA Travel ☎09/366 6673, 04/385 0561 or 03/379 9098.

Thomas Cook ☎03/379 6600.

OUTDOOR SPECIALISTS IN AUSTRALIA AND NEW ZEALAND

Adventure World Australia ☎02/9956 7766 or 1-800/221 931; New Zealand ☎09/524 5118.

Eurolynx New Zealand ☎09/379 9716; no Australian office.

France Ski International ☎02/683 5185.

French Bike Tours ☎03/9531 8787.

Walkabout Gourmet Adventures ☎03/5159 5556.

RED TAPE AND VISAS

Citizens of EU countries, Australia, Canada, Israel, New Zealand, Norway and the United States do not need visas to enter France, and can stay for up to three months.

Other passport holders (including British Travel Document holders, but excluding Bermuda) must obtain a visa before arrival in France. Obtaining a visa from your nearest French consulate is fairly routine, but check their hours before turning up, and leave plenty of time, since there are often long queues. Those who are living as non-residents of the country in which they are applying for a visa may have to wait for a fifteen day period

whilst their documents are forwarded to their country of residence for validation. Note that the British Visitor's Passport is no longer valid.

Three types of **visa** are currently issued: a **transit visa**, valid for one to five days and for one or two entries; a **short-stay** (*court séjour*) visa, valid for ninety days after the date of issue and good for multiple entries; and a **long-stay** (*long séjour*) visa, which allows for multiple stays of ninety days in any one six-month period over three years, but which is issued only after an examination of an individual's circumstances. Non-visa citizens who stay longer than three months are officially supposed to apply for a **Carte de Séjour**, for which you'll have to show proof of income at least equal to the French minimum wage; EU passports are rarely stamped, so there is no evidence of how long you've been in the country. If your passport does get stamped, you can cross the border to Switzerland and re-enter for another ninety days legitimately.

Visa requirements for Monaco (an independent principality) are identical to those of France; there are no border controls between the two.

CUSTOMS

With the Single European Market you can bring in and take out most things as long as you have paid

FRENCH EMBASSIES AND CONSULATES

Australia 492 St Kilda Rd, Melbourne, Vic 3001 (☎03/820 0921); 31 Market St, Sydney, NSW 2000 (☎02/9261 5779); 6 Perth Ave, Yarralumla, Canberra, ACT 2600 (☎02/6216 0100).

Canada Embassy: 2 Elysée, pl Bonaventure, Montréal, QUE H5A 1B1 (☎514/878 4381); Consulates: 1 pl Ville Marie, Bureau 22601, Montréal, QUE H3B 4S3 (☎514/878 4381); 1110 av des Laurentides, QUE G1S 3C3 (☎418/688 0430); 130 Bloor St W, Suite 400, Toronto, ONT M5S 1N5 (☎416/925 80441); 1201 736 Granville St, Vancouver, BC V6Z 1H9 (☎604/681 2301); 42 Sussex Drive, Ottawa, ON K1M 2C9 (☎613/789 1795).

Ireland 36 Ailesbury Rd, Ballsbridge, Dublin 4 (☎01/260 1666).

New Zealand 1–3 Willeston St, PO Box 1695, Wellington (☎04/720 200).

Norway Drammensveien 69, 0224 Oslo 2 (☎022/441 820).

Sweden Narvavägen 28, Stockholm 115–23 (☎08/663 0270).

UK French Consulate General (Visas Section): 6a Cromwell Pl, PO Box 67, London SW7 2EW; 7–11 Randolph Cres, Edinburgh (both ☎0891/887733, fax 0891/669932; *www.ambafrance.org.uk*).

USA Embassy: 4101 Reservoir Rd NW, Washington, DC 20007 (☎202/944-6195); Consulates: 3 Commonwealth Ave, Boston MA 02116 (☎617/266-1680); 737 N Michigan Ave, Olympia Center, Suite 2020, Chicago, IL 60611 (☎312/787-5359); 10990 Wilshire Bd, Suite 300, Los Angeles, CA 90024 (☎310/235-3200); 934 5th Ave, New York, NY 10021 (☎212/606-3621); 540 Bush St, San Francisco, CA 94108 (☎415/397-4330).

tax on them in an EU country and they are for personal consumption. Customs may be suspicious if they think you are going to resell goods. Limits still apply to drink and tobacco bought in **duty-free** shops: 200 cigarettes, 250g of tobacco or 50 cigars; 1l of spirits or 2l of fortified wine, or 2l of sparkling wine and 2l of table wine; 60ml of perfume and 250ml of toilet water.

COSTS, MONEY AND BANKS

The Côte d'Azur has a reputation for being excessively expensive and it certainly will be if you indulge in the quayside-cocktail-sipping, haute cuisine and nightclub-larking lifestyle that this coast notoriously caters for. Many, but by no means all, of the hilltop villages in Provence are equally geared up to the indulgences of the very rich. The major cities, including those on the coast, have budget options for accommodation and eating out that, as in the rest of France, are relatively low cost by northern European standards. However, prices do go up considerably in July and August, and the Côte d'Azur and Riviera are more expensive than the rest of the region.

For a comfortable existence, with a hotel room for two, a light restaurant lunch and a proper restaurant dinner plus moving around, café stops and museum visits, you need to **allow about 600–700F a day per person**.

However, if you are careful, staying at a hostel (45–100F) or camping (25–60F a head) and being strong-willed about not sitting down in cafés, **you could manage on 180–250F**, including a cheap restaurant meal.

For two or more people **hotel accommodation** can be almost as cheap as the hostels, though a sensible average estimate for a double room would be around 270F. As for food, you can spend as much or as little as you like. There are large numbers of reasonable **restaurants** with three- or four-course menus for between 90F and 120F, with midday meals almost always cheaper than in the evening. **Picnic food**, obviously, is much less costly, especially when you buy in the markets and cheap supermarket chains. **Wine** and **beer** are both very cheap in supermarkets; buying wine from the barrel at village coop cellars will give you the best value for money. The mark-up on wine in restaurants is high, though the house wine in cheaper establishments is still very good value. **Drinks** in cafés and bars are what really make a hole in your pocket – you have to accept that you're paying for somewhere to sit. Black coffee, draught lager and pastis are the cheapest drinks to order.

Transport need not be a large item of expenditure, unless you're planning to drive a lot on the autoroutes in a gas-guzzling **car**. The French autoroutes still have **tolls**, and these are particularly high in Provence. Petrol prices are around 6F a litre for leaded, around 5.5F for unleaded, and around 4.4F a litre for diesel; note that there are 3.8 litres to the US gallon.

French **trains** are good value (a typical return-trip fare between Marseille and Nice costs around 230F; and from Nice to Menton is around 52F), with many discounts available. **Buses** are cheaper, though prices vary enormously from one operator to another. **Bicycles** cost between 60F and 80F per day to rent.

Museums and **monuments** can make considerable dents in budgets. **Reduced admission** is often available for those over sixty, under eighteen, and for students under 26. Several towns operate a global ticket for their museums and monuments. These are detailed in the Guide.

CURRENCY AND THE EXCHANGE RATE

French currency is the **franc** (abbreviated as F or sometimes FF), divided into 100 centimes. Francs come in notes of 500, 200, 100, 50 and 20F, and there are coins of 20, 10, 5, 2, and 1F, and 50, 20, 10 and 5 centimes. At the time of writing, the exchange rate for sterling is a healthy 9.8F, making France a more affordable option once again. The exchange rate for the US dollar, however, remains at around 5F while the Canadian dollar and Australian dollar hover miserably around 3.25F and 2.95F respectively.

CHANGING MONEY

Standard **banking hours** are 9.30am–noon and 2–4pm, although you may find some places that don't close for lunch. Banks are always closed Sunday and either Monday or, less usually, Saturday. **Rates of exchange** and **commissions** vary from place to place – a 30F charge for changing 200F is not uncommon; the Banque Nationale de Paris usually offers the best rates and takes the least commission. There are **money-exchange counters** at airports and the train stations of all big cities, and usually one or two in town centres as well; these often keep much longer hours than the high-street banks. You'll also find automatic money **exchange machines** which take dollars and notes of all European currencies but give a very poor rate of exchange. It would be a sensible precaution to buy some French francs before leaving. For cash advances, see below.

TRAVELLERS' CHEQUES AND CREDIT CARDS

Obtaining **French franc travellers' cheques** can be worthwhile: they can often be used as cash, and French banks are obliged by law to give you the face value of the cheques when you change them, so commission is only paid on purchase.

It is worth getting a selection of denominations of travellers' cheques. Make sure you keep the purchase agreement and a record of cheque serial numbers safe and separate from the cheques themselves. In the event that cheques are lost or stolen, the issuing company will expect you to report the loss straightaway to their office in France; most companies claim to replace lost or stolen cheques within 24 hours.

THE EURO

France is one of eleven European Union countries who on January 1, 1999, formed an economic and monetary union (EMU) and started using a single currency, the **euro**. Initially, however, it will only be possible to make paper transactions in the new currency (if you have, for example, a euro bank or credit-card account), and the franc will remain, in effect, the normal unit of currency in France. Euro notes and coins will be issued at the beginning of 2002, and will replace the franc entirely by July of that year.

Credit cards are also widely accepted for goods and services; check the window stickers to see which ones are accepted. Visa is the most universally recognized; American Express, Mastercard/Access and Eurocard less so. It's always worth checking, however, that restaurants and hotels will accept your card; smaller ones often don't, and even train stations in small towns may refuse them. Be aware that French cards have a smart chip and machines may reject the magnetic strip of British, American or Australasian cards, even if they are valid. If your card is refused because of this, you can explain to the assistant by saying: "*Les cartes britanniques/américaines/canadiennes/de Nouvelle-Zélande ne sont pas cartes à puce, mais à piste magnetique. Ma carte est valable et je vous serais très reconnaissant(e) de demander la confirmation auprès de votre banque ou de votre centre de traitement.*"

Credit cards can also be used to get **cash advances** from banks and from cash-dispensing machines where the appropriate sign is displayed. For Visa cards (*Carte Bleue*), you can use the same PIN number as in Britain and the US. For Mastercard/Access, you need to apply for a special European PIN number before you go. If your credit card is also a **direct debit card**, you can use that facility where the cash dispensers show the Delta or Switch signs. This is the best way of getting money, with no commission charged, although you may be charged a handling fee in the region of 15F.

Europeans can use **Eurocheques**, backed up with a card, which can be used for paying shop and restaurant bills in the same way as an ordinary cheque at home. With a PIN number, you can also use them in cash machines which show the same symbol as on your card. Although there is only two percent commission on each cheque, you have to pay an annual fee for the service of around £10, and you must apply for a card in advance. On the positive side, you can specify the exact amount you want and use the cheques in some places where credit cards are not accepted (though you'll have to write out the sum in French). It can take between two days and six weeks for the money to be deducted from your account.

Before leaving home, ask your bank or credit card company for the number to ring if your credit card is **lost or stolen**.

HEALTH AND INSURANCE

Citizens of all EU countries are entitled to take advantage of French health services under the same terms as residents, if they have the correct documentation. British citizens need form E111, available from post offices. North American and other non-EU citizens have to pay for most medical attention and are strongly advised to take out some form of travel insurance.

Under the French social security system, every hospital visit, doctor's consultation and prescribed medicine is charged. Although all employed French people are entitled to a refund of 75–80 percent of their medical expenses, this can still leave a hefty shortfall, especially after a stay in hospital (accident victims even have to pay for the ambulance that takes them there).

To find a **doctor**, stop at any *pharmacie* and ask for an address. Consultation fees for a visit should be around 75–85F and in any case you'll be given a *Feuille de Soins* (Statement of Treatment) for later documentation of insurance claims. Prescriptions should be taken to a **pharmacie** which is also equipped – and obliged – to give first aid (for a fee). The medicines you buy will have little stickers (*vignettes*) attached to them, which you must remove and stick to your *Feuille de Soins* together with the prescription itself. In serious emergencies, you will always be taken to the **local hospital** (*Centre Hospitalier*), either under your own power or by ambulance.

As getting a refund entails a complicated bureaucratic procedure and in any case does not cover the full cost of treatment, it's always a better idea to take out ordinary **travel insurance**, which generally allows full reimbursement, less the first few pounds or dollars of every claim, and also covers the cost of repatriation.

If you're travelling in your own car you may want to get breakdown cover which includes **personal insurance**.

BRITISH COVER

Competitive travel insurance schemes covering **medical expenses** and **theft or loss** are sold by all travel agents and banks, from around £25 a month: ISIS policies, from STA Travel or branches of Endsleigh Insurance, are usually good value; Columbus Travel Insurance also does an annual multi-trip policy which offers twelve months' cover for £70. The RAC and AA offer **car breakdown** cover, including towing costs, labour, dispatch of spare parts and repatriation of the vehicle, plus medical expenses and loss of luggage or money, from around £100 for a family for fifteen days.

If you're going to ski, rock-climb or engage in any other **high-risk activities**, the premiums will be higher, but definitely worth it – the cost of a mountain rescue can run into hundreds of thousands of francs; check carefully that any insurance policy you are considering will cover you in case of an accident.

Most **travel agents** and **tour operators** will offer you insurance when you book your flight or

TRAVEL INSURANCE COMPANIES AND AGENTS

BRITAIN

AA ☎0191/226 0033.

Columbus Travel Insurance, 17 Devonshire Square, London EC2M 4SQ (☎0171/375 0011).

Endsleigh, 97–107 Southampton Row, London WC1B 4AG (☎0171/436 4451).

RAC ☎0800/550055.

STA Travel, 86 Old Brompton Rd, London SW7 3LH (☎0171/361 6161).

NORTH AMERICA

Access America, PO Box 90310, Richmond, VA 23230 (☎1-800/284-8300).

Carefree Travel Insurance, PO Box 310, 120 Mineola Blvd, Mineola, NY 11501 (☎1-800/323-3149).

Council Travel, 205 E 42nd St, New York, NY 10017 (☎800/743-1823).

Desjardins Travel Insurance, Canada only ☎1-800/463-7830.

International Student Insurance Service (**ISIS**) through **STA Travel**, 48 E 11th St, New York, NY 10003 (☎1-800/777-0112).

Travel Assistance International, 1133 15th St NW, Suite 400, Washington, DC 20005 (☎1-800/821-2828).

Travel CUTS, 187 College St, Toronto, ON M5T 1P7 (☎416/979-2406).

Travel Guard, 1145 Clark St, Stevens Point, WI 54481 (☎1-800/826-1300).

Travel Insurance Services, 2930 Camino Diablo, Suite 300, Walnut Creek, CA 94596 (☎1-800/937-1387).

AUSTRALIA AND NEW ZEALAND

AFTA, 144 Pacific Hwy, North Sydney (☎02/9264 3299).

Cover More, Level 9, 32 Walker St, North Sydney (☎02/9202 8000 or 1-800/251 881).

Ready Plan, 141–147 Walker St, Dandenong, Victoria (☎1300/555 017); 10th Floor, 63 Albert St, Auckland (☎09/300 5333).

UTAG, 347 Kent St, Sydney (13/1398)

holiday, and some will insist you take it. These policies are usually reasonable value, though as ever, you should check the small print. If you feel the cover is inadequate, or you want to compare prices, any travel agent, insurance broker or bank should be able to help. If you have a good "all risks" **home insurance policy** it may well cover your possessions against loss or theft even when overseas, and many private medical schemes also cover you when abroad – make sure you know the procedure and the helpline number.

Bank and credit cards also offer certain levels of medical or other insurance cover, especially if you use them to pay for your trip. This can be quite comprehensive, anticipating anything from lost or stolen baggage and missed connections to charter companies going bankrupt.

NORTH AMERICAN COVER

Before buying an insurance policy, check that you're not already covered. Canadians are usually covered for medical mishaps overseas by their **provincial health plans**, although they are unlikely to pick up the full tab in the event of an accident. Holders of official **student and youth cards** (see p.19) are entitled to accident coverage and hospital in-patient benefits. **Students** will often find that their student health coverage extends during the vacations and for one term beyond the date of last enrollment. **Bank and credit cards** often provide certain levels of medical or other insurance, and travel insurance may also be included if you use a major credit or charge card to pay for your trip. **Homeowners' or renters'** insurance often covers theft or loss of documents, money and valuables while overseas, though conditions and maximum amounts vary from company to company.

After exhausting the possibilities above, you still might want to contact a specialist **travel insurance** company; your travel agent can usually recommend one, or see the box above. Policies are comprehensive (accidents, illnesses, delayed or lost luggage, cancelled flights, etc), but maximum payouts tend to be meagre. Check whether the policy pays medical costs up front or reimburses you later, and whether it provides for medical evacuation to your home country. For policies that include lost or stolen luggage, check exactly what is and isn't covered, and ensure the per-article limit will cover your most valuable possession.

Premiums vary, so shop around. The best deals are usually available through student/youth travel agencies – **ISIS** policies, for example, cost $48–69 for fifteen days (depending on coverage), $80–105 for a month, $149–207 for two months, or up to $510–700 for a year. If you're planning to do any "dangerous sports" (skiing, mountaineering, etc), figure on a surcharge of twenty to fifty percent.

Most North American travel policies apply only to items lost, stolen or damaged while in the custody of an identifiable, responsible third party – hotel porter, airline, luggage consignment, etc. Even in these cases you will have to contact the local police within a certain time limit to have a complete report made out so that your insurer can process the claim. Note also that very few insurers will arrange on-the-spot payments in the event of a major expense or loss; you will usually be reimbursed only after going home.

Full-time students in North America are entitled through the **International Student Identity Card (ISIC)** to up to $3000 in emergency medical coverage and $100 a day for sixty days in the hospital, plus there's a 24-hour hotline to call in the event of a medical, legal or financial emergency. The card, which costs US$16 for Americans and CN$15 for Canadians, is available from Council Travel, STA and Travel CUTS (see p.10 for addresses).

AUSTRALASIAN COVER

Travel insurance is put together by the airlines and travel agent groups (see box on p.13) in conjunction with insurance companies. They are all comparable in premium and coverage. Adventure sports are covered – except mountaineering with ropes, bungee jumping (some policies), and unassisted diving without an Open Water licence; check the small print of any policy.

The policies on offer are all similar in premium and coverage: UTAG, for example, offers one-month's cover for A$196/NZ$220, two months' for A$271/NZ$320 and three months' for A$335/NZ$400.

As with all policies, make sure that you are covered for any activities you might be planning, especially if you are trekking or skiing.

DISABLED VISITORS

France has no special reputation for providing facilities for disabled travellers, and for people in wheelchairs the haphazard parking habits and stepped village streets are serious obstacles. In the major cities and coastal resorts, there are accessible hotels, and ramps or other forms of access are gradually being added to museums and other sites. Public toilets with disabled access are rare. APF, the French paraplegic organization, has an office in each *département* which will be the most reliable source of information on accommodation with disabled access.

Public transport is certainly not wheelchair-friendly, and although many train stations now have ramps to enable wheelchair users to board and descend from carriages, at others it is still up to the guards to carry the chair. In Marseille there is a special office which operates a transport system (see p.154). At the time of writing, cars with hand controls are not available for rent in Provence.

As far as **airlines** go, British Airways has a better-than-average record for treatment of disabled passengers; from North America, Virgin and Air Canada come out tops in terms of disability awareness (and seating arrangements) and might be worth contacting first for any information they can provide.

PLANNING A HOLIDAY

There are **organized tours and holidays** specifically for people with disabilities – the contacts (see box below) will be able to put you in touch with any specialists for trips to France. It's important to become an authority on where you must be self-reliant and where you may expect help,

CONTACTS FOR TRAVELLERS WITH DISABILITIES

FRANCE

APF (Association des Paralysés de France), 21 bd Mantega, Nice (☎04.92.15.78.70); HLM Les Serrets, Manosque (☎04.92.72.34.37); 279 av de la Capelette, Marseille (☎04.91.79.99.99); 90 av du Général-Nogués, Toulon (☎04.94.62.97.75), 3 rue du Marquis-de-Calvières, Avignon (☎04.90.89.41.92).

BRITAIN

Access Project, 39 Bradley Gardens, London W13 8HE. Information service giving details of disabled facilities throughout the world.

Holiday Care Service, 2nd floor, Imperial Building, Victoria Rd, Horley, Surrey RH6 7PZ (☎01293/774535). Information on all aspects of travel.

RADAR, 12 City Forum, 250 City Rd, London EC1V 8AS (☎0171/250 3222; Minicom ☎0171/250 4119). A good source of advice on holidays and travel.

Tripscope, The Courtyard, Evelyn Rd, London W4 5JL (☎0345/585641; Minicom ☎0181/994 9294). Phone-in travel information and advice service.

NORTH AMERICA

Information Center for People with Disabilities, Fort Point Place, 27–43 Wormwood St, Boston, MA 02210 (☎617/727-5540; TDD ☎617/345-9743). Clearing house for information, including travel.

Jewish Rehabilitation Hospital, 3205 Place Alton Goldbloom, Montréal, PQ H7V 1R2 (☎514/688-9550 ext 226). Guidebooks and travel information.

Kéroul, 4545 ave Pierre-de-Coubertin, CP 1000, Station M, Montréal, PQ H1V 3R2 (☎514/252-3104). Organization promoting and facilitating travel for mobility-impaired people. Annual membership $10.

Mobility International USA, PO Box 10767, Eugene, OR 97440 (☎541/343-1284). Information and referral services, access guides, tours and exchange trips. Annual membership $35 (includes quarterly newsletter).

Society for the Advancement of Travel for the Handicapped (SATH), 347 5th Ave, Suite 610, New York, NY 10016 (☎212/447-7284 or 447-0027). Non-profit travel-industry referral service that passes queries on to its members as appropriate; allow plenty of time for a response.

Travel Information Service, Moss Rehabilitation Hospital, 1200 West Tabor Rd, Philadelphia, PA 19141 (☎215/456-9603). Telephone information and referral service.

Twin Peaks Press, Box 129, Vancouver, WA 98666 (☎206/694-2462 or 1-800/637-2256). Publisher of the *Directory of Travel Agencies for the Disabled* ($19.95), listing more than 370 agencies worldwide; *Travel for the Disabled* ($14.95); the *Directory of Accessible Van Rentals* and *Wheelchair Vagabond* ($9.95), loaded with personal tips.

Wheels Up! (☎1-888/389-4335). Provides discounted airfare, tour and cruise prices for disabled travellers, and also publishes a free monthly newsletter.

AUSTRALASIA

ACROD (Australian Council for Rehabilitation of the Disabled), PO Box 60, Curtin ACT 2605 (☎02/6282 4333); 24 Cabarita Road, Cabarita NSW 2137 (☎02/9743 2699). Provides lists of travel agencies and tour operators for people with disabilities.

Disabled Persons Assembly, PO Box 10, 138 The Terrace, Wellington (☎04/472 2626). Provides details of tour operators and travel agencies for people with disabilities.

especially regarding transport and accommodation. It is also vital to be honest – with travel agencies, insurance companies and travel companions. Know your limitations and make sure others know them. If you do not use a wheelchair all the time but your walking capabilities are limited, remember that you are likely to need to cover greater distances while travelling (often over rougher terrain and in hotter temperatures) than you are used to. If you use a wheelchair, have it serviced before you go and carry a repair kit.

Read your **travel insurance** small print carefully to make sure that people with a pre-exisiting medical condition are not excluded. And use your travel agent to make your journey simpler: airline or bus companies can cope better if they are expecting you, with a wheelchair provided at airports and staff primed to help. A **medical certificate** of your fitness to travel, provided by your doctor, is also extremely useful; some airlines or insurance companies may insist on it. Make sure that you have extra supplies of drugs – carried with you if you fly – and a prescription including the generic name in case of emergency. Carry spares of any clothing or equipment that might be hard to find; if there's an association representing people with your disability, contact them early in the planning process.

INFORMATION AND MAPS

The French Government Tourist Office gives away maps and glossy brochures as well as lists of hotels and campsites for the Provence-Alpes-Côte d'Azur region and for the five départements: Alpes-de-Haute Provence, Alpes-Maritimes, Bouches-du-Rhône, Var and Vaucluse. Some of these, like the footpath maps, lists of festivals and so on, can be particularly useful.

TOURIST OFFICES

In Provence itself you'll find a **tourist office** – usually an Office du Tourisme (OT) but sometimes a Syndicat d'Initiative (SI) – in practically every town and many villages (addresses and opening hours are detailed in the Guide). For the practical purposes of visitors, there is little difference between them: SIs have wider responsibilities for encouraging business, while OTs deal exclusively with tourism.

From these offices you can get specific local information, including listings of hotels and restaurants, leisure activities, car and bike rental, walks, laundries and countless other things. Always ask for the free town plan. In the Alps they display daily meteorological information and have contacts for walking and climbing guides and ski schools. In the big cities you can usually also pick up free what's-on listings guides. In small villages where there is no OT or SI, the *mairie*, or town hall, will often offer a similar service. The regional or departmental tourist offices also offer useful practical information (for addresses see "Sports and Outdoor Activities" on p.49).

MAPS

In addition to the various free leaflets – and the maps in this guide – you'll probably need a reasonable **road map**. For most purposes, certainly for driving, the most convenient is the IGN red series no. 115 (scale 1:250,000) which charts the entire area or the larger Michelin 1:200,000 no. 245. In the same scale in Michelin's yellow series you need no. 84 for the coast and Alpes-Maritimes and no. 81 for inland Provence.

For exploring a particular area, and for **walking or cycling**, the larger IGN maps – their green (1:100,000 and 1:50,000) and blue (1:25,000) series – are invaluable. For even greater detail IGN also do a 1:10,000 series (10cm on the map for every 1km on the ground). These maps can be bought at almost all newsagents and bookshops, and from some tourist offices.

WEBSITES

FRENCH GOVERNMENT TOURIST OFFICES

Australia BNP Building 12th floor, 12 Castlereagh St, Sydney NSW 2000 (☎612/231 5244).

Canada 1981 av McGill College, Suite 490, Montréal, QUE H3A 2W9 (☎514/288 4264); 30 St Patrick St, Suite 700, Toronto ONT M5T 3A3 (☎416/593 6427).

Ireland 35 Lower Abbey St, Dublin 1 (☎01/703 4046).

Netherlands Prinsengr. 670, 1017 KX Amsterdam (☎020/627 33 18).

Norway Storgaten 10A, 0155 Oslo 1 (☎22/42 33 87).

Sweden Normalmstorg 1 Av, S11146 Stockholm (☎08/679 79 75).

UK 178 Piccadilly, London W1V 0AL (☎0891/244 123).

USA 610 5th Ave, Suite 222, New York, NY 10020-2452 (☎212/757-1125); 645 N Michigan Ave, Chicago, IL 60611-2836 (☎312/337-6301); 9454 Wilshire Blvd, Beverly Hills, CA 90212-2967 (☎213/271-7838); Cedar Maple Plaza, 2305 Cedar Springs Blvd, Dallas, TX 75201 (☎214/720-4010).

MAP OUTLETS

UK

London: Daunt Books, 83 Marylebone High St, W1 (☎0171/224 2295); National Map Centre, 22–24 Caxton St, SW1 (☎0171/222 4945); Stanfords, 12–14 Long Acre, WC2 (☎0171/836 1321); The Travel Bookshop, 13–15 Blenheim Crescent, London W11 2EE (☎0171/229 5260).

Scotland: Nicolson Maps, 3 Frazer St, Largs (☎01475/689242); John Smith and Sons, 57–61 St Vincent St, Glasgow G2 5TB (☎0141/221 7472).

Ireland: Hodges Figgis Bookshop, 56–58 Dawson St, Dublin 2 (☎01/677 4754); Waterstone's, Queens Bldg, 8 Royal Ave, Belfast BT1 1DA (☎01232/247 355); 7 Dawson St, Dublin 2 (☎01/679 1415); 69 Patrick St, Cork (☎021/276 522).

Note: Maps by mail or phone order are available from Stanfords, London (☎0171/836 1321).

NORTH AMERICA

Chicago: Rand McNally, 444 N Michigan Ave, IL 60611 (☎312/321-1751).

New York: British Travel Bookshop, 551 5th Ave, NY 10176 (☎1-800/448-3039 or 212/490-6688); The Complete Traveler Bookstore, 199 Madison Ave, NY 10016 (☎212/685-9007); Rand McNally, 150 E 52nd St, NY 10022 (☎212/758-7488); Traveler's Bookstore, in the lobby of the Time Warner building, 22 W 52nd St, NY 10019 (☎212/664-0995).

San Francisco: Sierra Club Bookstore, 6014 College Ave, Oakland, CA 94618 (☎510/658-7470); The Complete Traveler Bookstore, 3207 Filmore St,

CA 94123 (☎415/923-1511); Rand McNally, 595 Market St, CA 94105 (☎415/777-3131).

Santa Barbara: Map Link Inc, 25 E Mason St, Santa Barbara, CA 93101 (☎805/9650-4402); Pacific Traveler Supply, 529 State St, CA 93101 (☎805/963-4438; phone orders on ☎805/965-4402).

Seattle: Elliot Bay Book Company, 101 S Main St, WA 98104 (☎206/624-6600).

Toronto: Open Air Books and Maps, 25 Toronto St, M5C 2R1 (☎416/363-0719).

Vancouver: World Wide Books and Maps, 1247 Granville St, V6Z 1E4 (☎604/687-3320).

AUSTRALASIA

Adelaide: The Map Shop, 16a Peel St, SA 5000 (☎08/8231 2033)

Auckland: Specialty Maps, 58 Albert St (☎09/307 2217).

Melbourne: Map Land, 372 Little Burke St, Vic 3000 (☎03/9670 4383)

Perth: Perth Map Centre, 884 Hay St, WA 6000 (☎08/9322 5733).

Sydney: Travel Bookshop, Shop 3, 175 Liverpool St (☎02 92618200).

If you're driving to Provence the Michelin map no. 989 is the best for the whole of France. A useful free map, obtainable from French filling stations and traffic information kiosks, is the Bison Futé, showing alternative back routes to the congested main roads.

GETTING AROUND

If you want to visit the main cities then travelling by train will be the most reliable and economical means. You can then use the bus network to radiate out from the towns, though this is much easier in western Provence than the less populated east. By far the best way of getting around, however, is with your own transport, preferably motorized as much of the terrain is daunting for all but the most super-fit and super-muscled cyclist. Approximate journey times and frequencies for public transport can be found in the "Travel details" at the end of each chapter and local peculiarities are also pointed out in the text of the Guide.

TRAINS

The main **rail line** in Provence and the Côte d'Azur links all the major cities of the coast and the Rhône Valley, with Marseille as its hub. From here a second major line runs north along the Durance Valley to Manosque and Sisteron on its way to Gap. From Nice a line runs north through Tende to Turin. From Avignon trains head west into Languedoc and to Marseille via Cavaillon. Nice and Digne are linked by the **Chemin de Fer de Provence** (a narrow-gauge line), which is a brilliant ride in itself, and connects with the main rail network north of Digne by bus. **InterRail** passes give you only a fifty percent reduction on this line – the French rail passes are fully valid.

The French national rail company, the **SNCF**, deserves its reputation for efficiency. Trains are fast, frequent and reliable, and the system is

more or less idiot-proof. All but the smallest stations have an information desk and *consignes automatiques* – coin-operated lockers big enough to take a rucksack.

Fares are reasonable. The ultra-fast TGVs (Trains à Grande Vitesse), which should soon be running at full speed to Marseille, require a supplement at peak times and compulsory seat reservations costing between 20F and 92F depending on the journey and the time of day. When buying tickets, whether from automatic machines or the counter service, note that TGV ticket prices vary according to demand so, for example, a later train may be cheaper.

All **tickets** – but not passes (see below) – must be date-stamped in the orange machines at station platform entrances, and it is an offence not to "*Compostez votre billet*". Train journeys may be broken at any point for up to 24 hours.

Regional **rail maps** and complete **timetables** are on sale at tobacconist shops. Leaflet timetables for a particular line are available free at stations. *Autocar* at the top of a column means it's an SNCF bus service, on which rail tickets and passes are valid.

DISCOUNTS AND PASSES

Within France, the SNCF itself offers **discounted fares** for over 60s and under 26s on standard rail prices on *Période Bleue* and *Période Blanche* days; a leaflet showing both discount periods is given out at Gares SNCF (train stations). A quota of discounted seats, which must be booked in advance, is available on all TGV trains, irrespective of the "period".

In addition to these discounts, couples are entitled to an **aller-retour à deux**, 25 percent discount on return journeys on TGVs or on other trains if they start their journey on a blue-period day. Over 60s can get the **Carte Senior**, which costs 285F, is valid for one year for unlimited travel with up to fifty percent off tickets on TGVs as well as other journeys starting in blue or white periods. The same terms are available for 12- to 25-year-olds with a **Carte 12–25** pass, which costs 270F, and for 4- to 12-year-olds with the **Carte Enfant Plus**, which costs 350F. The last also entitles the cardholder to secure the same ticket reductions for up to three travelling companions also aged between 4 and 12. These train passes can be bought through most travel agents in France or from main SNCF stations and in Britain from **French Railways**, 179 Piccadilly, London W1V 0BA (☎0990/848848). For Europe-wide train passes, see p.11. For anyone planning to travel **from Britain** to Provence, the **Eurodomino** pass is worth considering (see p.6). It is available from accredited British Rail travel agents, the International Rail Centre at London Victoria, or from the French Railways office (see above).

BUSES

Provence is not as badly served by **buses** as many regions in France, with good networks radiating out from Aix and Nice, plus inland services between the two and along the coast between Toulon and St-Raphaël which do not duplicate train routes. In the least touristy areas timetables tend to be geared to **school and market needs** which usually means getting up at the crack of dawn to catch them. You may need to time your visit for a particular day of the week and fix up accommodation in advance.

SNCF buses are useful for getting to places on the rail network where the trains no longer stop; they are included on rail timetables. The rest of the bus network is run by a plethora of **private companies** that rarely manage to coordinate their services. Although most towns have a **gare routière** (bus station) – usually near the Gare SNCF – it's not necessarily used by all the operators. Instead of wading through the reams of different timetables, get the ticket office to help you or ask at the local tourist office.

DRIVING

Provence is superb **driving** country, whether on the coastal corniches or the zigzagging mountain routes. Driving allows you to explore remote villages and the most dramatic landscapes which are otherwise inaccessible, and roads like the **Route Napoléon**, the **Corniche Sublime** and the **Grande Corniche** were built expressly to give breathtaking views.

With a full complement of passengers the costs need not be excessive and the added ease of camping with a car or motorbike to carry the gear can allow you to save on the price of accommodation. **Fuel** costs around 6F a litre for leaded, 5.5F for unleaded, and 4.4F a litre for diesel; prices are lower at supermarket chains such as Intermarché.

All the **highways** (*autoroutes*) in Provence have tolls except for the urban stretches, the A51

between Marseille and Aix, and the A55 from Marseille to Martigues. Some sample charges are: Aix to Nice 87F; Aix to Sisteron 45F; Aix to Toulon 37F. The toll for the spur into Monaco is particularly dear (22F from Nice). For up to date information on traffic conditions on the autoroutes call ☎08.36.68.09.79.

Car rental costs upwards of £120/$170 a week. It is usually cheaper to arrange from Britain or the US before you leave – Budget offers competitive deals on pre-paid car rental in France. You'll find the big firms – Hertz, Avis, Europcar and Budget – at airports and in most big cities, with addresses detailed throughout the Guide. Local firms can be cheaper but you need to check the small print and be sure of where the car can be returned to. It's normal to pay an indemnity of around 2000F against any damage to the car – they will take your credit card number rather than cash. You should return the car with a full tank. Extras are often pressed on you, such as medical cover, which you may already have from travel insurance. The cost of car rental includes the compulsory car insurance.

All the major car manufacturers have service stations in France – you'll find them in the Yellow Pages (*Pages Jaunes*) of the phone book under *Garages d'automobiles*. For **breakdown services** look under *Dépannages*. If you have **an accident or break-in**, you should make a report to the local police (and keep a copy) in order to make an insurance claim.

In **mountainous areas** fuel stations are few and far between so it's wise to carry a can. Many of the high passes are closed from mid-October to May, June or even July. Notices give you good warning. In **July and August** the traffic jams on the coastal roads can be horrendous, in particular between Hyères and Cannes, and Nice and Menton. For recorded information on **road conditions** call Inter Service Route on ☎04.91.78.78.78.

Car **parking** is usually free in towns between midday and 2pm; otherwise charges vary from 5F to 15F an hour.

And finally, if you smoke, never throw your cigarette-end out of the window. The undergrowth of Provence and the Côte d'Azur in summer is bone-dry kindling wood, and a single spark can start a raging **fire**.

RULES OF THE ROAD

British, EU and US **driving licences** are valid in France, though an International Driver's Licence

CAR RENTAL AGENCIES

UK

Avis ☎0990/900500.
Budget ☎0171/935 3518.
National Car Rental ☎01895/233300.

Europcar ☎0345/222525.
Hertz ☎0990/996699.
Holiday Autos ☎0990/300454.

NORTH AMERICA

Alamo ☎1-800/522-9696.
Auto Europe ☎1-800/223-5555.
Avis ☎1-800/331-1084.
Budget ☎1-800/527-0700.
Dollar ☎1-800/421-6868.
Europe by Car US ☎1-800/223 1516, in NY 212/581-3040; Canada ☎1/800-252-9401.

Hertz US ☎1-800/654-3001; Canada ☎1-800/26-0600, in Toronto ☎416/620-9620.
Holiday Autos ☎1-800/422-7737.
National ☎1-800/CAR-RENT.
Thrifty ☎1-800/367-2277.

AUSTRALASIA

Avis Australia ☎1-800/225 533; NZ ☎09/525 1982.
Budget Australia ☎13/2848; NZ ☎09/275 2222.
Citroën Peugeot Euro Lease ☎02/9949 1711.

Hertz Australia ☎13/1918; NZ ☎09/309 0989.
Renault Eurodrive ☎02/9299 3344.
Fly and Drive Holidays NZ ☎09/529 3709.

makes life easier if you get a police officer unwilling to peruse a document in English. The vehicle's registration document (*carte grise*) and the insurance papers must be carried. If your car is right-hand drive, you must have your headlight dip adjusted to the right before you go – it's a legal requirement.

The law of **priorité à droite** – giving way to traffic coming from your right, even when it is coming from a minor road – is being phased out as it is a major cause of accidents. It still applies in built-up areas, so you still have to be vigilant in towns, keeping a look out along the roadside for the yellow diamond on a white background that gives you right of way – until you see the same sign with an oblique black slash, which indicates vehicles emerging from the right have right of way. "*STOP*" signs mean stop completely: "*CÉDEZ LE PASSAGE*" means "Give way".

Fines for driving violations are exacted on the spot, and only cash is accepted. Exceeding the speed limit by 1–30kmph can cost as much as 5000F. Speed limits are: 130kmph (80mph) on the tolled *autoroutes*; 110kmph (68mph) on two-lane-highways; 90kmph (56mph) on other roads; and 60kmph (37mph) in towns.

HITCHING

Provence is one of the few areas in France where **hitching** is still fairly common, particularly along

the coast in summer. Inland Provence is less easy, though in the remote areas it's an accepted way for locals to get around.

In general, looking as clean, ordinary and respectable as possible makes a very big difference, and hitching the less frequented **D-roads** paradoxically gets you to your destination more quickly. In **mountain areas** a rucksack and trekking gear often ensure lifts from fellow aficionados. When leaving a city it's easier to find a train station on the road a few miles out and go there by rail.

Autoroutes are a special case; hitching on the highway itself is strictly illegal, but you can make excellent time going from one service station to another. If you get stuck at least there's food, drink and shelter. It helps to have Michelin's *Guide des Autoroutes*, showing all the rest stops, service stations, tollbooths (*péages*) and exits. All you need apart from that is a smattering of French and not too much luggage. Remember to get out at the service station before your driver leaves the *autoroute*. The tollbooths are a second best (hitching there is legal), but ordinary approach roads are very difficult.

CYCLING

The French have a great respect for **cycling** – it's a national sport and passion. This shows in the warm reception given to cyclists and to the care and courtesy extended by French drivers (except

A CYCLING VOCABULARY

to adjust	ajuster	to deflate	gonfler	rack	le porte
axle	l'axe	dérailleur	le dérailleur		-bagages
ball-bearing	le roulement	frame	le cadre	to raise	relever
	à billes	gears	les vitesses	to repair	réparer
battery	la pile	grease	la graisse	saddle	la selle
bent	tordu	handlebars	le guidon	to screw	visser
bicycle	le vélo	to inflate	gonfler	spanner	la clef
bottom	le logement	inner tube	la chambre à air		(mécanique)
bracket	du pédalier	loose	dévissé	spoke	le rayon
brake cable	le cable	to lower	baisser	to straighten	rédresser
brakes	les freins	mudguard	le garde-boue	stuck	coincé
broken	cassé	pannier	le pannier	tight	serré
bulb	l'ampoule	pedal	le pédale	toe clips	les cale-pieds
chain	la chaîne	pump	la pompe	tyre	le pneu
cotter pin	la clavette	punctured	la crevaison	wheel	la roue

in large cities where bikes are not normally used as a means of transport and on the corniche roads where everyone drives crazily fast). In Provence you'll see cyclists beetling up **mountains**, often overtaking heavy vehicles, but if you're not up to such strenuous pedalling the **Rhône Valley** is the only area that is consistently easy-going. The other things to bear in mind are the high summer **temperatures** and relentless frazzling sun. If you are willing to tackle inclines, however, cycling is a wonderfully sensual way to explore the region, and will get you fit very quickly.

Restaurants and hotels along the way are nearly always obliging about looking after your bike, even to the point of allowing it into your room. Most large towns have well-stocked retail and **repair shops**, where parts are normally cheaper than at home. However, if you're using a foreign-made bike, it's a good idea to carry spare tyres, as French sizes are different. Inner tubes are not a problem, as they adapt to either size, though make sure you get the right valves.

The **train network** runs various schemes for cyclists, all of them covered by the free leaflet *Train et Vélo*, available from most stations. On *autorails* (when marked with a bicycle in the timetable) you can travel with a bike as free accompanied luggage. On TGVs and Corail coaches folding bikes or bikes with the wheels removed and packed in covers no bigger than 120 x 90cm (which you can buy at cycle shops) can be carried. Otherwise, you have to send your bike as registered luggage (195F). Although it may well arrive in less time, the SNCF won't guarantee delivery in

under five days; and you do hear stories of bicycles disappearing altogether. British Airways and Air France both take bikes free. You may have to box them though, and you should check with the airlines first.

Bikes for rent – usually mountain bikes (*vélos tous terrains* commonly abbreviated to *VTTs*) – are often available from campsites, youth hostels and *gîtes d'étape*, as well as specialist cycle shops, some tourist offices and train stations. Costs are between 60F and 80F per day and around 240F a week. Deposits of between 1000F and 2300F are required – you can give them credit card details rather than cash but make sure you get a proper receipt. The bikes are often not insured and you will be presented with the bill for its replacement if it's stolen or damaged so check whether you are covered for this by your travel insurance.

The best **maps** are the contoured IGN 1:10,000 series. In the UK, the Cyclists Touring Club, Cotterell House, 68 Meadow, Surrey GU7 3HS (☎01483/417217), will suggest routes and supply advice for a small fee, and they run a particularly good insurance scheme.

MOPEDS AND SCOOTERS

Mopeds and **scooters** are relatively easy to find: everyone in France, from young kids to grandmas, rides one of these, and although they're not built for any kind of long-distance travel, they're ideal for shooting around town and nearby. Places that rent out bicycles will often also rent out mopeds; you can expect to pay 200F a day for a 50cc Suzuki, for example, or 250F for an 80cc motorbike. Crash helmets are compulsory only on machines over 125cc, but you'd be a fool not to wear one even on a moped.

WALKING

Provence has an extensive network of **footpaths** and some of the most rewarding **trekking country**, both in the mountains and in the coastal hinterland. There's the national network of long distance footpaths, known as *sentiers de grande randonnée* – GR for short – marked by horizontal red and white striped signs, of which numbers 4, 5, 6 and 9 plus various offshoots run through the region. The national and regional parks – the Camargue, the Lubéron and the Mercantour – have additional networks, and then there are the smaller paths and forest tracks, all usually well signed. Coastal paths exist but only in short stretches.

Each GR is described in a **Topo guide** (available from Stanfords in London, see p.22, and from bookshops and newsagents in Provence), which gives a detailed account of the route (in French), including maps, campsites, refuge huts, sources of provisions, etc. In addition, tourist offices can put you in touch with guides and organizations for **climbing and walking expeditions**.

Specialized walking maps are produced by Didier Richard on a 1:50,000 scale. These include *Alpes-de-Provence* (no. 1), *Mercantour* (no. 9), *Haute-Provence* (no. 19), *Au Pays d'Azur* (no. 26) and *Maures et Haut Pays Varois* (no. 25); they are available in most major bookshops in the region and from Stanfords in London (see p.22). For **French guidebooks** on walking, the best publishers are Editions Edisud. Many of the paths are mentioned in this Guide, too, and some walks are detailed.

In July and August it's important to book a bed at the **mountain refuge huts** in advance. Phone numbers for many of the Alpine refuges are given in the Guide; you can also get lists from local tourist offices. Several are run by the Club Alpin Français which takes bookings from its office in Nice (☎04.93.62.59.99).

The warning to drivers about cigarette ends applies to walkers too. If you stub one out on the ground you must make sure that it is completely extinguished. Equally never light **fires**, however much you think a clearing is big enough for safety. You may find many paths and tracks have *défense d'entrée* signs in summer. These restrictions are to protect the forest from the risk of fire and should be respected – you can also be heavily fined if you're found on out-of-bounds paths.

ON THE WATER

You don't have to own a yacht to **sail** into the Côte d'Azur resorts. There are companies offering transport services from the gares maritimes (maritime ports) of many coastal towns, either out to islands or to neighbouring ports. Though not the cheapest way to get about, this can sometimes be the quickest when the summer traffic jams on the coastal roads are at their worst.

Trips down the Rhône are always slow and expensive. The boats tend to be of the Parisian *bateaux-mouches* variety – huge and ugly – and the deals often involve overpriced dinner-dance affairs. Inland, the **rivers of Provence** are harnessed to hydroelectric power stations and an extensive irrigation system. There are numerous barrages and water levels change at the flick of a switch (and with no warning). **Canoeing and rafting**, though possible in many stretches, should not, therefore, be undertaken without local guidance.

Details about boat trips and centres for canoeing and rafting are listed in the Guide.

ACCOMMODATION

Finding accommodation on the spot in the main cities of Provence and the Côte d'Azur is not a major problem except in July and August. At any time of year, though, booking a couple of nights in advance can be reassuring, saving the effort of trudging round and ensuring that you know what you'll be paying.

The summer season in the **coastal resorts** lasts from around mid-May to mid-September, and hotels, youth hostels and campsites are all stretched beyond their limits. The worst time of all is between July 15 and August 15 when the French take their holidays en masse. Your chances of finding anything then without advance booking become very slim indeed, though most tourist offices will do their best to help.

The problems are rather different **inland**, where the villages are often dominated by *résidences secondaires* (second homes) rather than hotels; those **hotels** that there are, and **bed and breakfast** in private houses (chambres d'hôtes), can get booked up well in advance. **Campsites**, however, are plentiful and rarely full once you're north of the Autoroute La Provençale.

Aside from the summer, the one bad month is **November** when almost all hoteliers take their holidays and most campsites are closed.

Phone numbers as well as addresses have been given in the Guide and the "Language" section at the back should help you make a reservation, though many hoteliers and campsite managers, and almost all youth hostel managers, will speak some English.

HOTELS

Hotel recommendations are given in the text of the Guide for almost every town or village mentioned with a price range for each (see box below). Many hotels, particularly those in smaller resorts and the inland villages, are **closed for one day of the week** – this means that you can't check in or out on the day in question, but if you're already installed you'll be supplied with a key and expected to look after yourself. Where applicable, these days are also noted in the text.

If you're travelling in peak season it's worth having as many addresses as possible. Local **accommodation lists** are available from tourist offices and lists for the Provence-Alpes-Côted'Azur region and each individual *département* can be obtained before you leave from any French Government Tourist Office.

A very useful option, especially if it's late at night, is the **Formule 1 chain**, well signposted on the outskirts of several towns. Characterless motels, they provide box-like rooms for up to three people for 140F. With a Visa, Mastercard, Eurocard or American Express credit card, you can let yourself into a room at any hour of the day or night. Reservations can be made on ☎08.36.68.56.85 (premium rate call at 2,23F a minute). The hotels are not difficult to find as long as you're travelling

---

ACCOMMODATION PRICE CATEGORIES

Throughout this guide, all hotels and guesthouses have been priced on a scale of ①–⑧, indicating the lowest price you could expect to pay for a double room in high season. What you get for your money varies enormously between establishments, but in the lower-priced hotels you should expect to pay considerably more for en-suite facilities. If you are staying anywhere for more than three days it's often possible to negotiate a lower price, particularly out of season.

① Under 160F	④ 300–400F	⑦ 600–700F
② 160–220F	⑤ 400–500F	⑧ Over 700F
③ 220–300F	⑥ 500–600F	

by car, and a brochure with full details can be picked up at any one.

All French hotels are **graded** from **zero to four stars**. The price more or less corresponds to the number of stars, though the system is a little haphazard, often having more to do with ratios of bathrooms to guests than quality; ungraded and single-star hotels are often very good. At the cheapest level, what makes a difference in cost is whether a room contains a **shower**: if it does, the bill will be around 30–50F more. **Breakfast**, too, can add 25–80F per person to a bill – you will nearly always do better at a café but some hotels will insist on providing it. **Single rooms** are only marginally cheaper than doubles so sharing always cuts costs considerably. Most hotels willingly provide rooms with extra beds, for three or more people, at good discounts.

In high season many hotels demand **demi-pension** (half board) which is not necessarily a bad deal, though it can get very boring eating in the same place all the time. Though it's illegal for hotels to insist on you taking meals when the cost is separate from the price of the room, many do and you may have little option but to agree. One plausible way out worth trying is to say you are *invité/e* (invited out).

CHAMBRES D'HÔTES

Chambres d'hôtes (bed and breakfasts in private houses) are fairly widespread, particularly in small villages. They vary in standard but are rarely an especially cheap option – usually costing the equivalent of a two-star hotel. However, if you're lucky, they may be good sources of traditional home-cooking. A selection are listed in the Guide; full lists are available from tourist offices and you can also find them detailed with Gîtes de France and gîtes d'étape (see below) by *département* in leaflets available from French Government Tourist Offices and the larger tourist offices.

HOSTELS, GÎTES D'ÉTAPE AND REFUGES

At between 50F and 100F per night for a dormitory bed, **youth hostels** – *auberges de jeunesse* – are invaluable for single travellers on a budget. Some offer double rooms for around 100F, but it can be cheaper for couples, and certainly for groups of three or more people, to share a room in a hotel – particularly if you have to pay a bus fare out to the edge of town to reach the local hostel. However, many hostels are beautifully sited, and

they allow you to cut costs by preparing your own food in their kitchens, or eating in their cheap canteens. To stay at many of the hostels you must be a member of **Hostelling International (HI)**, which currently costs £10/$25 for over 18s, £5/free for under 18s. Head offices are listed in the box on p.30. You can also join at Fédération Unie des Auberges de Jeunesse (FUAJ) hostels (100F for over 26s, 70F for under 26s) or buy a 19F "Welcome Stamp" which, once you've collected six, gives you international membership. If you don't have your own sleeping bag you'll have to pay around 17F to rent bedding.

You'll find independent hostels that do not belong to the HI, and in the main cities there are **foyers** or *résidences* – residential hostels for young workers and students – which often have age limits or are women only, and university accommodation, usually available only in July and August. Prices are rarely more than 100F for a single or double room and all are detailed in the Guide.

A third hostel-type alternative is the **gîtes d'étape** found in rural Provence. These are less formal than other youth hostels, often run by the local village or municipality (whose mayor will probably be in charge of the key), and provide bunk beds and primitive kitchen and washing facilities for around 40F. Designed primarily for people trekking or on bikes or horses, they are marked on the large-scale IGN walkers' maps and listed in the individual GR Topo guides, as well as in the *département* leaflets available from French Government Tourist Offices and local tourist offices.

In the mountains there are **refuge huts** on the main GR routes, normally open only in summer. They are extremely basic and not always very friendly places, and must be booked in advance in high summer (see "Walking" on p.27). Costs per night are between 35F and 90F depending on facilities. A list of refuge huts in the Alpes-Maritimes *département* is available from the Comité Régional de Tourisme, 55 promenade des Anglais, Nice (☎04.93.37.78.78) and for the Alpes-de-Haute-Provence *département* from the Comité Départemental de Tourisme, 19 rue du Dr-Honnorat, Digne-les-Bains (☎04.92.31.57.29).

RENTED ACCOMMODATION: GÎTES DE FRANCE

If you are planning to stay a week or more in any one place it might be worth considering **renting**

YOUTH HOSTEL ASSOCIATIONS

Australia
Australian Youth Hostels Association, 422 Kent Street, Sydney, NSW 2000 (☎02 9261 1111).

Canada
Hostelling International/Canadian Hostelling Association, 205 Catherine St, Suite 400, Ottawa, ON K2P 1C3 (☎613/237 7884 or ☎1-800/663 5777, except Newfoundland).

England and Wales
Youth Hostels Association (YHA), Trevelyan House, 8 St Stephen's Hill, St Albans, Herts AL1 2DY (☎01727/855215; for booking youth hostels abroad ☎01629/581418, fax 01629/581062).

France
Fédération Unie des Auberges de Jeunesse, 27 rue Pajol, 75018 Paris (☎01.44.89.87.27).

Ireland
An Oige, 61 Mountjoy St, Dublin 7 (☎01/830 4555); Youth Hostel Association of Northern Ireland, 22 Donegall Rd, Belfast BT12 5JN (☎01232/324 733).

New Zealand
Youth Hostels Association of New Zealand, Cnr Tce & Wakefield Sts, Wellington (☎04/801 7280).

Scotland
Scottish Youth Hostels Association, 7 Glebe Crescent, Stirling, FK8 2JA (☎01786/451181).

USA
Hostelling International-American Youth Hostels (HI-AYH), 733 15th St NW, Suite 840, Washington, DC 20005 (☎202/783-6161).

---

a house. You can do this by checking adverts placed by private and foreign owners in British Sunday newspapers *(The Observer* and *Sunday Times*, mainly), or trying one of the many firms that market travel and accommodation packages (see the box on p.5)

The easiest and most reliable method, however, is to use the official French Government service, the **Gîtes de France**, based in Britain at 178 Piccadilly, London W1V 9DB (☎0171/399 3500), or in Australia, through Explore Holidays, PO Box 256, Carlingford, NSW 2118. Their guide contains properties all over France, listed by *département*. The houses vary in size and comfort, but all are basically acceptable holiday homes; there is a description of each one, and the computerized booking service means that you can instantly reserve one for any number of full weeks. Costs vary with seaview houses on the Côte d'Azur and Riviera inevitably commanding very high prices. Inland you should be able to rent a comfortable house in the countryside with room for four or five people for around 2000–2500F a week in July and August. *Gîtes Accessible à Tous*, also available from Gîtes de France (£7 plus postage) lists the gîte accommodation especially equipped for the disabled.

CAMPING

Most towns and villages have at least one **campsite** (notable exceptions being Marseille which

has none, and Nice which has only one a long way out). Camping is extremely popular with the French and for those from the north of the country Provence is a favourite destination. The cheapest sites – at around 25F per person per night – are usually the **camping municipal**, run by the local municipality. They are always clean and have plenty of hot water, and are often situated in prime positions. Some youth hostels also have space for tents.

On the **Côte d'Azur** campsites can cost three times regular prices for few (or no) extra facilities, and tend to be monstrously big. At full capacity in July and August they can be far too crowded for comfort. Most of the sites recommended in the guide are the smaller ones. Inland, *camping à la ferme* – on somebody's farm – is another (generally facility-less) possibility. Lists of sites are detailed in the French Tourist Board's *Accueil à la Campagne* booklet and are available from local tourist offices. You should make sure of what you'll be charged before you pitch up – it's easy to get stung the following morning.

Phone numbers for campsites are given in the text of the Guide so you can check ahead for space availability. We also give the French grading from one to four stars which indicates the sophistication of the facilities. As a rough estimate for a family of four with a car and caravan or tent, **prices** should be from 40F to 60F for one-star sites, 50F to 70F for two-star sites, 90F to

110F for three-star sites and 100F to 120F for four-star sites.

Camping rough (*camping sauvage*, as the French call it) is possible but you must ask permission from the owner of the land first. Farmers can be very nasty if you don't and their weapons include guns as well as dogs. In the remote areas of northeastern Provence, where it may not be clear who owns the land, you'll probably be OK but don't camp within the protected area of the Parc de Mercantour. Nor should you ever camp in the forests in summer: however careful you think you might be, it takes only one stray spark to start a galloping inferno, and both local people and police are vigilant.

Camping **on the beach** is standard practice only on certain stretches in the Camargue; elsewhere

you'll be vulnerable to theft and mugging. If the police find you, it's possible that you could be arrested.

If you're planning to do a lot of camping, an **international camping carnet** is a good investment, available from home motoring organizations, or from one of the following: the Camping and Caravan Club, Greenfields House, Westwood Way, Coventry, CV4 8JH (☎01203/694995); Family Campers and RVers (FCRV), 4804 Transit Rd, Building 2, Depew, NY 14043 (☎1-800/245-9755).

The carnet serves as useful identification, covers you for third-party insurance when camping and is good for discounts at member sites. FCRV annual membership costs $25, and the carnet an additional $10.

FOOD AND DRINK

Food is as good a reason as any for going to Provence. The region has one of the great cuisines of France and some very fine wines in the Vaucluse, on the coast and at Châteauneuf-du-Pape.

For experiencing food and wine at their best, there's a phenomenal number of top gourmet **restaurants**, matched only in the rest of the country by Lyon and Paris. Many of these are cheap by British standards, their extravagance only relative to the prices of less elaborate but still gorgeously gluttonous meals you can have. Inevitably, quality can suffer in some of the tourist hotspots, but if you take your time – treating the business of choosing a place as an interesting

appetizer in itself – you should be able to eat consistently well without spending a fortune.

The **markets** of Provence (the best ones are detailed in the Guide) are a great sensual treat as well as lively social events. *Marchés paysans*, where *paysans* (smallholders, the backbone of French farming) sell directly to the public, are common.

Provence is also the homeland of **pastis**, the cooling aniseed-flavoured drink traditionally served with a bowl of olives before meals.

BREAKFAST AND SNACKS

A croissant, *pain au chocolat* (a choc-filled croissant) or a sandwich in a bar or café, with hot chocolate or coffee, is generally the best way to eat **breakfast** – at a fraction of the cost charged by most hotels. Croissants and sometimes hard-boiled eggs are displayed on bar counters until around 9.30 or 10am. If you stand – cheaper than sitting down – you just help yourself to these with your coffee, the waiter keeps an eye on how many you've eaten and bills you accordingly.

At **lunchtime**, and sometimes in the evening, you may find cafés offering a **plat du jour** (chef's daily special) at between 40F and 70F or *formules*, a limited or no-choice menu. The *croque-monsieur* or *croque-madame* (variations on the toasted-cheese sandwich) is on sale at cafés,

PROVENCAL CUISINE

Intense sunshine combined with all-important irrigation make Provence one of the great food regions of France. Just about everything flourishes here but pride of place must go to the olive tree, introduced to Provence by the ancient Greeks two and a half thousand years ago, and perfectly suited to the warm, dry climate. Olives accompany the traditional Provençal aperitif of pastis; they appear in sauces and salads, on tarts and pizzas, and mixed with capers in *tapenade* paste spread on bread or biscuits. **Olive oil** is the starting point for almost all Provençal dishes. Spiced with chillies or **Provençal herbs** (wild thyme, basil, rosemary and tarragon) it is also poured over pizzas, sandwiches, and used to make vinaigrette and mayonnaise for all the varieties of salad, including the bitter leaves of the Niçois *mesclum*.

The ingredient most often mixed with olive oil is the other classic of Provençal cuisine, **garlic**. Whole markets are dedicated to strings of white and pale purple garlic. Two of the most famous concoctions of Provence are *pistou*, a paste of olive oil, parmesan cheese, garlic and basil, and *aïoli*, a garlic mayonnaise and the traditional Friday dish in which it's served with salt cod and vegetables.

Vegetables and fruit have double or triple seasons in Provence, often beginning while Northern France is still in the depths of winter. **Ratatouille** ingredients — tomatoes, peppers, aubergines, courgettes and onions — are the favourites, along with purple-tipped asparagus and baby potatoes. Courgette flowers fritters stuffed with *pistou* is one of the most exquisite Provençal delicacies. As for **fruits**, the melons, white peaches, apricots, figs, cherries and Muscat grapes are unbeatable. **Almond** trees grow on the plateaux of central

Provence (eaten when they are still green in summer) along with lavender, which gives Provençal **honey** its distinctive flavour.

Sheep, taken up to the mountains in the summer months, provide the staple meat, of which the best is *agneau de Sisteron*. But it is **fish** that features most on traditional menus. The fish soups of **bouillabaisse**, famous in Marseille, and *bourride*, served with a chilli-flavoured mayonnaise known as *rouille*, are served all along the coast, as are whole sea bream, monkfish, sea bass or John Dory, covered with Provençal herbs and grilled over an open flame. **Seafood**, from spider crabs to clams, sea urchins to crayfish, crabs, lobster, mussels and oysters, is piled onto huge *plateaux de fruits de mer*, not necessarily representing Mediterranean harvests, more the luxury associated with this coast. October to April is the prime seafood season.

The one source of food unsuited to the dry heat of Provence is cattle, which is why olive oil rather than butter and cream dominate Provençal cuisine, and why the **cheeses** are invariably made from goats' or ewes' milk. Famous *chèvres* (goats' cheeses) are Banon, wrapped in chestnut leaves and marinated in brandy, the aromatic Picadon from the foothills of the Alps, Poivre d'Ain, pressed with wild savory, and Lou Pevre with a pepper coating.

Provençal cuisine is extremely healthy. A traditional meal should leave you feeling perfectly able to dance the night away, or, more prosaically, to pig yourself without fear of heart attack. Except of course for the famous chocolates, candied fruit and chestnuts, almond sweets and nougat, plus all the gluttonous ice-cream concoctions served with cocktails on the promenade cafés.

brasseries and many street stands, along with *frites*, crêpes, *galettes* (buckwheat pancakes), *gaufres* (waffles), *glaces* (ice creams) and all kinds of fresh sandwiches. For variety, there are Tunisian snacks like *brik à l'œuf* (a fried pastry with an egg inside), *merguez* (spicy North African sausage) and Middle Eastern falafel (deep-fried balls of chickpea with salad). Local specialities include the Niçois *pan bagnat*, an oil-dripping bun stuffed with salad and fish, and *pissaladière*, an onion, black olives and anchovy flan.

Crêperies, serving filled pancakes from around 35F upwards, are very popular. But quality is variable, as it is with the ubiquitous **pizzerias** *au feu de bois* (wood-fire baked).

For **picnics**, the local outdoor market or supermarket will provide you with almost everything you need from tomatoes and avocados to cheese and pâté. Cooked meat, prepared snacks, ready-made dishes and assorted salads can be bought at *charcuteries* (delicatessens), which you'll find everywhere — even in small villages, though the same things are cheaper at supermarket counters. You purchase by weight, or you can ask for *une tranche* (a slice), *une barquette* (a carton), or *une part* (a portion). You'll also find hot, whole spit-roasted chicken on every high street and at most markets.

Salons de thé, which open from mid-morning to late evening, serve brunches, salads, quiches and the like, as well as gâteaux, ice cream and a wide selection of teas. They tend to be a good deal pricier than cafés or brasseries – you're paying for the posh surroundings. At **pâtisseries**, along with the usual cakes, breads and pastries, you'll find *fougasse* or *fougassette*, a five-finger-shaped bread containing olives, anchovies, sausage or cheese, or flavoured with orange, lemon or rose water. *Chichi* (a light, scented doughnut) are sold from street stalls; the region's other classic sweet nibble is nougat.

FULL-SCALE MEALS

There's no difference between **restaurants** (*auberges* or *relais*) and **brasseries** in terms of quality or price range. The distinction is that brasseries, which resemble cafés, serve quicker meals at most hours of the day, while restaurants tend to stick to the traditional meal times of noon to 2pm and 7 to 9.30 or 10.30pm. After 9pm or so, restaurants often serve only à la carte meals – invariably more expensive than eating the set menu. In touristy areas in high season and for all the more upmarket places it's wise to make reservations – easily done on the same day. In small towns it may be impossible to get anything other than a bar sandwich after 10pm or even earlier; in major cities, town-centre brasseries will serve until 11pm or midnight and one or two may stay open all night.

Since restaurants change hands frequently and have their ups and downs, it's always worth asking local people for recommendations. This is the conversational equivalent of commenting on the weather in Britain and will usually elicit strong views and sound advice.

Prices and what you get for them are posted outside restaurants. Normally there is a choice between one or more **menus** where the number of courses has already been determined and the choice is limited. The *carte* (menu) has everything listed. *Service compris* or *s.c.* means the service charge is included. *Service non compris*, *s.n.c.* or *service en sus* means that it isn't and you need to calculate an additional fifteen percent. **Wine** (*vin*) or a drink (*boisson*) may be included, though rarely on menus under 90F. When ordering wine, ask for *un quart* (quarter-litre), *un demi-litre* (half-litre) or *une carafe* (a litre). You'll normally be given the house wine unless you specify otherwise; if you're worried about the cost ask for *vin ordinaire*. In the Guide the lowest-price menu or the range of menus is given; where average à la carte prices are given it assumes you'll have three courses and half a bottle of wine.

In the French sequence of **courses**, any salad (sometimes vegetables, too) comes separate from the main dish, and cheese precedes a dessert. You will be offered coffee, which is always extra (as much as 20F or more) to finish off the meal. You can specify if you like it strong (*serré*) or weak (*léger*).

At the bottom of the price range, **menus** revolve around standard dishes such as steak and fries (*steack-frites*), chicken and fries (*poulet-frites*), stews (*daubes* or a whole variety of other terms) and various concoctions involving innards such as *pieds et paquets* (feet and tripe of sheep). If you're simply not that hungry, just go for the plat du jour.

Going **à la carte** offers much greater choice and, in the better restaurants, access to the chef's specialities. You pay for it, of course, though a simple and perfectly legitimate ploy is to have just one course instead of the expected three or four. You can share dishes or just have several starters – a useful strategy for vegetarians. There's no minimum charge.

The French are much better disposed towards **children** in restaurants than other nationalities, not simply by offering reduced-price children's menus but in creating an atmosphere, even in otherwise fairly snooty establishments, that positively welcomes kids; some even have in-house games and toys for them to occupy themselves with. It is regarded as self-evident that large family groups should be able to eat out together.

Less self-evident is the thinking behind allowing **dogs** in, too; it can be quite a shock to realize that some of your fellow diners are attempting to keep their pets under control beneath the tables.

VEGETARIANS

On the whole, **vegetarians** can expect a somewhat lean time in Provence and the Côte d'Azur. A few towns have specifically vegetarian restaurants (which are detailed in the text), but elsewhere you'll have to hope you find a sympathetic restaurant (crêperies can be good standbys). Sometimes restaurants are willing to replace a meat dish on the *menu fixe* with an omelette; other times you'll have to pick your way through the *carte*. Remember the phrase: "*je suis végétarien(ne); il y a quelques plats sans viande?*" (I'm a vegetarian; are there any non-meat dishes?).

FOOD AND DISHES

Basic terms

Pain	Bread	*Sel*	Salt	*Couteau*	Knife
Beurre	Butter	*Sucre*	Sugar	*Cuillère*	Spoon
Céréale	Cereal	*Vinaigre*	Vinegar	*Cure-dent*	Toothpick
Lait	Milk	*Moutarde*	Mustard	*Table*	Table
Huile	Oil	*Bouteille*	Bottle	*L'addition*	Bill
Confiture	Jam	*Verre*	Glass	*Offert*	Free
Poivre	Pepper	*Fourchette*	Fork		

Snacks (*Casse-croûtes*)

Un sandwich/	**A sandwich…**	*Cru*	Raw
une baguette…		*Emballé*	Wrapped
au jambon/fromage	with ham/cheese	*À emporter*	Takeaway
au jambon beurre/	with ham & butter/	*Fumé*	Smoked
fromage beurre	cheese & butter	*Salé*	Salted/spicy
au pâté (de campagne)	with pâté (country-style)	*Sucré*	Sweet
Croque-monsieur	Grilled cheese and ham sandwich		
Croque-madame	Grilled cheese, ham or bacon and fried egg sandwich	***Oeufs***	**Eggs**
		au plat	Fried eggs
		/sauté à la poêle	
Pan bagnat	Bread roll with egg, olives, salad, tuna, anchovies and olive oil	*à la coque*	Boiled eggs
		durs	Hard-boiled eggs
		brouillés	Scrambled eggs
Tartine	Buttered bread or open sandwich	*poché*	Poached eggs

And some terms		***Omelette*** …	**Omelette** …
(Re)chauffé	(Re)heated	*nature/aux fines herbes*	plain/with herbs
Cuit	Cooked	*au fromage*	with cheese

Soups (*soupes*) and starters (*hors d'œuvres*)

Bisque	Shellfish soup	*Rouille*	Red pepper, garlic and saffron mayonnaise served with fish soup
Baudroie	Fish soup with vegetables, garlic and herbs		
Bouillabaisse	Soup with five fish and other bits to dip	*Velouté*	Thick soup, usually fish or poultry
Bouillon	Broth or stock		
Bourride	Thick fish soup with garlic, onions and tomatoes	**Starters**	
		Assiette	Plate of cold meats
Consommé	Clear soup	*anglaise*	
Pistou	Parmesan, basil and garlic paste or cream added to soup	*Crudités*	Raw vegetables with dressings
		Hors d'œuvres	Combination of the above
Potage	Thick vegetable soup	*variés*	plus smoked or marinated fish

Pasta (*pâtes*), pancakes (*crêpes*) and flans (*tartes*)

Pâtes fraîches	Fresh pasta	*Socca*	Thin chickpea flour pancake
Nouilles	Noodles	*Panisse*	Thick chickpea flour pancake
Raviolis	Pasta parcels of meat or chard, a Provençal, not Italian invention	*Pissaladière*	Tart of fried onions with anchovies and black olives
Crêpe au sucre	Pancake with sugar/eggs		
/aux œufs			

Fish (*poisson*), seafood (*fruits de mer*) and shellfish (*crustaces or coquillages*)...

Aiglefin	Small haddock or fresh cod	*Crabe*	Crab	*Maquereau*	Mackerel
		Crevettes grises	Shrimp	*Merlan*	Whiting
Anchois	Anchovies	*Crevettes roses*	Prawns	*Morue*	Salt cod
Amande de mer	Small sweet-tasting shell fish	*Daurade*	Sea bream	*Moules*	Mussels (with
		Écrevisse	Freshwater crayfish	*(marinière)*	shallots in white wine sauce)
Anguilles	Eels				
Araignée de mer	Spider fish	*Éperlan*	Smelt or whitebait	*Oursin*	Sea urchin
				Pageot	Sea bream
Baudroie	Monkfish or anglerfish	*Escargots*	Snails	*Palourdes*	Clams
		Favou(ille)	Tiny crab	*Poissons*	Fish from shore-
Barbue	Brill	*Flétan*	Halibut	*de roche*	line rocks
Bigourneau	Periwinkle	*Friture*	Assorted fried fish	*Poulpe*	Octopus
Brème	Bream			*Poutine*	Small river fish
Bulot	Whelk	*Gambas*	King prawns	*Praires*	Small clams
Cabillaud	Cod	*Girelle*	Type of crab	*Raie*	Skate
Calmar	Squid	*Grenouilles*	Frogs (legs)	*Rascasse*	Scorpion fish
Carrelet	Plaice	*(cuisses de)*		*Rouget*	Red mullet
Chapon de mer	Mediterranean fish (related to Scorpion fish)	*Grondin*	Red gurnard	*Rouquier*	Mediterranean eel
		Hareng	Herring		
		Homard	Lobster	*St-Pierre*	John Dory
		Huîtres	Oysters	*Saumon*	Salmon
Claire	Type of oyster	*Langouste*	Spiny lobster	*Sole*	Sole
Colin	Hake	*Langoustines*	Saltwater cray-fish (scampi)	*Telline*	Tiny clam
Congre	Conger eel			*Thon*	Tuna
Coques	Cockles	*Limande*	Lemon sole	*Truite*	Trout
Coquilles St-Jacques	Scallops	*Lotte de mer*	Monkfish	*Turbot*	Turbot
		Loup de mer	Sea bass	*Violet*	Sea squirt

... and fish terms

Aïoli	Garlic mayonnaise/or the dish when served with salt cod and vegetables	*Darne*	Fillet or steak
		En papillote	Cooked in foil
		Estocaficada	Stockfish stew with tomatoes, olives, peppers, garlic and onions
Anchoïade	Anchovy paste or sauce		
Arête	Fish bone		
Assiette de pêcheur	Assorted fish	*La douzaine*	A dozen
Béarnaise	Sauce of egg yolks, white wine, shallots and vinegar	*Frit*	Fried
		Friture	Deep-fried small fish
Beignets	Fritters	*Fumé*	Smoked
Bonne femme	With mushroom, parsley, potato and shallots	*Fumet*	Fish stock
		Gelée	Aspic
Brandade	Crushed cod with olive oil	*Gigot*	Baked fish pieces,
Colbert	Fried in egg with breadcrumbs	*de mer*	usually monkfish
Croûtons	Toasted bread, often rubbed with garlic, to dip or drop in fish soups	*Goujon*	Several types of small fish, also deep-fried pieces of larger fish coated in breadcrumbs

Meat (*viande*) and poultry (*volaille*)

Agneau (de pré-salé)	Lamb (grazed on salt marshes)	*Boudin noir*	Black pudding
		Caille	Quail
Andouille, andouillette	Tripe sausage	*Canard*	Duck
Bœuf	Beef	*Caneton*	Duckling
Bifteck	Steak	*Cervelle*	Brains
Boudin blanc	Sausage of white meats	*Châteaubriand*	Porterhouse steak

Meat (*viande*) and poultry (*volaille*) (cont)

Cheval	Horse meat	*Mouton*	Mutton
Contrefilet	Sirloin roast	*Museau de veau*	Calf's muzzle
Coquelet	Cockerel	*Oie*	Goose
Dinde, dindon,	Turkey of different	*Os*	Bone
dindonneau,	ages and genders	*Pintade*	Guinea fowl
Entrecôte	Ribsteak	*Porc, pieds de porc*	Pork, pig's trotters
Faux filet	Sirloin steak	*Poulet*	Chicken
Fricadelles	Meatballs	*Poussin*	Baby chicken
Foie	Liver	*Ris*	Sweetbreads
Foie gras	Fattened (duck/	*Rognons*	Kidneys
	goose) liver	*Rognons blancs*	Testicles
Gésier	Gizzard	*Sanglier*	Wild boar
Magret de canard	Duck breast	*Saucisson*	Dried sausage
Gibier	Game	*Steack*	Steak
Graisse	Fat	*Tête de veau*	Calf's head (in jelly)
Jambon	Ham	*Toro*	Bull meat
Langue	Tongue	*Tournedos*	Thick slices of fillet
Lapin, lapereau	Rabbit, young rabbit	*Travers de porc*	Spare ribs
Lard, lardons	Bacon, diced bacon	*Tripes*	Tripe
Lièvre	Hare	*Veau*	Veal
Merguez	Spicy, red sausage	*Venaison*	Venison

Meat and poultry terms – dishes . . .

Aïado	Roast shoulder of lamb, stuffed with garlic and other ingredients	*Coq au vin*	Chicken cooked until it falls off the bone with wine, onions, and mushrooms
Bœuf à la gardiane	Beef or bull meat stew with carrots, celery, onions, garlic and black olives, served with rice	*Gigot (d'agneau)*	Leg (of lamb)
		Grillade	Grilled meat
		Hâchis	Chopped meat or mince hamburger
Canard à l'orange	Roast duck with an orange-and-wine sauce	*Pieds et paquets*	Mutton or pork tripe and trotters
Canard périgourdin	Roast duck with prunes, pâté de foie gras and truffles	*Steak au poivre (vert/rouge)*	Steak in a black (green/red) peppercorn sauce
Cassoulet	A casserole of beans and meat	*Steak tartare*	Raw chopped beef, topped with a raw egg yolk
Choucroute	Pickled cabbage with peppercorns, sausages, bacon and salami		

. . . and terms

Blanquette, civet, daube, estouffade, hochepôt, navarin and ragoût	All are types of stew	*Épaule*	Shoulder
		Mariné	Marinated
		Médaillon	Round piece
		Pavé	Thick slice
Aile	Wing	*En croûte*	In pastry
Blanc	Breast or white meat	*Farci*	Stuffed
Broche	Spit-roasted	*Au feu de bois*	Cooked over wood fire
Brochette	Kebab	*Au four*	Baked
Carré	Best end of neck, chop or cutlet	*Garni*	With vegetables
Civit	Game stew	*Grillé*	Grilled
Confit	Meat preserve	*Marmite*	Casserole
Côte	Chop, cutlet or rib	*Mijoté*	Stewed
Cou	Neck	*Rôti*	Roast
Cuisse	Thigh or leg	*Sauté*	Lightly cooked in butter

... and terms (cont)

For steaks:

Bleu	Almost raw
Saignant	Rare
À point	Medium
Bien cuit	Well done
Très bien cuit	Very well cooked

Garnishes and sauces:

Américaine	White wine, Cognac and tomato
Arlésienne	With tomatoes, onions, aubergines, potatoes and rice
Au porto	In port
Auvergnat	With cabbage, sausage and bacon
Beurre blanc	Sauce of white wine and shallots, with butter
Bonne femme	With mushroom, bacon, potato and onions
Bordelaise	In a red wine, shallots and bone-marrow sauce
Boulangère	Baked with potatoes and onions
Bourgeoise	With carrots, onions, bacon, celery and braised lettuce
Chasseur	White wine, mushrooms and shallots
Châtelaine	With artichoke hearts and chestnut purée
Diable	Strong mustard seasoning
Forestière	With bacon and mushroom
Fricassée	Rich, creamy sauce
Galantine	Cold dish of meat in aspic
Mornay	Cheese sauce
Pays d'Auge	Cream and cider
Piquante	Gherkins or capers, vinegar and shallots
Provençale	Tomatoes, garlic, olive oil and herbs
Véronique	Grapes, wine and cream

Vegetables (*légumes*), herbs (*herbes*) and spices (*épices*), etc

Ail	Garlic	*Épinards*	Spinach	*Pélandron*	Type of string bean
Anis	Aniseed	*Épis de maïs*	Corn on the cob		
Artichaut	Artichoke	*Estragon*	Tarragon	*Persil*	Parsley
Asperges	Asparagus	*Fenouil*	Fennel	*Petits pois*	Peas
Avocat	Avocado	*Férigoule*	Thyme (in Provençal)	*Piment*	Pimento
Basilic	Basil			*Pois chiches*	Chickpeas
Betterave	Beetroot	*Fèves*	Broad beans	*Pois mange-tout*	Snow peas
Blette/bette	Swiss chard	*Flageolets*	White beans		
Cannelle	Cinnamon	*Fleur de courgette*	Courgette flower	*Pignons*	Pine nuts
Câpre	Caper			*Poireau*	Leek
Cardon	Cardoon, a beet related to artichoke	*Genièvre*	Juniper	*Poivron (vert, rouge)*	Sweet pepper (green, red)
		Gingembre	Ginger		
		Haricots	String (French)	*Pommes de terre*	Potatoes
Carotte	Carrot	*verts*	beans		
Céleri	Celery	*rouges*	kidney	*Radis*	Radishes
Champignons:	Mushrooms of	*beurres*	butter	*Raifort*	Horseradish
cèpes,	various kinds	*blancs*	white	*Riz*	Rice
chanterelles,		*Laitue*	Lettuce	*Romarin*	Rosemary
girolles, morilles		*Laurier*	Bay leaf	*Safran*	Saffron
Chou (rouge)	(Red) cabbage	*Lentilles*	Lentils	*Sarrasin*	Buckwheat
Choufleur	Cauliflower	*Maïs*	Corn	*Sauge*	Sage
Ciboulettes	Chives	*Marjoline*	Marjoram	*Serpolet*	Wild thyme
Concombre	Cucumber	*Menthe*	Mint	*Thym*	Thyme
Cornichon	Gherkin	*Navet*	Turnip	*Tomate*	Tomato
Échalotes	Shallots	*Oignon*	Onion	*Truffes*	Truffles
Endive	Chicory	*Panais*	Parsnip		

Dishes and terms

Beignet	Fritter	À la vapeur	Steamed
Farci	Stuffed	Je suis végétari-	I'm a vegetarian. Are
Gratiné	Browned with cheese or butter	en(ne). Il y a	there any non-meat
Jardinière	With mixed diced vegetables	quelques plats	dishes?
À la parisienne	Sautéed in butter (potatoes); with white wine sauce, and shallots	sans viande?	
		Biologique	Organic
À l'anglaise	Boiled	Raclette	Toasted cheese served with potatoes, gherkins and onions
À la grecque	Cooked in oil and lemon		
Râpé(e)s	Grated or shredded		
Pistou	Ground basil, olive oil, garlic and parmesan	Salad niçoise	Salad of tomatoes, radishes, cucumber, hard-boiled eggs, anchovies, onion, artichokes, green peppers, beans, basil and garlic (rarely as comprehensive, even in Nice)
Primeurs	Spring vegetables		
Salade verte	Lettuce with vinaigrette		
Gratin dauphinois	Potatoes baked in cream and garlic		
Mesclum	Salad combining several different leaves		
		Duxelles	Fried mushrooms and shallots with cream
Pommes château, fondantes	Quartered potatoes sautéed in butter	Fines herbes	Mixture of tarragon, parsley and chives
Pommes lyonnaise	Fried onions and potatoes	Frisé(e)	Curly
Ratatouille	Mixture of aubergine, courgette, tomatoes and garlic	Gousse d'ail	Clove of garlic
		Herbes de Provence	Mixture of bay leaf, thyme, rosemary and savory
Rémoulade	Mustard mayonnaise, sometimes with anchovies and gherkins, also salad of grated cerleriac with mayonnaise	Petits farcis	Stuffed tomatoes, aubergines, courgettes, peppers
		Tapenade	Olive and caper paste
Parmentier	With potatoes	Tomates à la provençale	Tomatoes baked with breadcrumbs, garlic and parsley
Sauté	Lightly fried in butter		

Fruits (*fruits*), nuts (*noix*) and honey (*miel*)

Abricot	Apricot	Marrons	Chestnuts
Acajou	Cashew nut	Melon	Melon
Amandes	Almonds	Miel de lavande	Lavender honey
Ananas	Pineapple	Mirabelles	Small yellow plums
Banane	Banana	Myrtilles	Bilberries
Brugnon, nectarine	Nectarine	Noisette	Hazelnut
		Noix	Nuts
Cacahouète	Peanut	Noix	Walnut
Cassis	Blackcurrants	Orange	Orange
Cérises	Cherries	Pamplemousse	Grapefruit
Citron	Lemon	Pastèque	Watermelon
Citron vert	Lime	Pêche (blanche)	(White) peach
Dattes	Dates	Pistache	Pistachio
Figues	Figs	Poire	Pear
Fraises (de bois)	Strawberries (wild)	Pomme	Apple
Framboises	Raspberries	Prune	Plum
Fruit de la passion	Passion fruit	Pruneau	Prune
Grenade	Pomegranate	Raisins	Grapes
Groseilles	Redcurrants	Reine-Claude	Greengage
Mangue	Mango		

. . . and terms

Agrumes	Citrus fruits
Beignet	Fritter
Compôte	Stewed fruit, sometimes just the juice
Coulis	Sauce of puréed fruit
Crème de marrons	Chestnut purée
Flambé	Set aflame in alcohol
Fougasse	Bread flavoured with orange flower water or almonds, can also be savoury
Frappé	Iced

Desserts (*desserts* or *entremets*), pastries (*pâtisseries*) and confectionery (*confiserie*)

Bombe	A moulded ice-cream dessert
Brioche	Sweet, high-yeast breakfast roll
Calissons	Almond sweets
Charlotte	Custard and fruit in lining of almond fingers
Chichis	Doughnuts shaped in sticks
Clafoutis	Heavy custard and fruit tart
Crème Chantilly	Vanilla-flavoured and sweetened whipped cream
Crème fraîche	Sour cream
Crème pâtissière	Thick eggy pastry-filling
Crêpes suzettes	Thin pancakes with orange juice and liqueur
Fromage blanc	Cream cheese
Gaufre	Waffle
Glace	Ice cream
Île flottante	Soft meringues floating on
œufs à la neige	custard
Macarons	Macaroons
Madeleine	Small sponge cake
Marrons	Chestnut purée and cream on a
Mont Blanc	rum-soaked sponge cake
Mousse au chocolat	Chocolate mousse
Nougat	Nougat
Palmiers	Caramelized puff pastries
Parfait	Frozen mousse, sometimes ice cream
Petit Suisse	A smooth mixture of cream and curds

Petits fours	Bite-sized cakes/pastries
Poires Belle Hélène	Pears and ice cream in chocolate sauce
Tarte Tropezienne	Sponge cake filled with custard cream topped with nuts
Tiramisu	Mascarpone cheese, chocolate and cream concoction
Truffes	Truffles
Yaourt, yogourt	Yoghurt

Terms:

Barquette	Small boat-shaped flan
Bavarois	Refers to the mould, could be a mousse or custard
Biscuit	A kind of cake
Chausson	Pastry turnover
Chocolat amer	Unsweetened chocolate
Coupe	A serving of ice cream
Crêpes	Pancakes
En feuilletage	In puff pastry
Fondant	Melting
Galettes	Buckwheat pancakes
Génoise	Rich sponge cake
Pâte	Pastry or dough
Sablé	Shortbread biscuit
Savarin	A filled, ring-shaped cake
Tarte	Tart
Tartelette	Small tart

Cheese (*Fromage*)

The cheeses produced in Provence are all either *chèvre* (made from goats' milk) or *brébis* (made from sheeps' milk). The most renowned are the *chèvres*, which include Banon, Picodon, Lou Pevre, Pelardon and Poivre d'Ain.

Le plateau de fromages is the cheeseboard, and bread, but not butter, is served with it. Some useful phrases: *une petite tranche de celui-ci* (a small piece of this one); *je peux le gouter?* (may I taste it?).

Basics

Pain	Bread	Huile	Oil	Vinaigre	Vinegar	Couteau	Knife
Beurre	Butter	Poivre	Pepper	Bouteille	Bottle	Cuillère	Spoon
Œufs	Eggs	Sel	Salt	Verre	Glass	Table	Table
Lait	Milk	Sucre	Sugar	Fourchette	Fork	L'addition	Bill

And one final note: always call the waiter or waitress Monsieur or Madame (Mademoiselle if a young woman). **Never** use garçon, no matter what you've been taught at school.

Many vegetarians swallow a few principles and start eating fish and shellfish on holiday. **Vegans**, however, should probably forget about eating in restaurants and plan to cook for themselves.

Wherever you can eat you can invariably drink and vice versa. **Drinking** is done at a leisurely pace whether it's as a prelude to food (*apéritif*), a sequel (*digestif*), or the accompaniment, and **cafés** are the standard places to do it. Every bar or café displays the full **price list**, usually without the fifteen per-cent service charge added, for drinks at the bar (*au comptoir*), sitting down (*la salle*), or sitting on the terrace (*la terrasse*) – each progressively more expensive. You pay when you leave and you can sit for hours over just one cup of coffee.

WINE

Wine is drunk at just about every meal or social occasion. *Vin de table* or *vin ordinaire* – **table wine** – is generally drinkable and always cheap. **A.O.C.** (*Appellation d'Origine Contrôlée*) wines are better quality and considerably more expensive: even buying direct from the vineyard you won't get a bottle of Châteauneuf-du-Pape for less than 60F, a Gigondas or Vacqueras for less than 45F or a Bandol for less than 35F. But there are plenty of Côtes du Ventoux, Côtes du Luberon and Côtes de Provence wines that can be bought for 15–20F a bottle. Restaurant mark-ups on A.O.C. wines can be outrageous.

The basic **wine terms** are: *brut*, very dry; *sec*, dry; *demi-sec*, sweet; *doux*, very sweet; *mousseux*, sparkling; *méthode champenoise*, mature and sparkling. There are grape varieties as well but the complexities of the subject take up volumes. A glass of wine is simply *un rouge, un rosé* or *un blanc*. If it is an A.O.C. wine you may have the choice of *un ballon* (round glass) or a smaller glass (*un verre*). *Un pichet* (a pitcher) is normally a quarter-litre.

The best way to **buy bottles** of wine is directly from the producers (*vignerons*), either at vineyards, at *Maisons* or *Syndicats du Vin* (representing a group of wine-producers), or at *Coopératifs Vinicoles* (wine-producer coops). At all these places (for which you'll find details in the Guide) you can sample the wines first. It's best to make clear at the start how much you want to buy (if it's only one or two bottles) and you will not be popular if you drink several glasses and then leave without making a purchase. The most economical option is to buy *en vrac* – which you can also do at some wine shops (*caves*) – taking an easily obtainable plastic five- or ten-litre container (usually sold on the premises) and getting it filled straight from the barrel. In cities supermarkets are the most economical places to buy your wine.

SPIRITS

Stronger alcohol is drunk from 5am as a pre-work fortifier, and then at any time through the day according to circumstance, though the national reputation for drunkenness has lost much of its truth. Cognac or Armagnac **brandies** and the dozens of *eaux de vie* (brandy distilled from fruit) and **liqueurs** are made with the same perfectionism as is applied to the cultivation of vines. Among less familiar names, try *Poire William* (pear brandy), *marc* (a spirit distilled from grape pulp), or just point to the bottle with the most attractive colour. Local specialities in Alpine

---

WINES OF PROVENCE

The most famous wine of the region is **Châteauneuf-du-Pape**, grown on the banks of the Rhône just north of Avignon. To the northwest, around the Dentelles, a clutch of villages have earned their own *appellations* within the Côtes du Rhône Villages region. They include the spicy and distinctive **Gigondas** and the sweet Muscat from **Beaumes-de-Venise**.

Further west are the light, drinkable but not particularly special wines of the Côtes du Ventoux and Côtes du Luberon.

Many of the vineyards in central Provence and along the coast were planted in World War I in order to supply, as speedily as possible, every French soldier with his ration of a litre a day. In the last 25 years, as the money to be made from property has soared, wine producers have had to up their quality in order for vineyards to compete with building as a profitable use of land. The Côtes de Provence *appellation* now has some excellent wines, in particular the rosés around the Massif des Maures.

The best of the coastal wines come from **Bandol**, with some gorgeous dusky reds; **Cassis** too has its own *appellation*; and around Nice the **Bellet** wines are worth discovering.

areas include herb liqueurs that go by various names, and *gentiane*, distilled from the flower. Measures are generous, but they don't come cheap: the same applies for imported spirits like whisky, often called Scotch.

The aniseed drink **pastis**, served with ice (*glaçons*) and water is a Provençal invention and one of the most popular **aperitifs** of the region. Pastis 51, Ricard and Pernod are all common brands whose names adorn every other glass and ashtray in Provence.

Cocktails are served at most late-night bars, discos and music places, as well as at upmarket hotel bars.

BEERS AND SOFT DRINKS

The familiar light Belgian and German brands, plus French brands from Alsace, account for most of the **beer** you'll find in Provence. Draught beer (*à la pression*, usually Kronenbourg) is the cheapest drink you can have next to coffee, wine and pastis – ask for *un demi* (1/3 litre). For a wider choice of draught and bottled beer you need to go to the special beer-drinking establishments or English-style pubs found in most coastal cities.

On the **soft drink** front, you can buy cartons of unsweetened fruit juice in supermarkets, although in the cafés the bottled (sweetened) nectars such as apricot (*jus d'abricot*) and blackcurrant (*cassis*) still hold sway. You can also get fresh orange and lemon juice (*orange/citron pressé*) – at a price. Otherwise there's the standard canned lemonade, cola (*coca*) and so forth.

Bottles of **spring water** (*eau minérale*) – either sparkling (*pétillante*) or still (*eau plate*) – are readily available, from the big brand names to the obscurest spa product. But there's not much wrong with the tap water (*l'eau du robinet*).

COFFEE AND TEA

Coffee is invariably espresso and very strong. *Un café* or *un express* is black; *une crème* is with milk; *un grand café* or *une grand crème* is a large cup. In the morning you could also ask for *un café au lait* – espresso in a large cup or bowl filled up with hot milk. *Un déca* (decaf) is widely available.

Ordinary **tea** (*thé*) is usually Lipton's; to have milk with it, ask for *un peu de lait frais* (some fresh milk). **Herb teas** (*infusions* or *tisanes*), served in every café, can be soothing; the more common ones are *verveine* (verbena), *tilleul* (lime blossom), *menthe* (mint) and camomile. *Chocolat chaud* – **hot chocolate** – lives up to the high standards of French fare and can be had in any café.

POST AND PHONES

French **post offices** – *postes* or *PTT*s – are generally open Mon–Fri 9am–noon and 2–5pm & Sat 9am–noon. Don't depend on these hours, though: in the larger towns you'll find a main office open throughout the day (usually 8am–8pm), while in the villages, lunch hours and closing times can vary enormously.

You can **receive mail** at any post office; it should be addressed (preferably with the surname underlined and in capitals) **Poste Restante**, followed by the name of the town and its postcode, detailed in the Guide for all the main cities. To collect your mail you need a passport or other verifiable ID and there may be a charge of around a couple of francs. You should ask for all your names to be checked, as filing systems are not brilliant.

For **sending letters**, the quickest international service is by *aérogramme*, sold at all post offices. You can buy ordinary stamps (*timbres*) at any *tabac* (tobacconist). If you're sending **parcels** abroad, try to check prices in various leaflets available: small *postes* don't often send foreign mail and may need reminding, for example, of the reductions for printed papers and books. **Faxes** can be sent and received from all main post offices and from many newsagents, though receiving a number of pages can work out to be quite expensive: the official French word is *télécopie*, but everyone understands *fax*.

You can make domestic and international phone calls from any telephone box (or *cabine*) and can receive calls where there's a blue logo of a ringing bell. Most call boxes only take **phone cards** (*télécartes*), obtainable from post offices, FNAC shops, train stations and some *tabacs*; the cheapest card is 40F for 50 units. Many call boxes also take credit cards. **Coin-only** boxes can still be found in cafés, bars and rural areas and take 1F, 2F, 5F and 10F pieces; put the money in after lifting up the receiver and before dialling. You can keep adding more coins once you are connected. You can also make calls from **booths at main post offices**. You apply at the counter to be assigned a number and then dial. The disadvantage with these – odd considering the French obsession with technology – is that you can't tell how much you're spending. It's worth counting your units and checking – mistakes are sometimes made.

For **calls** within France – local or long distance – simply dial all ten digits of the number.

Cheap rates operate between 7pm and 8am on weekdays, after noon on Saturday and all day Sunday. A local six-minute call will cost around 60 centimes.

The major **international calling codes** are given in the box below; remember to omit the initial 0 of the local area code from the subscriber's number. **Calling cards** available in Britain for use all over the world, tend to be an expensive option. The cheapest way to call home from France is to buy a pre-paid calling card once you're in France; there's a whole host of telecommunications companies offering cheap international phone calls, with cards starting at 50F and available from *tabacs*. You dial a free number, your account number and then the number you wish to call. The drawback is that the free number is often engaged and you have to dial a great many digits.

To avoid payment altogether, you can, of course, make a reverse-charge or **collect call** – known in French as "*téléphoner en PCV*". You can also do this through the operator in the UK, by

---

TELEPHONING

IDD CODES

From France dial ☎00 + IDD code + area code minus first 0 + subscriber number

Britain ☎44   Ireland ☎353   USA and Canada ☎1   Australia ☎61   New Zealand ☎64

From Britain to Provence: dial ☎00 33 + subscriber number minus the first 0
(this should then be a nine-digit number)

From the USA and Canada to Provence: dial ☎011 33 + eight-digit number

From Australia to Provence: dial ☎011 33 + eight-digit number

From New Zealand to Provence: dial ☎044 33 + eight-digit number

From Provence to Paris: dial ☎16/1 + number

TIME

France is one hour ahead of British time, except for a short period during October, when it's the same. It is six hours ahead of New York, and nine hours behind Sydney. This also applies during daylight savings seasons from the end of March to the end of September.

USEFUL NUMBERS WITHIN FRANCE

Telegrams By phone: internal ☎36.55; external ☎08.00.33.44.11 (all languages).

Time ☎36.99.

International operator For Canada and US ☎01; for all other countries ☎08.00.99.00 followed by IDD number.

International directory assistance For Canada and US ☎001 + area code + 555-1212; for all other countries ☎00.33.12 followed by IDD number.

French operator ☎10.13.

French directory assistance ☎12.

dialling ☎08.00.99.00.44 and asking for a "reverse-charge call". To get an English-speaking AT&T operator for North America, dial ☎08.00.99.00.11.

Some British **mobile phones** will work in Provence.

MINITEL

Phone subscribers in most French cities have a **minitel**, an on-line computer allowing access through the phone lines to all kinds of directories, databases, chat lines, etc. You will also find them in post offices. Most organizations, from sports federations to government institutions to gay groups, have a code consisting of numbers and letters to call up information, leave messages and make reservations. Dial the number on the phone, wait for a fax-type tone, then type the letters on the keyboard, and finally, press *Connexion Fin* (the same key ends the connection). If you're at all computer literate and can understand basic keyboard terms in French (*retour* – return, *envoi* – enter, etc), you shouldn't find them hard to use; but be warned that most services cost more than phone rates.

THE MEDIA

Most **British newspapers** plus the *International Herald Tribune*, are on sale in the large cities and resorts the day after publication.

Of the national **French daily papers** *Le Monde* is the most respected, with no concessions to entertainment (such as pictures) but a correctly styled French that is probably the easiest to understand. *Libération* is moderately left-wing, independent and more colloquial, with good, if choosy, coverage.

Regional newspapers enjoy much higher circulation than the Paris nationals and, though not brilliant for news, are useful for listings. The right-wing *La Provence* and the very tabloid *Nice Matin* are the two big ones in Provence, followed by *Var-Matin* and *Le Dauphiné Vaucluse*. There's also *La Marseillaise* (available everywhere except the Alpes-Maritimes *département*) which originated as a Resistance paper during the war, and is firmly left-wing.

National weeklies include the wide-ranging and left-leaning *Nouvel Observateur* and its right-wing counterpart *L'Express*. The best and funniest investigative journalism is in the weekly satirical paper, *Le Canard Enchaîné*. *Charlie Hebdo* is a sort of *Private Eye* or *Spy Magazine* equivalent. For really in-depth analysis of national and international events and trends there's the **monthly** independent *Le Monde Diplomatique* or *Le Monde*'s own monthly *Le Monde Dossiers Documents*.

The *Riviera Reporter* is a free **English-language magazine** with a mix of culture and politics, which you can pick up at any of the English bookshops on the Riviera. A newish French cultural magazine for the Alpes-Maritimes is *Le Pitchoun*, available free from cultural venues and bookshops.

French TV broadcasts six channels, three of them public, along with a good many more cable and satellite channels, which include CNN and the BBC World Service. The main French TV **news** is at 8pm on TF1 and Antenne 2. Arte, the fifh channel (after 7pm), shows undubbed movies. Best French documentaries are on the cable channel Planète.

If you've got a **radio**, you can tune into English-language news on the BBC World Service between 6.195 and 12.095MHz shortwave at intervals throughout the day and night. The Voice of America transmits on 90.5, 98.8 and 102.4FM. For **news** in French, there are the state-run France Inter (97.40 MHz), Europe 1 (FM 94.9) or round-the-clock news on France Infos (FM 105.2). **Local radio stations** include the English-language Riviera Radio (FM106.3 and 106.5) with news at 6–7am and 11am, and the BBC World Service overnight.

BUSINESS HOURS AND PUBLIC HOLIDAYS

Almost everything – shops, museums, tourist offices and most banks – closes for a couple of hours at midday. The basic working hours are 8am to noon and 2 to 6pm, with shops usually open till 7pm. In summer the midday break often extends to 3pm.

There is of course some variation. **Food shops** often don't reopen till halfway through the afternoon, closing just before dinner time between 7.30 and 8pm. Sunday and Monday are the standard closing days; in villages you may not even find a single *boulangerie* (bakery) open. **Banks** close at 4pm and in small towns may be closed on Monday. Small hotels often close on Sunday or Monday, restaurants likewise.

Museums and monuments tend to open at around 10am and close between 5 and 6pm. Summer times may differ from winter times; if they do, both are indicated in the listings through the book. Don't forget **closing days** – usually Tuesday or Monday, sometimes both.

Churches and cathedrals are almost always open all day, with charges only for the crypt, treasuries or cloister and little fuss about how you're dressed. Where they are closed you may have to take a look during Mass on Sunday morning or

PUBLIC HOLIDAYS

There are thirteen national holidays (*jours fériés*), when most shops and businesses, though not all museums or restaurants, are closed. They are:

January 1
Easter Sunday
Easter Monday
Ascension Day (40 days after Easter)
Whitsun (seventh Sunday after Easter, plus the Monday)
May 1 (May Day)
May 8 (Victory in Europe Day)
July 14 (Bastille Day)
August 15 (Assumption of the Virgin Mary)
November 1 (All Saints' Day)
November 11 (1918 Armistice Day)
Christmas Day

   Monaco, in addition to the above, takes days off on January 27 (Fête de Ste-Dévote) and November 19 (Fête Nationale Monégasque).

during other services for which times are usually posted up on the door. In small towns and villages, however, getting the key is not difficult – ask anyone nearby or hunt out the priest, whose house is known as the *presbytère*.

CULTURE AND FESTIVALS

Every town of any size in Provence or on the Côte d'Azur has its summer festival season, commonly called *Les Estivales*, which, more

often than not, is pure tourist hype, bearing little or no relation to local customs or history. In the Camargue and the Crau, however, and throughout inland Provence, particularly in the remoter mountain areas, there are numerous small-scale fêtes which are genuine manifestations of traditional village life. The region continues to attract visual artists and their customers; the other arts, though not so dominant, are well catered for in the long-established festivals and in the theatres, opera houses and concert venues of the major cities.

THE ARTS

Marseille is the city for **all-round culture**, from classic theatre to experimental performance,

SANTONS

Santons are painted pottery Christmas nativity figures, a speciality of Provence. Their uniqueness is in representing not just the holy family and shepherds but every nineteenth-century village character. So you'll have the olive-oil presser, the wine grower, the butcher, baker, soap maker and market gardener, women baking and carrying water, a gypsy band, plus the priest and mayor and even groups of *pétanque* players, all in imaculate detail. The figures are about 12cm high and their setting is a Provençal village with model houses, hillsides of pebbles and moss, twig vines and lime trees. In Aubagne, one of the main centres of *santon* art along with Aix and Marseille where they originated, scenes from Pagnol's novels are represented with *santons*.

You can visit *santonnier* workshops, see displays in museums or special exhibitions, attend the great *santon* fair in Marseille, or buy them from every craft and souvenir shop.

major art retrospectives to contemporary photography, video and multi-media, opera and acid jazz, plus football, political demonstrations and street happenings.

Avignon and Aix are the next most innovative cities on the arts front. Like Marseille they have their own resident theatre companies and orchestras; the most renowned **drama and dance festival** in France takes place in **Avignon** with a large fringe component; and Aix has dance, contemporary music (including rock and jazz) festivals, and an excellent new cultural centre, the Cité du Livre. Monaco, like Nice, Avignon and Marseille, has its own opera house and attracts world-class musicians; it also hosts a circus festival. **Juan-les-Pins** has the best **jazz festival**, closely followed by Nice; Châteauvallon near **Toulon** is famous for **dance** and **Orange** for its **classical music festival** in the Roman theatre. Classical concerts are performed in many churches, often with free or very cheap admission; **Menton** has one of the most beautiful outdoor venues for its **festival of chamber music**.

Cinema is treated very seriously. The **Cannes film festival** has the highest status, both nationally and internationally; it is, though, very much a credentials-only event. Better to try the Festival of Cinema in **La Ciotat** where the techniques of film-making were originated by the Lumière brothers in 1895. On a day-to-day level, there are good cinemas throughout Provence and the Côte d'Azur where you can see undubbed **foreign films** (*version originale* or *v.o.*).

But of all the arts, it's **painting, sculpture** and **ceramics** that Provence is most famous for; as well as all the superb art collections and exhibitions there are also numerous **art galleries** in the cities and coastal villages.

All the major cultural festivals are described in the Guide with details of where to get programme information and make bookings. For full listings, try the local **listings magazines**, available free from the tourist offices: the best ones are *Taktik*, which covers Marseille, Aix and the rest of the Bouches-du-Rhône; *César*, covering Avignon to Arles; and *Scènes d'Azur* gives wide coverage of the Alpes-Maritimes (available from cultural venues and bookshops). Otherwise the local papers, which have separate sections for the different areas, will be your best bet. The regional tourist office's magazine *Provence-Alpes-Côte d'Azur* is good for an overall round-up of events and where to go. Annual brochures *Musées Galeries d'Art Côte d'Azur* and *Itinéraire Officiel de l'Art*, available from most of the Riviera tourist offices, list all the art museums, galleries and the big art exhibitions.

TRADITIONAL FESTIVALS

Special days celebrate **wine-making, transhumance** (the movement of sheep between their winter and summer pastures), **olive** and other **harvests** – chestnuts, lavender, jasmine, for example. Plus there are one or two annual **village festivals**, for which local pipe bands, children in traditional costumes and the church with all its medieval superstitions trappings process to various shrines. These days they culminate with a beanfeast, much drinking and the sense of age-old community duly reaffirmed. Ever since the poet **Frédéric Mistral** and friends started the Provençal revival in the nineteenth century, these local traditions have been kept going, not as tourist attractions and not entirely as photo-opportunities for the mayor. Their original meanings may have lost relevance, but they're still a real part of contemporary village life, and fun. As an outsider, the events may just look quaint but watching people enjoy themselves can be a pleasure in itself and the festive spirit usually induces extra hospitality.

CALENDAR OF EVENTS

Dates change fom year to year so it's always worth checking with local tourist offices.

January
Circus Festival (sometimes held in Dec or Feb) – Monaco

Monte-Carlo Car Rally (end of month) – Monaco

Science Festival (last week) – Cavaillon

February
Classical Music Festival (end of Feb to March) – Cannes

Dance Festival (end of Feb to beginning of March) – Avignon

Lemon Festival (end of Feb to March) – Menton

Mardi Gras Carnival (week before Lent) – Nice

Mimosa Procession (third Sun) – Bormes

Olive Oil Festival (first Sun) – Nyons

March
Dance Festival – Cannes

April
Arts Festival (mid-April to mid-May) – Monaco

Fête des Gardians (bull and horse herdsmen; last Sun in month to May 1) – Arles

Ski Grand Prix – Isola 2000

Tennis Open – Monaco

Tennis Open – Nice

Wine Festival (25) – Châteauneuf-du-Pape

May
Arts Festival (end of May to mid-July) – Châteauvallon

Film Festival (second week) – Cannes

Formula 1 Grand Prix (Ascension weekend) – Monte-Carlo

Gypsy Festival (24–25) – Les Stes-Maries-de-la-Mer

Processions (May 16–18 & June 15) – St-Tropez

Rose Festival (second weekend) – Grasse

June
Bottle procession (1) – Boulbon

Cinema Festival (mid-June) – La Ciotat

Classical Music Festival – Vence

Comedians Festival – Cannes

Contemporary Music Festival (mid-June to first week July) – Aix

Dance Festival – Châteauvallon

Dance, Music, Folklore and Theatre Festival (end of June and beginning of July) – Arles

Fête de St-Jean (24)

Jazz and Chamber Music Festival (last 2 weeks) – Aix

Music Festival (Whitsun) – Apt

Sacred Music Festival – Nice

Sculpture Symposium (last 2 weeks) – Digne

Tarasque Festival (last full weekend) – Tarascon

Transhumance Festival (Whit Monday) – St-Rémy

Transhumance Festival (last weekend of month) – St-Étienne-de-Tinée

Triathalon (beginning of month) – Nice

July
Bastille Day (14)

Chorègies (operatic and choral music; mid-July to early Aug) – Orange

Dance Festival (mid-month) – Aix

Fête de St-Éloi (second Sun or penultimate Sun) – Graveson, Châteaurenard and Maillane

Firework Festival (July & Aug) – Monaco

Folklore Festival – Nice

Food Festival (around third weekend) – Carpentras

Gypsy Festival (mid-month) – Arles

Jazz Festival (last 2 weeks) – Juan-les-Pins

Jazz Festival (first 2 weeks) – Nice

Jazz Festival (third week) – Salon

Music Nights in the Citadel (end of July and beginning Aug) – Sisteron

Music, Theatre and Dance Festival – Carpentras

Olive Festival (weekend before July 14) – Nyons

Opera and Music Festival (mid-July to mid-Aug) – Aix

Painting Festival – Cagnes-sur-Mer

Photography Show (second week) – Arles

Provençal Festival (end July to early Aug) – Avignon and neighbouring towns

Sorgue Festival of music, theatre and dance – L'Isle-sur-la-Sorgue and neighbouring villages

Theatre, Dance and Music Festival plus Fringe Festival (mid-July to early Aug) – Avignon

Theatre, Dance and Music Festival – Marseille

Theatre, Jazz and Classical Music Festival (last 2 weeks) – Gordes

Theatre, Music and Art Festival (mid-July to end Aug) – Apt

CALENDAR OF EVENTS (CONT)

Theatre, Music and Art Festival (mid-July to end Aug) – Vaison

Venetian Festival (first Sat) – Martigues

Wine Festival (14) – Vacqueyras

August

Chamber Music Festival – Menton

Garlic Festival (end of month) – Poilenc

Graphic Arts (last week) – Lurs

Harvest Festival (15) – St-Rémy

Haute-Provence Festival (first 2 weeks; arts and crafts) – Forcalquier and neighbouring villages

Jasmine Festival (first Sun) – Grasse

Lavender Festival (end of month) – Digne

Square *Boules* championship – Cagnes-sur-Mer

September

Rice Harvest (mid-month) – Arles

Sheep Fair – Guillaumes

October

Sea procession and blessing (Sun nearest to 22) – Les Stes-Maries-de-la-Mer

November

Côtes du Rhône wine festival – Avignon

Santons Fair (last Sun to end of Dec) – Marseille

December

Provencal Midnight Mass (24) – Aix, Les Baux, Fontveille, Lucéram, St-Michel-de-Frigolet, St-Rémy, Ste-Baume, Séguret, Tarascon

Wine and Traditions Festival (first Sun) – Séguret

The Tarasque festival in **Tarascon** is a good one for kids. The gathering of the gypsies in **Les Stes-Maries-de-la-Mer** is one of the strangest and most exciting: it attracts vast crowds and, these days, a heavy police presence. The **folklore festivals** of Arles and Nice have rather more commercial origins, but can be very enjoyable nonetheless.

Bonfires are lit and fireworks set off for **Bastille Day** and for the **Fête de St Jean** on June 24, three days from the summer solstice. **May Day** is also commonly celebrated. **Mardi Gras** – the last blow-out before Lent – is far less of an occasion than in other Roman Catholic countries, and where it is celebrated – in Nice and other Riviera towns – it's designed for commercial interests and municipal prestige.

Finally, at **Christmas**, Mass is celebrated in many Provençal churches, with real shepherds offering real sheep, and the crib scene enacted by parishioners in traditional garb. A thirteen-course non-meat supper is traditionally served on Christmas Eve.

You'll find details of the most popular events as well as many small, lower-key traditional festivities throughout the Guide.

SPORTS AND OUTDOOR ACTIVITIES

Football is the most popular spectator sport in Provence, with motor racing famous in Monaco and enthusiasm over cycle races as great as in the rest of France. The most typically Provençal competitive pastime is *pétanque*. Outdoor activities in the region include hang-gliding, skiing, all types of water sport, climbing and mountain trekking.

SPECTATOR SPORTS

On every town or village square in Provence, in every park, or sometimes in a specially built arena, you'll see *pétanque*, the Provençal version of *boules*, being played. The principle is the same as bowls but the terrain is always rough, never grass, and the area much smaller. The metal ball is usually thrown upwards from a distance of 10m or a little more, to land and skid towards the marker (*cochonnet*). In Provence, uniquely, the players are allowed to move as they "point" (the first throw) or "aim" (the adversary's throw). There are café or village teams, endless championships, and, on the whole, it's very male-dominated.

The spectator sport most passionately followed in Provence is *le foot* – **football**. The best team is Olympique de Marseille; after a few setbacks, including a conviction for cheating in a European match, the club was bought by Adidas and is back in the First Division and the UEFA European Cup. Marseille has spawned two famous football players: Eric Cantona and, the national hero after the French victory in the World Cup in 1998, Zinedine Zidane.

The **Tour de France** cycling race in July generally has a stage in Provence; as does the **Paris–Nice** race in March. Cycling combined with running and swimming brings in the crowds for Nice's and Antibes' **triathalons**.

In and around the **Camargue**, the number-one sport is **bullfighting** (described in the Guide on p.104). Though not to everyone's taste it is at least considerably less gruesome than the variety practised by the Spanish.

The famous **Formula One Grand Prix** takes place in Monaco and some of the remote inland routes are used for **rally-driving**. Monaco and Nice also host international **Tennis Open** championships.

PARTICIPATORY SPORTS

Water sports on the **Côte d'Azur** are practised on the whole for the glamour factor rather than for competition. The waters and winds of the Mediterranean are far too temperate to exercise high-powered sailing or windsurfing skills. But for learning and just playing about in the warm water, it's potentially ideal. The problem, though, is congestion, and no one following the rules of the water. So beware the madcap jet skiers and power-boat racers. The other great drawback is inevitably the cost of renting the equipment. Every resort has several outlets – for sailing, windsurfing, water-skiing, wet-biking, scuba-diving – so you can shop around for the best prices, but it will still take a major chunk out of your budget, and prices go up every year.

Airborne sports, particularly **hang-gliding**, are extremely popular in Provence. Fayence is the main centre for **gliding** and St-André-les-Alpes one of many places with an excellent hang-gliding centre. *Baptêmes* (initiations) are not too expensive.

More and more health-conscious holiday-makers are taking to **trekking** in the mountains, with most ski resorts now catering for summer activities – like pony-trekking and climbing – in a big way. The main areas for **climbing** are the Alps, the Dentelles and the Luberon; contact the Club Alpin Français, 14 av Mirabeau, Nice (☎04.93.62.59.99) or 7 rue St-Michel, Avignon (☎04.90.82.34.82) for more information.

Horse-riding is catered for by numerous *Centres Equestres* throughout Provence, particularly in the Camargue. Normally what's offered is an accompanied ride in a group but there are some places where you can gallop off on your own; tourist offices will be able to supply more details.

The rivers and artificial lakes of Provence also provide opportunities for **canoeing**, **rafting**, and more gently paddling about in **boats**, windsurfing and yachting. Details of helpful organizations and centres catering for these pursuits are given in the Guide.

Skiing – whether downhill, cross-country or mountaineering – is enthusiastically pursued in Provence. There are over a dozen ski-resorts within two hours' drive of the coast, the three

All the Comités Départementals de Tourisme (CDT's), the departmental tourist boards, produce helpful brochures on all leisure activities, with useful addresses of specialist organizations. The big city tourist offices are likely to have these, or you can go to the CDT office for more detailed information. Addresses are:

Alpes-de-Haute-Provence: 19 rue du Dr-Honnorat, Digne (☎04.92.31.57.29).

Alpes-Maritimes: 55 Promenade des Anglais, Nice (☎04.93.37.78.78).

Bouches-du-Rhône: 13 rue Roux de Brignoles, Marseille (☎04.91.13.84.13).

Hautes-Alpes: 2 rue de Béal, Gap (☎04.92.51.03.41).

Var: 5 av Vauban, Toulon (☎04.94.09.00.69).

Vaucluse: 12 rue Collège de la Croix, Avignon; (☎04.90.80.47.00).

biggest being **Auron**, **Valberg** and **Isola 2000**, though recent weather changes have affected snowfalls in the lower Alps. It can be an expensive sport to pursue on your own and the Provence resorts are rarely covered by the international package operators, though some, like La Foux d'Allos, are much cheaper in terms of ski-lift charges than the higher resorts north of Provence. Local deals are available; the Comités

Départementals de Tourisme in Digne or Nice (see box above) and the Club Alpin Français (14 av Mirabeau, Nice; ☎04.93.62.59.99) will be the best sources of information.

Finally, two highly promoted activities of the Côte d'Azur, one with a long history and potentially ruinous, the other newly fashionable and environmentally suspect, are **gambling** and **golf**.

TROUBLE AND THE POLICE

Petty theft is endemic along the Côte d'Azur and pretty bad in the crowded hangouts of the big cities. It makes sense to take the normal precautions: don't wave money or travellers' cheques around; carry your bag or wallet securely; and never let cameras and other valuables out of your sight. But the best security of all is having a good insurance policy and keeping a separate record of cheque numbers, credit card numbers and the phone numbers for cancelling them, and the relevant details of all your valuables.

Drivers face the greatest problems, most notoriously break-ins – though having your vehicle stolen, particularly in Nice or Marseille, is not uncommon. It's always best to park overnight in guarded car parks; where that's not possible try to park in a busy street or in front of a police station. Never leave anything in the boot and remove your tapedeck if you can. It's not just foreign number plates that attract thieves; rented cars are also favourite prey.

If you need to **report a theft**, go along to the local *commissariat de police* (addresses are given for all the main cities), and make sure you get the requisite piece of paper for a claim. The first thing they'll ask for is your passport, and vehicle documents if relevant.

If you have an **driving accident**, officially you have to fill in and sign a *constat à l'aimable* (jointly agreed statement); car insurers should give you this with a policy, though in practice few seem to have heard of it. For non-criminal

EMERGENCIES
Ambulance ☎15
Police ☎17
Fire Service ☎18
Note: It's common for the fire brigade, les sapeurs pompiers, to be called for medical problems; they all have paramedical training and equipment.

driving violations such as speeding, the police can impose an on-the-spot fine. If you don't have the necessary cash you could find yourself passing several unpleasant hours at the police station.

By law you are supposed to carry ID with you at all times and the police have the right to stop and ask to see it.

COMMITTING CRIMES

Camping outside authorized sites can bring you into contact with the authorities, though it's more likely to be the landowner who tells you to move off. Police have been known to stalk the beaches, sweating in their uniforms, telling everyone to cover up their bottom halves and in Cannes there are on-the-spot fines for toplessness on the street, but there's no equivalent of the British public decency laws. **Topless sunbathing** is universally acceptable; nudity is in principle limited to specifically naturist beaches.

More seriously, anyone caught smuggling or possessing **drugs**, even a few grammes of marijuana, is liable to find themself in jail and consulates will not be sympathetic. This is not to say that hard-drug consumption isn't a visible activity: there are scores of kids dealing in *poudre* (heroin) in Marseille and Nice and the authorities are unable to do much about it.

Should you be arrested on any charge, you have the right to contact your consulate (see "Listings" for Marseille, Nice or Monaco).

RACIAL AND SEXUAL HARASSMENT

The large industrial cities of Provence and the Côte d'Azur towns have the highest proportion of extreme right-wing voters in France. **Racist attitudes** in the populace and the police are rife. Being black, or particularly if you are Arab or look as if you might be, makes your chances of avoiding unpleasantness very low. Hotels claiming to be booked up, police demanding your papers, and abuse from ordinary people is horribly frequent. In addition, even entering the country can be difficult. Changes in passport regulations have put an end to outright refusal to let some British holidaymakers in, but customs and immigration officers can still be obstructive and malicious. In North-African-dominated areas of cities, identity checks by the police are very common and not pleasant. If you suffer a racial assault, you're likely to get a much more sympathetic hearing from your consulate than from the police. The national antiracism organization, Ligue Internationale Contre le Racisme et Anti-Semitisme (LICRA), has an office in Marseille at 46 rue Ste-Victoire, ☎04.91.81.59.69.

Sexual harassment is generally no worse or more vicious than anywhere else, but it can be a problem making judgements about situations without the familiar linguistic and cultural signs. A "*Bonjour*" or "*Bonsoir*" on the street is usually a pick-up line. If you return the greeting, you've left yourself open to a persistent monologue and a difficult brush-off job. On the other hand, topless bathing doesn't usually invite bother and it's quite common, if you're on your own, to be offered a drink in a bar and not to be pestered even if you accept. Hitching is a risk, though some women do hitch alone in the more built-up areas of the Côte d'Azur.

If you need help, go to the police, although don't expect too much from them. The *mairie/hôtel de ville* (town hall) will have addresses of women's organizations (Femmes Battues, Femmes en Détresse or SOS Femmes), though this won't be much help outside business hours. The national **rape crisis** number, Viol Femme Information, is ☎08.00.05.95.95 (Mon–Fri 10am–6pm), but it may not have English speakers. Again your consulate may be the best source of sympathetic assistance.

GAYS AND LESBIANS

France is more liberal on homosexuality than most other European countries. The legal age of consent is fifteen and, in general, the French consider sexuality to be a private matter.

The dominance of extreme-right sympathies in many parts of Provence, however, means gays tend to be discreet. Marseille is the only place where gay and lesbian pride is celebrated, though Nice has a thriving gay club scene. As in many Mediterranean cultures, physical contact between women or men is seen as "natural" but kissing in public may raise hackles. Addresses for clubs and bars are listed in the Guide – mainly in Marseille, Nice and Aix.

GAY CONTACTS AND INFORMATION

Centre Gai et Lesbien, 3 rue Keller, Paris 11e (☎01.43.57.21.47; Mᵒ Ledru-Rollin). A gay and lesbian community centre. They also run a gay doctors' association ☎01.48.05.81.71.

David & Jonathan, 92 bis rue Picpus, Paris 12e (☎01.43.42.09.49; Mᵒ Michel-Bizot). 24hr answerphone for gay Christians.

Maison des Femmes, 163 rue de Charenton, Paris 12e (☎01.43.43.41.13; Mᵒ Reuilly-Diderot). Run by Paris Féministe, this is the home of the Groupe des Lesbiennes Féministes and the Mouvement d'Information et d'Expression des Lesbiennes, ARCL (Archives, Recherches et Cultures Lesbiennes). A cafeteria operates on Friday nights (8pm–midnight), and there are occasional events organized.

Minitel. 3615 GPS is the Minitel number to dial for information on groups, contacts, messages, etc. The service was set up by _Gai Pied_. There are also any number of chat lines.

Gay media

Radio FG (98.2 FM). 24hr gay and lesbian radio station with music, news, chat, information on groups and events.

Illico. A monthly with lonely hearts and Minitel numbers.

Lesbia. The most widely available lesbian publication, available from most newsagents. Each monthly issue features a wide range of articles, listings, reviews, lonely hearts and contacts.

Spartacus International Gay Guide. Guidebook focusing mainly on gay travel in Europe.

Têtu. Gay monthly magazine with intelligent, wide-ranging articles.

Gay/lesbian travel contacts

Detour Guides, 1016 3rd Ave, Sacramento, CA 95818 (☎916/448-4120). Series covers London, Paris, Amsterdam and several American cities.

Different Drummer Tours, PO Box 528, Glen Ellyn, IL 60137 (☎1-800/645-1275). Scheduled and customized international tours.

Different Strokes Tours, 1841 Broadway, New York, NY 10023 (☎1-800/688-3301). Customized international tours.

International Gay Travel Association, PO Box 4974, Key West, FL 33041 (☎1-800/448-8550 or 305/292-0217). Trade group that can provide a list of gay-owned or gay-friendly travel agents, accommodation and other travel businesses.

Man Around Ltd, 89 Wembley Park Drive, Wembley, Middlesex HA9 8HS (☎0181/902 7177). Gay tour operator.

WORK AND STUDY

Temporary agricultural work in Provence and the Côte d'Azur is hard to come by and, in summer, catering work or work in the tourist industry is a better bet. For longer-term employment, au-pair positions and English teaching are distinct possibilities if you take time to plan and make contact in advance.

If you're looking for something secure, it's important to plan well in advance. The best **general sources for all jobs in France** are the publications *Summer Jobs Abroad* (Vacation Work, 9 Park End St, Oxford, UK), *Work Your Way Around the World* (Vacation Work, 1507 Dana Ave, Cincinnati, Ohio, USA) and *1000 Pistes de Jobs* (*L'Étudiant*, 27 rue du Chemin-Vert, 75011 Paris). *Working Holidays* (Central Bureau, Seymour Mews House, Seymour Mews, London W1H 9PE) is also useful. In Provence, the two main papers, *Nice Matin* and *La Provence* carry job ads.

By law all EU nationals are entitled to exactly the same pay, conditions and trade-union rights as French nationals. France has a **minimum wage** (the SMIC), currently around 40F an hour. Employers, however, are likely to pay lower wages to temporary foreign workers who don't have easy legal resources.

The **University of Aix and Marseille** has its science faculties in Marseille and arts faculties in Aix, very popular with American students. Nice also has a university.

TEMPORARY WORK

Grape-picking during the wine harvest in September is possible, though many vineyards are automated and others too small to take on outsiders. Youth hostels in wine-growing areas sometimes recruit grape-pickers or you could always try asking at the local Agence Nationale de l'Emploi (ANPE) whose address you'll find in the phone book.

Getting a temporary job as a deck-hand or skivvy **on a yacht** is also feasible, but you'll have to hang about the ports, and getting on board will be very much a matter of luck. Pay and conditions are likely to be abysmal – it's assumed that you're there for the glamorous ride and you'll certainly be made to work for it. Another casual option, if you speak some French, is **bar work** in the many clubs run by American, Dutch, English or Irish managers on the coast. Again it's a matter of being in the right place at the right time.

Temporary jobs in the **travel industry** revolve around courier work – supervising and working on bus tours or summer campsites. You'll need good French (and maybe even another language) and should write to as many tour operators as you can, preferably in early spring. Getting work as a courier on a campsite is slightly easier. It usually takes in putting up tents at the beginning of the season, taking them down again at the end, and general maintenance and trouble-shooting work in the months between. Canvas Holidays (☎01383/644000) or Riviera Holidays (☎01482 448905) in Britain are worth approaching, as is the Union Française des Centres de Vacances (☎01.45.39.22.23) in Paris. Competition is fairly intense.

LONGER-TERM EMPLOYMENT

Teaching English is one of the easier ways of getting a job in France. It's best to apply from Britain; check the ads in *The Guardian*'s "Education" section (every Tuesday), or in the weekly *Times Educational Supplement*. Late summer is usually the best time. You don't need fluent French to get a post, but a TEFL (Teaching English as a Foreign Language) qualification may well be required. If you apply from home, most schools will fix up the necessary papers for you. It's also quite feasible to find a teaching job when you're in France, but you may have to accept semi-official status and no job security. For the addresses of schools, look under *Écoles de*

Langues in the Professions directory of the local phone book. Offering **private lessons** (via university noticeboards or classified ads), you'll have lots of competition, and it's hard to reach the people who can afford it, but it's always worth a try, particularly in Marseille where there are fewer native English-speakers around. Aix University is full of Americans, who tend to get most of what's available in that city – and elsewhere, particularly on the coast, there are all the kids of the English and American residents to compete with.

Au-pair work is usually arranged through one of a dozen agencies, all of which are listed in *Working Holidays*. In Britain, *The Lady* is the best magazine for classified adverts for such jobs. It's also worth contacting the Accueil Familial des Jeunes Étrangers (☎01.42.22.50.34) in Paris, or the American Institute for Foreign Study (☎1-800/727-AIFS) in the US; both place female au pairs only. Any agency will fill you in on the general terms and conditions (never very generous), and the state of the market; as a general rule, you shouldn't get paid less than 1000F a month (on top of board and lodging). It is wise to have an escape route (like a ticket home) in case you find the conditions intolerable.

Euroyouth (☎01702/341434), in Britain, runs a **summer holiday scheme**, placing people in French families for two to three weeks, where you get free board and lodging in exchange for English lessons.

CLAIMING BENEFIT

If you're an EU citizen – and you do the paperwork in advance – you can sign on for **unemployment benefit**. To do so, you must collect form E303 before leaving home, available in Britain from any DSS office. The procedure is first to get registered at an ANPE office (Agence Nationale pour l'Emploi), then take the form to your local ASSEDIC (benefits office) and give them an address, which can be a hostel or a hotel, for the money to be sent to. You sign once a month at the ANPE and receive benefit a month in arrears, in theory. In practice payments can be delayed in small towns for up to three months. After three months, you must either leave the country or get a *carte de séjour*. EU pensioners can arrange for their pensions to be paid in France.

STUDYING IN FRANCE

It's relatively easy to be a **student** in France. Foreigners pay no more than French nationals (around 1800F a year) to enrol for a course, and the only problem then is to support yourself. Your *carte de séjour* and – if you're an EU citizen – social security will be assured, and you'll be eligible for subsidized accommodation, meals and all the student reductions. In general, French universities are much less formal than British ones and many people perfect their fluency in the language while studying. There are strict entry requirements, including an exam in French for undergraduate degrees. For full **details and prospectuses**, contact the Cultural Service of any French embassy or consulate (see p.14).

Language schools all along the coast provide **intensive French courses** for foreigners; some are detailed in the Guide. The most popular is the summer Language and Civilization course at Aix. A complete list is given in the leaflet *Cours de Français, Langue Etrangère. Repertoire des Centres de Formation en France*, also obtainable from embassy or consular cultural sections. Finally, it's worth noting that if you're a full-time student in France, you can get a **work permit** for the following summer as long as your visa is still valid.

STUDYING FOR NORTH AMERICANS

Most universities have semester-abroad programmes to certain countries; the following are independent organizations that run programmes in France.

American Institute for Foreign Study, 102 Greenwich Ave, Greenwich, CT 06830 (☎1-800/727 2437). Language study and cultural immersion for the summer or school year.

Council on International Educational Exchange (CIEE), 205 E 42nd St, New York, NY 10017 (☎1-888/COUNCIL). The non-profit parent organization of Council Travel and Council Charter, CIEE runs summer, semester and academic-year programmes.

DIRECTORY

ALARM CALLS ☎36.88 or with a digital phone dial ☎*55* then the time (for example 0715 for 7.15); the cost is 3.65F.

BEACHES are public property within 5m of the high-tide mark, so you can kick sand past private villas and hotel sunbeds. Under a different law, however, you can't camp. Getting to many beaches and parking a car often requires entry through *terrain privé* (private land). In some instances, such "private beaches" charge a daily fee of 50F or 60F per car, but in return you may find facilities such as showers, beach bars and restaurants.

CAMERAS AND FILM Film is considerably cheaper in North America than France or Britain, so stock up if you're coming from there. If you're bringing a video camcorder, make sure any tapes you purchase in France are VHS. The normal French format, PAL, will only give black and white when played on VHS machines. Again, American videotape prices are way below French prices.

CHILDREN AND BABIES pose few travel problems. They're generally welcome everywhere, including most bars and restaurants. **Hotels** charge by the room, with a small supplement for an additional bed or cot, and family-run places will usually babysit or offer a listening service while you eat or go out. Many **restaurants** have children's menus or will cook simpler food on request. You'll have no difficulty finding disposable nappies (*couches à jeter*), but nearly all baby foods have added sugar and salt, and French milk powders are very rich indeed. SNCF charge nothing on **trains and buses** for under-fours, and half-fare for four- to twelve-year-olds (see p.23 for other reductions). Most local tourist offices have details of specific activities for children; along the coast there are a great number of classy funfairs, marinelands, zoos, go-karting tracks etc, all designed to extract the maximum amount of money off you. But almost every town has a municipal **children's playground** with a good selection of activities. Something to beware of – not that you can do much about it – is the difficulty of negotiating a child's **buggy** over the cobbles and steps of many of the hilltop villages.

ELECTRICITY is 220V out of double, round-pin wall sockets.

FISHING You need to become a member of a fishing club to get rights – this is not difficult, and any tourist office will give you a local address.

FOREST FIRES Every summer forest fires in Provence and the Côte d'Azur hit the international headlines. Vast tracts become blazing infernos long before the sprayers from Nice or Marseille can reach the area. Loss of life is common and people's homes are frequently destroyed. So always take the utmost care. The emergency number for the fire service is ☎18.

LAUNDRY Laundries are common in French towns, and some are listed in the Guide – elsewhere look in the phone book under *Laveries Automatiques*. The alternative *blanchisserie* or *pressing* services are likely to be expensive, and hotels in particular charge very high rates. If you're doing your own washing in hotels, keep quantities small as most forbid doing any laundry in your room.

LEFT LUGGAGE At the time of writing, left-luggage lockers at train stations are closed as a precaution against terrorist attacks.

SWIMMING POOLS Swimming pools (*piscines*) are well signposted in most French towns and reasonably priced. Tourist offices have their addresses.

TIME France is one hour ahead of British time for most of the year, except for a short period during October when it's the same. It is six hours ahead of Eastern Standard Time, nine hours ahead of Pacific Standard Time. This also applies during daylight-saving seasons, which are observed in France (as in most of Europe) from the end of March until the end of September.

TOILETS are usually to be found downstairs in bars, along with the phone, or there are the automatic concrete monsters on the streets costing 2F. Dirty, hole-in-the-ground, squatting loos are still common. The usual euphemism for toilet is "WC", pronounced "vé-sé".

WATER The fountains in the squares of towns and villages of Provence are there to provide water. Unless a notice says *Eau non potable* – a very rare occurrence – the water is drinkable and deliciously cool.

WEATHER Recorded information on weather conditions is available in each *département*.

Alpes-de-Haute-Provence ☎08.36.68.02.04.

Alpes-Maritimes ☎08.36.68.02.06.

Bouches-du-Rhône ☎08.36.68.02.13.

Hautes-Alpes☎08.36.68.02.05.

Var ☎08.36.68.02.83.

Vaucluse ☎08.36.68.02.84.

PART TWO

THE

GUIDE

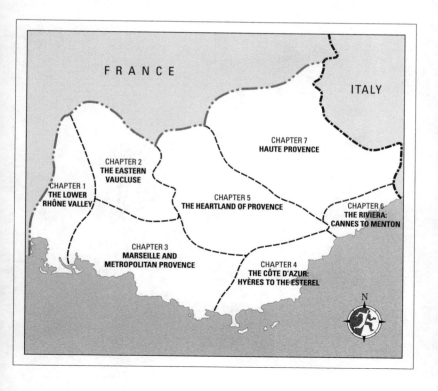

FRANCE

ITALY

CHAPTER 7
HAUTE PROVENCE

CHAPTER 2
THE EASTERN VAUCLUSE

CHAPTER 1
THE LOWER RHÔNE VALLEY

CHAPTER 5
THE HEARTLAND OF PROVENCE

CHAPTER 6
**THE RIVIERA:
CANNES TO MENTON**

CHAPTER 3
**MARSEILLE AND
METROPOLITAN PROVENCE**

CHAPTER 4
**THE CÔTE D'AZUR:
HYÈRES TO THE ESTEREL**

N

CHAPTER ONE

THE LOWER RHÔNE VALLEY

The lower stretch of the **Rhône Valley**, long a frontier between the rest of France and Provence, has seen centuries of fortification on its banks – at **Beaucaire** and **Villeneuve-lès-Avignon** on the French side, at **Tarascon**, **Boulbon** and **Barbentane** in Provence. It has been the north–south route of ancient armies, of medieval traders and of modern rail and road, and its river has been a vital trading route, bringing wealth and fame to the cities that line its banks.

Today, the prime city of the Provençal stretch is **Avignon**, the great city of the popes from medieval times until the Revolution and a major centre of art and architecture. To the north lies **Orange**, famous for its Roman amphitheatre, and the vineyards of the **Châteauneuf-du-Pape**, both drawing visitors into an otherwise heavily industrialized stretch of the valley.

The countryside attractions begin on the the modest rural plains to the south of Avignon, **La Petite Crau** and **La Grande Crau** – the stretch of land enclosed by the River Durance and the Rhône and separated by the abrupt ridge of the **Alpilles**. Here the villages and small towns have retained a nineteenth-century charm, living out the old customs and traditions revived by the great Provençal poet **Frédéric Mistral**, a native of La Petite Crau. This is the countryside that **Van Gogh** painted when he spent a year at Arles and then sought refuge in St-Rémy. Both towns pay tribute to his tragic brilliance.

Arles lies to the south, at the mouth of the Rhône delta. It was the centre of Roman Provincia, which stretched from the Pyrenees to the Alps and became the capital of Gaul towards the end of the Roman era; the city's great amphitheatre, like that in the Roman city of **Orange**, still seats thousands for summer entertainments. Further evidence of Roman occupation is apparent at **Glanum**, outside **St-Rémy-de-Provence**, where you can see the overlaid remains of Greek and Roman towns, and between Arles and St-Rémy, where the Romans' brilliant use of water power is in evidence in the **Barbegal mill**.

ACCOMMODATION PRICE CATEGORIES

Throughout this guide, all hotels and guesthouses have been priced on a scale of ①–⑧, indicating the lowest price you could expect to pay for a double room in high season. What you get for your money varies enormously between establishments, but in the lower-priced hotels you should expect to pay considerably more for en-suite facilities. If you are staying anywhere for more than three days it's often possible to negotiate a lower price, particularly out of season.

① Under 160F	③ 220–300F	⑤ 400–500F	⑦ 600–700F
② 160–220F	④ 300–400F	⑥ 500–600F	⑧ Over 700F

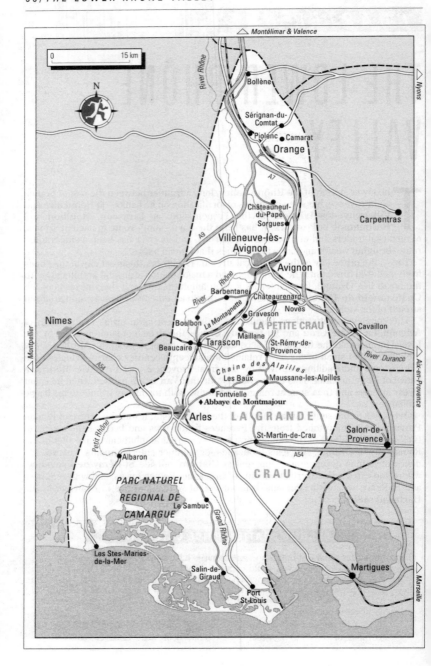

Below Arles, where the Rhône divides, is the strange watery land of the **Camargue**, with a natural history and way of life quite distinct from surrounding regions. The wet expanses sustain flocks of flamingoes and a multitude of other birds, while black bulls and wild white horses graze on the edges of the marshes and lagoons. The Camargue also provides a sanctuary for unique social traditions – it is here, to the town of **Les Stes-Maries-de-la-Mer**, that **gypsies** come every May from all over the Mediterranean to celebrate their patron saint's day.

Orange and around

The major routes south into the Rhône Valley all pass through **ORANGE**, best known for its spectacular **Roman theatre**. The city is the former seat of the counts of Orange, a title created by Emperor Charlemagne in the eighth century, and passed to the Dutch crown of Nassau in the sixteenth century. Its most memorable member was the Protestant Prince William, who ascended the English throne with his consort Queen Mary in 1689; the Protestant Orange Order in Ireland was founded to support William's military campaign against his Catholic predecessor, James II, which ended with the Battle of the Boyne.

Orange has never been the friendliest of towns, though its medieval street plan, Thursday market, fountained squares and houses with ancient porticoes and court-yards are attractive enough. Aside from the theatre, the triumphal **Roman arch**, and **museum**, there's not much to detain you, and you may feel that, however distant, the parallels between Roman culture and today's neo-fascists are such that you can give the whole place a miss with a clear conscience. If you're happy to linger, however, there is a surprising treat in the old residence of the nineteenth-century scientist, the **Harmas** of **Jean-Henri Fabre**, in Sérignan-du-Comtat, just north of the city.

Today, the city is host to a major summer **music festival** (see box on p.63), held in the Roman theatre. However, the quality of this festival has been put in jeopardy by Le Pen's *Front National* victory in the municipal elections of 1995. Opinions of French artists are split, with many of Arab or African origin arguing that it's now more impor-tant than ever for them to perform here, while others declare they will have nothing to do with events that increase the town hall's income and prestige. The **strip cartoon festival**, which used to bring in weird and wonderful characters, has already been pushed out of the city due to similar political differences.

Arrival, information and accommodation

The **gare SNCF** is about 1.5km east of the centre, at the end of av Frédéric-Mistral. The nearest bus stop is at the bottom of rue Jean-Reboul, the first left as you walk from the station towards the city centre. Bus #2 (direction Nogent) will take you to the Théâtre Antique, opposite which there's a seasonal **tourist office** (April–Sept Mon–Sat 10am–1pm & 2–6pm, Sun 10am–6pm); the **main tourist office** is a stop fur-ther on (Gasparin) on av Charles-de-Gaulle (April–Sept Mon–Sat 9am–7pm, Sun 10am–6pm; Oct–March Mon–Sat 9am–5pm; ☎04.90.34.70.88). The **gare routière** is close to the centre on place Pourtoules, just east of the Roman theatre. There's under-gound **parking** here too.

You'll have no problem finding **accommodation** in Orange, except during the Chorégies festival in July.

Hotels

Arcotel, 8 pl des Herbes (☎04.90.34.09.23, fax 04.90.34.09.23). Overlooking the pretty pl des Herbes, this is a small, appealing place. ②.

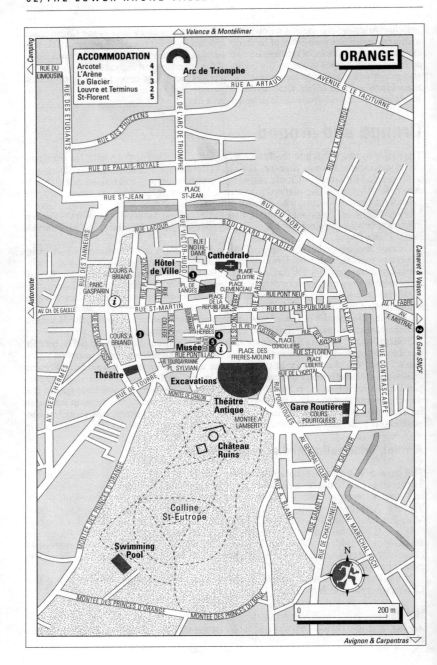

ORANGE

△ Valence & Montélimar

△ Camping

◁ Autoroute

Camaret & Vaison ▷
② & Gare SNCF ▷

ACCOMMODATION
Arcotel   4
L'Arène   1
Le Glacier   3
Louvre et Terminus 2
St-Florent   5

Arc de Triomphe

RUE DU LIMOUSIN
RUE DES ÉTUDIANTS
RUE DES PROCEENS
RUE DE PALAIS-ROYALE
RUE ST-JEAN
RUE LACOUR
RUE DES TANNEURS
AV. CH. DE GAULLE
RUE DES VILLASSES
AV. DES THERMES
RUE DE TOURRE

RUE A. ARTAUD
AVENUE G. LE TACITURNE
AV. DE L'ARC DE TRIOMPHE
AV. VICTOR-HUGO
RUE DU NOBLE
BOULEVARD DALADIER
RUE DE LA CONCHOIE
RUE CARISTIE

PLACE ST-JEAN
RUE J NOTRE-DAME
Cathédrale
Hôtel de Ville ❶
PLACE CLOITRE
PLACE CLEMENCEAU
RUE PONT NEUF
RUE DE LA RÉPUBLIQUE
PL. DE LANGES
PLACE DE LA RÉPUBLIQUE
PL. AUX HERBES
R. R. PETIT FUSTERIE
RUE DES AVESNES
RUE ST-FLORENT
AV. H. FABRE
AV. F. MISTRAL
RUE CONTRASCARPE
BOULEVARD DALADIER

COURS A BRIAND
PARC GASPARIN
i
COURS A BRIAND ❸
RUE ST-MARTIN
RUE ANCIEN COLLÈGE
RUE POURMANNE
PL. AUX HERBES
RUE SECOND
Musée ❹❺ *i*
RUE PONTILLAC
R. TOURGAYRANNE
PL. SYLVIAN
Théâtre
Excavations

PLACE DES FRERES-MOUNET
PLACE CORDELIERS
PLACE LIBERTE
RUE DE L'HOPITAL
RUE POURTOULES

Théâtre Antique
MONTEE DE CHALON
MONTEE A LAMBERT

Gare Routière
COURS POURTOULES

Château Ruins

Colline St-Eutrope

AV. GENERAL LECLERC
RUE BLANC
BD DALADIER
RUE GAMBETTA
RUE DE CHATEAUNEUF
AV. MARECHAL FOCH

Swimming Pool

N

MONTEE DES PRINCES D'ORANGE
MONTEE DES PRINCES D'ORANGE
MONTEE DES PRINCES DU VAUX

0   200 m

△ Avignon & Carpentras

L'Arène, pl de Langes (☎04.90.11.40.40, fax 04.90.11.40.45). Spacious rooms with all mod cons, on a quiet pedestrianized square. ④.

Le Glacier, 46 cours Aristide-Briand (☎04.90.34.02.01, fax 04.90.51.13.80). One of the most comfortable of the town's hotels. ③.

Louvre et Terminus, 89 av Frédéric-Mistral (☎01.90.34.10.08, fax 04.90.34.68.71). Useful if you don't want to shift your luggage far from the train station. ③.

St-Florent, 4 rue du Mazeau (☎04.90.34.18.53, fax 04.90.51.17.25). Rather kitsch decor, but central and cheap. ②.

Campsite

Le Jonquier, 1321 rue Alexis-Carrel (☎04.90.34.19.83, fax 04.90.34.86.54). Three-star site northwest of the centre, with tennis courts, pool and mini golf. Closed Nov to mid-March.

The Town

Orange is not a very big town and can be easily covered on foot. Its old streets lie north of the enormous Roman theatre which, with the hill of St-Eutrope behind, is the dominating feature.

The theatre

Days off in Orange circa 5 BC were entertainingly spent at the **theatre**, where an audience of ten thousand could watch farce, clownish improvisations, song and dance and, occasionally, for the sake of a visiting dignitary, a bit of heavy Greek tragedy, usually in Latin. Today, although the action is mainly limited to summer music, the theatre (April–Sept daily 9am–6.30pm; Oct–March 9am–noon & 1.30–5pm; 30F combined ticket with museum) is still the focus of the town, an awesome shell at the heart of the old medieval centre, which survived periods as a fortification, slum and prison before its careful reconstruction in the last century. In 1879 the first performance in 350 years was staged, initiating the Orange **Chorégies**, a festival of musical and dramatic arts (see box belolw).

Said to be the best-preserved Roman theatre in existence, Orange's theatre is the only one with the stage wall still standing – a massive 36m high and 103m across. The outer face, viewed from place des Frères-Mounets, resembles some monstrous prison wall, despite the ground-level archways leading into the backstage areas. Near the top you can see the blocks that held the poles of the awning which once hung over the stage and the front rows. Those at the back were protected from the sun by the hill of St-Eutrope into which the seats are built. Rows were allocated strictly by rank; an

---

FESTIVALS

In July Orange is packed with opera fanatics, here for the **Chorégies** or **choral festival**, performed in the Roman theatre. If you're interested in going, you'll need to make a reservation well in advance; details are available from the Bureau des Chorégies, 18 place Silvain, 84107 Orange (☎04.90.34.24.24) and from FNAC shops across the country. Ticket prices range from 90F to 900F.

The theatre is also used for jazz, film, folk and rock concerts. Prices range from 90F to 150F, and some performances are free; details are available from the Service Culturel de la Ville, 14 place Silvain (☎04.90.51.57.57) as well as from FNAC shops.

Between 1986 and 1996 Orange also hosted a **Festival BD** (*Bandes-Dessinées* or cartoon strips) during May. However, due to political differences between the producers and the *Front National* politicians in the town hall, this festival has been pushed out of Orange.

inscription "EQ Gradus III" (third row for knights) is visible near the orchestra pit. The enormous **stage** could accommodate vast numbers of performers, and the acoustics, thanks to the complex projections of the stage wall, allowed a full audience to hear every word. Though missing most of its original decoration, the inner side of the stage wall is an extremely impressive sight. Columned niches, now empty of their statues, run the length of the wall; below them a larger-than-life-size statue of Augustus, raising his arm in imperious fashion, looks down centre stage.

If the spectators grew bored during the day-long performances they could slip out of the west door to a complex in a semicircle cut into the rock. According to some archeologists, this contained baths, a stage for combats and a gymnasium equipped with three 180-metre running tracks alongside the wall of rue Pontillac, parts of which still stand. Others say it was the forum, or even a circus. There are widely differing views on how the excavations should be interpreted, though all agree that the massive capital was part of a temple.

The best view of the theatre in its entirety, and one for which you don't have to pay, is from **St-Eutrope hill**. You can follow a path up the hill either from the top of cours Aristide-Briand, montée P. de Chalons, or from cours Pourtoules, montée Albert-Lambert, until you are looking directly down onto the stage. The **ruins** around your feet are those of the short-lived seventeenth-century **château** of the princes of Orange. Louis XIV had it destroyed and the principality annexed to France, a small setback for William of Orange who was to become William III of Britain and Ireland.

The museum and Arc de Triomphe

Orange's **Musée Municipal** stands across the road from the theatre entrance (daily: April–Sept 9.30am–7pm; Oct–March 9.30am–noon & 1.30–5.30pm; 30F combined ticket with the theatre). Its various documents concerning the Orange dynasty include a suitably austere portrait of the very first Orangeman, William (Guillaume) the Taciturn, grandfather to William III. The museum also has an interesting – for classical historians at least – property register and land survey of the city in 77 AD, and a display of various bits and pieces from the theatre. The rest of the collection is rotated on a yearly basis, but contains diverse items such as the contents of a seventeenth-century apothecary and a collection of pictures portraying British workers from early this century by Frank Brangwyn, a Welsh painter who learnt his craft with William Morris.

To the north of the centre, on the main road into Orange, stands the town's second major monument, the **Arc de Triomphe**, whose intricate friezes and reliefs celebrate imperial victories against the Gauls. Classicists rave about it as one of the largest, best-preserved and oldest triple-bayed Roman arches in existence. However, its position in the middle of such a major road makes looking at pictures of the arch a more attractive option than studying the real thing.

Eating and drinking

Eating out in Orange is unlikely to prove an exceptional experience but there's no shortage of choice. *La Fringale*, 10 rue de Tourre (closed Wed & Sat midday, plus Sun midday out of season) is a cheap fast-food resto. At *Le Yaca*, in an old vaulted chamber at 24 place Silvain (closed Tues eve, all Wed & Nov) there's a generous choice of dishes for under 100F. Next door, *L'Aigo Boulido* (℡04.90.34.18.19; closed Sun and first two weeks of Oct) stays open after festival performances and has a 70F menu; and *Le Galois*, opposite, does midday salads for under 50F. *La Roselière*, 4 rue du Renoyer (closed Wed & Thurs midday; ℡04.90.34.50.42), by the hôtel de ville, is a lovely little **restaurant**, offering a menu at around 100F out of season, rising to 150F in summer.

For **drinking**, head for place de la République in the centre, where you'll find *Les Négociants*, the *Commerce* and the less expensive *Café de l'Univers*; these places are lively when the shops are open but much quieter at night. The *Café des Thermes* (8pm–1am) at 29 rue des Vieux-Fossés, to the west of cours Aristide-Briand, has a good selection of beers, a pool table and a youngish clientele, and is a better bet for evening entertainment.

Sérignan-du-Comtat and Camarat

There are three **buses** daily from Orange to **SÉRIGNAN-DU-COMTAT**, 8km north-east of the city, whose celebrated resident, **Jean-Henri Fabre** (1823–1915), spent the last 36 years of his life here. A remarkable self-taught scientist, Fabre is famous primarily for his insect studies; he also composed poetry, wrote songs and painted his specimens with artistic brilliance as well as scientific accuracy. As a boy his family's poverty consistently interrupted his education, but with the help of scholarships and, later, with pure, stubborn self-discipline, he attained diplomas in mathematics and the sciences. In his forties, with seven children to support, he was forced to resign from his teaching post at Avignon because parents and priests thought his lectures on the fertilization of flowering plants to be licentious if not downright pornographic. His friend John Stuart Mill eventually bailed him out with a loan, allowing him to settle in Orange. Darwin was also a friend with whom he had lengthy correspondence, though Fabre was too religious to be an evolutionist.

There's a **statue of Fabre** beside the red-shuttered buildings of the *mairie*. Fabre's house, which he named the **Harmas** (Latin for fallow land), is on the edge of the village on the N976 from Orange (May–Sept Mon & Wed–Sun 9am–noon & 2–6pm, Nov–April closes 4pm; 15F). Here, you can see his study with various specimens of insects and other invertebrates and his complete classification of the herbs of France and Corsica. The room gives a strong sense of a person in love with the world he researched, an impression echoed in the selection on the ground floor of Fabre's extraordinary **watercolours** of the fungi of the Vaucluse. The stunning colours and almost hallucinogenic detail make these pictures more like holograms than plastic art. After visiting the house you're free to wander round the **garden** where over a thousand species grow in wild disorder, exactly as Fabre wanted it.

Sérignan has a very smart **hotel-restaurant**, *L'Hostellerie du Vieux Château*, set in large grounds on rte de Ste-Cécile-les-Vignes (☎04.90.70.05.58, fax 04.90.70.05.62; ⑤).

For those with a car, it's an enjoyable drive from Orange to Sérignan; along the way are beautiful views of the smooth lower slopes of Mont Ventoux, and if you take the minor roads (D975, then D43) you pass the tiny wine-producing village of **CAMARAT**, guarded by a round-towered gateway topped with a campanile; Camarat's one claim to fame was a black Virgin Mary holding Jesus on her lap rather than to her breast, which was burnt in 1736 on the orders of the bishop of Orange who considered the pose to be indecent.

Châteauneuf-du-Pape

CHÂTEAUNEUF-DU-PAPE, a large village on the backroad from Orange to Avignon, takes its name from the ruins of the fourteenth-century Avignon popes' summer château, but neither this nor the medieval streets around **place du Portail**, the hub of the village, give Châteauneuf its appeal. It is the local **vineyards** that produce the magic, with grapes warmed at night by the large pebbles that cover the ground and soak up the sun's heat by day. Their rich ruby red wine is one of the most renowned in France, but the white, too, is exquisite.

If you can coincide your visit with the first weekend of August you'll find free *dégustation* stalls throughout the village, as well as parades, dances, equestrian contests, folkloric floats and so forth, all to celebrate the reddening of the grapes in the **Fête de la Véraison**. As well as wine, a good deal of grape liqueur (*marc*) finds its way down people's throats. For a casual introduction at other times, the best bet is the Cave Père Anselme on av Bienheureux-Pierre-de-Luxembourg, which has a **Musée des Outils de Vignerons** (daily 9am–noon & 2–6pm; free admission), plus free tasting of its own and other Rhône wines.

The Châteauneuf-du-Pape *appellation* does not, alas, come cheap, nor is there a centre where you can taste a good selection from the scores of *domaines*. If you're intent on buying, check the lists at the tourist office on place du Portail or the Fédération des Syndicats de Producteurs at 12 av Louis-Pasteur. You could also ask for the details of the winner of the previous April 25 competition when the village celebrates the day of Saint Marc, patron saint of wine-growers, with a procession from the church and a tasting by professionals to determine the best wines from the last vintage. Otherwise, you can visit an *Association de Vignerons* such as Prestige et Tradition, 3 rue de la République (Aug & Sept daily 8am–noon & 2–6pm; rest of year closed Sun), Reflets, 2 chemin du Bois de la Ville (Mon–Fri 8am–noon & 2–6pm), or La Vinothèque, 9 rue de la République (daily 10am–6pm), who group together several producers.

Practicalities

Buses from Orange arrive at the bottom of av des Bousquets which leads up to place Jean-Moulin, rue de la République and place Portail. The **tourist office** is on place du Portail (July & Aug Mon–Sat 9am–7pm, Sun 10am–5pm; rest of year Mon–Sat 9am–12.30pm & 2–6pm; ☎04.90.83.71.08).

There are just three **hotels** to choose: the tiny *La Garbure,* 3 rue Joseph-Ducos (☎04.90.83.75.08, fax 04.90.83.52.34; ④; closed mid-Oct to mid-Nov), which has only five rooms; *La Mère Germaine*, av Cdt-Lemaître (☎04.90.83.54.37, fax 04.90.83.50.37; ④; closed Wed) close to place du Portail and with just seven rooms; or the four-star *Hostellerie du Château des Fines Roches*, a ten-minute walk out of town on the rte d'Avignon (☎04.90.83.70.23, fax 04.90.83.78.42; ⑨; closed Sun & Mon out of season) also with seven rooms. There are also two **chambres d'hôtes** – chez Mme Melchor, La Font du Pape (☎04.90.83.73.97; ③; closed Dec–Feb) and chez Mme Dexheimer, Clos Bimard, rte de Roquemaure (☎04.90.83.73.16, fax 04.90.83.50.54; ②; closed Dec–Feb) – and a two-star **campsite**, Islon St-Luc (☎04.90.83.76.77), about 2km down chemin de la Calade, south from place Portail.

You can **eat** well for around 100F at the brasserie *La Mule du Pape* at 2 rue de la République, which also has a gastronomic restaurant on the first floor (☎04.90.83.79.22; restaurant closed Mon), but for a more extravagant blowout, the place to go is *La Mère Germaine* hotel (closed Wed), which offers panoramic views over the vineyards, all the best local wines and exquisite cooking; there's a weekday lunch menu for 200F.

Avignon and around

AVIGNON, great city of the popes and for centuries one of the major artistic centres of France, can be very daunting. Its monuments and museums are huge, and the city is always crowded in summer and can be stiflingly hot. But it has an immaculately preserved medieval centre with a multitude of impressively decorated buildings, ancient churches, chapels and convents, and more places to eat and drink than you could cover in a month. The city is at its busiest during July and early August, when the **Festival d'Avignon** – a medley of theatre, dance, lectures, exhibitions and concerts – draws people from all over the country.

Old Avignon is only a small corner of a large modern industrial city whose suburbs reach out to the neighbouring towns along the Autoroute du Soleil 8km east. Among the main attractions are the cultivated open countryside on the Île de la Barthelasse, and the much less crowded town of **Villeneuve-lès-Avignon**, on the opposite bank and, as such, technically outside of Provence.

The papal city: some history

Avignon's monuments, and most of its history, are bound up almost entirely with the status it acquired in the fourteenth century as the residence of the popes. **Pope Clement V**, taking refuge from anarchic feuding in Rome and northern Italy, first moved the papal headquarters here in 1309, a temporary act that turned out to last over seventy years, and a few decades longer, if you count the city's last flurry in defence of its antipope pretenders.

Though the town, unlike nearby Châteauneuf-du-Pape, did not originally belong to the papacy, it had the advantage of excellent transport links and a good Catholic landlord. Clement was not entirely confident about his security, however, even in France, and shifted his base between here, Vienne and Carpentras. His successor, **Jean XXII**, had previously been bishop of Avignon, so he re-installed himself quite happily in the episcopal palace Clement V had established. The next Supreme Pontiff, **Benoît XII**, acceded in 1335; accepting the impossibility of returning to Rome he demolished the bishop's palace to replace it with an austere fortress, now known as the **Vieux Palais**.

Number four of the nine Avignon popes, **Clement VI**, managed to buy Avignon off Queen Jeanne of Naples and Provence, apparently in return for absolution for any possible involvement she might have had in the assassination of her husband. He also built a **new palace** adjoining the old one, a much more luxurious affair showing distinctly worldly tastes. The fifth and sixth Avignon popes further embellished and fortified the papal palace, before the seventh, **Gregory XI**, after years of diplomacy, and an appeal from Catherine of Siena, moved the Holy See back to Rome in 1377. This did not please the French cardinals who promptly voted in the **Antipope Clement VII** to take up residence in Avignon, thus initiating the division in the Catholic Church known as the Great Schism. The courier business in excommunications and more worldly threats between Rome and Avignon flourished. **Antipope Benoît XIII**, who replaced Clement VII, became justifiably paranoid with the shifting alliances of the Schism. It was he who built the **city walls** and ordered all the houses surrounding the Palais des Papes to be destroyed, creating the space that is now the **place du Palais**. Benoît was hounded out by the French king in 1403 and thereafter Avignon had to be content with mere cardinals, though it remained papal property right up to the Revolution.

The **period of the popes** made a lasting impression on the city's population. Along with the Holy Fathers came a vast entourage of clerks, lawyers, doctors, flatterers, merchants and wheeler-dealers of Italian, French, Catalan, Languedocian and German origin, not to mention pilgrims from all over Europe. Jews were given sanction, and so too, during the Schism, were heretics fleeing papal bulls from Rome. The diverse, multicultural population flourished – as did the criminal community, drawn to the papal enclave to escape prosecution in the neighbouring domains. While the popes entertained visiting monarchs and ambassadors with spectacular candle-lit processions and banquets, every vice flourished. The **Black Death** struck in 1348 and was followed by intermittent periods of plague and famine, and in between times the appalling overcrowding took its toll. But Avignon remained a very lively city – "a sewer where all the filth of the universe has gathered", as Petrarch, a contemporary, described it.

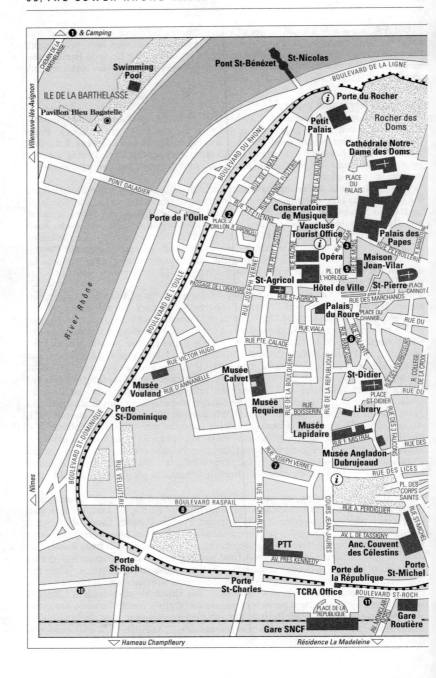

△ ❶ & Camping

CHEMIN DE LA BARTHELASSE

Swimming Pool

Pont St-Bénézet   St-Nicolas

BOULEVARD DE LA LIGNE

ⓘ Porte du Rocher

Rocher des Doms

ILE DE LA BARTHELASSE

Villeneuve-les-Avignon ◁

Pavillon Bleu Bagatelle ⊙

▲

Petit Palais

Cathédrale Notre-Dame des Doms

PLACE DU PALAIS

PONT DALADIER

BOULEVARD DU RHÔNE

RUE DE L'HAS

RUE GRANDE FUSTERIE

RUE DE LA BALANCE

Porte de l'Oulle ❷ PLACE CRILLON R. BARONCELLI

RUE ST-ÉTIENNE

Conservatoire de Musique

Vaucluse Tourist Office ⓘ ❸

Palais des Papes

RUE PEYROLLERIE

R. BANASTERIE

River Rhône

BOULEVARD DE L'OULLE

RUE PETIT FUSTERIE

RUE RADINE

RUE JOSEPH VERNET

❹

Opéra

PL. DE L'HORLOGE

❺

Maison Jean-Vilar

RUE DE MONS

PASSAGE DE L'ORATOIRE

St-Agricol

RUE ST-AGRICOL

Hôtel de Ville

St-Pierre PLACE CARNOT

RUE DES MARCHANDS

Palais du Roure

PLACE DU CHANGE

RUE DU

RUE VIALA

RUE PTE. CALADE

RUE DE LA RÉPUBLIQUE

RUE GALANTE

RUE BANCASSE

❻

RUE VICTOR HUGO

RUE DE LA BOUQUERIE

St-Didier

R. COLLÈGE DE LA CROIX

RUE DES FOURBISSEURS

Musée Vouland

RUE D'ANNANELLE

Musée Calvet

RUE DU

PLACE ST-DIDIER

RUE DES 3 FAUCONS

Porte St-Dominique

BOULEVARD ST-DOMINIQUE

Musée Requien

RUE BOISSERIN

Library

RUE DES

Musée Lapidaire

RUE F. MISTRA

RUE VELOUTERIE

Musée Angladon-Dubrujeaud

RUE JOSEPH VERNET

❼

RUE DES LICES

ⓘ

PL. DES CORPS SAINTS

Nîmes ◁

△

BOULEVARD RASPAIL

❽

RUE ST-CHARLES

RUE A. PERDIGUIER

COURS JEAN-JAURÈS

RUE ST-MICHEL

AV. L. DE TASSIGNY

PTT

Anc. Couvent des Célestins

Porte St-Michel

Porte St-Roch

⓾

AV. PRÉS KENNEDY

Porte St-Charles

Porte de la République

BOULEVARD ST-ROCH

AV. MONCLAR NORD

⓫

TCRA Office

PLACE DE LA RÉPUBLIQUE

Gare Routière

Gare SNCF

▽ Hameau Champfleury   Résidence La Madeleine ▽

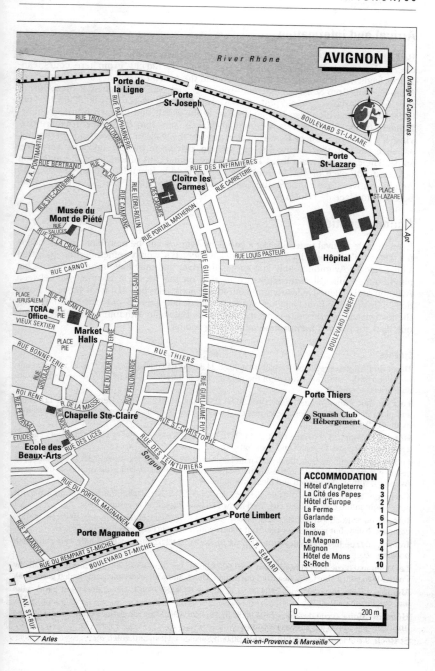

River Rhône

AVIGNON

Orange & Carpentras

N

BOULEVARD ST-LAZARE

Apt

Porte de la Ligne

Porte St-Joseph

Porte St-Lazare

RUE TROIS COLOMBES

RUE PALAPHARNERIE

RUE DES INFIRMIERES

PLACE ST-LAZARE

R.A. PONTMARTIN

RUE BERTRAND

RUE 3 PILATS

RUE STE CATHERINE

RUE LEDRU-ROLLIN

RUE DES CARMES

P. DES CARMES

RUE CARRETERIE

Cloître les Carmes

RUE PORTAIL MATHERON

Musée du Mont de Piété

RUE SALUCES

RUE CAMPANE

RUE LOUIS PASTEUR

Hôpital

RUE DE LA CROIX

RUE CARNOT

RUE PAUL-SAIN

RUE GUILLAUME PUY

BOULEVARD LIMBERT

PLACE JERUSALEM

RUE ST-JEAN LE VIEUX

PL PIE

TCRA Office

VIEUX SEXTIER

Market Halls

PLACE PIE

RUE DU FOUR DE LA TERRE

RUE THIERS

RUE BONNETERIE

RUE GRIVOLAS

RUE PHILONARDE

RUE GUILLAUME PUY

Porte Thiers

ROI RENE

R. DE LA MASSE

Squash Club Hébergement

RUE PETRAMALE

Chapelle Ste-Claire

RUE ST-CHRISTOPHE

ETUDES

RUE DES LICES

Ecole des Beaux-Arts

RUE DES TEINTURIERS

Sorgue

RUE DU PORTAIL MAGNANEN

RUE J. MANIVEL

9

Porte Limbert

AV. P. SEMARD

Porte Magnanen

RUE DU REMPART ST-MICHEL

BOULEVARD ST-MICHEL

AV. ST-RUF

ACCOMMODATION	
Hôtel d'Angleterre	8
La Cité des Papes	3
Hôtel d'Europe	2
La Ferme	1
Garlande	6
Ibis	11
Innova	7
Le Magnan	9
Mignon	4
Hôtel de Mons	5
St-Roch	10

0   200 m

Arles

Aix-en-Provence & Marseille

Arrival and information

Both the **gare SNCF**, on bd St-Rochand, and the **gare routière**, on av Montclar, are close to Porte de la République, on the south side of the old city. From here, cours Jean-Jaurès leads north into the old town; you'll find the **tourist office** at no. 41 (April–Sept Mon–Fri 9am–1pm & 2–6pm, Sat 9am–1pm & 2–5pm, Sun 9am–1pm & 2–5pm; during the festival daily 10am–7pm; Oct–March closed Sun; ☎04.90.82.65.11, fax 04.90.82.95.03), which also has an annexe at the north end of town by the Pont St-Bénézet (daily: April–Sept 9am–6pm, Oct–March 9am–1pm & 2–5pm). If you're **driving**, it's best to park near Pont Daladier, outside the walls on the west side of the city, as, once stuck in the narrow one-way system, driving in the city becomes very tiresome. The city's two main **local bus stations**, with TCRA offices for route maps and tickets (6.50F each or 48F for ten), are by Porte de la République (stops Poste, Cité Administrative, Gare routière and Gare) and place Pie. From Cité Administrative all buses go to place de l'Horloge.

Accommodation

Even outside festival time, finding a **room** in Avignon can be a problem: cheap hotels fill fast so it's a good idea to book in advance. It's worth remembering, too, that Villeneuve-lès-Avignon is only just across the river and may have rooms when its big neighbour is full. All **campsites** are located on the Île de la Barthelasse between Avignon and Villeneuve-lès-Avignon, an idyllic spot; take bus #10 from Poste to Porte de l'Oulle opposite Pont Daladier and then walk or take bus #20 onto the island. During the festival a temporary site is set up behind the Bagatelle with minimal facilities. Look out, also, for the odd **farmhouse** advertising rooms.

Hotels

Hôtel de l'Angleterre, 29 bd Raspail (☎04.90.86.34.31, fax 04.90.86.86.74). Located in a quiet neighbourhood in the southwest corner of the old city, this is a traditional hotel with some very reasonably priced rooms. ③.

La Cité des Papes, 1 rue J-Vilar (☎04.90.86.22.45, fax 04.90.27.39.21). Between pl de l'Horloge and pl du Palais with the best views reserved for the most expensive rooms, but comfort assured in all. ⑤–⑧.

Hôtel d'Europe, 12 pl Crillon (☎04.90.14.76.76, fax 04.90.85.43.66). A very classy hotel, set back in a shaded courtyard. Peaceful and luxurious. ⑨.

La Ferme, chemin du Bois, Île de la Barthelasse (☎04.90.82.57.53, fax 04.90.27.15.47). A sixteenth-century farm on the island in the Rhône (signed right off Pont Daladier as you cross over from Avignon), with well-equipped and pleasant rooms. ④.

Garlande, 20 rue Galante (☎04.90.85.08.85, fax 04.90.27.16.58). Delightful location on a narrow street right in the centre of the city. Well-known so booking ahead is essential. ④.

Ibis, 42 bd St-Roch (☎04.90.85.38.38, fax 04.90.86.44.81). Chain hotel located in the train station complex. Noisy, but worth it for the front rooms which offer great views over the city. ④.

Innova, 100 rue Joseph-Vernet (☎04.90.82.54.10, fax 04.90.82.52.39). Small, friendly, and well worth booking. ②.

Le Magnan, 63 rue Portail Magnanen (☎04.90.86.36.51, fax 04.90.85.48.90). Just inside the walls by Porte Magnanen a short way east from the station. Quiet, and with a very pleasant shaded garden. ④.

Mignon, 12 rue Joseph-Vernet (☎04.90.82.17.30, fax 04.90.85.78.46). Dated decor but good value and comfortable. ③.

Hôtel de Mons, 5 rue de Mons (☎04.90.82.57.16, fax 04.90.85.19.15). A thirteenth-century chapel imaginatively converted and very central. ③.

St-Roch, 9 rue Paul-Mérindol (☎04.90.16.50.00). Spacious, clean and quiet. ③.

Hostels

Hameau Champfleury, 33 av Eisenhower (☎04.90.85.35.02). A social centre which offers individual rooms for around 105F including breakfast, doubles for 85F per person and triples for 70F per person. Southwest of the gare SNCF; bus #1 or #2 to Champfleury stop.

Pavillon Bleu Bagatelle, camping Bagatelle, Île de la Barthelasse (☎04.90.86.30.39, fax 04.90.27.16.23). Rather basic facilities, but set in a pleasant shady campsite with rooms for four to eight people for 55F, or 75F including breakfast. Bus #10 from Poste to Porte de l'Oulle, then bus #20 to the Bagatelle stop.

Résidence La Madeleine, 4 impasse des Abeilles, 25 av Monclar-Nord (☎04.90.85.20.63). Studios with kitchenette for two people from around 180F, 220F for three or four – although prices jump considerably during the festival. Turn right out of the station and first right, away from the old town.

Squash Club Hébergement, 32 bd Limbert (☎04.90.85.27.78). This squash club also has three dormitories; 60F a night. Bus #2 east along the city walls from the gare SNCF to the Thiers stop. Closed Sun in winter and for Christmas holidays.

Campsites

Camping Bagatelle (☎04.90.86.30.39, fax 04.90.27.16.23). The closest site to the city centre. A three-star complex, visible as you cross the Daladier bridge from Avignon; bus #20 to Bagatelle stop.

Camping Municipal Pont St-Bénézet (☎04.90.82.63.50). A four-star site about 3km from the centre overlooking Pont St-Bénézet; bus #20 (Bénézet stop). Closed Nov–Feb.

Les Deux Rhônes, chemin de Bellegarde, Île de la Barthelasse (☎04.90.85.49.70, fax 04.90.85.91.75). Around 4km from the city and smaller than the other three; bus #20 (Traille stop).

Parc des Libertés, Île de la Barthelasse (☎04.90.85.17.73, fax 04.90.86.36.62). The cheapest of the four. Closed mid-Sept to mid-April.

THE FESTIVAL D'AVIGNON

Though the **Festival d'Avignon**, which runs from mid-July to early August, is dominated by theatre, there is plenty more on offer, including classical music and dance, lectures and exhibitions. The 1998 festival saw theatrical interpretations of Sophocles, Corneille, Shakespeare and Chekhov, with directors and companies as diverse as Jacques Lassalle and Cheek by Jowl – as well as a whole host of events celebrating the centenary of Brecht's birth. Each year a non-European country or region is invited to bring the best of its performing arts, traditional, modern and avant-garde, to the festival. In 1998 it was the turn of Southeast Asia, with an adaptation of Shakespeare's *Macbeth* in the style of the Peking Opera and shadow theatre among the offerings.

The **main festival** uses all of the city's great buildings as stages, the best being the Cour d'Honneur of the Palais des Papes. The programme, including details of how to book, is available from the second week in May from the Bureau du Festival d'Avignon, 8 bis rue de Mons (☎04.90.27.66.50) or from the tourist office. Ticket prices are reasonable (130–190F) and go on sale from the second week in June; you can buy them over the phone (11am–7pm; ☎04.90.14.14.14) or from FNAC shops in all major French cities. During the festival, tickets are available until 4pm for the same day's performances.

The fringe programme, **Festival Off**, takes place in eighty different venues and on the streets from 10am to midnight. The programme is available from the end of June from Avignon Public Off, BP5, 75521 Paris Cedex 11 (☎01.48.05.01.19). During the festival the office is in the Conservatoire de Musique on place du Palais. Ticket prices range from 50F to 80F and a *Carte Public Adhérent* (75F, or 50F if bought before the festival) gets you a thirty percent reduction on ticket prices for all of these shows.

During festival time there are up to two hundred thousand visitors and getting around or doing anything beyond the festival becomes virtually impossible.

The City

Avignon's **walls**, which still form a complete loop around the city, appear far too low to be a serious defence. In fact half their full height is now buried beneath the city, as is its moat – though all the gates and towers were restored during the nineteenth-century and there's still a strong sense of being in an enclosed space quite separate from the modern spread of the city.

Running north from the wall gate, cours Jean-Jaurès becomes **rue de la République**, the main axis of the old town, leading straight up to **place de l'Horloge**, the central square. Beyond that is **place du Palais**, the **Rocher des Doms** park and the **Porte du Rocher** overlooking the Rhône by the Pont d'Avignon, or Pont St-Bénézet as it's officially known. Avignon's major monuments occupy a compact quarter inside the northern loop of the walls. The **Palais des Papes**, northeast of the square and home of the medieval popes, is obviously the city's major sight, but there are other palaces dotted about the centre and, as you'd expect, a fair smattering of churches (most with very limited opening hours). The best of the **city's museums** are the **Petit Palais** and the **Musée Calvet**, and, for a break from the monumental, there are the pedestrian streets east of the papal palace towards place des Carmes, and to the southeast of the centre, the atmospheric **rue des Teinturiers**.

Palais des Papes

Serious sightseeing is bound to start off in the place du Palais, a huge cobbled square dominated by the **Palais des Papes** (daily: April–July 9am–7pm; during the festival 9am–9pm; early Aug to Oct 9am–8pm; Nov–March 9am–5.45pm; guided tours in English 11.30am & 4.45pm; last ticket issued 1hr before closing; 40F, including an audio-guide or guided tour). The palais is a monster of a building, best viewed from the rue Peyrolerie to its south; inside, so little remains of the original decoration and furnishings that you can be deceived into thinking that all the popes and their retinues were as pious and austere as the last official occupant, Benoît XII. The denuded interior certainly gives sparse indication of the corruption and decadence of fat, feuding cardinals and their mistresses, the thronging purveyors of jewels, velvet and furs, the musicians, chefs and painters competing for patronage, the riotous banquets and corridor schemings which took place here during the period of the popes.

Tours begin in the **Pope's Tower**, otherwise known as the Tower of Angels, entered via the **Treasury**, a vaulted room in the tower. Here the serious business of the church's deeds and finances went on and, beneath the flagging of the lower treasury, the papal gold and jewels were stored in four large safe holes. The same cunning storage device can be seen in the Chamberlain's quarters, in the **Chambre du Camérier**, just off the Jesus Hall. As the pope's right-hand man, the Chamberlain would originally have had lavishly decorated quarters, but successive occupants have left their mark and what is now visible is a confusion of layers. The other door in this room leads into the Papal Vestiary, where the pope would dress before sessions in the consistory. He also had a small library here and could look out onto the gardens below.

A door on the north side of the Jesus Hall leads to the **Consistoire** of the Vieux Palais, where sovereigns and ambassadors were received and the cardinals' council was held. The original flooring and the frescoes were destroyed by fire in 1413 and today it contains fragments of frescoes moved here from the cathedral plus a series of nineteenth-century paintings of the popes, all nine looking remarkably similar – unsurprisingly, given that the artist used the same model for each.

If it's medieval artistry you're after, however, go to the **Chapelle St-Jean**, off the Consistoire, and the **Chapelle St-Martial** on the floor above, reached via the cloisters. Both were richly decorated by the Sienese artist Matteo Giovanetti, and commissioned by Clement VI. The frescoes were damaged in the nineteenth century by soldiers using the building as barracks – they tried to chip off all the heads of the figures in order to sell them.

The **kitchen**, also on this floor, gives an idea of medieval times, and a hint of the scale of papal gluttony – its square walls becoming an octagonal chimneypiece for a vast central cooking fire. Major feasts were held in **Le Grand Tinel** which was also part of the conclave in which the cardinals were locked up in order to elect a new pope; clearly visible are the arches that led to additional rooms in the south and west in which the cardinals conspired and schemed in isolation from the world.

In the adjoining **Palais Neuf**, Clement VI's bedroom and study are further evidence of the pope's secular concerns, with wonderful food-oriented murals and painted ceilings. Beautifully restored, they illustrate in detail fishing, falconry, hunting and other courtly pursuits. However, austerity resumes in the cathedral-like proportions of the Grande Chapelle, or **Chapelle Clementine**, and in the Grande Audience on the floor below.

When you've completed the circuit, which includes a heady walk along the roof terraces, you can watch a glossy but informative film on the history of the palace (English headphones available). **Concerts** are also held here: programmes are available from the ticket office. During evening visits or concerts the illuminations give the palais a truly Gothic atmosphere.

North to Pont St-Bénézet

Opposite the entrance to the palais is the beautiful seventeenth-century **Hôtel des Monnaies**, the old mint, now the music conservatory, with a facade of griffons, cherubs, eagles and swathes of fruit. To the north stands the **Cathédrale Notre-Dame-des-Doms** (daily 7.30am–7.30pm), which might once have been a luminous Romanesque structure, but the interior has had a bad attack of Baroque. In addition, nineteenth-century fanatics mounted an enormous gilded Virgin on the belfry, which would look silly enough anywhere, but, when dwarfed by the fifty-metre towers of the popes' palace, is absurd. To the west of the square is the redeveloped **Quartier de la Balance**, now teeming with souvenir shops, but once home to the gypsies in the nineteenth century.

Behind the cathedral is the **Rocher des Doms park**, a relaxing spot with lovely views over the river to Villeneuve and beyond. To the west is the **Petit Palais** (July & Aug daily 10.30am–6pm; rest of year Mon & Wed–Sun 9.30am–noon & 2–6pm; 30F; free on Sun Oct–March), a former episcopal palace now housing a dauntingly huge gallery. There are almost a thousand paintings and sculptures here and it's easy to get stuck, with more than a dozen rooms still to go, on the mastery of colour and facial expressions of a Simone Martini or Fabriano, or to be fatigued by a surfeit of the Madonna and Child before you've reached Botticelli's masterpiece on the subject or the Niçois painter, Louis Bréa's *Assumption of the Virgin*. Anyone intrigued by labyrinths should look out for *Theseus and the Minotaur*; the labyrinth in the foreground is identical to the one on the floor of Chartres cathedral, and is thought by some to have mysterious powers of healing.

North of the Petit Palais, and well signposted, is the broken span of **Pont St-Bénézet** (April–Sept daily 9am–6.30pm; rest of year Tues–Sun 9am–1pm & 2–5pm; 15F; 31F combined ticket with Musée en Images); most of the bridge was swept away by floods in the seventeenth century and today only four of the original twenty-two arches remain. This is the bridge of the popular rhyme *Sur le pont d'Avignon* – though one theory has it that the lyrics are really "Sous le pont" (under the bridge), rather than "Sur le pont" (on the bridge), and refer to the thief and trickster clientele of a tavern on the Île de la Barthelasse (which the bridge once crossed) dancing with glee at the arrival of more potential victims. The bridge can be walked, danced or sat upon, but if you take small children, beware the precipitous, barely protected drops on either side.

To the right of the entrance to the bridge is the **Musée en Images** (April–Sept 9am–7pm; Oct to mid-Nov & Feb–March Tues–Sun 10am–5pm; 26F; 31F combined ticket with bridge), a twenty-minute slide show telling the history of the city (English tapes available). It's a bit pricey and predictable but a pleasantly lazy way of seeing some of the glories of the city's art and architecture.

Around place de l'Horloge

South of the Palais des Papes is the busy, café-lined **place de l'Horloge**, site of the city's imposing nineteenth-century **Hôtel de Ville** with its Gothic **clock tower**, and of the **Opéra**. Around the square, on rues de Mons, Molière and Corneille, famous faces are painted on the windows of the buildings. Many of these figures from the past were visitors to Avignon, and of those who recorded their impressions of the city, it was the sound of over a hundred bells ringing that stirred them most. Though there's not quite so many today, on Sunday mornings, traffic lulls permitting, you can still hear myriad different peals from churches, convents and chapels in close proximity. Many ecclesiastical buildings were knocked down during the Revolution and in the years up to 1815, when a minority of Avignonnais were still fighting against union with France. It was a bloody time: in 1791 a supporter of the new order was murdered in church; in response sixty counter-revolutionaries were buried alive in the icehouse of the papal palace.

The restored fourteenth-century **Église St-Agricol**, just behind the hôtel de ville, is one of Avignon's best Gothic edifices, with a beautifully carved fifteenth-century facade; inside, there's a Renaissance altarpiece of Provençal origin, and paintings by Nicolas Mignard and Pierre Parrocel (Wed 10am–noon, Sat 4–6pm, Sun 8–10pm). Beyond here lie the most desirable addresses in Avignon. High, heavy facades dripping with cupids, eagles, dragons, fruit and foliage range along **rue Petite-Fusterie** and **rue Joseph-Vernet**, where you'll find the most expensive shops selling chocolate, haute couture and baubles, with restaurants and art galleries to match.

To the south of the square, just behind rue St-Agricol on rue Collège du Roure, is the elegant fifteenth-century **Palais du Roure**, a centre of Provençal culture, whose gateway and courtyard are definitely worth a look; it is often host to temporary art exhibitions, and if you want a rambling tour through the attics to see Provençal costumes, publications and presses, photographs of the Camargue in the 1900s and an old stage coach, you need to turn up at 3pm on Tuesday (or make an appointment ☎04.90.80.80.88; 20F).

On rue de Mons, to the east, the seventeenth-century Hôtel de Crochans is home to the **Maison Jean Vilar** (Tues–Fri 9am–noon & 1.30–5.30pm, Sat 10am–5pm; free; ☎04.90.86.59.64), named after the great theatre director who set up the "Week of Dramatic Art" in 1947, which became the annual festival in the following year. The building houses festival memorabilia, an excellent library dedicated to the performing arts, and a collection of videos on everything from Stanislavski to last year's street theatre. These are sometimes shown in the foyer, or at special screenings, but you can also arrange your own viewing, with one day's notice – the catalogue is at the main desk. The Maison also puts on temporary exhibitions, workshops and public lectures with renowned theatre people.

THE FESTIVAL PROVENÇAL

The Palais du Roure is the main Avignon venue for the **Festival Provençal**, which for over two decades has been celebrating the Provençal language and traditions in poetry, theatre, dance and song. It takes place during July and early August, with events in several Vaucluse cities. Details from the Palais du Roure on ☎04.90.80.80.88.

The Banasterie and Carmes quartiers

The **quartier de la Banasterie**, to the east of the Palais des Papes, is mostly seventeenth- and eighteenth-century. The heavy wooden doors with highly sculptured lintels bear the nameplates of lawyers, psychiatrists and dietary consultants. It's worth poking your nose into the courtyard of the Hôtel de Fonseca, built in 1600 at 17 rue Ste-Catherine, to admire its mullioned windows and old well. Between Banasterie and place des Carmes are a tangle of tiny streets guaranteed to get you lost. Pedestrians have priority over cars on many of them, and there are plenty of tempting cafés and restaurants along the way. At 6 rue Saluces you'll find the peculiar **Musée du Mont de Piété** (Mon–Fri 8.30–11.30am & 1.30–5.30pm; free), an ex-pawnbroker's shop and now the town's archives, which has a small display of papal bulls and painted silk desiccators for determining the dry weight of what was the city's chief commodity.

Beyond, the Carmelite convent of the **Église St-Symphorien** once spread over the whole of place des Carmes, right down to the bell tower on rue Carreterie, built in the 1370s with the bell cage added in the sixteenth century. Today, all that remains is the church (Mon–Fri 8–9am & 6.30–7.30pm, Sat 5–7pm, Sun 8.45am–noon), which contains a stunning painting of *St Éloi* by Nicolas Mignard. The cloisters have become a theatre for Avignon's oldest permanent company, the Théâtre des Carmes, run by André Benedetto.

Further up, at 155 rue Carreterie, you'll find Avignon's English bookshop which also serves as a tearoom, meeting place and venue for readings and performances (Tues–Sat 9.30am–12.30pm & 2–6.30pm; sometimes open Fri eve & Sun pm).

From St-Pierre to the rue des Teinturiers

To the south of rue Banasterie, on **place St-Pierre**, stands one of the most spectacular of Avignon's churches, the Renaissance **Église St-Pierre** (Fri 2.30–5.30pm, Sat 9–11am, Sun 8.30–11.30am). When closed you can still admire its greatest artwork, the doors, carved in 1551; the Annunciation is depicted on the right, and St Jerome and St Michael on the left. Nearby, the **Musée Aubanel**, 7 place St-Pierre (by appointment only; ☎04.90.86.35.02; free) is dedicated to Provençal literature and to printing – a significant activity in the city prior to the Revolution, since the French censors had no jurisdiction here.

To the south is the city's main pedestrian precinct, which centres on **place du Change**, and the old **Jewish quarter** around rue du Vieux-Sextier and place Jérusalem, where, during the time of the popes, Jews had to wear yellow caps and were locked in every night. To the east is **place Pie**, site of the grimly functional modern **market halls** and an open flower market. Just to the south, on rue du Roi-Réné is the **Chapelle St-Clare**, where, during the Good Friday service in 1327, the poet Petrarch first saw and fell in love with Laura, as recorded in a note on the pages of the poet's copy of Virgil.

From place Pie, rue Bonneterie heads southeast, becoming **rue des Teinturiers**, the most atmospheric street in Avignon. Its name refers to the eighteenth- and nineteenth-century business of calico printing. The cloth was washed in the Sorgue, which still runs alongside the street, turning the wheels of long-gone mills. It's also an excellent street for restaurant-browsing, though the water tends to get a bit smelly as you reach the ramparts.

Place St-Didier and around

A short way south of place de l'Horloge and just east of the main drag, rue de la République, is **place St-Didier**. The square is dominated by the **Église St-Didier** (Mon–Sat 9am–noon & 2–7pm, Sun 10am–noon). Check out the altarpiece in the first chapel on the left which depicts Mary's pain with such realism that it has acquired the somewhat uncomfortable name of "Notre-Dame-du-Spasme". There are also some four-teenth-century frescoes in the left-hand chapel.

Between the noisy rue de la République and place St-Didier, on rue Labourer, is the impressive fourteenth-century former cardinal's residence, now the municipal library, the **Mediathèque Ceccano** (Mon 1–6pm, Tues–Sat 10am–6pm); occasional exhibitions are held in the beautifully decorated interior, or you could spend a tranquil afternoon reading in its quiet gardens. Opposite, the **Musée Angladon-Dubrujeaud** (Wed–Sun: April–Sept 1–6pm; Oct–March closes at 7pm; 30F) displays the remains of the private collection of Jacques Doucet. It was once a mighty collection, containing such treasures as Picasso's *Demoiselles d'Avignon* and Douanier-Rousseau's *The Snake Charmer* (now in the Musée d'Orsay), but much of it was either given away or sold bit by bit. Testimony to grander days can be found in the first room, where photographs of Jacques Doucet's house, with rooms decorated according to the style of the paintings therein, reveal a man ahead of his time. The rest of the downstairs room shows what is left of his contemporary collection; *Portrait of Mme Foujita* and a self-portrait by Foujita, Modigliani's *The Pink Blouse*, various Picasso's, and Van Gogh's *Railway Wagons*, the only painting from Van Gogh's stay in Provence to be on display in Provence. The theme of decorating rooms around a style has been taken up in the rest of the museum with a room dedicated to the medieval and Renaissance periods, three dedicated to the eighteenth century (Doucet's first passion) and a Far East room.

Musée Calvet and Musée Vouland

West of rue de la République are two museums that are well worth checking out. The first, the excellent **Musée Calvet** (Mon & Wed–Sun 10am–1pm & 2–6pm; 30F), is at 65 rue Joseph-Vernet. Housed in an impressive eighteenth-century palace, the museum is undergoing a restoration programme due to be completed in 2002, which means that some of the collection is reshuffled from time to time. However, the Galerie des Sculptures, the first room, is completed and set to stay where it is. A better introduction to a museum couldn't be wished for; the handful of languorous nineteenth-century marble sculptures, including Bosio's *Young Indian*, are perfectly suited to this elegant space, lit from either side. The end of the gallery houses the Puech collection with a large selection of silverware, Italian and Dutch paintings, but more unusually a Flemish curiosities cabinet, painted with scenes from the story of Daniel. Upstairs, the Provençal dynasties of the Mignards and the Vernets are well represented. Nicolas Mignard sets off with a fine set of Seasons in the Joseph Vernet room, whilst Joseph Vernet himself sticks to representing the different times of the day. Further down Horace Vernet donated the subtle *The Death of young Barra* by Jacques-Louis David as well as Géricault's *Battle of Nazareth*. On the way out don't miss the Victor Martin collection, including Vlaminck's *Sur le Zinc*, Bonnard's *Jour d'Hiver*, and the haunting portrait of *The Downfall* by Chaïm Soutine. The rest of the eclectic collection – from an Egyptian mummy of a five-year-old boy to intricate wrought-iron work, taking in Gallo-Roman pots and Gothic clocks along the way – is due to be on show again once restoration work is completed.

The **Musée Vouland** lies further west, at the end of rue Victor-Hugo, near Porte St-Dominique (Tues–Sat June–Sept 9am–noon & 2–6pm; Oct–May 2–6pm only; 20F). Here you can feast your eyes on the fittings, fixtures and furnishings that French aristocrats once indulged in. There's some brilliant Moustiers faïence, exquisite marquetry and Louis XV ink-pots with silver rats holding the lids.

Eating and drinking

Good-value midday **meals** are plentiful in Avignon and eating well in the evening needn't break the bank. The large terraced **café-brasseries** on place de l'Horloge, rue de la République, place du Change and place des Corps-Saints will all serve quick basic meals. Rue des Teinturiers and the streets of the Banasterie and Carmes are good places to try if you're on a tight **budget**, and the streets between place de Crillon and place du Palais if you're not.

Restaurants, cafés and bars

Les Apprentis de la Bonneterie, 26 rue de la Bonneterie (☎04.90.27.37.97). Taking its name from a Perec novel and retaining the original fixtures and fittings of the shop that once stood here, this restaurant has an easy charm. Tasty, well-presented food on the 78F menu.

Le Belgocargo, 10 pl des Châtaignes (☎04.90.85.72.99). Belgian restaurant specializing in mussels and beer. Midday menu with drink for under 50F. Closed Sun out of season.

Brunel, 46 rue de la Balance (☎04.90.85.24.83). Superb regional dishes. Menus from 200F. Closed Sun & Mon, and mid-July to mid-Aug.

Les Célestins, pl des Corps-Saints. 7am–1am. Café-bar with a young, fairly trendy clientele. Closed Sun.

Christian Étienne, 10 rue Mons (☎04.90.86.16.50). One of Avignon's best restaurants, housed in a fourteenth-century mansion and offering exotic combinations such as fennel sorbet with a saffron sauce plus some great fish dishes. From 300F; midday 170F menu. Last orders 9.30pm. Closed Sun & Mon.

La Cintra, 44 cours Jean-Jaurès. Dependable brasserie with a menu under 80F. Daily till midnight.

Côté Jardin, 7 rue des Trois-Carreaux (☎04.90.82.26.70). Tiny, attractive resto and very good value. Booking advisable. Around 100F.

L'Entrée des Artistes, 1 pl des Carmes (☎04.90.82.46.90). Small, friendly bistro serving traditional French dishes; 120F menu. Closed Sat midday, all Sun & first two weeks Sept.

L'Épicerie, pl St Pierre (☎04.90.82.74.22). A quiet spot in which to try out a selection of cheeses (65F) or starters (75F), or go for a relaxed meal (around 150F). Closed Sun.

La Ferme, chemin du Bois, Île de la Barthelasse (☎04.90.82.57.53) A traditional farmhouse with well-prepared simple dishes from 100F. Closed Sat midday & Mon out of season.

La Fourchette, 17 rue Racine (☎04.90.85.20.93). The basic fixed menu (around 150F) offers marinated sardines, vegetable terrine, stuffed tomatoes and excellent meat and fish stews. Last orders 9.30pm. Closed Sat, Sun & last two weeks in Aug.

Grand Café du Commerce, 21 rue St-Jean-le-Vieux. Pleasant café serving beer, coffee and snacks. Daily till 1am.

Hiély-Lucullus, 5 rue de la République (☎04.90.86.17.07). Avignon's top gastronomic palace, serving beautiful Provençal cuisine – gratin of mussels and spinach, stuffed rabbit, sole in red pepper sauce, lamb grilled in rosemary, scallop salad, a huge selection of goats' cheese and wonderful puddings – all washed down with the best local wines. Menus from 220F. Last orders 9.15pm. Closed Mon, Tues midday out of season & last two weeks of June.

Koala Bar, 2 pl des Corps-Saints. Loud and popular music played in this bar which attracts a young and mainly English-speaking crowd.

Mon Bar, 17 rue du Portail Matheron. Pleasant bar with a laid-back atmosphere.

Le Petit Bédon, 70 rue Joseph-Vernet (☎04.90.82.33.98). According to fellow chefs the "pot-belly" does the best meal for under 250F anywhere in the city. Last orders 10pm. Closed Mon eve, Sun & last two weeks in Aug.

Shakespeare, 155 rue Carreterie. English bookshop and *salon de thé*. Closed evenings and all Sun & Mon.

La Tache d'Encre, 22 rue des Teinturiers (☎04.90.85.46.03). The food is cheap (under 100F), yet not brilliant, but the musicians – jazz, rock, *chansons*, African or salsa – usually are. Congenial atmosphere, with live music Fri & Sat nights, plus occasional weekdays; booking advisable. Closed Mon & Tues eve, & Sun lunch.

Les Trois Clefs, 26 rue des Trois-Faucons (☎04.90.86.51.53). Inventive dishes based around seasonal vegetables, game and fish. The hare in *tapenade* and the *sandre au jus de ratatouille* are recommended. Menu, including wine, for 140F. Last orders 10pm. Closed Wed.

Venaissin, 16 pl de l'Horloge (☎04.90.86.20.99). In the height of summer you'd be very lucky to get a table here. It's the only cheap brasserie on pl de l'Horloge serving more than just *steack-frites*. Menu under 100F.

Woolloo Mooloo, 16 bis rue des Teinturiers (☎04.90.85.28.44). An old printshop with all the presses still in place. Now serves dishes from around the world and a good selection of teas. Menu under 100F. Occasional theme nights. Closed Mon & Sun lunch.

Nightlife and entertainment

Though a lot of the city's energy is saved up for the festival, there's a fair amount of **nightlife and cultural events** in Avignon all year round, particularly café-theatre. For more information, try at the tourist office which hands out a free bi-monthly calendar, *Rendez-Vous*. They may also have the free, weekly arts, events and music magazine, *César*, also available in arts centres.

Live music and discos

Le 5/5, 1 rempart St-Roch (☎04.90.82.61.32). Mainstream disco, popular with the locals. Thurs–Sat from 11pm.

AJMI Jazz Club, c/o La Manutention, rue Escalier Ste-Anne (☎04.90.86.08.61). Hosts major acts and some adventurous new groups. Thurs is jazz night.

Le Bistroquet, Quartier du Mouton, Île de la Barthelasse (☎04.90.82.25.83). Rock bar with live gigs. Closed Mon & June.

L'Esclave Bar, 12 rue du Limas. Gay bar and disco. Open daily; shows Wed & Sun; drinks from 40F.

Le Privé, rte de Tavel, Les Angles (☎04.90.25.90.99). Club hosting international DJs and playing mainly house music. Admission 50F before midnight, 70F after. Fri & Sat from 11pm.

Pub Z, corner of rue Bonneterie and rue Artaud. Rock bar, decorated in black and white in honour of the zebra. Open till 1.30am; closed Sun & first three weeks Aug.

Le Red Zone, 25 rue Carnot (☎04.90.27.02.44). Trendy bar with DJs and weekly concerts. Thurs–Sat 7pm–1.30am.

Les Sources, 24 bd St-Michel, by Porte Magnanen (☎04.90.86.32.76). Venue hosting theatre, jazz nights, flamenco and rock nights. Food available, too.

La Tache d'Encre, 22 rue des Teinturiers (☎04.90.85.46.03). Live music – jazz, rock, *chansons*, African or salsa – Fri & Sat, plus occasional weekdays; booking advisable. Closed Mon & Tues eve & Sun lunch. Menus for under 100F.

Tapalocas, 10 rue Galante (☎04.90.82.56.84). Spanish music, sometimes live. Tapas at 12F each. Daily 11.45am–1.30am.

Theatre and cinema

Théâtre du Balcon, 38 rue Guillaume-Puy (☎04.90.85.00.80). A venue that has put on African music, twentieth-century classics and contemporary theatre.

Le Cercle, 15 rue Galante (☎04.90.86.44.83). The former Utopia cinema is now used for a variety of events, including "Les Rendez-Vous Galante" where people perform, recite and tell stories.

Théâtre du Chêne Noir, 8 bis rue Ste-Catherine (☎04.90.86.58.11). May have mime, a musical or Molière on offer.

Opéra, pl de l'Horloge (☎04.90.82.23.44). Classical opera and ballet.

Péniche Dolphin Blues, chemin de l'île Piot (☎04.90.82.46.96). One-person shows and café-theatre in a barge moored on the Île Piot.

Utopia, 5 rue Figuière & 4 rue Escalier Ste-Anne (☎04.90.82.65.36). Cinemas showing avant-garde, obscure or old-time favourites, always in the original language. The tourist office has programmes.

Listings

Airport Aéroport Avignon-Caumont (☎04.90.81.51.15). Internal flights only.

Bike rental Aymard, 80 rue Guillaume-Puy (☎04.90.86.32.49); Masson Richard, pl Pie (☎04.90.82.32.19); Transhumance Voyages has a desk at the tourist office (☎04.90.95.57.81).

Boat trips Le Mireio, allée de l'Oulle (☎04.90.85.62.25); year-round trips upstream towards Châteauneuf-du-Pape and downstream to the Camargue – two-week advance booking recommended. Le Cygne, quai de la Ligne, 300m upstream from Pont St-Bénézet (☎04.66.59.35.62); trips to Beaucaire and Tarascon, Aigues-Mortes and Arles.

Bookshops Shakespeare, 155 rue Carreterie (closed Mon); Maison de la Presse, 36 cours Jean-Jaurès; FNAC, 19 rue de la République.

Bus Local buses: Urban Tourelle de la République (☎04.90.82.68.19) and place Pie (☎04.90.85.44.93). Long-distance buses: 5 av Montclar (☎04.90.82.07.35).

Car parks Guarded parking (24hr) at 16 bd St-Roch, near the train station and at 1 rue P-Mérindol; free, unguarded parking by Porte d'Oulle.

Car rental Budget, 89 rte de Montfavet (☎04.90.87.50.80); A.S.L 3 bd St-Ruf (☎04.90.86.06.61); AAC 15 bd St-Ruf (☎04.90.85.69.11); Europcar 27 bd St-Ruf (☎04.90.14.40.80).

Currency exchange Chaix Conseil, 43 cours Jean-Jaurès (Mon–Fri 10.10am–1pm & 3–7pm, Sat 9.40am–12.30pm & 1.30–7pm); 24hr automatic exchange at CIC, 13 rue de la République and at Caixa Bank, 64 rue Joseph-Vernet.

Emergencies For doctor/ambulance call: ☎15 or Médecins de Garde ☎04.90.87.75.00. Hospital: Centre Hospitalier H-Duffaut, 305 rue Raoul-Follereau (☎04.90.80.33.33).

Laundry 24 rue Lanterne; 27 rue Portail Magnanen; 66 pl des Corps-Saints; and 9 rue Chapeau-Rouge.

Markets Antiques: place Crillon (Sat morning); flea market on pl des Carmes (Sun morning). Books and records: cours Jean-Jaurès (July 1 to Aug 5 every Sat; rest of year first Sat of the month). Flowers: pl des Carmes (Sat morning). Food: in the covered halls on place Pie (Tues & Sun) and on rue rempart St-Michel, between portes St-Michel and Magnanen (Sat & Sun).

Pharmacy Call police at bd St-Roch on ☎04.90.16.81.00 for addresses of late-opening pharmacies.

Police Municipale 10 pl Pie (☎08.00.00.84.00).

Post office cours Président-Kennedy (Mon–Fri 8am–7pm, Sat 8am–noon).

Swimming pool Piscine de la Barthelasse, Île de la Barthelasse (May–Aug 10am–7pm; 24F/20F). Do not attempt to swim in the Rhône.

Taxis ☎04.90.82.20.20.

Trains ☎08.36.35.35.35.

Villeneuve-lès-Avignon

VILLENEUVE-LÈS-AVIGNON rises up a rocky escarpment above the west bank of the river, looking down upon its older neighbour from behind far more convincing fortifications. In the thirteenth and fourteenth centuries, when its citadel and bridge defences were built, the Rhône at Avignon was the French border, not just with the papal enclave but with the county of Provence, whose allegiances shifted between the many different rivals of the king of France. Despite that, and the French king's habit of claiming land, and therefore taxes, in areas of Avignon that the river flooded, Villeneuve operated largely as a suburb to Avignon, with palatial residences constructed by the cardinals and a great monastery founded by Pope Innocent VI.

To this day Villeneuve is, strictly speaking, part of Languedoc not Provence, and would score better in the hierarchy of towns to visit were it further from Avignon, whose monuments it can almost match for colossal scale and impressiveness. In summer, at least, it benefits, providing venues for the festival, as well as accommodation overspill; it's certainly worth a day, whatever time of year you visit.

Arrival, information and accommodation

From Avignon's gare SNCF, the #11 bus (direction Les Angles) runs every thirty minutes direct to place Charles-David (Bellevue stop) in Villeneuve; after 7pm you'll have to take a taxi or walk the 3km. The **tourist office** is on place Charles-David (July & Aug daily 8.45am–12.30pm & 2.30–6.30pm; rest of year Mon–Sat 8.45am–12.30pm & 2–6pm;

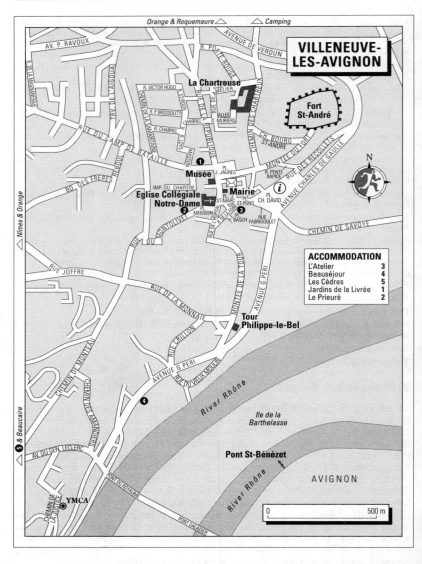

π04.90.25.61.33). They can help you with **accommodation**, though outside the festival period you shouldn't have too many difficulties finding your own.

HOTELS

L'Atelier, 5 rue de la Foire (π04.90.25.01.84, fax 04.90.25.80.06). A sixteenth-century house with huge open fireplaces and a walled garden. Excellent value. ③.

Beauséjour, 61 av Gabriel-Péri (☎04.90.25.20.56). Close to the bridge into Avignon, overlooking the river near the Pont du Royaume; avoid the rooms on the road side, as they're a bit noisy. ③.

Les Cèdres, 39 av Pasteur (☎04.90.25.43.92, fax 04.90.25.14.66). A converted Louis XIV mansion with pool and restaurant. ④.

Jardins de la Livrée, 4 bis rue Camp de Bataille (☎04.90.26.05.05). Bed and breakfast, plus excellent-value midday and evening meals; very friendly hosts and clean, comfortable rooms. The only drawback is the noise – all night – of passing trains. No credit cards. ④.

Le Prieuré, 7 pl du Chapitre (☎04.90.15.90.15, fax 04.90.25.45.39). If money is no object, then this is indisputably the first choice – if you fancy being surrounded by tapestries, finely carved doors, old oak ceilings and other baronial trappings, that is. The restaurant has a very good reputation. ⑧.

HOSTELS

YMCA hostel, 7 bis chemin de la Justice (☎04.90.25.46.20). Beautifully situated overlooking the river by Pont du Royaume, with balconied rooms for two to six people, and an open-air swimming pool. 96F, including breakfast; full or half board obligatory for stays of more than one night. Bus #1 (direction Villeneuve–Les Angles, stop Pont d'Avignon), or bus #10 (direction Les Angles–Villeneuve, stop Général-Leclerc).

CAMPSITE AND SELF-CATERING

Camping Municipal de la Laune, chemin St-Honoré, off the D980 (☎04.90.25.76.06). Near the sports stadium and swimming pools. Pleasant three-star site with plenty of shade and disabled facilities. Bookings can be made through the tourist office. Closed Oct–March.

Les Logis St-Éloi, 14 pl de l'Oratoire (☎04.90.25.40.36). A complex of studio apartments with kitchenettes situated in sixteenth- and seventeenth-century buildings. ③.

The Town

Villeneuve clusters around rue de la République which runs north from the Collègiale Notre-Dame church on pl St-Marc. The **Fort St-André** lies on a rise to the east.

For a good overview of Villeneuve – and Avignon – make your way south of place St-Marc to the **Tour Philippe-le-Bel** at the bottom of montée de la Tour (bus stop Philippe-le-Bel). This tower was built to guard the French end of Pont St-Bénézet, and a climb to the top (April–Sept Tues–Sun 10am–12.30pm & 3–7pm; Oct–Jan & March 10am–noon & 2–5.30pm; 10F) rewards with stunning views.

Even more indicative of French distrust of its neighbours is the enormous **Fort St-André** (access to the towers: April–Sept daily 10am–noon & 2–5pm; Oct–March 10am–noon & 2–6pm; 25F), whose bulbous, double-towered gateway and vast white walls loom over the town. Inside, refreshingly, there's not a hint of a postcard stall or souvenir shop, just tumbled-down houses and the former abbey, with its gardens of olive trees, ruined chapels, lily ponds and dovecotes (Tues–Sun same hours as the towers; 20F). Its cliff-face terrace is the classic spot for artists and photographers to compose their views of Avignon. You can reach the approach to the fortress, montée du Fort, from place Jean-Jaurès on rue de la République, or by the "rapid slope" of rue Pente-Rapide, a cobbled street of tiny houses leading off rue des Recollets on the north side of place Charles-David.

Almost at the top of rue de la République, on the right, allée des Muriers leads from place des Chartreux to the entrance of **La Chartreuse du Val de Bénédiction**

MUSEUMS AND MONUMENTS IN VILLENEUVE

The **Passeport pour l'Art** (45F) gives you entry to the Fort St-André, Tour Philippe-le-Bel, La Chartreuse du Val de Bénédiction, Collégiale Notre-Dame and its cloister and the Musée Pierre-de-Luxembourg. It is available from each of the sites covered and from the tourist office.

(April–Sept 9am–6.30pm; Oct–March 9.30am–5.30pm; 32F), one of the largest Charterhouses in France and founded by Innocent VI, the sixth of the Avignon popes, whose sharp profile is outlined on his tomb in the church. The buildings, which were sold off after the Revolution and gradually restored this century, are totally unembellished. With the exception of the Giovanetti frescoes in the chapel beside the refectory, all the paintings and treasures of the monastery have been dispersed, leaving you with a strong impression of the austerity of the strict practices of the Carthusian order. The only communication allowed was one hour of conversation a week plus the rather less congenial public confessions. Monks left the enclosure for one three-hour walk per week; within, their time was spent as much on manual labour as on prayer, and their diet was strictly vegetarian.

You are free to wander round unguided, through the three cloisters, the church, chapels, cells and communal spaces; there's little to see but plenty of atmosphere to be absorbed. It is one of the best venues in the Festival d'Avignon, and so is the four-teenth-century **Église Collégiale Notre-Dame** and its cloister on place St-Marc (April to mid-June Tues–Sun 10am–12.30pm & 3–7pm; mid-June to Sept daily Tues–Sun 10am–12.30pm & 3–7pm; Oct–Jan & March 10am–noon & 2–5.30pm; cloister 7F, otherwise free). The church is decorated with paintings of the Avignon School and with caring cupids tending Christ's hands and feet on the altar. However, Notre-Dame's most important treasure, a rare fourteenth-century smiling Madonna and Child made from a single tusk of ivory, allegedly carved by a convert from Islam, is now housed, along with many of the paintings from the Chartreuse, in the **Musée Pierre-de-Luxembourg** just to the north along rue de la République (same hours as Église Collégiale Notre-Dame; 20F).

The museum's spacious layout includes a single room, with comfortable seats and ample documentation, given over to the most stunning painting in the collection, *Le Couronnement de la Vierge*, painted in 1453 by Enguerrand Quarton as the altarpiece for the church in the Chartreuse. With fiercely contrasting red, orange, gold, white and blue, the statuesque and symmetrical central figures of the coronation form a powerful and unambiguous subject. To either side of them, in true medieval style, the social hierarchy is defined, using a greater variety of form and colour. Along the bottom of the painting the scale of detail leaps several frames, with flames engulfing sinners, devils and their assistant beasts carrying away victims, walled towns with pin-size figures, and in the distance Mont St-Victoire and the cliffs of Estaque. No other painting in the collection matches Quarton's work and many are too obviously public relations pieces for their patrons, placing the pope, lord or bishop in question beside the Madonna or Christ.

Eating and drinking

Villeneuve's centre has a good choice of **eating** places, both for reasonable run-of-the-mill meals and for gourmet blowouts in beautiful surroundings. Cave St-Marc, just up to the right as you approach place St-Marc from place Charles-David (9.30am–12.15pm & 3.30–7.15pm; closed Wed & Sun), is a good place for **wine buying**.

Aubertin, 1 rue de l'Hôpital (☎04.90.25.94.84). A sumptuous restaurant, serving a midday menu (120F; à la carte from 300F) in the shade of the old arcades by the Collégiale Notre-Dame. Closed Mon out of season.

La Banaste, 28 rue de la République (☎04.90.25.64.20). Good-value Provençal fare but better to eat indoors rather than on the noisy roadside. Menus from around 100F. Closed Tues out of season.

La Calèche, 35 rue de la République (☎04.90.25.02.54). Traditional dishes. Menus from around 98F. Closed Sun out of season.

La Magnaneraie, 37 rue Camp de Bataille, off rue de la Magnanerie (☎04.90.25.11.11). Very posh and very good; courgette flowers stuffed with cream of mushrooms and a *gâteau d'agneau* are the specialities. Menu for 170F; à la carte from 400F.

La Mamma Lucia, pl V-Basch (☎04.90.25.00.71). Italian specialities with pavement tables from which to watch the world go by. Menus from 80F. Closed Sun out of season.

Café de l'Univers, pl J-Jaurès. Ordinary café set in the heart of Villeneuve on a picturesque square.

La Petite Crau and La Montagnette

A short way downstream from Avignon, the Rhône reaches its confluence with the Durance. Between the two rivers and the Chaîne des Alpilles to the south is an area that was once a swampy wasteland. The rocky outcrop of **La Montagnette**, running parallel to the Rhône for 10km, and the hill at **Châteaurenard** were the only extensive bits of solid ground. However, the plain, known as **La Petite Crau**, has been steadily irrigated since Roman times, and today it is a richly cultivated area, with cherries and peaches as its main crops. It is criss-crossed with water channels, while row upon row of cypresses and poplars form windbreaks for the fruit trees. Villages in the area are few and far between, built on the scattered bases of rock, and many retain their medieval elements of fortified walls and churches and tangled narrow streets. This is this Provence that inspired **Frédéric Mistral** and Vincent Van Gogh.

If you have your own **transport**, La Petite Crau and La Montagnette can easily be reached as day-trips from Avignon, and from Tarascon or St-Rémy further south. By **bus**, it's more problematic, as bus links between the villages are sporadic. Buses from Avignon to Châteaurenard are most frequent, going on to Graveson and Maillane. Boulbon, Barbentane and Tarascon are served by buses to Nîmes. There are no train services.

Châteaurenard and Noves

CHÂTEAURENARD, just south of Avignon, is the main town in La Petite Crau and host to a massive wholesale fruit and vegetable market each Sunday; the produce is all locally grown and on market days the town is packed. Dominating the town's physical features are the two remaining towers of its Romanesque and Gothic medieval **castle** (July & Aug daily 10am–noon & 3–6.30pm; rest of year Mon–Thurs & Sun 10am–noon & 3–5pm, Sat 3–5pm; 20F), described by Frédéric Mistral as "twin horns on the forehead of a hill". Even if you're only passing through, it's worth taking the time to climb the castle's **Tour du Griffon** for the views across La Petite Crau to the Alpilles and La Montagnette. In a recess within the castle is engraved a 700-year-old troubadour poem, in Provençal, praising the beauty of the new building erected "by such a wise king".

Buses arrive on av Roger-Salengo at the east end of which is the **tourist offices** (July–Sept Mon–Sat 8.45am–noon & 3–7pm, Sun & public hols 10am–noon; Sept–June Mon–Sat 8.45am & 2–6pm; ☎04.90.94.23.27). For cheap and basic **accommodation** you could try *Le Central*, 27 cours Carnot (☎04.90.94.10.90; ②); *Les Glycines*, 14 av Victor-Hugo (☎04.90.94.10.66, fax 04.90.94.78.10; ②); or *Le Rustic,* place Victoire (☎04.90.94.13.36; ①). *La Roquette* **campsite** on av J-Mermoz (☎04.90.94.27.02; closed Nov–March) is small and inexpensive. For **food**, *La Buvette des Tours*, just below the castle, serves cheap salads, grills and pizzas on summer evenings (Thurs–Sun). Alternatively, there's the *Brasserie des Producteurs* at 4 rue R-Ginoux (☎04.90.94.04.61; menu from 70F; closed Sun).

Five kilometres east of Châteaurenard, the little village of **NOVES** is typical of the area, with its fourteenth-century gateway. It is also where Laura, the subject of Petrarch's besotted sonnets, is reputed to have lived. If you fancy splashing out on a luxury stopover, head for the *Auberge de Noves* (☎04.90.94.19.21, fax 04.90.94.47.76; ⑧) just outside Noves on the Châteaurenard road; this is a seriously expensive hotel-restaurant in a beautiful farmhouse with exquisite furnishings and impeccable service;

in its restaurant you can dine on such delicacies as oysters cooked in Châteauneuf-du-Pape and duck en croûte with herbs and acacia honey (weekday menu 200F; 250F menu with wine, otherwise over 450F). For more basic comforts, Noves' **campsite** *Le Pilon d'Agel*, on the rte de Mollégès (☎04.90.95.16.23; closed Oct–March), offers a pool, disabled facilities and horses to hire.

Maillane and La Montagnette

The poet Frédéric Mistral was born in **MAILLANE** in 1830 and buried there in 1914. Primarily responsible for the turn-of-the-century revival of all things Provençal, he won the Nobel Prize for Literature, a feat no other writer of a minority language has ever achieved. The house that he built and lived in from 1876 till the end of his life has been preserved intact as the **Museon Mistral**, 11 rue Lamartine (Tues–Sun 10–11.30am & 2.30–6.30pm; 20F).

La Petite Crau was Mistral's "sacred triangle", and its customs and legends were very often his primary source of inspiration. Black Madonnas and various saints feted in these villages were, and often still are, bestowed with the power to bring rain or cure diseases. In his memoirs Mistral describes the procession of St Anthime from **Graveson**, just north of Maillane, to **LA MONTAGNETTE**, where on reaching the abbey church of **St-Michel-de-Frigolet**, the people spread out a feast on the perfumed grass and knocked back bottles of local wine for the rest of the day. If it hadn't rained by the time they reached home, they punished the saint by dipping him three times in a ditch.

The name of the abbey derives from *ferigoulo*, Provençal for thyme, which grows profusely in these hills, hence the perfumed grass of the feast. The thyme is also used to make a liqueur, Le Frigolet, which can be bought at the end of a guided tour of the **abbey church** (Mon–Fri 2.30pm; Sun & hols 4pm; free). Mistral went to school in these buildings before they returned to ecclesiastical use in the mid-nineteenth century. The highlight of the visit is the series of fourteen paintings on the *Mysteries of the Virgin Mary* by Mignard in the main church, but you may find the cloisters (free access – ask at the shop by the entrance) more spiritually inspiring.

The valleys that cut through the scrubbed white rock of La Montagnette are shaded by olive, almond and apricot trees, oaks and pines. The heights never extend above 200m, and the smell of thyme is omnipresent; easy and exhilarating walking country.

Boulbon and Barbentane

One footpath from St-Michel-de-Frigolet takes you over the ridge and, after 5km or so, down to **BOULBON**. As a strategic site overlooking the Rhône, Boulbon was heavily fortified in the Middle Ages, and today the ruins of its enormous fortress, built half within and half above a rocky escarpment, are like some picture-book crusader castle.

MARKETS

If you're in La Petite Crau on a Friday, the **Marché Paysan in Graveson**, place du Marché (mid-May to Oct 4–8pm) is not to be missed with *paysans* from La Grande and La Petite Crau, the Camargue and from across the Durance selling their goats' cheeses, honey and jams, rice, olives and olive oil, flowers and aromatic plants as well as fruit and veg picked the same morning.

The ordinary morning markets here are on Friday in **Graveson**, Thursday in **Maillane** and **Noves**, Sunday in **Châteaurenard**, Wednesday in **Barbentane** and Tuesday in Rognonas, the village just across the Durance from Avignon.

THE FÊTE DE SAINT-ÉLOI

Boulbon celebrates the **Fête de Saint-Éloi** on the last Sunday of August. This involves chariots drawn by teams of horses in Saracen harness doing the rounds of the village, and much drinking by all the villagers. Elsewhere, notably in Graveson, Châteaurenard and Maillane, this saint, whose role is protector of beasts of burden, is feted on the penultimate Sunday of July.

Here, on the first day of June the men gather with a bottle of wine apiece and process to St-Marcellin chapel in the cemetery, one of Boulbon's six Romanesque places of worship. At the end of the service the wine is blessed, the bottles are lifted first in homage to the *Seigneur* and then to the lips. But some of the wine must remain undrunk, to be corked and preserved as an antidote to illness and misfortune.

Eight kilometres from Boulbon, at the northern edge of La Montagnette in **BARBENTANE**, the fourteenth-century **Tour Anglica** keeps watch on the confluence of the Rhône and Durance. The town has two medieval gateways and a beautifully arcaded Renaissance building, the **Maison des Chevaliers**, plus a much more recent **Château** (guided tours July–Sept 10am–noon & 2–6pm; April–June & Oct closed Wed; Nov–March Sun only; 35F), designed for grandeur rather than defence. This is a seventeenth-century ducal residence with gorgeous grey and white Tuscan marble floors, and all the vases, painted ceilings, chandeliers and delicate antique furniture that you would expect of a house still owned by generations of the same family of aristocrats. The Italianate gardens are the best part.

For **hotel** accommodation in Barbentane there are the rudimentary comforts of *Hôtel St-Jean*, le Cours (☎04.90.95.50.44; ②), or the *Castel Mouisson*, quartier Castel Mouisson (☎04.90.95.51.17; ③); closed mid-Oct to mid-March) with good facilities and a pleasant garden and pool. There are two **restaurants** worth going out of your way for: the hotel-restaurant *Auberge de Noves* (see p.83); and *L'Oustalet Maianen* in Maillane (☎04.90.95.76.17; closed Mon, Sun eve & mid-Oct to March), with an excellent-value midweek menu for under 100F, and a wonderful four-course menu for 145F.

St-Rémy-de-Provence and around

The scenery of La Petite Crau changes abruptly with the eruption of the **Chaîne des Alpilles**, whose peaks look like the surf of a wave about to engulf the plain. At the northern base of the Alpilles nestles **ST-RÉMY-DE-PROVENCE**, a dreamy place where Van Gogh sought psychiatric help and painted some of his most lyrical works. St-Rémy is a beautiful place, as unspoilt as the villages around, and its old town (the Vieille Ville) is contained within a circle of boulevards no more than half a kilometre in diameter. Outside this ring, the modern town is sparingly laid out, so you don't have to plough your way through dense developments before you reach the heart of the city. Outside the old town, all the attractions lie to the south: the **Roman arch**, the hospital of **St-Paul-de-Mausole** and the **Mas de la Pyramide** farmhouse in the old Roman quarries.

St-Rémy is ideally situated for exploration of the hills or, indeed, of La Petite Crau, and easy to get to by bus. A short way south are the remains of the ancient city of **Glanum**, and along the ridge of the Alpilles is the medieval stronghold of **Les Baux**, a place dedicated to luxury tourism; both are difficult to get to by public transport.

Arrival, information and accommodation

Arriving by **bus** you'll be dropped at **place de la République**, the main square abutting the Vieille Ville to the west. The **tourist office** (June–Sept Mon–Sat 9am–noon &

2–7pm, Sun 9am–noon; Oct–May Mon–Sat 9am–noon & 2–6pm; ☎04.90.92.05.22) is just south of the centre on place Jean-Jaurès, situated between av Pasteur and av Durand-Maillane and reached by following bd Marceau until it becomes av Durand-Maillane; it provides excellent free guides on **cycling** and **walking** routes in and around the Alpilles and has addresses for hiring **horses** and for **gliding** at a club that claims to hold the world record for the longest flight. If you want to **rent a bicycle**, **tandem** or **car**, go to Ferri, 35 av de la Libération, the road to Cavaillon (☎04.90.92.10.88). For a **taxi**, call ☎04.90.92.48.20, 04.90.92.25.71 or 04.90.92.46.92. The *Maison de la Presse* opposite *La Brasserie des Alpilles* stocks some **English-language newspapers** and paperbacks.

The town has a fairly wide choice of **accommodation**, though real bargains are quite hard to come by. You may prefer to use one of the three campsites close by.

Hotels

Hôtel des Antiques, 15 av Pasteur (☎04.90.92.03.02, fax 04.90.92.50.40). A nineteenth-century mansion close to the tourist office with huge grounds, pools and wonderfully aristocratic furnishings in the dining room and salons. Closed Nov–March. ⑤.

Les Arts–La Palette, above the *Café des Arts* at 30 bd Victor-Hugo (☎04.90.92.08.50, fax 04.90.92.55.09). An excellent location and very friendly. Closed Tues & Feb. ③.

Canto Cigalo, chemin de Canto Cigalo (☎04.90.92.14.28, fax 04.90.92.24.48). By the canal to the southeast of the old town; quiet and comfortable. ④.

Le Castellet des Alpilles, 6 pl Mireille (☎04.90.92.07.21, fax 04.90.92.52.03). South of the old town, past the tourist office; small and friendly, and some rooms with great views. Closed Nov–March. ⑤.

Mexican Café, 4 rue du 8 Mai 1945 (☎04.90.92.17.66). A Mexican-style hotel and restaurant in the middle of town with just five rooms. ③.

Nostradamus, 3 av Taillandier (☎04.90.92.13.23, fax 04.90.92.49.54). Studios for two to the north of the old town by the municipal pool. Not particularly atmospheric, but cheap. ③.

Villa Glanum, 46 av Vincent-van-Gogh (☎04.90.92.03.59, fax 04.90.92.00.08). Next door to the archeological site; pleasant, not too overpriced and has a swimming pool. Most rooms with disabled facilities. Half board only. Closed mid-Nov to Feb. ④.

Ville Verte, av Fauconnet/pl de la République (☎04.90.92.06.14, fax 04.90.92.56.54). Central location with a garden and pool and seven rooms with disabled facilities. It also organizes walking, climbing and cycling trips. ③.

Campsites

Le Mas de Nicolas, av Plaisance du Touch (☎04.90.92.27.05, fax 04.90.92.36.83). A four-star municipal site, with its own pool, 2km along the rte de Mollèges to the northeast. Closed Nov–Feb.

Monplaisir, chemin Monplaisir (☎04.90.92.22.70 or 04.90.92.12.91, fax 04.90.92.18.57). Two-star and by far the cheapest of the campsites, 1km to the north along the route de Maillane. Closed Nov–Feb.

Pegomas, rte de Noves (☎04.90.92.01.21, fax 04.90.92.56.17). Three-star, with pool, 1km east on the road to Cavaillon. Closed Nov–Feb.

The Town

St-Rémy's compact centre makes it a pleasant place for relaxed strolling round the picturesque streets and their stylish shops, galleries and restaurants. Rue Carnot cuts through the old town from bd Mirabeau to bd Marceau to place Favier, where the **Musée des Alpilles** and the **Musée Archéologique** can be found.

The impressive archeological sites of **Glanum** and **Les Antiques** along with St-Rémy's other attractions, including St-Paul-de-Mausole, the psychiatric hospital whose most famous former patient is **Van Gogh**, lie south of the old town along av Pasteur, which becomes av Vincent-van-Gogh after the canal.

The Vieille Ville

The **Vieille Ville** is encircled by boulevards Marceau, Gambetta, Mirabeau and Victor-Hugo. To explore the old town take any of the streets leading off these boulevards and start wandering up alleyways and through immaculate leafy squares. From place de la République, on av de la Résistance, you'll pass the town's main church, the **Collégiale St-Martin**, a Neoclassical lump of a building of interest only for its much renowned organ, painted in a surreal lime-green (recitals every Sat from July to Sept at 5pm). The route from **rue du Parage** off bd Gambetta is particularly appealing with its central stream of clear water. Several ancient stately residences line its route as the street meanders up to the fountained **place Favier**, where you'll find St-Rémy's two main museums.

For an introduction to the region, the **Musée des Alpilles**, on place Favier, is a good first visit. Housed in the Hôtel Mistral de Mondragon, a Renaissance mansion with a romantic interior courtyard (July & Aug 10am–noon & 2–7pm; April–June & Sept–Oct 10am–noon & 2–6pm; Nov & Dec 10am–noon & 2–5pm; 18F; 40F combined ticket with the Musée Archéologique and Glanum), the museum features interesting displays on folklore, festivities and traditional crafts, plus intriguing local landscapes, some creepy portraits by Marshall Pétain's first wife, and souvenirs of local boy Nostradamus.

The collection in the neighbouring **Musée Archéologique** housed in the fifteenth-century Hôtel de Sade on rue du Parage (guided tours Tues–Sun: April–Sept 10am–noon & 2–6pm; Feb–March & Oct–Dec 10am–noon & 2–5pm; closed Jan; 18F; 40F combined ticket with the Musée des Alpilles and Glanum), comes from the archeological digs at the Greco-Roman town of Glanum (see p.88). Its primary function is for categorization of the finds and the hour's tour may be a bit much for the casual visitor, but there are some stunning pieces, in particular the well-coiffeured heads of two women, possibly Livia and Octavia, wife and sister of Augustus.

To the east of place Favier, rue Millaud leads into **rue Hoche** where a fountain topped by a bust marks the house where **Nostradamus** was born on December 14, 1503. Only the facade of the house is contemporary with the futuristic savant, and it's not open to visitors. Heading south from here brings you to the eighteenth-century Hôtel d'Estrine, at 8 rue L'Estrine, now home of the **Centre d'Art Présence Van Gogh**. The centre hosts contemporary art exhibitions and has a permanent exhibition of Van Gogh reproductions and extracts from letters plus an audiovisual presentation on the painter (Tues–Sun 10.30am–12.30pm & 2.30–6.30pm; 20F). A wide selection of Van Gogh books, prints and postcards is available from the shop.

There are many **art galleries** scattered throughout St-Rémy: Le Grand Magasin, 24 rue de la Commune (summer daily 10am–12.30pm & 2.30–7pm; winter closed Mon) combines contemporary works of art with jewellery, accessories and household objects of a stylish and original nature; Lézard'Ailleurs, 12 bd Gambetta (variable opening hours; call ☎04.90.92.47.44 for details), is an antique shop and often hosts contemporary art exhibitions.

ST-RÉMY'S FÊTES

The best time to visit St-Rémy is for the **Fête de Transhumance**, on Whit Monday, when a two-thousand-strong flock of sheep, accompanied by goats, rams and donkeys, does a tour of the town before being packed off to the Alps for the summer. There's also the **Carreto Ramado** on August 15, a harvest thanksgiving procession in which the religious or secular symbolism of the floats reveals the political colour of the various village councils. Other festivals include a pagan rather than workers' **Mayday** celebration, with donkey-drawn floral floats on which people play fifes and tambourines, while, on July 14, August 15 and the fourth Sunday in September, the intrepid local youth attempt to set loose six **bulls** that are herded round the town by their mounted chaperons.

South of the Vieille Ville

Outside the old town enclosure, a short way south of the tourist office on rue Jean-de-Nostredame, is the beautiful Romanesque **chapel of Notre-Dame-de-Pitié** (April–June & Sept 2–6pm; July & Aug 10am–noon & 3–7pm; March & Oct–Dec 1.30–5.30pm; free), which exhibits the art of the twentieth-century Greek painter, Mario Prassinos, who settled in the village of Eygalières, near St-Rémy. Tree forms, a favourite motif of his work, become a powerful graphic language in the series of oil paintings created for the chapel, *Les Peintures du Supplice*, provoked by Prassinos' horror of torture.

If you keep heading south, following av Vincent-van-Gogh, you'll come to **Les Antiques**, a triumphal arch celebrating the Roman conquest of Marseille and a mausoleum thought to commemorate two grandsons of Augustus. Save for a certain amount of weather erosion, the mausoleum is perfectly intact. The arch is less so, but both display intricate patterning and a typically Roman sense of proportion. Les Antiques would have been a familiar sight to **Vincent van Gogh**, who, in 1889, requested that he be put away for several months. The hospital chosen by his friends was in the old monastery **St-Paul-de-Mausole**, a hundred yards or so east of Les Antiques, which remains a psychiatric clinic today. Although the regime was more prison than hospital, Van Gogh was allowed to wander out around the Alpilles and painted prolifically during his twelve-month stay. The *Champs d'Oliviers*, *Le Faucher*, *Le Champ Clôturé* and *La Promenade du Soir* are among the 150 canvases of this period. The church and cloisters can be visited (daily 9am–6pm); take av Edgar-Leroy or allée St-Paul from av Vincent-van-Gogh, go past the main entrance of the clinic and into the gateway on the left at the end of the wall.

Heading east along chemin des Carrières from the hospital you'll see signs to the right for the **Mas de la Pyramide** (daily: June–Aug 9am–noon & 2–7pm; rest of year noon & 2–5pm; worth waiting if there's no immediate answer to the bell at the gate; 20F), an old troglodyte farm in the Roman quarries of Glanum with a field of lavender and a cherry orchard surrounded by cavernous openings into the rock filled with ancient farm equipment and rusting bicycles. Standing in the centre of the lavender field is a twenty-metre slice of rock – the pyramid that gives the farm its name – revealing the depth of the ancient quarrying works. The farmhouse is part medieval, part Gallo-Roman and has some fascinating pictures of the owner's family who have lived here for generations.

Glanum

One of the most impressive ancient settlements in France, **GLANUM**, 500m south of Les Antiques, was dug out from the alluvial deposits at the foot of the Alpilles (April–Sept daily 9am–7pm; Oct–March daily 9am–noon & 2–5pm; 32F; 40F combined ticket with Musée des Alpilles and Musée Archéologique). The site was originally a Neolithic homestead until the Gallo-Greeks, probably from Massalia (Marseille), built a city here between the second and first centuries BC. The Gallo-Romans constructed yet another town here from the end of the first century BC to the third century AD.

Glanum can be very difficult to get to grips with. Not only were the later buildings moulded on to the earlier ones, but the fashion at the time of Christ was for a Hellenistic style. You can distinguish the Greek levels from the Roman most easily by the stones: the earlier civilization used massive hewn rocks while the Romans preferred smaller, more accurately shaped stones. The leaflet at the admission desk is helpful, as are the attendants if your French is good enough.

Where the site narrows in the ravine at the southern end you'll find a Grecian edifice around a **spring**, the feature that made this location so desirable. Steps lead down to a pool, with a slab above for the libations of those too sick to descend. An inscription records that Agrippa was responsible for restoring it in 27 BC and for dedicating it to Valetudo, the Roman goddess of health. But **altars** to Hercules are still in evidence, while up the hill to the west are traces of a prehistoric settlement which also depended on this spring. The Gallo-Romans directed the water through canals to heat houses and, of course, to the **baths** that lie near the entrance to the site. There are superb sculptures on the Roman **Temples Geminées** (twin temples), as well as fragments of mosaics, fountains of both periods, and first-storey walls and columns.

Eating and entertainment

Throughout the year, you'll find plenty of **brasseries** and **restaurants** open in and around old St-Rémy. *Le Jardin de Frédéric*, 8 bd Gambetta (☎04.90.92.27.76; closed Wed), has a 130F midday menu, and usually some interesting dishes on offer. There are a few good options on rue Carnot (leading from bd Victor-Hugo east through the old town to bd Marceau) including *La Gousse d'Ail* at no. 25 (☎04.90.92.16.87; closed Wed) where veggies can feast on pasta with *pistou* and almonds; *Le Gaulois* at no. 57 (☎04.90.92.11.53) which, though not brilliant, is at least generous with a menu under 100F; and *La Maison Jaune* at no. 15 (☎04.90.92.56.14; closed Mon & Sun eve) with polenta and pigeon roasted in Baux wines on the 245F menu, and grilled aubergines and *bourride de lotte* on the 120F lunchtime menu. *Lou Planet* at 7 place Favier is a scenic spot to dine on crêpes and *Le Bistrot des Alpilles*, 15 bd Mirabeau (☎04.90.92.09.17; till midnight; closed Sun), is the popular brasserie for *gigot d'agneau* and *tarte au citron* (75F midday menu, evening 165F).

For **café lounging** head for the *Café des Arts*, 30 bd Victor-Hugo (open till 12.30am; closed Tues & Feb) where the works of local painters are exhibited. Next door is the Librarie des Arts, a good bookshop with lovely picture books on the region. If you're after **picnic fare**, do your shopping at the Wednesday morning **market** on the pedestrian streets of the old town or at the Saturday market in place de la Mairie. The *boulangerie* at 5 rue Carnot sells the special *épis de St-Rémy*, spiky baguettes. In season you'll see and smell great bunches of basil and marjoram which are grown in abundance around St-Rémy; aromatic oils are another speciality of the town, which are produced and sold Chez Florame at 34 bd Mirabeau (Easter–Sept Mon–Fri 9am–noon & 2–6pm, Sat & Sun 10am–noon & 3–6pm; Oct–Easter closed Sun).

The Ciné Palace on av Fauconnet sometimes screens undubbed English-language films (programme from the tourist office), but if you fancy something a little more lively, try the two **discos**, *La Haute Galine,* quartier de la Galine (☎04.90.92.00.03) and *La Forge,* av de la Libération (☎04.90.92.31.52), or the *Cocktail Clun* **bar** on rue Roger-Salengro (running north from place de la République), which has a karaoke night.

Les Baux

At the top of the Alpilles ridge, 10km southwest of St-Rémy, lies the distinctly unreal fortified village of **LES BAUX**. Unreal partly because the ruins of the eleventh-century citadel are hard to distinguish from the edge of the plateau whose rock is both foundation and part of the structure. And unreal, too, because this Ville Morte (Dead City) and a vast area of the plateau around it are accessible only via a turnstile from the living village below, which remains a too-perfect collection of sixteenth- and seventeenth-century churches, chapels and mansions.

Les Baux once lived off the power and wealth of its medieval lords, who owed allegiance to none. When the dynasty died out at the end of the fourteenth century, the town, which had once numbered six thousand inhabitants, passed to the counts of Provence and then to the kings of France, who in 1632, razed the feudal citadel to the ground and fined the population into penury. From that date until the nineteenth century both citadel and village were inhabited almost exclusively by bats and crows, until the discovery of bauxite (the aluminium ore takes its name from Les Baux) in the neighbouring hills, which gradually brought back some life to the village. Today tourism is the most important industry, with around 1.5 million visitors a year descending on the population of four hundred.

The village

The lived-in village has a great many beautiful buildings, among them those housing its half-a-dozen or so museums. One of the best museums is the **Musée Yves Brayer** in the Hôtel des Porcelets (April–Sept daily 10am–12.30pm & 2–6.30pm; Oct–March Mon & Wed–Sun 10am–12.30pm & 2–5pm; 25F), showing the paintings of the twentieth-century figurative artist whose work also adorns the seventeenth-century **Chapelle des Pénitents Blancs** on place de l'Église. Changing exhibitions of the work of contemporary Provençal artists are displayed in the **Hôtel de Manville** (hours vary, check with the tourist office; free). The museum of the **Fondation Louis Jou** in the fifteenth-century Hôtel Jean de Brion (visit by appointment only; ☎04.90.54.34.17; 20F) contains the presses, wood lettering blocks and hand-printed books of the master typographer whose workshop opposite is still used for manual printing (products on sale in the boutique). The **Musée des Santons** in the old hôtel de ville (daily 8am–7pm; free) displays traditional Provençal nativity figures.

Follow the signs to the château for the entrance to the **Citadelle de la Ville Morte**, (March–Nov 9am–7.30pm, Nov–Feb 9am–5pm; 35F), where there are several museums among the ruins. Pick of the bunch is the **Musée de l'Olivier** in the Romaneque Chapelle St-Blaise, featuring slide shows of paintings of olive trees by Van Gogh, Gauguin and Cézanne. The **Musée d'Histoire des Baux** in the vaulted space of Tour de Brau has a collection of archeological remains and models to illustrate the history from medieval splendour to bauxite works. The most impressive ruins are those of the feudal castle demolished on Richelieu's orders; there's also the partially restored **Chapelle Castrale** and the **Tour Sarrasine**, the cemetery, ruined houses half carved out of the rocky escarpment, and some spectacular views, the best of which is out across La Grande Crau from beside the statue of the Provençal poet Charloun Riev at the southern edge of the plateau.

Practicalities

The **tourist office** is at the beginning of La Grande Rue (March–Sept daily 9am–7pm; Oct–April 9am–6pm; ☎04.90.54.34.39). You have to park – and pay– before entering the village and, as you'll soon discover, nothing in Les Baux comes cheap, least of all **accommodation**. There is just one moderately priced option, the *Hostellerie de la Reine Jeanne* (☎04.90.54.32.06, fax 04.90.54.32.33; ④) by the entrance to the village, which has very friendly staff and good **food** with menus starting from 100F. If you feel like treating yourself, try the beautiful hotel-restaurant *Oustau de Baumanière* (☎04.90.54.33.07; ⑨), just west of Les Baux on the road to the Val d'Enfer, which is spectacularly situated and simply luxurious. It is possible to get crêpes, pizzas and other **snacks** without breaking the bank along rue du Château.

The Val d'Enfer

Within walking distance of Les Baux, along the D27 leading north, is the valley of quarried and eroded rocks that has been named the **Val d'Enfer** (Valley of Hell). Dante, it is thought, came here while staying at Arles, and took his inspiration for the nine circles of the *Inferno*. Jean Cocteau used the old bauxite quarries and the contorted rocks for his film *Le Testament d'Orphée*, which also has scenes in Les Baux itself.

More recently, the very same quarries have been turned into an audiovisual experience under the title of the **Cathédrale des Images** (signposted to the right downhill from Les Baux's car park; June–Aug daily 10am–7pm; mid-Feb to May & Sept to mid-Nov daily 10am–6pm; looped film; 43F). You are surrounded by images projected all over the floor, the ceilings and the walls of these vast rectangular caverns, and by music that resonates strangely in the captured space. The content of the show, which changes yearly, doesn't really matter; it is just an extraordinary sensation, wandering on and through these changing shapes and colours. As an inventive use for an erstwhile worksite it can't be bettered.

Tarascon and Beaucaire

To the south of La Montagnette, the castles of **Beaucaire** and **Tarascon** face each other across the Rhône, the former in Languedoc on the west bank, the latter on the Provence side. Although the castles are regarded as classics, neither of the towns set below them is wildly alluring but both are useful bases for excursions into Languedoc with Nîmes and the Pont du Gard close at hand. Tarascon has one of the most famous Provençal carnivals, based on an amphibious monster known as the *Tarasque*, and is home to the **Souleïado** textile company. Near Beaucaire a reconstructed **Roman winery** has been put back to work.

Arrival, information and accommodation

Both towns are served by Tarascon's **train station** and have good **bus links** with Avignon, Arles, St-Rémy and Nîmes. The **gare SNCF** is south of Tarascon's centre on bd Gustave-Desplaces (☎08.36.35.35.35). **Buses** arrive at the *Café des Fleurs* stop, in front of the station. Opposite the station, on the other side of bd Gustave-Desplaces, is a **car park**, beyond which cours Aristide-Briand leads north to the road bridge across the Rhône. The **tourist office** is at 59 rue des Halles (summer Mon–Sat 9am–12.30pm & 2–6pm, Sun 10am–noon; winter Mon–Fri 9am–12.30pm & 2–6pm; ☎04.90.91.03.52), which leads right off cours Aristide-Briand. You can **rent bikes** in Tarascon at MBK, 1 rue E-Pelletan and **boats** at very reasonable prices in Beaucaire from the Capitainerie du Port on the south side of the canal opposite the tourist office on cours Sadi-Carnot.

Beaucaire is bounded to the south by the Canal du Rhône which provides a pleasure port for the town before joining the river just below the bridge to Tarascon. The **tourist office** is at 24 cours Gambetta, overlooking the canal 300m from the bridge (July Mon–Fri 8.45am–noon & 2–6pm, Sat 9.30am–12.30pm & 2.15–6.15pm, Sun 9am–noon; April–June, Aug & Sept closed Sun; Oct–March closed Sat & Sun; ☎04.66.59.26.57).

Tarascon has more **accommodation** to offer than Beaucaire, including a youth hostel, but it should be easy to find a room in either town, and as the centre of Beaucaire is just a kilometre's walk away from that of Tarascon, across the bridge, it doesn't really matter which of the two you choose.

Hotels

Les Échevins, 26 bd Itam, Tarascon (☎04.90.91.01.70, fax 04.90.43.50.44). Reasonable rooms in a handsome town house. Closed Nov–April. ③.

Napoléon, pl Frédéric-Mistral, Beaucaire (☎04.66.59.05.17). An inexpensive option by the river with very low-priced singles. Closed Mon. ②.

Le Provençal, 12 cours A-Briand, Tarascon (☎04.90.91.11.41). Paper-thin walls but each room has en-suite facilities. ②.

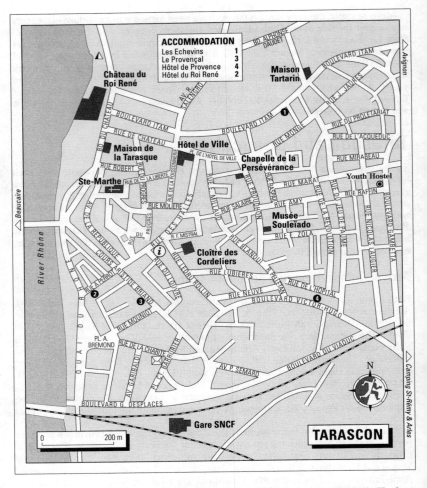

Hôtel de Provence, 7 bd Victor-Hugo, Tarascon (☎04.90.91.06.43, fax 04.90.43.58.13). The best choice in Tarascon with spacious air-conditioned rooms and balconies for breakfasting. Closed Fri out of season. ⑤.

Hôtel du Roy René, 13 rue André-Perrot, Tarascon (☎04.90.91.05.34). Old-fashioned and basic but excellent value. ②.

Robinson, rte de Remoulins, Beaucaire (☎04.66.59.21.32, fax 04.66.59.00.03). Two kilometres north of Beaucaire on D986, with pool and tennis court, and a warm welcome. ④.

Hostels and campsites

HI youth hostel, 31 bd Gambetta, Tarascon (☎04.90.91.04.08). About 500m northeast of the gare SNCF. Well-maintained town house with 65 dormitory beds; 11pm curfew. Closed mid-Dec to Feb. 46F per person, breakfast (19F) is compulsory on first night.

Camping St-Gabriel, Mas Ginoux, quartier St-Gabriel, Tarascon (☎04.90.91.19.83). A two-star site 5km southeast of town off the Arles road. Closed Oct–March.

Camping Tartarin, rte de Vallabrègues, Tarascon (☎04.90.91.01.46, fax 04.90.91.10.70). A two-star site right beside the river, just north of the castle. Closed Nov to mid-March.

Le Rhodanien, rue du Champ de Foire, Beaucaire (☎04.66.59.25.50). A three-star site centrally located on the riverbank. Closed Nov–March.

Tarascon

The **Château du Roi René** (Easter–Sept daily 9am–7pm; Oct–Easter Mon & Wed–Sun 9am–noon & 2–5pm; closed public hols; guided tours every hour; 32F), to the north of the centre, is the obvious site to head for, a vast impregnable mass of stone, beautifully restored to its determinedly defensive fifteenth-century pose. Its towers facing the enemy across the river are square, those at the back round, and nowhere on the exterior is there any hint of softness. Inside, however, is another matter. The castle was a residence of King René of Provence, and of his father who initiated the building, and was designed with all the luxury that the period permitted. The mullioned windows and vaulted ceilings of the royal apartments and the spiral staircase that overlook the **cour d'honneur** all have graceful Gothic lines and in the **Salle des Festins** on the ground floor and the **Salle des Fêtes** on the first floor the wooden ceilings are painted with monsters and other medieval motifs. Tapestries of a later date (François I) hang in the king's chambers and in several rooms graffiti dating from the fifteenth to the twentieth century testify to the castle's long use as a prison. There's an inscription by an eighteenth-century English prisoner in the **Salon du Roi**, and in the **Salles des Gallères** are carvings of boats, some dating from the crusades, made by prisoners awaiting judgement. In the **Salle des Gardes** the base of one vault column shows a man reading a book, sculpted at a time when such an activity was truly novel. A visit ends with a climb up to the **roof**, from which revolutionaries and counter-revolutionaries were thrown in the 1790s. It's likely to be a bad experience for anyone with vertigo, and sometimes, depending on the winds, unpleasant for everyone due to the fumes from Tarascon's paper mill just downstream. You can clearly see the polluting culprit, and, to the west, the far less substantial but still dramatic castle of Beaucaire.

THE TARASAQUE AND TARTARIN

The **Tarasque** is said to have been tamed by Saint Martha after a long history of clambering out of the Rhône, gobbling people and destroying the ditches and dams of the Camargue with its long crocodile-like tail. On **the last full weekend of June** it storms the streets of Tarascon in the fashion of a Chinese dragon, 6m long with glaring eyes and shark-size teeth, the tail swishing back and forth to the screaming delight of all the kids. The monster serves as a reminder of natural catastrophe, in particular floods, kept at bay in this region by the never totally dependable drainage ditches and walls.

Tartarin, another legend of an entirely different and much more recent origin, plays his part in the life of the town. The Tarascon character is a mid-nineteenth-century literary creation, the work of Alphonse Daudet who came from this part of Provence. For a long time the writer dared not set foot in the city, thanks to the garrulous, bragging caricature of a Provençal petty bourgeois he had invented. Tartarin makes out he is the great adventurer, scaling Mont Blanc, hunting leopards in Algeria, bringing back exotic trees for his garden at 55 bis bd Itam. The address is real, and is dedicated to the fictional character: **Maison de Tartarin** (June–Aug 10am–noon & 2–7pm; Sept to mid-Dec & mid-March to May 10am–noon & 1.30–5pm; 10F) with a waxwork figure waiting gun in hand in the hall. During the Tarasque procession, a local man, chosen for his suitably fat-bellied figure, strolls through the town as Tartarin.

The **Collégiale Royale Sainte-Marthe** (daily: 8am–noon & 2–6pm; free), which stands across from the castle, contains the tomb of Martha, the saint who saved the town from the Tarasque monster in its crypt; St Martha also appears in the paintings by Nicolas Mignard and Vien that decorate the Gothic interior along with works by Pierre Parrocel and Van Loo.

It's apparent from a wander round **the town** that the castle creams off most of the budget for old-building restoration, but it can be quite a pleasant change not to be surrounded by immaculate historic heritage. The streets of Renaissance hotels interspersed with older houses with Gothic decoration, the classical town hall and medieval arcades along rue des Halles are all very subdued, with just the shutters adding a soft diversity of colour. The town really only comes to life during the Tuesday morning **market**.

In the centre of the town, on place Frédéric-Mistral off rue Ledru-Rollin, the sixteenth-century **Cloître des Cordeliers** (mid-Feb to Sept daily 10am–noon & 2–6pm; free) has had its three aisles of light cream stone beautifully restored. It's used for exhibitions, sometimes of contemporary paintings, often by young artists. Other exhibitions are organized alongside a permanent collection of crib figures in the **Chapelle de la Persévérance** at 8 rue Proudhon (hours and price depend upon the exhibition; check at the tourist office), part of an erstwhile "refuge" for securing women and girls suspected of living "bad lives". Further down rue Proudhon, at no. 39, is the **Musée Souleïado** (summer Mon–Fri 10am–6pm by appointment only; ☎04.90.91.08.80; 30F), tribute to a family business which revived the 200-year-old Tarascon tradition of making brightly coloured and eye-dancing patterned, printed fabrics, now sold in shops all over Provence. The museum houses the eighteenth-century wood-blocks from which many of the patterns are still made, and tastefully displayed products including a table setting dedicated to the bulls of the Camargue.

Beaucaire

A statue of a bull standing at the head of the Canal du Rhône greets you as you arrive in **BEAUCAIRE** from Tarascon. To the north, between the castle and the river, is a bullring and a theatre on the site of the old **champs de foire**. The fair, founded in 1217, was one of the largest in medieval Europe, attracting traders from both sides and both ends of the Mediterranean as well as merchants from the north along the Rhône. The fairs reached their heyday in the eighteenth century but died out in the nineteenth with the onset of rail freight.

The faded facades of the classical mansions and arcades around **place de la République**, **rue de la République** and **place Clemenceau** speak of former fortunes but are gradually being restored. The Mansart-designed **Hôtel de Ville** and the much more modern market halls on place Clemenceau are very attractive, as is the seventeenth-century house at 23 rue de la République. Between the two is the eighteenth-century church of **Notre-Dame-des-Pommiers** with a frieze from its Romanesque predecessor embedded in the eastern wall, visible from rue Charlier.

To reach the **Château Royale de Beaucaire**, which is also undergoing extensive restoration, follow the ramparts north of the bridge and then cut into town on rue Victor-Hugo, cross place de la République and follow rue de la République until you reach place du Château. Every afternoon a **falconry display** with medieval costumes and music is staged here (hourly: March–June Mon, Tues & Thurs–Sun 2–5pm; July & Aug daily 3–6pm; Sept–Nov daily 2.30–4.30pm; 45F). It's great for kids, and the birds perform very well, but it's a shame that this has replaced the free ramble around the ruins, including the climb to the top of the tower that allowed you to appreciate the great advantage it had over Tarascon, whose castle lies far below. Only the **gardens** are open (April–Sept Mon & Wed–Sun 10am–noon & 2.15–6.45pm, Tues 1.15–6.45pm; Oct

Mon & Wed–Sun 10am–noon & 2.15–6.45pm; Nov–May 10am–noon & 2.15–5.15pm; closed public hols; free). In the gardens, the **Musée Auguste-Jacquet** (same hours; 12.50F) has a small but interesting collection of Roman remains, mostly from a mausoleum, and documents relating to the medieval fair.

The castle was destroyed in 1632 on Richelieu's orders when the town gave support to one of the cardinal's rivals, the duc de Montmorency. However, one irregular-sided tower still stands intact with the battlements and machicolations typical of thirteenth-century military strategy and, despite Richelieu's efforts, most of the walls overlooking the river have survived, as has the monumental staircase linking the upper and lower sections of the castle and a Romanesque chapel.

A much more enlivening Roman find is the winery with its original oak trunk press and amphorae containers at **La Mas des Tourelles** (July & Aug 10am–noon & 2–7pm; March–June, Sept & Oct daily 2–6pm; rest of year Sat only 2–6pm; 20F, includes a tasting), 4km along the road to Bellegarde. The wine-maker and archeologist proprietor has put the Roman cellars to work again, using precise classical methods and recipes. Some of these are rather strange; apparently the Romans liked fortifying their wine with honey or seasoning it with fenugreek, dried iris bulbs, quince and pigs' blood.

Eating, drinking, markets and festivals

Eating cheaply in Tarascon and Beaucaire is not a problem, but eating well is another matter. A good bet is the *Bistrot des Anges*, on pl du Marché in Tarascon, which usually has an interesting plat du jour (55F). The *Hôtel Terminus* by Tarascon's station on place Col-Berrurier (☎04.90.91.18.95; closed Wed & Sat midday) offers a wide but unexciting selection of starters and main dishes on a 70F menu. Beaucaire's quai Gén-de-Gaulle, on the north side of the canal, is where you'll find the best concentration of restaurants and cafés. Both towns are very quiet most evenings – *El Souleale* **bar** on rue des Halles in Tarascon is one of the few bars to stay open after 10pm.

Market day in Tarascon is on Tuesday and takes place along rue des Halles; in Beaucaire there's a market on Thursday and Sunday in the covered halls on place Clemenceau and cours Gambetta. On the first Friday of the month Beaucaire also has a **bric-à-brac** market on cours Gambetta.

Tarascon's end-of-June **Tarasque festival** (see box on p.93) involves public balls, bull and equestrian events and a firework and music finale. Beaucaire has its summer **Estivales**, a week of bullfighting, medieval processions, music, fireworks and so forth around July 21, plus its own Rhône monster legend, the **Drac**, feted on the first weekend in June and followed by a jazz concert.

La Grande Crau

La Grande Crau (or just plain La Crau) stretches south from the Alpilles and east from the Rhône delta to Salon, and was once, a very long time ago, the bed of the Rhône and the Durance. The name Crau derives from a Greek word for "stony", certainly a dominant feature of this landscape. Legend has it that Hercules, having trouble taking on local Ligurians and the Mistral wind both at once, called on Zeus for aid, which arrived in the form of a pebblestone storm, water off a duck's back to the classical hero.

Much of the area, like La Petite Crau, is irrigated and planted with fruit trees protected by windbreaks of cypresses and poplars. But other parts are still a stony desert in summer when the grass between the pebbles shrivels up. As winter approaches sections of the old Roman Via Aurelia are used as drove roads for sheep leaving their summer pastures in the mountains. In winter there are only the winds to contend with; in summer it is unbearably hot and shadeless.

There are some interesting stopoffs in the more amenable countryside between the western end of the Alpilles and Arles. The first is the extremely old **Chapelle St-Gabriel**, just 5km from Tarascon on the D33 to Les Baux, immediately after the junction with the main Avignon–Arles road. It's built on the site of a Gallo-Roman settlement, with a very appealing facade, possibly sculpted by the same artists responsible for St-Tromphime's tympanum in Arles; Tarascon's tourist office has the keys, but there's not that much to see inside. Between the chapel and a ruined medieval tower the GR6 footpath heads up towards the Alpilles ridge and Les Baux (see p.89). For a ten-kilometre round walk you could follow the GR6 until you hit a small road, turn left down to **St-Étienne-du-Grès** and left again along the D32.

South of St-Gabriel is **FONTVIEILLE**, a popular pilgrimage for the French as the place where the writer Alphonse Daudet used to stay. The road past the small literary museum, **Moulin de Daudet** (April–Sept daily 9am–7pm; Feb, March & Oct–Dec daily 10am–noon & 2–5pm; Jan Sun 10am–noon & 2–5pm; 10F), leads south to the crossroads with the D82 where the remains of two Roman aqueducts are visible. A little further south a left turning, signposted *Meunerie Romain*, brings you to the dramatic excavation of the **Barbegal mill**, a sixteen-wheel system powered by water from one of the aqueducts and constructed in 3 or 4 BC; it is estimated that the mill produced up to three tonnes of flour a day.

The road from Fontvieille to Arles takes you past the Romanesque ruins of the **Abbaye de Montmajour** (April–Sept daily 9am–7pm; Oct–March Mon & Wed–Sun 10am–noon & 2–5pm; 32F), a five-minute bus ride from Arles itself. Take heed when you climb the 124 steps of the fortified watchtower, as you will undoubtedly be surprised by dozens of pigeons startled by your arrival; the view from the top of La Grande Crau, the Rhône and the Alpilles is stunning. Below, in the **cloisters**, an excellent stone menagerie of beasts and devils enlivens the bases of the vaulting. Just 200m from the abbey, back in the direction of Fontvieille, the eleventh-century funerary chapel of **Ste-Croix** with its perfect proportions and frieze of palm fronds stands amid tombs cut out of the rock in a farmyard.

Arles

ARLES, on the east bank of the Rhône, is a major town on the tourist circuit, its fame sealed by the extraordinarily well-preserved Roman arena, **Les Arènes**, at the city's heart, and backed by an impressive variety of other stones and monuments, both Roman and medieval. Roman Arles provided grain for most of the western empire and was one of the major ports for trade and shipbuilding; under Constantine, it became the capital of Gaul, Britain and Spain. After the Roman Empire crumbled the city, along with Aix, refound its fortunes as a base for the counts of Provence before unification with France. For centuries it was Marseille's only rival, profiting from the inland trade route up the Rhône whenever France's enemies were blocking the port of Marseille. Arles began to decline when the arrival or train routes put an end to this advantage, and it was an inward-looking, depressed town that **Van Gogh** came to in the late nineteenth century. It was a prolific though lonely and unhappy period for the artist, ending with his self-mutilation and asylum in St-Rémy-de-Provence (see p.88). The **Fondation Vincent Van Gogh** pays tribute to him through the works of modern artists.

Today, Arles is a staid and conservative place, whatever the political colours of its mayors, but it comes to life for the **Saturday market** that brings everyone from the Camargue and La Crau into town. It also fills the year with a crowded calendar of festivals, of which the best are the **Rencontres Internationales de la Photographie**, based around the National School of Photography in July; the dance, music, folklore and theatre **Fêtes d'Arles** at the end of June and beginning of July; and the **Mosaïque**

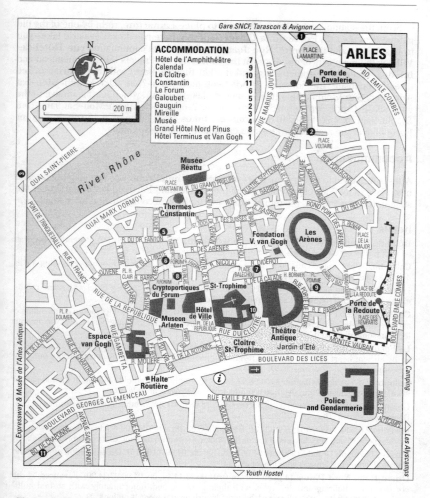

Gitanes with gypsy and flamenco dance and song in mid-July. For the locals, who say the photographic festival is only for Parisians, the key events are the annual opening of the bullfighting season with the **Fête des Gardians** on May 1, the crowning of the **Reine d'Arles**, once every three years – the last one took place in May 1999 – and the **rice harvest** festivities in mid-September.

Arrival and information

The **gare SNCF** is conveniently located a few blocks to the north of Les Arènes. Most **buses** also arrive here at the adjacent **gare routière** (☎04.90.49.38.01), though some, including all local buses, use the *halte-routière* on the north side of bd Georges-Clemenceau, just east of rue Gambetta.

From the station, av Talabot leads south to **place Lamartine**, right by one of the old gateways of the city, **Porte de la Cavalerie**. From here rue de la Cavalerie takes you to Les Arènes and the centre. **Rue Jean-Jaurès**, with its continuation **rue Hôtel-de-Ville**, is the main axis of old Arles. At the southern end it meets bd G-Clemenceau and **bd des Lices**, the promenading and market thoroughfare, with the **tourist office** directly opposite the junction (April–Sept daily 9am–7pm; Oct–March Mon–Sat 9am–6pm, Sun & public hols 10am–noon; ☎04.90.18.41.20), which has an annexe in the gare SNCF (April–Sept Mon–Sat 9am–1pm & 2–6pm; Oct–March Mon–Sat 9am–1pm & 1.30–5pm; ☎04.90.49.36.90). You can rent **bikes** from Peugeot at 15 rue du Pont or Europbike at the newspaper kiosk on esplanade Charles-de-Gaulle.

Accommodation

Arles is well used to visitors and there are plenty of **hotel rooms** to suit all budgets. The best place to look for cheap rooms is in the area around Porte de la Cavalerie near the station. If you get stuck, the tourist office will find you accommodation for a small fee.

Hotels

Hôtel de l'Amphithéâtre, 5 rue Diderot (☎04.90.96.10.30, fax 04.90.93.98.69). Recently redecorated with plenty of warm colours, tiles and wrought-iron work. Close to Les Arènes. ④.

Calendal, 22 pl Pomme (☎04.90.96.11.89, fax 04.90.96.05.84). Generous rooms overlooking a garden in a quiet square near Les Arènes. ③.

Le Cloître, 16 rue du Cloître (☎04.90.96.29.50, fax 04.90.96.02.88). A cosy hotel with some rooms giving views of St-Trophime. Closed mid-Nov to Feb. ③.

Constantin, 59 bd de Craponne, off bd Clemenceau (☎04.90.96.04.05). Pleasant, well maintained and comfortable, with prices kept down by its close proximity to the busy Nîmes highway and its location some distance from the centre. ③.

Le Forum, 10 pl du Forum (☎04.90.93.48.95, fax 04.90.93.90.00). Spacious rooms in an old house at the ancient heart of the city, with a swimming pool in the garden. A bit noisy and hot but very welcoming. Closed Nov–March. ⑥.

Galoubet, 18 rue du Dr-Fanton (☎04.90.93.18.11). Lovingly restored old building in the old part of town. Simply furnished and decorated rooms in rustic Provençal style. ③.

Gauguin, 5 pl Voltaire (☎04.90.96.14.35, fax 04.90.18.98.87). Comfortable, inexpensive and well run. Booking advisable. ②.

Mireille, 2 pl St-Pierre (☎04.90.93.70.74, fax 04.90.93.87.28). On the other side of the river with the more expensive and very luxurious rooms overlooking a swimming pool. Closed mid-Nov to Feb. ⑦.

Musée, 11 rue du Grand-Prieuré (☎04.90.93.88.88, fax 04.90.49.98.15). Quiet location opposite the Musée Réattu, small rooms with lots of charm. ③.

Grand Hôtel Nord Pinus, 14 pl du Forum (☎04.90.93.44.44, fax 04.90.93.34.00). Favoured by the *vedettes* of the bullring and decorated with their trophies, and, unfortunately, with stuffed bulls' heads. Despite all this, it's still one of the most luxurious and elegant options. ⑧.

Hôtel Terminus & Van Gogh, 5 place Lamartine (☎04.90.96.12.32). The Van Gogh theme is rather overplayed but at least colourful. A cheap option just outside one of the city gates, close to the train and bus stations. ①.

Hostel and campsites

HI youth hostel, 20 av Maréchal-Foch (☎04.90.96.18.25). Nearly 2km from centre; take bus #5 from pl Lamartine (direction Fourchon, stop Fournier). Basic facilities and an 11pm curfew. Reception 7–10am & 5–11pm. Closed Jan.

La Bienheureuse, on the N453 at Raphèle-lès-Arles, (☎04.90.98.48.06). Two-star campsite 7km out, but with regular buses from Arles (direction Aix, stop Raphèle). This is the best of the local campsites. The restaurant is furnished with pieces similar to those on display in the Museon Arlaten, and is full of pictures of popular Arlesian traditions.

Camping City, 67 rte de Crau (☎04.90.93.08.86, fax 04.90.93.91.07). Two-star site close to town on the Crau bus route (direction Aix, stop Crau). Closed Nov–Feb.

The City

The centre of Arles fits into a neat triangle between bd É-Combes to the east, bds Clemenceau and des Lices to the south, and the Rhône to the west. The main square, with the cathedral and town hall, is **place de la République**; while the hub of popular life is **place du Forum**. Apart from the **Musée de l'Arles Antique**, south of the expressway, and **Les Alyscamps**, across the train lines to the south, the city's **Roman and medieval monuments** are all within easy walking distance of the centre.

Les Arènes and around

The amphitheatre, known as **Les Arènes** (see box below for hours and price), in the centre of the city, is the most impressive of the Roman monuments. It dates from the end of the first century and, to give an idea of its size, it used to shelter over two hundred dwellings and three churches, built into the two tiers of arches that form its oval surround. This medieval *quartier* was cleared in 1830 and Les Arènes was once more used for entertainment. Today, though not the largest Roman amphitheatre in existence and missing its third storey and most of the internal stairways and galleries, it is a very dramatic structure and a stunning venue for performances, seating 20,000 spectators.

Facing Les Arènes from the west, at 26 Rond-Point des Arènes, the Palais de Luppé houses the **Fondation Vincent Van Gogh** (daily: mid-March to Nov 10am–7pm, rest of year 9.30am–noon & 2–5.30pm; 30F) which exhibits works by contemporary artists inspired by Van Gogh. Francis Bacon was the first to contribute with a painting based on Van Gogh's *The Painter on the Road to Tarascon* that had been destroyed during World War II. Roy Lichtenstein repaints *The Sower*, Hockney, Christo, César and Jasper Johns also pay their homage as do musicians, poets, photographers and the fashion designer Christian Lacroix who grew up in Arles. The collection sometimes goes on tour at which times it is replaced by an exhibition on one of the contributors.

The **Théâtre Antique** (see box below for hours and price), just south of Les Arènes, comes to life in July during the dance and theatre festival and for the *Fête du Costume*, in which local folk groups parade in traditional dress. A resurrected Roman, however, would be appalled at the state of this entertainment venue, with only one pair of columns standing, all the statuary removed and the sides of the stage littered with broken bits of stone. It was built a hundred years earlier than Les Arènes and quarried for stones to build churches not long after the Roman Empire collapsed; it then became part of the city's fortifications, with one of the theatre wings being turned into the **Tour Roland** whose height gives you an idea of where the top seats would have been. A convent and houses

---

MUSEUMS AND MONUMENTS

If you're planning on visiting several of the city's sites, it's worth considering the **global ticket** (55F), which covers entry to Les Arènes, Théâtre Antique, Museon Arlaten, Musée de l'Arles Antique, Cloître St-Trophime, Cryptoportiques, Les Alyscamps, Thermes de Constantin and the Musée Réattu. Global tickets can be purchased from any of the sites covered. Individual tickets for the sites cost 15F. All sites, except the Museon Arlaten and the Musée de l'Arles Antique, have the same **opening hours** (daily: July & Aug 9am–7pm; April–June & Sept 9am–12.30pm & 2–7pm; March & Oct 10am–12.30pm & 2–5.30pm; Feb & Nov 10am–noon & 2–5pm; Jan & Dec 10am–noon & 2–4.30pm; last tickets issued 30min before closing).

were later built over the area and it was only excavated at the turn of the twentieth century. Below the theatre the pleasant **Jardins d'Été** lead down to bd des Lices.

The quiet and attractive southeast corner of the city between bd Émile-Combes, Les Arènes and the theatre has vestiges of the ramparts built over the Roman walls down montée Vauban and in the gardens running alongside the boulevard past the old Roman gateway, the **Porte de la Redoute**. Just by the gate you can see where the aqueduct from Barbegal brought water into the city.

Place de la République and around

West of Les Arènes stands the **place de la République**, dominated by the **Cathédrale St-Trophime**, whose doorway boasts one of the most famous bits of twelfth-century Provençal stone carving in existence. It depicts the Last Judgement, trumpeted by angels playing with the enthusiasm of jazz musicians while the damned are led naked and in chains down to hell; the blessed, all female and draped in long robes, processing upwards.

The cathedral itself was started in the Dark Ages on the spot where, in 597 AD, Saint Augustine was consecrated as the first bishop of the English. It was largely completed by the twelfth century. A font in the north aisle and an altar in the north transept illustrating the parting of the Red Sea were both originally Gallo-Roman sarcophagi. The high nave is decorated with d'Aubusson tapestries; while you'll find more Romanesque and Gothic stone carving, this time with New Testament scenes enlivened with other myths such as Saint Martha leading away the tamed Tarasque, in the extraordinarily beautiful **cloisters**, accessible from place de la République to the right of the cathedral (see box on p.99 for hours and price).

An obelisk of Egyptian granite, that may once have stood in the middle of the Cirque Romaine (see below), stands in front of the cathedral, placed there by Louis XIV who fancied himself as a latter-day Augustus. Across place de la République from the cathedral stands the palatial seventeenth-century **Hôtel de Ville**, inspired by the Palace of Versailles. You can walk through its vast entrance hall with its flattened vaulted roof, designed to avoid putting extra stress on the **Cryptoportiques** below (see box on p.99 for hours and price). This is a huge, dark, dank and wonderfully spooky horseshoe-shaped underground gallery, built by the Romans, possibly as a food store, possibly as a barracks for public slaves, but certainly to provide sturdy foundations for the forum above. Access is currently from the Jesuits' church on rue Balze, although it may be incorporated into the Museon Arlaten in the near future.

The **Museon Arlaten** stands on nearby rue de la République (April & May Tues–Sun 9.30am–12.30pm & 2–6pm; June–Aug daily 9.30am–1pm & 2–6.30pm; Sept daily 9.30am–12.30pm & 2–6pm; Oct–March 9.30am–12.30pm & 2–5pm; 20F), set up in 1896 by Frédéric Mistral with his Nobel Prize money. In the room dedicated to the poet, a cringing notice piously instructs you to salute the great man's cradle. That apart, the collections of costumes, documents, tools, pictures and paraphernalia of Provençal life are extensive and intriguing. The evolution of Arlesian dress is charted in great detail for all social classes from the eighteenth century to World War I and includes a scene of a dressmaking shop. Two other life-size scenes portray a visit to a mother and new-born child, and a bourgeois Christmas dinner, not to be looked at if you're hungry. The room devoted to Provençal mythology, including a Tarasque from the Tarascon procession, is entertaining if not very enlightening.

Heading down rue du Président-Wilson from the Museon Arlaten and right into rue P.F-Rey brings you to the **Espace Van Gogh**, the former Hôtel-Dieu where Van Gogh was treated. It now houses a *mediathèque* and university departments, with a bookshop and a *salon de thé* in the arcades. The flowerbeds in the courtyard are a recreation of the hospital garden based on Van Gogh's painting and the descriptions he wrote of the plants in letters to his sister.

Place du Forum to the river and Van Gogh

North of place de la République, is **place du Forum**, still the centre of life in Arles today. In the square, you can see the pillars of an ancient archway and the first two steps of a monumental stairway that gave access to the Roman forum, now embedded in the corner of the *Nord-Pinus* hotel. The statue in the middle of the square is of Frédéric Mistral.

Heading north towards the river you reach the **Thermes de Constantin** (see box on p.99 for hours and price), the considerable ruins of what may well have been the biggest Roman baths in Provence. You can see the heating system below a thick Roman concrete floor and the divisions between the different areas but there's nothing to help you imagine the original. The most striking feature, an apse in alternating brick and stonework, which sheltered one of the baths, is best viewed from outside on place Constantin.

To the right, along rue du Grand Prieuré, is the entrance to the **Musée Réattu** (see box on p.99 for hours and price) where, beside the rigid eighteenth-century classicism of works by the museum's founder and his contemporaries, there are some stunning twentieth-century pieces. Of the moderns, Picasso is the best represented with the sculpture *Woman with Violin* and 57 ink and crayon sketches from between December 1970 and February 1971 which he donated to the museum. Amongst the split faces, clowns and hilarious Tarasque, is a beautifully simple portrait of Picasso's mother. Zadkine's study in bronze for the two Van Gogh brothers, Mario Prassinos' black and white studies of the Alpilles, Cesar's *Compression 1973* and works by contemporary artists are dotted about the landings, corridors and courtyard niches of this very beautiful fifteenth-century priory; there are also some very good temporary exhibitions.

If you walk to the back of the building, you'll see its gargoyles jutting over the river. There are lanterns along the river wall (and some wonderful sunsets), though much of the river front and its bars and bistros, where weary workers once drank and danced away their woes, was destroyed during World War II.

Another casualty of the bombing was the "Yellow House", on place Lamartine to the north of the centre, where **Van Gogh** lived before entering the hospital at St-Rémy. However, the café painted in *Café de Nuit* is still open for business in place du Forum. Van Gogh had arrived by train in February 1888 to be greeted by snow and a bitter Mistral wind. But he started painting straightaway, and in this period produced such celebrated canvases as *The Sunflowers*, *Van Gogh's Chair*, *The Red Vines* and *The Sower*. He used to wander along the riverbank wearing candles on his hat, watching the light of night-time; *The Starry Night* is the Rhône at Arles.

Van Gogh was desperate for Gauguin to join him, though at the same time worried about his friend's dominating influence. From the daily letters he wrote to his brother Théo, it was clear that the artist found few kindred souls in Arles. Gauguin did eventually come and moved in with Van Gogh. The events of the night of December 23, when Vincent cut off his ear after rushing after Gauguin brandishing a razor blade, were recorded by the older artist fifteen years later. No one knows the exact provocation. Van Gogh was packed off to the Hôtel-Dieu hospital where he had the fortune to be treated by a young and sympathetic doctor, Félix Rey. Van Gogh painted Rey's portrait while in the hospital as well as the hospital itself, in which the inmates are clearly suffering, not from violent frenzy, but from inexpressible unhappiness.

Musée de l'Arles Antique and the Cirque Romaine

The **Musée de l'Arles Antique** (daily: April to mid-Sept 9am–7pm; mid-Sept to March 9.30am–noon & 1.30–6pm; 35F) stands on the spit of land between the Rhône and the Canal du Rhône just west of the city centre. The triangular building, designed by Peruvian architect Henri Ciriani, is positioned on the axis of the **Cirque Romaine**, an enormous race-track currently being excavated, that stretched for 450m from the museum to the town side of the expressway. Built in the middle of the second century, the track was 101m wide and allowed an audience of 20,000 to watch the chariot races. You can look down into the digs crossed by av de la 1er Division Française Libre, the road in front of the museum, but the models inside the museum will give you a much better idea of Roman Arles' third major entertainment venue.

Inside, the museum is a treat: open plan, flooded with natural light and immensely spacious. It covers the prehistory of the area and then takes you through the centuries of Roman rule from Julius Caesar's legionnaire base and the development during the reign of Augustus through to the Christian era from the fourth century when Arles was Emperor Constantine's capital of Gaul, to the fifth century, the height of the city's importance as a trading centre when Emperor Honorius could say "the town's position, its communications and its crowd of visitors is such that there is no place in the world better suited to spreading, in every sense, the products of the earth". The exhibits are arranged chronologically as well as thematically, so, for example, there are sections on medicine, on the use of water power (with more details on the Barbegal mill; see p.96), on industry and agriculture. Fabulous mosaics are laid out with walkways above; and there are numerous sarcophagi with intricate sculpting depicting everything from music and lovers, to gladiators and Christian miracles.

Les Alyscamps

The Romans had their burial ground, **Les Alyscamps** (see box on p.99 for hours and price), southeast of the centre and it was used by the well-to-do Arlesians well into the Middle Ages. Now only one alleyway, foreshortened by a rail line, is preserved; to reach it follow av des Alyscamps from bd des Lices. Sarcophagi still line the shaded walk, whose tree trunks are azure blue in Van Gogh's rendering. Some of the tombs have an axe engraved on them which is thought to have been the contemporary equivalent of a notice warning "Burglar alarm fitted". There are numerous tragedy masks, too, though any with special decoration have long since been removed to serve as municipal gifts, as happened often in the seventeenth century, or to reside in the museums. But there is still magic to this walk which ends at the church of **St-Honorat** where more sarcophagi are stored.

Eating, drinking and entertainment

Arles has a good number of excellent-value **restaurants**. If you're looking for quick meals, or just want to watch the world go by, there's a wide choice of **brasseries** on the main boulevards, of which the most appealing is *La Grande Brasserie Arlésienne*, 14 bd des Lices (closed Tues).

Saturday is the big day of the week in Arles for the **market** that extends the length of bd Georges-Clemenceau, bd des Lices and bd Émile-Combes and many of the adjoining streets. The atmosphere is festive with all the brasseries full of friends having their weekly get-together, and stunning displays of local produce, in particular the cheeses and olives. A smaller food market takes place every Wednesday on bd É-Combes and bric-à-brac stalls spread down bd des Lices the first Wednesday of the month.

For all-round **entertainment**, go to *Le Méjan-Actes Sud*, on quai Marx-Dormoy (☎04.90.93.33.56), which offers **classical concerts** and **films**, along with meals and a bookshop.

Restaurants

L'Affenage, 4 rue Molière (☎04.90.96.07.67). A choice of over 25 different starters and Provençal specialities with generous portions in the stables of an eighteenth-century coach house. Menus at 90F and 140F. Closed Sun.

Hostellerie des Arènes, 62 rue du Réfuge (☎04.90.96.13.05). The service may be a bit abrupt but the food is real French family cooking. Two menus under 100F. Closed Tues.

Le Cloître & Lou Marquès, *Hôtel Jules César*, bd des Lices (☎04.90.93.43.20). *Le Cloître* has something to suit most budgets with a midday menu at around 100F (closed Nov & Dec). But the real gourmet delight is the far more expensive *Lou Marquès*, where the specialities include *baudroie* (monkfish), langoustine salad and Camargue rice cake, all served with the utmost pomposity; menus from 210F to 420F, à la carte over 400F; closed Nov & Dec.

Le Galoubet, 18 rue du Dr-Fanton (☎04.90.93.18.11). Pleasant, vine-covered terrace on which to taste the modern Provençal cuisine on a good-value 105F menu. Closed Sun.

Le Grillon, corner of rond-point des Arènes & rue Girard-le-Bleu (☎04.90.96.70.97). Pleasant place overlooking Les Arènes with menus from 82F. Closed Wed.

La Gueule de Loup, 39 rue des Arènes (☎04.90.96.96.69). Cosy restaurant serving traditional dishes with one menu under 120F. Closed Sun & Mon lunch.

L'Olivier, 1 bis rue Réattu (☎04.90.49.64.88). Small, elegant and very agreeable restaurant serving wine by the glass and with a delicious 150F menu.

La Paillote, 28 rue Dr-Fanton (☎04.90.96.33.15). Excellent quality at very low prices and a chance to try the local speciality of bull steak. Closed Thurs & Sat out of season.

Poisson Banane, 6 rue Forum (☎04.90.96.02.58). Serves the Caribbean speciality of fish and banana and other fruit and meat mixtures with a menu at 79F before 9.30pm. Open evenings only to 12.30am.

Saveurs Provençales, 65 rue Amédée-Pichot (☎04.90.96.13.32). Good traditional Provençal cooking in a pleasant atmosphere. Menus under 100F. Closed Mon & Sun eve.

Le Vaccarès, 9 rue Favorin (☎04.90.96.06.17). Overlooks pl du Forum and serves both new and old dishes in a light, inventive fashion. The lamb with *tapenade* and the fish *à la poutargue* (pressed in millet roe) are exceptional; menus from 135F, à la carte over 300F. Closed Mon & Sun eve.

Cafés, bars and ice cream

Cargo de Nuit, 7 av Sadi-Carnot. A new café-bar with an excellent line-up of live jazz and world music concerts. Open Thurs–Sat, food served till 2am, drinks till 5am.

Boitel, 4 rue de la Liberté. A *salon de thé* with a whole pâtisserie full of goodies to go with the Earl Grey. Closed Sun.

Le Café La Nuit, pl du Forum. If you sit on the terrace of this café you'll find yourself in quite a few holiday snaps, as this is the famous café in Van Gogh's *Café La Nuit*.

Bistrot Arlésian, pl du Forum. Young and noisy, its waiters greeted by each new arrival with kisses on both cheeks. The best of the pl du Forum bars.

L'Entrevue, quai Marx-Dormoy. Has a pleasant terrace frequented by the arty types from the arts centre next door.

Listings

Car parks Parking des Lices, off bd des Lices; free parking off bd E-Combes.

Car rental Avis at the gare SNCF (☎04.90.96.82.42); Europcar, bd Victor-Hugo (☎04.90.93.23.24); Eurorent, bd Victor-Hugo (☎04.90.93.50.14); Hertz, bd Victor-Hugo (☎04.90.96.75.23).

Currency exchange Rond-point des Arènes; several banks on pl de la République.

Emergencies ☎15; Centre Hospitalier J-Imbert, quartier Fourchon (☎04.90.49.29.29).

Pharmacy For a list of late-night pharmacies, call the gendarmerie on ☎04.90.96.02.04.

Police On bd des Lices opposite the Jardins d'Été (☎04.90.18.45.00).

Post office 5 bd des Lices, 13200 Arles (Mon–Fri 8.30am–7pm, Sat 8.30am–noon).

Swimming pool Stade Municipal off av Maréchal-Foch (June to mid-Sept Tues–Sun).

Taxis ☎04.90.96.90.03, 04.90.49.69.59 or 04.90.93.31.16.

Trains ☎08.36.35.35.35.

The Camargue

The Camargue is one of those geographically enclosed areas that are separate and unique in every sense. Its ever-shifting boundaries, the **Petit Rhône**, the **Grand Rhône** and **the sea**, are invisible until you stumble upon them; its horizons infinite because land, lagoon and sea share the same horizontal plain. And both animal and human life have traits peculiar to this drained and ditched and now protected delta land.

The region is home to the **bulls** and the **white horses** that the Camargue _gardians_ or herdsmen ride. Neither animal is truly wild though both run in semi-liberty. In recent times new strains of bull have been introduced because numbers were getting perilously low. The Camargue horse remains a distinct breed, of origin unknown, that is born dark brown or black, and turns white around its fourth year. It is never stabled, surviving the humid heat of summer and the wind-racked winter cold outdoors. The **gardians** likewise are a hardy community. Their traditional homes, or _cabanes_, are thatched and windowless one-storey structures, with bulls' horns over the doors to ward off evil spirits. They still conform, to some extent, to the popular cowboy myth, and play a major role in guarding Camarguais traditions. Throughout the summer, with spectacles involving bulls and horses in every village arena, they're kept busy and the work carries local glamour. Winter is a good deal harder, and fewer and fewer Camarguais property owners can afford the extravagant use of land that bull-rearing requires.

The two towns of the Camargue are as distant and as different as they could possibly be. **Les Stes-Maries-de-la-Mer** is the area's overcrowded resort, famous for its gypsy gathering, while **Salin-de-Giraud** is linked to the industrial complex around the Golfe de Fos. Such villages as are found are little more than hamlets. The rest of the habitations are farmhouses, or _mas_, set well back from the handful of roads, and not within easy walking distance of their neighbours.

There's really no **ideal time** for visiting the Camargue. If you have the sort of skin that attracts **mosquitoes**, then the months from March to November could be unbearable. Staying right beside the sea will be okay, but otherwise you'll need serious chemical

---

BULLFIGHTING IN ARLES AND THE CAMARGUE

Bullfighting in Arles and the Camargue is not the Spanish-style _mise-à-mort_, and it's usually the bullfighters, or _razeteurs_, who get hurt, not the beast. The sport remains a passion with the locals, who treat the champion _razeteurs_ like football stars, while the bulls are feted and adored – before retirement they are given a final tour around the arena while people weep and throw flowers.

The **shows** involve various feats of daring and, being much closer to the scene, you will feel more involved than with other dangerous sports. The most common show is where the bull has a cockade at the base of its horns and ribbons tied between them. Using blunt razor-combs (a recent regulation), the _razeteurs_ have to cut the ribbons and get the cockades. The drama and grace of the spectacle is the stylish way the men leap over the barrier away from the bull. For some shows involving horsemen arrows are shot at the bull, though these don't go in deep enough to make the animal bleed.

All this may leave you feeling cold, or sick, but it is your best way of experiencing **Les Arènes in Arles**. It may help to know that no betting goes on; people just add to the prize money as the game progresses. The tourist office, local papers and publicity around the arena will give you the details; be sure to check shows are not _mise-à-mort_.

WILDLIFE, AGRICULTURE AND INDUSTRY

The bulls and horses are just one element in the Camargue's exceptionally rich **wildlife**, which includes flamingoes, marsh- and seabirds, waterfowl and birds of prey; wild boars, beavers and badgers; tree frogs, water snakes and pond turtles; and a rich **flora** of reeds, wild irises, tamarisk, wild rosemary and famous juniper trees, which grow to a height of 6m, and form the Bois des Rièges on the islands between the Étang du Vaccarès and the sea, part of the central **National Reserve** to which access is restricted to those with professional research credentials. The whole of the Camargue is a Parc Naturel Régional, with great efforts made to keep an equilibrium between tourism, agriculture, industry and hunting on the one hand, and the indigenous ecosystems on the other.

After World War II the northern marshes were drained and re-irrigated with fresh water. The main crop planted was rice, established so successfully that by the 1960s the Camargue was providing three-quarters of all French consumption of the grain – although these days the industry is struggling to hold its own against cheaper imports. Vines were also reintroduced, and in the nineteenth century they survived the infestation of phylloxera that devastated every other wine-producing region because their stems were under water. There are other crops – wheat, fruit orchards and the ubiquitous rapeseed – as well as trees in isolated clumps. To the east, along the last stretch of the Grand Rhône, the chief business is the production of salt, first organized in the Camargue by the Romans in the first century AD, and now one of the biggest saltworks in the world. The salt pans and pyramids cannot help but add an extraterrestrial aspect to the Camargue landscape.

Though the Étang du Vaccarès, the Réserve des Impériaux and the central islands are out of bounds, there are paths and sea dykes from which their inhabitants can be watched, and special nature trails (detailed overleaf). The ideal months for bird-watching are the mating period of April to June, with the greatest number of flamingoes present between April and September.

weaponry. Biting flies are also prevalent and can take away much of the pleasure of cycling around this hill-less land. The other problem is the winds, which in autumn and winter can be strong enough to knock you off your bike. Conversely, in summer the weather can be so hot and humid that the slightest movement is an effort. For this reason, it may be better to make Arles your base and visit the Camargue on day-trips

Transport

There are fairly frequent **bus services** between Arles and Stes-Maries, but fewer between Arles and Salin and there's no direct service between the two. Timetables are available from Les Cars de Camargue on rue J-M-Artaud or the gare routière in Arles. For **drivers and cyclists** the main thing to be wary of is taking your car or bike along the dykes. Maps and road signs show which routes are closed to vehicles and which are accessible only at low tide, but they don't warn you about the surface you'll be driving along. The other problem is **theft** from cars. There are well-organized gangs of thieves with a particular penchant, as locals will testify, for British licence plates. You can **rent bikes** at Stes-Maries at Le Vélociste, pl des Remparts and pl des Gitans (☎04.90.97.83.26 or 04.90.97.86.44), and at Le Vélo Saintois at 19 av de la République (☎04.90.97.74.56). The other means of transport to consider is **horse-riding**. There are around thirty farms that hire out horses, by the hour, half-day or whole day.

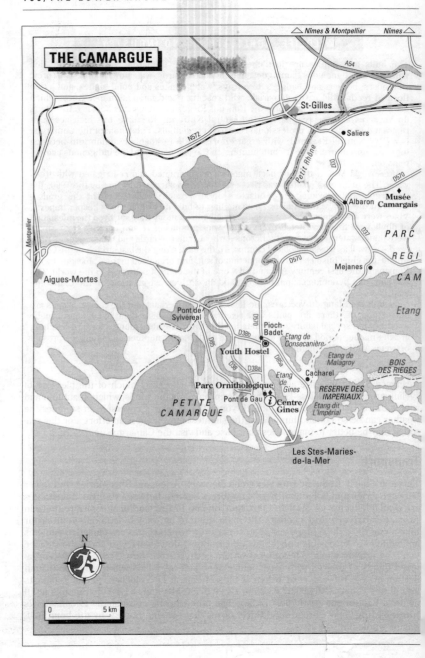

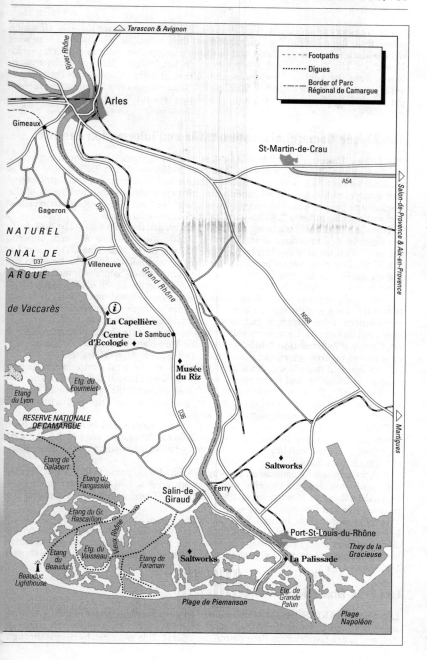

For transport as an end in itself, there's the **paddle steamer** *Le Tiki III* which leaves from the mouth of the Petit Rhône, off the route d'Aigues-Mortes 2.5km west of Stes-Maries (☎04.90.97.81.68), and operates trips up-river from mid-March to mid-November. The *Soleil*, a much less pretty vessel but designed for very shallow water, leaves from the port in Stes-Maries and follows the shoreline to the Petit Rhône (April–Sept; 1hr 30min trips; ☎04.90.97.85.89). Other boats offer fishing expeditions – get details from the **tourist office** in Stes-Maries (see p.109), which can also provide addresses.

The Musée Camarguais, nature trails and information centres

The **Musée Camarguais** (July & Aug daily 9.15am–6.45pm; April–June & Sept daily 9.15am–5.45pm; Oct–March Mon & Wed–Sun 10.15am–4.45pm; 25F), on the way to Stes-Maries from Arles halfway between Gimeaux and Albaron, gives a straightforward introduction to the area. It documents the history, traditions and livelihoods of the Camarguais people in the old sheep barn of a working farm. The displays are excellent and you can also follow a 3.5-kilometre trail through the farmland.

There are three main **trails** around the central area of the Camargue. The first skirts the Réserve des Impériaux along a drover's path, the *draille de Méjanes*, between Cacharel, 4km north of Ste-Maries, and the D37 just north of Méjanes. The second is one of the best observation points for **flamingoes** and follows the dyke between the Étangs du Fangassier and Galabert, starting 5km west of Salin-de-Giraud. Between these two is the *Digue à la Mer* running just back from the beach of Stes-Maries' bay. Cars are not permitted on these stretches, nor are you allowed on the sand dunes. In fact, you'll see a great many "no entry" signs; they're there to protect the fragile eco-environment of the Camargue and, as such, should definitely be respected.

At Pont de Gau, on the western side of the Camargue, 4km short of Les Stes-Maries, the **Centre d'Information Ginès** is one of the Parc Naturel Régional de Camargue's information centres (April–Sept 9am–6pm; Oct–March Mon–Thurs, Sat & Sun Fri 9.30am–5pm). It has videos, slides and exhibitions on the local environment, its eco-systems and fragility, and is the place to go for detailed maps of paths and dykes. Just down the road is the **Parc Ornithologique** (10am–sunset; 33F) with examples of some of the less easily spotted birds kept in aviaries, plus trails across a thirty-acre marsh and a longer walk, all with ample signs and information.

On the eastern side of the Camargue, the main nature trail is at **La Capelière** (Mon–Sat 9am–noon & 2–5pm; free) on the D36b on the eastern edge of the Étang du Vaccarès. There are exhibitions on Camargue wildlife, information on the best means of seeing it, plus initiation trails and hides.

A short way past Le Sambuc on the way to Salin, the Domaine Petit Manusclat has a small **museum** dedicated to **rice** with waxwork scenes, tools and other dusty para-phernalia (Mon–Sat 10am–noon & 1.30–5.30pm; 15F) plus a shop where you can buy the local rice and rice cakes.

Further south, 7km beyond Salin-de-Giraud just off the D36d beside the Grand Rhône, **La Palissade** (daily except public hols 9am–5pm; 15F) concentrates on the fauna and flora of its neighbouring lagoons, with a small and rather boring exhibition but a good nine-kilometre trail past duck and flamingo nesting grounds, and a shorter 1.5-kilometre path.

Les Stes-Maries-de-la-Mer

LES STES-MARIES-DE-LA-MER is the town most people head for in the Camargue, and is best known for its annual festival on May 24 and 25, when gypsies converge on the town to ask favours from their patron saint Sarah. It is swamped by people through-

THE LEGEND OF SARAH AND THE GYPSY FESTIVALS

Sarah was the servant of Mary Jacobé, Jesus's aunt, and Mary Salomé, mother of two of the apostles, who, along with Mary Magdalene and various other New Testament characters, were driven out of Palestine by the Jews and put on a boat without sails and oars – or so the story goes.

The boat subsequently drifted effortlessly to the island in the mouth of the Rhône where the Egyptian god Ra was worshipped. Here Mary Jacobé, Mary Salomé and Sarah, who was herself Egyptian, settled to carry out conversion work while the others headed off for other parts of Provence. In 1448 their relics were "discovered" in the fortress **church** of Stes-Maries on the erstwhile island, around the time that the Romanies were migrating into western Europe from the Balkans and from Spain. It's thought the two strands may have been reunited in Provence.

Whatever the explanation, the gypsies have been making their **pilgrimage** to Stes-Maries since the sixteenth century. It's a time for weddings and baptisms as well as music, dancing and fervent religious activities. On May 24, after Mass, the shrines of the saints are lowered from the high chapel to an altar where the faithful stretch out their arms to touch them. Then the statue of Black Sarah is carried by the gypsies to the sea. On the following day the statues of Mary Jacobé and Mary Salomé, sitting in a wooden boat, follow the same route, accompanied by the mounted *gardians* in full Camargue dress, Arlesians in traditional costume, and all and sundry present. The sea, the Camargue, the pilgrims and the gypsies are blessed by the bishop from a fishing boat, before the procession returns to the church with much bell ringing, guitar playing, tambourines and singing. Another ceremony in the afternoon sees the shrines lifted back up to their chapel.

In recent years the authorities have considered the event to be getting out of hand and there's now a heavy police presence and the all-night candle-lit vigil in the church has been banned. There is a certain amount of hostility between some townspeople and the *gitans* though the municipality has actively countered the racism. It's a wonderful event to be part of, but inevitably makes finding accommodation in the town impossible. Another pilgrimage takes place on the Sunday closest to October 22, dedicated solely to Mary Jacobé and Mary Salomé and without the participation of the gypsies.

out the summer and, as the Camargue's only real resort, is becoming grossly overdeveloped, catering for every leisure activity. Apart from peace and quiet you're not going to want for anything here. There are miles of beaches; a new pleasure port with boat trips to the lagoons; horses to ride; water sports; and the arenas for bullfights, cavalcades and other entertainment (events are posted on a board outside).

Arrival and accommodation

Buses from Arles arrive at the end of av d'Arles. The **tourist office** is on the seafront at 5 av van-Gogh (daily: summer 9am–8pm; winter 9–6pm; ☎04.90.97.82.55), five minutes' walk from the bus stop.

Rooms should be booked in advance between April and October, particularly in May, when the gypsy festival takes place. **Accommodation** tends to be more expensive here than in Arles, though there are several budget options to choose from. There are also some inexpensive places within easy reach of the resort. The regions only two campsites are also close to Stes-Maries; both are huge and expensive.

HOTELS

La Brise de Mer, 31 av G-Leroy (☎04.90.97.80.21, fax 04.90.97.71.10). Overlooking the sea, with a moderately priced restaurant. Obligatory half board in July & Aug. ⑨.

Camille, 13 av de la Plage (☎04.90.97.80.26). Characterless interior, but great sea views. ②.

L'Estable Chez Kiki, 13 rte de Cacharel (☎04.90.97.83.27, fax 04.90.97.87.78). Nothing very special but serviceable and inexpensive. Closed Nov–March. ③.

Le Flamant Rose, in Albaron between Arles and Stes-Maries (☎04.90.97.10.18, fax 04.90.97.12.47). Acceptable hotel-restaurant with some bargain rooms. ③.

Mangio Fango, rte d'Arles (☎04.90.97.80.56, fax 04.90.97.83.60). About 600m from Stes-Maries, overlooking the Étang des Launes with pool and patios. Closed mid-Nov to mid-Dec & Jan. ⑥.

Hostellerie du Mas de Cacharel, rte de Cacharel, 4km north on D85a (☎04.90.97.95.44, fax 04.90.97.87.97). Expensive rooms in one of the oldest Camargue farms, with horses to ride. ⑥.

Mas des Rièges, rte de Cacharel, Stes-Maries (☎04.90.97.85.07, fax 04.90.97.72.26). Down a track signed off the D85a close to Stes-Maries. An upmarket hotel in an old farmhouse, with swimming pool and garden. Closed Dec–Feb. ⑤.

Le Mediterranée, 4 rue Frédéric-Mistral (☎04.90.97.82.09, fax 04.90.97.76.31). Centrally located, inexpensive rooms. Closed mid-Nov to mid-Dec & Jan. ②.

Hôtel de la Plage, 95 bd de la République (☎04.90.97.85.09, fax 04.90.97.71.32). Not on the sea (as the name would suggest), but centrally located. Closed Jan. ③.

Le Sauvageon, petite rte du Bac (☎04.90.97.89.43, fax 04.90.97.74.49). Pretty little *auberge* in its own garden 9km north on the D38b linking the D38 and D570. ②.

Les Vagues, 12 av T-Aubunal (☎04.90.97.84.40). A low-priced option overlooking the sea on the rte d'Aigues-Mortes. Closed Feb. ②.

HOSTEL, CAMPSITES AND CHAMBRE D'HÔTES

HI hostel, in Pioch-Badet hamlet, 10km north of Stes-Maries on the Arles–Stes-Maries bus route (☎04.90.97.51.72, fax 04.90.97.54.88). Set in an old school, with rooms holding three to ten beds; 120F per person. Horse rides organized and bikes for rent.

Mas de Pioch, Pioch-Badet, 10km north of Stes-Maries (☎04.90.97.50.06, fax 04.90.97.55.51). Chambre d'hôte c/o Mme Cavallini; pool and large rooms; excellent value but needs booking well in advance. ③.

Camping La Brise, rue Marcel-Carrière on the east side of the village (☎04.90.47.84.67, fax 04.90.97.72.01). On the Arles to Stes-Maries bus route (stop La Brise). Three-star campsite.

Camping Le Clos du Rhône, at the mouth of the Petit Rhône, 2km west of the village on the rte d'Aigues-Mortes (☎04.90.97.85.99, fax 04.90.97.78.85). Only two of the Arles to Stes-Maries buses continue to here (stop Clos du Rhône). Four-star campsite. Closed Oct–Easter.

The Town

Though grossly commercialized, Stes-Maries is still an extremely pretty town with its streets of white houses and the grey-gold Romanesque **church**, fortified in the fourteenth century in response to frequent attacks by pirates. Inside, at the back of the crypt is the tinselled and sequined statue of Sarah (see box on p.109) always surrounded by candles and abandoned crutches and calipers. The church itself has beautifully pure lines and fabulous acoustics, and during the time of the Saracen raids it provided shelter for all the villagers and even has its own fresh-water well. Between March and Oct the church tower is open (10am–12.30pm & 2pm–sunset; 10F); affording panoramic views over the Camargue.

The local **Musée Baroncelli** (April to mid-Nov daily 10am–noon & 2–6pm; rest of year closed Wed; 10F), on rue Victor-Hugo, is named after the man who, in 1935, was responsible, along with various *gardians*, for initiating the gypsies' procession down to the sea with Sarah. This was motivated by a desire to give a special place in the pilgrimage to the Romanies. The museum covers this event, other Camarguais traditions and the region's fauna and flora.

Eating and drinking.

On summer evenings every other bar and restaurant has flamenco guitarists playing on the *terrasses* while the streets are full of buskers with a crazy variety of instruments. The atmosphere can be carnival or tackily artificial, depending on your mood.

As you might expect, there are few inexpensive **restaurants** in Stes-Maries, though there are plenty to choose from, and out of season the quality improves, and the prices come down. The specialities of the Camargue include *tellines*, tiny shiny shellfish served with garlic mayonnaise; *bœuf gardian*, bull's meat; eels from the Vaccarès; rice, asparagus and wild duck from the district; and *poutargue des Stes-Maries*, a mullet roe dish. The town **market** takes place on place des Gitans every Monday and Friday.

Les Alizés, 36 bis av T-Aubanel (☎04.90.97.71.33). Local specialities including bull sausage and Vaccarès eels. Good views over the port. Two menus under 100F. Closed Tues out of season & middle two weeks of Dec.

L'Impérial, 1 pl des Impériaux (☎04.90.97.81.84). Good fish dishes with interesting sauces. Menus from 130F. Open daily July & Aug, rest of year closed Tues & all Nov–March.

Le Kahlua, 1 rue Jean-Roche (☎04.90.97.98.56). Tapas, pizzas, grills and cheap wine on the *terrasse* overlooking pl des Gitans. Open daily till 1am.

Les Montilles, 9 rue du Capitaine-Fouque (☎04.90.97.73.83). Inexpensive menus, sometimes including a delicious duck mousse. Closed Jan.

Salin-de-Giraud and around

In total contrast to Stes-Maries, **SALIN-DE-GIRAUD** is an industrial village, based on the saltworks company and its related chemical factory, with workers' houses built on a strict grid pattern during the Second Empire.

If you want to take a look at the lunar landscape of the **salt piles**, there's a viewing point with information panels just south of Salin off the D36d. The saltworks here are the world's highest-capacity salt-harvesting site, covering an area of 110 square kilometres and producing 800,000 tonnes a year for domestic use and export. Across the Grand Rhône (there's a daily ferry at Salin; every 20min; 28F) and downstream you can see **Port-St-Louis**, where the rice and salt of the Camargue are loaded onto ships, and where, surprisingly, a small fishing fleet still operates.

There are two moderately priced **hotels** in the village: *Les Saladelles*, 4 rue des Arènes (☎04.42.86.83.87; ②), a traditional, family-run hotel with a popular restaurant; and *La Camargue*, 58 bd de la Camargue (☎04.42.86.88.52, fax 04.42.86.83.95; ③), with a little less character, but more mod cons. The centre of social life is the *Bar des Sports*, next to the *Saladelles* hotel, where *belote* (a card game) championships are held and where the local fan club for Marseille's football team is based. Original paintings by local artists are on the walls, there's a model ship crystallized in salt, pinball, bar football and arcade games, and a normally gregarious clientele. On Friday evenings in July and August, entertainment shifts to the *arènes* between the main road and the river.

In summer three of the Arles–Salin buses continue on to the long, sandy **Plage d'Arles** which stretches westwards from the mouth of the Grand Rhône. Due west of Salin a tortuous route of dyke-top tracks takes you to the **Pointe de Beauduc**, a wide spit of sand facing Stes-Maries across the bay. Amidst the shacks and caravans you'll find *Chez Juju* (closed Oct–April) and *Chez Marc et Mireille* (closed Wed), two fish **restaurants** where you can try freshly scooped *tellines*. It's a bit like barbecueing on the beach, and not cheap, but it's the best Camarguais dining experience.

travel details

Trains

Of the **ordinary direct trains** on the main line **between Paris and the Côte d'Azur** only 1 daily stops at Orange and Avignon (15–20min from Orange) and 3 daily at Arles (10–15min from Avignon). The main line from **Marseille to the Spanish border** stops at Arles (15–25min).

TGV

Avignon to: Marseille (8 daily; 1hr); Montpellier (8 daily; 1hr); Paris (10 daily; 4hr).

Orange to: Avignon (1 daily; 15min); Paris (1 daily; 3hr 30min).

Ordinary trains

Arles to: Narbonne (3 daily; 2hr); Nîmes (hourly; 30min); Tarascon (frequent; 10min).

Avignon to: Arles (hourly; 20min); Tarascon (frequent; 10min); Toulouse (2 daily; 4hr 10min).

Buses

Arles to: Les Baux (4 daily; 30min); Salin (Mon–Sat 6 daily, Sun 2 daily; 1hr), stopping at Le Sambuc (35min); Salon (6 daily; 1hr), some of which stop at Raphèle (5min); Stes-Maries (7 daily; 1hr), stopping at Albaron (30min).

Avignon to: Arles (frequent; 1hr 10min); Châteaurenard (hourly; 20min); Les Baux (2 daily; 1hr); Maillane (2 daily; 1hr), stopping at Graveson (50min); Manosque (2 daily; 2hr 30min); Marseille (4 daily; 2hr 10min), stopping at Aix (2hr); Montélimar (3 daily; 2hr); Nîmes (3 daily; 1hr 30min), stopping at Beaucaire (45min), Barbentane (20min), Boulbon (30min) and Tarascon (40min); St-Rémy (8 daily; 40min), some stopping at Noves (15min); Tarascon (frequent; 40min).

Orange to: Avignon (hourly; 45min–1hr 10min), stopping at Châteauneuf-du-Pape (4 daily; 15min); Sérignan (5 daily; 20min).

Tarascon to: Arles (3 daily; 20min); St-Rémy (3 daily; 20min).

CHAPTER TWO

THE EASTERN VAUCLUSE

As an area with a distinct identity the **Vaucluse département** dates only from the Revolution. It was created to tidy up all the bits and pieces: the papal territory of the Comtat Venaisson that became part of France in 1791, the principality of Orange won by Louis XIV in 1713, plus parts of Provence that didn't fit happily into the initial three *départements* drawn up in 1791. It's still a bit untidy, with the **Papal Enclave** surrounded by the Drôme *département*, but that apart, it has the natural boundaries of the Rhône, **Mont Ventoux**, the limit of the **Vaucluse plateau** and the **River Durance**. The Rhône Valley is covered in Chapter 1; this chapter deals with everything Vauclusian to the east.

The main urban centres of **Vaison-la-Romaine**, **Cavaillon**, **Carpentras** and **Apt** were once part of the imperial Roman belt, while the outlying villages remained tribal strongholds. During the Wars of Religion Carpentras was strongly papal, whereas the settlements of the southern Luberon supported the new religion. To this day there is very little unifying character to the area, save that its people have always been Provençal, whether ruled by Rome, Holland or France.

Today, Cavaillon, Carpentras and Apt are basically market towns, with life centred on the seasons of the best fruit and vegetables in Provence. Of far greater appeal are the villages and countryside. The jagged rocky teeth of the **Dentelles**, the panorama from the windswept heights of Mont Ventoux and the great green surge of the **Luberon** give three complete landscape contrasts. Then there are the multi-hued ochre mines of **Rustrel** and **Roussillon**, and the **River Sorgue** with its many channels and mysterious source at **Fontaine-de-Vaucluse**.

The villages are just as diverse: the dedicated wine-producing communities of the Dentelles, the chic medieval hilltop habitats surrounding Apt, the abandoned villages at **Buoux** and **Oppède-le-Vieux**, romantic **Fontaine**, and **Cucuron**, which is strongly Provençal in character; while you'll find great examples of twelfth-century Cistercian monasteries at **Sénanque** and **Silvacane**.

The Enclave des Papes and Nyons

The **Enclave des Papes**, centred on the town of **Valréas**, is not part of the Drôme *département* that surrounds it, but part of Vaucluse, an anomaly dating back to 1317

ACCOMMODATION PRICE CATEGORIES

Throughout this guide, all hotels and guesthouses have been priced on a scale of ①–⑧, indicating the lowest price you could expect to pay for a double room in high season. What you get for your money varies enormously between establishments, but in the lower-priced hotels you should expect to pay considerably more for en-suite facilities. If you are staying anywhere for more than three days it's often possible to negotiate a lower price, particularly out of season.

① Under 160F	③ 220–300F	⑤ 400–500F	⑦ 600–700F
② 160–220F	④ 300–400F	⑥ 500–600F	⑧ Over 700F

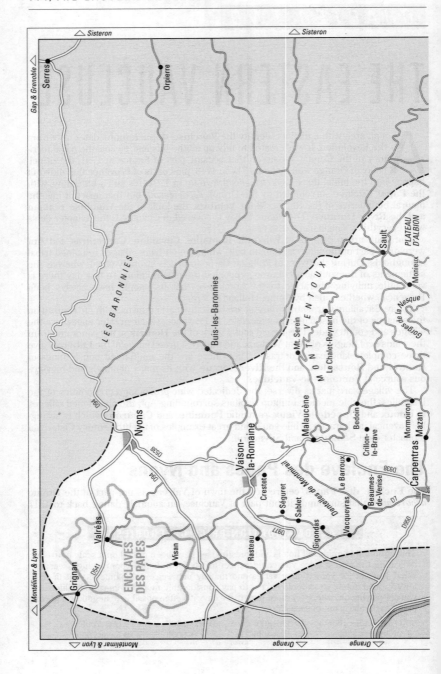

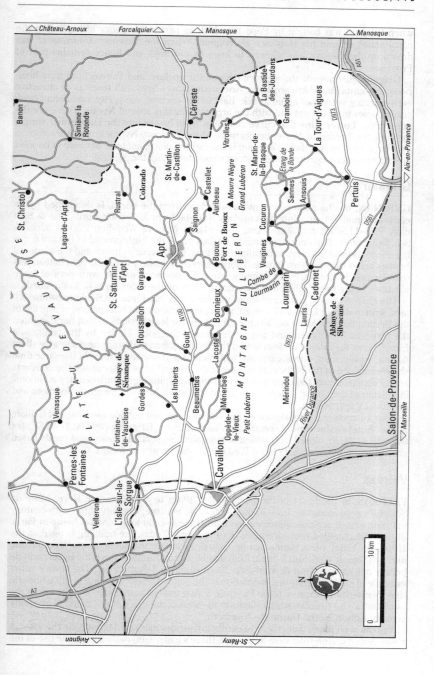

when the land was bought by Pope Jean XXII as part of his policy of expanding the papal states around his Holy See at Avignon. When the Vaucluse *département* was drawn up the enclave was allowed to keep its old links and hence remains part of Provence.

Grignan, just outside the western edge of the enclave, and Valréas both have luxurious **châteaux**, and there are many **vineyards**, most edged with roses as an attractive early-warning system of aphid attack. East of the enclave, the pretty, undulating landscape comes to an abrupt end with the arc of mountains around **Nyons**. These are the edge of the **Lower Alps** that curve southeast from Nyons into the **Baronnies range**, forming the border of Provence north of Mont Ventoux. Nyons is not, therefore, a Provençal city but it feels like one and is a delightful place, not least because of its solid protection against northern and eastern winds, including the Mistral.

Grignan

GRIGNAN, on the main route into the enclave from the north, is dominated by its **château** (guided tours: July & Aug daily 9.30–11.30am & 2–6pm; April–June & Sept daily 9.30–11.30am & 2.30–5.30pm; Nov–March daily 9.30–11.30am & 2–5.30pm; 30F). The enormous building takes up all the high ground of the town, rising above the heavy towers and walls of the town's St-Saveur's church and the medieval houses below the southern facade. Though eleventh-century in origin, the château was transformed in the sixteenth century into a Renaissance palace, with tiers of huge windows facing the south and statues lining the roof; the older parts lie to the north.

The château's most famous resident was the writer **Madame de Sévigné**, whose letters, written during Louis XIV's reign, are a popular source of information on the life of the French nobility. Mme de Sévigné came here for long periods to visit her daughter, the countess of Grignan, and her letters record the good life led by the family and friends: how they dined on fowl fed on thyme, marjoram and other herbs to give them flavour, on succulent doves, exquisite figs, melons and muscat grapes. At the same time she complained of the bitter cold whenever the Mistral blew. You can see the comforts and craftsmanship of the contemporary furnishings, plus eighteenth-century additions, in the tour of the *salons*, galleries and grand stairways, Mme de Sévigné's bedroom and the count's apartments.

Four kilometres from Grignan on the Valréas road, just outside the village of Grillon, is the **hotel-restaurant** *Auberge des Papes,* rte de Grignan (☎04.90.37.43.67, fax 04.90.35.51.28; ⑤; closed Oct) which offers quiet, comfortable rooms and meals based around truffles (restaurant closed Wed out of season; menus from 120F).

Valréas

VALRÉAS, at the heart of the enclave, lies 10km beyond Grignan. Here, Mme de Sévigné's granddaughter lived in the Château de Simiane, a mainly eighteenth-century mansion whose arcades, windows and balustrades would look more at home in Paris, though the pan-tiled roofs are distinctly Provençal. Today, the building is used as the **Hôtel de Ville**; a few rooms can be visited, including the *salon de mariage* and the library (Mon & Wed–Sun 3–5pm; free) and in July and August the hôtel hosts contemporary art shows (Mon & Wed–Sun 10am–noon & 2–8pm; free). The town's other example of *ancien régime* ornamentation is the painted wooden ceiling of the **Chapelle des Pénitents Blancs** on place Pie (July & Aug guided tours twice-weekly; ask at the tourist office for details), which stands to the west of the much more subdued eleventh-century **Église Notre-Dame-de-Nazareth**.

Valréas is an important centre of cardboard production and, just outside the town in a warehouse on the road west to Orange, there's a museum dedicated to the use of the product: the **Musée du Cartonnage et de l'Imprimerie** (April–Oct Mon & Wed–Sat 10am–noon & 3–6pm, Sun 3–6pm; 20F), a rather intriguing museum of packaging.

Valréas is at its busiest on June 23 and 24, for the night-time procession and show of the **Nuit de Petit St-Jean**, and on the first Sunday in August, when the **Fête des Vins de l'Enclave** takes place. At other times, it's a pleasant, if quiet, place to spend some time. The most interesting diversions lie in buying local **wines**. As well as the Côtes du Rhône appellation there's also Valréas Villages and Visan Villages, distinctive enclave wines, with flavours of violet, red fruits and pepper; it's said that these distinctive wines were what persuaded Pope Jean XXII to buy this area in the first place. The **Cave Coopérative** is at the Caveau St-Jean, av de l'Enclave des Papes; you can also visit the private cellars (full list from the tourist office).

The **tourist office** is on place Aristide-Briand (July & Aug Mon–Sat 9.15am–12.15pm & 2–7pm, Sun 9.15am–12.15pm; rest or year Mon–Sat 9.15am–12.15pm & 2–6pm; ☎04.90.35.04.71). The best places **to stay** are the *Grand Hôtel*, 28 av Gén-de-Gaulle (☎04.90.35.00.26, fax 04.90.35.60.93; ④) on the outskirts of town, and the more moderate *Camargue*, 49 cours Jean-Jaurès (☎04.90.35.01.51; ③) – both with reasonable restaurants. There's also a two-star **campsite**, *Camping de la Couronne*, by the river on the rte du Pègue (☎04.90.35.03.78; closed Nov–Feb).

A good place **to eat** is *La Ferme Champ-Rond*, chemin des Anthelmes (☎04.90.37.31.68; closed Sun eve & Mon), off rte de St-Pierre to the southeast of town; it uses local produce and is not too expensive with menus from 70F. In town, *L'Oustau*, 2 cours Tivoli (☎04.90.35.05.94; closed Sun eve & Mon) has menus starting from around 100F and a seafood menu at 130F. You can sample the **local wines** at the beautiful *Café de la Paix* on rue de l'Hôtel-de-Ville. The **market** is held on Wednesday on place Cardinal-Maury and cours du Berteuil on the eastern side of town, with local truffles figuring prominently between November and March.

Nyons

After Grignan and Valréas, **NYONS**, on the River Aigues, seems like a metropolis, though its population is well under ten thousand. It is an extremely attractive place, perfect for lazing about in cafés or strolling through, with its medieval centre and riverside aromatic gardens. If Nyons is on your route into Provence you can begin to appreciate the essentials of the region's cooking here: olives and olive oil, garlic, wild mushrooms, and countless varieties of fruit and vegetables, with seasons quite different to the north. If Nyons is on your way out, then this is the place to do the final shopping.

Arrival and accommodation

Nyons has no train links but is served by a regular bus service from Montélimar and Avignon. **Buses** arrive at place Buffaven on the edge of the old town, just northeast of the large central square, place de la Libération, where you'll find the **tourist office** (July & Aug Mon–Sat 9am–12.30pm & 2.30–7pm, Sun 10am–12.30pm; rest of year Mon–Sat 9am–12.30pm & 2–6.30pm; ☎04.75.26.10.35). **Accommodation** is easy to find: as well as the two excellent campsites – the four-star *Camping des Clos*, 1km along the road to Gap (☎04.75.26.29.90), which has its own pool; and the municipal site on promenade de la Digue (☎04.75.26.22.39; closed Oct to mid-March) – there are plenty of hotel rooms. Inexpensive options include *Le Petit Nice*, 4 av Paul-Laurens (☎04.75.26.09.46; ①), just to the west of pl de la Libération; *Lou Caleu*, on pl de la République (☎04.75.26.08.20; ②); and *Les Oliviers*, 2 rue A-Escoffier (☎04.75.26.11.44, fax 04.75.26.05.03; ①), a small, pleasant hotel with a garden bordering the old town to the north. For a bit more luxury, try *La Caravelle*, 8 rue des Antignans (☎04.75.26.07.44, fax 04.75.26.23.29; ④; closed mid-Nov to mid-Dec), a small hotel, looking out over gardens to the river, close to the town centre; or *La Picholine,* promenade de la Perrière (☎04.75.26.06.21, fax 04.75.26.40.72; ④), a quiet, secluded and comfortable place in the hills north of the town, with its own swimming pool and a good restaurant.

The Town

The pavement terraces of **place de la Libération**'s cafés and brasseries are a pleasant place to while away an afternoon, people-watching against a background of fountains, plane trees, palms and curly wrought-iron lampposts, and taking in the views beyond of steep wooded slopes that never block out the sun. On Thursdays the square and its neighbour to the northeast, place Buffaven, are taken over by a huge and wonderful **market**. A smaller one takes place on Monday – and in July and August there's a Sunday morning market in the old town.

East of place de la Libération, the arcaded **place du Dr-Bourdongle** leads into a web of streets, covered passages and stairways running up to the **quartier des Forts**, so named for the now ruined feudal castle; the fourteenth-century **Château Delpinal**, of which three towers remain; and the extraordinary **Tour Randonne**, which houses a nineteenth-century chapel, with a neo-Gothic pyramid supporting a statue of the Madonna, sitting delicately on the heavy crenellated base of a thirteenth-century keep.

Towards the river, which is crossed by a single-spanned Romanesque bridge, the Pont Romain, there are pleasantly untouristy streets, scattered with bars, restaurants and some highly unusual **shops**, such as the Galerie du Pontias at 20 rue des Bas Bourgs, selling the sort of traditional crafts and antiques normally seen only in folklore museums. Just beside the bridge, at 4 av de la Digue, are **Les Vieux Moulins** (July & Aug daily 10am–noon & 2.30–6pm; rest of year closed Sun; 20F), an old artisanal complex of two eighteenth- and nineteenth-century oil presses, an eighteenth-century soap works, and a traditional Provençal kitchen.

About 500m west of the bridge, along the river, is the small but sensual **Jardin des Arômes**, a garden of aromatic plants from which essential oils are made.

Eating and drinking

In addition to the many **brasseries** on place de la Libération there's *Le Petit Caveau*, 9 rue Victor-Hugo (☎04.75.26.20.21; set menu for 110F, à la carte from 250F; closed Sun eve & Mon out of season), which serves some very good, classic Provençal food and wines. The best place for *steack-frites* is the *Bar du Pont*, with great views over the old Pont Romain from the old town. At the hotel-restaurant *Les Alpes*, 9 rue des Déportés, you can get paella and couscous (☎04.75.26.04.99), while, on the same street, there's a

---

OLIVE PRODUCE

Nyons is famous for its **olives**. Black eating olives are a speciality, as is *tapenade* (a paste of olives, capers and herbs), but the biggest business is making olive oil, a process you can watch between December and February. Among firms that welcome visitors are **J Ramade**, av P-Laurens (just before place Oliver-de-Serres on the left), who have a video explaining all the subtleties, and **Moulin à Huile Autrand-Dozol**, on av de la Digue by the Pont Romain. The tourist office can provide more addresses; there's also a small **museum** on the subject on rue des Tilleuls (July & Aug Mon–Sat 10am–11.30am & 3–6pm; rest of year Tues–Sat 3–6pm, Sun 2.30–6pm; 12F).

The **Coopérative Agricole du Nyonsais** on place Oliver-de-Serres (July & Aug Mon–Sat 8.30am–1pm & 2–7.30pm, Sun 9.30am–12.30pm & 3–6.30pm; rest or year Mon–Sat 8.30am–1pm & 2–7pm, Sun 9.30am–12.30pm & 3–7pm) sells a full range of the olive products under the trademark "Nyonsolive", as well as nut and chilli oils, wines and honey.

choice of Tex-Mex at *Tequila Sunrise*, pizzas at *L'Alicoque*, or large open **sandwiches** and salads for around 45F at *La Tartinière*.

Vaison-la-Romaine and around

VAISON-LA-ROMAINE lies between Nyons and Orange to the southeast of the Enclave des Papes. The most dramatic approach, however, is from the southeast along the Malaucène road, from where the first glimpse of the town is of a ruined twelfth-century castle outlined against the sky. As you get closer you see the storeys of old pale stone houses and towers beneath it, and the eighteenth-century town laid around its Roman predecessor. The two are linked by a Roman bridge, spanning the River Ouvèze in a single arch. The population of Vaison began to settle on both sides of the river only late this century. The original Celtic Voconces, like the late medieval Vaisonnais, chose the high ground, for defensive reasons. Their eighteenth-century descendants moved back to the right bank, abandoning the citadel to wait for twentieth-century romantics to bring it back into fashion.

The older generation in Vaison recalls the days when shops were little more than front rooms and you would interrupt the cooking or other household chores when you went in to be served. They talk of a barber who played the violin and would always finish the final bars before getting out the soap and towels. These days the population of the town and its tourist visitors can keep several dozen bars, hotels and restaurants busy, as well as numerous souvenir and sports shops.

Vaison hit the headlines in 1992 when the River Ouvèze burst its banks, killing thirty people, and destroying riverside houses, the modern road bridge, and an entire industrial quarter. Though the town has recovered remarkably, its character has changed. It seems much more commercialized, and less friendly, perhaps because of the mass of ghoulish "tourists" who flocked to the town to see the damage.

Today, its main attractions are the medieval **Haute Ville** with a ruined cliff-top castle, the **Pont Romain** that held out against the floods, a cloistered former cathedral and the exceptional excavated remains of two **Roman districts**. Just south of Vaison there are sculptures in natural settings to be discovered at the **Crestet Centre d'Art**.

Arrival, information and accommodation

Buses to and from Avignon, Orange and Carpentras stop at the **gare routière** on av des Choralies, near the junction with av Victor-Hugo east of the town centre on the north side of the river. Heading down av Victor-Hugo you'll come to the main square, **place de Montfort**, from where it's a short walk further to **Grande Rue** which leads left to the **Pont Romain** and right, becoming av Général-de-Gaulle, to **place du Chanoine-Sautel**. The **tourist office** is on pl du Chanoine-Sautel (July & Aug daily 9am–12.30pm & 2–6.45pm; rest of year Mon–Sat 9am–noon & 2–5.45pm; ☎04.90.36.02.11) between the two Roman archeological sites.

Accommodation is thin on the ground and consequently is fairly expensive.

Hotels

Le Beffroi, rue de l'Evêché in the Haute Ville (☎04.90.36.04.71, fax 04.90.36.24.78). Stylish lodgings in a sixteenth-century residence; the rooms are furnished to befit the building and are not outrageously expensive. Closed mid-Nov to mid-Dec & mid-Feb to mid-March. ⑨.

Le Burrhus, pl Montfort (☎04.90.36.00.11, fax 04.90.36.39.05). The cheapest rooms in town and noisy at weekends as it's above the terraced cafés. ③.

Hôtel des Lis, cours Henri-Fabre (☎04.90.36.00.11, fax 04.90.36.39.05). Right in the centre, with some very large rooms. ⑥.

Le Logis du Château, Les Hauts de Vaison (☎04.90.36.09.98, fax 04.90.36.10.95). Along montée du Château south of the river and to the west of the Haute Ville; spacious rooms with lovely views. ④.

Hostel and campsite

Centre Culturel à Coeur Joie, Le Moulin de César, rte de St-Marcellin (☎04.90.36.00.78, fax 04.90.36.09.89). Just 1km east of town down av Geoffroy from the Pont Romain, with basic but adequate rooms for two to four people at 220F per person.

Camping du Théâtre Romain, chemin du Brusquet, off av des Choralies, quartier des Arts (☎04.90.28.78.66). Small three-star with good facilities. Closed Nov to mid-March.

The Town

Of all the distinctive periods in Vaison's history, it is the style and luxuries of the **Roman** population that are the most intriguing. The two excavated Roman residential districts in Vaison lie to either side of av Général-de-Gaulle: the **Fouilles Puymin** to the east and the **Fouilles de la Villasse** to the west (March–May & Oct daily 10am–12.30pm & 2–6pm; June–Sept daily 9.30am–12.30pm & 2–7pm; Nov–Feb Mon & Wed–Sun 10am–noon & 2–4.30pm; 40F, including the Puymin museum and the cathedral cloisters).

The Puymin excavations (*fouilles*) contain the theatre, several mansions and houses thought to be for rent, a colonnade known as the *portique de Pompée* and the museum for all the items discovered. The Villasse site reveals a street with pavements and gutters with the layout of a row of arcaded shops running parallel, more patrician houses (some with mosaics still intact), a basilica and the baths. The houses require a certain amount of imagination, but the street plan of La Villasse, the colonnade with its statues in every niche, and the theatre, which still seats seven thousand people during the July festival, make it easy to visualize a comfortable, well-serviced town of the Roman ruling class.

Most of the detail and decoration of the buildings is displayed in the **museum** (June–Sept daily 10am–1pm & 2.30–7.30pm; March–May & Oct daily 10am–12.30pm & 2.30–6pm; Nov–Feb Mon & Wed–Sun 10–11.30am & 2–4pm; admission covered by ticket for the excavation sites) in the Puymin district. Tiny fragments of painted plaster have been jigsawed together with convincing reconstructions of how whole painted walls would have looked. There are mirrors of silvered bronze, lead water pipes, taps shaped as griffins' feet, dolphin door knobs, weights and measures, plus household and building implements. The busts and statues are particularly impressive: among them a silver head of one of the Villasse villas' owners; the emperor Domitian, under whose reign the conquest of Britain was completed, wearing a breast-plate of Minerva and the Gorgon's head; and a statue of another famous emperor, Hadrian.

The former **Cathédrale Notre-Dame** lies west down chemin Couradou which runs along the south side of La Villasse. The apse of the cathedral, which was badly flooded, is a confusing overlay of sixth-, tenth- and thirteenth-century construction, some of it using pieces quarried from the Roman ruins. The **cloisters** (admission covered by ticket for the excavation sites) are fairly typical of early medieval workmanship, pretty enough but not wildly exciting. The only surprising feature is the large inscription visible on the north wall of the cathedral, a convoluted instruction to the monks to bring peace upon the house by loving the monastic rule and following God's grace.

Just south of the Roman districts, the **Pont Romain** leads across the river to the Haute Ville. The bridge has undergone extensive repair works since its battering in the 1992 flood but it says a lot for Roman engineering that it fared better than the modern road bridge to the west. Its new casings need weathering to return it to its former picturesqueness, but the grace of the high-arched structure remains.

From the bridge rue du Pont climbs upwards towards place des Poids and the fourteenth-century gateway to the medieval **Haute Ville**. More steep zigzags take you past the Gothic gate and overhanging portcullis of the belfry and into the heart of this sedately quiet, uncommercialized and rich *quartier*. There are fountains and flowers in all the squares, and right at the top, from the twelfth- to fifteenth-century **Castle**, you'll have a great view of Mont Ventoux. In summer the Haute Ville livens up every Tuesday when Vaison's **market** spreads up here.

Eating and drinking

The **restaurant** to head for in Vaison is *Le Bateleur* at 1 place Théodore-Aubanel, downstream from the Pont Romain on the north bank (☎04.90.36.28.04; lunch menu 98F; evening menu 142F; à la carte from 200F; closed Mon, Sun eve & mid-Nov to mid-Dec). The lamb stuffed with almonds and the *rascasse* soufflé are highly recommended. *L'Auberge de la Bartavelle*, 12 place Sus-Auze (☎04.90.36.02.16; closed Mon) has specialities from southwest France, for around 100–200F. Imaginative salads and savoury tarts are to be had at *Laure y Est*, 5 rue Buffaven (☎04.90.28.81.11; closed Sun, & Mon–Wed pm) as well as traditional *plats* for around 60F. There are more menus to consider on cours Taulignan and place de la Poste.

In the Haute Ville the restaurant at *Le Beffroi* hotel has a surprisingly inexpensive menu, and the food is very acceptable though served with stiff formality. At the far end of rue de l'Evêché on place du Vieux-Marché, *La Fête en Provence* (☎04.90.36.16.05; closed Wed out of season) has good game dishes on the 150F menu and a decent menu for around 100F. Otherwise there's a crêperie and pizzeria on place des Poids.

Standard **brasserie fare** is available on place de Montfort, which is also the best place to head for **drinks**. If you want to be in a more "local" ambience try *Vasio Bar* on cours Taulignan. The Maison des Vins in the same building as the tourist office has all the wines from the vineyards of the Dentelles and Ventoux.

Le Crestet

South of Vaison, 3.5km down the Malaucène road, a turning to the right leads up to **LE CRESTET**, a tiny hilltop village with a private château at the top and a little snack bar, *Le Panorama* (summer daily till 9pm; winter Sat & Sun only) from where you can admire the fantastic view, taking in the ruined château of Entrechaux, the Barronnies range and Mont Ventoux. From the village, signs direct you to the nearby **Crestet Centre d'Art** from where you can discover sculptures placed within the surrounding forest of oak, pine and honeysuckle. You can go at any time and there's no charge; though the centre won't provide you with a map, there is one on the wall at the entrance. From behind the building head right and then turn sharp left within 20m; the path then makes a clockwise loop – if you reach a dirt road you've gone too far. None of the sculptures are titled or signed and most are off the main path. Some are formed from the trees themselves, others are startling metal structures like a mobile and a Meccano cage. One of the first ones you're likely to come across is Parvine Curie's *La Grande Tête*, concrete cubes positioned so that Vaison's ruined château is framed directly behind.

South of Le Crestet, signed off the D76 to the Vaison–Malaucène road, is a lovely **hotel** in the middle of nowhere, *Le Mas de Magali* (☎04.90.36.39.91; ④; closed mid-Oct to mid-March) run by a Dutch couple, with its own pool and a *terrasse* looking eastwards to the mountains.

The Dentelles

The jagged hilly backdrop of the **DENTELLES DE MONTMIRAIL** is best appreciated from the contrasting landscape of level fields, orchards and vineyards lying to their south and west. The range is named after lace (*dentelles*), its pinnacles slanting, converging, standing parallel or veering away from each other, like the the the contorted pins on a lace-making board – though the alternative connection with "teeth" (*dents*) is equally appropriate. For geologists the Dentelles are Jurassic limestone folds, forced upright and then eroded by the wind and rain.

The Dentelles run northeast to southwest between Vaison and Carpentras. On the western and southern slopes lie the **wine-producing villages** of **Gigondas, Beaumes-de-Venise, Sablet, Séguret, Vacqueyras** and, across the River Ouzère, **Rasteau**. Several carry the distinction of having their own individual *appellation contrôlée*, within the Côtes du Rhône or Côtes du Rhône Villages areas. In other words their wines are exceptional and they are well feted. If you're in the region over the July 14 holiday head straight for Vacqueyras for the bacchanalian **Fêtes des Vins**. At any time of the year a more sober introduction to the subject is on offer at Rasteau's museum.

Besides wine-tasting and bottle-buying, the area is good for long **walks** in the Dentelles, happening upon mysterious ruins or photogenic panoramas of Mont Ventoux and the Rhône Valley. The pinnacles are also favourite destinations for apprentice **rock-climbers**: the Col de Cayron is one of the favourite pinnacles for serious climbing; the Dent du Turc needs only decent shoes and a head for heights to give a thrill. To the east of the range lies the *village perché* of **Le Barroux**, with a fine twelfth-century château.

Although it's possible to get to the villages by public transport from Vaison or Carpentras, having your own vehicle is definitely an advantage. You can **rent bikes** at the *Café du Court* in the centre of Vacqueyras; for **walking and climbing information** go to the Gîte d'Etape des Dentelles in Gigondas (☎04.90.65.80.85). Edisud publishes a good guide, *Randonnées au Ventoux et dans les Dentelles* by I. & H. Agresti, available from most tourist offices.

Rasteau

If the art and science of wine and the whole business of wine-tasting is a mystery to you, then head for **RASTEAU** and the **Musée du Vigneron** (Mon & Wed–Sun: July & Aug 10am–6pm; April–June & Sept 2–6pm; 15F). The museum is on the D975 between Rasteau and Roaix and belongs to the Domaine de Beaurenard which also has vineyards in Châteauneuf-du-Pape. Along with a fairly predictable collection of bottles and nineteenth-century implements, there's a half-hour video on the whole Côtes du Rhône area. The charts and panels are rather harder work, but instructive on geology, soil, vine types, fossils, parasites and wine-growing throughout the world. There's also a free wine-tasting with no obligation to buy.

If you need somewhere **to stay**, try the *Belle Rive* (☎04.90.46.10.20; ⑤; closed mid-Nov to March), a quiet hotel with a fine view from its terrace, and good food, including a rosemary-flavoured *crème brûlée*. For walkers there's the *Centre Départemental d'Animation et d'Accueil*, rte du Stade (☎04.90.46.15.48), which offers dormitory accommodation for 50F per night, plus three two-bed rooms, with full pension, for under 180F.

Séguret

There is a fair amount of cosmetic hype about the star Dentelles village, **SÉGURET**, but for all that it is alluring. Among its many medieval charms is a one-handed clock on the belfry and, on Christmas Eve, in place of the standard Provençal crib, there's a living re-enactment of the Nativity in which people play the parts their grandparents and great-grandparents played before them. The **Fête des Vins et Festival Provençal Bravade** in the last two weeks of August is a relatively recent publicity creation incorporating processions for the Virgin Mary and the patron saint of wine-growers.

Séguret has two very posh **hotels**, *Domaine de Cabasse*, rte de Sablet (☎04.90.46.94.12; ④; closed Dec–March), and *La Table du Comtat* in the village (☎04.90.46.91.49; ⑦), both with very few rooms and good restaurants. A slightly cheaper and a more rustic option is the *Bastide Bleue*, rte de Sablet (☎04.90.46.83.43; ④; closed Wed), 500m from the village on the Vaison road. For **food**, try *Le Mesclun*, rue des Poternes (☎04.90.46.93.43; closed Mon & Nov–Easter); it's quite expensive but renowned for the fresh local ingredients in its dishes.

Just south of Séguret lies **SABLET**, the largest of the villages, and the least obviously chic. One road spirals up the dome on which the oldest houses are built; near the summit stands the *Café des Sports*, which can feed you from its no-frills menu for under 100F. There's also a **campsite**, *Le Panoramic* (☎04.90.46.96.27; closed Nov–March), 2km from the village on the rte d'Orange.

Gigondas

GIGONDAS has the most reputed **wine** in the Dentelles. It is almost always red, quite strong, has a back taste of spice or nuts and is best aged at least four or five years. Sampling the varieties could not be easier since the **Syndicat des Vins** runs a *caveau des vignerons* (daily 10am–noon & 2–5.30pm) in place de la Mairie where you can taste and ask advice about the produce from forty different *domaines*. It's also a good place to buy as the bottles cost exactly the same as at the vineyards.

Gigondas' **tourist office** is on place du Portail (Easter–Sept Mon–Fri 10am–noon & 2–6pm, Sat & Sun 10am–noon; Oct–Easter Mon–Fri 10am–noon & 2–5pm, Sat 10am–noon; ☎04.90.65.85.46). It can provide lists of particular *domaines* or *caves* grouping several *vignerons* for the other villages. There's a charming **hotel**, *Les Florets*, 2km from the village towards the Dentelles (☎04.90.65.85.01; half board obligatory in season; ⑤) with an excellent Provençal restaurant (menus from 100F; closed Wed, also Tues out of season). As an alternative **eating** option try *L'Oustalet*, on place du Portail (☎04.90.65.85.30; closed Sun eve & Mon), which has a pleasant shaded terrace and serves reasonably priced food.

VACQUEYRAS, to the south, is home to an annual **wine festival** on July 14 and a wine-tasting competition on the first weekend of June, but its main claim to fame is as the birthplace of a troubadour poet **Raimbaud**, who wrote love poems to Beatrice in Provençal and died in the Crusades in 1207. You'll see plenty of signs for wine producers to visit around the village.

For accommodation, there's the very upmarket *Hôtellerie de Montmirail* just south of the centre on the road to Vacqueyras (☎04.90.65.84.01; menus from 100F; ⑦) with an excellent Provençal restaurant. There's also a campsite, the *Municipal Roquefiguier* (☎04.90.62.95.07; closed Nov–March), just outside the village on the raod to Violès.

Beaumes-de-Venise

The most distinctive wine, and elixir for those who like it sweet, is Beaumes-de-Venise muscat. Pale amber in colour and with a hint of roses and lemon following the muscat flavour, it can usually convince the very driest palates of its virtue. The place to buy it is at **BEAUMES-DE-VENISE**, in the Cave des Vignerons (Mon–Sat 8.30am–noon & 2–6pm, Sun 9am–12.30pm & 2–6pm), a huge low building on the D7 overlooked by the Romanesque bell tower of Notre-Dame-d'Aubune. The *cave* also sells red, rosé and white Côtes du Rhône Villages, and the light Côtes du Ventoux. The **church** in Beaumes reflects the key concern of the area in the trailing vines and classical wine containers sculpted over the door. The **tourist office** (June–Sept daily 9am–noon & 2–7pm; Oct–May Mon–Sat 9am–noon & 2–5pm; ☎04.90.62.94.39), near the church, can also provide lists of *domaines* or *caves* for the area.

The village has two quiet, old-fashioned **hotels**: the *Auberge St-Roch*, av Jules-Ferry (☎04.90.65.08.21; ②; closed Tues eve & Wed); and, a little way out, *Le Relais des*

Dentelles (☎04.90.62.95.27; ②; closed Mon), past the old village and over the river. There's also a **campsite** on the edge of the village, the *Municipal les Quierades* (☎04.90.65.84.24; closed Sept–March), out towards Malaucène.

Le Barroux

On the east side of the Dentelles, on the Vaison–Malaucène road, the largely untourist-ed **LE BARROUX** is a perfect *village perché* with a twelfth- to eighteenth-century **château** at the top that was restored just before World War II, burnt by the Nazis and restored again from 1960 to 1990 (April–May Sat & Sun 10am–8pm; June daily 2.30–8pm; July–Sept daily 10am–8pm; Oct daily 2.30–8pm; 20F).

Les Géraniums on place de la Croix (☎04.90.62.41.08, fax 04.90.62.56.48; ③; closed Jan & Feb), in Le Barroux, is a very peaceful, comfortable and unpretentious **hotel** in the heart of the village with views of the Dentelles; its *terrasse* restaurant serves very decent food with menus from 90F.

Mont Ventoux and around

From the Rhône, Luberon and Durance, the summit of **MONT VENTOUX** repeatedly appears on the horizon. White with snow, black with storm-cloud shadow or reflecting myriad shades of blue, the barren pebbles of the final 300m are like a coloured weath-er vane for all of western Provence. From a distance the mountain looks distinctly allur-ing, a suitable site for what was the first recorded notion of landscape in European thought. The fourteenth-century Italian poet Petrarch climbed the heights simply for the experience; the local guides he chartered for the two-and-a-half-day hike consid-ered him completely crazy.

Meteorological information is gathered, along with TV transmissions and Mirage fighter jet movements, from masts and dishes at the top. The tower directing the con-glomeration of receptors is in consequence no beauty, its essential design characteristic being to withstand winds from every direction, including the northern Mistral that can accelerate to 250km per hour across Ventoux. Wind, rain, snow and fearsome sub-zero temperatures are the dominant natural accompaniments to this tarmacked mountaintop.

The deforestation of Mont Ventoux dates from Roman times, and by the nineteenth century it had got so bad that the entire mountain appeared shaved. Oaks, pines, box wood, fir and beech have since been replanted and the owls and eagles have returned but the greenery is unlikely ever to reach the summit again. The road that zigzags up the 1900m and down again with such consummate, if convoluted, ease was built for the purposes of testing prototype cars, an activity that continued up till the mid-Seventies. Mont Ventoux is also a sporadic highlight of the Tour de France, hence its appeal in summer for passionately committed cyclists. Around the treeline is a memorial to the great British cyclist Tommy Simpson, who died here from heart failure in 1967, on one of the hottest days ever recorded in the race; legend has it that his last words were – "Put me back on the bloody bike."

But the chief human endeavour here is to mark the surface of the road with giant rows of graffiti of cosmopolitan individuals' names, local wines, the CGT, and, predictably for this part of the world, FN and Le Pen. Despite the unpromising envi-ronment, rest assured that from the summit, you have one of the most wonderful **panoramas**, not just in France, but in the whole of Europe. Between **November and May** all the road graffiti is covered by snow, with only the tops of the black and yellow poles beside the road still visible; then, people ascending Mont Ventoux will be on **skis**, leaving base either at Mont Serein on the north face or from the smaller southern station of Le Chalet-Reynard.

If you want to make the **ascent on foot** the best path to take is from Les Colombets or Les Fébriers, hamlets off the D974 east of **BEDOIN** whose **tourist office**, on Espace M.L-Gravier (July–Aug Mon–Fri 9am–1pm & 2–6pm, Sat 9–noon & 2–6pm, Sun 9am–noon; rest of year Mon–Fri 9am–12.30pm & 2–6pm, Sat 9am–noon; ☎04.90.65.63.95), can give details. They also organize a **night-time ascent**, once a week in July and August, leaving around 10pm to camp near the summit and await the sunrise; check with the tourist office for the day. La Passe Montagne (☎04.90.65.60.25), opposite Bedoin's tourist office, rents out **bikes** if you want to join the superfit cyclists in braving the gusts and horribly long steep inclines. In **Mont Serein** the Chalet d'Accueil Mt-Serein (☎04.90.63.42.02) can provide info on **ski-rental**, runs and lifts.

Bedoin has several **campsites**, including the two-star *Camping Pastory* on the Malaucène road (☎04.90.65.60.79; closed mid-Oct to mid-March) and over a dozen **gîtes ruraux** for anyone considering spending a week or more in the area.

Le Chalet-Reynard on the south face has a small **restaurant** (☎04.90.61.84.55; menus from 80F), filled with walkers in the summer and skiers in the winter. There's a very good gîte d'étape, *Les Écuries de Ventoux* (☎04.90.65.29.20; ①), 2km outside Malaucène, down a track off the road to Beaumont-de-Ventoux. At the other end of the scale, the *Hostellerie de Crillon le Brave*, place de l'Église (☎04.90.65.61.61, fax 04.90.65.62.86; ⑨) in **Crillon-le-Brave** just west of Bedoin, offers exquisitely tasteful luxury.

The Nesque Gorge

The **NESQUE GORGE** lies to the south of Ventoux, on the D942 from Carpentras to Sault. The River Nesque is dry most of the year and invisible from most of the road which clings to the rocks above it – a feat of engineering even more impressive than the geological fault itself. It's a barren area with just one landmark, located on the southern side before the gorge turns northeast again towards the village of Monieux. The 200-metre-high **Rocher du Cire** is coated in wax from numerous hives that wild bees have made, and supposedly provided the men of the nearby village with the reputation-enhancing exploit of abseiling down it to gather honey. This may well be a macho myth; certainly no one does it now. In **MONIEUX**, there's a cheap **gîte d'étape** for walkers, the *Ferme St-Hubert* (☎04.90.64.04.51; ①; closed Mon–Thurs), and a little **restaurant**, *Les Lavandes* (☎04.90.64.05.08; around 120F; closed Mon out of season).

The Plateau d'Albion

At **SAULT**, 6km northeast of Monieux, the steep forested rocks give way to fields of lavender, cereals and grazing sheep. Wild products of the woods, lactaire and grisel mushrooms, truffles and game, as well as honey and other lavender products are bought and sold at its Wednesday **market**; autumn is the best time for these local specialities. If you miss the market, La Maison des Producteurs on rue de la République can sell you all the goodies. Sault also has **fairs** on the Wednesday before Palm Sunday, St John's feast day (June 23) and on August 16.

At the **PLATEAU D'ALBION**, south of Sault, Mount Ventoux recedes from view. A ring of hills guards this treeless, undulating plain in which the chalky ground is riven by fissures, subterranean caverns and tunnels. Habitation is almost nonexistent and it's a shock when the narrow, badly surfaced and traffic-less D30 suddenly becomes a three-lane, superbly smooth highway which continues through St-Christol and down to Lagarde d'Apt. Part of the reason for this change is the enormous **airforce base** with its massive hangars and tall, rectangular, khaki-coloured blocks just north of St-Christol. Until recently, it was the base for France's eighteen land-based nuclear missiles, all of which have now been disarmed.

Carpentras and south

CARPENTRAS, with a population approaching thirty thousand, is one of the larger towns of the Vaucluse with a history dating back to around 5 BC, when it was the capital to a Celtic tribe. The Greeks, who founded Marseille, came here to buy honey, wheat, goats and skins. But the town really flourished in the fourteenth century, during the period of the popes when it briefly became the papal headquarters and gave protection to Jews expelled from France. Aside from its history, which is a major draw for tourists, Carpentras is worth visiting for its **Friday market** and for its **festival** in the last two weeks of July (see boxes below and on p.128). The town also serves as a good base for excursions into the Dentelles, Mont Ventoux, the Nesque Gorge and the towns and villages south towards Cavaillon and Apt.

Arrival, information and accommodation

Buses arrive either on av Victor-Hugo or on place Terradou, from where it's a short walk to av Georges-Clemenceau and right on to av Victor-Hugo and place Aristide-Briand. The train station is for freight only. The **tourist office** is at 170 allée Jean-Jaurès (July & Aug daily 9am–7pm; rest of year Mon–Fri 9am–12.30pm & 2–6.30pm, Sat closes 6pm; ☎04.90.63.00.78), halfway along av Jean-Jaurès which runs northeast from place Aristide-Briand. The town proper is small enough to cover easily on foot, but if you need a **bike** try Terzo Sports on av Mistral (☎04.90.67.31.56) or Egobike in the Complexe Sportif on av P. de Coubertin (☎04.90.65.22.15).

Most of Carpentras' **hotels** are on the boulevards which circle the old town; there are plenty of bargains to be had, but don't expect to find anywhere particularly quiet. On bd Albin-Durand try the basic *Le Théâtre* at no. 7 (☎04.90.63.02.90; ②); or *La Lavande*, 282 bd A-Rogier (☎04.90.63.13.49; ②); with just twelve beds it soon fills up, so booking is recommended. A rather kitsch but central option is *Le Malaga* on place Maurice-Charretier, (☎04.90.60.57.96; ②), all rooms en-suite facilities. For a bit more luxury, try *Le Fiacre*, 153 rue Vigne (☎04.90.63.03.15, fax 04.90.60.49.73; ③) close to the tourist office, in an old town house with a garden; or *Safari Hotel*, 1 av JH-Fabre (☎04.90.63.35.35, fax 04.90.60.49.99; ③), which, though lacking in character, has good amenities, including a pool and tennis courts.

The nearest **campsite** is the two-star *Camping Le Brégoux,* chemin du Vas, just outside the village of Aubignan, 5km north on the D7 towards Beaumes-de-Venise (☎04.90.62.62.50; closed Oct to mid-March).

The Town

A bird's-eye view of Carpentras shows clearly the perimeter line of the town in the Dark Ages (rues Vigne, des Halles, Raspail, du Collège and Moricelly), enclosed in the ring of boulevards that follow the line of the medieval town wall. Of this only the massive,

---

CARPENTRAS MARKET

Friday is the major **market** day in Carpentras. The local **fruit and vegetables** that appear so early in the lowlands of Vaucluse are available all round the town; **flowers and plants** are sold on av Jean-Jaurès; **antiques and bric-à-brac** on rue Porte-de-Monteux and place Colonel-Mouret; while, from the annual St-Siffrein fair (November 27) to the beginning of March, place Aristide-Briand and place du 24 Août 1944 are given over to the selling of **truffles**, the rooted not the chocolate kind.

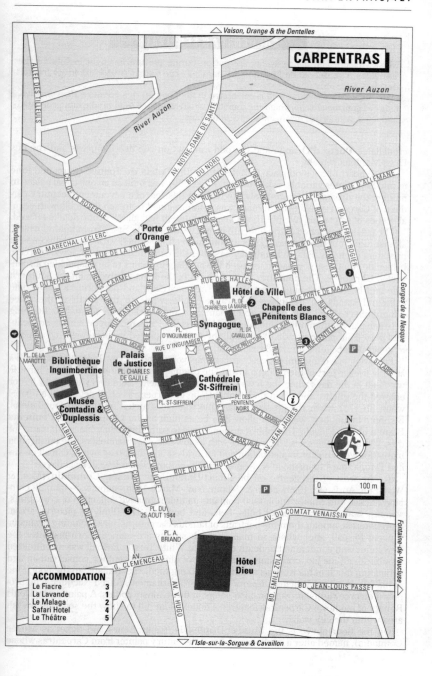

△ Vaison, Orange & the Dentelles

CARPENTRAS

River Auzon

River Auzon

Porte d'Orange

Hôtel de Ville

Chapelle des Pénitents Blancs

Synagogue

Palais de Justice

Cathédrale St-Siffrein

Bibliothèque Inguimbertine

Musée Comtadin & Duplessis

Hôtel Dieu

Camping ◁

Gorges de la Nesque ▷

Fontaine-de-Vaucluse ▷

0 — 100 m

N

P

P

PL. DU 25 AOUT 1944

PL. A. BRIAND

ACCOMMODATION

Le Fiacre	3
La Lavande	1
Le Malaga	2
Safari Hotel	4
Le Théâtre	5

▽ l'Isle-sur-la-Sorgue & Cavaillon

CARPENTRAS FESTIVALS

Music, theatre and dance events are put on during the last fortnight in July for the **Estivales**. The Bureau du Festival, La Charité, 77 rue Cottier (☎04.90.63.46.35) has full details.

On August 15, Vaucluse food is celebrated in the **Festival des Saveurs Provençales**, a day of gourmandise in which the minutiae of old-fashioned food production is debated and feted, with prizes given and plenty of tastings.

crenellated **Porte d'Orange** and the odd rampart on rue des Ramparts and rue des Lices-Monteux remain.

At the heart of town on place Gén-de-Gaulle, the **Palais de Justice** (tours mid-June to mid-Sept; times variable, ask at tourist office; 25F) was built as an episcopal palace to indulge the dreams, or more likely the realized desires, of a seventeenth-century cardinal of Carpentras. Nicolas Mignard was commissioned to fresco the walls with sexual scenes of satyrs and nymphs, but a later incumbent had all the erotic details effaced.

The palais is attached to the fifteenth-century **Cathédrale St-Siffrein** behind which, almost hidden in the corner, stands a **Roman arch**, inscribed with imperial scenes of prisoners in chains. Fifteen hundred years after the cathedral's erection, Jews, coerced, bribed or otherwise persuaded, entered the building in chains to be unshackled as converted Christians. The door they passed through, the **Porte Juive**, is on the southern side and bears the strange symbolism of rats encircling and devouring a globe. The cathedral stands on the place Général-de-Gaulle, while to the north is the place d'Inguimbert, lined with plane trees, lanterns and black swan fountains. Running between place d'Inguimbert and rue des Halles is the **Passage Boyer**, a high and beautiful glazed shopping arcade. It was built by the unemployed in the short-lived scheme to generate jobs after the 1848 revolution.

Following rue d'Inguimbert eastwards brings you to the ancient **Jewish ghetto** and a slightly livelier part of the modern town. The original **synagogue** on place de la Juiverie was built in the days when the Jews had to pay movement taxes every time they left or entered the ghetto, and when their rights to be in Carpentras at all depended on papal whim. In 1741 when the present synagogue was constructed on the old foundations, Bishop d'Inguimbert would not allow it to be as high as the **Chapelle des Pénitents Blancs** on rue Bidault. The rabbi's response was to paint the ceiling blue with stars "for then I'll have all the skies". This, along with its low hanging chandeliers, the purification baths (for women after menstruation and for brides) and the bread ovens, can all be visited (Mon–Thurs 10am–noon & 3–5pm, Fri closes 4pm; closed Jewish feast days).

To the west of the centre on bd Albert-Durand, the **Musée Comtadin** (Mon & Wed–Sun: April–Oct 10am–noon & 2–6pm; Nov–March 10am–noon & 2–4pm; 2F combined ticket with Musée Duplessis) contains an unimaginative collection of keys, guns, *santons*, seals, ex-votos, papal bulls, bells and bonnets. The dimly lit pictures are of more interest, among them the portraits of famous Carpentrassiens including François-Vincent Raspail, after whom so many French streets are named. Born just after the Revolution and condemned to death during the White Terror, Raspail was a committed republican all his life, criticising every brand of nineteenth-century conservatism and dedicating much of his work as a doctor to making medicine available to the poor. One of his fellow radical Vaucluse *députés* in the 1876 parliament, Alfred Nacquet, who proposed divorce rights for women, also hangs in these musty rooms. A painting by Denis Bonnet of medieval Carpentras features a nonexistent hill to show the separate Jewish area within the city walls.

On the floor above is the **Musée Duplessis** (same hours and ticket as Musée Comtadin), named after a mediocre eighteenth-century painter from Carpentras whose wealth and influence had much to do with the people he painted. Along with the paintings, Roman artefacts, an Egyptian tablet with a pharaonic scene captioned in Aramaic, and some very wonderful Renaissance miniatures are on display. Also in the complex, on the left as you enter the courtyard, is the **Bibliothèque Inguimbertine**, where several hundred thousand volumes on the history of Provence, Books of Hours, musical scores and early manuscripts are available for consultation (Mon 2–6.30pm, Tues–Fri 9.30am–6.30pm, Sat 9.30am–noon; closed July). Contemporary art is displayed in changing exhibitions at the nearby **Chapelle du Collège** on rue du Collège (Mon–Sat 9.30am–12.30pm & 2–6pm; free).

To the south of the centre, just beyond place Aristide-Briand, is the huge eighteenth-century **Hôtel-Dieu** building, which still functions as a hospital though you can visit its original opulent **pharmacy** (Mon, Wed & Thurs 9–11.30am; 4F). As well as gorgeously decorated vials and boxes containing cat's foot extract, Saturn salt, deer antler shavings and dragon blood, the painted lower cupboards tell a very "Age of Reason" moral tale of wild and happy monkeys ending up as tame and dutiful labourers.

Eating, drinking and entertainment

One of the best places to **eat** in Carpentras is *Le Marijo* at 73 rue Raspail (☎04.90.60.42.65; closed Sun), which has excellent menus for under 130F. *Les Halles* (☎04.90.63.24.11; closed Sun), at 41 rue Galonne off rue des Halles, is a cheaper option with menus under 80F; while *Le Vert Galant*, 12 rue Clapies (☎04.90.67.15.50; closed Sat midday & Sun), serves more sophisticated fare, with a weekday lunchtime menu for around 100F. You'll find crêpes at *La Magnane* on impasse G-Braque. Takeaway Thai, Chinese and Vietnamese food is available from *La Perle d'Asie* on place du Théâtre and quick pizzas from *La Garrigue*, 90 rue Cottier (daily till 11pm).

For **drinking** the *Pub Peter Polo* on the corner of place Aristide-Briand attracts a trendy crowd. There are several more café-brasseries on the square and, during the truffle season, the buyers, middlemen and *truffiers* do great business in the bar of the *Univers* hotel. There are some good cafés on place Charles-de-Gaulle, including *Le Siècle*, but all of them close by 7.30pm. For late-night drinking, head for *Le Petit Montmartre*, 40 rue David-Guillabert, popular with locals. Alternatively there's the bar at the *Hôtel Malaga* (closed Sun) on the corner of rue Juiverie and place Maurice-Charretier, which is usually a lively place.

Pernes-les-Fontaines

South of Carpentras, on the road to L'Isle-sur-la-Sorgue, lies the exquisite small town of **PERNES-LES-FONTAINES**. The fountains for which it's named (36 in all), the ramparts, gateways, castle, towers, covered market hall, Renaissance streets and half a dozen chapels all blend into a single complex structure, and the passages between its squares feel more like corridors between rooms.

Approaching from Carpentras you cross the River Nesque before reaching place Gabriel-Moutte on the left, the site of Pernes' Saturday market and tourist office; from here av Jean-Jaurès follows the line of the fourteenth-century ramparts, of which only three gates now remain. Second on the left is the Park Villeneuve, dating from 1550, which leads to rue Gambetta and the old town. At the end of rue Gambetta is the **Tour Ferrande** (guided tours arranged by the tourist office) which contains the town's great medieval artwork – **frescoes** dating from the era of the Bayeux tapestry and similar in style; they portray religious scenes of the Virgin and Child as well as scenes from the legend of William of Orange and the life of Charles of Anjou.

Heading down rue Victor-Hugo and along rue de la Halle brings you to the sixteenth-century Porte Notre-Dame and the **cormorant fountain** with the seventeenth-century market hall. From this gateway, rue Raspail heads south past the fifteenth-century **reboul fountain**, the oldest of Pernes' fountains, and onto the other remaining gate, the Porte St-Gilles.

Practicalities

The **tourist office** is on place Gabriel-Moutte (May–Sept Mon–Sat 9am–noon & 2.30–7pm, Sun 9am–noon; Oct–April Mon–Sat 9am–noon & 2–5.30pm; ☎04.90.61.31.04). An afternoon's wander may well be enough to sample Pernes-les-Fontaines' charms, but, if you find yourself seduced, some **hotel** possibilities include *La Margelle*, place Aristide-Briand on the boulevard ring to the south of the village (☎04.90.61.30.36; ②), with a rambling back garden and inexpensive menus; or *Prato-Plage* (☎04.90.61.37.75; ③), just outside the town on the Carpentras road on the edge of an artificial lake. The municipal **campsite** is in the quartier Coucourelles (☎04.90.66.45.55; closed mid-Sept to mid-April); campervans can park overnight on quai de Verdon (not Fri).

There's a delightful **restaurant**, *Au Fil de Temps* (☎04.90.66.48.61; closed Wed; lunch menu 95F; evening menu from 180F) on place L-Giraud, serving exquisite food. *Lou Cigalou* (closed Wed eve, Sat & Sun lunch), on place Aristide-Briand, serves wood-fire **pizzas** at a reasonable price.

Venasque

VENASQUE, 9km east of Pernes just before the roads start to wind over the Plateau de Vaucluse towards Apt, is a perfectly contained village on a spur of rock. At its highest end are three round towers and a curtain wall, at its lowest end a sixth-century baptistry, built on the site of a Roman temple which is though to have been dedicated to Venus. Like most Provençal villages it swings between a sleepy winter state and a tourist honey pot in summer. The best time to visit is in May and June, before the main tourist season begins, and when the daily **market** concentrates exclusively on the sale of local cherries.

Besides its location, Venasque's attractions lie in its food. **Haute cuisine**, with all the ingredients fresh from the market, is to be had at the *Auberge de la Fontaine* on place de la Fontaine (☎04.90.66.02.96; from 200F; closed Wed eve); you'll need to book for the main restaurant but on the ground floor *Le Bistro* (closed Sun eve & Mon) serves less expensive and less sophisticated dishes of the same high quality. The hotel-restaurant, *Les Remparts* (☎04.90.66.02.79; around 120F; closed mid-Nov to early March), at the top of the main street, rue Haute, also has a good restaurant, with an excellent dish of fish with citrus fruits (*dorade des agrumes*) usually on the menu.

The **tourist office** is on Grande Rue (mid-March to May & Oct Mon–Thurs, Sat & Sun 10am–12.30pm & 2–6pm, Fri 2–6pm; June–Sept Mon–Thurs, Sat & Sun 10am–12.30pm & 3–7pm, Fri 3–7pm; ☎04.90.66.11.66). It can help with **accommodation**, which is fairly thin on the ground: aside from rooms at the *Auberge* (⑧) and *Les Remparts* (④), the only other **hotel** in town is *La Garrigue*, rte de l'Appiè (☎04.90.66.03.40; ④; closed mid-Oct to Easter).

L'Isle-sur-la-Sorgue

L'ISLE-SUR-LA-SORGUE, not to be confused with Sorgues on the Rhône, lies 23km east of Avignon, halfway between Carpentras and Cavaillon. The town straddles five branches of the River Sorgue, its waters once full of otters and beavers, eels, trout and crayfish, and its currents turning the power wheels of a **medieval cloth industry**. Tanneries, dyeing works, and, in the eighteenth century, silk production, all ensured considerable prosperity for "the Island".

Those times are largely past. An epidemic killed off all the crayfish a hundred years ago and the eels and aquatic animals have long since gone, while the huge blackened wheels of the cloth industry turn now only as mementoes, the mills and tanneries standing empty, plants growing through the crumbling brickwork. But in summer fishing punts continue to crowd the streams and L'Isle is a cheerful place, particularly on Sundays, when people arrive for its well-known **antiques market**. L'Isle is also a useful, less expensive base for visiting nearby **Fontaine-de-Vaucluse**.

Arrival, information and accommodation

Trains from Avignon and Cavaillon arrive at the **gare SNCF**, southwest of the town centre, and **buses** arrive by place Gambetta. The **tourist office** is in the former granary on place de l'Eglise (April–Sept Mon & Sun 9.30am–12.30pm, Tues–Sat 9am–12.30pm & 2.30–7pm; Oct–March Mon & Sun 9am–12.30pm, Tues–Sat 9am–12.30pm & 2.30–6pm; ☎04.90.38.04.78). **Bikes** can be rented from MBK Comtat on place Gambetta (☎04.90.38.07.54).

L'Isle-sur-la-Sorgue is not a major tourist destination, so **rooms** tend to be fairly cheap – but watch out for water-loving midges. *Au Vieux Isle*, 15 rue Danton (☎04.90.38.00.46; ①), in one of the narrow alleyways of the old town, is pretty basic but has a pool table, bar football and occasional concerts. Other inexpensive rooms can be found at 33 rue Carnot (☎04.90.20.68.59; ①; closed Fri eve & Sat), above the restaurant *La Saladelle*. A little way out of town is *Le Pescador* in Partages-des-Eaux 1.5km upstream of the town (☎04.90.38.09.69; ③; closed Mon, Jan & Feb), in an idyllic spot at the point where the waters divide – follow signs to Carpentras and turn right immediately after crossing the main branch of the river. Or you could stay in an eighteenth-century coach house out in the countryside, *Le Mas de Cure Bourse*, chemin de la Serre (☎04.90.38.16.58; ⑥), a few kilometres southwest of town signed left off the D25 to Caumont, the continuation of av de l'Égalité. The rooms are decorated in traditional Provençal style and the restaurant is very good.

The municipal three-star **campsite**, *La Sorguette*, 41 Les Grandes Sorgues (☎04.90.38.05.71; closed Nov to mid-March), is by the river on the Apt road.

The Town

Though L'Isle-sur-la-Sorgue's claim to be the Venice of Provence stretches a point, it is a pleasant waterside location in which to spend an afternoon. The central **place de l'Église** and **place de la Liberté** provide reminders of past prosperity, most obviously in the Baroque seventeenth-century **church** (Tues–Sat 10am–noon & 3–6pm), by far the richest religious edifice for miles around. Each column in the nave supports a sculpted Virtue: whips and turtledoves are Chastity's props, a unicorn accompanies Virginity, and medallions and inscriptions carry the adornment down to the floor. Above the west door, angels, Christ, the Supreme Being and Mary veer heavenwards in gilded relief like flying ducks. Only the ceiling is bare. Heading north of the place de l'Église, you'll come to the eighteenth-century **Hôtel Donadeï de Campredon** at 20 rue du Docteur-Tallet (April–Sept Tues–Sun 10am–1pm & 3–6pm; Oct–March Tues–Sun 9.30am–noon & 2–5.30pm; 30F), which hosts temporary exhibitions of modern sculpture and painting.

The **Hôpital** on quai des Lices at the western edge of the old town is in the much more restrained style of the eighteenth century. Its monumental staircase carries de Sade's arms, and its chapel, fountained garden and pharmacy can usually be visited, though it will remain closed until 2000 for restoration work; check with the tourist office for the latest details. The pharmacy, though not as impressive as the one at Carpentras, has beautiful Moustiers porcelain vases and painted boxes containing such things as calcium extracted from crayfish eyes (a remedy for syphilis) and an epileptic cure so potent that a drop too many could kill.

Every year the Isle fishermen retain their medieval guild tradition of crowning a king of the Sorgue, whose job is to oversee the rights of catch and sale. The **Festival de la Sorgue** at the end of July sees all of them out in traditional gear and two teams battling from boats in an ancient jousting tournament. On the **spring equinox** the people of Velleron, 5km downstream, process down to the river and launch a fleet of tiny luminous rafts to celebrate the start of spring. If you want to get on the river yourself Canoë Evasion (☎04.90.38.26.22), signed right off the D25 towards Fontaine-de-Vaucluse, organizes **canoe trips**.

The Sunday market of **antiques** and secondhand goods centres on the Village des Antiquaires on av de l'Égalité spilling out onto the boulevards. Interesting **bric-à-brac** is also for sale at La Petite Curieuse, 23 impasse de la République, off the main shopping street of rue de la République.

Eating and drinking

Traditional **local specialities** include *écrevisse* (crayfish) *en coquille* and an omelette flavoured with a certain Sorgue weed, but today grilled trout is the staple, to be had at *La Saladelle*, 33 rue Carnot (☎04.90.20.68.59; closed Fri eve & Sat; 70F menu). For something more special, try *La Prévôté*, 4 rue JJ-Rousseau (☎04.90.38.57.29; weekday lunchtime menu around 130F, otherwise from 200F; closed Sun eve & Mon) behind the church. *Le Pescador* hotel in Partages-des-Eaux (see "Arrival"; closed Mon, Jan & Feb; menu from 100F) serves good fish dishes, or you can eat and drink at *La Guinguette* next door (☎04.90.38.10.61; menu around 100F). The *Mas de Cure Bourse* hotel (see "Arrival"; closed Mon & Tues lunch; menu around 165F) also has a reputable restaurant.

Café de l'Industrie, on quai de la Charité by place E-Char, serves excellent coffee and plats du jour for 60F, and there's the busy **brasserie**, *Café de la Sorgue*, on quai Jean-Jaurès. Good cakes and ice creams can be had at the *salon de thé Heyraud* at 36 av de la République. For **drinking**, head for place de l'Église, to the *Bar Le César* with its faded mirrors or at the swish fin-de-siècle *Café de France*.

Thursday is **market** day but the best place to buy food is at nearby Velleron where producers sell their goods direct at a busy *marché paysan* (summer Mon–Sat 6–8pm; winter Tues, Fri & Sat 4.30–6pm). For inexpensive **wine**, Le Caveau de la Tour de l'Isle at 12 rue de la République is the place to go (closed Sun & Mon).

Fontaine-de-Vaucluse

The diverging streams of L'Isle-sur-la-Sorgue have their source only 6km to the east in a mysterious tapering fissure deep below the sheer 230-metre cliffs barricading its opening at the top of a gorge above **FONTAINE-DE-VAUCLUSE**. Fascination with the **source**, one of the most powerful natural springs in the world, coupled with the beauty of the ancient riverside village where the fourteenth-century poet Petrarch pined for his Laura, makes this a very popular tourist spot – well over a million visitors a year converge here. But despite the crowds, Fontaine is still a supremely romantic place.

The source and the village

In spring, the waters of the Sorgue often appear in spectacular fashion, bursting down the gorge, at other times they seep stealthily through subterranean channels to meet the riverbed further down. The best time to admire them is in the early morning before the crowds arrive.

Palais des Papes, Avignon

Cathédrale St-Trophime, Arles

Pont St-Bénézet and the Petit Palais, Avignon

Abbaye de Sénanque

Oppède-le-Vieux

Etange de Vaccares, the Camargue

The Nesque Valley

Architectural detail, Aix-en-Provence

Gordes

Cassis harbour

Mont Ste-Victoire

View from the Cap Canaille, near Cassis

If you're intrigued by the source, and understand French, visit the **Norbert-Casteret Musée de Spéléologie** (April–Aug daily 10am–noon & 2–6pm; Sept–Nov, Feb & March Wed–Sun 11am & 2–5pm; 30F) in the underground commercial centre alongside chemin de la Fontaine. It's run by volunteers eager to communicate their passion for crawling about in the bowels of the earth. If such activity is on a par for you with spider or rat fraternizing, all the more reason to follow this tour through mock-up caves and passages. The museum winds up with a collection of underworld concretions gathered by Casteret, one of France's most renowned cavers, ranging from huge, jewellery-like crystals to pieces resembling fibre optics. Displays also document the intriguing history of the exploration of the spring, from the first 23-metre descent in 1878 to the robotic camera that reached the bottom a few years ago, its blurry pictures apparently showing a horizontal passage disappearing into the rock. It's thought that water seeping through a vast plateau of chalk (stretching as far north as Banon) hits an impermeable base that slopes down to Fontaine.

However the water arrives, it has long been put to use in turning the wheels of manufacturing. The first paper mill was built at Fontaine in 1522, and the last, built in 1862, ceased operations in 1968. The medieval method of pulping rags to paper has been re-created at the far end of the complex in the **Moulin à papier Vallis Clausa** (daily 9am–12.20pm & 2–6.20pm; Sun opens 10.30am; free). Flowers are added to the pulp and the resulting paper is printed with all manner of drawings, poems and prose from Churchill's "Blood, Sweat and Tears" speech to the legend of how God created Provence, on sale in the vast Vallis Clausa shop. There are other quality craft shops in the complex, including one selling household objects carved in olive wood, and an exhibition of *santons*.

Further along chemin de la Fontaine is the impressive and intense **Musée de la Résistance** (mid-April to mid-Oct & school hols Mon & Wed–Sun 10am–noon & 2–6pm; mid-Oct to Dec & March to mid-April Sat & Sun only; 20F). The overriding purpose of the museum is not to judge or apologize, but to remind people of the humanity of resistance. In so doing it acknowledges the extent to which the war period still perturbs the collective memory of the French. The museum looks at Marshall Pétain's anti-Semitic laws, which were not instructions from Berlin, and stresses how many French people must have opposed them since three-quarters of the French Jewish population escaped deportation. The re-created classroom and other displays of daily life bring home the authoritarian, anti-intellectual and patriarchal nature of France's fascist regime, its insistence on work, family and *patrie*, and the military cult of Pétain. A section is dedicated to the artists who refused to collaborate, another to the German Resistance.

In total, and grotesque, contrast, the **Musée de la Justice et des Châtiments** (daily: July & Aug 10am–8pm; rest of year 10am–7pm; 10F) a few doors down displays torture equipment and the methods of carrying out the death penalty based around the collection of the official French executioner in occupied Algeria from 1949 to 1953. There are appropriate statements by sociologists, but no mention that the horrors it evokes continued after the 1950s.

Across the river, through an alleyway just past the bridge, is the **Musée de Pétrarque** (mid-April to mid-Oct Wed–Sun 9.30am–noon & 2–6.30pm; winter Sat & Sun only; 15F) with beautiful old books dating back to the fifteenth century and pictures of Petrarch, his beloved Laura and of Fontaine where he passed sixteen years of his unrequited passion. The museum also hosts temporary art exhibitions.

Practicalities

Buses from L'Isle-sur-la-Sorgue drop you by the car park just before the church. The **tourist office** is on chemin de la Fontaine (May–Oct daily 9am–8pm; Nov–April Mon–Sat 10am–7pm; ☎04.90.20.32.22) off to the left towards the source.

Rooms in Fontaine are likely to be fully booked in summer, so booking ahead is advisable, or try in L'Isle-sur-la-Sorgue which should be more promising. Fontaine's **place de la Colonne** is particularly pleasant spot to stay, with hotel balconies, terraced restaurants and cafés overhanging the river. The cheapest and most characterful **hotel** is the *Grand Hôtel des Sources* (☎04.90.20.31.84; ②) with a whole variety of *vieille France* rooms. On the road back to L'Isle, about 3km from Fontaine and on the right, are two hotels worth trying: the excellent-value *L'Ermitage* (☎04.90.20.32.20; ③) and the smaller, more basic *Font de Lauro* (☎04.90.20.31.49; ③; closed Oct–March) down a track just past the other. The HI **youth hostel**, about 1km from the village on chemin de la Vignasse (reception 8–10am & 5–11pm; ☎04.90.20.31.65; closed Dec & Jan), is very pleasant. *Les Prés* **campsite** (☎04.90.20.32.38) is 500m downstream from the village with tennis courts and swimming pool.

The **restaurant** at *L'Ermitage* has better food than anything you're likely to be served in Fontaine, though for scenic *terrasses*, *Pétrarque & Laure* on the main square, by the bridge (☎04.90.20.31.48) is hard to beat. If you arrive early, the *boulangerie Le Moulin de la Fontaine* near the church does breakfasts, and a few doors down there's a crêperie. **Market** day is on Tuesday.

On the north side of the river, above the aqueduct, is a little hut called *Pêche de la Truite* where you can rent rods and lines. Just upstream *Kayak Vert* (☎04.90.20.35.44) rents **canoes** for a half-hour or hour's paddling, or for a fairly effortless eight-kilometre trip down to L'Isle-sur-la-Sorgue (where the canoes can be handed over).

Cavaillon

Approaches to **CAVAILLON** pass through fields of fruit and vegetables, watered by the Durance and Coulon rivers. Market gardening is the major business of the city and to the French, Cavaillon, its Roman origins notwithstanding, is known simply as a melon town. The **melon** in question is the Charentais, a small pale green ball with dark green stripes and brilliant orange flesh, in season from May to September. Together with asparagus and early spring vegetables, they are sold every weekday morning at one of the largest **wholesale markets** in Europe.

In the last week of January Cavaillon hosts a **science festival**, bringing together serious boffins, journalists, artists and celebrities with events free and open to all. Otherwise, there are a couple of events combining commercialism with festivities that could cheer up a visit: the *Foire St-Véran* in the second week in November and the *Fête de St-Gilles* in the first week of September. It must be said, however, that this doesn't make Cavaillon very interesting for much of the year, although it's certainly a useful stopover, with train and bus connections to Avignon, Salon, Aix and Carpentras, as well as to the Luberon to the east.

Arrival, information and accommodation

The **gare SNCF** and the **gare routière** are on av P-Semard on the east side of town. The **tourist office** (summer Mon–Sat 9am–12.30pm & 2–7pm, Sun 9.30am–12.30pm; winter Mon–Sat 9am–12.30pm & 1.30–6.30pm; ☎04.90.71.32.01) is on pl François-Tourel on the opposite side of town and can be reached by taking av du Mal-Joffre, opposite the train station, turning right at the end, then taking the first left onto cours Bournissac and following it to the end. **Bikes** can be rented from Cycles Rieu, 25 av Mal-Joffre (☎04.90.71.45.55).

In the centre of town, the most attractive budget **hotel** is *Le Parc*, 183 place F-Tourel (☎04.90.71.57.78; ②), followed by *Le Grenouillet*, 133 av Berthelot (☎04.90.78.08.08; ②; closed Dec–March), which is very agreeable for the price. *Le*

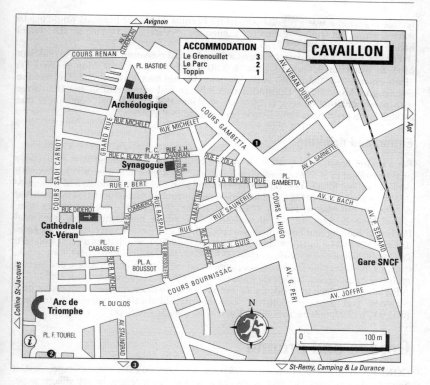

Relais Mercure, digue des Grands Jardins, quartier Boscodomini (☎04.90.71.07.79; ⑤), is a modern, luxurious hotel overlooking the Durance, with pool and tennis courts; while *Toppin*, 70 cours Gambetta (☎04.90.71.30.42; ④), is dependable, with rustic-style, comfortable rooms.

For **camping**, there's the three-star *Camping de la Durance*, digue des Grands Jardins, in the direction of the *autoroute* (☎04.90.71.11.78; closed Oct–March), is invariably crowded in the summer months.

The Town

All that remains of Roman Cavaillon is the **triumphal arch** on place du Clos, which on Mondays is surrounded by the weekly **market**. The **Cathédrale St-Véran** (April–Sept Mon 3–6pm, Tues–Sat 10am–noon & 3–6pm; Oct–March Mon 2–4pm, Tues–Sat 10am–noon & 2–4pm), due north of place du Clos, is Cavaillon's chief monument, an archaic-looking building, on the south side of which God appears above a sundial looking like a winged and battered Neptune. Inside, in the St-Véran chapel, an exuberant nineteenth-century marble altar glorifies the edible produce of the town, while in the rear chapel there's a painting of Saint Véran hauling off a slithery reptile known as Couloubre, who terrorized the locality in 6 AD.

For a panoramic view of the surrounding countryside you can climb the steep path from behind the Roman arch to the **Chapelle Saint-Jacques**. Built on the site of a temple to Jupiter it was a regular outpost for hermits whom the peasants would pay to warn them of impending storms (or Couloubre appearances) by ringing the chapel bell.

For glimpses into the past there's an **archeological museum** (mid-April to mid-Sept Mon & Wed–Sun 9.30am–12.30pm & 2.30–6.30pm; rest of year Mon & Wed–Fri 10am–noon & 2–4.30pm; 20F) in the chapel of the old hospital on Grand Rue, and the **Synagogue/Musée Juif Comtadin** (same hours and admission) in rue Hebraïque with plenty of ritual objects, but few insights into the small Jewish community that established a precarious right to existence in medieval Cavaillon.

Eating and drinking

For a **melon feast**, *Prevot*, 353 av de Verdon (☎04.90.71.32.43; closed Mon & Sun eve) on the road out to St-Rémy, does a "melon menu" from June to September: lobster with petals of melon, fillet of beef on dried melon and iced melon with nougat and Beaumes-de-Venise muscat for 360F. Cavaillon's best **restaurant** is *Alain Nicolet*, 3km southeast of town on the road to Pertuis at **Cheval Blanc** (☎04.90.78.01.56; last orders 9pm; closed Mon & Sun eve out of season; 250F), which has immaculate, traditional Provençal cooking and home-made sorbets. For a lighter meal, you could try *La Faim de Loup*, 129 av Mal-Joffre (☎04.90.78.31.68; around 110F), which does a great leek tart; *Le Grillon*, 50 cours Victor-Hugo (☎04.90.71.33.87; from 89F; closed Tues), for tagines, coucous, pastillas plus Provençal specialities and excellent Algerian wines, or charcoal grills at *Le Pantagruel*, 5 place de Cabassole (☎04.90.76.11.30; menus from 100F).

For a stylish place to **drink** try *Le Fin de Siècle*, 46 place du Clos, with heavy gold cornices and fantasy pictures, and an excellent-value restaurant upstairs (☎04.90.71.12.27; menus from 89F; closed Wed, plus Aug & Sept).

Gordes and around

GORDES, 6km north of the main Avignon–Apt road, and the same distance east of Fontaine-de-Vaucluse (but only as the crow flies) is a picturesque hilltop village, popular with film directors, media personalities, musicians and painters, many of whom have added a Gordes address to their main Paris residence. As a result, the place is full of expensive restaurants, cafés and art and artisanal shops.

There are good reasons for its popularity with the rich and famous. The approach at sunset is picture perfect, with the ancient stone turning gold as you climb the winding roads towards the centre. In addition there's a superb array of dry-stone architecture in the nearby **Village des Bories**. Gordes is also close to the **Abbaye de Sénanque** and to a couple of museums dedicated to glass and to olive oil. There's also a **festival** in the last two weeks of July when the village is awash with theatrical performances, jazz and classical music concerts.

The village

In the past, near-vertical staircases hewn into the rock gave the only access to the summit, where the church and houses surround a twelfth- to sixteenth-century **castle** with few aesthetic concessions to the business of fortification. At the turn of the century most of Gordes' villagers had abandoned the old defensive site and the place was in ruins. A centre of resistance during World War II, Gordes was rediscovered by various artists, including Chagall and the Hungarian scientist of art and design, Victor Vasarely. Vasarely undertook the restoration of Gordes castle and, in 1970, opened his Didactic Museum within its Renaissance interior. However, on his death in 1995, the collection was reclaimed by his family (although the Aix-en-Provence collection remains in situ) and the space devoted to the very different and less accessible **Musée Pol Mara** (July & Aug daily 10am–noon & 2–6pm, rest of year closed Tues; 25F). The career of the Belgian artist, also seduced by the beauty of Gordes, moves from Post-Expressionism to Pop Art with one dominant theme – the female body.

Practicalities

There are infrequent **buses** covering the 16km from Cavaillon to Gordes; they drop you at place du Château. **Bikes** can be rented at the Elf station at Les Imberts on the D2 halfway between Gordes and the Avignon–Apt road.

Gordes **tourist office** in the Salle des Gardes of the castle (daily 9am–noon & 2–6pm; Oct–March opens at 10am; ☎04.90.72.02.75) is helpful and has lists of accommodation and details of whatever's on. It also displays an extraordinary model of the village made out of matchsticks. Finding **accommodation** is particularly difficult during the summer festival. One very reasonably priced hotel in the village is *Le Provençal* on place du Château (☎04.90.72.10.01, fax 04.90.72.04.20; ③) with just seven rooms. *Les Romarins*, overlooking the village on the rte de Sénanque (☎04.90.72.12.13, fax 04.90.72.13.13; ⑤), is an old country house with traditionally styled comfortable rooms; similar is *La Gacholle*, rte des Murs (☎04.90.72.01.36, fax 04.90.72.01.81; ⑦; closed mid-Nov to mid-March), with unbeatable views over the Luberon. The most luxurious option is *Domaine de l'Enclos* (☎04.90.72.08.22, fax 04.90.72.03.03; ⑥) set in a terraced garden with spacious rooms on the rte de Sénanque. Halfway between Gordes and Murs on the D15 there's a very pleasant two-star **campsite**, *Camping des Sources* (☎04.90.72.12.48, fax 04.90.72.09.43; closed Nov–March); early booking is advisable.

There are two excellent **restaurants** within easy reach of Gordes: *Le Bistrot à Michel* on Grande Rue in Cabrières d'Avignon, on the winding road to Fontaine (☎04.90.76.82.08; last orders 9.15pm; closed Tues, also Mon out of season), is a favourite with the second-home-owning Parisians and serves up exquisitely simple food in a dining room decorated with Pagnol film posters, or in the garden (à la carte from 250F); and *Le Mas Tourteron* in Les Imberts, chemin de St-Blaise (☎04.90.72.00.16; closed Sun eve & Mon; weekday lunchtime menu 150F, otherwise 280F), where you can eat gorgeous Provençal specialities in a shaded garden or much cheaper quick lunches in *Le Petit Comptoir* bistro in the same establishment. In Gordes itself, the most popular place to eat is the *Comptoir du Victuailler*, place du Château (☎04.90.72.01.31; closed Tues eve & Wed out of season; from 175F), always full of Parisians in summer. The restaurant at *La Gacholle* hotel is pleasant but pricey (190F menu); *Tante Yvonne* (☎04.90.72.02.54; closed Sun eve & Wed out of season) on place du Château is a bit less expensive (menus from 135F).

Village des Bories

About 4km east of Gordes, signed off the D2 to Cavaillon, is an unusual rural agglomeration, the **Village des Bories** (daily 9am–sunset; 30F). This walled enclosure contains dry-stone houses, barns, bread ovens, wine stores and workshops constructed in a mix of unusual shapes: curving pyramids and cones, some rounded at the top, some truncated and the base almost rectangular or square. Cleverly designed, rain runs off their exteriors and the temperature inside remains constant whatever the season. To look at them, you might think they were prehistoric, and neolithic rings and a hatchet have been found on the site, but most of these buildings in fact date from the eighteenth century and were lived in until about one hundred years ago. Some may well have been adapted from or rebuilt over earlier constructions, and there are extraordinary likenesses with a seventh- or eighth-century oratory in Ireland, and with huts and dwellings as far apart as the Orkneys and South Africa.

Abbaye de Sénanque

Abbaye de Sénanque (March–Oct Mon–Sat 10am–noon & 2–6pm, Sun 2–6pm; Nov–Feb Mon–Fri 2–5pm, Sat & Sun 2–6pm; 25F), about 4km north of Gordes, predates both the *bories* and the castle and has been reinhabited and returned to its former use. It is one of a trio of twelfth-century monasteries established by the Cistercian order in Provence and stands alone, amid fields of lavender in a hollow of the hills, its weathered stone sighing with age and immutability.

The interior is huge, silent and cold. In 1969 the monks departed, retaining the title deeds, and Sénanque became a kind of "Cultural Encounter Centre", favouring all the world's major religions. A hundred years earlier the Sénanque monks had resuscitated the old Benedictine monastery on St-Honorat (see p.295) and it is from there that they recently returned to follow the austere regime of work and prayer at Sénanque.

From the abbey, the loop back to Gordes via the D177 and D15 reveals the northern Luberon in all its glory.

Les Bouilladoires

The area around Gordes was famous for its olive oil before severe frosts killed off many of the trees. A still-functioning Gallo-Roman press made from a single slice of oak two metres in diameter, as well as ancient oil lamps, jars and soap-making equipment, can be seen at the **Moulin des Bouillons** (May–Sept Mon & Wed–Sun 10am–noon & 2–6pm; Feb–April & Oct Mon & Wed–Sun 10am–noon & 2–5pm; 30F) in **LES BOUILLADOIRES**, on the D148 just west of St-Pantaléon, 3.5km south of Gordes, and well signed from every junction. The Gordes bus from Coustellet, on the main Avignon–Apt road, stops just outside.

The ticket for the Moulin also gives you access to the **Musée du Vitrail Frédérique Duran** (April–Oct Mon & Wed–Sun 10am–noon & 2–5pm), signalled by a huge and rather gross sculpture by Duran and housed in a semi-submerged bunker next door to the Moulin. Duran's contemporary stained-glass creations are extremely garish but if you want to learn about the long history of stained glass, you can, though perhaps the most attractive items are the gorgeous, strutting fowl and hedges of rosemary in the gardens around the two museums.

The Petit Luberon

The great fold of rock of the Luberon runs for fifty-odd kilometres between the Coulon and the Durance valleys from **Manosque** to Cavaillon. It is divided by the **Combe de Lourmarin**, the only way to cross the mountain for 20km on either side, into the Grand Luberon to the east and the **Petit Luberon** to the west. Though many forestry tracks cross the ridge, they are barred to cars (and too rough for bikes), and where the ridge isn't forested it opens into table-top pastures where sheep graze in summer. The northern slopes have Alpine rather than Mediterranean leanings: the trees are oak, beech and maple; and cowslips and buttercups announce the summer. But it is still very hot and there are plenty of **vines** on the lower slopes.

The Luberon has long been popular as country escape for Parisians, Germans, the Dutch and the British – it was the setting for Peter Mayle's *A Year in Provence* – and *résidences secondaires* are everywhere. Ruins, like **de Sade**'s **château** in **Lacoste** and the **Abbaye de St-Hilaire** near Bonnieux, are also being restored by their private owners.

There are few **hotels** in these parts, and, as a consequence, those that there are, are fairly expensive. Basing yourself at Cavaillon or Apt may be the most sensible option.

Oppède-le-Vieux

OPPÈDE-LE-VIEUX, above the vines on the steeper slopes of the Petit Luberon, remains relatively free of the yuppie invasion. There are a couple of cafés, the *Petit Café* being the most pleasant, and a quirky shop on the road alongside selling stones and fossils, oddments made from lavender, *santons*, postcards and good books on the locality. The square in front of the ramparts suggests, with its Renaissance gateway, a monumental town within. But behind the line of restored sixteenth-century houses there are only ruins which go up and up until you reach the remains of the medieval **castle**.

The locals used to have the reputation of being a bunch of crazies living among these ruins. There is certainly a madness to the place but the lunacy is the ease with which you can break your neck: there are no fences or warning signs, steps break off above gaping holes, paths lead straight to precipitous edges and at the highest point of the castle you can sit on a foot-wide ledge with a drop of ten or more metres below you. Be warned for yourself but particularly if you have children of clambering age.

For **accommodation** in the village try *M et Mme Bal* (☎04.90.76.93.52; ③); it's very popular so you really need to book months in advance. There are no restaurants in the village, but for **food** you could try the *Petit Café*.

Ménerbes

Heading east from Oppède-le-Vieux, **MÉNERBES** is the next hilltop village you'll come to. Shaped like a ship, its best site, on the prow as it were, is given over to the dead. From this cemetery you look down onto an odd jigsaw of fortified buildings and mansions, old and new. In the other direction houses with exquisitely tended terraces and gardens, and shuttered up outside holiday time, ascend to a mammoth wall that completely bars the way. It's the citadel and now another *résidence secondaire*.

Outside Ménerbes, left off the D103 towards Beaumettes, is the wine-producing Domaine de la Citadelle's **museum of corkscrews** (April–Sept Mon–Fri 9am–noon & 2–7pm, Sat, Sun & hols 10am–noon & 3–7pm; Oct–March Mon–Fri 9am–noon & 2–6pm, Sat 9am–noon; 20F), dating back to the seventeenth century. The fascinating collection includes a Cézar compression, a corkscrew combined with pistol and dagger, others with erotic themes and many with beautifully sculpted and engraved handles. You can also visit the wine cellars where you'll be offered a complimentary tasting. Between Ménerbes and Lacoste, on the D109, you can admire the seventeeth-century cloisters, exquisite Renaissance stairway and ancient dovecotes of the **Abbaye de St-Hilaire** (daily 10am–noon & 2–5pm).

Just outside Ménerbes, on rte des Baumettes, is the *Hostellerie Le Roy Soleil* (☎04.90.72.25.61, fax 04.90.72.36.55; ⑥), a quiet and very agreeable **place to stay**.

THE WARS OF RELIGION IN THE LUBERON

During five days in April 1545 a great swathe of the Petit Luberon, between **Lourmarin** and **Mérindol**, was burnt and put to the sword. Three thousand people were massacred and six hundred sent to the galleys. Their crime was having Protestant tendencies in the years leading up to the devastating Wars of Religion. Despite the complicity of King Henri II, the ensuing scandal forced him to order an enquiry which then absolved all those responsible: the Catholic aristocrats from Aix.

Lourmarin (see p.145) itself suffered minor damage but the castle in Mérindol was violently dismantled, together with every house. Mérindol's remains, on the hill above the current village on the south side of the Petit Luberon, are a visible monument to those events, and to this day the south face of the Petit Luberon remains sparsely populated.

Lacoste

LACOSTE and its **château** are visible from all the neighbouring villages. If daylight views have enticed you, you should see it in moonlight while a wind rocks the hanging lanterns on the narrow cobbled approaches to the château whose most famous owner was the Marquis de Sade. This was his retreat when the reaction to his writings got too hot, but in 1778, after seven years here, he was locked up in the Bastille and the castle destroyed soon after. Some people say the current owner, who has been repairing the building for over three decades, is looking for hidden treasure. It's open only by appointment, for large groups (☎04.90.75.80.39).

For **accommodation** in the village, there are eight rooms above the excellent *Café de France* (☎04.90.75.82.25; ③); the **café** itself provides copious helpings at midday of omelettes and fries, lamb and fries, and *salade niçoise*, for under 80F. **Market** day is on Tuesday.

Bonnieux and around

From the *terrasse* by the old church on the heights of the steep village of **BONNIEUX** you can see Gordes, Roussillon and neighbouring Lacoste, 5km away. Halfway down the village, on rue de la République, there's a museum of traditional bread-making, the **Musée de la Boulangerie** (April–Sept Mon & Wed–Sun 10am–noon & 3–6.30pm; Oct Sat, Sun & hols same hours; 20F); and on av des Tilleuls the **Église Neuve** exhibits four fifteenth-century wood paintings (summer 3–6.30pm; free).

From Bonnieux the D149 joins the Apt–Avignon road just after the triple-arched **Pont Julien** over the Coulon which dates back to the time when Apt was the Roman base of Apta Julia. Before you reach the bridge you'll see signs for the **Château La Canorgue**, a good place to try the light and very palatable Côtes de Luberon wines (Mon–Sat 9am–noon & 3–6pm).

For **accommodation** in Bonnieux try the *César* (☎04.90.75.80.18; ④) on place de la Liberté at the top of the village, or the *Hostellerie du Prieuré* (☎04.90.75.80.78, fax 04.90.75.96.00; ④) in the centre; though neither is particularly exceptional. The best option is *La Bouquière*, quartier St-Pierre (☎04.90.75.87.17; ⑤); however, it's very popular, so you'll need to book months in advance. For **eating**, try *Le Fournil*, overlooking the fountain of place Carnot (☎04.90.75.83.62; menus from 125F; winter closed Mon & Tues), which serves lovely Provençal dishes laced with olive oil and garlic. Friday is **market** day.

Apt and around

APT, the main settlement in the Luberon, lies to the east of the Combe de Lourmarin in the Grand Luberon. It is best known for its crystallized fruit and preserves. The town itself is not much of a place for sightseeing; its large confectionery factory spews mucky froth into a concrete-channelled River Coulon and in early spring, when mimosa is blossoming down on the coast, the temperature around Apt can drop to well below freezing. It's nevertheless a useful base, if you have your own transport, for visiting the surrounding villages: **Rustrel** and **Roussillon** to the north, with their **ochre mines**, and to the south, the hilltop villages of **Saignon** and **Buoux** with its fascinating **abandoned village** are all within a ten-kilometre radius of the town. Apt itself has excellent shops and a very lively Saturday **market** and from mid-July through August a **festival**, *Les Tréteaux de Nuit*, provides a choice of shows with concerts, plays, café-theatre and exhibitions.

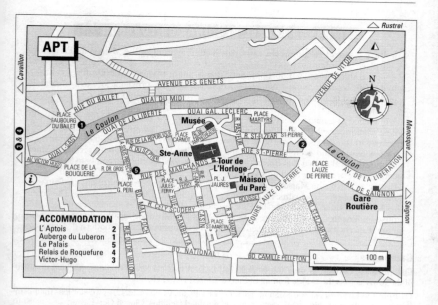

Arrival, information and accommodation

Buses drop you off either at the main **place de la Bouquerie** or at the **gare routière** on av de la Libération at the eastern end of the town; the train station is for freight only. The **tourist office** is at 20 av Philippe-de-Girard (July & Aug Mon–Sat 9am–1pm & 3–7pm, Sun 9am–noon; rest of year Mon–Sat 9am–noon & 2–6pm; ☎04.90.74.03.18), just up to your left as you face the river from place de la Bouquerie. Arriving by **car**, you may have to try the quays for parking space but place de la Bouquerie is still the focal point to head for. You can **rent bikes** from Guy Agnel, 86 quai Général-Leclerc (☎04.90.7417.16), or Cycles Peugeot, 44 quai de la Liberté (☎04.90.74.16.43).

There's a reasonable choice of **accommodation** in and around Apt; hotels in the town are less likely to be booked up here than in the more scenic hilltop villages.

Hotels

L'Aptois, 289 cours Lauze-de-Perret (☎04.90.74.02.02, fax 04.90.74.64.79). In the old town, at the end of place de la Bouquerie, with a streamlined modern exterior belying the clashing decor within. ②.

Auberge du Luberon, 8 place Faubourg du Ballet (☎04.90.74.12.50, fax 04.90.04.79.49). Directly across the river, with pleasant rooms and a quiet setting, this is probably the most desirable hotel in town. ③.

Le Palais, 24 pl Gabriel-Péri (☎04.90.04.89.32). The lowest-priced rooms to be had, bang in the centre above a rather uninspired pizzeria. Closed mid-Oct to March. ②.

Relais de Roquefure, Le Chêne, 6km from Apt on the N100 towards Avignon (☎04.90.04.88.88, fax 04.90.74.14.86). Good value, with horse and cycle outings organized. ④.

Victor-Hugo, 67 av Victor-Hugo (☎04.90.04.74.60). Opposite the old train station and flanked by gas stations, but pleasant enough if you get a room looking out on the courtyard. ③.

PARC NATUREL RÉGIONAL DU LUBERON

The **Parc Naturel Régional du Luberon** is administered by the Maison du Parc in Apt at 60 place Jean-Jaurès (April–Sept Mon–Sat 8.30am–noon & 1.30–7pm; Oct–March Mon–Fri 8.30am–noon & 1.30–6pm, Sat 8.30am–noon; ☎04.90.04.42.00). It's a centre of activity with laudable aims – nature conservation and the provision of environmentally friendly tourist facilities – though many people have misgivings about the practicalities of the project.

Any glance at a map will show the area covered by the park to be shot through with holes, *communes* where the local mayor has chosen to opt out. This makes a bit of a mockery of the park's key purpose of protecting the environment. In fact, the park has very few powers and even less money and mostly has to be content with giving technical and architectural advice that doesn't have to be followed. Certain attempts to assist small local producers have, according to the park's critics, backfired badly.

Be that as it may, the Maison du Parc is the place to go for information about the fauna and flora of the Luberon, footpaths, cycle routes, pony-trekking, gîtes and campsites. The centre also houses a small **Musée de la Paléontologie** (10F) which is specifically designed to amuse children. A submarine-type "time capsule" door leads down to push-button displays that include magnified views of insect fossils and their modern descendants.

Campsites

Camping les Cèdres, av de Viton (☎04.90.74.14.61). A two-star site within easy walking distance of the town, across the bridge from pl St-Pierre. Closed Dec–Feb.

Camping le Luberon, rte de Saignon (☎04.90.04.85.40, fax 04.90.74.12.19). Two-star less than 2km from town, with swimming pool, restaurant and disabled facilities. Closed Oct–Easter.

The Town

Saturday is the best day to visit Apt, when cars are barred from the town centre to allow artisans and cultivators from the surrounding countryside to set up stalls. As well as featuring every imaginable Provençal edible, including 200-year-old species of vegetables grown by one trader (see "Saignon", p.144), the **market** is accompanied by barrel organ, jazz musicians, stand-up comics, aged hippies and notorious local characters. Everyone, from successful Parisian artists with summer studios here, to military types from the St-Christol base, serious ecologists, rich foreigners and local Aptois, will be found milling around the central **rue des Marchands** for this weekly social commerce.

The great local speciality of fruits – crystallized, pickled, preserved in alcohol or turned into jam – features at the market but during the rest of the week you can go to La Bonbonnière on the corner of rue de la Sous-Préfecture and rue de la République for every sort of sweet and chocolate and the Provençal speciality *tourron*, an almond paste flavoured with coffee, pistachio, pine kernels or cherries. If you're really keen on sticky sweets you can ring Aptunion, the **confectionery factory** in quartier Salignan, 2km from Apt on the Avignon road (Mon–Sat 9am–noon & 2–6pm; ☎04.90.76.31.31) for a tour or just to visit the shop which sells all the possible fruit concoctions.

Other **shops** worth looking at are Tamisier on rue du Docteur-Gros selling kitchenware and the traditional fly-proof open boxes for storing cheese and sausage; Station Peintre on place de la Bouquerie with artists' materials at very good prices; Jean Faucon's ceramics on av de la Libération; and the Librarie Dumas, on the corner of rue des Marchands and place G-Péri, with some English books for sale.

While window-shopping along rue des Marchands take time to admire the **bell tower** spanning the street and the former **Cathédralé de Ste-Anne**, which has several relics and ancient objects (Tues–Sat 10am–noon & 3–7pm, Sun 10am–noon; guided tour of the treasures July to mid-Sept Tues–Sat 11am & 5pm; rest of year Sat 11am;

free). The **Musée Archéologique** at 4 rue de l'Amphithéâtre (June–Sept Mon & Wed–Sat 10am–noon & 2–5pm; Oct–May Mon & Wed–Fri 2.30–4.30pm, Sat 10am–noon & 2.30–5.30pm; 11.20F) is not wildly exciting, with a few remains of a Roman theatre in the basement. Temporary exhibitions of contemporary art are sometimes held in the **Chapelle de Recollets** at 26 rue Louis-Rousset, organized by Artifices, 47 rue de la République (☎04.90.74.01.26), which groups together some of the best artists based in the Luberon and arranges visits to studios.

Eating and drinking

For **food**, if you haven't already stuffed yourself with chocolates and candied fruit, try the traditional cuisine at *Le Chat qui Pêche* on cours Louze-de-Perret (closed Sun), or *Dame Tartine*, on place du Septier, which serves a variety of home-made flans and salads. Of the hotels, the *Victor-Hugo* does plats du jour for under 50F and you can eat very well at the *Auberge du Luberon*, where there's a superb choice of desserts, for around 155F (closed Mon & Sun eve out of season). Pricey Argentinian specialities and much cheaper pizzas are available at *Argentin*, 170 quai Général-Leclerc (☎04.90.74.53.09), with live music at weekends. In the industrial zone on the Avignon road opposite the turning to Gargas, the Tex-Mex restaurant *Pub 66* doubles up as a disco with theme nights. Further out on the Avignon road, at Le Chêne, there's extremely good food and a chance to try all the local goats' cheeses plus a lavender *crème brûlée* at *Bernard Mathys* (☎04.90.04.84.64; menus from 160F; closed Tues & Wed).

Roussillon

Perching precariously above soft-rock cliffs 10km northwest of Apt, the buildings of **ROUSSILLON** radiate all the different shades of the seventeen ochre tints once quarried here. A spiralling tour past potteries, antique shops and restaurants leads up to the summit viewing table which is worth the effort for the views over the Luberon and Ventoux, but if your interest is in seeing the **ochre quarries** themselves, a well-signed footpath leads from the car park on place de la Poste where you'll also find the tourist office and a Centre Social et Culturel with occasional art exhibitions. Just outside Roussillon, on the Apt road, an old **ochre factory**, the Usine Mathieu, has been rehabilitated and can be visited (tours daily: July & Aug 10am–7pm; March–June & Sept–Nov 11am & 2–5pm; 20F). The tour takes you round the various washing, draining, settling and drying areas of the process, the simplicity of which is appealing. Finally, excellent yearly exhibitions are organised on themes related to the use and production of ochre, with accompanying workshops for both adults and children.

Roussillon's **tourist office** is on pl de la Poste (Easter–Nov Mon–Sat 10am–noon & 2.30–7pm, Sun 2.30–7pm; Dec–Easter daily 2–6pm; ☎04.90.05.60.25). If you need somewhere to stay, try the *Rêves d'Ocres* hotel, on rte de Gordes (☎04.90.05.60.50, fax

---

OCHRE QUARRYING

Ochre quarrying has been practised in the Vaucluse since prehistoric times, producing the natural dye that gives a range of colours, which don't fade in sunlight, from pale yellow to a blood red. By the nineteenth century the business was considerable. First overloaded donkeys, then horses hauling trucks and then, by the 1880s, trains, carried the dust to Marseille to be shipped round the world. In 1929 forty thousand tonnes of ochre were exported from the region. Twenty years later it was down to 11,500 tonnes, and in 1958 production was finally stopped, in part because of reduced demand with competition from synthetic dyes, but also because the foundations of Roussillon were being undermined.

04.90.05.79.74; ④), which is warm, welcoming and with some rooms offering good views of the Luberon. There's also a very pleasant two-star **campsite**, *Camping L'Arc en Ciel*, in pine woods 2km along the D104 to Goult (☎04.90.05.73.96; closed Oct to mid-March). For **meals**, try Roussillon's *La Treille*, 1 rue du Four (☎04.90.05.64.47), which serves a mixture of North African, Turkish and Scandinavian specialities with one menu from 110F, or you can get a crêpe at *La Gourmandine* on place l'Abbé-Avon.

Rustrel and around

RUSTREL, 10km northeast of Apt, is a very sweet little village with far fewer *résidences secondaires* than Roussillon. There's a small and welcoming **hotel** in the village, the *Auberge de Rustréou*, 3 pl de la Fête (☎04.90.04.90.90; ④) and a convivial **bar-restaurant** *Les Platanes* (☎04.90.04.93.99; menus from 140F), with good beers and a basement for live music most Saturday nights.

The dramatic quarries, known as the **Colorado Provençal**, near the village are signed off the D22 towards Gignac, just before you reach Rustrel from Apt. The track round the quarries begins at the car park entrance. Having passed the remains of old settling tanks that look like unearthed foundations and a small ruined building, take the track on the right marked with white. The full, circular, route takes about 1hr 30min to walk and the **map** (15F), available from the snack bar in the car park, will prove useful, as the route can be quite hard to follow – particularly when the stream meanders onto the creamy ochre sand of the path. Persevere and you will end up in an amphitheatre of coffee, vanilla and strawberry ice-cream coloured rock, whipped into pinnacles and curving walls. If you continue up above a little waterfall, you can turn left, then left again onto a wider path, which soon brings you to the gods' seats over the quarry. Continue and you'll end up back on the same route leading back to the settling tanks. There are further routes branching off this walk if you feel the urge.

Saignon

SAIGNON is only 4km from Apt but already high enough up the Luberon to have an eagle's-eye view of the town. From below, the village rises like an immense fort with natural turrets of rock; on closer inspection it turns out to be a mix of crumbling farmhouses and perfectly restored summer residences. The gardener, Monsieur Danneyrolles, whose ancient, organically grown species of vegetables are on sale in Apt's markets, lives here at La Molière; if you phone him (☎04.90.74.44.68), he may show you round his fabulous **garden**.

There's a pleasant **hotel** in the centre of the village, the *Auberge du Presbytère*, pl de la Fontaine, (☎04.90.74.11.50, fax 04.90.04.68.51; ④), offering some wonderful views; and 2.5km north, just before Auribeau, is the *Auberge de Jeunesse Le Regain*, 2.5km north of Saignon just before Auribeau (☎04.90.74.39.34; 75F per night; closed mid-Jan to mid-Feb), open to non-members for one-night stays. The hostel also has plenty of information on local **walks**.

Buoux

The fortified, abandoned hilltop village known as the **Fort de Buoux**, 10km south of Apt, stands on the southern edge of a canyon, forged by the once powerful River Aiguebrun at the start of its passage through the Luberon. To reach the fort follow the road signed off the D113 to the gateway at the end, beyond which it's a ten- to fifteen-minute walk to the entrance (daily sunrise till sunset; 10F).

Numerous relics of prehistoric life have been found in the Buoux Valley and in the earliest Christian days anchorite monks survived against all odds in tiny caves and niches in the vertical cliff face. In the 1660s, Fort de Buoux was demolished by command of Richelieu for being a centre of Protestantism, but the remains of old Buoux – including water cisterns, storage cellars with thick stone lids, arrow-slitted ramparts, the lower half of a Romanesque chapel and a pretty much intact keep – still give a good impression of life here over the centuries. Today, the spot is popular with **climbers**, many of whom can be seen clinging to the cliff face as you approach the fort. Most of them will be denizens of the corporate or municipal holiday homes that cluster round the road into the valley.

Returning to the junction with the D113, going left takes you past the slender Romanesque tower of the former Prieuré de St-Symphorien and onto the Lourmarin road, while going right brings you to the present-day village of **BUOUX** (the "x", by the way, is pronounced). For **accommodation** try the *Auberge des Seguins*, quartier de la Combe (☎04.90.74.16.37, fax 04.90.74.16.37; ①; closed mid-Nov to March); run by the mayor of Buoux, an expert on the history and wildlife of the Luberon and the man responsible for most of the footpaths, it is a popular stop with climbers and walkers. Just outside the village is the *Auberge de la Loube* **restaurant** (☎04.90.74.19.58; closed Thurs & Wed eve out of season), which has a considerable local reputation: some say it's pretentious and over-priced, others that it's *génial* and delicious. You can judge for yourself with the midday 125F menu.

From Buoux, or indeed from Apt, there are fabulous views west from the road to the Combe de Luberon; in the gorge itself you can stop off by the river, at its most spectacular in spring.

From the Luberon to the Durance

The **southern slopes of the Luberon** come into the climatic sphere of the Mediterranean. They are filled with the smell of pines and wild thyme, the yellow and gold of honeysuckle and immortelle, and the quick movements and stillnesses of sun-basking reptiles. Unlike the humid northern face, here it is hot and dry. The lower slopes are taken up by vines, grown both for wine and the grapes, and cherry orchards. Where the land levels out, 12km or so back from the Durance, the ground is highly fertile and all the classic crops of Provence are grown. The smaller holdings, divided more aesthetically and greenly by organic windbreaks, specialize in one or other of the ingredients for ratatouille. Because of the importance of agriculture, the villages here are still very Provençal in character, with far fewer Parisians and other foreigners than in the northern Luberon.

The beautiful villages of **Lourmarin**, **Vaugines** and **Cucuron** sit amidst vineyards and the unspoilt countryside of the Grand Luberon foothills; **La Tour d'Aigues** has an elegant ruined château; **Ansouis** an inhabited aristocratic castle; **Cadenet** has a certain charm; and **Pertuis** has the best transport links and accommodation possibilities in the area. Across the Durance is the ancient **Silvacane Abbey**.

Lourmarin

LOURMARIN stands at the bottom of a *combe*, its Renaissance **château** guarding with nonchalant ease a small rise to the west. A fortress once defended this strategic vantage point but the current edifice dates from the sixteenth century when comfort was beginning to outplay defence; hence the generous windows.

Since 1929 the château has belonged to the University of Aix, who use it to give summer sabbaticals to artists and intellectuals of various scientific and philosophical persuasions. Those that do more than just think usually leave behind a creation, and you can see these works on the 45-minute **guided tour** (July–Sept daily 10.30am–noon &

2.30–6.30pm; rest of year Mon & Wed–Sun 2.30–5.30pm; 20F), which takes you through the vast rooms with intricate wooden ceilings, massive fireplaces and beautifully tiled floors where the favoured cultural workers socialize. **Concerts** are held in the château every Saturday evening during July and August, and throughout the summer **exhibitions** of all sorts are staged (contact the tourist office for more information).

The most famous literary figure associated with Lourmarin town is the writer Albert Camus, who spent the last years of his life here and is buried in the cemetery.

Practicalities

Lourmarin's **tourist office** is at 9 av Philippe-de-Girard (Mon–Sat 10.30am–12.30pm & 4–6pm; closed Jan; ☎04.90.68.10.77). There are several **restaurants** around the fountained squares of the village. Good and reasonably priced *paysan* dishes can be had at *La Récréation*, 15 rue Philippe-de-Girard (☎04.90.68.23.73; closed Wed), with one menu around 110F. Further out of town, the expensive but excellent *La Fenière* on rte de Cadenet (☎04.90.68.11.79; menus from 190F; closed Mon lunch, and first two weeks of Jan) can be trusted to use absolutely fresh ingredients in seriously gourmet combinations. As for places **to stay**, there's the wonderfully situated *Hostellerie Le Paradou* on the D943 at the start of the *combe* (☎04.90.68.04.05, fax 04.90.08.54.94; ④) and back towards Lourmarin, *Le Four à Chaux*, a gîte with dormitory beds and a few rooms (☎04.90.68.24.28, fax 04.90.68.11.10; ③). There's a three-star **campsite**, *Les Hautes Prairies*, on rte de Vaugines (☎04.90.68.02.89, fax 04.90.68.23.83; March–Dec), with a pool, bar and restaurant. **Bikes** can be rented at Freestyle on rue du Temple (☎04.90.08.53.46).

East to Pertuis

If you take the minor D56 road east from Lourmarin, the first place you come to is **VAUGINES**, a gorgeous little village with a nice old-fashioned café, *Café de la Fontaine*, opposite the *mairie*, and a **hotel** with great views, the *Hostellerie du Luberon* (☎04.90.77.27.19, fax 04.90.77.13.08; ④). Vaugines is the meeting point of the GR97 from the Petit Luberon and the GR9 which crosses the Grand Luberon to Buoux in one direction and in the other loops above Cucuron and skirts the Mourre-Nègre summit before running along the eastern end of the ridge.

The neighbouring village of **CUCURON** is a bit larger and almost as fetching, with some of its ancient ramparts and gateways still standing and a bell tower with a delicate campanile on the central place de l'Horloge. Cucuron had a glimpse of fame when it was taken over by the film industry for the shooting of Rappeneau's *The Horseman on the Roof*, based on a Giono novel, and, at the time, the most expensive French film made. The village's main business, however, is olive oil and it has a sixteenth-century mill in a hollow of the rock face on rue Moulin à l'Huile that is still used to press olives. At the top of the rock a **park** surrounds the site of the former citadel. At the other end of the village is the **Église Notre-Dame-de-Beaulieu** which contains a sixteenth-century painting on wood amongst its art treasures. From the end of May to the middle of August a huge felled poplar leans against the church, a tradition dating back to 1720 when Cucuron was spared the plague. On rue de l'Église, a short way from the church is a small **museum** (10am–noon & 3–7pm; closed Tues morning; free) on local traditions and early history plus a collection of daguerreotypes.

On the north side of the village, by the reservoir bordered by plane trees, you'll find the **hotel-restaurant** *L'Étang* (☎04.90.77.21.25, fax 04.90.77.10.98; ③) which serves very pleasant food (menus from 110F). There are two **campsites**: *Lou Badareu* at La Rasparine, to the southeast of the village towards La Tour d'Aigues (☎04.90.77.21.46; closed Dec to mid-March) next to a rather expensive gîte d'étape, and *Le Moulin à Vent* on chemin de Gastoule off the D182 to Villelaure (☎04.90.77.25.77; closed Oct–March). A Tuesday **market** is held on place de l'Étang.

Halfway between Cucuron and Pertuis, the perched village of **ANSOUIS** has a **château** (May–Oct daily 2.30–6pm; Nov–April closed Tues; 30F) lived in since the twelfth-century by the same family; the mother of the current ducal resident wrote a bestseller called *Bon Sang Ne Peut Mentir* (Good Blood Cannot Lie). The real attractions of this superb castle, however, are its remarkably rich furnishings, from Flemish tapestries and silver chandeliers to kitchen pots and pans. In the village below, the **Musée Extraordinaire** (daily: June–Sept 2–7pm; Oct–May Oct–May 2–6pm; 22F) is dedicated to underwater life and has some extremely kitsch touches. The village **market** is held on Thursday.

The seventeenth-century **Château de Sannes**, just south of the D27 before the Bonde lake between Cucuron and La Motte-d'Aigues, produces Côtes de Luberon wines *au naturel* – in other words with no fertilizers, pesticides or additives – as it would have been done when the eighteenth-century château was first inhabited; the wines are for sale in the château's shop (daily 8am–noon & 2–7pm). The set-up is somewhat snooty, and if you don't fancy this you could try the Vins Coopératives in La Motte d'Aigues or in Grambois. For picnic food, **ST-MARTIN-DE-LA-BRASQUE** has a smallholders' **market** every Sunday between May and October as well as a rather surprising trompe l'oeil mural of Roman ruins.

Pertuis and La Tour d'Aigues

The one sizeable place this side of the Durance is **PERTUIS**, which hasn't a great deal to offer except for places to stay. Like so many Vaucluse towns, it really comes to life on **market** day, Friday in this case. At the beginning of May the **festival** of street theatre and strip cartoons can be fun, too.

The nearest **train station** is in the nearby town of Meyrargues and SNCF **buses** make the ten minute journey to Pertuis, dropping you at the **gare routière** on place Garcin, within easy walking distance of the centre: leave the square on the opposite side from the bus station and turn left up rue Henri-Silvy. The town centres around **place Parmentier**, where you'll find flowers for sale on Friday, **rue Colbert**, the main clothes shopping street leading up to **place Jean-Jaurès**, and **place du 4 Septembre** and **place Mirabeau** just to the north. The **tourist office** is on place Mirabeau (Mon–Fri 9am–noon & 2–6pm, Sat 9.30am–noon & 2.30–6pm; ☎04.90.79.15.56) in the old keep, all that remains of Pertuis' castle. The narrow streets of the Vieille Ville to the north are, for the most part, low lit and lifeless.

Of the **places to stay**, the best central options are the *Hôtel du Cours*, place Jean-Jaurès (☎04.90.79.00.68, fax 04.90.79.14.22; ③), which is small and friendly, and *L'Aubarestiero* on place Garcin (☎04.90.79.14.74, fax 04.90.79.00.57; ③), a very quiet hotel where the only disturbances are on Wednesday and Saturday mornings when vegetable stalls are set up in the square. The *Sévan*, on av de Verdon on the way out towards Manosque (☎04.90.79.19.30, fax 04.90.79.35.77; ⑥), is the most expensive option; it belongs to a chain and is unappealing from the outside, but the rooms and the swimming pools are rather pleasant. The three-star municipal **campsite** *Les Pinèdes*, av Pierre-Augier (☎04.90.79.10.98), has excellent facilities.

You'll find plenty of **brasseries** and **restaurants** on the main squares and streets, but nothing wildly special. The *bar-tabac, Hunycl*, on rue Voltaire, is a pleasant place to hang out. For getting around, **bikes** can be rented at Cycles Genin, 73 rue Giraud (☎04.90.79.49.43).

Heading northeast from Pertuis towards Grambois brings you to **LA TOUR D'AIGUES** where a vast shell of a **château** dominates the village centre. The castle was half destroyed during the Revolution but the most finely detailed Renaissance decoration, based on classical designs including Grecian helmets, angels, bows and arrows and Olympic torches, has survived on the gateway arch. You can admire most of the ruins' glories from the outside but there's also a **Musée de Faïence**, and a **Musée de** l'Histoire du Pays d'Aigues (July & Aug daily 10am–1pm & 3.30–6.30pm; April–June & Sept daily 9.30–11.30am & 3–6pm; Oct–March Mon & Wed–Fri 9.30–11.30am & 2–5pm, Tues 9.30–11.30am, Sat & Sun 2–5pm; 25F), covering every academic aspect of this region's development from prehistoric times to the present, plus temporary exhibitions and a video on the southern Luberon to be seen inside. There's a shaded **café** on the far side of the main road from the castle and one **hotel**, *Les Fenouillets*, not far from the centre on the Pertuis road (☎04.90.07.48.22; ④).

Cadenet and around

The main road heading south from Lourmarin detours round **CADENET**. If you feel like stopping make sure you go to the central place du Tambour d'Arcole to see the statue of the manic drummer-boy, hair and coat tails flying as he runs; André Étienne is so commemorated for his inspired one-man diversion that confused the Austrians and allowed Napoléon's army to cross the River Durance in 1796.

Cadenet's **tourist office** on place du Tambour d'Arcole (Mon–Sat 9.30am–noon & 2.15–6.15pm; ☎04.90.68.38.21) also rents out **bikes**. There's an excellent four-star **campsite** by a lake, the *Val de Durance* (☎04.90.68.37.75; closed Oct–March), and a **restaurant**, *Stéfani*, 35 rue Gambetta (☎04.90.68.07.14; closed Tues–Thurs eve), which offers a midday weekday menu with wine for under 80F. **Market** day is Monday.

Silvacane Abbey

On the other side of the Durance from Cadenet stands the **Abbaye de Silvacane**, built by the same order and in the same period as the abbeys of Sénanque and Le Thoronet, although the "wood of rushes", from which the name Silvacane derives, had already been cleared by Benedictine monks before the Cistercians arrived in 1144. As at the other two great monasteries, the architecture of Silvacane reflects precisely the no-nonsense, no-frills rule of Saint Benedict (Benoît) in which manual work, intellectual work and worship comprised the three equal elements of the day.

The buildings that remain look pretty much as they did seven hundred years ago, with the exception of the refectory, rebuilt in 1423 and given Gothic ornamentation that the earlier monks would never have tolerated. The windows in the church would not have had stained glass either; and the only heated room was the *salle des monies* where the work of copying manuscripts was carried out. The daily reading of "the Rule" and public confession by the monks took place in the *salle capitulaire* and the *parloir* was the only area where conversation was allowed. You can still visit the stark, pale-stoned splendour of the church and its compact surrounding buildings and cloisters (April–Sept daily 9am–7pm; rest of year Mon & Wed–Sun 10am–1pm & 2–5pm; closed public hols; 25F)

travel details

Trains

Cavaillon to: Avignon (5–9 daily; 30min); L'Isle-sur-la-Sorgue (7–9 daily; 10min); Marseille (5 daily; 1–2hr).

L'Isle-sur-la-Sorgue to: Avignon (6–8 daily; 15–30min); Cavaillon (7–9 daily; 10min); Marseille (change at Miramas; 5 daily; 1hr 10min–2hr 10min).

Meyrargues to: Aix (3 daily; 20min); Marseille (3 daily; 50min); Sisteron (3 daily; 1hr).

Buses

Apt to: Aix (2 daily; 2hr 20min); Avignon (4 daily; 1–2hr); Bonnieux (1 daily; 20min); Cadenet (2 daily; 45min); Carpentras (3 weekly school term; 1hr); Digne (2 daily; 3hr 10min); Lourmarin (2 daily; 30min); Pertuis (2 daily; 1hr); Roussillon (1 daily; 20min); Rustrel (5 weekly; 40min); Sault (2 weekly; 1hr).

Carpentras to: Aix (3 daily; 1hr 50min); Apt (3 weekly school term; 1hr); Avignon (frequent; 45min); Beaumes-de-Venise (2 daily; 15min); Bedoin (2–3 daily; 40min); Cavaillon (4 daily; 35–45min); Gigondas (2 daily; 40min); L'Isle-sur-la-Sorgue (3 daily; 15–30min); Malaucène (2 daily; 30min); Marseille (4 daily; 2hr 15min); Orange (4 daily; 30min); Pernes-les-Fontaines (1 daily; 10min); Sablet (2 daily; 45min); Sault (1 daily; 1hr 30min); Vacqueyras (2 daily; 30min);

Vaison (2 daily; 45min); Venasque (2 daily; 30min).

Cavaillon to: Aix (3 daily; 1hr 10min); Apt (2 daily; 45min); Avignon (frequent; 45min); Bonnieux (3 weekly; 1hr); Carpentras (2 daily; 30–45min); Gordes (2 daily; 45min); L'Isle-sur-la-Sorgue (4 daily; 15min); Lacoste (3 weekly; must be booked in advance; 40min); Oppède-le-Vieux (3 weekly; must be booked in advance; 20min); Pernes-les-Fontaines (2 daily; 30min).

L'Isle-sur-la-Sorgue to: Avignon (10 daily; 30–40min); Carpentras (3 daily; 15–30min); Cavaillon (4 daily; 15min); Fontaine-de-Vaucluse (10 daily; 15min).

Nyons to: Avignon (2 daily; 1hr 40min–2hr); Grignan (4 daily; 40min); Vaison (4 daily; 30min); Valréas (4 daily; 20min).

Pertuis to: Aix (6 daily; 30min); Ansouis (1 daily; 10min); Apt (2 daily; 1hr); Cucuron (1 daily; 20min); Meyrargues (3 daily; 15min); La Tour d'Aigues (3 daily; 10min).

Vaison to: Avignon (2 daily; 1hr 15min); Camaret (3–4 daily; 40min); Carpentras (2 daily; 45min); Nyons (5 daily; 30min); Orange (2 daily; 1hr); Rasteau (1 daily; 15min); Séguret (4 daily; 15min); Sablet (3–4 daily; 20min).

Valréas to: Avignon (3 daily; 1hr 30min); Grignan (4 daily; 20min); Nyons (4 daily; 20min); Orange (3 daily; 45min).

CHAPTER THREE

MARSEILLE AND METROPOLITAN PROVENCE

Encompassing Marseille, Aix and Toulon, "Metropolitan Provence" is by far the most populated and industrial part of the region, and indeed of southern France. It's cosmopolitan, culturally dynamic and wields considerable political and economic influence, not least for the way it dramatizes the severe consequences of dated industries and recession. But the area also has vast tracts of deserted mountainous countryside and a shoreline of high cliffs, deep jagged inlets and sand beaches with stretches still untouched by the holiday industry.

The two great poles of attraction are the contrasting cities of **Marseille** and **Aix-en-Provence**. Marseille, a vital commerical port for more than two millennia and France's second largest city, is, for all its notorious reputation, a wonderful place with a distinctive, unconventional character that never ceases to surprise. The charms of Aix, with one of the most perfect old town centres in all of France, are much more commonly sung. It glories in the medieval period of independent Provence and the riches of its seventeenth- and eighteenth-century growth.

The first foreigners to settle in Provence, the ancient **Greeks** from Phocaea and their less amiable successors from **Rome**, left evidence of their sophistication around the **Étang de Berre**, at **Les Lecques**, and most of all at Marseille. Museums in Marseille and Aix guard reminders of the indigenous peoples of Provence whose civilization the Romans destroyed.

Military connections are strong in this region. **Salon-de-Provence** trains French airforce pilots and **Toulon** is home to the French navy's Mediterranean fleet. Until very recently the planes for the one and the ships for the other, plus the freighters for Marseille, were all built at **Istres**, **La Seyne** and **La Ciotat**.

But between the battleships of Toulon and the petrochemical industries and tanker terminals around the Étang de Berre there are still great **seaside attractions**: the pine-covered rocks of the **Estaque**; the *calanques* (rocky inlets) between Marseille and **Cassis**; the sand beaches of La Ciotat bay and the coastal path to **Bandol**; and the

---

ACCOMMODATION PRICE CATEGORIES

Throughout this guide, all hotels and guesthouses have been priced on a scale of ①–⑧, indicating the lowest price you could expect to pay for a double room in high season. What you get for your money varies enormously between establishments, but in the lower-priced hotels you should expect to pay considerably more for en-suite facilities. If you are staying anywhere for more than three days it's often possible to negotiate a lower price, particularly out of season.

① Under 160F	③ 220–300F	⑤ 400–500F	⑦ 600–700F
② 160–220F	④ 300–400F	⑥ 500–600F	⑧ Over 700F

heights from which to view the coast, close-up on the **route de Crêtes** or **Cap Sicié**, and at a distance from **Le Gros Cerveau** and **Mont Caume**.

For countryside, you can escape **inland** from the conurbations, following in Cézanne's steps from Aix to **Mont-Victoire**; in those of Pagnol's characters around **Aubagne**; or explore the legends of Mary Magdalene in the **Chaîne de la Ste-Baume**. In the last you'll find great expanses of hillside and forest, with only birds and squirrels for company, and little villages like **Signes**, where time seems to stand still.

The area also has great **wines** at Bandol and Cassis, and great **seafood** gourmandise, particularly in Marseille, home of the famous sea-fish dish, bouillabaisse.

Marseille

The most renowned and populated French city after Paris, **MARSEILLE** has, like the French capital, prospered and been ransacked over the centuries. It has lost its privileges to sundry French kings and foreign armies, refound its fortunes, suffered plagues, religious bigotry, republican and royalist terror and had its own Commune and

POWER, POLITICS AND FOOTBALL

Marseille has all the social, economic and **political ills** of France writ large. The white middle class constantly complain that their city centre has been taken over by North Africans, and racism is rife, as are poverty, bad housing and rising unemployment, particularly amongst the young. It's a socially explosive mixture, but one that Marseille shares with many other European cities. Yet Marseille also has to contend with its notoriety for protection rackets and shoot-outs, **corruption**, drug-money laundering and prostitution. It's impossible not to notice the glazed eyes of young kids and of the women lounging on cars by street corners. That said, however, to some extent the city's dangerous reputation is unfair. Shoot-outs by the *milieu*, as the Mafia is called, are rare, and underworld activities flourish just as much in the other towns of the Côte d'Azur. At least as far as casual visitors are concerned, there's no more reason to feel paranoid here than you would in any big European city.

One sphere of city life which has been as tumultuous and murky as its reputation would have it, however, is that of **politics**. There is plenty of grassroots support for the *Front National* and for Le Pen, who scored most votes in the first round of the presidential elections of 1995 but who, by 1998, was fighting a two-year national public ban for assaulting a left-wing political opponent. Marseille's most notorious politician during recent decades, however, was **Bernard Tapie**, a millionaire businessman with the common touch who entered politics in the 1980s with the express intention of seeing off Le Pen's *Front National*, and who won the hearts of the Marseillais by making their football team, **Olympique de Marseille** (OM), great again – in 1993 they became the first French team to win the European Cup. Charges of fraud and tax evasion failed to dent Tapie's popularity, and in the 1994 European elections he gained around seventy percent of the vote. However, under his ownership, OM's finances went haywire and both owner and team were embroiled in a notorious scandal when it was discovered that Marseille had been guilty of chicanery and match-fixing in the 1992 season, enabling them to clinch the national Championship and qualify for their "glorious" European run of 1993. OM was relegated to the second division as punishment, and was taken over by a consortium of private business interests in conjunction with the town hall. Tapie was declared bankrupt, jailed for eight months for bribery and match-rigging, and has been involved in litigation and lengthy appeals regarding his financial misdemeanours ever since. Whereas OM are now back to their flamboyant best and competing in Europe again, to the delight of their impassioned supporters, a political comeback by Tapie in the foreseeable future seems highly unlikely.

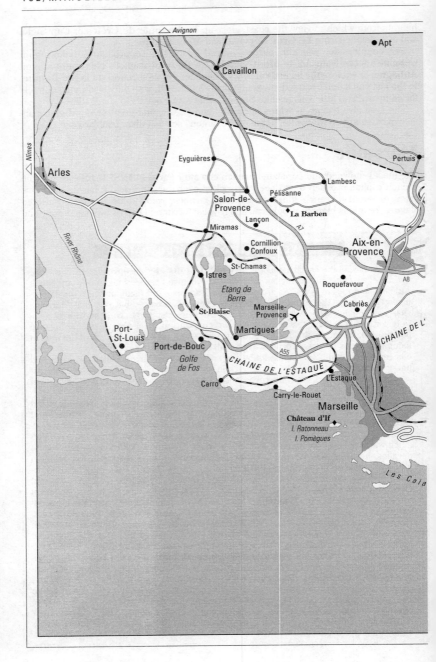

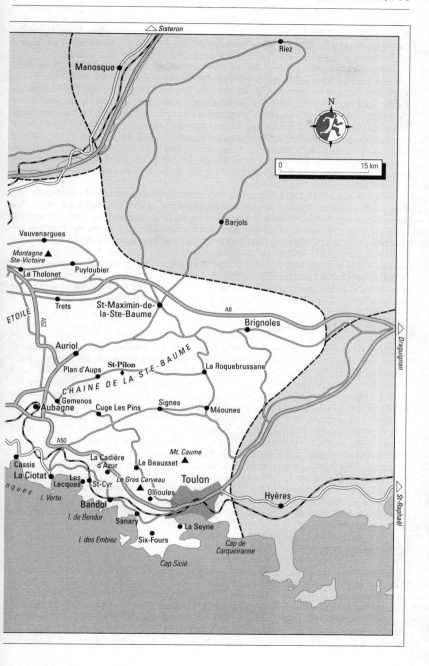

Bastille-storming. It was the presence of so many Revolutionaries from Marseille marching their way from the Rhine to Paris in 1792 which gave the name to the Hymn of the Army of the Rhine that became the national anthem, "La Marseillaise".

Marseille has been a trading city for over two and a half thousand years, ever since ancient Greeks from Ionia discovered shelter in the Lacydon inlet, today the Vieux Port, and came to an agreement with the local Ligurian tribe. The story goes that the locals, noticing the exotic cargo of the strangers' boats, sent them off to the king's castle where the princess's wedding preparations were in full swing. The Ligurian royal custom at the time was that the king's daughter could choose her husband from among her father's guests. As the leader of the Greek party walked through the castle gate, he was handed a drink by a woman and discovered that she was the princess and that he was the bridegroom. The king gave the couple the hill on the north side of the Lacydon and Massalia came into being. And there ends, more or less, Marseille's association with romance.

Which is not to say Marseille cannot be romantic. It has a powerful magnetism as a true Mediterranean city, surrounded by mountains and graced with hidden corners that have the unexpected air of fishing villages. It has its triumphal architecture, too, and the cosmopolitan atmosphere of a major port. But perhaps the most appealing quality is the down-to-earth nature of its inhabitants, who are gregarious, generous, endlessly talkative and unconcerned if their style seems provocatively vulgar to the snobs of Aix or the Côte d'Azur. Their animation makes this one of the most delightful European cities to visit. What's more, it is not a a typically touristy city. As a visitor, your status is no different from that of the people departing and arriving on the ships, those on business or fans of the city's mercurial football team, Olympique de Marseille, or OM as it is known.

Arrival and information

Arriving by **car**, you'll descend into Marseille from the surrounding heights of one of three mountain ranges. From any direction the views encompass the barricade of high-rise concrete on the lower slopes, the vast roadstead with docks stretching miles north from the central **Vieux Port** and Marseille's classic landmark, the **Basilique de Notre-Dame-de-la-Garde** perched on a high rock south of the Vieux Port. Follow signs for the Vieux Port to reach the city centre.

The city's **airport**, the Aéroport de Marseille-Provence, is 20km northwest of the city centre; a shuttle bus runs to the **gare SNCF St-Charles** (5.30am–9.50pm; every 20min; 45F), on the northern edge of 1er arrondissement on esplanade St-Charles. The **gare routière** stands to the right of the station entrance, on place Victor-Hugo. From esplanade St-Charles, a monumental staircase leads down to bd d'Athènes, which becomes bd Dugomier before reaching **La Canebière**, Marseille's main street. La Canebière runs to the head of the **Vieux Port**, a fifteen-minute walk to the right of the intersection. Marseille's main **tourist office** is at 4 La Canebière (June–Aug daily 9am–8pm; rest of year Mon–Sat 9am–7pm, Sun 10am–5pm; ☎04.91.13.89.00, fax 04.91.13.89.20).

City transport

The city's **bus**, **tram** and **métro** network is efficient, though not particularly cheap. You can get a plan of the **transport system** from RTM at 6–8 rue des Fabres, one street north of La Canebière near the Bourse, the city's stock exchange. **Tickets** are flat rate for bus, tram and métro and can be used for journeys combining all three as long as they take less than one hour. You can buy **single tickets** (9F) from the driver or at métro ticket offices, or **carnets** of six tickets (41F) from métro stations and RTM kiosks; a **day pass** (25F) is also available from métro ticket offices and automatic vending machines (press *autres titres* on the screen and then *carte journée*). Tickets need to be punched in the machines on the bus, on tramway platforms or at métro gates. The métro runs daily from 5am to 9pm, and until 12.30am when the football team are playing. **Night buses** run out from the centre from 9.25pm to 12.30am, from rue des Fabres, one block north of La Canebière, near the Bourse: pick up a timetable from the RTM office or métro sales points.

Accommodation

Since Marseille is not a great tourist city, **finding a room** in July or August is no more difficult than during the rest of the year. **Hotels** are plentiful with lots of very cheap options around the Opéra and on the streets running south from La Canebière. If you get stuck for a room, the main tourist office on La Canebière offers a free accommodation service. The most inexpensive options are the city's **youth hostels**, both quite a way from the centre. **Camping** is only possible at the Bois-Luzy hostel to the north of the city, which has room for twenty tents.

Hotels

Alizé, 35 quai des Belges, 1er (☎04.91.33.66.97, fax 04.91.54.80.06). Comfortable, soundproofed rooms, the more expensive looking out onto the Vieux Port. ④.

Athènes, 37 bd d'Athènes, 1er (☎04.91.90.03.83). Inexpensive hotel, right next to the train and bus stations; some of the top-storey rooms have balconies. ②.

Le Béarn, 63 rue Sylvabelle, 6e (☎04.91.37.75.83, fax 04.91.81.54.98). Pleasant, quiet hotel, close to the centre. ①.

Caravelle, 5 rue Guy-Mocquet, 1er (☎04.91.48.44.99). Friendly, quiet and close to La Canebière and cours Julien, just off bd Garibaldi. ②.

Le Corbusier, Cité Radieuse, 280 bd Michelet, 8e (☎04.91.77.18.15, fax 04.91.16.78.28). Stylish hotel on the third floor of the renowned architect's prototype high-rise; book in advance. ③.

Edmond-Rostand, 31 rue Dragon, 6e (☎04.91.37.74.95, fax 04.91.57.19.04). Helpful management, great charm and atmosphere, and well known, so you should book in advance. ③.

Esterel, 124 rue Paradis, 6e (☎04.91.37.13.90, fax 04.91.81.47.01). Pleasant place in a good, animated location with all mod cons. ③.

Frantour-Tonic Hotel, 43 quai des Belges, 1er (☎04.91.55.67.46, fax 04.91.55.67.56). Newly done-up and now the smartest of the Vieux Port hotels. Jacuzzi and steam bath in many rooms, from 560F for port view. ④.

Lutétia, 38 allée Léon-Gambetta, 1er (☎04.91.50.81.78, fax 04.91.50.23.52). Very central with pleasant rooms. ③.

Manon, 36 bd Louis-Salvator, 6e (☎04.91.48.67.01, fax 04.91.47.23.04). Pleasant place, though a little noisy, between the Préfecture and cours Julien. ②.

New Hotel Select, 4 allée Léon-Gambetta, 1er (☎04.91.50.65.50, fax 04.91.50.45.56). A clean and clinical modern hotel, but with a good central location. ④.

Hotel Pavillon, 27 rue Pavillon, 1er (☎04.91.33.76.90, fax 04.91.33.87.56). In a central location and very friendly. ②.

Le Richelieu, 52 Corniche Kennedy, 7e (☎04.91.31.01.92, fax 04.91.59.38.09). Friendly place, and one of the more affordable of the corniche hotels, overlooking the plage des Catalans. ③.

Le St Ferréol's Hôtel, 19 rue Pisançon, cnr rue St-Ferréol, 1er (☎04.91.33.12.21, fax 04.91.54.29.97). Pretty decor, marble baths with Jacuzzis, in a central pedestrianized area. ⑤.

Youth hostels, foyers and chambre d'hôtes

HI youth hostel, 76 av de Bois-Luzy, 12e (☎04.91.49.06.18). Bus #8 from Centre Bourse (direction St-Julien, stop Bois Luzy). Cheap, clean youth hostel in a former château a long way out from the centre. Camping also available. Curfew 11pm. Reception 7–10am & 5–10.30pm.

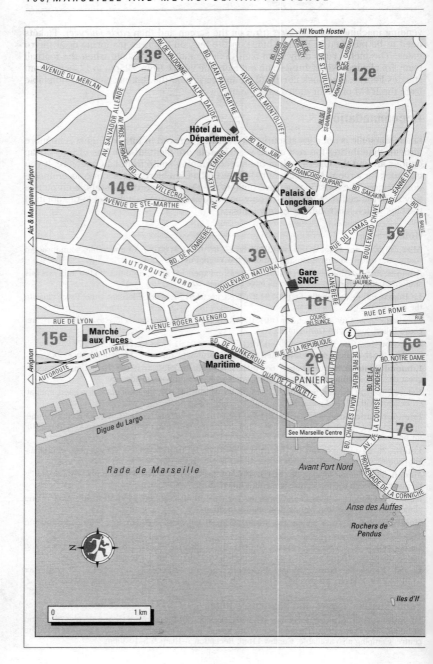

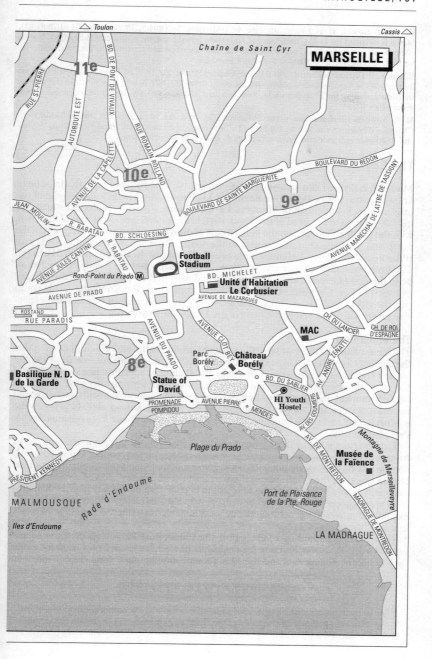

HI youth hostel, 47 av J-Vidal, impasse du Dr-Bonfils, 8e (☎04.91.73.21.81, fax 04.91.73.91.23). Métro Rond-point du Prado, then bus #44 (direction Roy d'Espagne, stop Place Bonnefon). Not so cheap or secure as the Bois Luzy hostel, but the lack of curfew and proximity to the beach make up for that. Reception 7.30–9.30am & 5–11pm. Closed Jan.

Résidence Darius Milhaud, 100 traverse Charles-Susini, 13e (☎04.91.61.44.39). Métro La Rose then bus #3 to Susini–Marie-Louise, and it's 100m down the hill. A long way north of the centre. Individual studios for 115F per night, available July and August only. Reception open Sat & Sun usual office hours.

M & Mme Schaufelberger, 2 rue St-Laurent, 2e (☎ & fax 04.91.90.29.02). Métro Vieux Port. Chambre d'hôtes on the fourteenth floor of a high-rise in Le Panier with great views from the balcony. Separate entrance and bathroom. English spoken by friendly owner. ③.

The City

Marseille is divided into sixteen arrondissements which spiral out from the focal point of the city, the **Vieux Port**. Due north lies **Le Panier**, the Vieille Ville and site of the original Greek settlement of Massalia. **La Canebière**, the wide boulevard starting at quai des Belges at the head of the Vieux Port, is the central east–west axis of the town, with the **Centre Bourse** and the little streets of **quartier Belsunce** bordering it to the north and the main shopping streets to the south. The main north–south axis is **rue d'Aix** becoming **cours Belsunce** then **rue de Rome**, **av du Prado** and **bd Michelet**. The lively, youngish quarter around **place Jean-Jaurès** and the trendy **cours Julien** lie to the east of rue de Rome. On the headland west of the Vieux Port are the villagey *quartiers* of **Les Catalans** and **Malmousque** from where the **Corniche** heads south past the city's most favoured residential districts towards the main beaches and expensive promenade bars and restaurants of the **Plage du Prado**.

The Vieux Port

The **Vieux Port** is, more or less, the ancient harbour basin, and the original inlet that the ancient Greeks sailed into. Historic resonances, however, are not exactly deafening on first encounter, drowned as they are by the stalling or speeding lanes of traffic. Yet the quayside cafés indulge the sedentary pleasures of observing street life; the morning **fish market** on the quai des Belges provides some natural Marseillais theatre; and the mass of cafés and seafood restaurants on the **pedestrianized streets** between the southern quay and cours Estienne d'Orves ensure that the Vieux Port remains the life centre of the city.

Two fortresses guard the harbour entrance. **St-Jean**, on the northern side, dates from the Middle Ages when Marseille was an independent republic, and is now only open when hosting exhibitions. Its enlargement of 1660, and the construction of **St-Nicolas** fort, on the south side of the port, represent the city's final defeat as a separate entity. Louis XIV ordered the new fort to keep an eye on the city after he had sent in an army, suppressed the city's council, fined it, arrested all opposition and, in an early example of rate-capping, set ludicrously low limits on Marseille's subsequent expenditure and borrowing.

The best view of the Vieux Port is from the **Palais du Pharo**, built on the headland beyond Fort St-Nicolas by Emperor Napoléon III for his wife and now used for major rock concerts, congresses and the like. Its surrounding park (8am–10pm) hides an

---

MUSEUMS PASSPORT

If you're planning on visiting several of Marseille's museums it makes sense to invest 50F in the **Museums Passport**, available from June to September from all the city's museums and valid for a fortnight.

underground *mediathèque* and exhibition space. For a wider-angle view, head up to **Notre-Dame-de-la-Garde**, the city's Second Empire landmark which tops the hill south of the harbour. Crowned by a monumental gold Virgin that gleams to ships far out to sea, the church itself is a monstrous riot of neo-Byzantine design (daily: summer 7am–8pm; winter 7.30am–5.30pm; bus #60).

There are two small museums on the south side of the port which are worth checking out. The **Musée du Santon**, 47 rue Neuve Ste-Catherine (Mon–Sat 9am–noon & 2.30–7pm; free), is part of the Carbonnel workshop, one of the most renowned producers of the crib figures for which Provence is famous. The **Maison de l'Artisanat et des Métiers d'Art**, 21 cours Estienne d'Orves (Tues–Sat 1–6pm; free), hosts excellent temporary exhibitions on Marseillais themes: from soap and olive oil production to the cultures of the different nationalities that make up the city's population. Two doors away is the intellectual haunt of *Les Arcenaulx*: a restaurant, *salon de thé* and bookshop.

A short way inland from the Fort St-Nicolas, above the Bassin de Carénage and the slip road for the Vieux Port's tunnel, is Marseille's oldest church, the **Abbaye St-Victor** (daily 8am–7pm; 10F entry for crypt). Originally part of a monastery founded in the fifth century on the burial site of various martyrs, the church was built, enlarged and fortified – a vital requirement given its position outside the city walls – over a period of two hundred years from the middle of the tenth century. It certainly looks and feels more like a fortress with the walls of the choir almost three metres thick, and it's no ecclesiastical beauty. You can descend to the crypt and catacombs, a warren of chapels and passages where the weight of stone and age, not to mention the photographs of skeletons exhumed, create an appropriate atmosphere to recall the horrors of early Christianity; Saint Victor himself, a Roman soldier, was slowly ground to death between two millstones.

Present Christian worship in the city has as its headquarters a less gloomy edifice but one of minimum aesthetic appeal. The **Cathédrale de la Major** (Tues–Sun 9am–noon & 2.30–5.30pm) on the north side of the Vieux Port overlooking the modern docks, is a striped neo-Byzantine solid block that completely overshadows its predecessor, the Romanesque **Vieille Major** (guided tours by appointment only; ☎04.91.90.53.57) that stands, much diminished, alongside.

Opposite the two cathedrals, on esplanade de la Touret, a mural illustrates the ancient Greeks arriving at Marseille, and at the end of the esplanade, opposite Fort St-Jean, is the small Romanesque **Church of St-Laurent**, built on the site of a Greek Temple of Apollo (Wed pm only).

Le Panier

Le Panier, the oldest part of Marseille, lies to the east of the cathedrals and stretches down to the Vieux Port. This is where the ancient Greeks built their Massalia, and where, up until World War II, tiny streets, steep steps and a jumble of houses irregularly connected, formed a Vieille Ville typical of this coast. In 1943, however, Marseille was under **German occupation** and the quarter represented everything the Nazis feared and hated, an uncontrollable warren providing shelter for *Untermensch* of every sort, including Resistance leaders, Communists and Jews. They gave the twenty thousand inhabitants one day's notice to leave. While the curé of St-Laurent pealed the bells in protest, squads of SS moved in; they cleared the area and packed the people, including the curé, off to Fréjus, where concentration camp victims were selected. Out of seven hundred children, only sixty-eight returned. Dynamite was laid, carefully sparing three old buildings that appealed to the Fascist aesthetic, and everything in the lower part of the quarter, from the waterside to rue Caisserie and Grande Rue, was blown sky high.

After World War II, archeologists reaped some benefits from this destruction in the discovery of the remains of a warehouse from the first-century AD Roman docks. You can see vast food-storage jars for oil, grain and spices in their original positions, and

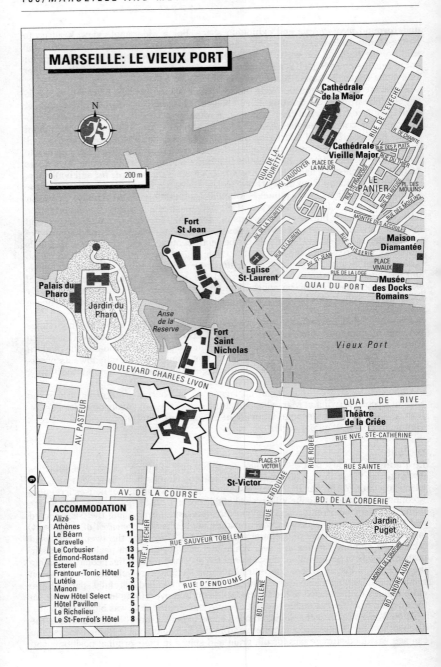

MARSEILLE: LE VIEUX PORT

N

0   200 m

Cathédrale de la Major

Cathédrale Vieille Major

RUE DE L'EVECHE

R. DE CHARITE

RUE DES P. PUITS

RUE DU THIER

LE PANIER

PL. DES MOULINS

QUAI DE LA TOURETTE

AV. VAUDOYER

PLACE DE LA MAJOR

RUE DES MOULINS

MONTEE DES ACCOULES

RUE CAISSERIE

Maison Diamantée

Fort St Jean

AV. DE LA TOURETTE

RUE ST-LAURENT

Eglise St-Laurent

AV. ST-JEAN

RUE DE LA LOGE

PLACE VIVAUX

Musée des Docks Romains

QUAI DU PORT

Palais du Pharo

Jardin du Pharo

Anse de la Reserve

Fort Saint Nicholas

Vieux Port

BOULEVARD CHARLES LIVON

QUAI DE RIVE

Théâtre de la Criée

RUE ROBER

RUE NVE. STE-CATHERINE

AV. PASTEUR

RUE SAINTE

PLACE ST-VICTOR

St-Victor

RUE D'ENDOUME

BD. DE LA CORDERIE

AV. DE LA COURSE

RUE J. RECHER

Jardin Puget

RUE SAUVEUR TOBELEM

ACCOMMODATION

Alizé	6
Athènes	1
Le Béarn	11
Caravelle	4
Le Corbusier	13
Edmond-Rostand	14
Esterel	12
Frantour-Tonic Hôtel	7
Lutétia	3
Manon	10
New Hôtel Select	2
Hôtel Pavillon	5
Le Richelieu	9
Le St-Ferréol's Hôtel	8

RUE D'ENDOUME

BD. TELLENE

MONTEE D'OREILLE

BD. ANDRE AUNE

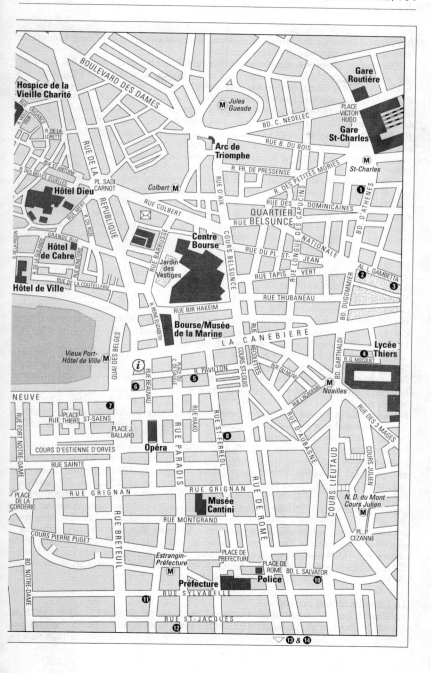

part of the original jetty, along with models, mock-ups and a video to complete the picture, can be viewed at the **Musée des Docks Romains** on place de Vivaux (Tues–Sun: summer 11am–6pm; winter 10am–5pm; 12F).

The quarter preserves some of its old identity at the top of the slope, but the quayside area is postwar quick-and-cheap-build concrete. Amongst all this are the landmark buildings that the Nazis spared: the seventeenth-century **Hôtel de Ville** on the quay; the half-Gothic, half-Renaissance **Hôtel de Cabre** on the corner of rue Bonneterie and Grande Rue; and the **Maison Diamantée** of 1620, so called for the pointed shape of its facade stonework, on rue de la Prison. Neighbouring building works have disturbed the Maison Diamantée's foundations and it is closed for repairs until the year 2000. It normally houses the **Musée de Vieux Marseille** (check with tourist office for new opening hours), a wonderful hotch-potch of mementoes celebrating old Marseille. One of the largest exhibits is a scale model of the central area across La Canebière, made to commemorate the insurrection of June 1848. The model shows miniature dead bodies, people falling and shooting, plus all the streets that disappeared soon afterwards when the **Palais de Bourse** was built, specifically to erase *quartiers* that the authorities could not trust. There are also moving photographs of Le Panier prior to the Germans' similar, though more drastic, action, including a model of the transporter bridge across the Vieux Port that went with the dynamite. Another section covers the plague that decimated the city in 1720: antidote recipes, doctors' bizarre costumes and implements for purifying letters.

Overlooking the small **place Daviel** nearby is an impressive eighteenth-century bell tower, all that remains of the Église des Accoules, destroyed in 1794 as it had served as a meeting place for counter-revolutionaries after the French Revolution. To the north of here, above the place Daviel, is the vast nineteenth-century **Hôtel Dieu**, now a nursing college. At the junction of rue de la Prison and rue Caisserie, the steps of montée des Accoules lead up and across to **place de Lenche**, site of the Greek agora, a few blocks south of the cathedrals and a good café stop.

What's left of old Le Panier is above here, though the fifteen windmills of place des Moulins disappeared in the nineteenth century, and if you climb rue du Réfuge you'll find yourself in a modern demolition clearing. The exposed inner walls of old tenement buildings have superb state-of-the-art **murals** of TV screens and loudspeakers, in violent contrast to the refined cultural centre at the far end of the clearing. This is the **Hospice de la Vieille Charité**, a seventeenth-century workhouse with a gorgeous Baroque chapel surrounded by columned arcades in pink stone. Only the tiny grilled exterior windows recall its original use.

The temporary exhibitions – usually brilliant – and evening concerts are popular, but at other times the hospice is extraordinarily deserted, despite its two museums, café and excellent bookshop. The **Musée d'Archéologie Méditerranéenne** (Tues–Sun: summer 11am–6pm; winter 10am–5pm; 12F; 18F for special exhibitions; 25F combined ticket with Musée des Arts) contains some very beautiful fourth- and fifth-century BC pottery and glass, an Egyptian collection with mummies and their accompanying boxes for internal organs plus a mummified crocodile. It also displays fascinating finds from a Celto-Légurian settlement at Roquepertuse, between Marseille and Aix, including a double-headed statue. The other permanent collection is the **Musée des Arts Africains, Océaniens et Amérindiens** (same hours and prices as Musée d'Archéologie), which is dark and spooky with a horrible collection of dried heads, and detailed descriptions of all, usually in French.

La Canebière and around

La Canebière, the famed broad boulevard that runs for about a kilometre east from Marseille's port, is the undisputed hub of the town, named for the hemp (*canabé*) that once grew here and provided the raw materials for the town's thriving rope-making trade. Fashioned originally with the Champs-Élysées in mind, La Canebière is more of a patchwork affair of hotels, cafés and shops, and, at the port end, two museums: the **Musée de la Marine et de l'Economie** (daily 10am–6pm; 10F), housed on the ground floor of the Neoclassical stock exchange and filled with intricate models and paintings of ships on the high seas; and the **Musée de la Mode**, a bit further up at no. 11 (Tues–Sun noon–7pm; 18F), with regular exhibitions of variable quality.

Behind the stock exchange is the **Centre Bourse** shopping centre and the **Jardin des Vestiges**, where the ancient port extended, curving northwards from the present quai des Belges. Excavations have revealed a stretch of the Greek port and bits of the city wall with the base of three square towers and a gateway, dated to the second or third century BC. The beautifully lit and spaced **Musée d'Histoire de Marseille**, inside the Centre Bourse (Mon–Sat noon–7pm; free), shows the main finds of Marseillaise excavations, of which the most dramatic is a third-century AD wreck of a Roman trading vessel. There are models of the city, reconstructed boats, everyday items such as shoes and baskets, and a beautiful Roman mosaic of a dolphin, plus a great deal of information on text panels and a video about the Roman, Greek and pre-Greek settlements. Laws that were posted up in Greek Massalia are cited, forbidding women to drink wine and allowing would-be suicides to take hemlock if the 600-strong parliament agreed. While you're in the Centre Bourse, you could check out the free debates and arts events hosted by the FNAC bookshop (Mon–Sat 10am–7pm; monthly programme available from the first floor).

The city's annual **garlic market** (mid-June to mid-July) takes place just east of the Centre Cours, on cours Belsunce and its continuation rue d'Aix. The thoroughfare stretches from La Canebière to **Porte d'Aix**, Marseille's Arc de Triomphe, modelled on the ancient Roman arch at Orange. This was part of the city's grandiose mid-nineteenth-century expansion which included the Cathédrale de la Major and the new Joliette docks, paid for with the profits of military enterprise, most significantly the conquest of Algeria in 1830. Today it's one of the North African community's meeting places.

The **quartier Belsunce**, the area between cours Belsunce/rue d'Aix, bd d'Athènes and St-Charles, is very much an Arab district, though not exclusively so. As well as hundreds of tiny shops selling North African food, music, household goods and clothes, trading takes place here on the streets from flattened cardboard boxes, of hi-fis, suits and jeans from France and Germany, and spices, cloth and metalware from across the Mediterranean. It's a huge and dynamic market without any French middlemen, hence the fear and anger it arouses in some quarters.

At the top end of bd d'Athènes, a monumental stairway leads up to **Gare St-Charles**. It was laid out in the 1920s with Art Deco railings, lamps and mammoth statues and has steps wide enough for people to sit and chat, play cards or, for some, simply to lie drunk without constituting an obstruction.

More Arab trading, on a smaller scale, takes place just south of La Canebière around the lively **Marché des Capucins** (Mon–Sat 8am–7pm) by the former Gare de l'Est, now the **Galerie des Transports**, a museum dedicated to the city's public tranport (Wed–Sat 10am–5pm; free). The streets around here are fairly seedy, with plenty of insalubrious hotels and, come nightfall, prostitutes on every corner.

The prime shopping quarter of Marseille, and a continuation of the red-light district, is encompassed by three streets running south from La Canebière: rue de Rome, rue Paradis and, between the two, rue St-Ferréol which terminates at the pseudo-Renaissance **Préfecture**, where demonstrations in the city traditionally converge. Side streets like rue du Pavillon are full of tempting café and *pâtissier* stops, making this is a good area for a midday meal.

Between rue St-Ferréol and rue de Rome, on rue Grignan, is the city's most important art museum, the **Musée Cantini** (Tues–Sun: summer 11am–6pm; winter 10am–5pm; 12F; 15–20F for exhibitions), housing paintings and sculptures dating from the end of the nineteenth century up to the 1950s. The Fauvists and Surrealists are well represented along with works by Matisse, Léger, Picasso, Ernst, Le Corbusier, Miró and Giacometti. Only a proportion of the permanent collection is displayed at any one time, and even less during the many excellent temporary exhibitions.

A few blocks east of rue de Rome, the streets between place Julien and cours Julien are full of bars and music shops, and the *cours* itself, with pools, fountains, and restaurant tables, is one of the most pleasant places to idle in the city. Madame Zaza of Marseille, an original and affordable Marseillaise couturier, has her shop at no. 73; there are bookshops and art galleries to browse in, plus a stamp market, with antiques and junk every second Sunday in summer months. The **daily market**, known as **La Plaine**, on place Jean-Jaurès is at its best on Saturday when there's a good mix of food and clothing, including bargain Italian shoes.

Palais de Longchamp and around

The **Palais de Longchamp**, 2km inland from the port (bus #80 or #41 from La Canebière, or métro Longchamp-Cinq-Avenues), went up in 1869, the year when the opening of the Suez Canal gave a crucial advantage to the Mediterranean ports, bringing a new boom for Marseillais trade. It was built as the grandiose conclusion of an aqueduct at Roquefavour (no longer in use) bringing water from the Durance to the city. Water is still pumped into the centre of the colonnade connecting the two palatial wings of the building. Below, an enormous statue looks as if it's honouring some great feminist victory: three well-muscled women stand above four bulls wallowing passively in a pool from which a cascade drops the four or five storeys to ground level.

The palace's north wing houses the city's **Musée des Beaux-Arts** (Tues–Sun: summer 11am–6pm; winter 10am–5pm; 12F), a hot and slightly stuffy place, but with a fair share of delights. Most unusual, and a very pleasant visual treat, are three paintings by Françoise Duparc (1726–76), whose first name has consistently found itself masculinized to François in both French and English catalogues. The nineteenth-century satirist from Marseille, Honoré Daumier, who served six months for his suitably vicious caricatures of Louis Philippe's government, has a whole room dedicated to his cartoons. Plans for the city, sculptures, and the famous profile of Louis XIV by the Marseille-born Pierre Puget are on display along with graphic contemporary canvases of the plague that decimated the city in 1720. The other wing of the palace is taken up with the **Musée d'Histoire Naturelle** (Mon–Sat noon–7pm; free) – mouldy stuffed animals and lots and lots of fossils.

Just before you reach the palace, at 140 bd Longchamp, is the **Musée Grobet-Labadi** (Tues–Sun: summer 11am–6pm; winter 10am–5pm; 15F), a typical late-nineteenth-century bourgeois town house filled with exquisite objects, but not wildly interesting. Northwest of the palace, at the end of bd Mal-Juin, stands the brand-new **Hôtel du**

Département (Metro St-Just). Deliberately set away from the centre of town in the run-down St-Just-Chartreux *quartier*, the new seat of local government for the Bouches-du-Rhône *département* is the biggest public building to have been erected in the French provinces in the twentieth century. It was designed by the English architect William Alsop, who used his hallmark ovoid glass tube shapes above and alongside vast rectangular blocks of blue steel and glass. In front of it, like a vast turtle's back, is the **Dôme**, a venue for shows and exhibitions. The hotel's great glass foyer is accessible during working hours and the tourist office can arrange architectural tours.

Parc Chanot, Cité Radieuse and beyond

Av du Prado, the continuation of rue de Rome, is an eight-lane highway, with impressive fountains and one of the city's biggest **daily markets** between métros Castellane and Perrier. At the rond-point du Prado, the avenue turns west to meet the corniche road.

Bd Michelet continues southwards past **Parc Chanot**, where you'll find Olympique de Marseille's ground. OM's reputation for occasional brilliance means that home matches are almost always sold out, but some tickets are available from the *OM Café* on the quai des Belges right on the Vieux Port, with prices ranging from 80F for the stands to 130F for the cheapest seats.

Beyond Parc Chanot, set back just west of the boulevard, is a mould-breaking piece of architecture, **Le Corbusier's Cité Radieuse**, designed in 1946 and completed in 1952. A seventeen-storey housing complex on stilts, the Cité fails to amaze now only because so many apartment buildings the world over have imitated Le Corbusier's revolutionary model. There are 23 different layouts for the apartments, to suit single people and varying sized families, the larger ones split across two floors and with balconies on both sides of the building with unhindered views of mountains and sea. Although there are still many private offices, the commercial side of the concept has been falling into a rather depressed state of late, and the restaurant and post office have closed, leaving only a small supermarket on one of the floors. The hotel remains (see p.157), and at the top you'll find sports and recreational facilities amid sculptural and ceramic decoration. The whole complex is surrounded by lawns: a "vertical garden city" Le Corbusier called it, and a "*unité d'habitation*" in which each element, and most crucially the individual tenant, has autonomy within the collective space. Many of the original tenants are still in residence. To reach the Cité take the métro to Rd-Pt du Prado, then bus #21 (direction Vaufrèges or Luminy).

Further south, at 69 av d'Haïfa, (bus #23 or #45 from métro Rd-Pt du Prado, stop Haïfa or Marie-Louise), is the contemporary art museum, **MAC** (Tues–Sun: summer 11am–6pm; winter 10am–5pm; 12F). The permanent collection, displayed in perfect, pure-white surroundings, is the continuation of the Cantini collection, with works from the 1960s to the present. The artists include the Marseillais César and Ben, along with Buren, Christo, Klein, Niki de St-Phalle, Tinguely and Warhol. There's also the Cinémac (☎04.91.25.01.07), a cinema showing feature films, shorts and videos on different themes each month.

Between av d'Haïfa and the sea, just off av Prado, is **Parc Borély**, with ponds, palm trees, a rose garden, botanical gardens (daily 8am–9pm; free) and no restrictions about walking or picnicking on the grass. It was originally the grounds of the **Château Borély**, an eighteenth-century mansion which the town hall keeps promising to turn into a decorative arts museum. Next to the park is the race-course with its old, elegant stands on the promenade by the Plage du Prado.

The corniche and south to Les Goudes

The most popular stretch of sand close to the city centre is the small plage des Catalans, a few blocks south of the Palais du Pharo. This marks the beginning of Marseille's **Corniche Président-Kennedy**, initiated and partly built after the 1848 revolution, giving work to eight thousand unemployed. Despite its inland bypass of the Malmousque peninsula, it's a corniche as good as any on the Riviera, with *belle époque* villas on the slopes above, the Îles d'Endoume and the Château d'If in the distance, cliffs below and high bridge piers for the road to cross the inlets of La Fausse-Monnaie and Les Auffes where the Monument aux Morts de l'Armée d'Orient frames its statue against the setting sun.

Prior to 1948, Malmousque and the **Vallon des Auffes** were inaccessible from the town unless you followed the "customs men's path" over the rocks or took a boat. There was nothing on Malmousque, but the Vallon des Auffes had a freshwater source and a small community of fishermen and rope-makers. Amazingly it is not much different today, with fishing boats pulled up around the rocks, tiny jumbled houses and restaurants serving the catch. Only one road, rue du Vallon-des-Auffes, leads out; otherwise it's the long flights of steps up to the corniche.

Malmousque is now a very desirable residential district, favoured by the champagne-socialist set, with Marseille's most expensive hotel-restaurant, *Le Petit Nice*, at one end and a military barracks at the other. Between the *terrain militaire* and the inlet of La Fausse-Monnaie there's a **coastal path** you can follow with views along the coast to Cap Croisette and out to the offshore islands. It's linked by steps to tiny bays and beaches: perfect for secluded swimming when the Mistral isn't whipping up the waves.

Behind La Fausse-Monnaie inlet, a path leads to the Théâtre Silvain, an open-air theatre set in a wilderness of trees and flowers. There's more greenery, of a formal nature, a short way further along the corniche in the **Jardin Valmer** (bus #83 stop Corniche J-Martin) and you can explore the tiny streets that lead up into this prime district of mansions with high-walled gardens.

The Corniche J-F Kennedy ends at the Plage du Prado, the city's main sand beach backed by a wide strip of lawns and the ugly Espace Borély complex of shops and restaurants. The promenade continues, however, with a glittering array, best seen at night, of restaurants, clubs and cafés all the way to Montredon. Marseille's newest museum, the **Musée de la Faïence** (Tues–Sun: June–Sept 11am–6pm; Oct–May 10am–5pm; 12F), is at 157 av de Montredon, in the elegant nineteenth-century Château Pastré, set in a huge park that extends to the foot of the Montagne de Marseilleveyre (bus #19 from métro Rd-Pt du Prado, stop Montredon-Chancel). The eighteenth- and nineteenth-century ceramics, many of them produced in Marseille, are of an exceptionally high standard, such as the vibrant productions of Théodore Deck, but there is also a small collection of novel modern pieces.

From Montredon to Les Goudes, where the gleaming white, beautifully desolate hills finally meet the sea and the coast road ends, there are easily accessible *calanques* (rocky inlets) that face the setting sun, ideal for evening swims and supper picnics. If you prefer to walk, the GR98 to Cassis starts from the top of av de la Grotte-Roland, off av de Montredon a short way beyond the Pastré park. It splits into the 98a which follows the ridge inland and 98b which descends to the sea at Callelongue, the last outpost of Les Goudes. *La Grotte* bar here is where walkers gather. A map of the paths is available from the tourist office: ask for their leaflet on the *calanques*.

The islands

> *Blacker than the sea, blacker than the sky, rose like a phantom the giant of granite, whose projecting crags seemed like arms extended to seize their prey.*

So the **Château d'If** appears to Edmond Dantès, hero of Alexandre Dumas' *The Count of Monte Cristo*, having made his watery escape after five years of incarceration as the innocent victim of treachery. In reality most prisoners of this island fortress died before they reached the end of their sentences – unless they were nobles living in the less fetid upper-storey cells, like one de Niozelles who was given six years for failing to take his hat off in the presence of Louis XIV, and Mirabeau who had run up massive debts with shops in Aix. More often, the crimes were political. After the revocation of the Edict of Nantes in 1685, thousands of Marseillais Protestants who refused to accept the new law were sent to the galleys and their leaders entombed in the Château d'If. Revolutionaries of 1848 drew their last breath here.

Apart from the castle, there's not much else to the Île d'If: just a small café-restaurant and clear seas in which to swim. Dumas fans will love it, others may raise an eyebrow at the cell marked "Dantès" in the same fashion as non-fictional inmates' names. But it's a horribly well-preserved sixteenth-century edifice and the views back towards Marseille are wonderful.

Boats leave from the quai des Belges at 6.45am and hourly from 9am to noon and 2 to 5pm, plus one at 6.30pm with slight seasonal variations. The château's opening hours fit the boat timetable and the journey takes fifteen minutes, costing 50F. Entrance to the castle costs an additional 25F. At rather more expense (80F) you can do a round trip taking in the other two islands of the Frioul archipelago, **Pomègues** and **Ratonneau**, which are joined by a causeway enclosing a yachting harbour. In days gone by these islands were used as a quarantine station, most ineffectually in the early 1720s when a ship carrying the plague was given the go-ahead to dock in the city, resulting in the decimation of half the population.

The **Îles d'Endoume**, the islands off Malmousque, with their abandoned monastery, cannot be visited.

Eating and drinking

Fish and seafood are the main ingredients of the Marseillais diet, and the superstar of dishes is the city's own expensive invention, **bouillabaisse**, a saffron- and garlic-flavoured fish soup with bits of fish, croûtons and *rouille* to throw in and conflicting theories about which fish should be included and where and how they must be caught. The other city speciality is the less exotic *pieds et paquets*, mutton or lamb belly and trotters.

The best, and most expensive, **restaurants** are close to the corniche, while for international choice cours Julien is the best place to head for. The pedestrian precinct behind the south quay of the Vieux Port is more upmarket and fishy, with plenty more restaurants between the Opéra and La Canebière. Cheap **snacks** are to be had in Le Panier as well as some good old-time bistros, and from the stands along cours Belsunce you can buy fries and sandwiches stuffed with meat for under 15F.

As Marseille is a Mediterranean city, people tend to stay up late in summer. Around the Vieux Port, from place Jean-Jaurès to cours Julien, and the Plage du Prado are the areas where there are always lots of people around and **cafés** and **restos** open well into the night. Be warned that many restaurants take very long summer breaks.

Restaurants, cafés and bars

L'Abri Côtier, 1 bd des Baigneurs, 8e (☎04.91.72.27.29). Lovely restaurant overlooking the sea in Montredon. Menus from around 150F. Closed Mon & Tues out of season, plus all Jan & Feb.

Chez Angèle, 50 rue Caisserie, 2e (☎04.91.90.63.35). Packed Le Panier local, with a bargain *menu fixe* for basic French food. Closed Sat eve, Sun & Aug.

Les Arcenaulx, 25 cours Estienne-d'Orves, 1er (☎04.91.54.77.06). Superb food for 250F to 300F a head in this intellectual haunt, which is also a bookshop. Cheap lunch menus during the week from 135F. Last orders 11.30pm. Closed Sun.

L'Art et les Thés, Centre de la Vieille Charité, 2er. The cultural centre's tearoom. Closed Tues.

L'Assiette Marine, 142 av Mendez-France, 8e (☎04.91.71.04.04). Serves fresh pasta in lobster sauce, aubergine and lamb with truffles, and other exquisite dishes, just north of the Plage du Prado. Menus at 135F and 300F.

Auberge "In", 25 rue du Chevalier-Roze, 2e (☎04.91.90.51.59). In a health-food shop on the edge of Le Panier. Vegetarian *menu fixe* served lunchtimes and early evenings. Closed Sun.

Le Byblos Prado, 61 promenade de la Plage, 8e (☎04.91.22.80.66). Lebanese mezzes and wine from 150F. Closed Sun eve.

Le Cadratin, 17 rue St-Saëns, 1er. Friendly and cheap bar with Sixties music playing on the jukebox and a great mix of people, both foreign and local.

Pizzaria des Catalans, 3 rue des Catalans, 7e (☎04.91.52.37.82). Excellent pizzas served just above the beach. Midday only out of season.

La Coupole, 5 rue Haxo, 1er. Elegant brasserie serving a midday plat du jour with a glass of wine for 100F. Seafood salads are a temptation.

Dar Djerba, 15 cours Julien, 6e. Excellent Tunisian restaurant with beautiful tiling – ignore the stuffed camel's head and tackle one of their excellent coucouses. Around 150F.

L'Épuisette, Vallon des Auffes, 7e (☎04.91.52.17.82). This is the place to eat the Auffes catch. From 200F. Closed Sun eve.

Chez Étienne, 43 rue Lorette, 2e. Another old-fashioned Le Panier bistro; hectic, cramped and crowded. Full meal 150–250F, but you can just have a pizza. No bookings. Closed Sun.

La Garbure, 9 cours Julien, 6e (☎04.91.47.18.01). Rich specialities from southwest France, including Bresse chicken. Menus around 150F. Closed Sat midday, Sun & mid-July to mid-Aug.

Chez Jimmy, rue Ste-Françoise, 1er. Unnamed Le Panier snack bar opposite the *Bar des 13 Coins* serving very cheap sandwiches of meatballs, stuffed tomatoes, and chips.

La Kahena, 2 rue de la République, 2er. Popular Moroccan resto, with grills and couscous from 60F. Closed Mon midday & Sun.

Bar de la Marine, 15 quai Rive-Neuve, 1er. A favourite bar for Vieux Port lounging and inspiration for Pagnol's celebrated Marseille trilogy. Closed Sun.

Le Marseillois, quai du Port. Restaurant on the deck of an old sailing vessel in the Vieux Port. Menus from 140F. Closed Sun.

Les Mets de Provence, 18 quai Rive-Neuve, 7e (☎04.91.33.35.38). A Marseille institution with authentic Provençal cooking and very reasonable midday menus. Closed Mon eve & Sun.

Chez Michel, 6 rue des Catalans, 7e (☎04.91.52.30.63). There's no debate about the bouillabaisse ingredients here. A basket of five fishes, including the elusive and most expensive one, the *rascasse*, is presented to the customer before the soup is made. Quite simply the place to eat this dish. Expect to pay 250F for the bouillabaisse alone.

Chez Neale, 36 cours Julien, 6e. Salads, cakes and English breakfast served all day from 10am; brunch at weekends. Under 100F. Closed Mon eve & Sun.

Le Panier des Arts, 3 rue du Petit-Puits, 2e (☎04.91.56.02.32). Reasonably priced Provençal specialities, to a background of classical music, close to the Vieille Charité.

Café Parisien, 1 pl Sadi-Carnot, 2e. Very beautiful, old-fashioned café, where people play cards and chess. Occasional painting exhibitions.

La Patalain, 49 rue Sainte, 1er (☎04.91.55.02.78). Restaurant serving local specialities, in particular *pieds et paquets*. Menus from 190F. Closed Sat midday, Sun & mid-July to end-Aug.

Bar Le Petit Nice, 26 pl Jean-Jaurès, 1er. The place to head for on Sat morning during the market.

Bar de la Samaritaine, 2 quai du Port, 2e. The sunniest port-side bar with comfy terrace chairs.

Brasserie des Templiers, 21 rue Reine-Elizabeth, 1er. Next to the Centre Bourse with quick eats and good beers.

Sur le Pouce, 2 rue des Convalescents, 1er. Very cheap, studenty Tunisian resto in the quartier Belsunce.

Markets and food shops

The city's copious **street markets** provide a feast of fruit and veg, olives, cheeses, sausages and spit-roast chickens – everything you'd need for a picnic except for wine, which is most economically bought at supermarkets. The markets are also good for cheap clothes, particularly shoes. La Plaine and av du Prado are the biggest; the Capucins the oldest. On Sunday afternoons, when all else is closed, there's the **Marché du Soleil** and a few food stalls along rue Longue des Capucins (métro Noailles).

Marseille's Sunday morning flea market, **Marché aux Puces**, is a brilliant spectacle, and good for serious haggling. There's a relaxed atmosphere, plenty of cafés, and everything and anything for sale, including very cheap fruit and veg.

The markets

Quai des Belges, Vieux Port, 1er; métro Vieux Port. Fish sold straight off the boats. Daily 8am–1pm.

Capucins, pl des Capucins, 1er; métro Noailles. Fish, fruit and veg sold here and in the Halles Delacroix on nearby rue Halles-Delacroix, towards rue de Rome. Mon–Sat 8am–7pm.

Place Carli, 1er; métro Noailles. Antiquarian books and records. Daily 10am–5pm.

Cours Julien, 6e; métro N.-D.-du-Mont-Cours Julien. Food Mon–Sat; stamps Sun; antiquarian books second Sat of month; bric-à-brac second Sun of month.

Allées de Meilhan, La Canebière, 1e; métro Réformés. Flowers Tues & Sat 8am–1pm.

La Plaine, pl Jean-Jaurès, 5e; métro N.-D.-du-Mont Cours Julien. Food daily; general goods Tues, Thurs & Sat; organic produce Fri. All 8am–1pm.

Prado, av du Prado, 6e; métro Castellane and Perrier. Food and general goods daily; flowers Fri. Both 8am–1pm.

Marché aux Puces, av du Cap-Pinède, 15e; bus #35 from the Vieux Port (stop Cap-Pinède) or buses #25, #26, #36, #70 from métro Bougainville (stop Lyon). Food Tues–Sun; antiques Thurs–Sun mornings; bric-à-brac Sat; flea market Sun. All 8am–7pm.

Marché du Soleil, rue du Bon-Pasteur, 1er; métro Colbert/Jules Guesde. Food. Daily 8am–7pm.

Shops

Le Carthage, 8 rue d'Aubagne, 1er. Best Tunisian pâtisseries and Turkish delight.

Castelmuro, 31 rue paradis, 1er & 137 rue Jean-Mermoz, 8e. One of the best upmarket *charcuterie*, chocolate and pâtisserie shops.

La Chaise Longue, 33 rue de Paradis, 1er. Stylish coffee cups and other household accessories.

Pâtisserie d'Aix, 1 rue Nationale, 1er. More excellent Tunisian sweetmeats.

Nightlife and entertainment

Marseille's **nightlife** has something for everyone, with plenty of live rock and jazz, nightclubs and discos, as well as theatre, opera and classical concerts. Theatre is particularly innovative and lively in Marseille. The Virgin Megastore at 75 rue St-Ferréol and the tourist office's ticket bureau are the best places to go for **tickets and information** on gigs, concerts, theatre, free films and cultural events. Virgin also stocks a wide selection of English books and runs a café on the top floor, open, like the rest of the store, seven days a week until midnight. Other places to head for information are the book and record shop FNAC on the top floor of the Centre Bourse, the travel agency and comic shop La Passerelle on rue des Trois-Mages, and the New Age music shop Tripsichord next door. At any of these places, you can pick up a copy of *Taktik*, Marseille's independent free weekly listings paper, which comes out on a Wednesday.

In an old abandoned abattoir just north of the Marché aux Puces (bus #25 or #26 stop Abattoirs) various alternative theatre groups, bands and artists hang out and perform. Events here are not widely advertised, and the only way to really find out what's going on is to pay a visit.

Live music

La Cave à Jazz, 24 quai de Rive-Neuve, 7e. Jazz club and an occasional venue for rock, fashion, theatre and dance events.

Cité de la Musique, 4 rue Bernard du Bois, 1er (☎04.91.39.28.28). Jazz cellar and auditorium.

Maison de l'Étranger, 9 av Général-Leclerc, 3e (☎04.91.28.24.01). A club not far from the gare SNCF St-Charles, which puts on regular world music gigs, especially Raï, but is threatened with closure due to financial problems.

La Maison Hantée, 10 rue Vian, 6e (☎04.91.92.09.40). Country music, R&B and rock. Closed Mon.

May Be Blues, rue Poggioli, 6e (☎04.91.42.41.00). Relaxed blues and jazz club. No entry charge, though drinks go up once the music starts. Closed Mon & Tues.

Au Moulin, 47 bd Perrin, 13e (☎04.91.06.33.94). Near métro St-Just, an obscure venue in the northwest of the city specializing in weird and wonderful European bands.

Pelle Mêle, 8 pl aux Huiles, 1er (☎04.91.54.85.26). Jazz bistro and piano bar. Closed Sun.

Le Stendhal, 92 rue Jean-de-Bernady, 1er (☎04.91.84.74.80). Bar with red and black interior, after Stendhal's novel. Wide selection of malt whiskies and beers. Live music Tues & Thurs.

Nightclubs

New Cancan, 20 rue Sénac, 1er (☎04.91.47.50.18). Gay club with high camp and transvestite shows.

Le New Orleans, 1 quai de Rive-Neuve, 1er (☎04.91.33.87.27). This venue plays everything from jazz be-bop to current chart toppers.

Palacio de la Salsa, 19 rue Neuve Ste-Catherine (☎04.91.33.92.57). Dance venue, playing mainly Latin vibes. Closed Mon–Wed.

Le Pourquoi Pas, 1 rue Fortia, 1er (☎04.91.33.50.54). Offers Caribbean music and punch to get drunk on.

Trolleybus, 24 quai de Rive-Neuve, 7e (☎04.91.54.30.45). Piano bar and disco in a series of vaulted rooms; mainly popular rock and techno. Closed Mon–Wed.

Film, opera, theatre and concerts

Ballet National de Marseille, 20 bd Gabès, 8e (☎04.91.71.03.03). The home base of Roland Petit's famous dance company.

Bastide de la Magalone, 245 bd Michelet, 9e (☎04.91.39.28.28). Classical music concerts.

Chocolat Théâtre, 59 cours Julien, 6e (☎04.91.42.19.29). Theatre, restaurant and exhibition space with shows ranging from male striptease to avant-garde improvisations.

Cinéma Paris, 31 rue Pavillon, 1er (☎04.91.33.15.59). The only cinema in Marseille which regularly shows undubbed English-language films (labelled *v.o. – version originale*).

Théâtre de la Criée, 30 quai de Rive-Neuve, 7e (☎04.91.54.70.54). Home of the Théâtre National de Marseille and Marseille's best theatre.

Espace Julien, 33 cours Julien, 6e (☎04.91.47.09.64). A mixed-bag arts centre, showing theatre, jazz, dance and exhibitions.

Théâtre de Marionettes Massalia, 41, rue Jobin, 3e (☎04.91.62.39.51). Lively puppet theatre with changing programme of adult (evening) and children's (matinee) shows.

Théâtre du Merlan, av Raimu, 14e (☎04.91.98.24.35). Set amid horrific high-rise housing in the north of the city, this cultural centre is remarkable for having a police commissariat on the ground floor. Occasional shows in English.

Opéra, 1 pl Reyer, 1er (☎04.91.55.00.70). Symphony concerts and operas.

Listings

Airlines Air France and Air Inter, both 14 La Canebière, 1er (☎08.02.80.28.02); British Airways (☎08.02.80.29.02) and Delta (☎04.91.90.07.90), both 41 La Canebière, 1er; El Al at the airport (☎04.42.14.35.00).

Airport information ☎04.42.78.21.00 or 04.42.89.09.74.

Bike rental Green Bike, 135 av Clot Bey, 8e (☎04.91.72.42.63).

Bookshops Fuéri-Lamy, 21 rue Paradis, 1er (closed Mon), sells English books; Librarie des Editions Parenthèse, 72 cours Julien, 6e, sells books on architecture, art, cinema, photography and music; and Maupetit, 140 La Canebière, 1er, is a good general French bookshop.

Bus information ☎04.91.08.16.40.

Car parks cours Estienne-d'Orves, 1er; cours Julien, 1er; allées Léon-Gambetta, 1er; pl Monthyon, 6e; Centre Bourse, 1er; Gare St-Charles, 1er; pl Félix-Baret, 6e; pl Gal-de-Gaulle, 1er.

Car rental Budget, 40 bd de Plombières (☎04.91.64.40.03); Citer, 96 bd Rabatau, 8e (☎04.91.83.05.05); Europcar, 7 bd Maurice-Bourdet, 1er (☎04.91.99.40.90); Thrifty, 6 bd Voltaire, 1er (☎04.91.05.92.18). All have main agencies at the airport.

Consulates Britain, 24 av du Prado, 6e (☎04.91.53.43.32); USA, 12 bd Paul-Peytral, 6e (☎04.91.54.92.00).

Currency exchange Comptoir de Change Méditerranéen, Gare St-Charles; Comptoir Marseillais de Bourse, 22 La Canebière.

Disabled information Office Municipal pour Handicappés, 128 av du Prado, 8e (☎04.91.81.58.80), has information on disabled access and facilities, and operates a transport service (call ☎04.91.78.21.67 a day ahead). See also Taxis below.

Emergencies ☎15; SOS Médecins (☎04.91.52.91.52); 24hr casualty departments: La Conception, 144 rue St-Pierre, 5e (☎04.91.38.36.52); SOS Voyageurs, Gare St-Charles, 3e (☎04.91.62.12.80).

Ferries SNCM, 61 bd des Dames (☎08.36.67.95.00), runs ferries to Corsica, Tunisia and Algeria.

Gay and lesbian information Centre Gai et Lesbien Méditerranéen, 1 rue du Châteauredon (☎04.91.33.72.65).

Lost property 18 rue de la Cathédrale, 2e (☎04.91.90.99.37); SNCF Trouvé (☎04.91.95.14.97); Commissariat Centrale (☎04.91.91.90.40).

Pharmacy Gare St-Charles (Mon–Fri 7am–10pm, Sat 7am–8pm).

Police Commissariat Centrale, 2 rue Antoine-Becker, 2e (daily 8am–noon & 2–6pm; ☎04.91.39.80.00).

Post office 1 pl de l'Hôtel-des-Postes, 1er.

Taxis ☎04.91.02.20.20; disabled facilities Monsieur P. Dahan (06.11.54.99.99); English-speaking ☎04.91.83.00.06 or 04.91.89.76.08.

Train information ☎04.91.08.50.50 or 08.36.35.35.35.

L'Estaque and westwards

Marseille's docks and its northern coastal sprawl finally end at **L'ESTAQUE**, an erstwhile fishing village much loved by painters in the last century, and easy to get to by train (10min on Miramas train). It was no rural paradise even in 1867 as a gouache by Cézanne of the factory chimneys of L'Estaque shows (originally given to Madame Zola and now exhibited in his studio in Aix). Yet it still has fishing boats moored alongside yachts, and the new artificial beaches to the west ensure that L'Estaque remains a popular escape from the city. For a good fish **dinner** try *La Réserve*, at 226 chemin de Riau (☎04.91.46.11.19; closed Sun). If you just want a snack, *chichis* (long, scented doughnut-like confections) from the Chichis Fruguis kiosk on the promenade are delicious.

Between L'Estaque and Carry-le-Rouet, the hills of the **Chaîne de l'Estaque** come right down to the coast, a gorgeous wilderness of white rock, pines and brilliant yellow scented broom. The shore is studded with *calanques* where the water is exceptionally clean and you can look across the roadstead of Marseille to the islands and the entrance of the Vieux Port. The train tunnels its way above the shore while the main road, the N568, then D5, takes an inland route through **La Rove** and **Ensues-la-Redonne**, with smaller roads looping down to the fishing villages and summer holiday homes of **Niolon**, **Mejean** and **La Redonne**. At Méjean simple meals of grilled fish and *petites fritures* are served overlooking the tiny port at *Le Mange Tout* (☎04.42.45.91.68; closed winter).

The charm of this stretch of coast ends abruptly at **CARRY-LE-ROUET**, with its crammed harbour. The **tourist office** here (July & Aug Mon–Sat 9am–noon & 2–6pm; rest of year Tues–Sat 10am–noon & 2–5pm; ☎04.42.13.20.36, fax 04.42.44.52.03) will give you a list of hotels and private rooms, but there's no real reason to stop other than to visit its wonderful **restaurant**, *L'Escale*, on a terrace above the right-hand side of Carry's port, where the *gâteau de poissons* is said to be divine (☎04.42.45.00.47; menus from 300F; closed Mon midday & Sun). If you're **camping**, you could head further west to Tamaris, a tiny village with several campsites including *Lou Cigalon*, Corniche des Tamaris (☎04.42.49.61.71; closed Oct–March), and *Les Tamaris*, Calanque des Tamaris (☎04.42.80.72.11; closed Oct–March).

Carry merges into its western neighbour Sausset-les-Pins, where the beaches are stony and artificial, without any break in the seaside houses and apartment buildings. For **beaches** it's best to head beyond Tamaris where there are long, sandy beaches around the pleasantly downmarket family resorts of **CARRO** and **LA COURONNE**, famous for its windsurfing competition held in April or May. Sumptuous seaside sunsets are assured thanks to the heavy dose of particles hovering above the monstruous petrochemical ports of Lavéra and Fos.

Around the Étang de Berre

The shores of the 22-kilometre-long and 15km-kilometre-wide **Étang de Berre**, northwest of L'Estaque, are not the most obvious holiday destination. The lagoon is heavily polluted, especially around the southern edges near Marseille's airport, and the sources are only too visible: oil refineries, petrochemical plants and tankers heading in and out of the Caronte Canal linking the lagoon with the vast industrial complex and port on the Golfe de Fos.

There are, however, some unexpected pockets worth exploring: the ancient remains at **St-Blaise**, the perched villages of **Miramas-le-Vieux** and **Cornillon-Confoux**, and, despite its close proximity to Europe's largest oil refinery, the town of **Martigues**.

Martigues

MARTIGUES straddles both sides of the Caronte Canal and the island in the middle, at the southwest corner of the Étang de Berre. In the sixteenth century when the union of three separate villages, Jonquières to the south, Ferrières to the north and the island, known simply as l'Île, created Martigues (and the French flag or so they claim), there were many more canals than the three that remain today. But Martigues has joined the long list of places with waterways to be dubbed the "Venice" of the region, and it deserves the compliment, however fatuous the comparison.

In the centre of l'Île, in front of the sumptuous facade of the airy Église de la Madeleine, a low bridge spans the Canal St-Sébastien where fishing boats moor and houses in ochre, pink and blue look straight down onto the water. This appealing spot is known as the **Miroir aux Oiseaux** and was painted by Corot, Ziem and others at the turn of the century. Some of these artists' works, including Ziem's *Vieux Port de Marseille*, can be seen in the **Musée Ziem** on bd du Juillet in Ferrières (July & Aug Mon & Wed–Sun 10am–noon & 2.30–6.30pm; rest of the year Wed–Sun 2.30–6.30pm; free); an entirely different artistic perspective is given upstairs, in the well-presented local history display, by the illuminating *ex voto* offerings to the town's Virgin featuring some graphic shipwrecks.

Behind the idle strolling quaysides of l'Île's canal, new housing has been designed on a pre-modern, acute-angled layout. From **quai Toulmond** the white, green, and mirror boxes of the ridiculously expensive municipal offices across the water and the towering highway bridge above the Caronte Canal contrast with the masts and bright hulls of the pleasure boats tied up along the quay.

A nineteenth-century swing bridge alongside a more dilapidated modern metal road bridge joins l'Île to **Ferrières**, whose tiny streets of shops and bars spread back from the relaxed focal point of place Jean-Jaurès. To the south, the tanker passage of the Canal Galiffet is spanned by a drawbridge taking you into **Jonquières**, the third and most lively of Martigues' centres, with the best concentration of bars and restaurants lining the main axis of cours du 4 Septembre and esplanade des Belges.

Practicalities

Buses from Marseille stop at the station bar on quai Tessé just to the right of the bridge. From the **gare SNCF** take bus #3 or #5 (direction Ferrières), to the centre. The **tourist office** is in Ferrières, just to the left of the road bridge on quai P-Doumer (July & Aug Mon–Sat 9am–7pm, Sun 10am–noon; rest of year Mon–Fri 8.30am–noon & 2–6.30pm, Sat 9am–noon & 2–6.30pm; ☎04.42.80.30.72).

The best of the **hotels** is the *St-Roch,* allée P-Signac, off av Georges-Braque, Ferrières (☎04.42.80.19.73; ⑤); *Le Provençal*, 35 bd du 14 Juillet, Ferrières (☎04.42.80.49.16; ③), is noisy but a lot cheaper.

A good time to visit is during July and August to see the spectacle of the *Sardinades*, when thousands of plates of grilled sardines are sold cheaply each evening along the quays in Jonquières (except during the folklore festival towards the end of July). Aside from these, the **food** to look out for is *poutargue*, a paste made from salted mullet, and *melets*, seasoned fish fry fermented in olive oil. Three **restaurants** to try, all on l'Île, are *Bouchon à la Mer*, 19 quai Toulmond (☎04.42.80.36.80; menus from 200F); the scenically sited *Le Miroir*, quai Brescon (☎04.42.80.50.45; menus from 110F); or *Chez Marraine*, 6 rue des Cordonniers (☎04.42.49.37.48; menus from 90F; closed Sun eve & Mon), where the fish soup is especially good.

St-Mître-les-Remparts, St-Blaise and Istres

About 6km beyond Martigues, on the road to Istres, lies the walled village of **ST-MÎTRE-LES-REMPARTS** with two original gateways allowing entrance to its minuscule, cramped heart. From the unusual church at the culmination of the corkscrew nest of streets you can see westwards over the Étang du Pourra and Étang d'Engenier towards the Fos complex.

From the main road the D51 leads away from St-Mître village up to a hill between two more lagoons, the Étang de Citis and Étang de Lavalduc. On the hill stands the twelfth-century Chapelle St-Blaise beside a thirteenth-century wall and the **Oppidum St-Blaise** archeological site (Mon & Wed–Sun 9am–noon & 2–5pm; 20F). The ancient inhabitants of this well-defended site left their mark throughout eight distinct periods, from 7 BC to the fourteenth century. If the site is closed you can still walk around it, see the extraordinary surviving Greek ramparts through the fence, watch red squirrels and butterflies, sit among the red flowers that grow in the sand by the edge of the Lavalduc lagoon and generally enjoy the woods and water, which can sometimes appear blood red because of the algae encouraged by a high salt content.

Back on the main road north, 6km beyond St-Mitre is **ISTRES**. The town, whose main business has been the construction of military jets, has a delightful Vieille Ville, with fine views from the terrace of the fortified **Notre-Dame-de-Beauvoir church** at the top of the hill, and numerous winding medieval streets to explore. Look out for the **dragon fountain** incongruously decorated with plastic flowertubs on place de Bourras, and the many ceramic *cigales* (cicadas) that are used to embellish exterior walls across Provence. Cicadas and their distinctive summery chirruping hold a place of affection in the hearts of most Provençals as they live only in the warm climes of the south. Istres' **Musée Archéologique** lies to the west of here on place du Puits Neuf (daily: June–Sept 2–7pm; Oct–May 2–6pm; 10F) and houses an impressive collection of Greek amphorae gathered from wrecks in the Golfe de Fos, many with their hand-painted destinations still visible. The museum also contains a unique bronze ship's figurehead of a boar. Abutting the bd Paul-Painlevé, part of the ring road around the old town, is the **Centre d'Art Contemporain** (Mon–Fri 9am–7pm, Sat 2–7pm, Sun 2–5.30pm; 15F) which mounts prestigious exhibitions of contemporary art.

The modern **tourist office** is at 30 allées Jean-Jaurès (mid-June to mid-Aug Mon–Fri 9am–noon & 2–7pm, Sat 9am–noon & 3–7pm, Sun 10am–noon & 2–6pm; rest of year Mon–Fri 9am–noon & 2–6pm, Sat 9am–noon & 3–6pm, Sun 10am–noon; ☎04.42.55.51.15), by the eighteenth-century Portail d'Arles archway at the northwest corner of the Vieille Ville; it has a complete list of hotels should you want to stay. There's a pleasantly situated **hotel**, *Le Castellan*, place Ste-Catherine (☎04.42.55.13.09, fax 04.42.56.91.36; ③), north of the Vieille Ville by the park over-looking the Étang de l'Olivier. There's also the three-star **campsite** *Camping Vitou* on rte de St-Charmas (☎04.42.56.51.57) for those with tents. There are several pleas-ant **cafés** on place Hôtel-de-Ville, close to the Centre d'Art Contemporain, while the best **restaurant**, *Le Saint-Martin* (☎04.42.56.07.12; menus around 200F; closed Tues eve & Wed), is over to the east by the *Des Heures Claires* pleasure port on the Étang de Berre.

Miramas-le-Vieux, St-Chamas and Cornillon-Confoux

The town of Miramas, to the north of the Étang de Berre, was a nineteenth-century creation tied to the expanding rail network. By the 1930s it had failed to develop any identity beyond its rail connections to the heavy industries of the coast, and was known simply as Miramas-Gare. Little has changed today, and you're really only likely to find yourself here if you're travelling by train between Arles and Avignon and Marseille, or using it as a stopoff for exploring the villages of **Miramas-le-Vieux**, **St-Chamas** and **Cornillon-Confoux** to the south.

MIRAMAS-LE-VIEUX, a typical Provençal medieval village, is perched on a hill 3km south of Miramas' train station. Narrow cobbled streets lead up past the pretty public gardens below place de la Marie to the immaculately restored **St-Vincent church** and its tiny predecessor, still standing in the churchyard. Beyond is place du Château and its **castle** ruins, the venue for musical soirées at the beginning of July. There are pottery shops and a couple of excellent ice-cream parlours, including *Le Quillé*, whose mouthwatering choice of flavours and fine terrace view attracts a small evening crowd from the towns in the area. For all the efforts made, though, the village remains attractive precisely for its lack of tourists.

Just to the south, on the Étang de Berre, is **ST-CHAMAS**, where portside workers' houses are separated from the rest of the town by an aqueduct between two high rocks, one of which is colonized by a scenic grid of tightly terraced houses. Here, on the Monté des Pénitents, is a helpful little **tourist office** (Mon–Sat: mid-June to mid-Sept 9am–noon & 3–7pm; rest of year 9am–noon & 1.30–5.30pm; ☎04.90.50.90.54). A few metres further on up the hill is the path that accesses the top of the nineteenth-century **Pont de l'Horloge aqueduct**, an astonishing creation that affords the best views of the town from alongside its hallmark clock. This unpretentious town has several other inter-esting monuments, including a seventeenth-century church with a severely cracked bell tower, and **La Poudrerie gunpowder factory** that Louis XIV initiated in 1690, and which was the economic mainstay of the town until shortly before its closure in 1974. A twenty-minute walk south of the centre brings you to the elegant **Pont Flavien**, a first-century BC Roman triumphal bridge spanning the River Touloubre – an unexpected sight in the wasteland to the left of the main road to Aix.

Though not on the lagoon itself, the neighbouring rock-perched village of **CORNILLON-CONFOUX**, 4km east of St-Chamas, gives even better views of the Étang de Berre, taking in the Alpilles, the Luberon and sometimes even Mont Ventoux as well.

Salon-de-Provence and around

The northern exit from the Autoroute du Soleil to **SALON-DE-PROVENCE** takes you past a memorial to **Jean Moulin**, the Resistance leader who was parachuted into the nearby Alpilles range in order to coordinate the different *maquis* groupings in Vichy France. He was eventually caught on June 21, 1943, tortured, deported and murdered by the Nazis. The bronze sculpture, by Marcel Courbier, is of a lithe figure landing from the sky like some latterday Greek god, very beautiful though somewhat perplexing if you're not aware of the invisible parachute.

In modern-day Salon, learning to fly Mirage jets is one of the principal activities, and, during some periods, they scream overhead day and night. The clientele of the town's bars and restaurants usually includes blue-uniformed cadets from the École de l'Air at the **airforce base** to the south of the town. Salon is very proud of its role in the nation's strategic forces, not least because the base has given a welcome boost to the local economy for the last fifty years. The tail-end of an aeroplane incongruously resting in a hole in the public gardens on place Général-de-Gaulle commemorates the 1987 anniversary of the school.

In the past, Salon's prosperity was due to the small black **olives** that produced an oil, *olivo selourenco*, of great gastronomic renown. By the end of the nineteenth century the Salonais were making soap from their oil, a highly profitable commodity manufactured in the most appalling conditions in subterranean mills. Those to whom the dividends accrued built spacious *belle époque* residences outside the old town walls, which today are the hotels, cafés, banks and offices on cours Pelletan, cours Carnot, cours Victor-Hugo and cours Gimon, encircling the Vieille Ville to the north and east.

The famous predictions of **Nostradamus** were composed in Salon, though the museum dedicated to him is less appealing than the mementoes of **Napoléon** in Salon's castle, the Château de l'Empéri. A good time to visit the town is mid-July when, on odd-numbered years, the **jazz festival** takes place, or in August for the annual **chamber music festival** in the château and open-air jazz and world music events in the place Morgan.

SALON AND LA CRAU

Salon lies at the eastern edge of Provence's most arid region, **La Crau**. In the face of perennial droughts, medieval Salon still managed to have successful tanneries, a saffron crop and flocks of sheep reputed for the quality of their mutton. In the mid-sixteenth century life dramatically changed when Adam de Craponne engineered a canal from the River Durance through the gap in the hills at Lamanon and across La Crau to the Étang de Berre, and today, the area west of Salon is criss-crossed with canals. A contemporary account describes the people of Salon greeting the arrival of the waters with "applause, astonishment and joyful incredulity". The project was financed by Salon's foremost famous resident, Michel de Nostradamus. The **Musée de Salon et de la Crau** (Mon & Wed–Fri 10am–noon & 2pm–6pm, Sat & Sun 2–6pm; 10F), on av Roger-Donnadieu, a short way east of the town on the D17 towards Pélissanne, presents the wildlife of La Crau, in stuffed form, and details the oil- and soap-making industries of Salon.

Arrival, information and accommodation

From the **gare SNCF** on av Émile-Zola, bd Maréchal-Foch leads you on to cours Pelletan, at the edge of the Vieille Ville. The **gare routière** is on place Morgan, adjoining bd Maréchal-Foch between the train station and the centre. The **tourist office** (July & Aug Mon–Sat 9am–noon & 2–7pm, Sun 10am–noon; rest of year Mon–Sat 9am–noon & 2.30–6.30pm, closed Sun; ☎04.90.56.27.60) is on the other side of the ring road around the Vieille Ville at 56 cours Gimon.

Finding **accommodation** should not be too difficult, whatever time of year you choose to visit. The *Regina*, 245 rue Kennedy (☎04.90.56.28.92, fax 04.90.56.77.43; ①), is the best of the budget options; the *Grand Hôtel de la Poste*, 1 rue Kennedy (☎04.90.56.01.94, fax 04.90.56.20.77; ③) and the *Hôtel de Provence*, 45 bd Maréchal-Foch (☎04.90.56.27.04, fax 04.90.56.99.76; ②), are well located, if nothing to write home about; and the *Vendôme*, 34 rue Maréchal-Joffre (☎04.90.56.01.96, fax 04.90.56.48.78; ③), has a pleasant courtyard setting. If you prefer to be out in the country, the *Domaine de Roquerousse* (☎04.90.59.50.11, fax 04.90.59.53.75; ⑤), in the opposite direction to Salon from the northern *autoroute* exit, has twenty rooms and ten self-contained units set in an extensive park. Otherwise, there's the seriously expensive *Hostellerie de L'Abbaye de Sainte-Croix*, 3km from Salon on the D16, route du Val-de-Cuech (☎04.90.56.24.55, fax 04.90.56.31.12; ⑧), an ancient abbey in beautiful surroundings.

The canal-bank three-star **campsite**, unimaginatively named *Camping Nostradamus* (☎04.90.56.08.36, fax 04.90.56.65.05; closed Nov–Feb), on the D17 towards Eyguières and the Arles bus route (rte d'Eyguières), also has some **dormitory accommodation**, and studios for around 200F.

The Town

In the mid-Sixties the town council decided that the **Vieille Ville** was falling apart and initiated a programme of demolition and rebuilding, completed in the late 1980s, amid proud mayoral slogans of "*Salon Renaissance, la Vitalité du Centre*". The effect, however, of having moved out the old inhabitants – save those in sixteenth-century houses with the money to renovate – has been to create a distressingly artificial space, full of new apartments and offices.

Given the lack of life in this part of town, you might as well concentrate on the dead in the **Château de l'Empéri**, the centrepiece of the Vieille Ville. This is a massive structure, a proper medieval fortress to suit the worldliness of its proprietors, the archbishops of Arles. It now houses, equally appropriately, a **museum of French military history** (Mon & Wed–Sun 10am–noon & 2.30–6pm; 15F) from the period of Louis XIV to World War I; the sections devoted to the Revolution and Napoléon are particularly fascinating.

Flights of gleaming steps run down the castle rock to place des Centuries, a wide open space of little obvious purpose, overlooked by the Centre Commerciale St-Michel which houses the **Musée Grévin de la Provence** (daily: summer 9.30am–noon & 2–6.30pm; winter 9am–noon & 2–6pm; 20F; 35F combined ticket with Maison de Nostradamus), a series of waxwork scenes illustrating episodes from the legends and history of Provence, with taped commentaries available in several different languages.

The **Église St-Michel**, with its twelfth-century tympanum and two belfries, on rue du Bourg-Neuf, opposite, squats oddly in the midst of this architectural model of a town centre. Cafés with high-tech chairs and shops selling windsurfing gear have rather greater pulling power than the naive representation of Saint Michael battling with two serpents above the church's west door. Some streets, such as **rue Moulin-d'Isnard**, are more consistently ancient but what is lacking throughout is precisely what was supposed to be introduced by all the upheaval of the 1980s, a bit of life.

To the north of here stands the **Maison de Nostradamus** (July & Aug daily 9.30am–noon & 2–6.30pm; rest of year Mon–Fri 9am–noon & 2–6pm, Sat & Sun 2–6pm; 20F; 35F combined ticket with the Musée Grévin), on the street now named after the soothsayer. Nostradamus arrived in Salon in 1547, already famous for his aromatic plague cure, administered in Aix and Lyon, and married a rich widow. After some fairly long Italian travels, he returned to Salon and settled down to study the stars, the weather, cosmetics and the future of the world. Translations in numerous languages of his *Centuries*, the famous predictions, are displayed in the house along with pictures of events supposedly confirming them. There are waxwork tableaux and visuals meant to fill you with wonder, but nothing particularly earth-shattering – the most interesting exhibit is the 1979 sculpture by François Bouché in the courtyard. Nostradamus died in Salon in 1566 and his tomb is in the Gothic Collégiale St-Laurent, at the top of rue du Maréchal-Joffre, north of the Vieille Ville.

To reach Collégiale St-Laurent from the museum, you'll pass through **Porte de l'Horloge**, the principal gateway to the Vieille Ville. This is a serious bit of seventeenth-century construction, with its Grecian columns, coats of arms, gargoyles and wrought-iron campanile. Through the arch is place Crousillat, which centres on a vast mushroom of moss concealing a three-statued fountain; a wonderful spot for a café break.

Eating and drinking

The best of Salon's **restaurants** is *La Salle à Manger*, 6 rue Maréchal-Joffre (☎04.90.56.28.01; closed Sun eve & Mon), with wonderful Italianate decor and lovely Provençal food at very reasonable prices – it's very popular so book ahead. The *Hostellerie de L'Abbaye de Ste-Croix* (see p.177) and *Le Mas du Soleil*, 38 chemin de St-Côme (☎04.90.56.06.53), are the two top-notch gourmet restaurants, the latter slightly more affordable with two menus under 200F. A more economical alternative is *La Brocherie des Cordeliers*, 20 rue d'Hozier (☎04.90.56.53.42; closed Sun midday & Mon), in a former thirteenth-century chapel, which has menus under 100F and excellent *magret de canard*. For cheap and filling couscous there's the *Restaurant Bleu*, 32 rue Palamard (☎04.90.56.51.93); or for late-night eats, try *La Boulangerie*, 13 rue Portalet (☎04.90.56.62.81; around 100F; open Tues–Sat 7pm–dawn).

The place for **café lounging** is around the marvellous mossy fountain on place Crousillat, where you'll find *Bar de la Fontaine*, *Nostradamus* and the *Café des Arts*. On rue A-Moutin, opposite the hôtel de ville, there's a piano bar, *Le Grenier d'Abondance*. The Vieille Ville also has plenty of cafés, brasseries and bars but locals tend to gravitate to the boulevards.

Salon's famous olive oil and other produce can be bought at the busy Wednesday **market** on place Morgan or the Sunday market on place de-Gaulle.

Around Salon

Ten kilometres north of Salon, the main road and highway pass through a narrow gap in the hills by **LAMANON**, a village which was never much more than a stopover on the transhumance routes (used for the moving of flocks, still followed by the Crau shepherds every June), though it does have a château. Above the village, hidden amongst rocks and trees, is a strange troglodyte village, the **GROTTES DE CALES**, which was inhabited from Neolithic times until the nineteenth century. Stairs lead down into grottoes, part natural, part constructed, with hooks and gutters carved into the rock; at the centre is a sacrificial temple. Access is free: follow the road going up to the right of the church which turns into a path, from which the Grottes are signed to the right.

EYGUIÈRES, just west of Lamanon, is a town of five thousand inhabitants with a fairly uninspiring eighteenth-century church, several old fountains and wash-houses, a ruined medieval castle, the remains of a Roman aqueduct, an eighteenth-century oil press and a Gallo-Grecian necropolis on the hill above. The countryside here is typical of the dry Crau region, but less predictably you may also see llamas grazing along with goats and horses. Llamas are excellent at keeping trim forest firebreaks – so, too, are goats, but goats are forbidden from running loose in the forests, thanks to an unrevoked Napoleonic law.

Bears, elephants, big cats, hippos and a host of other non-native mammals and birds are kept for more conventional purposes at the **Château de la Barben** (Château: Mon & Wed–Sun 10am–noon & 2–6pm; Zoo: daily 10am–6pm; Château 40F; Zoo an additional 55F), 12km east of Salon, just beyond Pélissanne. This is a place to take young children, with plenty of entertainment such as miniature train rides, as well as the standard zoo delights. The château was lived in for a while by Napoléon's sister, Pauline

Borghese, and her apartments are still decorated in imperial style, while the rest retains a seventeenth-century luxury.

Aix-en-Provence

AIX-EN-PROVENCE lies just 25km north of Marseille, but historically, culturally and socially it is moons apart from its neighbour. Aix is complacently conservative, and a stunningly beautiful town, its riches based on land owning and the liberal professions. Marseille's successful financiers, company directors and gangsters live in Aix; people dress immaculately; hundreds of foreign students, particularly Americans, come to study here; and there's a certain snobbishness, almost of Parisian proportions, in the air.

Aix began life as Aquae Sextiae, a Roman settlement based around its hot springs of sodium-free water – still used for cures in a thermal establishment on the site of the Roman baths in the northwest corner of the Vieille Ville. From the twelfth century until the Revolution Aix was the capital of Provence. In its days as an independent fiefdom, its most mythically beloved ruler, King René of Anjou (1409–80), held a brilliant court renowned for its popular festivities and patronage of the arts. René introduced the muscat grape to the region, and today he stands in stone in picture-book medieval fashion, a bunch of grapes in his left hand, looking down the majestic seventeenth-century replacement to the old southern fortifications, the cours Mirabeau.

The humanities and arts faculties of the university Aix shares with Marseille are based here, where the original university was founded in 1409. In the nineteenth century Aix was home to two of France's greatest contributors to painting and literature, Paul Cézanne and his close friend Émile Zola.

Arrival, information and accommodation

Cours Mirabeau is the town's main drag, with the multi-fountained place du Général-de-Gaulle, or La Rotonde, at its west end. The train and bus stations lie to the south and west of here: the **gare SNCF** (☎08.36.35.35.35) is on rue Gustavo-Desplace at the end of av Victor-Hugo, the avenue leading south from the *place*; the **gare routière** (☎04.42.27.17.91) is between the two western avenues, av des Belges and av Bonaparte, on rue Lapierre. The **tourist office** (daily: July & Aug 8.30am–10pm; Sept 8.30am–8pm; rest of year 8.30am–7pm; ☎04.42.16.11.61) is located at 2 place Général-de-Gaulle, between av des Belges and av V-Hugo. The main **post office** is also close by at 2 rue Lapierre.

If you are planning to visit during the summer, particularly during the festival which runs from mid-July to mid-August, your chances of getting an unbooked **room** are pretty slim – it's worth **reserving** a couple of months in advance at least. Rents and rates in central Aix are very high and reflected in the prices of hotels, as well as in shops and restaurants.

Hotels

Hôtel des Augustins, 3 rue de la Masse (☎04.42.27.28.59, fax 04.42.26.74.87). A stylish luxury hotel in a converted medieval monastery just off the cours Mirabeau. ⑧.

Hôtel des Arts-Sully, 69 bd Carnot (☎04.42.33.11.77). The cheapest rooms in the centre of Aix – a bit noisy, but very welcoming. It doesn't take bookings, so turn up early. ②.

La Caravelle, 29 bd Roi-René (☎04.42.21.53.05, fax 04.42.96.55.46). By the boulevards to the southeast of the city. The more expensive rooms overlook courtyard gardens. ③.

Hôtel Cardinal, 24 rue Cardinale (☎04.42.38.32.30, fax 04.42.26.39.05). A clean, peaceful and welcoming hotel. ③.

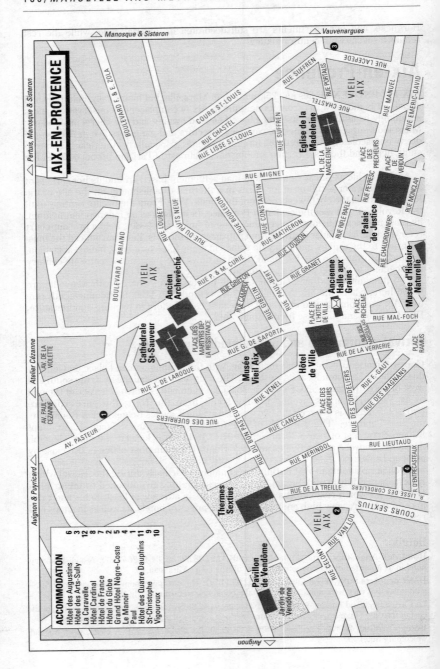

AIX-EN-PROVENCE

△ Manosque & Sisteron
△ Vauvenargues
△ Pertuis, Manosque & Sisteron
△ Avignon & Puyricard
△ Atelier Cézanne
△ Avignon

BOULEVARD F. E. ZOLA
RUE LACEPÈDE
VIEIL AIX
RUE SUFFREN
RUE MANUEL
RUE CHASTEL
RUE PORTALIS
COURS ST-LOUIS
RUE EMERIC-DAVID
RUE CHASTEL
RUE LISSE ST-LOUIS
Eglise de la Madeleine
RUE SUFFREN
PLACE DES PRÊCHEURS
PLACE DE VERDUN
RUE MIGNET
PL. DE LA MADELEINE
RUE PEYRESC
RUE MONCLAR
RUE DU PUITS NEUF
RUE CONSTANTIN
RUE RIFLE RAFLE
RUE LOUBET
RUE BRUEYS
RUE MATHERON
Palais de Justice
RUE CHAUDRONNIERS
BOULEVARD A. BRIAND
RUE LOUBON
Musée d'Histoire Naturelle
VIEIL AIX
RUE P. & M. CURIE
RUE GRANET
Ancien Archevêché
RUE GRIFFON
RUE PAUL-BERT
Ancienne Halle aux Grains
AV. DE LA VIOLETTE
RUE CARDERA
RUE GIBELIN
PLACE DE L'HÔTEL DE VILLE
PLACE DES MARSEILLAIS-RICHELME
RUE MAL-FOCH
Cathédrale St-Sauveur
PLACE DES MARTYRS DE LA RESISTANCE
Musée Vieil Aix
RUE G. DE SAPORTA
Hôtel de Ville
PLACE RAMUS
AV. PAUL CÉZANNE
RUE J. DE LAROQUE
RUE DE LA VERRERIE
RUE VENEL
PLACE DES CARDEURS
RUE F.-GAUT
AV. PASTEUR
RUE DES GUERRIERS
RUE DU BON PASTEUR
RUE CANCEL
RUE DES CORDELIERS
RUE DES MAGNANS
RUE MERINDOL
RUE LIEUTAUD
Thermes Sextius
RUE DE LA TREILLE
R. D'ENTRECASTEAUX
LISSE DES CORDELIERS
COURS SEXTIUS
RUE CELONY
VIEIL AIX
RUE VAN LOO
Pavillon de Vendôme
Jardin de Vendôme

ACCOMMODATION

Hôtel des Augustins 6
Hôtel des Arts-Sully 3
La Caravelle 12
Hôtel Cardinal 8
Hôtel de France 7
Hôtel du Globe 2
Grand Hôtel Nègre-Coste 5
Le Manoir 4
Paul 1
Hôtel des Quatre Dauphins 11
St-Christophe 9
Vigouroux 10

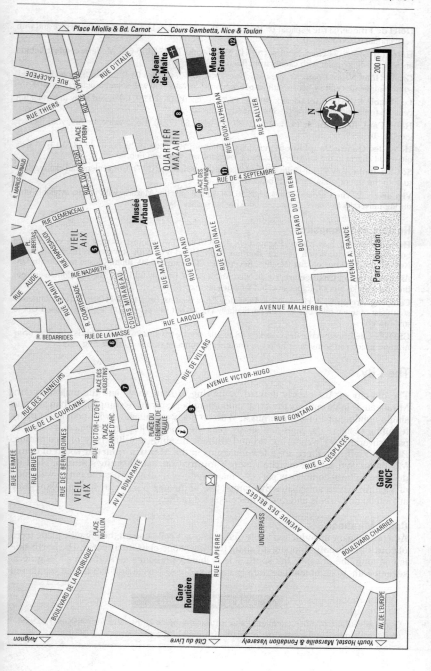

Place Miollis & Bd. Carnot △   △ Cours Gambetta, Nice & Toulon

200 m

RUE LACEPEDE
RUE D'ITALIE
RUE DE L'OPERA
RUE THIERS
R. MARIUS-REINAUD
PLACE FORBIN
RUE TOURNEFORT
St-Jean-de-Malte
Musée Granet
QUARTIER MAZARIN
RUE ROUX-ALPHERAN
RUE SALLIER
RUE CLEMENCEAU
PL. ALBERTAS
RUE PAPASSAUD
VIEIL AIX
Musée Arbaud
PLACE DES 4 DAUPHINS
RUE DE 4 SEPTEMBRE
BOULEVARD DU ROI RENE
RUE NAZARETH
RUE AUDE
RUE ESPARIAT
RUE COURTESSADE
RUE MAZARINE
RUE GOYRAND
RUE CARDINALE
AVENUE A. FRANCE
Parc Jourdan
R. BEDARRIDES
RUE DE LA MASSE
RUE LAROQUE
AVENUE MALHERBE
RUE DES TANNEURS
PLACE DES AUGUSTINS
RUE DE VILLARS
AVENUE VICTOR-HUGO
RUE DE LA COURONNE
RUE VICTOR-LEYDET
PLACE JEANNE D'ARC
PLACE DU GENERAL DE GAULLE
RUE GONTARD
RUE FERMEE
RUE BRUEYS
RUE DES BERNARDINES
VIEIL AIX
AV. N. BONAPARTE
RUE G.-DESPLACES
Gare SNCF
PLACE NIOLLON
AVENUE DES BELGES
BOULEVARD CHARRIER
BOULEVARD DE LA REPUBLIQUE
RUE LAPIERRE
UNDERPASS
Gare Routière
AV. DE L'EUROPE

Avignon △   △ Cité du Livre   Youth Hostel, Marseille & Fondation Vasarely △

Hôtel de France, 63 rue Espariat (☎04.42.27.90.15, fax 04.42.26.11.47). Right in the centre and with very comfortable rooms. ④.

Hôtel du Globe, 74 cours Sextius (☎04.42.26.03.58, fax 04.42.26.13.68). Modern comfort behind ancient facade, popular with clients from the nearby *baths*. ②.

Grand Hôtel Nègre-Coste, 33 cours Mirabeau (☎04.42.27.74.22, fax 04.42.26.80.93). Hotel in a handsome eighteenth-century house with an old-fashioned elevator and well-sound-proofed rooms. ④.

Le Manoir, 8 rue d'Entrecasteaux (☎04.42.26.27.20, fax 04.42.27.17.97). Tucked away in a quiet but central street, with agreeable air-conditioned rooms. ④.

Hôtel Paul, 10 av Pasteur (☎04.42.23.23.89, fax 04.42.63.17.80). Good value for Aix, with its own garden. ③.

Hôtel des Quatre-Dauphins, 54 rue Roux-Alphéran (☎04.42.38.16.39, fax 04.42.38.60.19). Warm, old-world charm in the quartier Mazarin. Closed for two weeks in Feb. ⑤.

St-Christophe, 2 av Victor-Hugo (☎04.42.26.01.24, fax 04.42.38.53.17). Convenient and classy, close to both the station and cours Mirabeau. ⑤.

Vigouroux, 27 rue Cardinale (☎04.42.38.26.42). In the quartier Mazarin with rooms available only during university holidays. Advanced booking necessary. ③.

Hostels and campsites

HI youth hostel, 3 av Marcel-Pagnol (☎04.42.20.15.99). Two kilometres west of the centre; take bus #8 or #12 (direction Jas de Bouffan, stop Vasarely). With its own restaurant (closed Nov–March), but no cooking facilities. Reception 7.30–10am & 5.30–10pm. Closed mid-Dec to Jan.

Airotel Camping Chanteclerc, rte de Nice, Val St-André (☎04.42.26.12.98). Three kilometres from the centre; take bus #3. Expensive, but facilities are excellent.

Camping Arc-en-Ciel, rte de Nice, Pont des Trois Sautets (☎04.42.26.14.28). Three kilometres southeast of town; take bus #3. Not particularly cheap, but has very good facilities. Closed Oct to mid-March.

CROUS, Cité Universitaire des Gazelles, 38 av Jules-Ferry (☎04.42.26.47.00). This is a student organization which can sometimes help you find cheap rooms on campus. July & Aug only.

The City

The old city of Aix, clearly defined by its ring of boulevards and the majestic cours Mirabeau, is in its entirety the great monument here, far more compelling than any one single building or museum within it. With so many streets alive with people, so many tempting restaurants, cafés and shops, plus the best markets in Provence, it's easy to pass several days wandering around without needing any itinerary or destination. Beyond **Vieil Aix**, there are a few museums in the **Mazarin quartier** south of **cours Mirabeau**, and, further out, the **Vaserely foundation** and **Cézanne's studio**. The Cité du Livre cultural complex is part of a major redevelopment across the entire west side of Vieil Aix which anticipates the completion of the new TGV train station, 20km away at Plateau de l'Arbois and due to be completed in the year 2000.

Cours Mirabeau

As a preliminary introduction to life in Aix, take a stroll beneath the gigantic plane trees of **cours Mirabeau**, stopping off along the way at one of its many cafés. The north side is one long line of cafés; the south side is lined with banks and offices, all lodging in seventeenth- to eighteenth-century mansions. These have a uniform hue of weathered

AIX'S MUSEUMS

Take advantage of Aix's excellent-value **museum pass** (40F; valid for one year) to visit the town's municipal museums. Available from all of the museums.

THE MARKET SQUARES

On **Saturdays** the whole of Vieil Aix is taken up with **markets**. Fruit and veg are sold on **place Richelme**, as they are every morning: purple, white and copper onions; huge sprigs of undried herbs; the orange flowers from young courgettes; and, according to season, different forest mushrooms or red fruits in mouthwatering displays. Fish stalls spread down rue des Marseillais and, behind the post office, **place de l'Hôtel-de-Ville** is filled with lilies, roses and carnations. Across rue Méjanes to the east you can buy clothes – new, mass-produced, hand-made or jumble – from stalls in rues Peyresc, Rifle-Rafle, Bouteilles, Chaudronniers and Monclar. Beyond the Palais de Justice, **place de Verdun** hosts its flea market with bric-à-brac and anything from real rabbit hats to plastic earrings, while the neighbouring **place des Prêcheurs** and **place de la Madeleine** display every edible from the region. Over to the west rue des Cordeliers is lined with more clothes stalls.

Moving at anything other than a snail's pace, let alone trying to admire achitectural rather than edible and perfumed details, is completely impossible. The same thing happens on a smaller scale on Tuesdays and Thursdays.

stone, with ornate wrought-iron balconies and Baroque decorations, at their heaviest in the tired old muscle-men holding up the porch of the Hôtel d'Espargnet at no. 38.

Opposite the hotel is Aix's most famous café, *Les Deux Garçons*, with a reputation dating back to World War II of serving intellectuals, artisticos and their entourage. The interior is all mirrors with darkening gilt panels and reading lights that might have come off the old *Orient Express*. The other cafés have a shifting hierarchy of kudos. All are pricey, though very tempting with cocktails, ice creams, and wicker armchairs from which to watch the milling street.

Vieil Aix

To explore the heart of Aix, wander north from cours Mirabeau and then anywhere within the ring of cours and boulevards. The layout of **Vieil Aix** is not designed to assist your sense of direction but it hardly matters when there's a fountained square to rest at every 50m and a continuous architectural backdrop of treats from the sixteenth and seventeenth centuries.

Starting from the eastern end of cours Mirabeau, heading north into place de Verdun, brings you to the **Palais de Justice**, a Neoclassical construction on the site of the old counts of Provence's palace. Count Mirabeau, the aristocrat turned champion of the Third Estate, who accused the États de Provence, meeting in Aix for the last time in 1789, of having no right to represent the people, is honoured here by a statue and allegorical monument. Just to the north, on place des Prêcheurs, is the **Église de la Madeleine** (closed Sun afternoon). The church's interior is decorated with paintings by Van Loo, born in Aix in 1684, and by Rubens, as well as a three-panel medieval Annunciation in which Gabriel's wings are owl feathers and a monkey sits with its head just below the deity's ray of light.

Further west, in place Richelme at the heart of Vieil Aix, a delicate though fairly massive foot hangs over the architrave of the old corn exchange, now the **post office**. It belongs to the goddess Cybele dallying with the masculine River Rhône. Just north of here, the **Hôtel de Ville** displays perfect classical proportions and embroidery in wrought iron above the door. Alongside stands a **clock tower** which tells the season as well as the hour of day.

Rue Gaston-de-Saporta takes you up from place de l'Hôtel-de-Ville to the **Cathédrale St-Sauveur**, a conglomerate of fifth- to sixteenth-century building works, full of medieval art treasures. The early sixteenth-century tapestries on the walls of the nave were originally hung in England's Canterbury Cathedral until they were sold by the Puritans and picked up in Paris for next to nothing by an Aix church official. On the south wall of the central nave is a painting commissioned by King René in 1475, *The Burning Bush*. The two side panels showing the king and his second wife are usually closed over the main picture. A notice in the south nave gives the times when the sacristan will open the picture and talk about it – very interesting if your French is up to it.

The painting focuses on Mary and babe sitting in the burning bush with castles, possibly Tarascon and Avignon, in the receding distance, and Moses surprised by an angel in the foreground. All the details – the Virgin's mirror, the trunks of the bush, Moses removing his slipper, the angel's medallion, the dog's collar, the snail in the bottom right-hand corner, the thimble-sized face reflected in the spiral of Saint Maurice's armour in the left-hand panel – are steeped in theological significance.

As part of the lecture, the sacristan also uncovers the panels protecting the west doors to reveal four Old Testament prophets and twelve sibyls – wise women of antiquity who supposedly prophesied Christ's birth, death and resurrection – beautifully sculpted by a Toulon carpenter in 1510. But the best sculpture of all is in stone, in the Romanesque **cloisters**, fashioned some 430 years earlier (access through the cathedral).

Nearby, at 24 rue Gaston de Saporta, the art gallery **La Galerie du Festival** has a permanent small collection of original prints and sketches by Cézanne, Renoir, Pissarro and others. Further down, through place des Martyrs-de-la-Résistance, is the former bishop's palace, the **Ancien Archevêché**, the setting, each July, for part of the grandiose music festival, and housing the **Musée des Tapisseries** (Mon & Wed–Sun 10am–noon & 2–6pm; 10F). The tapestries are all rather wonderful: musicians, dancers and animals in a 1689 series of *Grotesques*; nine scenes from the life of Don Quixote, woven in the 1740s, including one with the somewhat club-footed cat being divested of its armour by various *demoiselles*; and four *Jeux Russiens* (Russian Games) of a few decades later with superb miscellaneous detail to them. There's also a contemporary section with one exhibition a year, for which the definition of tapestry is broadened to include textiles made of rope, raffia or feathers.

The **Musée du Vieil Aix** at 17 rue Gaston-de-Saporta (Tues–Sun 10am–noon & 2.30–5pm; 15F) could be worth a glance while you're in this part of town. It has a set of marionettes that were a vital part of the old Fête-Dieu religious procession, and a huge collection of *santons*. Among the other odds and ends are paintings on velvet and a portrait of an Englishman receiving honorary citizenship for charitable works.

South of place de l'Hôtel-de-Ville is the elegant, cobbled eighteenth-century **place d'Albertas**, where, on summer evenings, concerts are held. The square is just off rue Espariat, which runs west to place du General-de-Gaulle and has a distinctly Parisian style. Aix's classiest couturier shops cluster in this area: Yves St-Laurent and Kenzo on rue Espariat, Chrisian Lacroix and others on rue Marius-Reinaud and rue Aude.

At 6 rue Espariat, a seventeenth-century mansion houses the **Musée de l'Histoire Naturelle** (Mon–Sat 10am–noon & 1–5pm; Sun 1–5pm; 10F). The cherubs and garlands decorating the ceilings are slightly at odds with the stuffed birds and beetles, ammonites and dinosaur eggs below; this is a rainy day – or sunstroke – refuge.

Quartier Mazarin

Taking rue Clemenceau south over cours Mirabeau, brings you into the heart of the **Quartier Mazarin**, built in five years in the mid-seventeenth century by the archbishop brother of the cardinal who ran France when Louis XIV was a baby. It's a very dignified district, and very quiet.

Before you reach the beautiful square of the four-dolphin fountain, you'll pass **Musée Paul Arbaud**, at 2a rue du 4-Septembre, a dark, musty old house, to which you are reluctantly granted admission after ringing the bell (Mon–Sat 2–5pm; 15F). The museum's main collection is of Marseillais and Moustiers ceramics, but there are more interesting items tucked away in the claustrophobic rooms of leather-bound books, silk wallpaper and painted and panelled ceilings. The best is a portrait by Pierre Puget of his mother. There are also portraits of Mirabeau and family and royalist trinkets such as nobles' rings that were offered as bail for Louis XVI while he was imprisoned in Paris.

A couple of blocks east of the dolphin fountain, on place St-Jean-de-Malte in the former priory of the Knights of Malta, is the most substantial of Aix's museums, the **Musée Granet** (Mon & Wed–Sun 10am–noon & 2–6pm; 10F). Covering art and archeology, it exhibits the ever-growing finds from the Oppidum d'Entremont (see p.190), a Celto-Légurian township 3km north of Aix, which flourished for about a hundred years, along with the remains of the Romans who routed them in 124 BC. The museum's paintings are a mixed bag: Italian, Dutch, French, mostly seventeenth- to nineteenth-century, not very well hung or lit. François Granet (1775–1849), whose collection initiated the museum, was an Aixois painter; his portrait by Ingres hangs here but his own works are better represented in the Musée Paul Arbaud. The portraits of Diane de Poitiers by Jean Capassin and Marie Mancini by Nicolas Mignard are an interesting contrast and there is also a self-portrait by Rembrandt. One wall is dedicated to the most famous Aixois painter, **Paul Cézanne**, who studied on the ground floor of the building, which at that date was the art school. Two of his student drawings are here as well as a handful of canvases, including *Bathsheba*, *The Bathers* and *Portrait of a Woman*.

The Atelier Paul Cézanne, the Vasarely Foundation and the Cité du Livre

Cézanne used many studios in and around Aix but at the turn of the century, four years before his death, he had a house built for the purpose at what is now 9 av Paul-Cézanne, overlooking Aix from the north. It was here that he painted the *Grandes Baigneuses*, the *Jardinier Vallier* and some of his greatest still-lifes. The **Atelier Paul Cézanne** (daily: April–Sept 10am–noon & 2.30–6pm; Oct–March 10am–noon & 2–5pm; admission 25F) has been left exactly as it was at the time of his death in 1906: coat, hat, wine glass and easel, the objects he liked to paint, his pipe, a few letters and drawings – everything save the man himself, who would probably have been horrified at the thought of it being public. To get to the house, take bus #1 (stop terminus Beisson) or the Coutheron–Puyricard bus (stop Cézanne).

Cézanne was born in Vieil Aix at 28 rue de l'Opéra, but grew up in a house to the southwest of the city on the slopes of the hill known as Jas de Bouffon. The hill is now dominated by the **Vasarely Foundation**, 1 av Marcel-Pagnol (Mon–Fri 10am–1pm & 2–7pm, Sat and Sun 10am–7pm; ☎04.42.20.01.09), a building in black and white geometric shapes created by the Hungarian-born artist in 1976. To get there take bus #8 or #12 (stop Fondation Vasarely). The seven hexagonal spaces of the ground floor are each hung with dramatic tapestries and paintings, while upstairs sliding showcases reveal hundreds of drawings, designs, collages and paintings related to all Vasarely's favourite themes; most importantly, the collective and social nature of art. The Foundation has only recently reopened after a long period of closure after its then director was imprisoned for selling off works privately and pocketing the cash.

Collective cultural life is the basis of the **Cité du Livre** in the old match-making factory at 8–10 rue des Allumettes (Tues, Thurs & Fri noon–6pm, Wed & Sat 10am–6pm; free), a short way south of the gare routière. It includes libraries, a cinema, theatre space, a *videothèque d'art lyrique* (where you can watch just about any French opera performance) and any number of exhibitions. But the most stunning features are the two entrances at the ends of the conglomerate of buildings: giant books leaning together as if on a shelf, a wonderful example of French imaginative design flair. The whole complex testifies to a continuing determination to keep culture safe from the free play of market forces by creating beauty in public places. It would have made Vasarely very happy.

Eating and drinking

Aix is stuffed full of **restaurants** of every price and ethnic origin. Place des Cardeurs, just northwest of the hôtel de ville, is filled with restaurant, brasserie and café tables, while rue de la Verrerie, running south from place Hôtel de Ville, and place Ramus have an immense variety of Indian, Chinese and North African restaurants. Rue des Tanneurs is a good street for those with low budgets. The **café-brasseries** on cours Mirabeau are also tempting, and in between them you'll find cheaper snacks and pedlars of delicious fresh fruit juice.

Cafés and restaurants

L'Aligôte, 6 pl des Cardeurs (☎04.42.63.00.26). Specialities from southwest France from 150F.

De l'Archevêché, pl des Martyrs-de-la-Résistance (☎04.42.21.43.57). Good midday pasta, tapas and salads for under 80F.

Les Bacchanales, 10 rue Couronne (☎04.42.27.21.06). Salmon with *cèpes*, rabbit with marjoram; inventive cooking with menus from 95F. Open till 1am in summer.

Le Basilic Gourmand, 6 rue du Griffon (☎04.42.96.08.58). Classic Provençal food on an 80F midday menu, accompanied by exhibitions of paintings by local artists.

Le Bistrot Latin, 18 rue Couronne (☎04.42.38.22.88). *Escargot* and black olive sauce, profiteroles and honey, and garlic rabbit are three of the top dishes here. Midday menu 89F, evening from 118F. Closed Mon midday & Sun eve.

La Bodéga, cnr rues de la Treille/Muletiers (☎04.42.96.54.00). Spanish resto serving paella valencienne for around 150F. Fri & Sat only.

Le Clos de la Violette, 10 rue de la Violette (☎04.42.23.30.71). Aix's most renowned restaurant with dishes that might not sound very seductive – stuffed lamb's feet and *pieds et paquets* – but are in fact gastronomic delights. More obviously alluring are the puddings: a clafoutis of greengages and pistachios with peach sauce and a tart of melting dark chocolate. 185F menu midday, otherwise menus from 300F and à la carte from 450F. Closed Mon midday & Sun.

Les Deux Garçons, 53 cours Mirabeau. The erstwhile haunt of Camus is done up in faded 1900s style and still attracts a motley assortment of literati. Good brasserie food, but not cheap.

Café Le Grillon, 49 cours Mirabeau. One of the biggest and best brasseries on the cours with a 120F menu.

L'Hacienda, cnr rue Mérindol/pl des Cardeurs (☎04.42.27.00.35). A 60F midday menu including wine, with delicious hacienda beef à la carte served al fresco.

Le Jasmin, 6 rue de la Fonderie (☎04.42.38.05.89). Iranian food for around 100F. Closed Sat & Sun eve.

Khéops, 28 rue de la Verrerie (☎04.42.96.59.05). Egyptian cuisine featuring falafel, stuffed pigeon and gorgeous milk-based desserts. Menus from 120F.

Pizzaria Malta, 28 pl des Tanneurs (☎04.42.26.15.43). Nice atmosphere and cheap plonk to accompany the pizzas or pasta.

Le Montmartre, cnr of rues Verrerie and Marseillais (☎04.42.96.28.82). Varied dishes and good choice on cheap fixed menus.

Bar Tabac du Palais, cnr rue Manuel/pl des Prêcheurs. Small, pleasant bar from which to view the market.

Café de Paris, 41 cours Mirabeau (☎04.42.26.04.51). A classic, expensive café on the cours.

Pizza Chez Jo/Bar des Augustins, pl des Augustins (☎04.42.26.12.47). Cheap pizzas and traditional plats du jour; usually packed, but you won't have to wait long for a table.

Le Platanos, 13 rue Rifle-Rafle (☎04.42.21.33.19). Very cheap and popular Greek resto with menus under 100F.

Tay Lai, 16 bis rue Marseillais (☎04.42.23.53.79). Popular and reasonably priced Vietnamese restaurant.

Nightlife and entertainment

Surprisingly, Aix does not have the variety of theatre and dance that you can find in Marseille, but there are some good **pubs** with **live music**, excellent **jazz** venues, and **classical concerts** given in the city's churches. If you fancy a trip to the cinema, then try La Mazarin, 6 rue Laroque (☎04.42.26.99.85), an independent **cinema** where most foreign films are shown in their original language.

A selection of concerts and other mainstream cultural events are listed in *Le Mois à Aix*, available free from the tourist office; the best place for bookings and for more information is the FNAC book and record shop on place Forbin. The best time for Aix nightlife is during the summer **festivals** (see below) when much of the entertainment happens in the street.

Blue Note, 10 rue de la Fonderie (☎04.42.38.06.23). American bar-restaurant with live jazz, blues, folk and country music on Tuesday and Thursday.

Bugsy, 25 rue de la Verrerie (☎04.42.38.25.22). Pub with billiards and rock videos. Daily 6pm–2am.

Cité du Livre, 8–10 rue des Allumettes (☎04.42.25.98.65). Concerts, plays, dance, poetry readings and films.

La Fontaine d'Argent, 5 rue de La Fontaine-d'Argent (☎04.42.38.43.80). Café-theatre with a diverse programme including dance.

Hot Brass, chemin de la Plaine-des-Verguetiers, rte d'Eguilles-Célony (☎04.42.21.05.57). The best jazz club in Aix, with afternoon tea dances on Sunday from 3 to 8.30pm. Mon–Sat 10.30pm onwards. Entry 100F, including first drink.

Le Richelme, 24 rue de la Verrerie (☎04.42.23.49.29). Mainstream disco. Daily from 9pm.

Le Scat Club, 11 rue de la Verrerie (☎04.42.23.00.23). All kinds of jazz, rock, funk – the best live music venue in Vieil Aix; reasonable prices. Daily from 10pm.

Théâtre de la Fonderie, 14 cours St-Louis (☎04.42.63.10.11). New plays and dance.

Shopping

Aix's **markets** provide the greatest shopping pleasures (see box on p.183), but there are some good specialists. For English-language **books** try Paradox Bookstore, 15 rue du 4-Septembre; or Les Bouquinists Obscurs, 2 rue Boulégon, which, apart from selling an obscure selection of English books and comic books, also has second-hand tapes and records. More **music** is sold at Compact Club, 12 rue Gaston de Saporta. If you're

---

AIX FESTIVALS

For much of June and July, Vieil Aix is taken over by its music festivals and the accompanying street entertainers of the alternative scene; street theatre, rock concerts and impromptu gatherings turn the whole area into one long party. The main events are the **Aix en Musique**, a rock, jazz, experimental and classical music event running from mid-June to early July; the **Festival International Danse**, covering everything from classical to contemporary dance in the middle two weeks of July); and the **Festival International d'Art Lyrique et de Musique**, dedicated to opera and classical concerts in the last two weeks of July.

Tickets for the music festivals' mainstream events range from 80F to 890F: for the Aix en Musique festival, they are available from Espace Forbin, 3 place John-Rewald (☎04.42.21.69.69); for the Festival International d'Art Lyrique et de Musique from the Palais de l'Ancien Archevêché in Vieil Aix (☎04.42.17.34.34); those for the dance festival, for which several public rehearsals and performances are free, are available from the Espace Forbin, 3 place John-Rewald off cours Gambetta (☎04.42.63.06.75).

looking for French-language books, Vents du Sud, on place du Petit-Marché, is the best. **Santons**, the Provençal crèche figures, are produced and sold at Fouque, 63 cours Gambetta.

Some of the best shops around, however, are those specializing in food. If you like your **bread** fresh and warm, the Boulangerie-Pâtisserie on rue Tournefort is open around the clock, even on Christmas day, and sells pizzas, pastries and other snacks as well as bread. Chez Poulain, on the corner of rue des Tanneurs and rue Espariat, also sells wonderful bread and cakes. There is a fantastic selection of **cheeses** at Gérard Paul on rue Marseillais. Should you want to try the local **wines**, contact the Maison des Agricultures, 22 av Henri-Pontier (☎04.42.23.57.14), for information; they can also advise you on where you can buy **olive oil**. On the last weekend in July, the Coteaux d'Aix **wines** are celebrated with a fair on cours Mirabeau.

Chocolates and sweets are sold at Puyricard, 7 rue Rifle-Rafle; *calissons*, Aix's speciality almond sweets, can be found at Du Roi René, 7 rue Papassaudi.

Listings

Bike rental Cycle Naddeo, 54 av de Lattre de Tassigny (☎04.42.21.06.93; closed Sun & Mon); Cycles Zammit, 27 rue Mignet (☎04.42.23.19.53; closed Sun & Mon).

Car rental ADA Discount, av Henri-Mouret (☎04.42.52.36.36); Avis, 11 bd Gambetta (☎04.42.21.64.16); Budget, 16 av des Belges (☎04.42.38.37.36); Europcar, 55 bd de la République (☎04.42.27.83.00); National Citer, 724 av du Club Hippique (☎04.42.17.22.50).

Currency exchange American Express, 15 cours Mirabeau; Change d'Or, 22 rue Thiers. Automatic machines at most banks.

Emergencies ☎15; Centre Hospitalier, chemin de Tamaris (☎04.42.33.90.28); SOS Médecins (☎04.42.26.24.00); Urgences (☎04.42.26.66.00).

Laundry 60 rue Boulégon; rue de la Fonderie; 28 rue des Bernardines; 4 rue de la Treille.

Pharmacy For the name and address of a late-night pharmacy, ring the police on ☎04.42.26.31.96; or check the notice on any pharmacy's door.

Police Emergency ☎17; Av de l'Europe (☎04.42.93.97.00).

Post office 2 rue Lapierre, 13100 Aix.

Taxis ☎04.42.26.29.30, 04.42.27.62.12 or 04.42.21.61.61; 24hr service: ☎04.42.27.71.11.

Around Aix

If city life begins to pall, there is gorgeous countryside to be explored around Aix, particularly to the east, where you'll find **Cézanne**'s favourite local subject, the **Mont Ste-Victoire**, which he painted over fifty times, and west where he also often painted, along the **Arc River**. Around are the diverse pulls of **Puyricard**'s wine and chocolates, the ancient sites at **Oppidum d'Entremont** and a strange artist's château in **Vauvenargues**.

Mont Ste-Victoire and around

If you're interested in **climbing Mont Ste-Victoire**, 8km east of Aix, the northern approach is a little easier than that of the southern face, which has a sheer 500-metre drop, though it'll still require some determination. Don't underestimate the fierce sun either: avoid attempting the walk between about 11am and 3pm, especially in the summer months when you should always wear a hat, and bring suncream and a minimum of two litres of water per person. The path leaves the D10 just before Vauvenargues, after a parking bay called Les Cabassols. The round trip to the monumental **Cross of**

Provence and back takes around three to four hours, depending on fitness, and the path is steep and poorly marked towards the top. Once at the top of the ridge, at 945m – marked by a chapel and the cross that doesn't figure in any of Cézanne's pictures – serious hikers can follow the path east to the summit of the Ste-Victoire massif at **Pic des Mouches** (1011m), along some breathtakingly vertiginous cliff faces. Just beneath the Pic des Mouches on the north side is the **Gouffre du Garagaï** chasm, that was once rumoured, among other things, to be the bottomless pit into hell. The path branches to the north about 200m past the summit, and after about fifty minutes rejoins the road at the **Col des Portes** pass (a good alternative starting point for climbing the massif). Otherwise stay on the ridge and descend southwards to **Puyloubier** (about 15km from the cross).

Vauvenargues

Leaving Aix via bd des Poilus, the D10 road to Vauvenargues passes the lake and barrage of Bimont from where you can walk south past Mont Ste-Victoire to Le Tholonet. If you want to drive, the sixty-kilometre circuit round the mountain offers wonderful views. At peaceful **VAUVENARGUES**, a perfect, weather-beaten, red-shuttered four-teenth-century **Château**, bought by Picasso in 1958, stands just outside the village with nothing between it and the slopes of the mountain. **Picasso** lived there till his death in 1973, and is buried in the gardens, his grave adorned with his sculpture *Woman with a Vase*. The château, still owned by his step-daughter, is strictly private, and the otherwise friendly locals are taciturn when it comes to discussing the connection. If the village appeals you can **stay** at a chambre d'hôtes, c/o Jacqueline Thery, *La Jacquière*, chemin des Mattes (☎04.42.66.01.79; ③; closed Oct–April); or at the pleasant, small hotel, *Au Moulin de Provence*, 33 av des Maquisards (☎04.42.66.02.22, fax 04.42.66.01.21; ②), with views over Mont Ste-Victoire and Picasso's château, a terrace restaurant, and friendly owners.

Le Tholonet

The D17 south of Ste-Victoire skirts the edge of woods leading up to the defensive face of the mountain. There are two parking places with confusing maps of paths. Heading upwards you soon get views of Ste-Victoire, from this angle looking like a wave with surf about to break. Modern aqueducts pass overhead, the responsibility of the Société du Canal de Provence which has its headquarters in the Italianate seventeenth-century château in **LE THOLONET**. The grounds are used for open-air concerts during the Aix music festival, but the château is otherwise closed to the public.

At the main crossroads there's an inexpensive, fairly basic **hotel-restaurant** *Les Relais de Cézanne* (☎04.42.66.91.91; ②); opposite, there's a popular restaurant, *Chez Thome* (☎04.42.66.90.43), with outdoor tables under the trees and menus starting at 130F. On the east side of the village, by an old windmill, is a bronze relief of Cézanne on a stele. About 1km south of the village, on rte de largesse Campagne Régis, is a won-derful **restaurant**, *La Petite Auberge* (☎04.42.66.84.24; menu around 100F; closed Sun eve & Mon). For those with lots of cash to blow, there's the **hotel-restaurant** *Relais Sainte-Victoire* in Beaurecueil (☎04.42.66.94.98, fax 04.42.66.85.96; restaurant closed Mon, Fri midday & Sun eve; menus from 200F; ⑤). There's also the *Ste-Victoire* **camp-site** (☎04.42.66.91.31, fax 04.42.66.96.43) in Beaurecueil, which can be reached by bus from Aix.

East of Le Tholonet, you drive beneath the mighty face of the massif, passing the **Maison de Ste-Victoire** (daily 10am–7pm), a tourist centre with information and hik-ing maps as well as a boutique and a restaurant, and on to **Puyloubier**, where military enthusiasts might like to visit the French Foreign Legion's Pensioners' Château. The small **museum** (Tues–Sun 10am–noon & 2–5pm; free) has a fairly uninspiring display of uniforms and regalia, whilst there is also a ceramics workshop and wine cellar.

From here, the road continues through vineyards towards **Pourrières**, before twisting up a marvellous wooded road, and looping back round to Col des Portes and Vauvenargues.

North of Aix: Oppidum d'Entremont

Three kilometres north of Aix is the archeological site of the **Oppidum d'Entremont** (Mon & Wed–Sun 9am–noon & 2–6pm; free), once the chief settlement of one of the strongest confederations of indigenous people in Provence. Built in the second century BC, it was divided into two parts: the upper town, where it's assumed the leading fighters lived; and the lower town, for artisans and traders. The site lay on an important trade crossroads from Marseille to the Durance Valley and from Fréjus to the Rhône and was protected by curtain walls and towers, within which streets were laid out on a grid pattern. It was the Marseille merchants who finally persuaded the Romans to dispose of this irritant to their expanding business (see Musée Granet on p.185).

The plateau on which this Celtic-Ligurian stronghold was built is as interesting for its views over Aix and across to the dramatic Mont Ste-Victoire, as for the ancient layout marked by truncated walls but denuded of all other objects. Take av Pasteur out of Aix centre; then turn right after 2.5km just before you cross the N296; bus #14 also runs here from av Pasteur (direction Puyricard, stop Entremont), as does a special tour bus (every 30min) from the Crédit Agricole on cours Sextius.

Puyricard

Continuing north along the D14, you'll pass **L'Usine de Puyricard** on your right, just before you reach Puyricard village. Here at the creative base and factory of the best chocolates in France, the methods used are traditional and artisanal; the ingredients are the best-quality butter, cream, nuts and liqueurs without a trace of preservatives or artificial colouring. You can buy Puyricard chocolates in Aix, and all the main Provençal cities, but you might as well drop in to the factory if you're passing. The smell and the sight of all the varieties are overwhelmingly wonderful for any dedicated chocolate eater and though they cost around 280F a kilo, a small box won't break the bank.

PUYRICARD itself is a pleasant little village with a twelfth-century church. If you want to sample some of the local **wines**, the Domaine de St-Julien-les-Vignes (on the tiny road 3km northwest of Puyricard by the Canal de Verdon – marked on the map as St-Julien ferme; ☎04.42.92.10.02) is open for individual buyers from 1 to 7pm daily. Further north, near the banks of the Durance, the northern limit of the *appellation*, the **Château de Fonscolombe** in Le Puy Sainte-Réperarde (by appointment only; ☎04.42.61.89.62) produces excellent wine.

Roquefavour and Cabries

The Arc River, which runs south of Aix, and inspired Cézanne's *Grande Baigneuse*, can be followed westwards to the **AQUADUC DE ROQUEFAVOUR**. Alternatively, take the D64 from Jas de Bouffan, which is good cycling terrain and offers several wine *dégustation* stops, to reach Roquefavour. The valley steepens as you approach the three-tiered aqueduct, built to take Durance water to Marseille. Further downstream, by the junction of the D10 and D65, is the site of the **Oppidum de Roquepertuse** whose finds are displayed in Marseille's history museum.

CABRIES, 13km south of Aix off the road to Marseille, is a totally untouristy *village perché*, with a **château** built in the Dark Ages for the counts of Provence and lived in several centuries later by the artist **Edgar Mélik**, who bought it in 1934. He used to play the role of a fiendish count, filling the château with wolf-like dogs, playing his blood-red piano all night long, and painting demonic figures on the walls. The château, which contains works by Mélik as well as temporary exhibitions of other artists, is open to visitors (Mon & Wed–Sat 10am–noon & 3–6pm, Sun 3–6pm).

The Chaîne de la Ste-Baume

Marseille's suburbs extend relentlessly east along the highway and N8 corridor north of the Chine de St-Cyr. You reach **Aubagne** before you realize you've left Marseille, even though the landscape is now dominated by mountains on all sides. The range to the east is the **Chaîne de la Ste-Baume**, a sparsely populated region of rich forests and one of the least spoilt areas in the region. Once you're up on the plateau to the north, it's wonderful territory for walks and for bicycling, the woods, flowers and wildlife of the northern face showing a profusion rare in these hot latitudes. All of the area north to St-Maximin, south to **Signes**, west to **Gémenos** and east to **La Roquebrussanne** is protected. You are not allowed to camp in the woods or light fires, and a still extant royal edict forbids the picking of orchids.

For details of the numerous **footpaths**, including the GR9, GR98 and GR99, the best guide is Gorgeon-Luchesi's *Randonnées pédestres dans la Ste-Baume*, published by Edisud and available in local tourist offices.

Aubagne

With a triangle of *autoroutes* around it, **AUBAGNE** is an easy place to pass by. It's the headquarters of the French Foreign Legion and not a wildly attractive place, but it does have some saving graces. Its other claim to fame is as the birthplace of writer and film-maker Marcel Pagnol (1895–1974) and the setting for his tales. This makes Aubagne highly significant for the French, though the international success in the 1980s of Claude Berri's films of Pagnol's *Jean de Florette* and *Manon des Sources*, starring Gérard Depardieu and Emmanuelle Béart, have widened the appeal. In *Jean de Florette* an out-sider inherits a property on the arid slopes of the Garlaban mountain, whose rocky crest rears like a stegasaurus's back, north of Aubagne. The local peasants who have blocked its spring watch him die from the struggle of fetching water, delighted that his new scientific methods won't upset their market share.

The soil around Aubagne is very good for flowers, fruit and vegetables and, on Tuesday, Thursday, Saturday and Sunday mornings, you can take your pick of the edible produce from the excellent **market** stalls on cours Voltaire. The soil also makes excellent pottery; hence the town's further renown, for *santons* and ceramics, and the only School of Ceramics in Provence. From mid-July to the end of August, and in December, a huge daily **market of ceramics** and **santons** takes place on the central street of cours Maréchal Foch. At any time of the year you can visit potters' workshops in the Vieille Ville to the east of cours Voltaire: rue F-Mistral beyond the hôtel de ville is a good street to try. Other interesting displays of the art can be found in the **Ateliers Thérèse Neveu** (Tues–Sun 9am–noon & 2–6pm; free), in the cour de Clastre behind the Vieille Ville's St-Saveur church.

The most impressive display of *santons* is to be found at **Le Petit Monde de Marcel Pagnol** (July & Aug Tues–Sun 9am–12.30pm & 2.30–6pm; Feb–June & Sept–Nov Tues–Sun 9am–noon & 2–6pm; free) in a diorama on Esplanade de Gaulle opposite the helpful **tourist office** (Mon–Sat 9am–noon & 2–6pm; ☎04.42.03.49.98). Pagnol's finely detailed little figures play out their parts on a model of the local district, complete with windmills, farms and villages; it might sound twee, but it isn't because these characters are no angels. From December to mid-January, a Christmas crib with figures repre-senting all the traditional trades and occupations replaces Pagnol's world. For real Pagnol fans, the tourist office supplies a map of all the places in his stories – check if any areas are closed in summer due to risk of fires – and offers a two-and-a-half-hour coach tour (July & Aug Wed & Sat 4pm).

Gémenos to Plan-d'Aups

GÉMENOS, 3km east of Aubagne, has a beautiful seventeenth-century château as its **Hôtel de Ville** and is a tempting place to stop. There's a good **restaurant**, *Le Baron Brisse*, 48 chemin Jouques (☎04.42.32.00.60; menus from 145F; closed Sun, Mon, late July & early Aug) and several good pâtisseries: try the Pan Doré on the place Georges-Clémenceau. For **accommodation**, there's a fantastic luxury hotel, the *Relais de la Magdeleine* (☎04.42.32.20.16, fax 04.42.32.02.26; meals from 250F; ⑦; closed Dec to mid-March); set in a lovely, vine-covered eighteenth-century manor house in a park designed by Le Nôtre, it lies on the N396 rte d'Aix on the way out of town. Two minutes' walk further along the N396 is a less expensive option, the friendly *Le Provence* (☎04.42.32.20.55; ②), which also has studios for up to four people.

From Gémenos the D2 follows the narrow valley of St-Pons, past an open-air municipal theatre cut into the rock and the **Parc Naturel de St-Pons** with beech, horn-bean, ash and maple trees around the ruins of a thirteenth-century Cistercian abbey, before beginning the zigzagging ascent to the Espigoulier pass. A footpath beyond the park soon links to the GR98 which climbs directly up the Ste-Baume and then follows the ridge with breathtaking views.

At **PLAN-D'AUPS** the dramatic climb levels out to a forested plateau running parallel to the ridge of Ste-Baume, which cuts across the sky like a massively fortified wall. A comfortable small **hotel**, *Lou Pèbre d'Aï* (☎04.42.04.50.42, fax 04.42.62.55.52; ③) in the quartier Ste-Madeleine, offers just about the only **restaurant** in this village of scattered buildings and one tiny Romanesque church. **Tourist information** is available from the *mairie* (office hours; ☎04.42.04.50.10).

Four kilometres on from Plan-d'Aups is the starting point for a **pilgrimage** based on Provençal mythology, or simply a walk up to the peaks. The myth takes over from the sea-voyage arrival in Stes-Maries-de-la-Mer of Mary Magdalene, Mary Salomé, Mary Jacobé and St-Maximin (see p.109). **Mary Magdalene**, for some unexplained reason completely at odds with the mission of spreading the gospel, gets transported by angels to a cave just below the summit of Ste-Baume. There she spends 33 years, with occasional angel-powered outings up to the summit, before being flown to St-Maximin-de-la-Ste-Baume (see below) to die.

The **paths** up from the *Hôtellerie*, a roadside pilgrimage centre run by Dominican friars and open for prayers or information (daily 9am–6pm; ☎04.42.04.50.21), are dotted with oratories, calvaries and crosses. The *grotte* itself has been closed due to dangerous rock falls, with wrangling between municipal and national authorities about who should pay for the necessary stabilization work. For information regarding its current status, phone the *Hôtellerie*. If open, you'll find the *grotte* is suitably sombre, while the path beyond to the **St-Pilon summit** makes you wish for some of Mary's winged pilots.

East to La Roquebrussane

The road east from Plan-d'Aups crosses the range through miles of unspoiled forest. The groves of spindly, stunted oaks and beeches have exerted a mystical pull since ancient times, and it is believed they were once a sacred Druidical forest. Around the village of **MAZAUGUES**, just before you reach La Roquebrussane, you pass huge, nineteenth-century covered stone wells, built to hold ice which could then be transported on early summer nights down to Marseille or Toulon; an industry which once gave livelihoods to many an inhabitant of the Ste-Baume. From Mazaugues the GR99 takes you, after an initial steep climb, on a gentle three- to four-hour walk down to Signes (it also links halfway with the GR98 from Ste-Baume); while continuing east by road will bring you to **LA ROQUEBRUSSANE**, where winged pilots can be arranged, after a fashion, in the form of **gliders**, quartier Le Riolet (☎04.94.86.97.52). There's also a large Saturday food **market** here and a pleasant **hotel**, *La Loube* (☎04.94.86.81.36, fax 04.94.86.86.79; ④).

Méounes-les-Montrieux

Continuing south by road to follow the southern face of the range, you pass through **MÉOUNES-LES-MONTRIEUX**, with a couple of **hotels**, including the small, welcoming *Hôtel de France* on place de l'Église (☎04.94.33.95.92; ②), and three **campsites** of which the best is *Camping Club Gavaudan* (☎04.94.48.95.34), 1.5km from the village at the Château de Gavaudan. The *Auberge de la Source* **restaurant** on the rte de Brignoles (☎04.94.33.98.08; menus from 145F) serves trout from its own pond in a beautiful garden.

Signes

From Méounes you can follow the lovely Gapeau stream which has its source just before **SIGNES**. This is yet another appealing little village, a place where palm trees and white roses grow around the war memorial, where the clock tower and fountains are at least five hundred years old, and where the people make their living from wine, olives, cereals and market gardening, or, in the case of two small enterprises, biscuits and nougat. At Lou Goustetto on the main road as you leave the village westwards, you can sample biscuits in a multitude of completely natural flavours that include Provençal herbs and nuts, lemon, cinnamon, cocoa and honey. They are hard and unsweetened and excellent to munch as you climb the Ste-Baume. The other delicious edible comes from Nougat Fouque, 2 rue Louis-Lumière, a honey overdose that manages not to stick to your teeth.

The village has a **tourist office** of sorts in the *mairie* (office hours; ☎04.94.90.88.03) on place du Marché where the Thursday **market** takes place, and there's a **campsite**, *des Promenades*, on the edge of the village on the road from Méounes (☎04.94.90.88.12). There are a few small **hotels**, the best of which is the *Auberge des Espéréguins* (☎04.94.90.87.35; ③) on the rte de Méones, but it's often full; as well as some gîtes d'étape (ask at the *mairie*). There's also a solid local **restaurant**, *Le Chaudron* at 6 rue Bourgade.

St-Maximin-de-la-Ste-Baume

Heading north from Chaîne-de-la-Ste-Baume, the first place of any interest is **ST-MAXIMIN-DE-LA-STE-BAUME**. Here, in 1279, the count of Provence claimed to have found the crypt with the relics of Mary Magdalene and Saint Maximin hidden by local people during a Saracen raid. The count started the construction of a **basilica** and **monastery** on place de l'Hôtel-de-Ville, which finally took their present shape in the fifteenth century, and have since seen lavish decoration of stone, wood, gold, silk and oil paint added, particularly during the reign of Louis XIV, one of many French kings to make the pilgrimage to the *grotte* and the crypt.

There is, therefore, plenty to look at in the **basilica** (daily: summer 8am–7pm; winter 8–11.45am & 2–6pm), from the beautifully detailed wood panelling in the choir and the paintings on the nave walls, to the wonderfully sculptured fourth-century sarcophagi and the utterly grotesque skull once venerated as that of Mary Magdalene, encased in a glass helmet framed by a gold neck and hair in the **crypt**. The building itself is a heavy Gothic affair, unusual for Provence, but the thirteenth-century **cloisters** and chapterhouse of the monastery (April–Oct Mon–Fri 10am–noon & 2–6pm; Sun 2–7pm; Nov–March Mon–Fri 10am–noon & 2–6pm; free) are much more delicate. Look down the well to see the escape route that the Dominican friars used on several occasions in the sixteenth century when the monastery was placed under siege. Today, the monastery is the setting for classical concerts (call ☎04.94.78.01.93 for details).

To the south of the church a covered passageway leads into the arcaded rue Colbert, a **former Jewish ghetto**. All the medieval streets of St-Maximin with their uniform tiled roofs at anything but uniform heights have considerable charm, and there's a reasonable choice of restaurants, and shops selling the work of local artisans.

Practicalities

The **tourist office** is in the hôtel de ville next to the basilica (daily: 9.15am–12.30pm & 2–6.45pm; ☎04.94.59.84.59). If you walk west along rue Général-de-Gaulle from the basilica you'll find a well-run, friendly **hotel**, *Plaisance*, at 20 place Malherbe (☎04.94.78.16.74, fax 04.94.78.18.39; ④), in a grand town house with spacious rooms; while the newly converted *Couvent Royal* on place Jean-Salusse (☎04.94.86.55.66, fax 04.94.86.82.82; ③), is a particularly atmospheric option, with clean, excellent-value rooms, some looking out over the cloister itself. The local three-star **campsite**, *Provençal* (☎04.94.78.16.97; closed mid-Oct to March), is 3km out along the chemin de Mazaugues, the road to Marseille. **Cafés** and **brasseries** congregate on place Malherbe, the present-day hub of St-Maximin.

Brignoles

BRIGNOLES, 16km east of St-Maximin, is a good base for a night or two's stay. For years the town made a living from its quarries, providing bauxite for the aluminium works in Marseille and Gardanne. Their near exhaustion and the emergence of foreign competition meant closure and major redundancies, but the place still has plenty of life in its centre, alongside a medieval quarter full of quiet, shaded squares and old facades with faded painted ads and flowering window boxes.

At the southern end of the old quarter is a thirteenth-century summer residence of the counts of Provence, now adapted as the **Musée du Pays Brignolais** (April–Sept Wed–Sat 9am–noon & 2.30–6pm, Sun 10am–noon & 3–6pm; Oct–March Wed–Sat 10am–noon & 2.30–5pm, Sun 10am–noon & 3–5pm; 20F). This fascinating, old-style museum dips into every aspect of local life that the town is proud of: from one of the oldest palaeo-Christian sarcophagi ever found to a reinforced concrete boat made by the inventor of concrete in 1840. There's a statue of a saint whose navel has been visibly deepened by the hopeful hands of misguided infertile women, a reconstruction of a bauxite mine, a crèche of *santons*, a fine collection of *ex voto* paintings, some Impressionist Provençal landscapes by Frédéric Montenard and the chapel of the palace, cluttered with ancient religious statuary from around the area. Climb the tower for the best view of the town and its surroundings.

Rue des Lanciers, with fine old houses where the rich Brignolais used to live, leads up from place des Comtes-de-Provence to **St-Sauveur**, a twelfth-century church in which, on the left-hand side, you can see the remains of an older church. Behind St-Sauveur the stepped street of rue Saint-Esprit runs down to rue Cavaillon and place Carami, the café-lined central square of the modern town.

Practicalities

Buses stop at place St-Louis. The excellent, friendly new **tourist office** (June–Sept Mon–Sat 9am–12.30pm & 2–8pm, Sun 10am–noon & 2.30–7pm; Oct–May Mon–Sat

9am–12.30pm & 2–7pm; ☎04.94.72.04.21) is on the north side of the River Carami by the carrefour de l'Europe roundabout. **Hotels** in Brignoles are very good value: try *Le Provence*, place du Palais de Justice (☎04.94.69.01.18; ②), or the *Hôtel des Ouvriers* on rue Ste-Ursule (☎ & fax 04.94.69.10.64; ①). In addition, there's a *Formule I* in the Ratan industrial quarter signed off the N7 to the west of town (☎04.94.69.45.05; ①). The two-star municipal **campsite** is 1km down the rte de Nice (☎04.94.69.20.10; closed mid-Oct to mid-March).

There's also a profusion of **eating and drinking** stops, none of which is very expensive. On place Carami you can get meals or snacks at *Le Central* bar-brasserie and the *Café de l'Univers,* and ice creams and cakes at *Treand. Le Pourquoi Pas* on rue Cavaillon (☎04.94.69.00.76; evenings only) serves pizzas and couscous, and does takeaway. *La Gousse d'Ail*, at 7 rue Louis-Maître (☎04.94.59.28.92), makes good-value Provençal dishes; while *Les Romarins*, at 5 rue St-Esprit (☎04.94.59.20.99), is a good, family-run place serving filling French fare prepared with great care. Across the bridge from the tourist office at 56 rue Barbaroux, *Lou Crespeu* (☎04.94.69.33.43; closed Sun midday & Mon) makes delicious, inexpensive crêpes – try the buckwheat *galettes de sarrasin* with any of the crêpe fillings.

For summer evening entertainment, you could check out the **open-air theatre** in an olive grove 3km south of town on the rte de Camps-la-Source (☎04.94.80.81.38) which puts on classical concerts, jazz, theatre and variety acts from late June to late August.

Cassis

It's hard to imagine the little fishing port of **CASSIS**, on the main coast road south from Marseille, as a busy industrial harbour in the mid-nineteenth century, trading with Spain, Italy and Algeria. Its fortunes had declined by the time Dérain, Dufy and other Fauvist artists started visiting at the turn of the century. In the 1920s Virginia Woolf stayed while working on *To the Lighthouse* and later Winston Churchill used to come to paint. These days it's packed out every summer, and the port bustles with activity at night: stalls sell artisans' handicrafts, guitarists busk round the port, and a smell of chip fat lingers in the air. But many people still rate Cassis the best resort this side of St-Tropez, its inhabitants most of all.

Arrival, information and accommodation

Buses from Marseille arrive at place Montmorin between the port and the beach, but the **gare SNCF** is 3km out of town with no bus connection. There are two **tourist offices**, a seasonal one on the port (July & Aug 10am–1pm & 3–10.30pm) and the main one on place Baragnon just south of av Victor-Hugo, the main street leading to the port (July to mid-Sept daily 9am–7.30pm; rest of year Mon–Sat 10am–1pm & 2–6pm, Sun 9am–12.30pm; ☎04.42.01.71.17). **Bikes** can be rented from Roue Libre (☎04.42.01.06.24) on quai St-Pierre.

Hotels

Le Clos de Arômes, 10 rue Paul-Mouton (☎04.42.01.71.84, fax 04.42.01.31.76). Charming, quiet hotel with a lovely garden. Closed Oct–April. ⑤.

Le Golfe, 3 place du Grand Carnot (☎04.42.01.00.21, fax 04.42.01.92.08). In the middle of all the bustle, overlooking the port. Closed Nov–March. ④.

Le Grand Jardin, 2 rue P-Eydin (☎04.42.01.70.10, fax 04.42.01.33.75). Close to the port and not bad for the price. ④.

Joli Bois, rte de la Gineste (☎04.42.01.02.68). Just off the main road to Marseille, 3km from Cassis. A bargain but it has only ten rooms, so it's best to book ahead. Half board only in high season. ②.

Laurence, 8 rue de l'Arène (☎04.42.01.88.78). Close to the port and market and the cheapest rooms in town. Closed mid-Nov to mid-March. ③.

Les Roches Blanches, av des Calanques (☎04.42.01.09.30, fax 04.42.01.94.23). Perfect position overlooking the bay with terraces and a pine wood leading down to the water. ⑧.

Le Commerce, 1 rue de Ste-Clair (☎04.42.01.09.10, fax 04.42.01.14.17). Next to the port and one of the least expensive options. Closed mid-Nov to mid-Jan. ③.

Hostel and campsite

HI youth hostel, *La Fontasse* (☎04.42.01.02.72). In the hills above the *calanques* west of Cassis and accessible only by foot. From the D559 (bus stop Les Calanques), a road leads down towards the Col de la Gardiole; at the point where it becomes a track, take the left fork, and after another 2km you'll find the hostel. The facilities are basic, but if you want to explore this wild, uninhabited stretch of limestone heights, the people running it will advise you enthusiastically. To get to Cassis you can descend to the *calanques* and walk along the coast (about 1hr). Reception 8–10am & 5–11pm.

Les Cigales (☎04.42.01.07.34). Campsite just off the D559 from Marseille before av de la Marne turns down into Cassis, 1km from the port. Closed mid-Nov to mid-March.

The Town

The white cliffs hemming it in and the value of its vineyards on the slopes above have stopped Cassis becoming a relentless sprawl; instead the modern development is all a bit toytown. Portside posing and drinking aside, there's not much to do except sunbathe and look up at the ruins of the town's medieval **Castle**. It was built in 1381 by the counts of Les Baux and refurbished this century by Monsieur Michelin, the authoritarian boss of the family tyres and guides firm, whose granddaughter is now the proprietor.

Cassis has a small **museum** (summer Wed, Thurs & Sat 3.30–6.30pm; winter 2.30–5.30pm; free) in the eighteenth-century presbytery on rue Xavier d'Authier just behind the tourist office. It has a bit of everything: nineteenth-century paintings and photographs of Cassis and Marseille, old furniture and costumes, Roman amphorae, and an anglophile curator who will give you an enthusiastic guided tour.

The favoured tourist pastime, though, is to take a **boat trip to the calanques** (45–80F), the long, narrow, deep, fjord-like inlets that have cut into the limestone cliffs. Several companies operate from the port, but check if they let you off or just tour in and out, and be prepared for rough seas. If you're feeling energetic, you can take the well-marked **footpath** from the rte des Calanques behind the western beach; it's about a ninety-minute walk to the furthest and best inlet, **En Vau**, where you can climb down rocks to the shore. Intrepid pine trees find root-holds, and sunbathers find ledges on

---

THE COSQUER CAVE

In 1991, **Henri Cosquer**, a diver from Cassis, discovered paintings and engravings of animals, painted handprints and finger tracings in a cave between Marseille and Cassis, whose sole entrance is a long, sloping tunnel which starts 37m under the sea. The cave would have been accessible from dry land no later than the end of the last ice age and carbon dating has shown that the oldest work of art here was created around 27,000 years ago. Over a hundred animals have been identified, including seals, auks, horses, ibex, bisons, chamois, red deer and a giant deer known only from fossils. Fish are also featured along with sea creatures that might be jellyfish. Most of the finger tracings are done in charcoal and have fingertips missing, possibly to convey a sign language by bending fingers.

Though the cave is unlikely ever to be made accessible to the public, Marseille's tourist office has run an exhibition on the cave two years running and may do so again.

the chaotic white cliffs. The water is deep blue and swimming between the vertical cliffs is an experience not to be missed.

Eating and drinking

Sea urchins accompanied by the delicious, crisp Cassis white wine are the speciality here. **Restaurant** tables are in abundance along the portside on quai des Baux, quai Calandal and quai Barthélemy; prices vary but the best bet is to follow your nose, and seek out the most enticing fish smells. The authentic Provençal ratatouille and freshly caught fish at *Chez Gilbert*, 19 quai Baux (☎04.42.01.71.36; 110F menu; closed Tues eve & Wed out of season), are hard to beat. *Nino*, on quai Barthélemy (☎04.42.01.74.32; menus from 130F; closed Sun eve & Mon out of season), serves pasta, bouillabaisse and wonderful grilled fish. *Le Romano*, 15 quai Barthélemy (☎04.42.01.08.16; menus from 120F), has a delicious fricassée of scallops and langoustines. The most beautiful gourmet restaurant is *La Presqu'île*, on rte des Calanques in the quartier de Port-Miou, overlooking both the *calanques* and the bay of Cassis and offering exquisite fish dishes and traditional Provençal fare (☎04.42.01.03.77; menus from 250F; booking essential; closed Sun eve & Mon). For **drinking**, the *Bar Canaille*, on the corner of quai Calandal and quai des Baux, has the best *terrasse*, under the shade of a plane tree.

Cassis **wines**, from grapes grown on the slopes above the D559, are very special. Mistral described the white as "shining like a limpid diamond, tasting of the rosemary, heather and myrtle that covers our hills". If you arrive by train you can stop off at two **vineyards** on your way down the D1: the Domaine des Quatres Vents (☎04.42.01.01.12) and Clos d'Albizzi (☎04.42.01.11.43). There are more along the D41 which loops east from the station, and along the D559 towards La Ciotat; the tourist office can supply a full list. For **picnic food** to go with the wine, head for the **market**, held around rue de l'Arène south of the port on Wednesday and Friday mornings.

The Corniche des Crêtes

If you have a car or motorbike, the **Corniche des Crêtes** road south from Cassis to La Ciotat (the D41a) is definitely a ride not to be missed. From Cassis the chemin St-Joseph turns off av de Provence, climbs at a maximum gradient to the Pas de la Colle, then follows the inland slopes of the Montagnes de la Canaille. Much of the landscape is often blackened by fire but every so often the road loops round a break in the chain to give you dramatic views over the sea. You can walk it as well in about three and a half hours: the path, beginning from *Pas de la Colle*, takes a precipitous straighter line passing the road at each outer loop.

La Ciotat and around

The shipbuilding town of **LA CIOTAT** has been most notable for its politics in recent years, having elected a Communist mayor at the head of a united left list in 1995. Since then, the mayor has been trying hard to get the shipyards – which closed in 1989 – open again, something that is being seriously considered at the regional level, but has still not happened here. You might not associate the building of 300,000-ton oil and gas tankers with the pleasures of a Mediterranean resort, but it is one of the surprising charms of **La Ciotat** that the **Vieux Port**, below a golden stone Vieille Ville, shelters the dramatic massive cranes and derricks of the shipyards as well as the fishing fleet and the odd yacht or two. It would be an enormous boost to the town if the changing shifts at the docks were once again to be an integral part of the same quayside scene as the pavement cafés and restaurants, and fishermen mending their nets.

In 1895 **Auguste and Louis Lumière** filmed the first ever moving pictures in La Ciotat and in 1904 went on to develop the first colour photographs. The town celebrates its relatively unknown status as the cradle of cinema with an annual **film festival** in mid-June.

Arrival, information and accommodation

The **gare SNCF** is 5km from the town centre but a bus meets every train and gets you to the Vieux Port in around thirty minutes. The Vieille Ville and port look out across the Baie de la Ciotat, whose inner curve provides the beaches and resort-style life of La Ciotat's beachside extension, **La Ciotat Plage**. The **gare routière** is at the end of bd Anatole-France by the Vieux Port right beside the **tourist office** (June–Sept Mon–Sat 9am–8pm, Sun 10am–1pm; Oct–May Mon–Sat 9am–noon & 2.30–6pm; ☎04.42.08.61.32). **Bikes** can be rented from Cycle Lleba at 1 av F-Mistral (☎04.42.83.60.30) and Cyclazur on av F-Gassion (☎04.42.08.90.74).

Hotels

Beaurivage, 1 bd Beaurivage (☎04.42.83.09.68). The more expensive rooms have sea views. ③.
Bellevue, 3 bd Guérin (☎04.42.71.86.01). Small, peeling hotel overlooking the port. ②.
Best Western Miramar, 3 bd Beaurivage (☎ & fax 04.42.83.33.79). Possibly the best hotel in the town, set amid pines by the sea. Half board compulsory in summer. ⑤.
La Marine, 1 av F-Gassion (☎04.42.08.35.11). Just above the Vieille Ville; modern, very pleasant place with little balconies. ②.
Hôtel de la Rotonde, 44 bd de la République (☎04.42.08.67.50, fax 04.42.08.45.21). Near the old port and good value. ③.

Camping

Belle-Plage, 14 av de Fonsainte (☎04.42.83.14.72). Take bus #4 (direction gare SNCF, stop Fonsainte) to reach this three-star site by the sea. Closed Oct–March.
St-Jean, 30 av St-Jean (☎04.42.83.13.01, fax 04.42.71.46.41). Take bus #4 (direction gare SNCF, stop St-Jean Village). Three-star site by the sea, the closest one to the centre. Closed Oct–March.

The Town

The resplendently ornate nineteenth-century former *mairie* at the end of quai Ganteaume now houses the **Musée Ciotaden** (June–Sept Wed–Mon 4–7pm; Oct–May 3–6pm; 15F), charting the history of the town back to its foundation by the ancient Greeks of Marseille when local shipbuilding began. Further down the quay is the

---

FILM IN LA CIOTAT

La Ciotat's train station has a commemorative plaque to the film *L'Arrivée d'un train en gare de La Ciotat*, which was one of a dozen or so films, including *Le déjeuner de bébé* and the comedy *L'Arroseur arrosé*, shown in the Château Lumière in September 1895. The audience jumped out of their seats as the image of the steam train hurtled towards them. Three months later the reels were taken to Paris for the capital's citizens to witness cinema for the first time.

The town's **Festival du Cinéma** is a public and affordable event which takes place mid-June, usually revolving around a particular theme or genre. The venues include the Eden Cinema and the Chapelle des Pénitents Bleus. A full programme for the festival, and films, theatre and music throughout the summer, is obtainable from the tourist office.

seventeenth-century church, **Notre-Dame-de-l'Assomption**, with its Baroque facade and a striking early-seventeenth-century painting by André Gaudion of the *Descent of the Cross* alongside modern works of art.

To the east along the seafront, on the corner of bd A-France and bd Jean-Jaurès, is the **Eden Cinema**, the world's oldest movie house. Further on, at plage Lumière, is a solid 1950s monument to Auguste and Louis Lumière who screened the world's first films in the château owned by their father which once stood at the top end of allée Lumière (see box on p.198). The brothers appear again in a mural on the covered market halls which house the modern cinema, visible as you walk up rue Régnier from bd Guérin north of the port.

The streets of the Vieille Ville, apart from rue Poilus, are uneventful and a bit run down. If you feel the need to do something you can take a **boat trip** from quai de Gaulle out to the tiny offshore **Île Verte**, where a small restaurant, the *Relais des Pêcheurs*, serves pizzas, grills and baked fish. Both *Vedette Voltigeur* (☎04.42.83.11.44) and *Vedette Monte Cristo* (☎04.42.71.53.32) make the 15-minute crossing to Île Verte daily; while *Vedette Provence* (☎04.42.08.63.55) makes trips to the *calanques* of Cassis and Marseille from quai Ganteaume.

Alternatively, you could explore the contorted rocks beyond the shipyards that the city's founders named "the eagle's beak" and which are now protected as the **Parc du Mugel** (daily: June–Sept 8am–8pm; Oct–May 9am–6pm). A path leads up from the entrance through overgrown vegetation and past scooped vertical hollows to a narrow terrace overlooking the sea. The cliff face looks like the habitat of some gravity-defying, burrowing beast rather than the erosions of wind and sea. To get there, take bus #3 (direction La Garde, stop Mugel); cars are allowed in the park only if providing access for the disabled.

If you continue on bus #3 to Figuerolles you can reach the **Anse de Figuerolles** *calanque* down the avenue of the same name, and its neighbour, the **Gameau**. Both have pebbly beaches and a completely different dominant colour from the *calanques* of Cassis.

Eating, drinking and entertainment

La Ciotat's **restaurants** are not gastronomically renowned, though *Coquillages Franquin*, at 13 bd Anatole-France (☎04.42.83.59.50), serves perfectly respectable fish dishes despite its unfortunate location by a petrol station. There are plenty of **cafés** and **brasseries** on the quays: *L'Escalet* has a very cheap fixed menu; *Le Goéland* has omelettes and Breton crêpes; and there's an ample selection of **beers** at the *Bar Continental*. The *Bar à Tin* and *L'Entracte Bar* overlooking the Cinema Lumière and the Tuesday market on place E-Gras are pleasant places to drink. Also on place E-Gras, the Atelier Convergences gives **jazz concerts** every Friday evening.

There's also a Sunday **market** on the quays. The main shopping street is rue des Poilus running back from the port. Lou Pecadou, a fishmonger's at no. 20, sells paella and other fish dishes from huge iron pans, and, if you've run out of reading matter, Wiesgrill newsagent's at no. 23 has a selection of second-hand English thrillers.

Les Lecques and St-Cyr

Across La Ciotat bay are the fine sand beaches and unremarkable family resort of **LES LECQUES**, an offshoot from the Vieille Ville of **ST-CYR-SUR-MER** behind. The one reminder of the far past here dates back to Caesar and Pompey's contest for the control of Marseille. The decisive naval battle, which Caesar won, took place near a town called Taureontum, whose precise location is unknown. On the rte de la Madrague at the east end of the bay are the remains of two **Roman villas**, dated first century AD. With three extant mosaics, patches of frescoes, a couple of interesting sarcophagi, numerous beautiful Greek and Roman vases and other household paraphernalia, the villas form the **Musée de Taureontum** (June–Sept Mon & Wed–Sun 3–7pm; Oct–May Sat & Sun only 2–5pm; 5F).

St-Cyr has two sites to detain you briefly: the small **Centre d'Art Sébastien** on bd Jean-Jaurès (June–Sept Mon & Wed–Sun 10am–noon & 3–7pm; Oct–May Mon & Wed–Sat 2.30–5.30pm, Sun 10am–noon & 2.30–5.30pm; 15F during temporary exhibitions, otherwise free), which displays the paintings and tender terracotta statues of this Parisian-born artist and friend of Picasso in a beautifully restored former caper storehouse; and a miniature, golden Statue of Liberty on the place de Portalis, sculpted by Bartholdi, the artist who created its better-known sister. Beyond these, the attractions are St-Cyr's **vineyards**, which belong to the excellent Bandol *appellation*. One of the best reds comes from the Château des Baumelles, a seventeenth-century manor house just out of St-Cyr to the right off the Bandol road, which can be visited by appointment only (☎04.94.26.46.59). The Domaine du Cagueloup on the D66 towards La Cadière d'Azur (Mon–Fri 8am–noon & 2–7pm; ☎04.94.26.15.70) has open *dégustations*. St-Cyr also has a food **market** on Sunday.

The **gare SNCF** lies midway between St-Cyr-sur-Mer and Les Lecques; from the station it is a twenty-minute walk down to Les Lecques. The **tourist office**, which caters for both towns, is on place de l'Appel du 18 Juin, off av du Port in Les Lecques (June to mid-Sept Mon–Sat 9am–7pm, Sun 10am–1pm & 3–7pm; rest of year Mon–Sat 9am–noon & 2–6pm; ☎04.94.26.73.73).

For **hotels**, the very small *Beau Séjour*, 34 av de la Mer, Les Lecques (☎04.94.26.54.06; ④; closed Jan to mid-June), offers some of the cheapest rooms to be found, or there's the comfortable *Grand Hôtel*, 24 av du Port, Les Lecques (☎04.94.26.23.01, fax 04.94.26.10.22; ⑥; closed Nov to mid-April), with a large garden leading down to the sea. Less expensive places can be found up the hill in St-Cyr, such as the *Auberge Le Clos Fleurie*, at 27 av du Gén-de-Gaulle near the train station (☎04.94.26.27.46; ②); and the *Hôtel de France* on place Portalis (☎04.94.26.22.55; ②), in the centre of town. Les Lecques has a large three-star **campsite**, *Les Baumelles* (☎04.94.26.21.27; closed Nov–Feb), on the beach right in the centre of the resort.

For a wide choice of **restaurants** try av du Port along the seafront. Alternatively, to find somewhere secluded to picnic you could explore the coastal path, which runs from La Madrague at the east end of Les Lecques' beach down to the Pointe du Déffend without passing a single house, and then on to Bandol (3hr 30min). To the east of Pointe du Déffend, on the calanque de Port-d'Alon, there's a gorgeous fish **restaurant**, *La Calanque* (☎04.94.26.20.08; menus from 160F; closed Tues).

Bandol and around

Continuing south on the coastal road to Toulon, the next stop is **BANDOL**, a smallish, unpretentious resort, rightly proud of its wines. Vineyards have kept much of its hinterland free of new building but the approaches to the town are a rash of cupboard houses, the hill above the centre is sliced by bands of condominiums, and bulldozers lurk at the ready by the patches of undeveloped land that forest fires have cleared. Bandol has some cheap accommodation on offer, as well as all the usual expensive accoutrements of casino, discotheques, cocktail bars and water sports, and it's a good coastal base from which to explore Toulon. Exploring the coast, the wines and the hinterland are the main attractions, however, along with the **Île de Bendor**, an offshore island, which, suitably enough, houses France's largest exposition of wines, spirits and alcohols.

The Île de Bendor

Île de Bendor was an uninhabited rocky island when it was bought by the rags-to-riches pastis man **Paul Ricard** in the 1950s, and today the atmosphere is somewhat surreal, with unlikely statues, an uneasy discrepancy between the people and the place, and a 1950s architectural style severely stamped on most of its buildings. Ricard himself died in 1997, but his family still own the place. Boats leave for the island from quai de l'Hôtel-de-Ville on the port. The crossing takes about seven minutes (June–Sept daily 7am–1am; Oct–May daily 8am–8.30pm; 26F return).

From March to the end of June, and from September to mid-November the island is taken over by business conferences and receptions. For the rest of the year activities revolve around the diving school, Club Nautique and Fondation Paul Ricard. The **Fondation** teaches dance and drawing, gives new artists a chance to show and sell their works, and hosts monthly exhibitions in the **Espace Culturel Paul Ricard** (Mon & Wed–Sun 10am–noon & 2.15–6pm). The **Club Nautique** organizes yacht races and windsurfing championships, and runs a hostel and a sailing school. The **diving school** (☎04.94.29.55.12, fax 04.94.29.83.34), where most of France's customs and police divers are trained, runs five-day PADI open water courses between April and October (2600F) and rents equipment.

Inland, there's also the cavernous **Exposition Universelle des Vins et Spiritueux** (Easter–Sept Mon 10.15am–noon & 3–7pm; closed Wed & Sat am; free) to the west of the port. Decorated with murals by art-school students, the hall has a comprehensive display of French wines and liquors and a slowly expanding selection of liquid intoxicants from the world over. The exposition's claim that no culture has ever failed to produce alcohol, is yet to be proved, but there are some wierd and wonderful items, including an evil bottle of Chinese spirit in which a large gecko floats.

The mainland

Back on the **mainland** the thing to do is hunt out drink that isn't yet a museum piece, in particular Bandol's own *appellation* produced in the area encompassing St-Cyr (see p.200). It's the best of the Côtes de Provence wines with the reds the most reputed, maturing for over ten years on a good harvest, and bouquets sliding between pepper, cinnamon, vanilla and black cherries; the rosé is equally wonderful.

Back from the port on allées Vivien you'll find the **Maison des Vins du Bandol** (☎04.94.29.45.03), which sells its own selection of wines and will give you lists of *propriétaires* to visit. For cheese, sausages and the like to go with the wine, there's a daily **market** in front of the church a few blocks back from quai de l'Hôtel-de-Ville, which spreads onto the quayside on Tuesdays.

Bandol's most scenic sandy **beach** is around the **Anse de Renécros**, an almost circular inlet just over the hill west of the port, reached via bd Louis-Lumière. Better still are the coves and beaches along the coastal path to Les Lecques which you reach from av du Maréchal-Foch on the western side of the Anse de Renécros (signed in yellow). There's good bicycling, too, in the countryside north of Bandol: you could head for the perched medieval village of **La Cadière d'Azur** (take the road above the station, left on the D559, then right), and then across the valley to the more touristy fortified hamlet of **Le Castellet** with its gloomy, crypt-like bastion of a twelfth-century church, perfumed boutiques and wonderful panorama of the vineyards below. Approximately 3km to the southeast of here lies **Le Vieux Beausset**, south of Le Beausset, where the Romanesque **Chapelle Notre-Dame** (Tues–Thurs 10am–6.30pm, Sat & Sun 2–6pm) gives a suberb panoramic view.

Practicalities

From Bandol's **train station**, head straight downhill and you'll reach the town centre above the port. The **tourist office** is on allées Vivien by the quayside (July & Aug daily 9am–1pm & 2–7pm; rest of year Mon–Sat 9am–noon & 2–6pm; ☎04.94.29.41.35). You can rent **bikes**, motorized or not, at Holiday Bikes on rte de Marseille

(☎04.94.32.21.89), west down av Loste on the other side of the rail lines from the station; or at Bandol Chlorophylle, av du 11 Novembre (☎04.94.29.54.67).

The three **hotels** on the **island** are priced for big company expense accounts; the *Soukana* (☎04.94.25.06.06, fax 04.94.25.04.89; ⑤; closed Oct–March) at the far end of the island is the best bet, but you'd still have to book months in advance. On the **mainland** the choice of cheap hotels includes *Le Provence* (☎04.94.32.32.25; ②), with a friendly restaurant and parking space, just beneath the station, where *pétanque* players gather to play and drink pastis; the *Commerce*, 5 rue des Tonneliers (☎04.94.29.52.19; ①; closed Nov–March); *Roses Mousses*, 22 rue des Écoles (☎04.94.29.45.14; ③; closed Oct–March); *Bourgogne*, rue Marçon (☎04.94.29.41.16; ③) close to the beach; and *La Brise*, 12 bd Victor-Hugo (☎04.94.29.41.70; ③). More expensive, but still good value, are the *Coin d'Azur*, 23 rue Raimu (☎04.94.29.40.93 ⑤), a well-run hotel looking onto the Anse de Renécros; and the very pleasant *Golf Hôtel*, right on Renécros beach (☎04.94.29.45.83, fax 04.94.32.42.47; ⑤). Bandol's top hotel, *Île Rousse*, 17 bd Louis-Lumière (☎04.94.29.33.00, fax 04.94.29.49.49; ⑤), has a terrace leading down to the sea from the west of the port and vast light rooms.

The *Club Nautique* on the Île de Bendor provides very cheap **HI youth hostel accommodation** in cramped, basic bunk-bed doubles (no membership necessary but book ahead; ☎04.94.29.52.91). If you're **camping**, try the three-star *Vallongue* (☎04.94.29.49.55; closed Oct–Easter), 2km out of town on the rte de Marseille.

In the centre of Bandol, you'll find plenty of **restaurants** in rue de la République and allée Jean-Moulin, running parallel to the portside promenade. The *Auberge du Port*, 9 allée Jean-Moulin (☎04.94.29.42.63), has nice fish dishes, with menus from 105F and à la carte over 300F; while *La Marmite* on rue F-Fabre (☎04.94.25.05.60) serves good-value dishes in a friendly atmosphere. The restaurant at the hotel *Île Rousse* (see above) is the place for seafood soup and a *crème brûlée* flavoured with lavender (menus from 150F; à la carte from 250F). Arguably as good is *Le Clocher*, 1 rue de la Paroisse (closed Wed out of season & Sun midday; ☎04.94.32.47.65; menus from 150F; à la carte from 250F).

Le Bourbon Street Café at 2 bd Victor-Hugo is a tapas **bar** with occasional live music, while for something a little more sophisticated, *Poupoune* and *L'Escale* on quai Charles de-Gaulle above the beach are obvious places for cocktail-sipping.

The Cap Sicié peninsula and Ollioules

The coastal approach to Toulon from Marseille takes you via the congested neck of the **Cap Sicié peninsula** On the western side, Six-Fours-les-Plage sprawls between Bandol's neighbour **Sanary-sur-Mer** and **Le Brusc** on the western tip where you can get boats to another Ricard-owned island, **Île des Embiez**. The eastern side of the peninsula merges with Toulon's former shipbuilding suburb of **La Seyne-sur-Mer** while at the southern end a semi-wilderness of high cliffs and forest reigns.

Approaching Toulon on the Aubagne road, you'll pass through the twisting **gorge d'Ollioules**, where the heights of **Le Gros Cerveau** and **Mont Caume** above it are well worth visiting.

Sanary-sur-Mer

The little fishing harbour of **SANARY-SUR-MER** is 7.5km east from Bandol on the Cap Sicié peninsula. With its palm trees, nineteenth-century church spire, pastel pink and yellow facades along the seafront, and fountains with statues representing agriculture and fishery, the harbour retains its charm despite the urban conglomoration it's now immersed in. Housed in the thirteenth-century **Tour Romane** by the port is a small **diving museum** (July & Aug daily 3–8pm; free), based around the collection of one of the pioneers of the modern sport, Frédéric Dumas, who worked with Jacques Cousteau.

Buses run frequently from Bandol's quai de l'Hôtel-de-Ville to Sanary. The town's **train station**, which it shares with Ollioules (see p.204), is 2.5km north of the centre, but the buses into town don't always link up with train arrivals: the bar in front of the station has a copy of the latest timetable. The **tourist office** is by the port in the Jardin de la Ville (☎04.94.74.01.04). In front of it is a plaque commemorating the German-speaking artistic community that made Sanary its base in the 1930s: people like Brecht, Stefan Zweig and Ferdinand Bruckner, many of whom were fleeing from the strictures of Hitler's NSDAP party. If you want **to stay**, the *Centre Azur* hostel, 149 av du Nid (☎04.94.74.18.87, fax 04.94.34.79.10), may have some rooms, or there's the *Hôtel de la Tour*, 24 quai Général-de-Gaulle (☎04.94.74.10.10, fax 04.94.74.69.49; ④), with a perfect location overlooking the port. There is a good three-star **campsite**, *Les Girelles*, on the chemin de Beaucours, by the sea on the Bandol road (☎04.94.74.13.18, fax 04.94.74.60.04; closed Oct–Easter).The **restaurant**, *Relais de la Poste*, place Poste (☎04.94.74.22.20; closed Sun eve & Mon), has interesting dishes with fresh ingredients; alternatively, for a low-priced delicious fish meal, head 1km west from the port along av Gallieni and av de Portissol to *Le Cabanon* (☎04.94.74.13.89) on the Plage de Portissol.

From Sanary the D559 and D63 head towards Toulon through Six-Fours-les-Plages which seems to be nothing but sprawling, suburbs littered with hoardings. A small road off the D63, to the north, however, takes you up to **Notre-Dame-de-la-Pépiole** (open 3–6pm; free), a stunning fifth- to sixth-century chapel in the midst of pines, cypresses and olive trees.

The southeast reaches of the peninsula are not exactly wilderness, but the sturdy sentinel of **Notre-Dame-de-Mai** (May, Easter Mon & mid-Aug to mid-Sept) once a primitive lighthouse, now a place of pilgrimage, provides a reason to **hike** for an hour or two up the pretty backroads here. The best route is the one that heads off the D16 2km east of the junction with the D559. Signs indicate the chapel, just beyond an Elf station. It's a four-kilometre hike up, worth it for heady views in every direction; it can get pretty windy up here, and even on a calm day, exploring the cliffs should be done with a certain amount of caution. There are easy alternatives back down again, east around the headland to La Seyne or west to **Le Brusc** where you can reward yourself with a generous fish dinner at *Le St-Pierre*, 47 rue de la Citadelle (☎04.94.34.02.52; weekday menu around 100F; closed Tues eve & Wed out of season).

Île des Embiez

Paul Ricard's second privately owned island, in fact a small archipelago, turns out to be as dubious in conception as Bendor. The **Île des Embiez** greets visitors with mock classical goddesses on pillars around the large **pleasure port** and scattered Greco-Roman picnic tables. The **Fondation Océanographique Ricard** (July & Aug daily 10am–12.30pm & 1.30–6.30pm; rest of year Mon, Tues, Thurs, Fri & Sun 10am–12.30pm & 1.30–5.45pm, Wed & Sat 1.30–6.30pm; 15F) has aquariums and exhibitions on underwater matter. There are pony and go-kart rides for the under-twelves and in summer a miniature road-train does the circuit of the island, all great fun for pre-teens. Away from the paying attractions, much of the island has been laid waste by various "works". In spring the more or less untrammelled south-facing cliffs are a riot of yellow flowers but the rest of the year they're covered in dull scrub and, with the exception of a few pocket-handkerchief-sized beaches of fine gravel and crystal water, there's not much to induce a lengthy stay.

There are frequent **ferry crossings** from Le Brusc (daily: July–Sept 7am–12.45am; rest of year 7am to 8.30pm; journey time 12min). You can also reach the island from

Sanary port from April to September (25min). **Accommodation** is pretty scarce: there's a small **youth hostel** (no membership needed but book well in advance; ☎04.94.74.93.90), one de luxe hotel and a few rented villas.

Ollioules

OLLIOULES, north of the peninsula, derives its name from "olive" and it's one of those Provençal small towns that, despite ruined medieval castle, arcaded streets, fountains and Romanesque church, still manages to have an economy not totally dependent on tourism. Much of this rests on its floral wholesale and export market, the biggest in France, though open to the public only during the *Foire aux Plantes* at the end of April on the central place Jean-Jaurès. Small-scale artisans are also much in evidence, earning their keep making barrels, pots, nougat or reeds for musical instruments, as well as wine and olive oil. And on the cultural front, the *commune* contains the **Centre National de Création et de Diffusion Culturelles** in the château of Châteauvallon (off the D92 towards north Toulon), with an impressive calendar of arts events as well as hosting an **international dance festival** every July (details from the centre ☎04.94.22.74.00 and from Ollioules or Toulon tourist offices).

Practicalities

Ollioules shares its **gare SNCF** with Sanary; it lies between the two, about 3.5km south of Ollioules. There's a regular bus service between the town and the station, and you can also catch a bus here direct from Toulon's train station. The **tourist office**, on 16 rue Nationale (July & Aug Mon–Sat 9am–noon & 3–6pm; rest of year closed Wed & Sat pm; ☎04.94.63.11.74). **Bikes** can be rented at Oki Bike, 5 rue Henri-Barbusse (☎04.94.63.46.37).

Very cheap **rooms** can be had at *L'Escale* hotel-bar-restaurant, 1 rue Hoche (☎04.94.63.21.07; ①); and *Au Bon Coin* hotel-crêperie, 11 rue Marceau (☎04.94.63.22.26, fax 04.94.63.30.45; ②), both run by friendly couples and both just above place Jean-Jaurès. For **meals**, *L'Estable Fleurie* on rte de la Seyne is distinguished by its seafood dishes, while omelettes and the like can be had from the *Bar-Tabac de la Mairie* on place Jean-Jaurès. A **market** takes place on place Jean-Jaurès on Thursday and Saturday mornings, and for some very special Bandol AOC wine head for the Domaine de Terrebrune, 724 chemin de la Tourelle, signed off the rte du Gros Cerveau (Mon–Sat 9am–noon & 2–7pm, Sun 2–7pm), which produces a wonderful deep and dusky red **wine** and has an expensive but very good Provençal restaurant, with menus from 200F (closed Mon eve & Sun out of season; ☎04.94.74.01.30).

Mont Caume and Le Gros Cerveau

Though less dramatic in their inclines than the Cap Sicié cliffs, the mountain ranges to the north of the peninsula give the best panorama of this complex coast. **Mont Caume** to the east is by far the highest point in the locality. Access at the top is restricted by the military but you can get a view northwards across acres of forest to the Chaîne de la Ste-Baume and the distinctively sharp drop of the Montagne de la Loube by La Roquebrussanne.

The road between Mont Caume and the gorges takes in the villages of **Le Broussan**, which has a small general store, and **Evenos**, perched up in the winds around a ruined castle.

West of the gorges, the **Gros Cerveau** ridge reveals the islands of Embiez and Bendor, the Toulon roadstead, Cap Sicié and La Ciotat's shipbuilding yards. From an abandoned military barracks you can look down northwards onto the strange rock forms. This is good walking country, though watch out in the hunting season for *chasse gardée* signs.

Toulon

Viewed from the distant heights of Mont Caume or Notre-Dame-du-Mai, it's clear why **TOULON** had to be a major port. The heart-shaped bay of the Petite Rade gives over fifteen kilometres of shoreline around Toulon and its suburb **La Seyne-sur-Mer** to the west. Facing the city, about three kilometres out to sea, is **St-Mandrier**, a virtual island, connected to the Cap Sicié peninsula by the isthmus of Les Sablettes and protecting the Grande Rade both northwards and eastwards.

Toulon was half-destroyed in World War II and its rebuilt whole is dominated by the military and associated industries. The arsenal that Louis XIV created is one of the major employers of southeast France and the port is home to the French Navy's Mediterranean fleet. The shipbuilding yards of La Seyne have, however, been axed, closing the book on a centuries-old and at times notorious industry. Up until the eighteenth century, slaves and convicts were still powering the king's galleys and, following the Revolution, convicts were sent to Toulon with iron collars round their necks for sentences of hard labour. After 1854 convicts were deported to the colonies that Toulon's ships had played a major part in winning.

Today, French nationals of non-European origin face the threat of second-class treatment in housing and provision of local services from the town hall, controlled since May 1995 by the *Front National* whose main policy plank is a "preference for the French". It was a victory that shocked France – and Toulon for that matter – with the city being the most significant electoral gain for the extreme-right party to date. The Front has subsequently lost its seat in the national assembly but remains in power at the local level.

Toulon has never been a particularly pleasant city. Its museums are dull; major gentrification works on the Vieille Ville are likely to be suspended after running up massive debts (plus financial scandals) under the previous administration; highway traffic crawls through the centre; it has all the paranoia of a big city with few of the charms; it's claustrophobic, ugly – in short, a place to avoid.

If you do get stuck in Toulon, there is at least cheap accommodation, good markets and cheap shops and restaurants, and you can escape the city centre by heading up **Mont Faron** or taking a boat across the roadstead to **La Seyne** or **St-Mandrier**.

Arrival, information and accommodation

The **gare SNCF** and **gare routière** are on place Albert-1er. Walking straight out of the station down av Vauban will bring you to the place d'Armes. Follow the busy avenue that runs east parallel to the coast and turn left into rue Letuaire, which leads onto the small place Raimu, where you'll find the **tourist office** (July & Aug Mon–Sat 9am–7pm, Sun 10am–noon; rest of year Mon–Sat 9am–6pm, Sun 10–noon; ☎04.94.18.53.00). A **bus map** is available from the RMTT kiosk on place de la Liberté, three blocks southeast of the station. To reach the seaside suburb of Le Mourillon, take bus #3 or #13 from the centre.

One of the cheapest **hotels** in Toulon is the *Hôtel des Allées*, 18 allée Amiral-Courbet (☎04.94.91.10.02; ①), where English is spoken and you can find rooms for up to four people; other inexpensive central options are the *Little Palace*, 6–8 rue Berthelot (☎04.94.92.26.62, fax 04.94.89.13.77; ②), and *La Molière*, 12 rue Molière (☎04.94.92.78.35, fax 04.94.62.85.82; ②) in the Vieille Ville by the theatre. In Le Mourillon, east of the centre, *La Corniche*, 17 littoral Frédéric-Mistral (☎04.94.41.35.12, fax 04.94.41.24.58; ④), has some very pleasant rooms, the more expensive ones with views over the sea. There's also a **hostel**, *Foyer de la Jeunesse*, 12 place d'Armes (☎04.94.22.62.00; booking essential), just west of the Vieille Ville, ten minutes' walk from the train station, with meals for 25F.

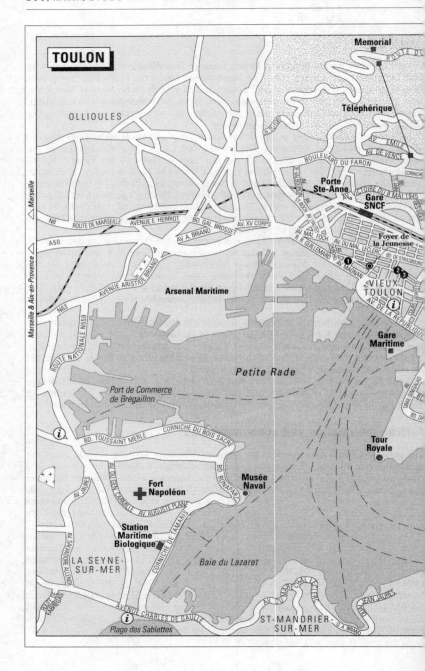

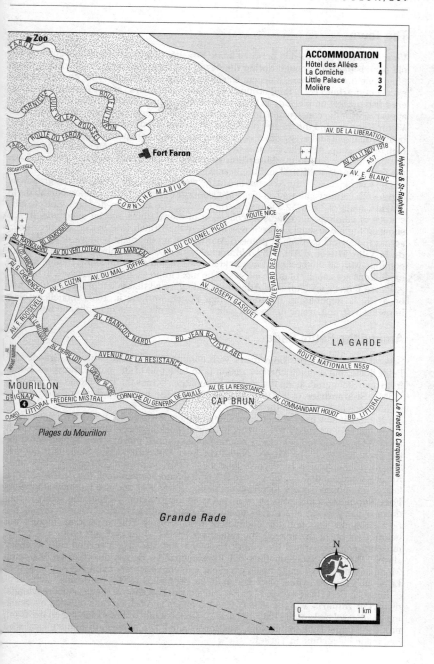

ACCOMMODATION

Hôtel des Allées	1
La Corniche	4
Little Palace	3
Molière	2

The Town

Vieux Toulon, crammed in between bd de Strasbourg and av de la République on the old port, is pleasant enough during the day. It has a fine scattering of fountains, more often than not of dolphins, a decent selection of shops, particularly for clothes, and an excellent **market** (Tues–Sun) around rue Landrin and cours Lafayette, as well as a covered fish market on place de la Poissonnerie. Big chunks of the Vieille Ville have disappeared with the construction of a gleaming new lycée and shopping centre, and place Victor-Hugo around the theatre is all cleaned up and full of café tables, but towards the quays you'll still find every other door leads to a cheap restaurant, bar, jazz dive, nightclub or sex shop. At night, the area becomes particularly seedy and you'd be better off heading further east to the **Mourillon quartier** where trendy nightlife glitters down the littoral Frédéric-Mistral and the beaches face the open sea.

The vast expanse of the **Arsenal** lies to the west of the Vieille Ville, with its grandiose eighteenth-century gateway on place Monsenergue leading to the **Musée Naval/de la Marine** (daily 9.30am–12.30pm & 3–7pm; 29F). The museum displays figureheads, statues of admirals, an extensive collection of model ships and an enormous fresco showing the old arsenal before it was burnt by the British (see below). To the north, across the formal gardens of **place d'Armes** and up the main boulevard, the **Musée de la Ville/Musée d'Art**, 113 bd Maréchal-Leclerc (daily 1–7pm; free), is very disappointing, with all the best paintings held in reserve and never on show; though special exhibitions are usually of more interest. The most impressive public artwork in the city is Pierre Puget's sculptures of **Atlantes**, holding up all that is left of the old town hall on av de la République. It's thought that Puget, working in 1657, modelled these immensely strong, tragic figures on galley slaves as allegories of might and fatigue.

Around the Petite Rade

Several companies offer **boat tours** with commentary around both the Grande and Petite Rade, but a much cheaper option is to take one of the public transport **boats** from quai Stalingrad, along the av de la République, across the Petite Rade to **La Seyne** (#8M); **St-Mandrier** (#28M); or **Les Sablettes**, the isthmus between them (#18M, which stops at Tamaris on the way).

Although it now has the merchant shipping port, the loss of **LA SEYNE**'s naval shipyards has taken a heavy toll on this industrial working-class community. However, it reverted to its old red colours by electing a Communist mayor when Toulon voted for the *Front National*. The **Musée Naval du Fort Balaguier** (Wed–Sun 10am–noon & 2–6pm; 10F) explores La Seyne's long association with naval history. In 1793, after Royalists had handed Toulon over to the British and Spanish fleet, the British set up a line of immensely secure fortifications between this fort and the fort now known as **Fort Napoléon**, a kilometre or so inland from the museum. Despite the ability to rain down artillery on any attacker, a Captain Bonaparte with a bunch of volunteers took the Fort Balaguier and sent the enemies of revolutionary France packing, though not before they burnt the arsenal, the remaining French ships and part of the town. The museum commemorates the young Napoléon and also has a section on the galley slaves. The Fort Napoléon (bus #81 from central La Seyne; direction Le Mai, stop Montplaisant) occasionally hosts excellent contemporary art exhibitions; check with La Seyne's **tourist office**, place Ledru-Rollin (☎04.94.94.73.09), for details.

Between Fort Balaguier and Les Sablettes is the shoreline of the peaceful residential district of **Tamaris**, with its rickety wooden jetties and fishing huts on stilts overlooking the mussel beds of the Baie du Lazaret. The beautiful oriental building on the front, now the Marine Biology Institute, was constructed by a nineteenth-century local who had made his fortune in Turkey.

At **Les Sablettes** you can lounge on the south-facing beach; beyond is the little port of **SAINT-MANDRIER-SUR-MER**, sandwiched between the high walls of *terrain militaire*, where you can look across the harbour, past all the battle ships, to the grim metropolis.

Mont Faron

Aside from the harbour boat trips, the best way to pass an afternoon in Toulon is to leave the town 542m below you by ascending to the summit of **Mont Faron**. By road, chemin du Fort-Rouge to the northwest of the centre becomes rte du Faron, snaking up to the top and descending again from the northeast, a journey of 18km in all. The road is a one-way, narrow slip of tarmac with no barriers on the cliff-edge hairpin bends, looping up and down through luscious vegetation. To reach the summit as the crow flies, take bus #40 (direction Super Toulon or Les Mas du Faron, stop Téléphérique) to bd Amiral-Vence where a **funicular** operates (summer daily 9am–7pm; ☎04.94.92.68.25; 34F return); it's a bit pricey but a treat.

At the top of Mont Faron there's a **memorial museum** to the Allied landings in Provence of August 1944 (June Tues–Sun 9.30am–12.15pm & 2.30–6.30pm; rest of year daily same hours; 25F) with screenings of original newsreel footage. In the surrounding park are two restaurants, and a little further up to the right, a **zoo** (☎04.94.88.07.89) specializing in big cats. Beyond the zoo you can walk up the hillside to an abandoned fort and revel in the cleanness of the air, the smell of the flowers and the views beyond the city way below.

Eating and drinking

Toulon's best rewards are mainly in **eating**. There are plenty of brasseries, cafés and restaurants along the quayside, some selling just sandwiches, others offering seafood-based fixed menus for under 100F. Good couscous for around 100F is to be had *Chez Mimi*, 83 av de la République (☎04.94.92.79.60; closed Wed); Toulon's oldest restaurant, *Au Sourd*, 10 rue Molière, in the Vieille Ville (☎04.94.92.28.52; closed Mon, Sun eve & most of July), specializes in fish dishes including bouillabaisse, with a good menu at 140F and à la carte at around 300F. North of bd Strasbourg, the *Pizzaria Luigi*, 40 rue Picot (☎04.94.92.89.14; closed midday Sat & Sun), serves pizzas and delicious raviolis until midnight. The littoral Frédéric-Mistral in Le Mourillon is chok-a-block with restaurants; try *Le Bistrot* in the *Hotel La Corniche* at no. 17 (☎04.94.41.35.12; closed Sun eve & Mon) which serves good-value *plateaux de fruits de mer* and Bandol wines, with menus from 120F.

East towards Hyères

Beyond Le Mourillon to the east, Toulon merges with **LE PRADET** where old houses with lovely gardens are shaded by pines above the cliffs leading to the **Pointe de Carquieranne**. A path follows the coast all the way round the headland to Carquieranne and steep steps lead down to beaches which are crowded during the day but lovely in the evening as they catch the sun setting over Toulon's harbour. At Plage de la Garonne, 10km east of Toulon (bus #23 or #39 to Pradet Place, then #91A/B to La Garonne), the beachside **restaurant** *El Plein Sud* serves grilled fish and cheap wine as night falls in summer.

Past Pointe de Carquieranne, between Pointe du Beau Rouge and the D559, a small road crosses the side of a hill guarded by two old forts with views of the Presqu'île de Giens and the Île de Porquerolles (see p.219). If you're **cycling** from Toulon to Hyères there's a proper track running beside the D559.

travel details

Trains

Aix to: Briançon (1–2 daily; 3hr 30min); Château-Arnoux–St Auban (3–4 daily; 1hr–1hr 30min); Marseille (frequent; 30–40min); Manosque (3–4 daily; 40min); Meyrargues (3 daily; 15min); Sisteron (3–4 daily; 1hr 15min–1hr 40min).

Aubagne to: Marseille (frequent; 15min); Toulon (every hour; 35 min).

Marseille to: Aix (frequent; 35min); Arles (frequent; 45min); Aubagne (every 30min; 20min); Avignon (frequent; 1hr–1hr 15min); Bandol (every 30min; 45min); Cannes (frequent; 1hr); Carry-le-Rouet (6–10 daily; 25–40min); Cassis (every 30min; 25min); Cavaillon (3–4 daily; 45min–1hr 10min); Hyères (2 daily; 1hr 30min); Istres (6–8 daily; 1hr); L'Estaque (10–14 daily; 15min); La Ciotat (every 30min; 30min); La Couronne (6–8 daily; 40min); La Redonne-Ensués (6–8 daily; 25min); La Seyne-Six Fours (every 40min; 1hr); Les Arcs-Draguignan (every hour; 1hr 20min–2hr 15min); Lyon (8 daily; 2hr 40min); Martigues (6–8 daily; 45min); Menton (8 daily; 3hr 30min–4hr) Miramas (frequent; 30min–1hr 20min); Nice (frequent; 2hr 20min–3hr 30min); Niolon (5–6 daily; 30min); Ollioules-Sanary (every 40min; 50min); Paris (10 daily; 4hr 20min–8 hr 40min); St-Chamas (4 daily; 40min); St Cyr-Les-Lecques (every 30min; 35–40min); St-Raphaël (frequent; 1hr 45min); Salon (3–4 daily; 25–50min); Sausset-les-Pins (6–8 daily; 35min); Tarascon (7 daily; 1hr); Toulon (frequent; 40min–1hr).

Miramas to: Arles (8–12 daily; 20min); Avignon (9–11 daily; 40min–1hr); Marseille (frequent; 25min–1hr 10min).

Salon to: Avignon (9 daily; 1hr); Marseille (4 daily; 50min); Miramas (6 daily; 10min).

Toulon to: Marseille (frequent; 1hr).

Buses (Sundays and holidays reduced services)

Aix to: Apt (2 daily; 2hr 20min); Arles (6 daily; 1hr 15min); Avignon (6 daily; 1hr–1hr 15min); Bandol (2 daily in summer; 1hr); Brignoles (2 daily; 50min); Carpentras (3 daily; 1hr 50min); Cavaillon (3 daily; 1hr 10min); Marseille (frequent; 25min); Nice (5 daily; 2hr 15min–4hr); St-Cyr (2 daily in summer; 1hr); St-Maximin (2 daily; 30min); Salon (12 daily; 40min); Sanary (2 daily in summer; 1hr 15min); Six-Fours (2 daily in summer; 1hr 30min); Toulon (4 daily; 1hr 15min).

Aubagne to: Aix (10 daily; 40min); Bandol (8 daily; 1hr); Brignoles (5 daily; 1hr–1hr 30min); Cassis (9 daily; 25min); Gémenos (hourly Mon–Sat; 20min); La Ciotat (5 daily; 20min); Marseille (frequent; 20–30min); St-Maximin (7 daily; 1hr–1hr 15min).

Marseille to: Aix (frequent; 30min); Arles (4 daily; 2hr 10min–2hr 30min); Aubagne (frequent; 20–30min); Bandol (6 daily; 1hr 30min); Barcelonnette (4 daily; 3hr 50min–4hr 30min); Brignoles (3 daily; 1hr 30min–1hr 50min); Carpentras (4 daily; 2hr 15min); Cassis (7 daily; 50min); Digne (4 daily; 2hr–3hr); Forcalquier (3 daily; 2 hr 10min–2hr 30min); Gémenos (4 daily; 45min); Grenoble (1 daily; 4hr); La Ciotat (8 daily; 1hr); Les Lecques (4 daily; 1hr 15min–1hr 30min); Manosque (6 daily; 1hr–1hr 30min); Martigues (10–11 daily; 1hr–1hr 30min); St-Chamas (3 daily; 1hr 20min); St-Maximin (6 daily; 1hr–1hr 30min); Salon (5 daily; 1hr 20min–1hr 40min); Sisteron (5–6 daily; 2hr 30min).

Martigues to: Istres (5 daily; 25min); Marseille (10–11 daily; 1hr 15min–1hr 30min); Salon (4 daily; 1hr 10min).

Salon to: Aix (12 daily; 40min); Arles (9 daily; 1hr–1hr 20min); Eyguières (7 daily; 15min); Istres (4 daily; 35min); La Barben (10 daily; 15min); Les Baux (2 daily; 30min); Marseille (10 daily; 45min–1hr 15min); Martigues (4 daily; 1hr 10min); Miramas (6 daily; 20min).

Toulon to: Aix (4 daily; 1hr 15min); Bandol (every 30min; 1hr); Brignoles (6 daily; 1hr 30min); Draguignan (5 daily; 2hr 10min); Hyères (every 30min; 35–50min); Le Brusc (6–7 daily; 25min); Le Pradet (every 30min; 20min); Méounes (2 daily; 50min); Nice (2 daily; 2hr 30min); St-Maximin (1 daily; 1hr 40min); St-Raphaël (4 daily; 2hr); St-Tropez (8 daily; 2hr 15min); Sanary (every 30min; 35–45min); Signes (2 daily; 1hr 15min); Six-Fours (frequent; 25min).

Ferries

Marseille to: Corsica (4–10 weekly; 8–12hr).

Toulon to: Corsica (2–5 weekly; 7–11hr).

Flights

Marseille to: Paris (21 daily; 1hr).

CHAPTER FOUR

THE CÔTE D'AZUR:
HYÈRES TO THE ESTEREL

The **Côte d'Azur** is the most desirable and at the same time most detestable stretch of Mediterranean coast. The glimmering rocks along its shore and the translucent sea, the February mimosa blossom, the springtime scents of pine and eucalyptus or the golden autumn chestnut crop and reddening vines are woven by the Mediterranean light into a compulsive sensual magic. It can still cast the spell that attracted the Impressionist and Post-Impressionist painters at the turn of the century – whose paintings can be seen at St-Tropez – their Bohemian successors and the 1950s film world. But in summer it also has the worst traffic jams and public transport, the most crowded quaysides, campsites and hitching queues, the most short-tempered locals – and outrageous prices.

Unlike the Riviera further east, or the Toulon–Marseille stretch to the west, the Côte d'Azur proper is off the main routes and has no major cities. Between the largest town, Hyères, and the conurbation of St-Raphaël-Fréjus, are a string of fishing villages turned yacht and pleasure ports. Pre-eminent among them is **St-Tropez**, or "St-Trop" as its aficionados like to call it, a brand-name for sea, sun, celebrity and sex.

There's such a tangle of resorts it's sometimes hard to distinguish one from another; but in **Cavalière**, **Pramousquier**, **Le Rayol** with its fabulous **garden**, and **Le Trayas** you can get glimpses of how this coast all once looked. There are even some stretches which have held out against the construction mania altogether: west of **Cap Bregançon**, the southern end of **St-Tropez's peninsula**, little snatches of the **Corniches des Maures** and along the **Corniche d'Esterel** west of Le Trayas below the dramatic red volcanic crags of the **Massif d'Esterel**. But for real coastal wilderness you need to head out to sea to the gorgeous **Îles d'Hyères**, also known as the Îles d'Or, where the region's rarest fauna and flora are seriously conserved and protected.

Hyères, which attracted foreign visitors in the eighteenth century while Cannes was still a fishing village, thrives on its horticulture as much as on its tourism and is an affordable place to stay. **Fréjus** is the most historical of the towns proper, dating back

ACCOMMODATION PRICE CATEGORIES

Throughout this guide, all hotels and guesthouses have been priced on a scale of ①–⑧, indicating the lowest price you could expect to pay for a double room in high season. What you get for your money varies enormously between establishments, but in the lower-priced hotels you should expect to pay considerably more for en-suite facilities. If you are staying anywhere for more than three days it's often possible to negotiate a lower price, particularly out of season.

① Under 160F	③ 220–300F	⑤ 400–500F	⑦ 600–700F
② 160–220F	④ 300–400F	⑥ 500–600F	⑧ Over 700F

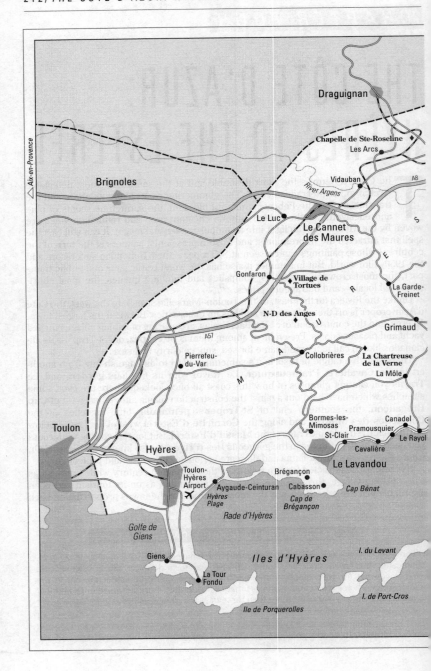

△ Aix-en-Provence

Draguignan

Chapelle de Ste-Roseline ◆
Les Arcs

Vidauban

River Argens

A8

Brignoles

Le Luc

Le Cannet
des Maures

S

Gonfaron

Village de
Tortues ◆

La Garde-
Freinet

N-D des Anges ◆

M A U R E S

Grimaud

A57

Pierrefeu-
du-Var

Collobrières

La Chartreuse
de la Verne ◆

La Môle

M

Bormes-les-
Mimosas
St-Clair

Canadel
Pramousquier

Le Rayol

Cavalière

Le Lavandou

Toulon

Hyères

Toulon-
Hyères
Airport ✈

Brégançon

Aygaude-Ceinturan
*Hyères
Plage*

Cabasson

Cap Bénat

*Cap de
Brégançon*

Rade d'Hyères

*Golfe de
Giens*

I. du Levant

Giens

Iles d'Hyères

La Tour
Fondu

I. de Port-Cros

Ile de Porquerolles

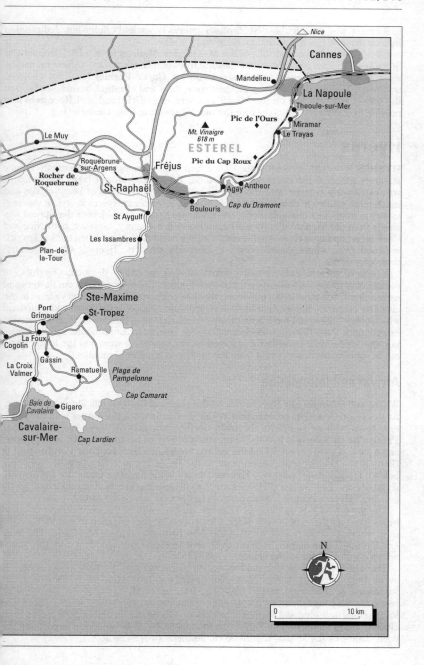

to Roman times; its neighbour **St-Raphaël** ignores its ancient origins but, dedicated to holiday-makers, has rooms and food for every budget.

Inland, the dark wooded hills of the **Massif des Maures** form a backdrop east to St-Raphaël. Hidden amid the sweet-chestnut trees and cork oaks are ancient monasteries and medieval villages. **Collobrières** and **La Garde-Freinet** have not forsaken traditional livelihoods and carry on their wine, cork and chestnut businesses beyond the tourist season while on the Massif's eastern edge **Grimaud** and **Rocquebrune** provide exclusive second homes for the more discerning Côte clientele.

Hyères

HYÈRES is the oldest resort of the Côte d'Azur, listing among its pre-twentieth-century admirers Empress Joséphine, Queen Victoria, Tolstoy and Robert Louis Stevenson. It was particularly popular with the British, having the advantages of being closer, and much more southerly, than its rival Nice. In order to winter at Hyères in style it was necessary to have one's own villa, hence the expansive gardened residences that spread seawards from the Vieille Ville. By the beginning of this century, however, both Nice and Cannes had upstaged Hyères in the clientele they could attract, and when the foreign rich switched from winter convalescents to quayside strutters, Hyères, with no central seafront, lost out.

It is, nevertheless, a very popular resort, and has the unique distinction on the Côte of not being totally dependent on the summer influx. The town exports cut flowers and exotic plants, the most important being the date palm, which graces every street in the city. The orchards, nursery gardens, vineyards and fields of vegetables, taking up land which elsewhere would have been developed into a rash of holiday units, are crucial to its economy. Even the saltworks are still going. Hyères is consequently rather appealing: the Vieille Ville is neither a sanitized tourist trap nor a slum and the locals aren't out to squeeze maximum profit from the minimum number of months.

Arrival and information

Walled and medieval **old Hyères** lies on the slopes of Casteou hill, 5km from the sea. Av des Îles d'Or and its continuation av Gén-de-Gaulle mark the border with the **modern town** with av Gambetta the main north–south axis. At the coast the peculiar **Presqu'île de Giens** is leashed to the mainland by an isthmus, known as **La Capte**, and a parallel sand bar enclosing the salt marshes and a lake. **La Tour Fondue** port at Giens is the closest embarkation point to the Île de Porquerolles (see Îles d'Hyères below); Hyères' **main port** is at **Hyères-Plages** at the top of La Capte. **Le Ceinturon**, **Ayguade** and **Les Salins d'Hyères** are the village-cum-resorts along the coast northeast from Hyères-Plages; **L'Almanarre** is to the west where the sand bar starts.

The **gare SNCF** is on place de l'Europe, 1.5km south of the town centre; frequent buses connect the station with place Clemenceau at the entrance to the Vieille Ville from where it's a short walk south to the **gare routière** on place Mal-Joffre. The modern Hyères-Toulon **airport** is between Hyères and Hyères-Plage, 3km from the centre with a regular shuttle to the centre.

The **tourist office** is near the bus station in the beautiful Rotunde Jean-Salusse on av de Belgique (July & Aug daily 8am–8pm; Sept–June Mon–Fri 8.30am–6pm, Sat 9am–noon & 2–5.30pm; ☎04.94.65.18.55). Its map of Hyères and the surrounding resorts is very useful and it can provide information on everything from archery and karate clubs to fishing and surfing competitions. **Bikes** and mopeds can be rented from Holiday Bikes on chemin du Palyvestre (☎04.94.38.46.08) between the airport and the train station, or the Mistral Centre on rte de Giens (☎04.94.58.26.87).

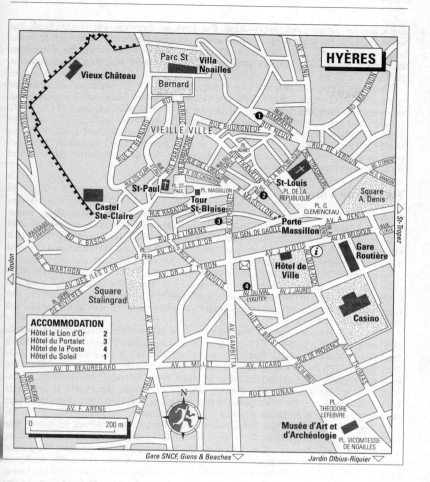

Accommodation

Hotels in Hyères are not expensive. There are only three in the Vieille Ville, but plenty in the modern town and even more on La Capte and along the seafront between Hyères-Plage and L'Ayguade. Outside July and August you can take your pick.

In the Vieille Ville, *Hôtel le Soleil*, on rue du Rempart (☎04.94.65.16.26, fax 04.94.35.46.00; ③), is well positioned high up at the foot of parc St-Bernard; *Hôtel du Portalet*, 4 rue de Limans (☎04.94.65.39.40, fax 04.94.35.86.33; ②), is less appealing but much more central; and *Au Lion d'Or*, 2 rue République (☎04.94.65.25.55; ②), has no pretentions to being anything but basic.

Right in the centre of the modern town, the *Hôtel de la Poste*, 7 av Lyautey (☎04.94.65.02.00; ②), is an inexpensive, reliable option. By the sea, you could try *Le Calypso* at 36 av de la Méditerranée, Hyères-Plage (☎ & fax 04.94.58.02.09; ④; closed

Dec); or *La Reine Jane*, overlooking the port at Ayguade (☎04.94.66.32.64, fax 04.94.66.34.66; ④; closed Jan). On the wooded slopes of Costabelle, 1km back from the sea at L'Almanarre, *La Québécoise*, 20 ch de l'Amiral (also called the *Hostellerie Provençale*; ☎04.94.57.69.24, fax 04.94.38.78.27; ④), is quiet and very pleasant with a pool and sea views.

There are plenty of **campsites** on Presqu'île de Giens, La Capte and all along the coast, some of them catering for over one thousand pitches. Some smaller, more pleasant ones are: *Camping-Bernard* in Le Ceinturon (☎04.94.66.30.54, fax 04.94.66.48.30; closed Oct–Easter), a two-star close to the beach; *Le Capricorne* on rte des Vieux Salins (☎04.94.66.40.94, fax 04.94.66.46.88; Oct–March), also a two-star and 1.5km from the beach at Les Salins; and *Clair de Lune*, av du Clair de Lune (☎04.94.58.20.19, fax 04.94.58.15.90), a three-star on Giens with diving facilities, windsurfs for rent and washing machines.

The Vieille Ville

To the west of place Clemenceau a medieval gatehouse, **Porte Massillon**, opens onto rue Massillon and the Vieille Ville. At **place Massillon**, you encounter a perfect Provençal square, with terraced cafés overlooking the twelfth-century **Tour St-Blaise** (Mon & Wed–Sun 10am–noon & 4–7pm; free), the remnant of a Knights Templar lodge, which now provides the space for contemporary art exhibitions – frequently less impressive than their dramatic setting. Don't miss the narrow staircase that leads up onto the roof-top terrace for a bird's-eye view of the medieval centre. To the right of the tower, a street leads uphill to place St-Paul, from where you have another panoramic view over a section of medieval town wall to Costabelle hill and the Golfe de Giens.

Wide steps fan out from the Renaissance door of the former collegiate church of **St-Paul** (April–Oct Wed–Sat 10.30am–noon & 3.30–6pm, Sun 10am–noon; Nov–March Wed–Sat 10.30am–noon & 3–5pm) whose distinctive belfry is pure Romanesque, as is the choir, though the simplicity of the design is masked by the collection of votive offerings hung inside. The decoration also includes some splendid wrought-iron candelabras and a Christmas crib with over-life-size *santons*. Today, the church is used only for special services – the main place of worship is the mid-thirteenth-century former monastery church of **St-Louis** on place de la République.

To the right of St-Paul's, a Renaissance house bridges rue St-Paul, its turret supported by a pillar rising beside the steps. Through this arch you can reach rue St-Claire which leads past the neo-Gothic Porte des Princes to the entrance of **parc Ste-Claire** (8am–dusk; free), the exotic gardens around **Castel Ste-Clair**. The castle itself was originally owned by the French archeologist Olivier Voutier, who discovered the Venus de Milo, was then home to the American writer Edith Wharton and now houses the offices of the Parc National de Port Cros.

Cobbled paths lead up the hill via Rue St-Bernard towards the **parc St-Bernard** (8am–dusk; free), full of almost every Mediterranean flower known. Alternatively, from St-Paul you can head up to the park via rue Paradis, where you'll find an exquisite Romanesque house at no. 6, now just an ordinary residence. In the upper part of the Vieille Ville all the houses have a slight backward tilt as if to let even more light play on their old undisturbed facades.

At the top of the park, above montée des Noailles – which can be reached by car from cours Strasbourg and av Long – is the **Villa Noailles**, a Cubist mansion designed by Mallet-Stevens in the 1920s and enclosed within part of the old citadel walls. All the luminaries of Dada and Surrealism stayed here and left their mark, including Man Ray who used it as the setting for one of his most inarticulate films, *Le Mystère du Château* *de Dé*. Restoration work is due to finish in the year 2000, and until then the villa is open only from late June to early September when it's the setting for a major art exhibition (10am–noon & 3–7pm; free).

To the west of the park and further up the hill you come to the remains of Hyères' **Vieux Château** whose keep and ivy-clad towers outreach the oak and lotus trees and give stunning views out to the Îles d'Hyères and east to the Massif des Maures.

The modern town

The switch from medieval to eighteenth- and nineteenth-century Hyères is particularly abrupt, with wide boulevards and open spaces, opulent villas, waving palm fronds and whitewashed walls instead of weathered stone. Erstwhile fantasy aristocratic residences now have administrative functions, a good example being the former palace-hotel behind the tourist office. One block south, however, the opulent **casino** has been restored to its glass-domed glory and to its original vice.

If you're keen on the ancient history of this coast, the **Musée d'Art et d'Archéologie** (Mon & Wed–Fri 10am–noon & 2.30–5.30pm; free) on the top floor of the city's administrative building on place T. Lefèbvre will be of interest. It displays the finds of the archeological digs at L'Almanarre, the point where the route de Sel from the Presqu'île de Giens joins the coast. L'Almanarre derives its name from the Arabic for "lighthouse", which is what the Saracens built higher up the slope after destroying a Benedictine monastery, leaving only the chapel of St-Pierre-de-la-Manarre. Merovingian graves have been unearthed, beneath them traces of a Roman city known from Classical texts by the wonderful name of Pomponiana, and beneath that the remnants of the Greek port of Olbia.

Down to the coast

There are plenty of beaches around Hyères' coastal suburbs, but some areas are plagued with hordes of mosquitoes, so bring insect repellent just in case. The eastern side of La Capte, the very built-up isthmus of the **Presqu'île de Giens**, is one long sand beach, with very warm and shallow water, and is packed out in summer. To the northeast, traffic fumes and the proximity of the airport take away the seaside charms between Hyères Plage and Le Ceinturon despite the pines and ubiquitous palms. It's far more pleasant further up by the little fishing port of **Les Salins d'Hyères**. East of Les Salins, where the coastal road finally turns inland, you can follow a path between abandoned saltflats and the sea to a naturist beach.

Alternatively, there's the less sheltered **L'Almanarre** beach to the west of the Presqu'île de Giens, where you can swim from a narrow crescent of sand: French sailing championships are sometimes held here. Just to the north of L'Almanarre is the Costabelle hill, topped by the 1950s **Notre-Dame-de-Consolation**. The church, a concrete, stone and stained-glass affair – a classic example of its architectural era – houses an ancient statue of Our Lady, the object of pilgrimage for almost a millennium. South of L'Almanarre the route du Sel leads down the sand bar on the western side of the Presqu'île, giving you glimpses of the saltworks and the lake with its flamingoes between the sand bar and the built-up La Capte.

Besides the peculiarity of Presqu'île's attachment to the mainland (last broken by storms in 1811) Giens is a fairly nondescript, over-populated and upmarket resort. **La Tour Fondue**, a Richelieu construction on the eastern side, overlooks the small port that serves the Îles d'Hyères.

Regular **buses** from Hyères' gare routière run to Giens, L'Almanarre, Hyères-Plage and Le Centurion.

Eating, drinking and markets

For **eating** and **drinking** in Hyères, there are the terraced café-brasseries in place Massillon and, all around this part of the Vieille Ville, a good choice of crêperies, pizzerias and little bistros that serve plats du jour for around 80F.

Restaurants worth trying include *Le Haut du Pavé*, 2 rue du Temple (☎04.94.35.20.98; closed Mon), where you can dine on mussels for under 50F and, on Saturday evenings, listen to jazz in the basement; *La Bergerie*, 16 rue de Limans (☎04.94.65.57.97; closed Sat & Sun midday, also Sun eve out of season), a friendly and down-to-earth pizzeria; *Les Jardins de Bacchus*, on the edge of the new town at 32 av Gambetta (☎04.94.65.77.63; menus from 145F; à la carte around 350F), which serves novel concoctions such as caramelized pears on salmon with prawns and bacon; and *La Parillada*, overlooking the Port d'Hyères in Hyères-Plages (☎04.94.57.44.82; menus from 150F; closed Nov–March), with Spanish specialities based on fresh fish. For the best **cakes and ice creams** try *Pâtisserie Blonna* at 1 place Clemenceau (closed Mon).

A food **market** is held on place de la République on Tuesday and Thursday mornings and along av Gambetta on Saturday morning; while organic produce is sold on place Vicomtesse de Noailles on Tuesday, Thursday and Saturday mornings; arts, crafts and food are sold on place Clemenceau on Saturday morning; there's a Wednesday food market at Ayguade; and a flea market takes place in La Capte on Sunday mornings.

The Îles d'Hyères

A haven from tempests in ancient times, then the peaceful habitat of monks and farmers, the **Îles d'Hyères** (also known as the Îles d'Or) from the Middle Ages onwards became a base for piracy and coastal attacks by a relentless succession of assorted aggressors, against which the tiny populations of the islands were ineffectual. Henri II hit upon an inspired solution to this problem in 1550: presumably intending to fight fire with fire he designated the islands to be penal colonies. Convicted criminals arrived in droves but Henri's plans were thwarted when they turned to piracy themselves and even attempted to capture a ship of the royal fleet from Toulon. The islands are covered in forts – some rebuilt, others left half-destroyed or abandoned – from the sixteenth century, when François I started a trend of under-funded fort building, to the twentieth

---

GETTING TO THE ÎLES D'HYÈRES

There are ferries to the Îles d'Hyères, some operating only in summer, from six ports along the Côte d'Azur. Departures are from:

Cavalaire (☎04.94.64.08.04, and 04.94.64.48.38). Summer-only services to Île de Levant (45min), Port Cros (1hr) and Porquerolles (1hr 30min).

La Londe Port de Miramar. Summer-only services to Port Cros (45min) and Porquerolles (30min).

Le Lavandou 15 quai Gabriel-Péri (☎04.94.71.01.02). Services to Île de Levant (daily; 30min) and Port Cros (daily; 35min) and Porquerolles (July & Aug daily; April–June & Sept 3 weekly; 50min).

Port d'Hyères (☎04.94.57.44.07). Year-round services to Île de Levant and Port-Cros (1hr 30min), plus summer-only service to Porquerolles (1hr 15min).

Toulon quai Stalingrad (☎04.94.62.41.14). Summer-only services to Île de Levant (1hr), Port Cros and Porquerolles.

La Tour Fondue Presqu'île de Giens (☎04.94.58.21.81; bus #66 from the Port d'Hyères). Year-round service to Porquerolles (20min), plus summer-only services to Île de Levant and Port Cros.

century, when the German gun positions on Port-Cros and Levant were knocked out of action by the Americans.

The islands are still not free of garrisons, thanks to the knack of the French armed forces for getting prime beauty sites for bases. In this case, the army only acquired its *terrain militaire* in 1971, when the French government bought most of the archipelago to save the islands from overdevelopment and to protect their unique fauna and flora. A contradictory move certainly, but it has prevented the otherwise inevitable Côte build-up, and in the non-military areas the government, through the Parc National de Port-Cros and the Conservatoire Botanique de Porquerolles, has taken some sound environmental initiatives. On **Porquerolles**, the largest island, water is recycled using the natural means of sun-bred micro-organisms; some electricity is generated from gas produced from cane; the fertilizers used are compost not chemical; and cars are strictly limited.

Port-Cros and its small neighbour Bagaud are just about uninhabited, so there the main problem is controlling the flower-picking and litter-dropping habits of visitors. On **Levant** the military rule all but a tiny morsel of the island.

Whatever measures are taken to protect them, the Îles d'Hyères still constitute a very fragile environment, situated as they are by one of the most overpopulated coastlines. But their hot, wild, scented greenery, fine sand beaches, sea and sun constitute the essence of what makes this part of the planet so desirable. If you want to **stay on them**, however, your only reasonably priced options are on Levant, and then you need to book months in advance. Accommodation on Porquerolles is limited to extremely pricey hotels and rented apartments; on Port-Cros it is almost nonexistent.

Porquerolles

PORQUEROLLES is the most easily accessible of the Îles d'Hyères and has a permanent village around the port, with a few hotels and restaurants, plenty of cafés, a market and seemingly endless games of *boules*. In summer its population explodes to over ten thousand, but there is some activity year-round. This is the only cultivated island and it has its own wine, the *appellation* Côtes des Îles.

The origins of the ancient **Fort Sainte-Agathe** which overlooks the village are unknown, but it already existed in 1200, and was refortified in the sixteenth century by François I, who built a tower with five-metre-thick walls to resist cannon-fire. The fort has a small **museum** (June–Sept daily 11am–6pm; 20F) dedicated to shipwrecks.

The **village** itself dates from a nineteenth-century military settlement. It still focuses around the central place d'Armes, named after its original function as a parade ground. Its first non-military notoriety came in the 1960s, when Jean-Luc Godard used the village, and the calanque de la Treille at the far end of the plage de Notre-Dame, for the bewildering finale of the film *Pierrot le Fou*. Recently, the island has taken to hosting an artist in residence with works on show during the summer months at one of the hotels in the village.

Porquerolles is big enough to find yourself alone amid its stunning landscapes. The **lighthouse** due south of the village and the **calanques** to its east make good destinations for an hour's walk, though it's not safe to swim on this side of the island. The southern shoreline is all cliffs with scary paths meandering close to the edge through heather and other exuberant Provençal growth. Gentle sandy **beaches** are to be found on either side of the village, with the nearest beach just 1km away (continue away from the port past the Arche de Noë and take the first, well-signed turn right), known as the **plage d'Argent**, a 500-metre strip of white sand around a curving bay, backed by pine forests and a single restaurant. The longest beach is the **plage de Notre-Dame**, 3km northeast of the village, just before the *terrain militaire* that takes up the northern tip.

If you don't want to get around on foot, you can rent a **bike** from one of the eight outlets in the village, including *La Becane*, to the left of the church (☎04.94.58.30.20), and *L'Indien*, on place d'Armes (☎04.94.58.30.39); a cheaper option is to pay for your bike with your ferry ticket in La Tour Fondue and pick it up when you disembark at Porquerolles. There's a small **information centre** (June–Sept daily 9am–12.30pm & 2.30–6pm; ☎04.94.58.33.76) by the harbour where you can get basic maps of the island.

Hotels in Porquerolles cost 500F upwards and need to be booked months in advance. The most luxurious is *Le Mas du Langoustier* (☎04.94.58.30.09, fax 04.94.58.36.02; ⑨; closed mid-Oct to April) at the western end of the island. *Sainte-Anne* (☎04.94.58.30.04, fax 04.94.58.32.26; ⑧; closed mid-Nov to mid-Feb); *Auberge des Glycines* (☎04.94.58.30.36, fax 04.94.58.35.22; ⑧; closed Jan to mid-Feb) and *Relais de la Poste* (☎04.94.58.30.26; fax 04.94.58.33.57; ⑥; closed Nov–March) are all on place d'Armes in the village, and, with the exception of the *Relais de la Poste*, offer full board only. The island has no **campsite** and *camping sauvage* is strictly forbidden.

Most of the **cafés** and **restaurants** in the village cater for the wealthier tourist, who can snack on lobster at *Le Mas du Langoustier* (see above; menus from 300F). Slightly more affordable is the grilled fish at the *Auberge des Glycines* (see above; menus from 120F). *La Plage d'Argent* (☎04.94.58.32.48; closed Oct–March), overlooking the d'Argent beach, has a good midday menu for around 100F.

Port-Cros

The dense vegetation and mini mountains of **PORT-CROS** make exploring this island considerably harder going than Porquerolles, even though it is less than half the size. Aside from ruined forts and the handful of buildings around the port, the only intervention on the island's wildlife are the classification labels on some of the plants and the extensive network of paths. You are not supposed to stray from these signposted routes and it would be very difficult to do so given the thickness of the undergrowth.

The entire island is a protected zone – no smoking outside the port area, no picking of flowers – and, as the only member of the archipelago with natural springs, has the richest **fauna and flora**. Kestrels, eagles and sparrowhawks nest here; there are shrubs that flower and bear fruit at the same time, and more common species such as broom, lavender, rosemary and heather flourish in abundance. If you come armed with a botanical dictionary, the leaflet provided by the **Bureau d'Information du Parc** at the port will reveal all the species to be seen, watched and smelled.

It takes a couple of hours to walk from the port to the nearest beach, **plage de la Palud**; a similar time to cross the island via the **Vallon de la Solitude** or **Vallon de la Fausse-Monnaie**. You can also follow a ten-kilometre **circuit of the island**. At the Fort de Lestissac, on the way to the plage de la Palu, there is an exhibition on the island's **marine life** (July–Sept 10am–6pm; free), which is also protected. The shallow waters between Palu beach and the tiny offshore island are full of diverting fishes to look at. More serious scuba divers explore the underwater world around the **Ilot de la Gabinière** off the southern shore. Alternatively, an expensive "submarine" trip in a glass-bottomed boat called the *Seascope* is on offer around the islands. Be warned, though, that, while enjoyable, it is not as exciting as its publicity makes out.

Staying on Port Cros, sadly, is not much of an option. The island's sole **hotel**, *Le Manoir* (☎04.94.05.90.52, fax 04.94.05.90.89; ⑨; closed mid-Sept to mid-May) is prohibitively expensive, as are the few **restaurants** around the port, though there are a few places where you can get a sandwich or a slice of pizza. Camping is forbidden.

Île de Levant

The **ÎLE DE LEVANT** – ninety percent military reserve – is almost always humid and sunny. Cultivated plantlife goes wild with the result that giant geraniums and nasturtiums climb three-metre hedges, overhung by gigantic eucalyptus trees and yucca plants.

The tiny bit of the island spared by the military is a **nudist colony**, set up in the village of **Héliopolis** in the early 1930s, and nudism is compulsorary on the beaches of Bain de Diane and Les Grottes. About sixty people live here year round, joined by thousands who come just for the summer and tens of thousands of day-trippers. The residents' preferred street dress is *"les plus petits costumes en Europe"*, on sale as you get off the boat.

Visitors who come just for a couple of hours tend to be treated as voyeurs. If you stay, even for one night, you'll generally receive a much friendlier reception, but in summer without advance booking you'd be very lucky to find a room or camping pitch. In the **hotels**, half board is usually compulsory in summer with rooms needing to be reserved well in advance. The best-value places near the port are *Le Gaëtan* on chemin de l'Ayguade (☎04.94.05.91.78, fax 04.94.36.77.17; ⑦; closed early-Oct to Easter); and *La Source*, on the same street (☎04.94.05.91.36, fax 04.94.05.93.47; ⑤; closed mid-Oct to March). *La Brise Marine* (☎04.94.05.91.15, fax 04.94.05.93.21; ⑤; closed Nov–April), in the centre of the village, is small and very charming. For more luxury, there's the cliff-top *Le Ponant* (☎ & fax 04.94.05.90.41; ⑦; closed Oct–May); and the very smart *Héliotel* (☎04.94.05.90.63, fax 04.94.05.90.20; ⑧; closed Nov–March). In addition, there are three naturist **campsites**: *Le Colombero* (☎04.94.05.90.29; closed Oct–Easter), *La Joie de Vivre* (☎04.94.05.90.49; closed Oct–Easter) and *La Pinède* (☎04.94.05.90.47; closed Nov–March).

Levant has a better choice of **restaurants** than the other islands; you can eat decently at *La Source* (see above; menus from 100F) and *La Brise Marine* (see above; menu at 130F), or snack at the *Brasserie Île de Beauté*.

The Corniche des Maures

The Côte d'Azur really gets going to the east of Hyères, with the resorts of the **Corniche des Maures**, the twenty-kilometre stretch of coast from Le Lavandou to the Baie de Cavalaire; multi-million-dollar residences lurk in the hills, even more pricey yachts in the bays, and seafront prices start edging up. This is where the rich and famous go to seed: Douglas Fairbanks Jr (a house in Bormes) and the late grand duke of Luxembourg to name but two, plus a whole host of titled names that *Tatler* readers are assumed to know. And though aristos and celebrities are not always known for their good taste, when it comes to locations for living, they can usually be relied upon.

The Corniche des Maures has beaches that shine silver from the mica crystals in the sand; tall dark pines, oaks and eucalyptus shading them and hiding garish villa balconies; glittering rocks of purple, green and reddish hue; and chestnut-forested hills keeping winds away. There are even stretches where it's possible to imagine what all this coast was like in bygone years, notably around **Cap de Brégançon**, at the **Domaine de Rayol gardens**, and between **Le Rayol** and the huge resort of **Cavalaire**.

Transport around the corniche is the biggest problem: the road itself is narrow and littered with hairpin bends and the buses that make the run (high season only) drive extremely slow, as do any cars that trail them. Cycling, too, is strenuous – and hair-raising – and doesn't get you very far unless you're Tour de France material. There are no trains.

Bormes-les-Mimosas

BORMES-LES-MIMOSAS, 16km west of Hyères, is indisputably medieval, with a restored castle at the summit of its hill, protected by spiralling lines of pantiled houses backing onto short-cut flights of steps. The castle itself is private property, but there is a public terrace alongside it which offers attractive views. Attractions in the village include a **Musée d'Art et d'Histoire** at 65 rue Carnot (June–Sept Mon & Wed–Sat 10am–noon & 2.30–7pm, Sun 10am–noon; rest of year Thurs & Sun 10am–noon & 3–5pm; 10F), with its turn-of-the-century regional painting; a mindlessly ugly pleasure port down by **La Favière**, flanked by spot-the-spare-foot-of-sand beaches; and oddly named addresses in the Vieux Village such as "alleyway of lovers", "street of brigands" "gossipers' way", and "arse-breaker street".

The mimosas here, and all along the Côte d'Azur, are no more indigenous than the people passing in their Porsches. The tree that flowers in February in myriad tiny yellow pom-poms was introduced from Mexico in the 1860s, and the extension to the place-name dates from 1968. Nonetheless, the display is spectacular, followed as it is by the bougainvillea and other luscious summer climbing flowers.

When you've had enough of exploring the immaculately paved alleyways or following the signed *circuits touristiques* up and down the steep slopes of the old village, you could head for the coast, but be prepared for *Defense d'entrée* and *Propriété privée* signs at every turn. Private housing estates have entirely blocked road-access to the extremity of **Cap Bénat** but you can reach it on foot along a coastal path from La Favière's beach. From Cap Bénat westwards to the hideous seaside extension of **La Londe**, vineyards and private woods will block your passage, as well as the security arrangements around the château at **Cap de Brégançon**, which is the holiday home of the president of the Republic. Note also that in summer you will be forced to pay for access to each of the three public tracks down to the shore from the La Londe–Cabasson road (cars around 35F; cyclists and pedestrians 5F). However, once you've reached the water you can wander along the gorgeous beaches as far as you like, with no apartment buildings amongst the pine trees, not even villas, just the odd mansion in the distance surrounded by its vineyards.

Practicalities

During July and August Bormes-les-Mimosas is served by a **minibus** connection (6 daily; 30min) from Le Lavandou; otherwise, it's a two-kilometre walk from Le-Pin-de-Bormes on the main Hyères–Le Lavandou road. Minibuses arrive at the top of the village, near place Gambetta, where you'll find the **tourist office** (July & Aug daily 9am–12.30pm & 3–8pm; June & Sept daily 9am–12.30pm & 2.30–7pm; rest of year Mon–Sat 9am–12.30pm & 2–6pm; ☎04.94.71.15.17). Two reasonable **hotels** in old Bormes are *La Terrasse*, 19 place Gambetta (☎04.94.71.15.22; ③), with ordinary, clean rooms; and the *Bellevue* also on place Gambetta (☎04.94.71.15.15; ②), a bit plain and old-fashioned. In Cabasson there's a very attractive and peaceful hotel, *Les Palmiers*, a 240 chemin du Petit Fort (☎04.94.64.81.94, fax 04.94.64.93.61; ⑥), with its own path to the beach. **Campsites** lie just below the main road or in La Favière, closer to Le Lavandou than to Bormes. These include *Le Camp du Domaine* right by the sea on the rte de Bénat (☎04.94.71.03.12, fax 04.94.15.18.67; closed Nov to mid-March); a much smaller four-star site, *Clos-Mar-Jo*, 895 chemin de Bénat (☎04.94.71.53.39; closed Oct–March); the two-star *La Célinette*, 30 impasse du Houx (☎04.94.71.07.98; closed early Oct to March); and the two-star *Les Cyprès* on av de la Mer (☎04.94.64.86.50, fax 04.94.15.21.01; closed Oct–March). Book in advance in high season.

This being the Côte proper, **restaurants** become rather interesting, though often more costly than a hotel room. Reasonably priced and excellent quality are: *La Tonnelle des Délices*, on place Gambetta (☎04.94.71.34.84; closed Wed), which has menus from

100F; and *L'Escoundudo*, 2 ruelle du Moulin (☎04.94.71.15.53; closed Mon & Tues mid-day out of season), which serves excellent, affordable Provençal specialities, with a delicious tomato and hot goats' cheese tart on the generous 160F menu and a lunchtime menu for under 100F. *Pâtes...et Pâtes* on place du Bazar (closed Tues) serves the best pasta for 100–150F. More run-of-the-mill meals can be had at the hotels listed above and at *La Pastourelle*, 41 rue Carnot (☎04.94.71.57.78).

Le Lavandou

One of many Mediterranean fishing villages turned pleasure port, **LE LAVANDOU**, to the south of Bormes, has nothing wildly special to recommend it, apart from some tempting shops and a general Azur atmosphere. From the central promenade of quai Gabriel Péri the sea is hardly visible for pleasure boats moored at the three harbours, and it's only the demand of the more upmarket restaurants that keeps the dozen or so fishing vessels still in business. The **beach**, that port construction has spared, is east-facing and backed by high-rise buildings to the west of town.

The whole conglomeration of the town, which merges with Bormes to the west and **St Clair** to the east (whose beach is more pleasant than Le Lavandou's), concentrates its charm in the tiny area between av du Gal-de-Gaulle and quai Gabriel-Péri where café tables, sporting multicoloured goblets of cocktails and ice creams, overlook the *boules* pitch and the traffic of the seafront road. Three narrow stairways lead back to rue Patron Ravello, place Argaud and rue Abbé-Helin, each lined with specialist shops and cafés.

If you're looking for something more energetic than window-shopping you could rent a surf-board or a boat, go water-skiing, take a trip to the Îles d'Hyères or try out deep-sea diving. But if you're after the fabled silver beaches you need to head east out of town to the string of villages between Le Lavandou and Cavalaire-sur-Mer.

Practicalities

Buses stop on the av de Provence, a short walk west of the **tourist office** on quai Gabriel-Peri (May–Sept Mon–Sat 9am–12.30pm & 2.30–7.30pm, Sun 10am–noon & 3.30–6.30pm; Oct–April Mon–Sat 9am–noon & 2.30–6pm; ☎04.94.71.00.61). The unexotic **quai des Îles d'Or**, a wide patch of tarmac dividing two of the ports, juts out from the tourist office. **Ferries** to the Îles d'Hyères (daily), to St-Tropez (every Tues) and to Brégançon (every Sun) leave from here; the École de Plongée offers initiation **deep-sea dives** (turn up at noon; around 150F); and Cap Sud on quai Gabriel-Peri (☎04.94.71.59.33) rents out **motor boats**. For escaping into the hills or attempting to hunt out secluded beaches you can rent **bikes** from Planète Glisse, 15 av des Ilaires (☎04.94.71.16.50) or Holiday Bike, av Vincent-Auriol (☎04.94.15.19.99).

In summer your chances of finding a **hotel room** are pretty slim. Prices are similar to Bormes, with rather less charm at the bottom end of the range. Some less pricey addresses to try, all in the centre, include: *L'Îlot Fleurie*, bd Front de Mer right next to the beach (☎04.94.71.14.82, fax 04.94.15.03.46; ④); *Neptune*, 26 av Gal-de-Gaulle (☎04.94.71.01.01, fax 04.94.64.91.61; ③); *Hôtel l'Oustaou*, 20 av Gal-de-Gaulle (☎04.94.71.12.18, fax 04.94.15.08.75; ③); and *L'Auberge Provençale*, 11 rue Patron Ravello (☎04.94.71.00.44, fax 04.94.15.02.25; ②). For several times as much you could have a charming room overlooking the sea at St-Clair in the *Belle-Vue*, chemin du Four des Maures (☎04.94.71.01.06; ⑦; closed Nov–March); or at *La Calanque*, 62 av du Gal-de-Gaulle (☎04.94.71.05.96, fax 04.94.71.20.12; ⑧; closed Oct, Nov & Jan) in a less attractive building but with views over the port and fishing and diving trips laid on. For **campsites**, there are those at Bormes (see p.222), or try *Caravaning St-Clair*, av André-Gide in St-Clair (☎04.94.71.03.38; closed Nov–Feb), a three-star for campervans and caravans only.

Sea-view gourmandise comes at a price at *L'Algue Bleue* (menus from 145F; à la carte from 300F; ☎04.94.71.01.95), *La Calanque* hotel's **restaurant**; the sea bass is particularly fine. The *Auberge Provençale*'s restaurant (menus from 130F; closed Mon, Tues & Wed midday) is central and busy, and the food is excellent if a touch expensive à la carte. At *Le Pêcheur*, quai des Pêcheurs (☎04.94.71.58.01; menus from 95F; closed Mon), you can dine on fish caught by the restaurant's owner. As for **café lounging** you can take your pick along quai Gabriel-Péri: *Le Rhumerie* has live music at weekends and the most comfy terrace chairs; *Chez Mimi* has good beers and perhaps the edge on the ice-cream front; *Le Pantheur Rose* is a smart piano-bar. There's also the *Brasserie du Centre* on place Ernest-Reyer, which serves cocktails in a stylish setting.

If you're determined to accelerate the rate your money parts company with you, Le Lavandou's **nightlife** will assist. *Le Paradis*, at résidence Marbello, bd du Front-de-Mer (10.30pm–5am; closed mid-Oct to March), is a **disco** which has been going strong for more than fifty years; *La Jamaïque*, quai Baptistin Pins (10.30pm–dawn), is a more laid-back nightclub with an older clientele and Afro-Caribbean sounds.

Along the corniche

The road east out of Le Lavandou and St-Clair (av André-Gide or the D559) is lined with pink oleander bushes interspersed with purple bougainvillea, a classic feature of the Côte d'Azur corniche as it curves its way through the steep wooded hills that reach right down to the sea. The pines and eucalyptus hiding the estates of holiday villas, the geographical impossibility of a constant shore-line road, and the scented flowers go some way to compensate for the loss of countryside. There's also the old railway track (*Ex-Voie Férée*), the lengths of which you can walk along, running from Pramousquier to Cavalaire-sur-Mer, which brought the rich and curious to these parts at the turn of the century. For all the modern build-up of this stretch, it is, along with the St-Tropez peninsula it leads to, the most beautiful part of the Côte d'Azur.

The **beaches** here really are silvery and from **PRAMOUSQUIER**, 7km from Le Lavandou, you can even look up from the turquoise water to woods undisturbed by roads and buildings. Between Aiguebelle and Cavalière, before you reach Pramousquier, a path through the pines above **Pointe du Layet** gives you access to the tiny *calanques* around the headland that extends out from Plage du Rossignol and Plage du Layet. **CAVALIÈRE** has a long, wide beach and hill horizons that easily outreach the highest houses. Though **LE CANADEL** and **LE RAYOL**, two joined villages 4km east of Pramousquier, have gradually colonized their upper slopes, they feel like villages and the climb up the sinuous D27 to the **Col du Canadel**, on the road to La Môle, has unbeatable views and beautiful cork-oak woodland.

The best place of all, however, where you can totally forget what has happened to this coast in the last forty years, is the huge **Domaine du Rayol gardens** in Le Rayol (daily: July & Aug 9.30am–12.30pm & 4.30–8pm; Feb–June & Sept to mid-Nov 9.30am–12.30pm & 2.30–6.30pm; 40F). The grounds extending down to the Figuier bay and headland originally belonged to a banker who went bust at the gaming tables of Monte Carlo in the 1930s. He built the Art Nouveau mansion through which you enter the gardens, the Art Deco villa, farmhouse and classical pergola to which a later owner added the dramatic long flight of steps lined with cypresses. Areas of the garden are dedicated to plants from different parts of the world that share the climate of the Mediterranean: Chile, South Africa, China, California, Central America, Australia and New Zealand. Apart from the extraordinary diversity in the forms and colours of the vegetation, some of which is left alone to spread and colonize at will, there's sheer brilliance in the landscaping that entices you to explore, to retrace your steps and get to know every path and every vista. In July and August you can take a snorkelling tour of the "Jardin Marine" (book at least a week in advance; ☎04.94.05.32.50; 70F). There are also highly informative and engaging guided tours (in French only) of the garden, given by its professional gardeners.

Heading east from Le Rayol and Le Canadel the corniche climbs away from the coast through 3km of open countryside, sadly scarred nearly every year by fires, where the only visible building is **La Maison Blanche**, a lone mansion donated by its heirless owner to the *commune* of Cavalaire, who have made all the land around it a protected site. As abruptly as this wilderness commences, it ends with sprawl of **CAVALAIRE-SUR-MER**. Here the tiny *calanques* give way to a long stretch of sand and level land that has been exploited for the maximum rentable space. In its favour, Cavalaire is very much a family resort and not too stuck on glamour.

Practicalities

In Le Rayol, the helpful **tourist office** is on place Le Rayol (July & Aug daily 9.30am–12.30pm & 3–7pm; Sept–June Mon–Sat 9.30am–12.30pm & 3–6pm; ☎04.94.05.65.69); it has details of possible walks including the *Ex-Voie Férée*. Cavalaire-sur-Mer's **tourist office** (mid-June to mid-Sept daily 8.30am–7.30pm; rest of year Mon–Sat 9am–12.30pm & 2–6pm; ☎04.94.01.92.10) is in the supremely ugly and unmissable Maison de la Mer, where av du Port meets promenade de la Mer; it has lists of hotels and campsites. **Bikes** can be rented nearby at Holiday Bikes (☎04.94.64.18.17).

Finding **rooms** in this area outside July and August should not present a problem; if you get stuck there are a number of hotels in Cavalaire-sur-Mer, where the **hotel** with the best view is *Les Cigales*, rue des Écoles (☎04.94.05.80.32, fax 04.94.05.74.94; ④). Above the main road in Pramousquier and within easy walking distance of the beach, the *Hôtel Beau Site* (☎04.94.05.80.08, fax 04.94.05.76.76; ④) has rooms with sea-view balconies, while *Le Mas* (☎ & fax 04.94.05.80.43; ⑤), one street behind, has a pool and even better views. Between Pramousquier and Le Canadel *Le Karlina*, on chemin du Plageron (☎04.94.05.61.65, fax 04.94.05.63.52; ⑦), has its own private beach front and boat. In Le Rayol you can stay in an apartment for four people from 320F to 480F a day at *Les Îles de la Mer*, close to the beach on av des Américains (☎04.94.05.63.76, fax 04.94.05.63.23), or there are simple low-priced rooms at the *Auberge des Silaques* on the main road (☎04.94.05.60.13; ③).

The place to **eat** and **drink** is *Le Maurin des Maures* on the main road at Le Rayol (☎04.94.05.60.11; Mon–Sat midday menu under 100F, otherwise 150F) serving fresh grilled fish, bouillabaisse and fried seafoods. For **nightlife**, head down to Le Canadel's beach where *La Tropicana* **disco** keeps the night young (from 10.30pm; ☎04.94.05.61.50; July & Aug only).

La Croix-Valmer

From Cavalaire-sur-Mer's seafront, another exceptional sight of coastline, the **Domaine de Cap Lardier**, dressed only in its natural covering of rock and woodlands, greets you from the other side of the Baie de Cavalaire. This is a wonderful coastal conservation area around the southern tip of the St-Tropez peninsula; access to it is the main reason why **LA CROIX-VALMER** is a preferable base to Cavalaire, though the resort's centre is some 2.5km from the sea. That too adds charm, however, since some of the land in between is taken up by vineyards which produce a very decent wine. Local legend maintains that Emperor Constantine stopped here with his troops on his way to Rome and had his famous vision of the sun's rays forming a cross over the sea which converted him, and therefore ultimately all of Europe, to the new religion; hence the "cross" in the name of the village which only came into existence in 1934.

La Croix-Valmer's **tourist office** in Les Jardins de la Gare, just up from the central junction place des Palmiers (mid-June to mid-Sept Mon–Sat 9am–7pm, Sun 9am–1pm;

rest of year Mon–Sat 9am–noon & 2–6pm, Sun 9am–noon & 2–6pm; ☎04.94.55.12.12), has a list of walks in the area. **Bikes** and scooters can be rented from Holiday Bikes, on rte 559 east of the village (☎04.94.79.75.12). A budget-priced **hotel** for this part of the world is *La Bienvenue* on rue L-Martin (☎04.94.79.60.23, fax 04.94.79.70.08; ③; closed Nov–Easter), right in the centre of the village. One of the least expensive options near the beach is the small, family-run *Hostellerie La Ricarde*, quartier de la Plage (☎04.94.79.64.07, fax 04.94.54.30.14; ③), whilst at the other end of the scale is *Le Château de Valmer* on rte de Gigaro (☎04.94.79.60.10, fax 04.94.54.22.68; ⑧), a seriously luxurious old Provençal manor house within walking distance of the sea. For a **campsite** with excellent facilities try the four-star *Sélection* site on bd de la Mer (booking essential in summer; ☎04.94.55.10.30, fax 04.94.55.10.39; closed mid-Oct to mid-March), 2.5km southwest of the town centre on the main road towards Cavalaire, and just 400m from the sea.

There are some extremely tempting **restaurants** along the beach, though none is particularly cheap; the best is *Souleïas* (☎04.94.55.10.55; menus from 200F). Good, inexpensive pizzas are guaranteed at *Le Coin de l'Italien* (☎04.94.79.67.16), almost the last commercial outlet before the conservation area. The local **wine** is for sale at the Cave Vinicole on bd de Tabarin by place des Palmiers.

To reach the **beach**, Plage du Gigaro, and the start of the paths to Cap Lardier, you need to take bd Georges Selliez from place des Palmiers (the D93), turn right into bd de Sylvabelle, then left along bd de la Mer. It's a four-kilometre walk, so you may prefer to catch the **shuttle bus** (*navette*), which runs hourly in summer from the tourist office in the the village to the beaches.

St-Tropez and its peninsula

The origins of **ST-TROPEZ** are not remarkable: a little fishing village that grew up around a port founded by the Greeks of Marseille, it was destroyed by the Saracens in 739 and finally fortified in the late Middle Ages. Its sole distinction from the myriad other fishing villages along this coast was its inaccessibility. Stuck out on the southern shores of the Golfe de St-Tropez, away from the main coastal routes on a wide peninsula that never warranted real roads, St-Tropez could be reached easily only by boat. This held true as late as the 1880s, when the novelist **Maupassant** sailed his yacht into the port during his final high-living binge before the onset of syphilitic insanity. The Tropeziens were a little shocked but it was the beginning of their induction to bizarre strangers seeing paradise in their commonplace home.

Soon after Maupassant's fleeting visit, the painter and leader of the Neo-Impressionists, **Paul Signac**, sailed down the coast in his boat named after Manet's notorious painting *L'Olympia*. Bad weather forced him to moor in St-Tropez and, being rich and impulsive, he decided to have a house there; *La Hune*, on what is now rue Paul-Signac, was built for him, designed by his fellow painter Henri van de Velde. Signac opened his doors to impoverished friends who could benefit from the light, the beauty and the distance from the respectable convalescent world of Cannes and Nice. **Matisse** was one of the first to take up his offer; the locals were shocked again, this time by Madame Matisse modelling in a kimono. **Bonnard**, **Marquet**, **Dufy**, **Derain**, **Vlaminck**, **Seurat**, **Van Dongen** and others followed, and by the eve of World War I, St-Tropez was fairly well established as a hang-out for Bohemians.

The 1930s saw a new influx of artists, this time writers as much as painters. **Jean Cocteau** came here. **Colette** bought a villa outside the village, where she lived for fourteen years, describing the main concerns of her life there as "whether to go walking or swimming, whether to have rosé or white, whether to have a long day or a long night". **Anaïs Nin**'s journal records "girls riding bare-breasted on the back of open cars... an

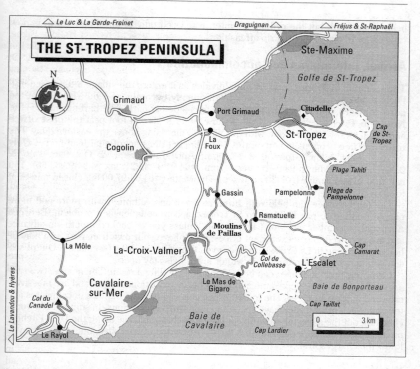

intensity of pleasure..." and undressing between bamboo bushes that rustled with concealed lovers.

After World War II, St-Tropez was ready for another burst of singular animation. In 1956 Roger Vadim arrived, with crew, to film **Brigitte Bardot** in *Et Dieu Créa La Femme*. The international cult of Tropezian sun, sex and celebrities took off; even the Sixties hippies who flocked to the revamped Mediterranean mecca of liberation managed to look glamorous, and the resort has been mainstream big-money ever since.

The star-studded list of St-Tropez **property owners** includes Elton John, George Michael and Jean-Paul Belmondo as well as high-profile business types such as Mohamad Al Fayad, owner of Harrods. Brigitte Bardot, for decades the most famous icon of the place, eventually carried out her threat and moved out in the late 1990s, though she still visits her animal sanctuary here. In the summer of 1989 she famously announced to the world that a "black tide of human filth" was physically and morally polluting her beloved village. Europe's media descended on the town where the beleaguered mayor said yes, the summer influx has quadrupled in the last few years, and yes, they have to collect the rubbish twice a day and still can't keep the streets clean. "It is true that St-Tropez is a dying village," concluded the mayor, "but who brought all this vice and indecency here in the first place?"

In 1991 another disaster struck with the discovery that the famous hundred-year-old **plane trees** on place des Lices were rotting. Several had to be chopped down; the remainder have undergone intensive surgery and their hollow trunks are now propped up with metal crutches. They are perhaps a fitting metaphor for St-Tropez itself. Rubbish bins have multiplied, and the clientele with titanium-plated credit cards has not been abandoned, but the ordinary punter, who used only to stroll and gawp, is now catered for in run-of-the-mill rip-off fashion.

Arrival, information and accommodation

The road into St-Tropez from La Foux divides as it enters the village into av Général-Leclerc and av Gal-de-Gaulle, which itself quickly becomes av 8 du Mai 1945 at the **gare routière**, and runs parallel to a vast port-side car park. The harbour here is the **Nouveau Port** for yacht overspill. Follow av du 8 Mai on foot past the **post office** and you'll hit the **Vieux Port**, with the Vieille Ville rising above the eastern quay. The **tourist office** is opposite you on the Vieux Port at the start of quai Jean-Jaurès (July & Aug daily 9.30am–1pm & 3–10.30pm; April–June, Sept & Oct 9am–1pm & 2.30–7pm; Nov–March 9am–1pm & 2–7pm; ☎04.94.97.45.21, fax 04.94.97.82.66). You can rent **bikes** from MAS, 3 rue Joseph-Quaranta (☎04.94.97.00.60; closed mid-Sept to March).

The tourist office can help with **hotel** reservations, although with more and more people wanting to pay homage to St-Tropez, accommodation is a problem. Between April and September you won't find a room unless you've booked months in advance and are prepared to pay exorbitant prices. If you have your own transport, you may be better off staying in La Croix-Valmer or even Cavalaire-sur-Mer (see p.225). Out of season you may be luckier, though in winter few hotels stay open.

Camping near St-Tropez can be as difficult as finding a room. The nearest two sites are on the plage du Pampelonne and both charge extortionate rates and are massively crowded in high summer. The tourist office can also provide full lists of campsites and tell you which official sites have space and help with reservations. In summer it's worth checking out the signs for **camping à la ferme** that you'll see along the D93. Pitching on a farm can be more pleasant that the overcrowded official sites, but make sure you know the charges first.

Hotels

Le Baron, 23 rue de l'Aïoli (☎04.94.97.06.57, fax 04.94.97.58.72). Overlooking the citadel, comfortable and a bit quieter than those in the centre. ⑤.

Les Chimères, quartier du Pilon (☎04.94.97.02.90, fax 04.94.97.63.57). One of the cheaper options a short way back from the gare routière towards La Foux. Closed mid-Nov to mid-Feb & over Christmas and New Year. ④.

L'Ermitage, av Paul-Signac (☎04.94.97.52.33). Above pl des Lices, charming and very comfortable. ⑧.

Les Lauriers, rue du Temple (☎04.94.97.04.88, fax 04.94.97.21.87). Small and very good value, close to pl des Lices. Closed last two weeks of Nov & all Feb. ⑦.

Lou Cagnard, 18 av Paul-Roussel (☎04.94.97.04.24, fax 04.94.97.09.44). Dreary-looking from the outside, but with a decent garden and night-time quiet. Closed Nov & Dec. ④.

La Ponche, 3 rue des Remparts (☎04.94.97.02.53, fax 04.94.97.78.61). An old block of fishers' houses luxuriously kitted out and with a host of famous arty names in its guest book. Closed Nov–March. ⑨.

Le Sube, 15 quai Suffren (☎04.94.97.30.04, fax 04.94.54.89.08). Unique views over the port for over 1500F a night; decor to make you think you're in a yacht and mirrors everywhere. ⑨.

Campsites

La Croix du Sud, rte des Plages (☎04.94.79.80.84, fax 04.94.79.89.21). A four-star site 3km from Ramatuelle towards the Plage de Pampelonne (see p.231). Closed Oct–April.

Camping Parc Montana, off the road to Bourrian near Gassin (☎04.94.55.20.20, fax 04.94.56.34.77). A three-star site which also has caravans for rent. Closed Oct–March.

Les Tournels on rte de Camarat (☎04.94.55.90.90, fax 04.94.55.90.99). Vast site but well situated, 1km from the sea.

The Town

Beware of coming to St-Tropez in high summer, unless by yacht and with limitless credit. The 5.5km of road from La Foux, the mainland as it were, has summer traffic jams as bad as Nice or Marseille, and the pedestrian jams to the port are not much better. The hotels and restaurants are full and too expensive, and the beaches, while not quite as bad as Bardot's description, are certainly not the cleanest on the coast. So save your visit, if you can, for a spring or autumn day and you may understand why this place has had such history and such hype.

St-Tropez has no need to advertise its medieval streets with *circuits touristiques* – in fact the soft-coloured ancient weathered buildings appear such a natural backdrop to the commerce that you hardly notice them.

The **Vieux Port** is where you get the classic St-Tropez experience: the quayside café clientele face-to-face with the yacht-deck Martini-sippers, and the latest fashion looks parading in between, defining the French word *frimer* (derived from sham) which means exactly this – to stroll ostentatiously in places like St-Tropez. You may well be surprised at just how entertaining this spectacle can be, especially when added to the jugglers, fire-eaters and mimics that trade their art in the streets.

The **yachts**, which in this restricted harbour space appear to share the scale of cross-Channel ferries, tend to be registered in Britain, the US, the Caribbean or France. Union Jacks normally predominate, though actual owners of these ugly floating fortunes are just as likely to be Manhattan or City of London banks as individual aristocrats or stars.

The other pole of St-Trop's life is **place des Lices**, southeast of the Vieux Port, with its sad but surviving plane trees and the benches and *boules* games underneath. The café-brasseries have become a bit too Champs-Élysées in style, and a new commercial block has been added near the northern corner, but you can still sit down for free and ponder the unchanged dusty surface that is so essential for the momentum of Provence's favourite pastime.

Between the port and place des Lices – rue Sibille, rue Clemenceau – and in the smaller lanes in the heart of the old village you can window-shop or buy haute couture, antiques, *objets d'art* and classy trinkets to your heart's content.

East from the port, from the top end of quai Jean-Jaurès, you pass the **Château Suffren**, originally built in 980 by Count Guillaume 1er of Provence – now home to an antique shop and occasional art exhibitions – and into place de l'Hôtel-de-Ville where the *mairie* with its attractive earthy pink facade and dark green shutters reminds you that this is a real town. A street to the left takes you down to the rocky **Baie de la Glaye**; straight ahead rue de la Ponche passes through an ancient gateway to place du Revelin above the **fishing port** with its tiny beach. Turning inland and upwards, struggling past shop fronts, stalls and café tables, you can finally reach the open space around the sixteenth-century **citadel** (summer Mon & Wed Sun 10am–5.30pm; winter Mon & Wed Sun 10am–4.30pm; closed all Nov). Its maritime museum is not much fun but the walk round the ramparts on an overgrown path has the best views of the gulf and the back of the town, views that have not changed since their translations into oil on canvas before World War II.

These paintings can be seen at the **Musée de l'Annonciade** (June–Sept Mon & Wed–Sun 10am–noon & 3–7pm; Oct & Dec–May Mon & Wed–Sun 10am–noon & 2–6pm; 25F), reason in itself for a visit to St-Tropez. It was originally Signac's idea to have a permanent exhibition space for the Neo-Impressionists and Fauvists who painted here, though it was not until 1955 that collections owned by various individuals were put together in the deconsecrated sixteenth-century chapel on place Georges-Grammont just west of the port. The museum features representative works by Signac, Matisse and most of the other artists who worked here: grey, grim, northern scenes of Paris, Boulogne and Westminster, and then local, brilliantly sun-lit scenes by the same brush. Two winter scenes of St-Tropez by Dufy contrast with Camille Camoin's springtime *Place des Lices* and Bonnard's boilingly hot summer view. The museum is a real delight for its contents, unrivalled outside Paris for the 1890 to 1940 period, for the way it displays them, and for the fact that it can sometimes be the least crowded place in town.

Eating and drinking

There are **restaurants** for every budget in St-Tropez, as well as plenty of **snack bars** and takeaway outfits, particularly on rue Georges-Clemenceau and place des Lices. Almost all are open daily from June to September; many close altogether for the winter months. Place aux Herbes has a Tuesday and Saturday morning fish **market** with some fruit and veg available.

Cafés and snacks

Café des Arts, pl des Lices. The number-one café-brasserie on the square. Old-timers still gather in the bar at the back. Menus from 200F.

Glaces Alfred, rue Sibille. Ice creams made on the premises.

Le Gorille, quai Suffren. Straightforward quayside fare. July & Aug open 24hr. Under 100F.

La Patate, rue Clemenceau. Snack bar serving omelettes, pasta, *pan bagnat* and so forth.

Café Sénéquier, on the port. The top quayside café, horribly expensive, but selling sensational nougat (also sold in the shop at the back).

Snack Thierry et Roland, cnr bd Vasserot and rue F-Sibille. Generous takeaway sandwiches for around 25F. In the same block of outlets you'll find pizzas, roast chicken and a *charcuterie*.

La Tarte Tropezienne, 1 rue G-Clemenceau. Pâtissier which claims to have invented this sponge and cream custard cake.

Restaurants

Auberge des Maures, rue du Dr-Boutin, off rue Aillard (☎04.94.97.01.50). Roast lamb, stuffed peppers and gooey chocolate cake at reasonable prices; menu from 130F.

Bistrot des Lices, 3 pl des Lices (☎04.94.97.29.00). *Fin-de-siècle* decor for traditional preening and spectacular food, from spider-crab soup to scallop *aïoli*, roasted turbot in ratatouille to stuffed shoulder of hare in a thyme sauce, and unbelievable chocolate puds; midday menu 175F, otherwise from 280F. The *Boeuf sur la Place* next door, under the same management, serves less exotic dishes for half the price.

La Citadelle, cnr rue Citadelle and rue Aire du Chemin. *Moules marinières*, fish soup, *pissaladières*, and other standard regional fare. Not brilliant, but reasonably priced with plats du jour for 58F.

L'Echalote, 35 rue du Gal-Allard (☎04.94.54.83.26). Rich, meaty dishes and a great scallop salad to enjoy in the tranquillity of the garden; midday menu under 100F, otherwise from 200F.

Joseph, 1 pl de l'Hôtel-de-Ville (☎04.94.97.01.66). Good bouillabaisse, *bourride* and desserts. Menus from 160F, à la carte from 300F.

Lou Revelen, 4 rue des Remparts (☎04.94.97.06.34). Grilled fish, *petits farcis*, fresh pasta and seafood dishes with a menu before 8.30pm for under 100F.

Le Petit Charron, 6 rue des Charrons (☎04.94.97.73.78). Tiny terrace and dining room serving beautifully cooked Provençal specialities. Menus from 150F. Closed Wed out of season.

Regis et Lolo, montée de la Citadelle (☎04.94.97.15.53). Small, friendly bistro; menus around 140F.

La Table du Marché, 38 rue Clemenceau (☎04.94.97.85.20). Hard to get a table here but worth the wait for true bistro-style gourmandise; lunchtime menu under 100F.

Nightlife

In season St-Tropez stays up late, as you'd expect. The **boules games** on place des Lices continue till well after dusk, the portside spectacle doesn't falter till the early hours and even the shops stay open well after dinner time. If you have pots of cash and want to see, and be seen with, the nightlife creatures, **clubs** to try include the current-ly young and fashionable *Le Papagayo* in the Résidence du Nouveau Port with world music and theme nights; and *L'Esquinade*, 2 rue du Four, which has been going strong for decades; *Les Caves du Roy* in the flashy *Hôtel Byblos* on rue Paul-Signac is the most expensive and exclusive; and there's the **gay** disco *Le Pigeonnier*, 13 rue de la Ponche. All are open every night in summer, and usually Saturday only in winter.

The beaches

The beach within easy walking distance of St-Tropez is **Les Graniers**, below the citadel just beyond the Port des Pêcheurs along rue Cavaillon. From here a path follows the coast around the **Baie des Canoubiers** which has a small beach, to Cap St-Pierre, Cap St-Tropez, the very crowded **Salins** beach and right round to **Tahiti-Plage** (about 11km). This eastern area of the peninsula is where the rich and famous have their vast villas with helipads and artificial lakes in acres of heavily guarded grounds.

Tahiti-Plage is the start of the almost straight five-kilometre north–south **Pampelonne** beach, famous bronzing belt of St-Tropez and initiator of the topless bathing cult. The water is shallow for 50m or so and exposed to the wind, and it's some-times scourged by dried sea vegetation, not to mention slicks of industrial pollutants. But spotless glitter comes from the unending line of beach bars and restaurants, all with patios and sofas, and all serving cocktails and gluttonous ice creams (as well as full-blown meals), in addition to renting out the luxurious beach mattresses and matching parasols. Though you'll find people in the nude on all stretches of the beach, only some of the bars welcome people carrying wallets and nothing else. *Club 55*, named for the year when Vadim's film crew scrounged food from what was then a family beach hut, is supposed to be a favourite with the celebrities (à la carte from 250F; closes at sundown).

The beach ends with the headland of **Cap Camaret**, beyond which the private resi-dential settlement of **Villa Bergès** grudgingly allows public access to the **Plage de l'Escalet**. Another coastal path leads to the next bay, the **Baie de Briande**, where you'll find the least populated beach of the whole peninsula. Beyond here the villas end and you can continue to **Cap Lardier** with a choice of paths upwards and downwards and along the gorgeous shore all the way round to La Croix-Valmer.

To **get to the beaches** from St-Tropez, there's a frequent minibus service from place des Lices to Salins and Pampelonne, and a bus from the gare routière to Pampelonne and L'Escalet. Tahiti can be reached by taking a bus to Pampelonne and walking along the beach, or from St-Tropez by bike. The other beaches make great bike rides too. If you're driving you'll be forced to pay high parking charges at all the beaches, or to leave your car some distance from the sea and prey to thieves.

The interior of the peninsula

Though the coast of the St-Tropez peninsula sprouts second residences like a cabbage patch gone to seed, the **interior** is almost uninhabited, thanks to government inter-vention, complex ownerships and the value of some local wines. The best view of this richly green, wooded and flowering countryside is from the hilltop village of **Gassin**, its lower neighbour **Ramatuelle**, or the tiny road between them, the beautiful route des Moulins de Paillas where three ruined windmills could once catch every wind.

Gassin

GASSIN is the shape and size of a small ship perched on a summit; once a Moorish stronghold, it is now, of course, highly chic. It's a perfect place for a blow-out dinner, sitting outside by the village wall with a spectacular panorama east over the peninsula. Of the handful of restaurants, *Bello Visto*, 9 place des Barrys (☎04.94.56.17.30, fax 04.94.43.45.36; restaurant closed Tues), has very acceptable Provençal specialities on a 120F menu and nine rooms at excellent prices for this brilliant setting (③). Cheapish crêpes and pizzas can be had at *Au Vieux Gassin* (☎04.94.56.14.26) nearby.

Ramatuelle

RAMATUELLE is bigger than its neighbour, though just as old, and is surrounded by some of the best Côte de Provence vineyards (the top selection of wines can be tasted at Les Maîtres Vignerons de la Presqu'île de St-Tropez by the La Foux junction on the N98). The twisting and arcaded streets are inevitably full of arts and crafts of dubious talent, but it is very pleasant none the less. The French actor, Gérard Philippe (1922–59), is buried in Ramatuelle's **cemetery** on the outskirts of the village. His ivy-covered tomb, shaded by a rose bush, is set against the wall on the right as you look down. The central Romanesque **Église Notre-Dame** that formed part of the old defences has heavy gilded furnishings from the Chartreuse de la Verne (see p.234) and an impressive early-seventeenth-century door carved out of serpentine.

Opposite the church on place de l'Ormeau is a small **tourist office** (July & Aug Mon–Sat 9am–1pm & 3–7.30pm, Sun 10am–1pm & 3–7pm; rest of year Mon–Fri 8.30am–12.30pm & 2.30–7pm, Sat 9am–12.30pm & 3–6.30pm; ☎04.94.79.26.04), with a good list of *campings à la ferme*. If you want a **room**, try *Chez Tony*, at 31 rue Clemenceau (☎04.94.79.20.46; ②), which is fairly basic, but one of very few **hotels** within the village. Alternatively, there is the *Lou Castellas* (☎ & fax 04.94.79.20.67; ③), outside the village on the road to Gassin, with panoramic views and its own restaurant. For something to **eat**, stop off for a dish of fresh pasta or the day's speciality at *Au Fil à la Pâte* at 27 rue Victor-Léon (☎04.94.79.13.88; under 100F; closed Wed & mid-Nov to mid-Dec).

The Massif des Maures

The secret of the Côte d'Azur is that despite the gross conglomeration of the coast, Provence is still just behind, old, sparsely populated, village-oriented and dependent on the land for its produce as much as for its value as real estate. Between Marseille and Menton, the most bewitching hinterland is the **Massif des Maures** that stretches from Hyères to Fréjus.

The highest point of these hills stops short of 800m but the quick succession of ridges, the sudden drops and views, and the curling, looping roads are pervasively mountainous. Where the lie of the land gives a wide bowl of sun-lit slopes, vines are grown. Elsewhere the hills are thickly forested, with Aleppo and umbrella pines; holly; tremendous gnarled cork oaks, their trunks scarred in great bands where their precious bark has been stripped; and sweet-chestnut trees. On a windy autumn day chestnuts the size of grenades explode upon your head, while water from a thousand springs cascades down each face of rock. In the heat of summer there is always the darkest shade alternating with one-way light – the rocks that compose this massif absorb rather than reflect – and it's hardly surprising that its name derives from the Provençal and Latin words for dark, *mauram* and *mauro*.

Much of the massif is inaccessible even to **walkers**. However, the GR9 follows the most northern and highest ridge from Pignans on the N97 past Notre-Dame-des-Anges, La Sauvette, **La Garde-Freinet** and down to the head of the Golfe de St-Tropez. There are other paths and tracks, such as the one following the Vallon de Tamary from north of La Londe-des-Maures to join one of the roads snaking down from the Col de Babaou to Collobrières. Some don't go very far and many are closed to the public in summer for fear of forest fires, but when the smaller backroads are open, this makes exceptional countryside for exploring by mountain bike or on foot.

For **cyclists**, the D14 that runs through the middle, parallel to the coast, from Pierrefeu-du-Var north of Hyères to **Cogolin** near St-Tropez, is manageable and stunning.

Collobrières and around

At the heart of the massif is the ancient village of **COLLOBRIÈRES**. It is reputed to have been the first place in France to learn from the Spanish that a certain tree plugged into bottles allows a wine industry to grow. From the Middle Ages until very recent times **cork** production has been the major business of the village, and it is still the best place in the region to buy items roughly fashioned from raw cork bark such as fruit platters and plant pots, sold from a couple of roadside stalls in the centre of the village by the rough-hewn old men who own the concessions to collect it. However, the main industry now is *marrons glacés* and every other confection derived from sweet chestnuts.

On the terrace of the main *bar-tabac* that overlooks the River Collobrier, you can imagine that the forests that surround you go on for hundreds of miles, shutting out all the world of cost-accounting time and space. The church, the *mairie* and the houses don't seem to have been modernized this century. Yet on the other side of the river, at the eastern end of the village, a streamlined, no-nonsense, gleaming bright-blue construction, the **Confiserie Azurienne**, exudes efficiency and modern business skills. Workers clock in and out, production schedules are met, profits are made, all from the conker's sister fruit. The factory itself can't be visited but there's a shop that sells chestnut ice cream, chestnut jam, chestnut nougat, chestnut purée, *chestnut glacées* and chestnut bonbons. For the fanatic, there's always the annual *Fête de la Châtaigne*, the **chestnut fair**, at the height of the harvest in early- to mid-October, with special dishes served in restaurants and roast chestnuts sold in the streets.

Practicalities

Collobrières' **tourist office** on bd Charles-Caminat (July & Aug Mon–Sat 10am–12.30pm & 3.30–6.30pm; rest of year Tues–Sat 10am–12.30pm & 2.30–6pm; ☎04.94.48.08.00) is very welcoming and can supply details of the **walks** through the massif (for 10F) and some excellent local gîtes d'étape in the fantastic surrounding hills. There are two **hotels**, both of them small so it is advisable to book in advance in summer: *Notre-Dame*, 15 av de la Libération (☎04.94.48.07.13, fax 04.94.48.05.93; ④), and the excellent-value *Auberge des Maures*, 19 bd Lazare-Carnot (☎04.94.48.07.10, fax 04.94.48.02.73; ② per person full board). There are also two great **chambres d'hôtes**: *L'Atelier du Rempart*, Colette Brésis's ceramic studio at Les Bonnaux, two kilometres west of the village along the D14 (☎04.94.48.05.92; ③; closed Nov–March); and Andrée Cécile's *La Bastide de La Cabrière*, six kilometres in the direction of Gonfaron on the D39 (☎04.94.48.04.31, fax 04.94.48.09.90; ⑤). The municipal **campsite**, the *St-Roch*, is open during July and August only. *Camping sauvage* is forbidden: you might just get away with camping in the woods in late autumn or early spring, but when it's hot and dry don't even consider it – one stray spark and you could be responsible for a thousand acres of burnt forest.

For food, other than chestnuts and the fare at *L'Auberge des Maures*, the **restaurant** *La Petite Fontaine*, 1 place de la République (☎04.94.48.00.12; last orders 9pm; closed Mon & Sun afternoon), is congenial and affordable with one menu around 110F – it books up fast. South of the village signed off the D41 to Bormes at the Col de Babaou, the *Chèvrerir du Peïgros* (☎04.94.48.03.83; midday only out of season) is an isolated farmhouse serving its own produce on a 120F menu. If you want to buy some local **wines**, head for *Les Vignerons de Collobrières* close to the *Hôtel Notre-Dame*; local **market** days are Thursday and Sunday.

Around Collobrières

Writing at the end of the nineteenth century, Maupassant declared that there was nowhere else in the world where his heart had felt such a pressing weight of melancholy as at the ruins of **La Chartreuse de la Verne** (June–Sept Mon & Wed–Sun 11am–6pm; Mon & Wed–Sun Oct & Dec–May 11am–5pm; 30F). Since then a great deal of restoration work has been carried out on this Carthusian monastery, abandoned during the Revolution and hidden away in total isolation, 12km from Collobrières on a winding, partially tarmacked track off the D14 towards Grimaud. It remains a desolate spot; the buildings of this once vast twelfth-century complex, in the dark reddish-brown schist of the Maures, combined for decorative effect with local greenish serpentine, appear gaunt and inhospitable, but the atmosphere is indisputable. However, if the nutty, chocolate-brown olive bread on sale in the shop is anything to go by, life here for the monks couldn't have been that deprived.

Another religious settlement concealed in these hills is **Notre-Dame-des-Anges**, to the north of Collobrières on the Gonfaron road, almost at the highest point of the Maures. As a place of worship it goes back to pagan times, but in its nineteenth-century remodelled form it lacks the atmosphere of La Verne. It is open only on certain days of pilgrimage and national holidays – it's equipped with a **hostel** to receive the faithful – but the main point of a visit for most people is to take in the views encompassing the Alps and the sea.

A rare creature which populated a third of France a million years ago and now only just survives in the Massif des Maures is cared for and protected in **Le Village des Tortues** (March–Nov daily 9am–7pm; 40F), a few kilometres east of Gonfaron on the D75 to Les Mayons. This is not just a tourist attraction but a serious conservation project to repopulate the native Hermann tortoise, under ever-increasing threat from urbanization, forest fires, theft of eggs and sale as pets. Other tortoises, like the yellow-shelled giant from Madagascar, have been rescued and brought here. The visit is both relaxed and educational. A leaflet (available in English) guides you round the large enclosures where you'll see the tiny babies, "juveniles" and those soon to be released back into the wild.

La Garde-Freinet

For almost a hundred years, from 888 to 975, the Massif des Maures was occupied by invaders from the eastern and southern Mediterranean. The dreaded Saracens, the name by which the people of Provence refer indiscriminately to Moors, Turks, Arabs or North Africans, and who are held responsible for everything that has failed to survive since the Dark Ages, had their headquarters in **LA GARDE-FREINET** less than 3km northeast of Collobrières and originally known as Le Fraxinet. The foundations of their **fortress**, from where attacks on the interior were made, are still visible above the village beside the ruins of a fifteenth-century castle. Follow the signs to the GR9 at the northern end of the village; a path leads from a car park down to a cross and then up to the fort, about 1km in all, and steep.

La Garde-Freinet also has the honour of a radical past in the insurrectionary days of Louis Napoléon's coup d'état. Not only did the cork workers form a highly successful cooperative in 1851, but in their struggle with the landowners, women played as strong a role as men. So much so that the prosecuting magistrate of Aix wrote to the minister of justice warning him that La Garde-Freinet, with its new form of socialism in which women took part, would encourage other villagers to abandon public morals and descend into debauchery.

Today the occupiers of the village include Oxbridge professors and other Anglos with time on their hands, but it still feels like it belongs to the locals, thanks to the regeneration of forestry business around cork and chestnut, and the number of young local children around is refreshing. It also has top-notch medieval charm; easy walks to stunning panoramas; markets each Wednesday and Sunday; a sweet-chestnut coopera- tive on the main road as you leave the village heading north, and tempting food shops such as *La Voute*, 38 rue St-Jacques, with organic produce and good local wines for sale; as well as reasonable accommodation possibilities. For hikers, the 21-kilometre GR9 **route des Crêtes** to the west of the village passes along a tremendously scenic forest- ed ridge. The going is good, as it used to be open to vehicles and half the route is sur- faced, but traffic has been banned due to fire risk and those attempting to drive it now face an 800F fine if they are caught.

Practicalities

The helpful **tourist office** operates from 1 place Neuve (July & Aug Mon–Sat 10am–12.30pm & 3–6pm, Sun 10am–12.30pm; rest of year Mon–Sat 10am–12.30pm & 3–6pm; ☎04.94.43.67.41), and provides information on all of the Maures region, includ- ing suggested walks. A small **museum** above the office displays archeological finds from the Saracen fortifications.

For **rooms**, *La Sarrazine*, on the D588 after it turns west at the top of the village (☎04.94.43.67.16; ②), *La Claire Fontaine* on place Vieille (☎04.94.43.60.36, fax 04.94.43.63.76; ②) and *Le Fraxinois* on rue François-Pelletier (reception at the *Tabac-Presse*; ☎04.94.43.62.84 or 04.94.43.69.65; ③; closed Mon) are incredibly good value for this part of the world. The two three-star **campsites** are close at hand: the munic- ipal *Saint-Éloi* (☎04.94.43.62.40; closed Oct–May) opposite the municipal pool, and *La Ferme de Bérard* (☎04.94.43.32.23; closed Nov–Easter) five kilometres along the D558 towards Grimaud, with its own pool and restaurant. **Walkers** can stay at a **gîte d'étape** on the GR51 towards the coast, the *Hameau de La Cour Basse* (☎04.94.43.64.63).

In the evenings *Le Lézard* **restaurant** and **bar** on the exquisite place du Marché is the place to be (☎04.94.43.62.73; menus from around 100F); concerts are held every other Saturday. More elaborate food is served up in the rampant garden of *La Faucado* on the main road to the south (☎04.94.43.60.41; midday menu Mon–Sat 110F, à la carte from 300F; booking essential; closed Tues out of season, Jan & Feb). Pigeon fanciers, in the culinary sense, should try *La Colombe Joyeuse* on the place Vieille (☎04.94.43.65.24; menus from 95F; closed Mon) for its à la carte birds with a flavour of true pedigree that are served up, complicitly, by the nephew of the gentleman who used to run a famous but now defunct pigeon museum and breeders' centre in the village.

La Môle

Another village with its own life and, in this case, singularly free of tourist concerns, is **LA MÔLE** on the fast N98 between Bormes and Cogolin, southeast of La Chartreuse de La Verne and north of Le Rayol and Le Canadel. It is in a fabulous bowl of meadows and vineyards with old farmhouses, rather than new villas, dotted along the lanes that lead into the hills. The three reasons to stop here are: the *Auberge de la Môle* **café** (closed Mon) serving good strong coffee and decked out with old wooden fittings, ancient framed posters and a wonderfully old-fashioned petrol pump; the *Relais d'Alsace* **restaurant** (☎04.94.49.57.02; closed Mon out of season & Sun eve) with hearty spe- cialities from northeast France on menus from 80F and dependable *steack-frites* for under 50F; and, best of all, the Boulangerie Simon (closed Nov–April) that stays open day and night, baking the most amazing olive and raisin breads, cakes and flans, and selling goats' cheeses and jam. As you leave Le Môle for Cogolin, the perfect four-turreted residence appears on the left – with an aerodrome for private planes on the right – and, more realistically, a small one-star **campsite**, *Les Caramagnols* (☎04.94.54.40.06; closed Oct–May) with caravans to rent.

Cogolin

COGOLIN, 10km west of St-Tropez, is not just a popular tourist destination. Its economy rests in several craft industries: reed-making for wind instruments, pipes for smoking, wrought-iron furniture, silk yarn and knotted wool carpets; all offering one-off, made-to-order, high-quality and high-cost goods for the Côte d'Azur market.

It's possible to visit some of the **craft factories**; the extremely helpful tourist office (see below) will provide you with a complete list of addresses and times, and help with making appointments. Alternatively, you can just wander down av Georges-Clemenceau and pop into the retail outlets. For **carpets**, the renowned Manufacture de Tapis just off av Clemenceau on bd Louis-Blanc (exhibition room only Mon–Fri 9am–noon & 2–6pm) re-creates designs by famous artists such as Léger and Mondrian. Every carpet is hand-made and can take up to a year to finish; the order book includes presidential residences, embassies and local palaces. The production of **pipes** from briar wood is on show at Courrieu, 58 av Clemenceau (Mon–Sat 8am–noon & 2–6pm). World-famous musicians visit Rigotti on rue Barbusse to replace the reeds of their oboes, bassoons and clarinets; unfortunately, they open their doors only to professionals.

Film buffs might like to visit the **Musée Espace Raimu**, 18 av G. Clemenceau (summer Mon–Sat 10am–noon & 4–7pm, Sun 4–7pm; winter Mon–Sat 10am–noon & 3–6pm, Sun 3–6pm; 20F), a place affectionately dedicated to the life and achievements of one of French cinema's greatest stars, and currently run by his granddaughter. From place Bellevue, at the top of the town away from the bustling centre, you can see across the St-Tropez peninsula to Gassin, Ramatuelle and St-Tropez itself. Having taken in that view, and seen enough of Cogolin's manufacturing businesses, the one thing left to do is try the **wines** which particularly pleased Julius Caesar; the Cave des Vignerons is on rue Marceau on the way out of town before you join the N98 heading westwards (closed Sun out of season).

Practicalities

From the **gare routière** on av Clemenceau head upwards to the central place de la République where you'll find the **tourist office** (July & Aug Mon–Sat 9am–12.30pm & 2.30–7pm, Sun 9.30am–12.30pm; rest of year Mon–Fri 9am–noon & 2.30–6.30pm, Sat 9am–noon; ☎04.94.55.01.10).

Hotels are reasonable and are a pleasant alternative to staying in congested St-Tropez: the best option is the comfortable, amiable *Le Coq* on place de la Mairie (☎04.94.54.13.71, fax 04.94.54.03.06; ③); the *Du Golfe*, 13 av Clemenceau (☎04.94.54.40.34, fax 04.94.54.14.48; ③), is fairly uninspiring; and *Le Clemenceau*, 1 rue Carnot (☎04.94.54.15.17, fax 04.94.54.42.78; ③), has some low-priced rooms but is on a very noisy junction. For **eats** you can choose your own menu for under 100F at *La Grange,* 7 rue du 11 novembre (☎04.94.54.60.97; closed Mon), or try *La Taverne du Siffleur*, 9 rue Nationale (☎04.94.54.67.02; menus from 90F), which overlooks a fountain on a very quiet street. If you want a **drink**, the *Bistrot de Cogolin* next to *Du Golfe* hotel has a fine beer selection and you can check what is being shown at the pretty **cinema** across the street, dedicated to the French film actor Jules Raimu.

Grimaud and around

GRIMAUD is a film set of a *village perché*, where the cone of houses enclosing the eleventh-century church and culminating in the spectacular ruins of a medieval castle appears as a single, perfectly unified entity, decorated by its trees and flowers. The most vaunted street in this ensemble is the arcaded **rue des Templiers** which leads up to the pure Romanesque **Église St-Michel** and a former house of the Knights Templars. The views from the château ruins are superb, and the monumental, sharply cut serpentine window frames of the shattered edifice stand in mute testimony of former glory.

It's an exclusive little village whose "corner shop" sells antiques and contemporary art. There's a small **tourist office** at 1 bld des Aliziers just off the main road passing the village (Mon–Sat: July & Aug 9am–12.30pm & 3–7pm; rest of year 9am–12.30pm & 2.30–6.30pm; ☎04.94.43.26.98). If you're on a budget and need food or a place to stay it's worth making the tortuous climb to La Garde-Freinet, although *Le Coteau Fleuri* (☎04.94.43.20.17, fax 04.94.43.33.42; menu from 120F; ④), on the place des Pénitents at the western edge of the village, offers a few reasonable **rooms** in addition to its good restaurant, and **campers** might like to try the *Camping Charlemagne* (☎04.94.43.22.90), at le Pont de Bois, two kilometres outside the village on the road to Collobrières. You can get crêpes and omelettes at *Le Boubou* on the fountained place du Cros (menus from 125F; closed Thurs & Oct–April); plats du jour at *L'Écurie de la Marquise* at 3 rue du Gacharel (☎04.94.43.27.26; menu from 78F; closed Sun eve & Wed); or more serious fare on the vine-covered terrace of the *Café de France* on place Neuve (☎04.94.43.20.05; 127F menu; closed mid-Nov to Feb). On the lower side of place Neuve the *Pâtisserie du Château* tearoom sells wonderful cakes and fresh nutty breads. There is a **market** on Thursday and Sunday.

Port Grimaud

Avoiding the St-Tropez traffic altogether is difficult if you're visiting **PORT GRIMAUD**, the ultimate Côte d'Azur property development that half stands and half floats at the head of the Golfe de St-Tropez just north of La Foux, and whose fortunate residents move around by boat not car.

It was created in the 1960s as a private lagoon pleasure city with waterways for roads and yachts parked at the bottom of every garden. All the houses are in exquisitely tasteful old Provençal style and their owners, amongst them Joan Collins, are more than a little well heeled. In a way it's surprising that the whole enclave isn't wired off and patrolled by Alsatian dogs. One can only assume that envious gawping tourists somehow add to the already over-inflated values.

The main visitors' entrance is 800m up the well-signed road off the N98. You don't have to pay to get in but you can't explore all the islands without renting a boat (about 35F per person for half an hour) or taking a crowded boat tour with Les Coches d'Eau (18F). Even access to the church tower for views is controlled by an automatic ticket barrier (5F). However, if you want to **eat** and **drink**, there are rows upon rows of brasseries, restaurants and cafés, clearly designed for the visiting public rather than the residents, and not particularly good value, though affordable enough.

Ste-Maxime and around

STE-MAXIME, which faces St-Tropez across its gulf, is an archetypical Côte conurbation: palmed corniche and enormous pleasure boat harbour, beaches crowded with confident bronzed windsurfers and waterskiers, a local history museum in a defensive tower that no one goes to, and an outnumbering of estate agents to any other businesses by about ten to one. It sprawls a little too far – like many of its neighbours – but the magnetic appeal of the water's edge is hard to deny.

To enjoy the resort, however, requires money. If your budget denies you the pleasures of promenade cocktail-sipping and seafood-platter picking, not to mention waterskiing, wet-biking and windsurfing, you might as well choose somewhere rather prettier to swim, lie on the beach and walk along the shore.

For the spenders, **Cherry Beach** or its five neighbours on the east-facing Plage de la Nartelle, 2km from the centre round the Pointe des Sardinaux towards Les Issambres, is the strip of sand to head for. As well as paying for shaded, cushioned comfort, you can enter the water on a variety of different vehicles, eat grilled fish, have drinks brought to your mattress, and listen to a piano player as dusk falls. A further 4km on, **Plage des Eléphants** has much the same facilities but is slightly cheaper.

In addition to the beaches, Ste-Maxime's Vieille Ville has several good **markets**: a covered flower and food market on rue Fernand-Bessy (July & Aug Mon–Sat 6am–1pm & 4.30–8pm); a Thursday morning market on and around place du Marché; bric-à-brac every Friday morning on place Jean-Mermoz; and arts and crafts in the pedestrian streets every afternoon and evening in summer (4–11pm).

Ten kilometres north of town on the road to Le Muy, the **Musée du Phonographe et de la Musique Mécanique** at parc St-Donat (Easter to mid-Oct Wed–Sun 10am–noon & 3–6pm; 15F) is the result of one woman's forty-year obsession with collecting audio equipment. This marvellous museum's facade resembles Hansel and Gretel's fantastical biscuit house but is actually modelled on an eighteenth-century Limonaire mechanical music machine. Inside, the owner has on display one of Thomas Edison's "talking machines" of 1878, the first recording machines of the 1890s and an amplified lyre (1903). One of the first saucer-shaped amplifiers, made of paper, is still in remarkably good condition, along with an astonishing 1913 audiovisual language teaching aid and the wonderfully neat portable record-players of the 1920s. In addition there's an extraordinarily wide selection of automata, musical boxes and pianolas. Almost half the exhibits still work, and you may find yourself listening to the magical, crackling sounds of an original wax cylinder recording from the 1880s played on the equipment it was made for. The main aim of the collection is to get kids to understand that their personal stereos didn't drop out of the sky after centuries of silence. If you get a tour from Madame herself (she speaks a little English) you'll find it hard to resist her enthusiasm for the history of this branch of twentieth-century technology.

Practicalities

Buses arrive in town along the seafront and stop in front of the **tourist office** on the promenade Simon-Lorière (July & Aug Mon–Sat 9am–8pm, Sun 10am–noon & 4–7pm; June & Sept Mon–Sat 9am–12.30pm & 2–7pm; Oct–May Mon–Sat 9am–12.30pm & 2–6pm; ☎04.94.96.19.24), which can give you all the relevant information on trips and pleasures. If you're heading for St-Tropez from Ste-Maxime, an alternative to the bus, and at not much greater cost, is to go by **boat**; the service from Ste-Maxime's **gare maritime** on the quai L-Condroyer runs daily from April to October with more frequent crossings in July and August (☎04.94.96.51.00; 64F). **Bikes** and **mopeds** can be rented at Rent Bike, 11 rue Magali (☎04.94.43.98.07) or Holiday Bikes, 8 av St-Exupéry (☎04.94.43.90.19).

The tourist office can advise on hotel vacancies, which are very rare in summer. Among the less expensive **hotels** are the good-value and welcoming *Auberge Provençale*, 49 rue Aristide-Briand (☎04.94.55.76.90, fax 04.94.55.76.91; ①), which also has studios for up to four people and its own restaurant; and the small *Castellamar*, 21 av G-Pompidou (☎04.94.96.19.97; ③; closed mid-Nov to Dec), on the west side of the river but still close to the centre and the sea. For more pleasant and more expensive surroundings, try the *Hôtel de la Poste*, 11 bd Frédéric-Mistral (☎04.94.96.18.33, fax

04.94.96.41.68; ⑤), an ugly modern construction but with very nice rooms and right in the centre; *Les Palmiers*, on rue Gabriel-Péri in a quieter location by the church and Tour Carrée (☎04.94.96.00.41, fax 04.94.96.74.30; ⑤); or the *Marie-Louise*, 2km west in the Hameau de Guerre-Vieille (☎04.94.96.06.05; ④), tucked away in greenery but within sight of the sea. For **camping**, *Les Cigalons*, in quartier de la Nartelle, is the three-star seaside option (☎04.94.96.05.51, fax 04.94.96.79.62; closed mid-Sept to May); or there's *La Baumette*, rte du Plan de la Tour (☎04.94.96.14.35, fax 04.94.96.35.38; closed mid-Sept to May) up in the hills off the D74.

For **eating**, the *Hostellerie de la Belle Aurore*, 4 bd Jean-Moulin (☎04.94.96.02.45; weekday midday menu 180F, otherwise from 240F; closed Wed midday & Oct–March), offers gourmet food on a sea-view terrace; or, for half the price, *Le Bistrot du Port*, 118 av Gal-de-Gaulle (☎04.94.96.17.77; menus under 100F), serves fish dishes. *Le Sarrazin*, 7 place Colbert (☎04.94.96.10.84; menus from 110F; closed Tues out of season & Jan), is not bad either. The pedestrian streets are jam-packed with restaurants; one way of choosing from those on rue Hoche is to check them from the kitchen side along rue Fernand-Bessy.

Coastwards to St-Aygulf

Distinguishing **Val d'Esquières**, a suburb of Ste-Maxime, **Les Issambres**, the seaside extension of Roquebrune, and **St-Aygulf**, belonging to the *commune* of Fréjus, is hardly worth the effort. They all merge into one continuous lesser clone of Ste-Maxime. For all that, this stretch still has its attractions, revealing traditional white-washed, pan-tiled Provence architecture amid the filing-cabinet condominiums, and a shoreline of rocky coves and *calanques* alternating with golden crescents of sand. In Les Issambres there's even a narrow band of pines that almost lets you pretend that the corniche apartments and villas don't exist. If the seaside development gets too much, you can always head up and away into the empty eastern extremity of the Massif des Maures.

Practicalities

Hotels worth trying include *La Quiétude*, set back from the corniche (☎04.94.96.94.34, fax 04.94.49.67.82; ④; closed Dec & Jan), and *La Bonne Auberge*, overlooking the sea (☎04.94.96.90.74; ②; closed Nov–March), both in Les Issambres; *Le Catalogne*, av de la Corniche d'Azur in St-Aygulf (☎04.94.81.01.44, fax 04.94.81.32.42; ⑦; closed mid-Oct to Easter) with a pleasant, shaded garden; *Motel Defillet* at 69 impasse Corot (☎04.94.81.21.15; ③; closed Nov–March), at the start of the long straight beach to St-Raphaël in St-Aygulf, plus *La Caravelle* (☎04.94.81.24.03, fax 04.94.81.78.21; ⑤; closed Oct to mid-May) near Plage de la Gaillarde between the two. **Campsites** are plentiful and well signed off the corniche. **Bikes** can be rented from Les Hippocampes, at 519 av Corniche d'Azur, the main road through St-Aygulf (☎04.94.81.35.94).

The *Villa St-Elme* is the fancy **restaurant** on the corniche des Issambres, with elaborate and delicate fish dishes to be consumed while admiring the Golfe de St-Tropez from an exotic 1930s building directly above the sea (☎04.94.49.52.52; menus from 190F). At the other end of the scale, *Le Pointu*, on place de la Galiote in St-Aygulf, produces a brilliant *moules marinières* for under 50F. The St-Aygulf resort has a good daily **market**, too, and great *poulets rôtis* from a permanent stall overlooking the main square on bd Honoré-de-Balzac.

Inland: the Argens Valley

The **River Argens** meets the Mediterranean in unspectacular style between St-Aygulf and St-Raphaël. It is an important source of irrigation for orchards and vines, but as a waterway it has little appeal, being sluggish, full of breeding mosquitoes and on the whole inaccessible. The geographical feature that dominates the lower Argens Valley, and acts as an almost mystical pole of attraction, is the **Rocher de Roquebrune** between the village of **Roquebrune-sur-Argens** and the town of **Le Muy**.

Roquebrune-sur-Argens

ROQUEBRUNE-SUR-ARGENS lies on the edge of the Massif des Maures, 12km from the sea, facing the flat valley of the Argens opening to the northeast. Some of its sixteenth-century defensive towers and ramparts remain, and almost every house within them is four hundred years old or more, joined together by vaulted passageways, arcades and tiny cobbled streets. The largest mulberry tree in Provence shades the central square, while at the bridge over the Argens, just north of the village, M Vacherot grafts the rarest **orchids** in his nursery (visits by appointment only; ☎04.94.45.48.59). You can taste beautiful red and rosé **wines** (phone first) at the Domaine de Marchandise (☎04.94.45.42.91), and at the Domaine des Planes (☎04.94.82.90.03); or fill up with quality plonk at the Coopérative Vinicole. Delicious nougat and chocolate can be bought from Courreau, 2 montée St-Michel, and there's a **market** Tuesday and Friday morning.

The **tourist office** is on rue Jean-Aicard (July & Aug daily 9am–7pm; April, June & Sept Mon–Fri 9am–noon & 2–6pm, Sat 9am–noon; ☎04.94.45.72.70) and can provide addresses for accommodation, as well as information on walks and sports. Between Roquebrune and Le Muy there's a *Formule I* hotel (☎04.94.81.61.61; ①). The *Villages Hôtel*, nearby on the D7 (☎04.94.45.45.00, fax 04.94.81.63.53; ①), is a similarly modern and impersonal establishment but has several rooms with facilities for the handicapped; otherwise two **chambres d'hôtes** worth trying are *L'Acacia* (☎04.94.45.71.92; ⑤) and *Vasken* (☎04.94.45.76.16; ⑤). Between the village and St-Aygulf the road is lined with mega **campsites**, but more pleasant pitches are to be had on local farms; ask at the tourist office. Of the **restaurants**, *La Table Provençal*, 37 Grande Rue (☎04.94.45.36.74; closed Tues out of season), has a lovely setting; or you can get a filling meal for 100F at *Le Mas des Oliviers* (☎04.94.81.25.81), 6km from the village along the D7 in the direction of St-Aygulf.

Rocher de Roquebrune

The rust-red mass of the **Roquebrune rock** erupts unexpectedly out of nothing, as if to some purpose. Even the Autoroute du Soleil thundering past its foot fails to bring it into line with the rest of the coastal scenery glimpsed from the fast lane. To reach it, coming from Roquebrune, take the left fork just after the village, signed to La Roquette; at the next fork you can go left or right depending which side of the mountain you want to skirt. The right-hand route runs alongside the highway giving you access to **Notre-Dame-de-la-Roquette**, an erstwhile place of pilgrimage. The southern side is quieter but steeper.

From either side of the mountain several **paths** lead into the ancient woods encircling the rock and up through the fissured and pot-holed face. The summit has recently been crowned by some basic metalwork resembling semaphore signals, the art of trendy sculptor Bernard Venet, who lives in **Le Muy** when he's not hobnobbing in Paris or New York. In case it isn't immediately obvious, these minimalist T, arrow and cross shapes are homages to three great crucifixion paintings by Giotto, Grunewald and El Greco.

Le Muy and around

LE MUY is not a wildly exciting place but it's interesting politically, having had one of the sole surviving Communist mayors of the Côte d'Azur in the 1980s, switching to a coalition of right-wing and *Front National* in 1989, and shifting in the late-1990s to a centrist administration.

The town's political history and ideological leanings are often mirrored in the names of its streets, its buildings and architecture. One street is named after Maurice Lachâtre, a revolutionary writer, publisher and printer who escaped from the 1871 Paris Commune and was sheltered in Le Muy. The *Provençal* bar that surrounds and hides the apse of the town's church was built during the 1930s period of militantly atheist socialism.

The **tour Charles-Quint** takes its name from the attempted assassination of the Emperor Charles V in 1536 by the people of Le Muy. Unfortunately they were not to know that the king was aware of his unpopularity and had rented a Spanish poet, Garcilaso de la Vega, to masquerade as him. Consequently the Muyoise killed the Spaniard, retreated to the tower, were told by the invader that they would be spared if they surrendered, came out with their hands up and were promptly massacred; the tower was renamed after their arch enemy. Today, the tower houses a **Musée de la Libération** (March–June Sun 10am–noon; July & Aug Sun & Thurs 10am–noon), commemorating events of 1944's Operation Dragoon, which opened a second front in the south of France against the Germans.

If you need a place to **stay**, try the *Hôtel les Allées*, 2 allée Victor-Hugo (☎04.94.45.08.30; ②), a fairly basic place in the centre of the village; or the *Horstel* (☎04.94.81.82.56, fax 04.94.45.96.11; ②), just outside the village on the rte de Fréjus with bungalows, a swimming pool and a good-value **restaurant** (menus from 70F).

Chapelle de Ste-Roseline

A short way up the road to Draguignan (see p.256) from Le Muy, the D91 leads left to the **Chapelle de Ste-Roseline** (March–May 2–6pm; June–Sept Tues–Sun 3–7pm; Oct–Feb 2–5pm; free; ☎04.94.73.37.30). The old abbey buildings of which the chapel is part are a private residence, belonging to a wine grower, and today you can visit the cellars and taste the *cru classé* named after the chapel (Mon–Fri 9am–noon & 2–7pm, Sat & Sun 10am–noon & 2–6.30pm).

The interior of the chapel is really rather ghoulish. Saint Roseline was born in 1263 and spent her adolescence disobeying her father by giving food to the poor. On one occasion he caught her and demanded to see the contents of her basket; the food miraculously turned into rose petals. She became the prioress of the abbey and when she died her body refused to decay. It was paraded around the faithful of Provence until it got lost. A blind man found it and, supposedly, it now lies in a glass case in the chapel, shrivelled and dark brown but not quite a skeleton. What's worse are her eyes – one lifeless, the other staring at you – displayed in a separate, gaudy frame on a wall. Louis XIV is said to be responsible for the dead eye. On a pilgrimage here he reckoned the staring eyes smacked of sorcery so had his surgeon pierce one. Life immediately left it. Horror objects apart, the chapel has a fabulous mosaic by **Chagall** showing angels laying a table for the saint; some beautifully carved seventeenth-century choir stalls; and an impressive Renaissance rood-loft in which peculiar things happen to the legs of the decorative figures.

Les Arcs-sur-Argens and beyond

LES ARCS is yet another picturesque medieval village, a Saracen lookout tower dominating its skyline, the sole standing remnant of its thirteenth-century castle. It is also one of the centres for the Var wine industry. On the main road from Le Muy, past the turning to the village and the bridge across the Argens, you'll see the **Maison des Vins**. Here you can taste and buy wine and cheeses and pick up details of local *vignerons* to visit and *routes du vin* to follow (July–Sept 10am–8pm; Oct–June 10am–7pm).

The **tourist office** on place Gal-de-Gaulle (Wed–Fri 8.30am–noon & 2.30–6pm; ☎04.94.73.37.30) has information on the surrounding area. For accommodation, there's the exclusive hotel *Le Logis du Guetteur* (☎ & fax 04.94.99.51.10; ⑤), which commands the only access to the panoramic views by the Saracen tower on place du Château. Less expensive rooms are available at *L'Avenir*, av de la Gare (☎04.94.73.30.58; ②), by the gare SNCF, situated halfway between the village and the N7, which also has some simple and filling menus from 60F. The **restaurant** in *Le Logis* is worth trying (menus from 135F), or you could always try the Maison des Vins' very beautiful restaurant serving Provençal specialities, *Le Bacchus Gourmand* (☎04.94.47.48.47; menus from 150F; closed Mon out of season & Sun eve). The best day to come to Les Arcs is Thursday for the busy **market** on the central square.

Vidauban

Following the road west from Les Arcs the next village you come to, **VIDAUBAN**, is as attractive as its neighbour, particularly at night when its old-fashioned lamps are lit. The village has a charming **restaurant**, *Le Concorde*, 9 place Clemenceau (☎04.94.73.01.19; menus from 145F, gourmand menu at 260F; closed Wed); and some wine *domaines* worth visiting including the Vieux Château d'Astros (to arrange an appointment, call ☎04.94.73.00.25) and the Château St-Julien d'Aille (to arrange an appointment, call (☎04.94.73.02.89).

St-Raphaël and Fréjus

The major conurbation of **St-Raphaël** on the coast and **Fréjus**, centred 3km inland, has a history dating back to the Romans. Fréjus was established as a naval base under Julius Caesar and Augustus, St-Raphaël as a resort for its veterans. The ancient port at Fréjus, or Forum Julii, had two kilometres of quays and was connected by a walled canal to the sea, which was considerably closer back then. After the battle of Actium in 31 AD, the ships of Antony and Cleopatra's defeated fleet were brought here.

The area between Fréjus and the sea is now the suburb of **Fréjus-Plage** with an unattractive 1980s development of a marina, **Port-Fréjus**. St-Raphaël merges with Fréjus and Fréjus-Plage, which in turn merge with **Boulouris** to the east.

Despite the obsession with facilities for the seaborne rich – there were already two pleasure ports at St-Raphaël before Port-Fréjus was built – this is no bad place for a stopover. There's a wide price range of hotels and restaurants, some interesting sightseeing in Fréjus, and good transport links with inland Provence and the coast eastwards along the Corniche d'Esterel.

Fréjus

The population of **FRÉJUS**, remarkably, was greater in the first century BC than it is today if you count only the residents of the town centre, which lies well within the Roman perimeter. But very little remains of the original **Roman walls** that once circled the city, and the **harbour** that made Fréjus an important Mediterranean port silted up early on and was finally filled in after the Revolution. It is instead the **medieval centre**, with its very lively shopping and café streets, that evokes a feel for this ancient town.

Arrival and information

About four trains a day stop at **Fréjus gare SNCF**, just three to four minutes' away from St-Raphaël. Buses between the two towns are much more frequent and take ten minutes on the St-Raphaël–Draguignan route. The Fréjus **gare routière** is at place Paul-Vernet on the east side of the town centre, opposite the small Fréjus **tourist**

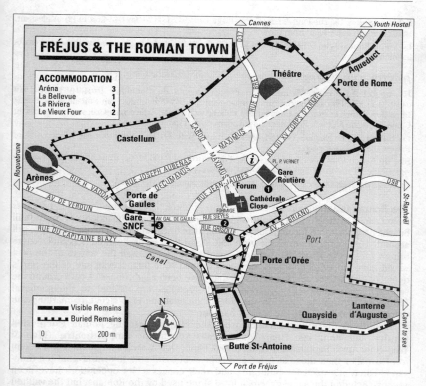

FRÉJUS & THE ROMAN TOWN

ACCOMMODATION

Aréna	3
La Bellevue	1
La Riviera	4
Le Vieux Four	2

office, 325 rue Jean-Jaurès (Mon–Sat 9am–noon & 2–6pm, Sun 10am–noon & 2.30–5.30pm; ☎04.94.17.19.19). **Bikes** can be rented in Fréjus from Holiday Bikes, 943 av de Provence (☎04.94.52.30.65).

Accommodation

Hotels are not as plentiful in Fréjus as in St-Raphaël, but it's generally a quieter place to stay. There are several **youth hostels** in the vicinity, and **campsites** close to the sea between Fréjus and St-Aygulf but they are all on a giant scale and neither cheap nor friendly. The campsites in the woods north of Fréjus are preferable but charges are still high in mid-summer.

HOTELS

Aréna, 145 av Général-de-Gaulle (☎04.94.17.09.40, fax 04.94.52.01.52). Pretty rooms, if a bit small, in a converted bank in Fréjus centre. Pleasant swimming pool. ⑤.

La Bellevue, pl Paul-Vernet (☎04.94.51.39.04, fax 04.94.51.35.20). Not the quietest location but convenient and inexpensive. ③.

Résidences du Colombier, 1239 rte de Bagnols (☎04.94.51.45.92, fax 04.94.53.82.85). A series of modern bungalows in a pine wood north of the town; all rooms have their own garden and terrace. Closed Nov–Feb. ⑥.

La Riviera, 90 rue Grisolle (☎04.94.51.31.46). Very small hotel in the centre of Fréjus. Not very modern, but clean and perfectly acceptable. ②.

Sable et Soleil, 158 rue Paul-Arène, Fréjus-Plage (☎04.94.51.08.70, fax 04.94.53.49.12). A pleasant, small, modern hotel 300m from the sea. ④.

Le Vieux Four, 49 rue Grisolle (☎04.94.51.56.38, fax 04.94.53.64.50). Small, centrally located establishment. ③.

HOSTEL AND CAMPSITES

HI hostel Auberge de Jeunesse de Fréjus, chemin du Counillier (☎04.94.53.18.75, fax 04.94.53.25.86). Two kilometres from Fréjus centre; bus #4, #8 or #9 from St-Raphaël or Fréjus (direction L'Hôpital, stop Les Chênes) and walk up av du Gal-d'Armée Jean-Calies – the chemin du Counillier is the first left. Reception closed 10am–6pm; 11pm curfew.

Le Dattier, rte de Bagnols (☎04.94.40.88.93, fax 04.94.40.89.01). A three-star site 3.5km north of Fréjus. Closed Oct–Easter.

Site de Gorge Vent, quartier de Bellevue, Fréjus (☎04.94.52.90.37, fax 04.94.44.41.24). A two-star site off the N7 towards Cannes, 3km from the town centre.

Auberge de Jeunesse de Fréjus, a large campsite alongside the hostel.

The Roman town

Doing a tour of the **Roman remains** gives you a good idea of the extent of Forum Julii, but they are scattered throughout and beyond the town centre and take a full day to get around. Turning right out of the gare SNCF and then right down bd Severin-Decuers brings you to the **Butte St-Antoine**, against whose east wall the waters of the port would have lapped, and which once was capped by a fort. It was one of the port's defences, and one of the ruined towers may have been a lighthouse. A path around the southern wall follows the quayside (odd stretches are visible) to the medieval **Lanterne d'Auguste**, built on the Roman foundations of a structure marking the entrance of the canal into the ancient harbour.

Heading in the other direction from the station, past the Roman **Porte des Gaules** and along rue Henri-Vadon, leads you to the **amphitheatre** (Mon & Wed–Sun: April–Sept 9.30am–noon & 2–6.30pm; Oct–March 9am–noon & 2–4.30pm; free), smaller than those at Arles and Nîmes, but still able to seat around ten thousand. Today it's used for bullfights and rock concerts. Its upper tiers have been reconstructed in the same greenish local stone used by the Romans, but the vaulted galleries on the ground floor are largely original. The Roman **theatre** (Mon & Wed–Sun: April–Sept 9am–6.30pm; Oct–March 9am–5pm; free) is north of the town, along av du Théâtre-Romain, its original seats long gone, though again it is still used for music and theatre shows during the *Nuits Aurélienne* **festival** in late July. Northeast of the theatre, at the end of av du XV Corps-d'Armée, a few arches are visible of the forty-kilometre **aqueduct**, which was once as high as the ramparts. Closer to the centre, where bd Aristide-Briand meets bd Salvarelli, are the arcades of the **Porte d'Orée**, positioned on the former harbour's edge alongside what was probably a bath complex.

The medieval town

The **Cité Episcopale**, or cathedral close, takes up two sides of **place Formigé**, the marketplace and heart of both contemporary and medieval Fréjus. It comprises the cathedral flanked by the fourteenth-century bishop's palace, now the hôtel de ville, the baptistry, chapterhouse, cloisters and archeological museum. Visits to the cloisters and baptistry are guided and leave approximately every hour (Mon & Wed–Sun: April–Sept 9am–7pm; Oct–March 9am–noon & 2–5pm; 25F including entrance to museum); access to the cathedral is free (9am–noon & 4–6pm) but you will have to peer through a glass partition to see the baptistry and will miss the fascinating seventeenth-century carved wooden portals with their depictions of a Saracen massacre unless you take the tour.

The oldest part of the complex is the **baptistry**, one of France's most ancient buildings, built in the fourth or fifth century and, as such, contemporary with the decline and fall of the city's Roman founders. Its two doorways are of different heights, signifying the enlarged spiritual stature of the baptized, and it was used in the days of early Christianity when adult baptism was still the norm. Parts of the early Gothic **cathedral** may belong to a tenth-century church, but its best features, apart from the coloured diamond-shaped tiles on the spire, are Renaissance: the choir stalls, a wooden crucifix on the left of the entrance, and the intricately carved doors with scenes of a Saracen massacre. By far the most beautiful and engaging component of the whole ensemble, however, is the **cloisters**. Slender marble columns, carved in the twelfth century, support a fourteenth-century ceiling of wooden panels painted with apocalyptic creatures. Out of the original 1200 pictures, 400 remain, each about the size of this page. The subjects include multiheaded monsters, mermaids, satyrs and scenes of bacchanalian debauchery. The **Musée Archéologique** on the upper storey of the cloisters has as its star pieces a complete Roman mosaic of a leopard and a copy of a renowned double-headed bust of Hermes. You can wander through the modern courtyard of the hôtel de ville but you get a better view of the orangy Esterel stone walls of the episcopal palace from rue de Beausset.

Rue Jean-Jaurès, at the top of rue de Fleury, curves down to the shaded **place de la Liberté** which **rue Sieyes** links with place Formigé. Clothes, souvenirs and food shops are interspersed with cafés, and commercial arty life draws people down **rue St-François-de-Paule** off the bottom end of rue Jean-Jaurès: Riquet Beaux-Arts at no. 69 sells artists' materials; a photo gallery has free exhibitions at no. 108; plus there are antique shops and attractive bistros. Beyond place Agricola on the main road out of town, wonderful old distillery buildings house La Fréjusienne **wine coop**.

Around Fréjus

About 2km north of Fréjus, there's a Vietnamese pagoda and an abandoned Soudanese-style mosque, both built by French colonial troops. The **Pagode Hong Hien** (daily: May–Sept 9am–noon & 3–6.30pm; Oct–April 9–noon & 2–5pm), still maintained as a Buddhist temple, is on the crossroads of the N7 to Cannes and rue Henri-Giraud (bus #3). The **Mosquée Missiri de Djeanne** is on rue des Combattants d'Afrique du Nord, to the left off the D4 to Bagnols 2km from the RN7 junction; a strange, guava-coloured, fort-like building of typical West African style, it is decorated inside with fading murals of desert journeys gracefully sketched in white on the dark pink walls.

Fréjus' **modern art gallery** (summer Tues–Sun 2–6pm; winter closed Tues–Sat 2–6pm) is bizarrely located in the Zone Industrielle du Capitou just by turn-off 38 from the highway; from place Paul-Vernet, take bus #2 to Z.I. Capitou. It has no permanent collection but some quite interesting temporary exhibitions. Another venue for temporary exhibitions, this time of photography, is the ugly Neoclassical **Villa Aurélienne** (Tues–Sun 2–6/7pm) in the Parc Aurélienne, north of av de l'Europe and reached by bus #4; details of what's on at both of these spaces are available from the tourist office.

There's a **water amusement park**, Aquatica (July & Aug daily 10am–7pm; June & Sept 10am–6pm; 98F, children 76F; bus #19 or #29), off the RN98 to St-Aygulf. Water scooters, toboggans and pedal boats, chutes into an enchanted river, lakes, a huge swimming pool with artificial waves, a beach for the less energetic, and an open-air cinema make up some of its main attractions. Aquatigolf, part of the same complex, has two 18-hole miniature-golf courses (June–Sept daily 4pm–1am; 40F). In the same entertainment zone there's a **funfair**, a **go-cart track**, Azur Karting (mid-June to mid-Sept daily 11am–midnight; rest of year Mon & Wed–Sun 11am–9pm; 80F, children 45F), and a one-kilometre motorbike and quad circuit (daily 11am–9pm; 80F).

Eating, drinking and nightlife

Fréjus is not a bad place for menu-browsing and café-lounging, with the cheaper **eateries** found on place Agricola, place de la Liberté and the main shopping streets. At Fréjus-Plage there's a string of eating houses to choose from, with more upmarket seafood outlets at Port-Fréjus. For **nightlife**, there is a plethora of fairly relaxed bars around Le Port de Fréjus, and clubbers should watch out for the Botafogo beach parties that are held on Friday nights in summer.

Aréna, 139 av Général-de-Gaulle (☎04.94.17.09.40). A hotel-restaurant (see p.243) which serves excellent fish dishes; menus start at 135F.

La Cave Blanche, on pl Calvini above the cathedral close (☎04.94.51.25.40). Offers a seafood cocktail on a menu of around 100F. Closed Sun eve & Mon.

Café de la Cité, 152 rue Jean-Jaurès. A nicely ordinary bar.

Bar du Marché, place de la Liberté. A classic café for snacks and sipping beers under the shade of plane trees.

Les Potiers, 135 rue des Potiers (☎04.94.51.33.74). Located in a tiny backstreet, this is one of the best restaurants in Fréjus; it serves dishes of fresh seasonal ingredients; à la carte only for around 220F. Closed Mon midday.

Chez Vincent, on rue Desaugiers below pl Formigé (☎04.94.53.89.89). Has a good goats' cheese salad, with menus from 120F. Closed Mon midday.

St-Raphaël

A large resort and now one of the richest towns on the Côte, **ST-RAPHAËL** became fashionable at the turn of the century. It lost many of its *belle époque* mansions and hotels in the bombardments of World War II; some, like the *Continental*, have recently been rebuilt, others have been restored more gradually. Meanwhile the tiny **old quarter** (*vieux quartier*) beyond place Carnot on the other side of the rail line seems to have been starved of municipal funds.

Arrival and information

St-Raphaël's **gare SNCF**, in the centre of the town, is the main station on the Marseille–Ventigmilia line; the **gare routière** is on av Victor-Hugo, just across the rail line behind the gare SNCF. For information on St-Raphaël and all the surrounding region, try the **tourist office**, conveniently situated on rue W-Rousseau (daily 8.30am–7pm; ☎04.94.19.52.52): turn left out of the gare SNCF and you'll see it in front of you. There is also a small **information booth** in front of the casino on the seafront (July & Aug 3pm–midnight). **Water-sports** enthusiasts can purchase a *Pass Nautique* for 50F at the tourist office, which gives a range of trial offers and discounts for activities such as kayaking, windsurfing and diving from a variety of sites along the St-Raphaël–Esterel coast. **Divers** might like to explore some of the numerous wartime wrecks and underwater archeological sites off the coast, with companies such as CIP St-Raphaël Odyssée (*La Plongée* boat on quai Albert-1er in the Vieux Port; ☎04.94.82.37.43) and Club Sous l'Eau (Port Santa Lucia just to the east of the town centre; ☎04.94.95.90.33) organizing trips. **Bikes** can be rented from Patrick Moto, 260 av Général-Leclerc (☎04.94.53.65.99).

Accommodation

There are plenty of **hotels** in St-Raphaël, from seafront palaces to backstreet budget options. They can all get extremely busy in summer, however, so it's worth booking in advance.

If you prefer to go **camping** try the area east of St-Raphaël along the Esterel coast (see p.249), although even here it's still a little pricey in mid-summer. *Le Val Fleury*, on the N98 at Boulouris (☎04.94.95.21.52), is a large four-star site close to the beach.

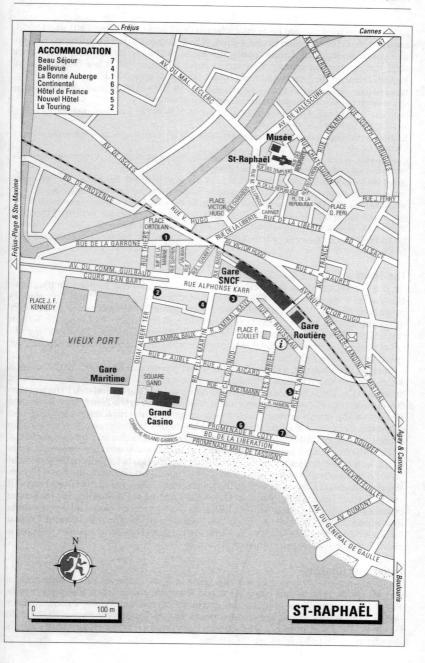

ACCOMMODATION

Beau Séjour	7
Bellevue	4
La Bonne Auberge	1
Continental	6
Hôtel de France	3
Nouvel Hôtel	5
Le Touring	2

ST-RAPHAËL

The Centre International Le Manoir, chemin de l'Escale, Boulouris (☎04.94.95.20.58, fax 04.94.83.85.06; reception closed 4–5pm; July & Aug only), is a luxurious and expensive **youth hostel** with double rooms, run by an extremely friendly and enthusiastic staff, and catering for groups of teenagers and a young crowd. It lies 5km east of St-Raphaël, close to the beach, and right by the Boulouris gare SNCF.

Beau Séjour, promenade René-Coty (☎04.94.95.03.75, fax 04.94.83.89.99). One of the less expensive seafront hotels with pleasant terrace. Closed Dec–March. ④.

Bellevue, 22 bd Félix-Martin (☎04.94.19.90.10, fax 04.94.19.90.11). Excellent value for its central location, but book well in advance. ③.

La Bonne Auberge, 54 rue de la Garonne (☎04.94.95.69.72). Inexpensive and close to the old port. Closed Dec. ③.

Continental, promenade René-Coty (☎04.94.83.87.87, fax 04.94.19.20.24). A classic seafront pile reconstructed to its *fin-de-siècle* ocean-liner glory. ⑥.

Hôtel de France, 25 pl Galliéni (☎04.94.95.19.20, fax 04.94.95.61.84). An inexpensive option and better than its unattractive exterior would suggest. Rather noisy, opposite the station. ③.

Nouvel Hôtel, 6 av Henri-Vadon (☎04.94.95.23.30). By the station, but nothing exceptional. ④.

Hôtel du Soleil, 47 bd du Domaine de Soleil, off bd Christian-Lafon (☎04.94.83.10.00, fax 04.94.83.84.70). A small, pretty villa with its own garden east of the centre. ③.

Le Touring, 1 quai Albert 1er (☎04.94.95.01.72, fax 04.94.95.86.09). Not very quiet but good value for the location. ④.

The Town

On rue des Templiers, to the north of the stations, a crumbling fortified Romanesque church has fragments of the Roman aqueduct that brought water from Fréjus in its courtyard. Nearby, there's an interesting local history and underwater archeology **museum** that no one really visits (mid-June to mid-Sept daily 10am–noon & 3–6pm; rest of year Mon–Sat 10am–noon & 2–5pm; free). The streets in this *vieux quartier* are full of shops to let or for sale, unable to compete with the shopping malls in the seafront apartment buildings and hotels.

Back on **the seafront**, a stroll along the broad promenade René-Coty to the junction with rue Henri-Vadon reveals St-Raphaël's preference for the loud and large in the grand hotels and the 1930s Résidence La Méditerranée at 1 av Paul-Doumer. Art Deco stucco flowers adorn La Rocquerousse apartment buildings next to the *Hôtel Beau Séjour* and vestiges of the town's prewar clientele appear amidst the characterless modern constructions along av des Chevrefeuilles – a blue-domed but surprisingly plain Russian church, and on av Paul-Doumer a rather pretty English church and a *fin-de-siècle* villa.

The **beaches** stretch between the Vieux Port in the centre and the newer Port Santa Lucia, with opportunities for every kind of water sport. **Boats** leave from the gare maritime on the south side of the Vieux Port to St-Tropez, Port Grimaud, the Îles d'Hyères and the islands off Cannes as well as the much closer *calanques* of the Esterel coast. If you're tired of sea and sand you could try some **bowling** at the Bowling Raphaëlois on promenade René-Coty (3pm–3am) or **billiards** close by at *Le Candy*; and if you want to lose whatever money you have left on slot machines or blackjack, the **Grand Casino** on Square de Grand overlooking the Vieux Port (daily 11am–4am) – whose director is also the mayor – will be only too happy to oblige.

Eating and drinking

You'll find reasonably priced **brasseries** and pizzerias, crêperies and **restaurants** of varying quality around Port Santa Lucia and along the promenades. **Cafés** such as *Le Victor-Hugo* on rue Victor-Hugo, which overlooks the market, are also a good, cheaper option. For **snacks**, cakes, ice creams, **beers** and cocktails try *L'Emeraude*, 3 bd du Gal-de-Gaulle. **Food markets** are held every day on place Victor-Hugo and place de la République, with fish sold on place Ortolan.

Le Pastorel, 54 rue de la Liberté (☎04.94.95.02.36). This place has been serving traditional dishes since 1922. Menus start around 160F. Closed Sun & Mon.

La Petite France, 57 rue Vauban (☎04.94.40.51.34). Friendly and inexpensive restaurant on a narrow street between rue Alphonse-Karr and rue de la Garonne. Menu from 69F.

Le Poussin Bleu, cnr of Promenade and rue Charles-Gounod (☎04.9495.25.14). Moderately priced seafront brasserie.

Le Sirocco, 35 quai Albert Ier (☎04.94 95 39.99). Quite a smart restaurant specializing in fish, with a good menu for around 120F plus a view of the sea. The wine is expensive.

Le Tisonnier, 70 rue de la Garonne (☎04.94.95.28.51). Offers a Provençal menu for 89F with ravioli and salmon cooked with fennel.

La Voile d'Or, 1 bd du Gal-de-Gaulle (☎04.94.95.17.04). The *bourride Raphaëloise à la rouille* (fillet of sea bream in a seafood and saffron sauce) is the best of the fishy dishes on offer. Menus from 140F. July & Aug closed Tues & Wed midday; rest of year closed all Tues & Wed.

Nightlife and entertainment

For **drinking**, try the selection of beers at *Blue Bar* on the Promenade above Plage du Veillat (open till 4am in summer), or for sipping expensive cocktails to piano accompaniment there's the *Madison Club* at the casino (7pm–4am) or *Coco-Club* at Port Santa Lucia (till dawn). *La Réserve* on promenade René-Coty is the stereotypical Côte d'Azur **disco**, with conventional red velvet and glitter decor and popular hits from the last twenty years. *Le Kilt*, 130 rue Jules-Barbier (11.30pm–dawn) is a little more exciting, but not much.

Around late June or early July St-Raphaël hosts an international competition of New Orleans **jazz** orchestras (the tourist office can supply details).

Listings

Boat rental Club Nautique at the western end of Port Santa Lucia (☎04.94.95.11.66).

Car rental ADA St-Raphaël Automobiles (☎04.94.83.11.41); Avis (☎04.94.95.60.42) and Europcar (☎04.94.95.56.87), are all on pl P-Coulet, St-Raphaël; also Holiday Bikes, 943 av de Provence, Fréjus (☎04.94.52.30.65).

Currency exchange Centre Commerciale de la Gare in the St-Raphaël train station (June–Sept Mon–Fri 4–10pm, Sat & Sun 9am–10pm); Change Service, 26 av du Commandant-Guilbaud on the Vieux Port, St-Raphaël (July & Aug daily 9am–9pm). Most banks have cashpoint machines.

Emergency ☎15; Hôpital Intercommunal Bonnet, av André-Léotard, Fréjus (☎04.94.40.21.21); SOS Médecins (☎04.94.95.15.25).

Laundry 5 rue Jules-Ferry; 34 av Général-Leclerc.

Pharmacy Call Police Municipale in St-Raphaël (☎04.94.95.24.24) for the name of a late-night pharmacy.

Police Commissariat, av Amiral-Baux, St-Raphaël (☎04.94.95.00.17).

Post office Poste Principale, av Victor-Hugo, St-Raphaël.

Taxi ☎04.94.95.04.25 or 04.94.51.51.12.

The Esterel

The 40km **Corniche de l'Esterel**, the sole stretch of wild coast between St-Raphaël and the Italian border, remains untouched by property development – at least between **Anthéor** and **Le Trayas** – its backdrop an arc of brilliant red volcanic rock tumbling down to the sea from the harsh crags of the **Massif de l'Esterel**. From the two major routes between Fréjus and **La Napoule**, the coastal N98 and rail line, and the inland N7, minor roads lead into this steeply contoured and once deeply wooded wild terrain. The **shoreline**, meanwhile, is a mass of little beaches, some sand, some shingle, cut by rocky promontories.

The inland route

The high, hairpin **inland route** is a dramatic but sometimes heart-rending drive; for every 2km of undisturbed ancient olive trees and gravity-defying rock formations, you have to suffer 1km of new motels and "residential parks" with real-estate hoardings. The Esterel is – or was – one of the most beautiful areas on the planet, as well as one of its oldest land masses. The interior had for centuries been uninhabited, save for reclusive saints, escaped convicts from Toulon and Resistance fighters. It has no water and the topsoil is too shallow for cultivation. Prior to the twentieth-century creation of the corniche, the coastal communities were linked only by sea routes. The inland route (N7), however, is ancient, following in parts the Roman Via Aurelia.

Many of the minor roads are barred to vehicles and even bicycles during the summer months, and some are closed throughout the year: phone the Office National des Forêts (☎04.94.24.00.83) for the most recent information. This makes **walking** even more enjoyable, even though camping is strictly forbidden. The tourist office in St-Raphaël (see p.246) can provide details of paths and of the peaks that are the most obvious destinations. The highest point is **Mont Vinaigre**, which you can almost reach by road, turning left 8km out of Fréjus on the N7; a short, signposted footpath leads up to the summit. At 618m it's not really a mountain – 600 million years of erosion have taken their toll – but the view is spectacular.

The corniche

With half a dozen train stations and hourly buses between St-Raphaël and La Napoule, this is a very accessible coastal stretch for non-drivers. Boats also run along the coast from St-Raphaël's gare maritime. Along the stretch between Anthéor and Le Trayas each easily reached beach has its summer snack-van, but by clambering over rocks you can usually find a near-deserted cove.

Le Dramont, Agay and Anthéor

The merest snatch of clear hillside and brasserie-less beach distinguishes Boulouris from **LE DRAMONT**, 9km east from St-Raphaël's centre, where the landing of the 36th American division in August 1944 is commemorated. A cliff-top path around the **Cap du Dramont** headland gives fine views out to sea, though looking inland the most severe and recent encroachment on the Esterel is revealed. This is the designer "village" of **Cap Esterel**, created out of nothing but pure profit motive and squatting smugly on the ridge between Le Dramont and Agay. Fenced off and with its security gates guarded night and day, it is a vast enclave of time-share apartments and hotels, huge swimming pools, a golf course, terraced gardens, "streets" of arty-crafty shops, and even a mock church divided into "studios" and "luxury apartments". All very tastefully done of course, pastel shades and pan-tiled roofs, but totally unreal. No one lives there permanently; there's no history past or present, no depth and no diversity. For the curious, there's free two-hour parking (no vehicles circulate in Cap Esterel) or you could get there by bus from St-Raphaël.

In contrast, Le Dramont's close neighbour **AGAY** is one of the least pretentious resorts of the Côte d'Azur, and beautifully situated around a deep horse-shoe bay edged by sand beaches, red porphyry cliffs and pines. Both Agay and its eastern neighbour **ANTHÉOR** suffer from the creeping contagion of housing estates with rural names like Mas and Hameaux edging ever higher up their hills, but once you do get above the concrete line, at the **Sommet du Rastel** for example (signed up Agay's av du Bourg or bd du Rastel), you can begin to appreciate this wonderful terrain.

There are at least nine **campsites** in this area. Along the Valescure road near the River Agay you'll find the four-star *Les Rives d'Agay* (☎04.94.82.02.74; closed Nov to mid-Feb) and *Agay-Soleil*, by the beach at 1114 bd de la Plage (☎04.94.82.00.79; closed mid-Nov to mid-March); or there's the *Azur Rivage*, around the headland in Anthéor-Plage (☎04.94.44.83.12; mid-March to mid-Oct). **Hotels** are also thick on the ground: Agay's *France Soleil* on bd de la Mer (☎04.94.82.01.93, fax 04.94.82.73.95; ⑤); closed Nov–Easter) and *Sol e Mar* (☎04.94.95.25.60, fax 04.94.83.83.61; ⑦; closed mid-Oct to March) in Le Dramont both have sea views; less expensive options are *Hôtel l'Esterella* (☎04.94.82.00.58, fax 04.94.82.02.05; ③) on the bd de la Plage in Agay, and *Les Flots d'Or* in Anthéor (☎04.94.44.80.21, fax 04.94.44.83.71; ④; closed mid-Oct to mid-Feb). **Bikes** can be rented at Mountain Bike, inland at the Domaine du Grenouillet on the rte de Valescure (☎04.94.82.81.89); from the *Vallée du Paradis* campsite off av du Gratadis in Agay and at nearby Holiday Bikes, on av du Gratadis in Agay.

Le Trayas

LE TRAYAS is on the highest point of the corniche and its shoreline is the most ragged, with wonderful inlets to explore. You can also trek to the Pic d'Ours from here (about 3hr; the path is signed from the gare SNCF).

The **hotel** *Relais des Calanques*, corniche d'Or (☎04.94.44.14.06, fax 04.94.44.10.93; ⑤; closed Nov & Dec) nestles above a cove, the water almost lapping at its terrace where good sea-fish is served. Less expensive rooms can be had at *L'Auberge Blanche*, 1061 rte des Calanques/RN98 (☎04.94.44.14.04, fax 04.94.44.17.27; ④), where the bus stops. Le Trayas also has an **HI youth hostel**, the *Villa Solange*, 9 av de la Véronèse (☎04.93.75.40.23, fax 04.93.75.43.45; reception closed 10am–5pm; closed Jan), a two-kilometre uphill slog from the stop outside the *Auberge Blanche* on the Cannes–St-Raphaël bus route or from Le Trayas' gare SNCF. Once you've arrived you won't regret it – just make sure you book in advance. Le Trayas' nearest **beach** is just beneath it at the little port of **La Figueirette**, which also has a comfortable **hotel**, *Le Mas Provençal* (☎04.93.75.40.20, fax 04.93.75.44.83; ⑤), at 10 av du Trayas, with good facili-ties, including a tennis court, swimming pool and restaurant.

Miramar and Théoule-sur-Mer

At **MIRAMAR** and especially in its neighbouring town of **THÉOULE**, further along the coast, the proximity of Cannes begins to show: you can see the city's outskirts, and the local architecture is infected with its style. From the Pointe de l'Esquillon you get an unhindered view of the private residential estate designed by Jacques Couelle at Porte-La-Galère on the neighbouring headland.

One **hotel** worth trying out in Miramar if you're not on a tight budget is *La Tour de l'Esquillon* (☎04.93.75.41.51, fax 04.93.75.49.99; ⑧), with a spectacular view from high up on the corniche, its own private beach, a swimming pool, and a good restaurant with menus from 150F. The coastline becomes less rugged at Théoule, where the most pre-cipitous of the cliff scenery finishes and the beaches begin again. Théoule's **tourist office**, at 1 corniche d'Or (Mon–Sat 9am–7pm, Sun 10am–5pm; ☎04.93.49.28.28), rents **bikes** for 70F per day.

La Napoule

The fantasy castle, built onto the three towers and gateway of a medieval fort, that announces **LA NAPOULE** and heralds the Riviera, appears on the point of sinking under its own weight. The **castle** ranks high amongst the classic pre-World War I follies built by foreigners on the Côte; the creators, in this instance, being the American sculp-tor Henry Clews and his wife. The lovely gardens and the interior can be visited (guid-ed tours only: July & Aug Mon & Wed–Sun 3pm, 4pm & 5pm; rest of year Mon & Wed–Sun 3pm & 4pm; 25F) with its collection of Clews' odd and gloomy works, repre-sented on the outside by the grotesques on the gateway.

On the eastern side of the village, the River Siagne flows into the sea. If you follow it a short way upstream, you'll see an elegant arched rail bridge, which could hardly offer a more telling contrast to the Clews château, in terms of lightness, grace, and economy of design. Its creator was Gustave Eiffel.

The **tourist offices** on av de Cannes by the *autoroute* exit (☎04.93.49.14.39), and av Henri-Clews opposite La Napoule's port (mid-April to June Mon–Sat 9am–12.30pm & 2–6pm; July to mid-Sept daily 9am–12.30pm & 3–7pm; mid-Sept to mid-April Mon–Fri 2–6pm; ☎04.93.49.95.31), will help with **accommodation**. There are two hotels worth approaching, *La Calanque* on bd Henri-Clews (☎04.93.49.95.11, fax 67.44; ⑤; halfboard compulsory in summer; closed Nov–March), which has rooms with views of the château and the sea and a restaurant serving some fine fish dishes in thee Provençal style (menus from around 100F); or the better-value and more peaceful *Villa Parisiana* (☎04.93.49.93.02, fax 04.93.49.62.32; ③), on rue de l'Argentière. If you get stuck, the characterless inland resort of Mandelieu-La Napoule has plenty of hotels, not to mention golf courses.

If you have the money to splash out on a meal, head for *L'Oasis* **restaurant**, rue Jean-Honoré-Carle (book in advance; ☎04.93.49.95.52); menus start at 500F, but it also offers a spectacular three-course lunch plus coffee, petits fours and wine for a more affordable 230F.

travel details

Trains

Les Arcs to: Draguignan (frequent; 5min); Fréjus (4 daily; 15min); Gonfaron (1–3 daily; 10min); St-Raphaël (frequent; 20min); Toulon (frequent; 40min–1hr); Vidauban (1–3 daily; 5min).

Hyères to: Toulon (4–6 daily; 20min).

St-Raphaël to: Agay (10 daily; 10min); Anthéor (10 daily; 15min); Boulouris (10 daily; 5min); Cannes (frequent; 25–35min); Les Arcs–Draguignan (frequent; 20min); Le Dramont (10 daily; 10min); Le Trayas (10 daily; 20min); Mandelieu-La Napoule (10 daily; 30min); Marseille (frequent; 1hr 45min); Nice (frequent; 1hr–1hr 20min); Théoule-sur-Mer (10 daily; 25min); Toulon (frequent; 1hr).

Buses

Hyères to: Bormes (frequent; 25min); La Croix-Valmer (8 daily; 1hr 15min); Le Lavandou (frequent; 35min); Le Rayol (8 daily;1hr); St-Tropez (8 daily; 1hr 30min–1hr 45min); Toulon (every 30min; 35–50min).

Le Lavandou to: Bormes (6 daily; 30min); Cavalaire-sur-Mer (8–9 daily; 30min); Cavalière (8–9 daily; 10min); Cogolin (2 daily; 40min); Grimaud (2 daily; 45min); Hyères (frequent; 35min); La Croix-Valmer (8–9 daily; 40min); La Garde-Freinet (2 daily; 1hr); La Môle (2 daily; 30min); Le Rayol (8–9 daily; 20min); St-Tropez (8 daily; 1hr); Toulon (frequent; 1hr 10min).

Ste-Maxime to: Plan-de-la-Tour (2–4 daily; 15min).

St-Raphaël to: Cannes (10–13 daily; 1hr 10min); Cogolin (7 daily; 1hr–1hr 30min); Draguignan (10–12 daily; 1hr 15min–1hr 30min); Grimaud (6 daily; 1hr); La Foux (9 daily; 1hr–1hr 15min); Le Muy (12–14 daily; 50min); Les Issambres (10 daily; 20–30min); Nice Airport (3 daily; 1hr); Rocquebrune (9–11 daily; 40min); Ste-Maxime (10 daily; 30–40min); Ste-Roseline (8–9 daily; 1hr); St-Tropez (8–10 daily; 1hr–1hr 30min).

St-Tropez to: Bormes (8 daily; 1hr–1hr 15min); Cavalaire-sur-Mer (8–9 daily; 30min); Cavalière (8–9 daily; 50min); Cogolin (8 daily; 15min); Gassin (1 daily; 30min); Grimaud (8 daily; 20–40min); Hyères (8 daily; 1hr 30min–1hr 45min); La Croix-Valmer (8 daily; 20min); La Garde-Freinet (1 daily; 45min); Le Lavandou (8 daily; 1hr); Le Rayol (8 daily; 40min–1hr); Les Issambres (8 daily; 1hr); Ramatuelle (1 daily; 30min); Ste-Maxime (8 daily; 45min); St-Raphaël (8–10 daily; 1hr–1hr 30min); Toulon (8 daily; 2hr–2hr 15min).

Flights

Hyères to: Corsica (2 daily; 50min); Lille (April–Sept 1 weekly; 1hr 30min); Paris (10 daily; 1hr 30min).

CHAPTER FIVE

THE HEARTLAND OF PROVENCE

This chapter takes in the Upper Var – the northern half of the Var *département* – and the western section of the Alpes-de-Haute-Provence. It is one of the least populated of France's non-mountainous areas and is the **heartland of Provence** not because it is geographically central, but because it is here that you can escape the region's over-commercialized resorts and begin to discover the individuality and true beauty of Provence.

Small towns and villages such as **Aups**, **Riez**, **Cotignac**, **Forcalquier** and **Simaine-la-Rotonde** still thrive on their traditional industries of cultivating lavender, making honey, tending sheep, digging for truffles and pressing olive oil; and in isolated places like **Banon** and the hamlets around Sisteron, it's hard to believe this is the same country, never mind province, as the Côte d'Azur.

True, foreigners have bought second homes in the idyllic **Haut Var villages** but the tidal wave of new-house building does not yet extend north of the Autoroute Provençale (A8). Nor has the Marseille–Gap highway, which follows the **River Durance**, encouraged major industrialization. Prices here remain much, much lower than on the coast or in western Provence.

Landscapes are exceptional, from the gentle countryside of the Haut Var or Pays de Forcalquier to the rolling plains and wide horizons of the **Plateau de Valensole** and the high harshness of the **Montagne de Lure**; the wild emptiness of the **Plateau de Canjuers**, the untrammelled forests east of Draguignan and, most spectacularly of all, Europe's largest ravine, the **Grand Canyon du Verdon**, matched only in grandeur by the snowcapped mountains on the northern horizons.

Food is fundamentally Provençal: lamb from the high summer pastures, goats' cheese, honey, almonds, olives and wild herbs. The soil is poor and water scarce, but the Côtes de Provence **wine** *appellation* extends to the Upper Var.

The towns, dull **Draguignan**, busy but parochial **Manosque** and **Sisteron**, the declining mountain gateway to Provence, are not the prime appeal. First and foremost this is

---

ACCOMMODATION PRICE CATEGORIES

Throughout this guide, all hotels and guesthouses have been priced on a scale of ①–⑧, indicating the lowest price you could expect to pay for a double room in high season. What you get for your money varies enormously between establishments, but in the lower-priced hotels you should expect to pay considerably more for en-suite facilities. If you are staying anywhere for more than three days it's often possible to negotiate a lower price, particularly out of season.

① Under 160F	③ 220–300F	⑤ 400–500F	⑦ 600–700F
② 160–220F	④ 300–400F	⑥ 500–600F	⑧ Over 700F

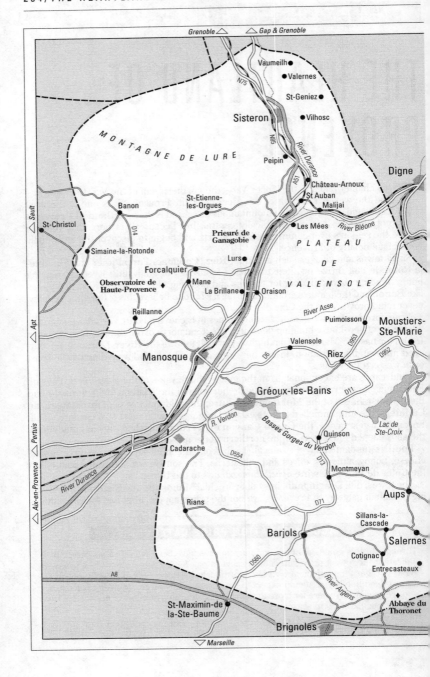

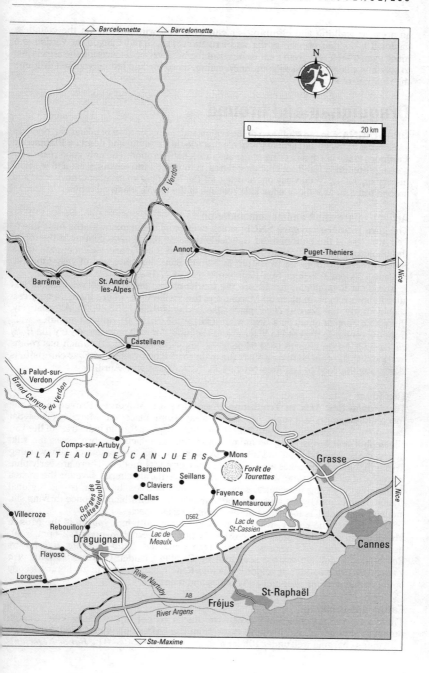

an area for **walking** and **climbing**, or **canoeing** and **windsurfing** on the countless dammed lakes that provide power and irrigation. The Grand Canyon du Verdon is a must, even if seen only from a car or bus. But the best way of discovering the area is just to stay in a village that takes your fancy, eating, dawdling and letting yourself drift into the rhythms of local life.

Draguignan and around

DRAGUIGNAN, in the southeast of the region and the major town of inland Var, revolves around the barracks and artillery schools that use the beautiful and desolate **Plateau de Canjuers** to the north as a firing range and mock battleground. The only good reason for passing through, apart from changing buses, is to visit its **museums** of art and of social history or, if it's a Wednesday or Saturday, for the benefit of an excellent **market** on and around place du Marché in what little remains of the town's medieval centre.

Arrival, information and accommodation

The **gare routière** and **gare SNCF**, which connects Draguignan with the main line at Les Arcs, are at the bottom of bd Gabriel-Péri, south of the town centre. At the top of the boulevard turn left to find the **tourist office** at 9 bd Georges-Clemenceau (mid-June to mid-Sept Mon–Sat 9am–1pm & 2–7pm, Sun 9am–1pm; rest of year Mon–Sat 8.30am–12.30pm & 2–6pm, Sun 10am–noon ☎04.94.47.10.76).

Rue de la République, just before the tourist office, and rue Georges-Clisson, just after it, both lead up to place du Marché and the Vieille Ville, where there's a very reasonable **hotel**, the *Touring Hôtel*, place Claude-Gay (☎04.94.68.15.46; ②). Alternatively, there's *La Pergola* on av du 4 Septembre (☎04.94.67.01.12; ③), only ten minutes' walk from the centre on the road to Flayosc and Lorgues. For a bit more luxury try the *Hôtel du Parc*, 21 bd de Liberté (☎04.94.68.53.84, fax 04.94.47.11.92; ④), which has rooms overlooking the courtyard as well as the main road. The two-star *La Foux* **campsite** is 2km along the road to Les Arcs (☎04.94.68.18.27; closed Nov–April).

The Town

The **Musée des Arts et Traditions Populaires de Moyenne Provence**, 15 rue Joseph-Roumanille, a couple of streets away from place du Marché (Tues–Sat 9am–noon & 2–6pm, Sun 2–6pm; 20F), beautifully displays the old industries of the Var. Nineteenth-century farming techniques and the manufacturing processes for silk, honey, cork, wine, olive oil and tiles are presented within the context of daily working lives – though some scenes are spoilt by rather dire wax models. There are early photographs of villages in the Var, many of which have hardly altered save for the means of transport crossing the central squares. The loss of trees, however, is one regional change highlighted by the museum: the mulberry tree, on which the once thriving silk industry depended, is today one of the region's rarest species.

Also close to the centre, with a showcase window to tempt you in, is the **Musée Municipale**, 9 rue de la République (Mon 2–6pm, Tues–Sat 9am–noon & 2–6pm; free), housed in a former bishop's palace. Treats include *Child Blowing Bubbles* by Rembrandt; a delicate marble sculpture by Camille Claudel; Greuze's *Portrait of a Young Girl*; two paintings of Venice by Ziem; a Renoir; and upstairs in the library, a copy of the *Romance of the Rose* and early bibles and maps.

Eating and drinking

There's a generous choice of inexpensive **places to eat** in the Vieille Ville, though nothing very special, but if you've come from the coast you'll be relieved to be back with **cafés** charging well under 10F for a sit-down terrace coffee. The *Bar de Négociants* amidst the flower stalls on place du Marché or *Les Mille Colonnes*, also serving food, on place des Herbes are recommended. If sugary things are your passion, seek out the De Neuville *confiserie* at 191 rue du Combat.

Rebouillon and Châteaudouble

About 5km northwest of town along av de Montferrat is **REBOUILLON**, an exquisitely peaceful village built around an oval field on the banks of the River Nartuby. Almost immediately the scenery changes dramatically with the start of the **Gorges du Châteaudouble**. Though a mere scratch compared to the great Verdon gorge, it has some impressive sites, not least the village of **CHÂTEAUDOUBLE** hanging high above the cliffs. Nostradamus predicted that the river would grind away at the base until the village fell; he is yet to be proved right. Almost deserted except during the summer holidays, Châteaudouble consists of little more than a ruined tower and ramparts, which you can reach from a path beside the *Bar du Château* (also offering accommodation), two churches, a handful of houses, a potter's workshop, a bee-keeper and his hives, and *La Tour* restaurant (☎04.94.70.93.08; menu under 100F) with a terrace overlooking the gorge.

Towards Lac de St-Cassien

If you're meandering eastwards towards Grasse from Draguignan a number of medieval villages north of the main Draguignan–Grasse road (the D562) might detain you. Sheltering below the inhospitable wilderness of the plateau of Canjuers to the north, the settlements of **Callas**, **Claviers**, **Bargemon**, **Seillans**, **Mons**, **Fayence**, **Tourettes** and **Montauroux** were all virtually inaccessible less than a hundred years ago. Not so now, though they are still a far cry from the mega-villages nearer the coast. To the south of the D562 is a wonderful, virtually uninhabited expanse of forest where, between January and June, you may see untended cattle with bells round their necks and sheep chewing away at the undergrowth. After a long period of campaigning, farmers have managed to persuade the authorities to allow the animals to roam some of the old pasturing grounds of the transhumance routes, which has the great ecological benefit of maintaining the diversity of the forest fauna.

Callas, Claviers and Bargemon

CALLAS, 12km northeast of Draguignan, is a pleasant place to stay. It has a lovely square by the church at the top of the village and, further down on the shaded place Georges-Clemenceau, a very reasonable **hotel-restaurant**, the *Hôtel de France* (☎04.94.76.61.02; ②). In the same *commune*, but 7km south, below the Draguignan–Grasse road on the D25 overlooking the Pennafort waterfalls, is the much grander *Hostellerie des Gorges de Pennafort* with its own pool, lake and olive grove (☎04.94.76.66.51, fax 04.94.76.67.23; ⑦).

Continuing north from Callas the steep narrow roads through luscious valleys lead to **CLAVIERS**, 3km away, where very little happens other than gentle games of *boules* and slow sipping of local Côtes de Provence wine, and on to **BARGEMON**, 3km further north. Within its four twelfth-century gates, Bargemon is kept in summer shade by towering plane trees on every fountained square and, in spring, the streets are filled with orange petals and mimosa blossom. The fifteenth-century **Église St-Étienne** which forms part of the defences is now a **museum-gallery** with exhibitions of local painters (daily: May–Sept 3–6pm; Oct–April 2.30–5.30pm; free). The two angel heads on the high altar are attributed to the great Marseillais sculptor Pierre Puget.

For **food** and **accommodation**, there's the excellent *Auberge des Arcades*, 12 av Pasteur (☎04.94.76.60.36, fax 04.94.76.68.33; menus from 160F; closed Tues & Wed out of season & all Nov; ③), which has a cosy sitting room, a piano-bar and a *salon de thé*.

Heading eastwards from Claviers, the road gently curves past woods and vineyards without a building in sight. If you turn right at the junction with the Draguignan–Grasse road you can stop after 1km and take a track to your left through more undisturbed woodland down to the **Lac de Meaulx**.

Seillans

Heading east from Bargemon to **SEILLANS**, 13km away, the long-distance view suddenly opens out to the mountains. Close-up you'll see the effects of Côte-style property inflation in an ugly rash of white villas. The Vieux Village, where the painter Max Ernst spent his last years, hides behind medieval walls. A small **collection** of lesser-known lithographs by Ernst, as well as some by his companion Dorothea Tanning, is on show a few doors down from the tourist office on rue de l'Église (Tues–Sat 2–6pm; 10F). Seillans' most spectacular piece of artistry, however, is 1km beyond the village on the road to Fayence. A Renaissance retable, attributed to an inspired Italian monk, is housed in the Romanesque **Chapelle de Notre-Dame-de-l'Ormeau** (mid-May to mid Sept Tues & Thurs 11am–noon; or by appointment at the tourist office in Seillans).

Seillans' **tourist office** is on place du Valat (May–Sept daily 9.30am–12.30pm & 2.30–6pm; Oct–April closed Sun; ☎04.94.76.85.91). The best place to **stay** or **eat** in Seillans is the *Hôtel de France Clariond* (☎04.94.76.96.10, fax 04.94.76.89.20; menus from 170F; ⑥; closed Wed out of season) with its own pool and panoramic views. A few cheaper rooms are available at the equally pleasant *Les Deux Rocs* on the fountained place Font-d'Amont by the old wash house (☎04.94.76.87.32, fax 04.94.76.88.68; ⑤; closed Nov–March); it also serves good Provençal food (menus from 120F; closed Tues & Thurs lunch).

Fayence and around

FAYENCE, one of the main centres for gliding in France, makes a sensible – if not the most inspiring – base for this part of the world. It's livelier than its smaller neighbours, has a good selection of places to eat, as well as bus connections with Draguignan, 33km to its southwest, Grasse, 25km east, and Cannes 40km southeast.

The **tourist office** is on place Léon-Roux (mid-June to mid-Sept Mon–Sat 9am–noon & 2.30–7pm, Sun 9am–noon; rest of year Mon–Sat 9am–noon & 2–6pm; ☎04.94.76.20.08); there's also the Castle bookshop at 1 rue St-Pierre (9am–12.30pm & 2.30–7pm; closed Mon am & Sun), near the car park, which stocks a reasonable selection of local guides and maps in English.

For **accommodation** try *La Sousto* on rue du Paty (☎04.94.76.02.16; ④), right in the centre of the village, which has five well-equipped studio rooms for two to four people, or the *Hôtel des Oliviers*, just below the village on the D19 (☎04.94.76.13.12, fax 04.94.76.08.05; ⑤), which is perfectly acceptable but a touch characterless. Alternatively, there's the *Auberge de la Fontaine* (☎04.94.76.07.59; ③), 3km away on the road to Fréjus, beyond the junction with the main Draguignan–Grasse road; here, Provençal cooking, with a menu under 100F, adds to the attraction of its isolation. For really special surroundings you need to book in at *Le Moulin de la Camandoule* (☎04.94.76.00.84, fax 04.94.70.10.40; ⑥), a converted mill on the little road out to Notre-Dame-des-Cyprès; it's run by an English couple, but the meals (menus from 185F) are prepared by a skilled and inventive French chef. Options for **camping** include the three-star *Lou Cantaire*, 7km out on the road to Draguignan (☎04.94.76.23.77; closed mid-Oct to mid-March), and the two-star *Le Grillon*, 4km towards Grasse, past the turning to Tourettes (☎04.94.76.02.96; closed Oct–March).

For **food** options other than hotels, there's *Le France* on the main street beyond the hôtel de ville gateway (☎04.94.76.00.14; closed Mon & Sun eve in winter), which has dependable chefs and menus starting at 130F. The tables below it belong to the café *Le Lord Byron* just opposite which does good ice creams. A few paces away on place Léon-Roux, the *Entracte* does a light lunch and snacks all day, although being on the main thoroughfare it can be quite noisy. For a quieter, more substantial meal head up to the top of the village, where *La Farigoulette* (☎04.94.84.10.49; closed all Mon & Tues lunch) has a good 120F lunch menu. Copious amounts of good food are served at the *Patin Couffin*, place de l'Olivier (☎04.94.76.29.96; 125F menu; closed Mon). For a gourmet treat try *Las Castellaras* (☎04.94.76.13.80; menus from 225F; closed Wed), signed off the Seillans road, where you can eat lobster, wild mushrooms, pigeon and courgette flowers by a rose garden. **Drinks** and bar billiards are on offer at the *Bar des Campagnes* on place de l'Église.

Tourettes and Mons

The distinctly un-medieval **château** in **TOURETTES**, Fayence's close neighbour 1km to the east, is a copy of an early nineteenth-century cadet school set up in St Petersburg for Tsar Nicholas I by a French colonel. He built this replica for his retirement and it's still a private residence and not open to the public.

For an energetic walk from Fayence, take the GR49 (off the D563 just north of town) through the Fôret de Tourettes, across the valley of La Siagnole River and up to the truly perched village of **MONS**. Once there, you can reward yourself with a drink at one of the cafés on place St-Sébastien and the tremendous views, which sometimes extend as far as Corsica and Italy.

Callian, Montauroux and the Lac de St-Cassien

CALLIAN, east of Fayence, and **MONTAUROUX**, its larger neighbour, have merged together, leaving only a tiny expanse of woods before the suburbs of Grasse begin. Callian is more obviously picturesque but Montauroux's large open place du Clos makes a pleasant change from narrow twisting medievalism, as does the grassy summit of the village with its fig tree, church and little chapel of St-Barthélemy whose ceiling and walls are covered in painted panels.

Montauroux's **tourist office** on place du Clos (May–Sept Mon–Sat 9am–12.30pm & 2.30–6.30pm; Oct–April Mon–Fri 9.30am–12.30pm & 3–6pm, Sat 9.30am–12.30pm; ☎04.94.47.75.90) can advise on the many inexpensive **hotels** and campsites in the vicinity. For a central option, *La Marjolaine* (☎04.94.47.72.78; ③), just off the main road directly below the tourist office, is nothing special but is reasonably priced and has good views, a pleasant terrace; and a **restaurant** (menus from 100F).

The **Lac de St-Cassien** reservoir lies 4km to the south of here. You can use the reservoir for swimming (best access from the D37 after you've crossed the lake), sailing or rowing, and eat pizzas, grills and ice creams at the various lakeside establishments. No motor boats are allowed and the water is very clean.

The Haut Var

The **Haut Var**, stretching west from Draguignan from the Argens Valley to the Verdon Gorge, is the true heart of Provence, with soft enveloping countryside of woods, vines, lakes and waterfalls, with streaks of cliffed hill ridges before the high plateaux and mountains further north. To the outsider, its picturesque medieval villages – amongst them, **Flayosc** and **Lorgues**, **Cotignac** and **Entrecasteaux** – merge together; to know them properly you'd have to live here for winter after winter, limiting your world to just

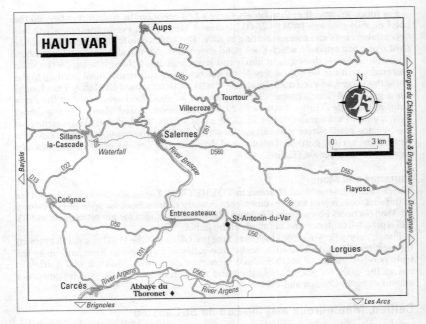

HAUT VAR

a few square miles. Familiarity would establish the individuality of each place and the stories of the older residents would connect the present with the past. For these villages, despite the proliferation of *résidences secondaires*, hold on to their identity, however guarded it is from the casual eyes of visitors. The region is also home to the **Abbaye du Thoronet**, the oldest of Provence's three surving Cistercian monasteries.

Flayosc and Lorgues

From Draguignan you can head west for 5km to **FLAYOSC** or 11km southwest to **LORGUES**; both are excellent **eating** stops. *L'Oustaou* on place Brémond, the main square of Flayosc (☎04.94.70.42.69; menus from 120F; closed Mon & Sun eve), has a rare genuine Provençal atmosphere to go with the local specialities. *Chez Bruno* on rte de Vidauban in Lorgues (☎04.94.73.92.19; menu at 280F, à la carte around 400F; closed Mon & Sun eve out of season) is considerably more expensive, but if you're prepared to pay the serious sums involved you can try wonderfully wild local ingredients in a chestnut and *chanterelle* soup and in the truffle and game dishes, followed by *crème brûlée* with figs in wine; the chef, M Bruno, is one of France's celebrity chefs and may well be away cooking dinners for presidents or royalty.

The Abbaye du Thoronet

Fifteen kilometres west of Lorgues, across the River Argens, deep in the forest of La Daboussière, is one of Provence's three great Cistercian monasteries, the **Abbaye du Thoronet** (April–Sept Mon–Sat 9am–7pm, Sun 9am–noon & 2–7pm; Oct–March 9am–noon & 2–5pm; 35F). Like Silvacane and Sénanque (see pp.148 & 138), it was founded in the first half of the twelfth century, but Thoronet is the oldest of the three and the one that was completed in the shortest time, giving it a tight unity that emphasises its graceful austerity. Finally abandoned in 1791, it was kept intact during the Revolutionary era as a remarkable monument to history and art. Restoration started in the 1850s, and a more recent campaign has brought it to clear-cut perfection. As with the other two, it's the spaces – here delineated by walls of pale rose-coloured stone – that are the essence of the experience. The *abbaye* is off the D79, between the hamlet of Le Thoronet and Cabasse; there are no buses so you'll need your own transport to get there.

Cotignac

Of all the Haut Var villages **COTIGNAC**, 20km to the north of Thoronet, would perhaps be the best to choose for a life of sensual exile. From its utterly photogenic place de la Mairie, rue de l'Horloge leads under the clock tower and on up to the church; from here a path takes you to the foot of the eighty-metre cliff that forms the village's back wall. At the summit stand two ruined towers of a long-abandoned castle, and in between the rock is riddled with caves and subterranean passages of white rock and stalactite formations. Rock falls have blocked the nerve-racking upward route of rusty iron rails and precarious ledges. Instead you can wander along the semi-abandoned gardens at the foot of the cliff or through the village's passageways and stairs bursting with begonias, jasmine and geranium before gravitating to the long, shaded **cours Gambetta** where life in Cotignac revolves.

Centre-stage in the history of Cotignac are the now defunct tanning works, once a major industry of the Haut Var, and the miraculous Virgin in the **Chapelle de Notre-Dame-des-Grâces**, on the summit across the valley to the south. Long called upon as a saviour from the plague, this Virgin finally hit the big time in 1638 when Louis XIII and Anne of Austria – married for 22 childless years – made their supplications to her. Nine months after the royal visit, the future Sun King let out his first demanding squall.

If you want to sample some of Cotignac's local produce, head for Les Ruchers du Bessillon at 2 rue des Naïfs which sells an exceptional variety of **honey**; René Vacca in quartier Nestuby for **olive oil**; and the Vignerons de Cotignac 100m out of town on the Salernes road (D13) for **wine**.

Practicalities

Cotignac's **tourist office** is just off the cours Gambetta at 2 rue Bonaventure (Mon–Sat 9.30am–12.30pm & 3–5pm, Sun 10am–noon; ☎04.94.04.61.87). The recently renovated *Du Cours*, 18 cours Gambetta (☎04.94.04.78.50; ③; closed mid-Nov to Jan), is a good place **to stay**, as is *Lou Calen* at the bottom of the *cours* (☎04.94.04.60.40, fax 04.94.04.76.64; ④), whose restaurant (closed Wed out of season) has a reasonable and filling 100F menu of simple local fare. The municipal **campsite** is on the Aups road on your right about 3km outside Cotignac (☎04.94.04.71.91).

For **food**, there's a good pizzeria, *Les Trois Marches*, on cours Gambetta; or out on the road to Carcès, you can indulge in duck in fig sauce by a pool at *Le Mas de Cotignac* (☎04.94.04.66.57). The community's various clans gather in the *Bar de l'Union* at the top of the *cours*: bee-keepers, *vignerons* and immigrants working as fig-packers or labourers. Cotignac's **market** is on Tuesday.

Entrecasteaux

Nine kilometres east of Cotignac towards Lorgues, **ENTRECASTEAUX** is almost too tiny to be called a village. Its château, the village's dominant feature, owes a lot to a Scotsman with an unlikely history. Ian McGarvie-Munn (1919–81) was a painter who trained as a naval architect after World War II and later became the head of the National

Workshops for Applied Arts in Colombia. Soon after his wife's father had become president of Guatemala, McGarvie-Munn took over as head of the Guatemalan navy, following that with a stint as the country's ambassador to London. In 1974, by now retired from diplomatic-military service, he found himself looking longingly at the ruined shell of Entrecasteaux's seventeenth-century château. He bought it, then spent the rest of his life and every last penny on the massive restoration job. The family continued the work after his death, then sold the castle off in 1995. It's still privately owned, but is back in French hands.

You can visit the **château** (July & Aug daily 11am–12.30pm & 2.30–6pm; April–June & Sept Mon, Tues & Thurs–Sun 11am–12.30pm & 2.30–6pm; Oct–March Mon, Tues & Thurs–Sun 11am–noon & 2.30–5pm; 30F), and the publicly owned **Le Nôtre** gardens, which separate the château from the village. The château's interior is spacious, light and charmingly rustic, typified by the terracotta tiles, a style that was all the rage when the Count and Countess of Grignan used the château as their summer residence. The minimal furnishings add to the general effect, but the reception room and the countess's bedroom give some idea of the status of the one-time inhabitants. Exhibitions on the first floor relate to later occupants, firstly Raymond Bruny, who charted part of the coast of western Australia and Tasmania; and secondly, photos of the sorry state in which McGarvie-Munn found the château before beginning his extensive restoration.

Practicalities

It's possible **to stay** in the château itself, at a price (☎04.94.04.43.95; ⑧), and there's a restaurant, too (menus from 95F; closed eve & all Wed). Or, if you're simply seeking a suitable base as an alternative to Cotignac, see if you can get one of the eight **rooms** in the very welcoming hotel-restaurant *Lou Cigaloun* in St-Antonin-du-Var, Entrecasteaux's even smaller neighbour to the west (☎04.94.04.42.67; ④); its restaurant (closed Mon out of season & Tues; weekday menu around 100F) offers simple but fine cooking.

Decent **meals** for around 125F can also be had at *La Forchette*, up beyond the Entrecasteaux's château entrance (☎04.94.04.42.78; closed Mon & Sun eve), and at *Lou Picateou*, below the château.

Salernes and Sillans

Compared with Cotignac, **SALERNES**, 7.5km north of Entrecasteaux, is quite a metropolis, with a thriving tile-making industry and enough near-level irrigated land for productive agriculture. Sunday and Wednesday are the best days to visit the **market** beneath the ubiquitous plane trees on the *cours*. There are also the pottery and tile workshops, selling a mix of designs you'd find in any home improvement shop as well as items with more local flair.

In the nineteenth century the workshops churned out the hexagonal terracotta floor tiles that have been reproduced in various synthetic materials ever since. You'll find shops in the centre of the town and larger *ateliers-magasins* on the outskirts: Maurice Emphoux, Jacques Polidori and Pierre Boutal on the road to Draguignan; Alain Vagh on the road to Entrecasteaux; and Ateliers de la Baume, 4km east on the D560. Remember if you want to carry home some originals, these are artisans' artefacts and priced accordingly.

For somewhere **to stay**, try the *Grand Hôtel Allègre* on the rte de Sillans (☎04.94.70.60.30; ③), a classic old-fashioned hotel with a pretty garden; or there's the fourteenth-century farmhouse, *La Bastide Rose*, across the River Bresque towards La Colle Riforan (☎04.94.70.63.30; ④). There's also a four-star campsite, *Les Arnauds*, just outside the town on the Sillans road (☎04.94.67.51.95; closed Oct–April). **Cheap eats** in Salernes include *La Fontaine*, place du 8 mai 1945 (☎04.94.70.64.51; closed Wed & Sun evening out of season), takeaway pizzas at *La Cuillère* on rue Pierre Blanc (closed Mon), a range of cafés on the *cours* and a **bar** with a good selection of beers opposite the tourist office.

   SILLANS, 6km west of Salernes, is not in itself overtly picturesque, but its **waterfall** down a delightful path signed from the main road (a 20-minute walk from the car park) is stunning. The water falls into a turquoise pool that makes for a brilliant swim. If you want to **stay** in Sillans, there's *Les Pins* hotel-restaurant (☎04.94.04.63.26; ③); *chambres d'hôtes* at *La Dame d'Argent* beyond the waterfall (☎04.94.04.63.23; ③) or the **campsite**, *Le Relais de la Bresque* (☎04.94.04.64.89), 1km out along the road to Aups, which has a restaurant, swimming pool, bar, horse-riding, *pétanque* and ping-pong.

Villecroze

Five kilometres northeast of Salernes, **VILLECROZE**, like Cotignac, sits beneath a water-burrowed cliff. The gardens around the base are delightfully un-Gallic and the same lack of formality extends throughout the town. It's an attractive place, with lovely vaulted arcades down rue des Arcades and rue de France, and a Romanesque church with a wall of bells.

   In the 1970s, an early radical ecologist by the name of Jean Pain ran his heating, lighting and 2CV on compost made from the undergrowth of the surrounding woods, material otherwise destroyed to avoid the risk of fire. Pain's compost gave back nutrients to the forest soil and agricultural land of this harsh terrain, and his methods of generating power from compost have been taken up in Canada, California and Senegal.

   If Villecroze tempts you to **stay**, try to get one of the eight rooms at the *Auberge des Lavandes* on place du Général-de-Gaulle (☎04.94.70.76.00; ③), one of the best deals in the region; or at the secluded and very comfortable *Au Bien Être* in quartier Les Cadenières (☎04.94.70.67.57; ④), 3.5km south along the D557. There are two three-star **campsites**, *Les Cadenières* (☎04.94.67.58.30; closed Nov–Feb) and *Le Ruou* (☎04.94.70.67.70; closed Nov–March), both on the D560 towards Flayosc. For food, the **restaurant** at the *Au Bien Être* has menus for around 155F (closed Mon, Tues & Weds lunch out of season). The other restaurant of some repute is *Le Colombier* on rte de Draguignan (☎04.94.70.63.23; midday menu around 115F; closed Mon out of season).

Tourtour

TOURTOUR sits 300m higher than Villecroze, atop a ridge from which the view extends to the massifs of Maures, Ste-Baume and Ste-Victoire. The village has a seemingly organic unity, soft-coloured stone growing into stairways and curving streets, branching to form arches, fountains, and towers. The ruin of an old mill looks as if it has always been like this; the elephant-leg towers of the sixteenth-century bastion stand around the *mairie* and the post office as if of their own volition, while the twelfth-century **Tour du Grimaldi** might have erupted spontaneously from the ground. The two elms on the main square, planted when Anne of Austria and Louis XIII visited Cotignac, are almost as enormous as the bastion towers, but are beginning to show signs of decrepitude.

   Having said that, Tourtour is all a bit unreal, full of *résidences secondaires* and *salons de thé* selling expensive fruit-juice cocktails. It also has this region's most upmarket **hotel-restaurant**, the *Bastide de Tourtour* (☎04.94.70.57.30, fax 04.94.70.54.90; menus from 160F; ⑧), specializing in classic local cuisine, and with Jacuzzis, tennis courts and a gym to go with the lavish rooms.

Aups

The village of **AUPS**, 10km north of Salernes, is an ideal base for visiting the villages of the Haut Var or the Grand Canyon du Verdon for those with their own transport. Though only 500m or so above sea level, it was considered by the ancients to be the beginning of the Alps; the Romans called it Alpibus which became Alps then Aups. The chief town of one of the Ligurian tribes and the location for a Roman army hospital, it then thrived in the Middle Ages, and by the eighteenth century its prosperity was inducing delusions of grandeur in the local abbot. Having mathematically proved Aups to be at the centre of Europe, he drew a map of the continent on the tiles of his house to illustrate the fact. He also erected a column in his garden inscribed with the scientific knowledge of his day and was responsible for one of the seven sundials that decorate the village.

Arrival, information and accommodation

Coming from Sillans, Salernes or Villecroze, you enter **Aups** along av Georges-Clemenceau which ends with place Frédéric-Mistral and place Martin-Bidouré. The very helpful **tourist office** is to your left in the former town hall (April–June & Sept Mon 3–6pm, Tues–Sat 10am–noon & 3–6pm; July & Aug Mon–Sat 9am–12.30pm & 3–7pm, Sun 9.30am–12.30pm; Oct–March Mon 2–4pm, Tues–Sat 10am–noon & 2–4pm; ☎04.94.70.00.80). The Vieille Ville is in front of you with the church to the right.

All the **hotels** in Aups are good value: the recently refurbished *Provençal* on place Martin-Bidouré (☎04.94.70.00.24; ④) is the most expensive; the *Grand Hôtel* on place Duchâtel (☎04.94.70.10.82; ②; closed Jan–March) is the cheapest. More luxury is to be had at *L'Escale du Verdon*, 1km out on the rte de Sillans-la-Cascade (☎04.94.84.00.04; ④; closed mid-June to Aug). There are two **campsites** close to town: the two-star *Camping Les Prés*, to the right off allée Charles-Boyer towards Tourtour (☎04.94.70.00.93), where you can also rent **bikes**; and the three-star *Saint Lazare* 2km along the Moissac road (☎04.94.70.12.86; closed Oct–March), which has a pool.

If you want to go **riding**, *Campagne de l'Estré* (☎04.94.84.00.45) about 3km along the road to Moustiers-Ste-Marie, will organize treks to the Gorges du Verdon and can put people up for the night. The tourist office also has details of local **walks**.

The Town

On place Martin-Bidouré a monument commemorates a period of republican resistance all too rarely honoured in France. Its inscription reads: "To the memory of citizens who died in 1851 defending the Republic and its laws", the year being that of Louis Napoléon's coup d'état. Peasant and artisan defiance was strongest in Provence, and the defeat of the insurgents, who flew the red flag because the tricolour had been appropriated by the usurper, was followed by a massacre of men and women alike. At Aups, the badly wounded Martin Bidouré escaped, but was found soon afterwards being succoured by a peasant, and shot dead on the spot.

This event might explain the strident "République Française, Liberté, Egalité, Fraternité" sign on the **Église St-Pancrace**, proclaiming the supremacy of state before religion – a common feature of French churches but usually more discreet. The church was designed by an English architect five hundred years ago and has had its doors restored in the last ten years by two resident British carpenters. The Renaissance portal is in good shape, there are some altarpieces inside and the attractive nineteenth-century stained-glass windows have all been cleaned up and repaired.

Another plus for Aups is its **museum of modern art** – the Musée Simon Segal – in the former convent chapel on av Albert-1er (mid-June to mid-Sept 10.30am–noon & 4–7pm; 15F). The best works are by the Russian-born painter Simon Segal, but there are interesting local scenes in the other paintings, such as the Roman bridge at Aiguines, now drowned beneath the artificial lake of Ste-Croix.

Unfortunately La Fabrique, the former abbot's house, is a private residence and can't be visited. But the old streets, the sixteenth-century clock tower with its campanile, and the Wednesday and Saturday morning **market** which fills place Martin-Bidouré, all make this a very appealing place to be. Aups has become more geared to tourism in recent years but its living still comes from agriculture and there's prime local produce to be had in the shops. Along with honey, the Aups speciality is truffles, and if you're here on a Thursday between November and mid-March you'll witness the **truffle market**. The local lamb has a gourmet reputation: marinaded and roasted with thyme is the traditional preparation. Other delicacies include small birds cooked with juniper berries; the gun shop in the main street explains the ready supply. For **food shopping**, Bernard Georges sells honey and truffles (in season) from his farm, Mas du Vieux Moulin, on rue de la Piscine east of place Martin-Bidouré; the Pâtisserie à la Claire Fontaine sells nougat and other local sweets; and, at 7 rue Maréchal-Foch, L'Herbier sells soaps, liqueurs and dried flowers. The best place for bread and cakes (olive oil *fougasses* in particular) is the Boulangerie-Pâtisserie Canut on place du Marché. On av Albert-1er the Domaine Valmoisine has a shop where you can buy wine *en vrac*.

Eating, drinking and entertainment

For **meals**, your first choice should be the hotel-restaurant *St-Marc* (☎04.94.70.06.08; ③; closed Tues eve, Wed & middle 2 weeks of June), a nineteenth-century mill on rue Aloisi. Serving local dishes, truffles and boar in season, it offers a very cheap midday menu and evening menus for around 100F. For standard, reliable food try the *Yucca* at 3 rue Mal-Foch (closed Mon eve & Tues), and for snacks, the *boulangerie-pâtisserie* at no. 20 av Albert-1er (closed Dec–April). The **bar** opposite the church is the place to sip pastis. The tourist office has details of theatre, film and other **entertainment** to be had at the Centre Culturel.

Barjols

For all its springs, streams and fountains, **BARJOLS**, 16km west of Cotignac, is a depressing place. The town has still not recovered from the closure of its tanneries, and many of the people at the Saturday **market** on place Émile-Zola seem as glum as characters from a Zola novel. The rickety buildings of the ancient tanning industry have been taken over by artists and craft workers; you can visit their studios (follow signs to Art-Artisanal) down the old road to Brignoles, east of the Vieille Ville. Looking back upwards from here at the industrial ruins is a good spooky night-time experience.

In January a strange **festival** takes place which commemorates the miraculous arrival of an ox during a famine, but is in honour of the town's patron saint, St-Marcel: the cow gets killed and roasted to the accompaniment of flutes and tambourines and the refrain "Saint Marcel, Saint Marcel, the little tripe, the little tripe".

Le Pont d'Or on allée Louis-Pasteur (☎04.94.77.05.23; ①) serves the best **food** in town with menus from 80F; it also has good-value **rooms**. Nightlife, such as it is, centres around the two squares with huge mossy fountains.

The Grand Canyon du Verdon

From Aups the road north skirts the military terrain of the Camp de Canjuers and crosses the River Verdon as it leaves the gorge to fill the vast artificial basin of the Lac de Ste-Croix. This is the quickest approach from the south to the **Grand Canyon du Verdon**, Europe's widest and deepest gorge, but not the most dramatic. The most heart-stopping approach is from Draguignan and the Gorges de Châteaudouble via Comps-sur-Artuby along one of the very few public roads through the military terrain of the Camp de

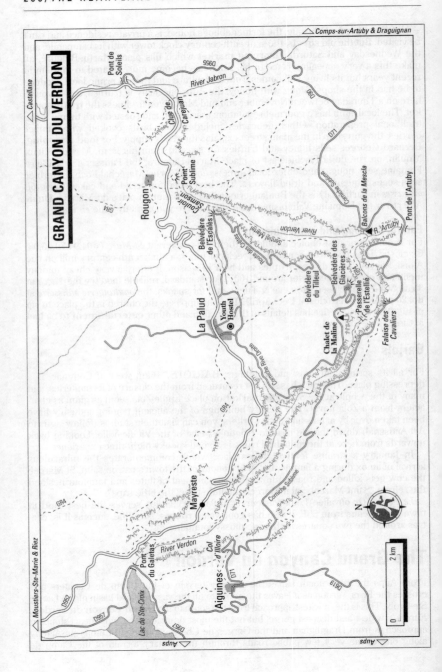

GRAND CANYON DU VERDON

INFORMATION AND GUIDES: A CHECKLIST

There are plenty of organizations and individual guides with whom you can arrange expeditions on foot, horseback, raft, canoe or by air. The Bureau des Guides and Le Perroquet Vert will also give advice if you don't want to be part of a group. Prices vary with the season and the number of people taking part, but they are reasonable.

Bureau des Guides, La Palud (Mon–Sat 10am–12.30pm & 2–5.30pm ☎04.92.77. 30.50). Information and guides on walks and rock-climbing.

Bruno Potié, La Palud (☎04.92.77.32.07). Professional walking guide and rock-climber.

Le Perroquet Vert, La Palud (☎04.92.77.33.39). Climbing shop.

Ranch Les Pioneers, La Palud (☎04.92.77.38.30). Horse-rides with your own guide.

UCPA, La Palud (☎04.92.77.30.29). Climbing, walking, canoeing and nautical trekking with a trained guide.

Verdon Animation Nature, La Palud (☎04.92.77.30.15). Canoeing and rafting with the help of a trained guide.

Verdon Passion, Moustiers (☎04.92.74.69.77). Hang-gliding and paragliding.

Canjuers. After Comps-sur-Artuby, the road turns westwards through 16km of end-of-the-earth heath and hills, with each successive horizon higher than the last. When you reach the canyon, it is as if a silent earthquake had taken place while you journeyed.

From the first vantage point on the route from Draguignan, the **Balcons de la Mescla**, it's a 250-metre drop to the base of the V-shaped, 21-kilometre gorge incised by the Verdon through piled strata of limestone. Ever-changing in its volume and energy, the river falls from **Rougon** to the east of the gorge, disappearing into tunnels, decelerating for shallow languid moments and finally exiting in full steady flow at the **Pont de Galetas** to fill the huge resevoir of the **Lac de Ste-Croix**.

Running west from the Balcons is the **corniche sublime**, built expressly to give the most breathtaking and hair-raising views. On the north side, the **Route des Crêtes** serves the same function, at some points looking down a sheer 800-metre drop to the sliver of water below. The entire circuit is 130km long and it's cycling country solely for the preternaturally fit. Even for drivers it's hard work, as the hidden bends and hairpins in the road are perilous and, in July and August, so is the traffic.

Public transport around the canyon is poor. There's one **bus** between Aix, Moustiers, La Palud, Rougon and Castellane (July to mid-Sept Mon, Wed & Sat; rest of year Sat only); and one other bus between La Palud, Rougon and Castellane (July & Aug Mon–Sat). **Drivers** should note that petrol stations are few and far between. By far the best way to explore the canyon, if your legs are strong enough, is to descend to the river and follow it by foot; to **walk** from Rougon to Mayreste on the sentier Martel takes two days and the trip should be made only as part of a **guided group** (see box above), as crossing the torrent by rope is no simple matter on your own. It's possible to walk just the section between Rougon and Les Malines, a trek of about eight hours. Unaccompanied shorter excursions into the canyon include the fairly easy descent from the **Falaise des Cavaliers** (west of the Balcons), crossing via the **Passerelle de l'Estellié** and ascending to the *Chalet de la Maline*, in about two hours. Another walk of similar length can be done from the **Point Sublime**, passing though the **Couloir Samson**, a 670-metre tunnel with occasional "windows" and a stairway down to the chaotic sculpture of the river banks.

Canoeing or **rafting** the entire length of the gorge should not be attempted unless you are very experienced and strong, as you will have to carry your craft for long stretches. However, you can pay (quite a lot) to join a group and tackle certain stretches of the river. Because of the electricity boards operations these trips aren't always possible, so be prepared for disappointment. A cheaper, though less exciting option, is to paddle about on the last stretch of the gorge: you can rent canoes and pedalos at the Pont du Galetas. **Rock-climbing** is also possible as is **horse-riding** on the less precipitous slopes around the gorge. Finally, for the ultimate buzz, there's **hang-gliding**.

La Palud-sur-Verdon

LA PALUD-SUR-VERDON is the closest village to the gorge and the best base in terms of information and organizations for exploring the area (see box on p.267).

The **tourist office** (June–Aug daily 10am–noon & 4–6pm; Easter–May and Sept to mid-Dec Thurs & Fri 10am–noon & 4–6pm Sat 10am–noon; ☎04.92.77.32.02), on the main road, will help with accommodation and information on **walking tours** of the gorge. You should also get details of the route and advice on **weather conditions** (recorded information ☎08.36.68.02.04) before you set out. You'll need drinking water, a torch/flashlight (for the tunnels), and a jumper for the cold shadows of the narrow corridors of rock. Always stick to the path and don't cross the river except at the *passerelles* as the EDF (electricity board; ☎04.92.83.62.68 for recorded information) may be opening dams upstream.

There is plenty of **accommodation** within easy reach of the village. Of the hotels *Le Provence*, rte de la Maline (☎04.92.77.36.50, fax 04.92.77.31.05; ④; closed Nov–March) has the most stunning position, just below the village; *Les Gorges du Verdon*, just beyond the youth hostel (☎04.92.77.38.26, fax 04.92.77.35.00; ⑥; closed Oct–April), has all mod cons and is beautifully isolated; and *Le Panoramic*, rte de Moustiers, La Palud (☎04.92.77.35.07, fax 04.92.77.30.17; ⑤; closed mid-Nov to March), whose views are not as panoramic, but it's an agreeable enough place; there's also the small *Auberge des Crêtes*, 1km east of La Palud (☎04.92.77.38.47, fax 04.92.77.30.40; ③; closed Oct–March), which has just 12 rooms. There's a youth hostel, *Le Trait d'Union*, half a kilometre below La Palud (☎04.92.77.38.72; closed Nov–March) and a two-star campsite 1km west of the village (☎04.92.77.38.13).

The centre of social life is *Lou Cafetie* **bar-restaurant** (menu 46F; closed Nov–March), where conversation is inevitably thick with stories of near-falls, near-drownings and near-death from exposure. For picnic provisions there's a **market** on Wednesday morning.

Aiguines

AIGUINES, at the western end of the Corniche Sublime, is perched high above the Lac de Ste-Croix, with an enticing château (closed to the public) of pepperpot towers that dazzle with their coloured tiles, and a history of wood-turning. The *boules* for *pétanque* made from ancient box-wood roots used to be Aiguines' speciality; in the 1940s the industry sustained a population of six hundred people. Women would bang the little nails into the *boules* to give them their metal finish, inventing intricate and personalized designs. There's a tiny **Musée des Tourneurs sur Bois** (mid-June to mid-Sept Mon & Wed–Sun 10am–noon & 2–6pm; 10F) devoted to the intricate art of wood-turning, and some very expensive and beautiful woodwork, as well as pottery and faïence, to be viewed at the **Galerie d'Art** opposite the tourist office. Walking around Aiguines you'll notice a great sense of openness and of being up in the air; even its old streets follow the ridge rather than clustering in the usual spiral.

Every conceivable water sport is practised on the nearby **Lac de Ste-Croix**, and you should find gear available for rental at Les Salles-sur-Verdon or Ste-Croix-du-Verdon and at other outlets around this enormous reservoir. Swimming is good with easy access from the D957 between Aups and Moustiers, though sometimes when the water levels are low it's a bit muddy round the edges.

There are plenty of places to stay around Aiguines. For central **hotels**, try *Du Vieux Château*, on the main road (☎04.94.70.22.95; ②); or *Altitude 823*, below the main road (☎04.94.70.21.09; ③; closed Nov–March). For a bit more style and comfort, there's *Le Grand Canyon* at Falaise des Cavaliers, halfway between Aiguines and Comps (☎04.94.76.91.31, fax 04.94.76.92.29; ④; closed mid-Oct to mid-April), with comfortable rooms, balconies and a dining terrace overlooking the 300-metre drop down the gorge; or the *chambre d'hôtes* in the *Château de Chanteraine*, signposted off the D19 1km before entering Aiguines from the Lac de Ste-Croix (☎04.94.70.21.01; ③). There's also a two-star **campsite**, *Le Galetas*, on the D957 (☎04.94.70.20.48; closed Nov–March), almost within diving distance of the lake, a long way down from the village.

Moustiers-Ste-Marie

Given the choice, the nearby resort of **MOUSTIERS-STE-MARIE** is one place to avoid, particularly in the height of summer. It's glutted with *ateliers* making and selling glazed pottery – Moustiers' traditional speciality – and with hotels, restaurants and souvenir stalls where service is given as a reluctant favour. The pottery, like the village before its commercial metamorphosis, is pastel and pretty; it's on sale in Liberty's and Bloomingdales but if you want to lug plates or jugs home with you, here's your chance. The **tourist office** (daily July & Aug 10am–12.30pm & 2–7.30pm; May–June & Sept 10.30am–12.30pm & 2–6pm; March–April & Oct 11am–noon & 2–5pm; Nov–Feb 2–5pm; ☎04.92.74.67.84) at the top of the village, will dole out leaflets by the bagful should you wish to do the rounds.

Riez and around

RIEZ, 20km from the Grand Canyon to the west of the Lac de Ste-Croix is one of the least spoilt small towns of inland Provence. There are a couple of pottery workshops, but the town's main business comes from the lavender fields that cover this part of the region. Just over the river, about a kilometre away on the road south, is a **lavender distillery**, a building strangely reminiscent of 1950s Soviet architecture, which produces essence for the perfume industry.

Arrival, information and accommodation

The **tourist office** is at 4 cours allées Louis-Gardiol (June–Sept Tues–Sun 9.30am–12.30pm & 2.30–6.30pm; rest of year Tues, Thurs & Fri 8.30am–noon & 2.30–5.30pm, Wed 8am–5pm, Sat 8am–4pm; ☎04.92.77.99.09); when closed try the Hôtel de ville, behind the tourist office (office hours; ☎04.92.74.99.00), which can also provide information.

Carina, the ugly, executive-style **hotel** across the river in the quartier St-Jean (☎04.92.77.85.43, fax 04.92.77.74.93; ④; closed mid-Nov to March), has lovely views from its rooms. Out-of-town options are limited to the *Hôtel Cigalou* (☎04.92.77.75.50; ③) on the rte de Roumoules or the *Château de Pontfrac* (☎04.92.77.78.77; ③) on the rte de Valensole. You'll also find the **restaurant** *Les Abeilles* on allées Louis-Gardiol (☎04.92.77.89.29; closed eve in winter), which is a real treat with specialities such as *aïoli* and imaginative menus including wine that start well below 100F. There's a two-star **campsite** on rue Edouard-Dauphin, across the river (☎04.92.77.75.45; closed Oct–May).

The Town

In size Riez is more a village than a town, but it soon becomes clear that it was once more influential than it is now. Some of the houses on Grande Rue and rue du Marché – the two streets above the main allées Louis-Gardiol – have rich Renaissance facades and the former hôtel de ville on place Quinconces was once an episcopal palace. The cathedral, which was abandoned four hundred years ago, has been excavated just across the river from allées Louis-Gardiol. Beside it is a **baptistry** (check with the tourist office for opening times), restored in the nineteenth century, but originally constructed, like the cathedral, around 600 AD. If you recross the river and follow it downstream you'll find the even older and much more startling relics of four **Roman columns** standing in a field.

A rather more strenuous **walk**, first heading for the clock tower above Grande Rue and then taking the path past the cemetery and on upwards (leaving the cemetery to your left), brings you to a cedar-shaded platform at the summit of the hill; this is the site of the Roman town, though the only building now occupying the site is the eighteenth-century **Chapelle St-Maxime**, with a patterned interior that is gaudy or gorgeous, depending on your taste.

The **Maison de l'Abeille**, 1km out of the village along the road to Digne (daily 10am–12.30pm & 2.30–7pm; free), is a research and visitors' centre where you can buy various **honeys** as well as hydromel, or mead – the honey alcohol of antiquity. If you show enthusiasm you will be regaled with fascinating accounts of bee physiology, bee anthropology, bee sociology, bee sexuality (the mating of French and English bees has yet to succeed), and get introduced to the bees themselves. The people here are very keen for you to share their obsession.

The Plateau de Valensole

Riez lies to the south of the **Plateau de Valensole**, which continues as far as the Bléone and Durance rivers and is cut in two by the wide stony course of the River Asse. Roads and villages north of the river are sparse. It's a beautiful landscape: a wide, uninterrupted plain whose horizons are the sharp high edges of mountains.

The most distinctive sight of the plateau is row upon row of **lavender** bushes, green in early summer, turning purple in July. Every farm advertises *lavandin* (a hybrid of lavender used for perfume essence) and *miel de lavande* (lavender honey). There are fields of golden grain, of almond trees blossoming white in early spring, and the gnarled and silvery trunks of olive trees. Even for Provence, the warm quality of the light is exceptional: the ancient town of Valensole, midway between Riez and Manosque, the village of Puimoisson on the road to Dignes, and the tiny hamlets along the Asse exude warmth from it even on wintry days.

This is well off the beaten track; hotels, though not thick on the ground, are unlikely to be booked up, and you can ask farmers if you can camp on their land.

The Lower Verdon

Southwest of Riez, along the Colostre and the last stretch of the Verdon, the land is richer and more populated. People commute to the Cadarache nuclear research centre at the confluence of the Durance and the Verdon, or to the new high-tech industries that are very gradually following the wake of the Marseille–Grenoble *autoroute*. Visitors tend to be the affluent ill, coming to take the cure at the long-established spa of Gréoux-Les-Bains.

On the much more attractive route south from Riez towards Barjols, **QUINSON** sits at the head of the **Basses Gorges du Verdon**. If you have not yet explored the

Verdon's Grand Canyon, these 500-metre depths should strike you as quite dramatic, although, unfortunately, they are not as accessible. The river, restrained upstream by barrages and artificial lakes, rushes down here to one last reservoir and dam before rolling resignedly past Gréoux and down to the Durance. From Quinson the path from the road where it crosses the Verdon shortly comes to an end with steps down to a bathing place. The GR99 makes a short detour to the south side of the gorge a couple of kilometres downstream, and there are paths from the road between Quinson and Esparron that lead to the edge and go no further.

There's a nicely old-fashioned **hotel**, the *Relais Notre-Dame* (☎04.92.74.40.01, fax 04.92.74.02.10; ③; closed mid-Dec to mid-March), on the main road just south of Quinson, close to the river before it enters the gorge. You can also rent **bikes** from here.

Seven kilometres south of Quinson, **MONTMEYAN** is a beautifully unspoilt Provençal village with fabulous views of the Valensole Plateau and the Alps. You'll find economical **accommodation** and **food** at the basic *Hôtel de France* (☎04.92.74.40.01; ②) in the centre of town.

Manosque

MANOSQUE, 33km west of Riez, is an ancient town, strategically positioned just above the right bank of the River Durance. Its small, compact old quarter is surrounded by ever-spreading industrial units linked by roads designed for container lorries. It is a major population centre in the *département* of Alpes-de-Haute-Provence and busy profiting from the new corridor of affluence that follows the river. Many of its residents work at the Cadarache atomic centre, or in Aix, or even in Marseille now that the highway gives speedy access.

For the French, Manosque is most famous as the home town of the author **Jean Giono** who was born here in 1895. As well as mementoes of the writer, the town also contains an extraordinary work of art on the theme of the Apocalypse by the Armenian-born painter, **Jean Carzou**.

Arrival, information and accommodation

The **gare SNCF** is 1.5km south of the centre with regular **buses** up av Jean-Giono, the main route into town which ends at Porte Saunerie. From the **gare routière** (☎04.92.87.55.99), on bd Charles-de-Gaulle, turn left and then right onto av Jean-Giono. The **tourist office** (mid-June to mid-Sept Mon & Wed–Sat 9am–12.15pm & 1.30–6pm, Tues 9–11.45am & 1.30–6.30pm, Sun 10am–noon; rest of year closed Sun; ☎04.92.72.16.00) is to the left on place du Dr-Joubert just before you reach Porte Saunerie.

Staying in Manosque presents few problems. For low-priced rooms in the centre, you could try *François 1er*, 18 rue Guilhempierre (☎04.92.72.07.99, fax 04.92.87.54.85; ③), or *Peyrache*, 37 rue Jean-Jacques-Rousseau (☎04.92.72.07.43; ③). Outside the Vieille Ville's ring of boulevards is the *Grand Hôtel de Versailles*, 17 av Jean-Giono (☎04.92.72.12.10; ③). The most pleasant, and costly, hotel is the *Hostellerie de la Fuste* (☎04.92.72.05.95; ⑦) across the Durance and 1km along the D4 towards Oraison. There's an **HI youth hostel** (☎04.92.87.57.44) 750m north of the Vieille Ville along bd Martin-Bret and av de l'Argile, in the Parc de la Rochette; take bus #2 (La Rochette stop). It's near a covered swimming pool and the three-star municipal **campsite** on av de la Repasse (☎04.92.72.28.08; closed Oct–March).

The Town

Vieux Manosque is scarcely half a kilometre across. You can enter it through two of its remaining fourteenth-century gates, Porte Saunerie from the south and Porte

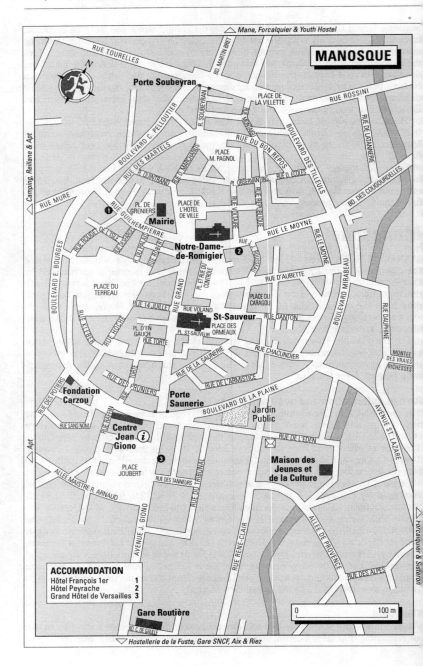

Soubeyran, which sports a tiny bell suspended within the iron outline of an onion dome, from the north. Midway between the two, another bell tower of more intricate design graces the **Église de Saint-Sauveur**. Neither this nor the **Église de Notre-Dame-de-Romigier** is a particularly stunning church, though the latter's Black Virgin (black due to the effect of gold leaf on wood) boasts a lengthy résumé of miracles. The charm of Manosque lies not in architectural set-pieces, but rather in its small decorative details, such as the pattern in brick and flints in front of the seventeenth-century **Hôtel de Ville**, the Renaissance door frame of Notre-Dame, and the superb statue, *Le Froid*, by Bloche on promenade Aubert-Millot.

There's nothing pretentious about the shops lining **rue Grande, rue des Marchands** and **rue Soubeyran** which link the two gates. The streets are busy with fruit and vegetable **markets** on Monday, Wednesday and Friday, and the big weekly market every Saturday, which is even bigger in the first week of the month. Stall-holders and bargain-seekers come in from all the surrounding villages and you'll find moving through the central streets a very slow but entertaining business. If you can find a seat in the **bar-tabac** *Le Cigaloun* beside the church on place Hôtel-de-Ville, grab it fast and watch the animation from there.

The attractive eighteenth-century house that is now the **Centre Jean Giono**, on bd Elémir-Bourges by Porte Saunerie (Tues–Sat 9am–noon & 2–6pm; 21F), was the first house to be built outside the old town walls. As well as manuscripts, photos, letters and a library of translations of Giono's work, the centre has an extensive video collection of films based on his novels, films he contributed to plus interviews and documentaries. Giono himself did not live here. His home was at **Le Paraïs** (guided tours by reservation only Fri 3–5.30pm; ☎04.92.87.73.03; free), off montée des Vrais Richesses 1.5km north of the Vieille Ville.

Giono was imprisoned at the start of World War II for his pacifism, and again after liberation because the Vichy government had promoted his belief in the superiority of nature and peasant life over culture and urban civilization as appropriate Nazi propaganda. In truth, far from being a fascist, Giono was a passionate ecologist who believed that to live close to nature was to be in touch with the cosmic essence of things and with essential human goodness. The countryside around Manosque, its hills and streams, its wildlife, sun, storms and winds do more than just feature in his novels, they actually play as strong a part as the characters that they shape. World War II embittered him, and his later novels are less idealistic. Giono never left Manosque and died here in 1970.

Jean Carzou, Giono's contemporary, confronts the issues of war, technology, dehumanization and the environmental destruction of the planet head on in an extraordinary monumental work, **L'Apocalypse**, composed of painted panels and stained-glass windows in the former church of the **Couvent de la Présentation**, on bd Elémir-Bourges just up from the Centre Giono (Fri–Sun 10am–noon & 2.30–6.30pm; check at the tourist office for latest times; 25F). Nuclear and chemical weaponry, Pol Pot's massacres, Stalin's gulags, Hitler's concentration camps, the genocide of the Armenians by the Turks, the extermination of the American Indians, the Terror of the French Revolution, cities in ruins, scorched earth, civilizations destroyed . . . it's all portrayed here in nightmarish style.

Eating, drinking and entertainment

Restaurants in the Vieille Ville are generally great value. Simple but satisfying meals for 100F or less can be had at *La Barbotine* on place de l'Hôtel-de-Ville (☎04.92.72.57.15; closed Sun) and *Restaurant le Luberon* at 21 place du Terreau (☎04.92.72.03.09; closed Mon & Sun eve out of season). If you want a change from Provençal cuisine, the Chinese *Le Royal Orient*, 12 bd Elémir-Bourges (☎04.92.72.42.57; closed Mon); Vietnamese *Le Viet-Nam*, 98 av de Lattre-de-Tassigny (☎04.92.72.16.49); and Thai

Thanh Binh, 7 bd Casimir-Pellloutier (☎04.92.87.36.83), are all excellent though not cheap. *La Source* on rte de Dauphin (☎04.92.72.12.79; closed Mon & Sat midday) serves a wonderful chocolate pudding.

Forcalquier and around

In contrast with Manosque, **FORCALQUIER**, 17km to the north, is a very low-key town. It's not on any rail line and it seems surprising that the main road that ascends to place du Bourguet should take the trouble at all. The *place* can be deserted, the bars empty, and the masonry of the ancient houses is fraying at the edges. So it comes as no surprise to learn that it is the past glories of the town, and the surrounding soft, hilly countryside, that are the real attraction.

That said, things are a good deal livelier on a Monday when it's **market day**, which on the first week in every month becomes a *foire* and really rouses this sleepy place. In July and August there's a flea market every Sunday and, over the first two weeks of August, a general glut of arts and crafts fairs and exhibitions in the *Festival de Haute-Provence*.

Arrival, information and accommodation

Buses drop you off at place du Bourguet, where you'll find the **tourist office** at no. 8 (mid-June to mid-Sept Mon–Sat 9am–12.30pm & 2–7pm, Sun 10am–1pm; rest of year Mon–Sat 9am–noon & 2–6pm; ☎04.92.75.10.02). You can **rent bikes** from Maxi Meca on bd de la République (☎04.92.75.12.47) and from the campsite (see below).

The best place **to stay** is the *Auberge Charembeau* (☎04.92.70.91.70, fax 04.92.70.91.83; ⑤; closed Dec & Jan) out of town at the end of a long drive signed off the road to Niozelles. *Le Colombier* (☎04.92.75.03.71, fax 04.92.75.14.30; ⑤) is another attractive countryside retreat, 3km south of Forcalquier off the D16. In town, the *Hostellerie des Deux Lions*, next door to the tourist office at 11 place du Bourguet (☎04.92.75.25.30; ④; closed Mon out of season & Sun eve) is a seventeenth-century coach house, with comfortable rooms and an excellent restaurant serving game and fowl dishes flavoured with all the herbs of Provence. *Le Grand Hôtel*, 10 bd Latourette (☎04.92.75.00.35; ③), is the low-budget option and perfectly acceptable. The municipal **campsite** (☎04.92.75.27.94; closed Nov–March) is on the road to Sigonce past the cemetery; it also rents out caravans.

The Town

Despite its slumbering air, Forcalquier's **public buildings** suggest that this was once a place of some significance. In the **twelfth century** the counts of Forcalquier rivalled those of Provence, with dominions spreading south and east to the Durance and north to the Drôme. Gap, Embrun, Sisteron, Manosque and Apt were all ruled from the **citadel** of Forcalquier, which even minted its own currency. When this separate power base came to an end, Forcalquier was still renowned as the *Cité des Quatre Reines*, since the four daughters of Raimond Béranger V, who united Forcalquier and Provence, all married kings. One of them, Eleanor, became the wife of Henry III of England, a fact commemorated by a modern plaque on the Gothic fountain of place Bourguet.

Not much remains of the ancient citadel at the summit of the rounded, wooded hill that dominates the southern half of the town. Beside the ruins of a tower, sole vestige of the counts of Forcalquier's castle, and the half-buried walls of the original cathedral, stands a nineteenth-century chapel, **Notre-Dame-de-Provence**.

On the opposite side of the town, along the road to Sigonce, is the town's **cemetery**, in a much better state of repair than the houses of the living. Many of the oddly conical vaults were used for habitation until this century, like the Neolithic *bories* they resemble.

The elegant staircase leading down to the geometric paths, the clipped yews and high box hedges, and the detailed inscriptions on many of the tombs make this an especially appealing place.

In the town centre stands the former **Cathédrale Notre-Dame** with its asymmetric and defensive exterior, a finely wrought Gothic porch and Romanesque nave which has recently been restored. South of the cathedral you enter the **Vieille Ville** where the houses date from the thirteenth to the eighteenth century. From place Vieille or rue Mercière you can bear right for place St-Michel and the ancient street fronts of Grande Rue, rue Béranger, place du Palais and rue du Collège. Place St-Michel has another fountain, whose decorative figures are embroiled in activities currently banned under biblical sanction in half the states of the USA.

At the top and to the left of rue Passère, running south off place Vieille, and with more crumbling historic facades, you reach the start of montée St-Mary, which leads up to the citadel. The one remaining gateway of the Vieille Ville, the Porte des Cordeliers, is further down, east of place Vieille. The old **synagogue** on rue des Cordeliers marks the former Jewish quarter of Forcalquier. The superior power of the Roman Catholic Church is represented by the **Couvent des Cordeliers** at the end of bd des Martyrs. Built between the twelfth and fourteenth centuries, it bears the scars of wars and revolutions but preserves a beautifully vaulted scriptorium and a library with its original wooden ceiling. It's used for concerts and exhibitions (programme from the tourist office) and is open for **guided tours** (July to mid-Sept daily 11am, 2.30, 4.30 & 5.30pm; May, June & mid-Sept to Oct Sun & hols 2.30pm & 4.30pm; 15F).

Eating and drinking

The best places to eat are the *Deux Lions* on place du Bourguet (☎04.92.75.25.30; menus from 160F) with its traditional fare; and the *Lapin Tant Pis* (☎04.92.75.38.88; closed Mon eve & Tues) on place Vieille offering more modern creations; the latter also has a shop where you can choose from a tempting array of olive oils and other local produce. There are cheaper menus at *La Crêperie*, 4 rue des Cordeliers, where you can get great salads, grills, ice creams and crêpes, and *Le Commerce* on place du Bourguet (closed Mon eve & Tues out of season) is a good place to try the wonderful local lamb.

Another product of the town, based on fruits and nuts from further south, is **exotic alcohol**. The Distillerie de Haute-Provence has its shop on av St-Promasse just down from the tourist office, where you can buy cherries, pears and mixes of different fruits and nuts pickled in liqueur. Of its fruit wines, the *de brut de pêche*, a sparkling peach aperitif, needs to be tasted to be believed. For ordinary **café drinking**, the *Brasserie La Fontaine* on place St-Michel is a friendly locals' watering hole and the *Café L'Hôtel de Ville*, on place Bourguet, is perfectly positioned for *pétanque*-watching.

Mane

The village of **MANE**, 4km south of Forcalquier at the junction of the roads from Apt and Manosque, still has its feudal citadel – now a private residence closed to the public – and Renaissance churches, chapels and mansions remarkably intact. The most impressive building is a former Benedictine priory, **Notre-Dame-de-Salagon**, half a kilometre out of Mane off the Apt road. It comprises fifteenth-century monks' quarters, seventeenth-century stables and farm buildings, and an enormous fortified twelfth-century Romanesque church with traces of fourteenth-century frescoes and sculpted scenes of rural life. Archeological digs in the choir have revealed the remnants of an earlier, sixth-century church. Three **gardens**, one of aromatic plants, another of medicinal plants, and one cultivated as the medieval monks would have used it, have been re-created to illustrate the way in which the monks used the land. A number of exhibitions and activities are organized each year by the Conservatoire du Patrimoine

Ethnologique of the Alpes-de-Haute-Provence *département* which runs the site (June–Sept daily 10am–noon & 2–7pm; rest of year daily 2–6pm; 25F). If you need somewhere to **stay** in Mane try *La Reine Rose*, on Grand Chemin (☎04.92.75.35.30; ④) with cold floor-tiles in the rooms but offering a friendly welcome.

Further along the Apt road, past a medieval bridge over the River Laye, you come to a palatial residence that has been called the Trianon of Provence. The pure eighteenth-century ease and luxury of the **Château de Sauvan** (guided tours July & Aug Mon–Fri & Sun 3.30pm; rest of year Thurs, Sun & hols 3.30pm; 30F) come as a surprise in this harsh territory, leagues from any courtly city. Though there are hundreds of mansions like it around Paris and along the Loire, the residences of the rich and powerful in Haute-Provence tend towards the moat and dungeon, not to French windows giving onto lawns and lake. The furnishings are predictably grand and the hall and stairway would take some beating for light and spaciousness, but what's best is the setting: the swans and geese on the square lake, the peacocks strutting by the drive, the views around and the delicate solidity of the aristocratic house.

The Observatoire de Haute-Provence

The tourist literature promoting the pure air of Haute-Provence is not just hype. Proof of the fact is the National Centre for Scientific Research **observatory** on the wooded slopes west of Mane, sited here because it has the fewest clouds, the least fog and the lowest industrial pollution in all France. Visible from miles around, it presents a peculiar picture of domes of gleaming white mega-mushrooms pushing up between the oaks. It's open for **guided tours** (April–Sept Wed 2–4pm; Oct–March Wed 3pm; 15F), so you get to see some telescopes and blank monitors, and the mechanism that opens up the domes and aims the lens. It's more fun than it sounds, but it's a shame you can't visit at night. As recompense you can buy wonderful postcards of stars, comets and nebulae.

Simaine-la-Rotonde, Banon and the Montagne de Lure

The gentle countryside of the Pays de Forcalquier gives way to the north to the great barrage of the **Montagne de Lure** and to the west, past **Simaine-la-Rotonde** and **Banon**, to the desolate Plateau d'Albion (see Chapter two). The more northern villages, including Banon, are where you're likely to hear Provençal being spoken and see aspects of rural life that have hardly changed over centuries. It was in a tiny place on the Lure foothills due north of Banon called Le Contadour where Jean Giono (see p.273) set up his summer commune in the 1930s to expostulate the themes of peace, ecology and the return to nature.

Simaine-La-Rotonde

The spiralling cone of **SIMAINE-LA-ROTONDE** marks the horizon with an emphasis greater than its size would warrant. However many *villages de caractère* (Simaine's official classification) you may have seen, this is one to re-seduce you. Neither over-spruce nor on the verge of ruin, it gives the feeling of a place that people love and are prepared to work for.

The modern town – post office, banks, *boulangerie* and bars – all lies in the plain by the D51, cleanly separated from the old village's winding streets of honey-coloured stone in which each house is part of the medieval defensive system. The zigzags end at the **Rotonde** (mid-June to mid-Sept Mon–Sat 10am–12.30pm & 3–7pm, Sun 3–7pm;

April to mid-June & mid- to late-Sept Mon & Wed–Sun 3–5.30pm; 10F), a huge domed building that was once the chapel of the castle but looks more like a keep. Nineteenth-century restoration work added smooth limestone to its rough-hewn fortress stones, but the peculiar feature is the asymmetry between its interior and exterior, being hexagonal on the outside and irregularly dodecagonal on the inside. The set of the stones on the domes is wonderfully wonky and no one knows what once hung from or covered the hole at the top. In July and August the Rotonde is used for diverse cultural functions.

Beyond the Rotonde there's a path to the chapel of **Notre-Dame-de-Pieté**, which stands amongst old windmills. As you head back down through the village you pass all sorts of architectural details which catch the eye: heavy carved doors with stone lintels in exact proportion, wrought-iron street lamps, the scrolling on the dark wooden shutters of the building opposite the **covered hall of the old market**, Simaine's most stunning building. With its columns framing open sky, the hall almost overhangs the hillside on the steepest section of the village; no longer used as a market-place, it's where people stop on their daily rounds to pass the time of day or stare into the middle distance, where cats stretch out in the sun, and where, each July 14, the **village dance** is held.

Tourism is not Simaine's main preoccupation, but it does have a **tourist office**, housed in the Rotonde (same hours as Rotonde); when the office is closed, go the *mairie* in the upper village for help and information. There's only one **hotel**, the *Auberge du Faubourg* (☎04.92.75.92.43; ②; closed Nov–Feb), which has just eight rooms and insists on half board. The only other accommodation options are a **gîte**, *Le Chaloux* (M Rider; ☎04.92.75.99.13; ①; closed Jan to mid-March), with horses to ride, and a two-star **campsite**, *Camping de Valsaintes*, on the main road (☎04.92.75.91.46; closed Oct–April). The only place to **eat** is *Chez Mimile/Le Restaurant St-Hubert* in the quartier des Gîtes in the *faubourg* (closed Wed & Sun eve).

Banon

Like Simaine, the houses of the Haute Ville of **BANON** form a guarding wall. Within the fortified gate, the protective huddling of the buildings is even closer, forcing one street to tunnel underneath the others.

Banon is famous for its **cheese**. The *plateau des fromages* of any half-decent Provence restaurant will include a round goats' cheese marinaded in brandy and wrapped in sweet chestnut leaves, but there's nothing like tasting different ages of the untravelled cheese, sliced off for you by the *fromager* at a market stall on place de la République. As well as ensuring that you taste the very young and the well-matured varieties, they may give you an accompaniment in the form of a sprig of savory, an aromatic local plant of the mint family. The *boulangerie* on the square sells the local variety of *fougasse* bread, stuffed with Banon cheese.

The only accommodation option here is the **campsite**, *L'Épi Bleu* (☎04.92.73.30.30) with a pool and **bikes** for rental. For a pleasant and reasonably priced meal try the **hotel-bar-restaurant** *Les Voyageurs* on the main square (☎04.92.73.21.02; ②); alternatively there's *La Braserade* pizzeria and *crêperie* (weekends only), also on the main square.

The Montagne de Lure

Roads north of Banon peter out at the lower slopes of the **Montagne de Lure**. To reach the summit of the Lure, by road or the GR6, you have to head east to St-Étienne-les-Orgues, 12km north of Forcalquier. The footpath avoids the snaking road for most of the way, but you're walking through relentless pine plantation and it's a long way without a

change of scenery (about 15km). Just below the summit you'll see **ski-lifts** and the
hotel-restaurant *Montagne de Lure* (☎04.92.73.00.05; ②; menus from 75F).

When the trees stop you find yourself on sharp and rubbly stones without a single soft-
ening blade of grass. The summit itself is a mass of telecommunications aerials and
dishes; a grimmer high-perched desert would be hard to find. That said, the point of the
climb is that the Lure has no close neighbours, giving you 360 degrees of mountainscape,
as if you were airborne. The view of the distant snowy peaks to the north is the best; those
with excessive stamina can keep walking towards them along the GR6 to Sisteron.

Up the River Durance

The Marseille–Grenoble *autoroute* now speeds along the River Durance, bypassing the
industrial town of **St-Auban** and its older neighbour **Château-Arnoux**, renowned for
its superb restaurant, *La Bonne Étape*. The views from the fashionable little village of
Lurs and the ancient **Prieuré de Ganagobie** have not been affected, nor has their isolation. La Brillane is the nearest gare SNCF to Lurs; Ganagobie is between La Brillane
and Peyruis with no public transport links.

Lurs

Situated on a narrow ridge above the west bank of the Durance, **LURS** is another *village de caractère*, but much more keen on its picturesque status than Simaine-
la-Rotonde. Immaculately restored houses stand amid immaculately maintained ruins;
commerce extends no further than two restaurants, a printer's, grocery shop, and a
café, all around the visitors' car park on place de la Fontaine. Once you surface at the
top of the village, however, you have to admit it's worth the fuss. Across the wide, multi-
branching river you have the abrupt step up to the Plateau de Valensole, with the snowy
peaks beyond. To the south the land drops before rising again in another high ridge
along the river. To the west and north the views are as extensive, from the rolling hills
around Forcalquier to the Montagne de Lure.

The best way to appreciate this geography is to follow the paths to the small chapel
of **Notre-Dame-de-Vie** along the narrowing escarpment. The right-hand path goes
through the woods and is less clearly defined than the eastern path, the **Promenade
des Evêques**, which is marked by fifteen small oratories.

In the late 1940s Lurs was deserted save for the passing bandit. With no electricity
or running water except that which poured through gaping roofs, it was well on its way
to joining the other ghost villages of Provence. It was not architects or builders who rescued Lurs, but graphic artists and printers, including the author of the universal
nomenclature for typefaces. Hence the *imprimerie* (printer) on place des Feignants,
and the **Rencontres Internationales de Lurs** that brings in practitioners of the
graphic arts from calligraphers to computer-aided-design consultants for the last week
in August.

For somewhere **to stay**, there's a hotel-restaurant, *Le Séminaire*, near the car park
on place de la Fontaine (☎04.92.79.94.19; ④; menus from 125F), housed in the old
summer residence of the bishops of Sisteron. Alternative eating options include the
nearby *La Bello Visto* **restaurant** (☎04.92.79.95.09; closed Wed) and a small café, also
on place de la Fontaine.

The Prieuré de Ganagobie

About 7km north of Lurs are examples of complex design skills that far predate the
invention of printing. The floor of the church of the twelfth-century **Prieuré de**

Ganagobie (Tues–Sun 3–5pm) is covered with mosaics composed of red, black and white tiles. They show fabulous beasts with tails looping through their bodies, and the four elements represented by an elephant (Earth), a fish (Water), a griffon (Air) and a lion (Fire). Interlocking and repeating patterns show a strong Byzantine influence, and there's a dragon slain by a St George in Crusader armour. The porch of the church is also an unusual sight, its arches carved to a bubbly pattern that's thought to be an imitation of medieval bunting.

If you're not in a hurry, you can pass the time walking through the oaks and broom, pines and lavender eastwards along the allée des Moines to the edge of the Plateau de Ganagobie on which the priory stands, 350m above the Durance, or westwards following the allée de Forcalquier for views to the Montagne de Lure and beyond Forcalquier to the Luberon.

St-Auban and Château-Arnoux

North of the priory, the impending confluence of the Durance and Bléone is announced by the **Pénitents des Mées**, a long line of pointed rocks on the east bank, said to be the remains of cowled monks, literally petrified for desiring the women slaves a local lord brought back from the Crusades. Beyond here, the approach to Château-Arnoux is not very promising. Petrochemical factories cover the right bank of the Durance at **ST-AUBAN**, a suburb of grid-plan barrack houses set up in 1916.

At **CHÂTEAU-ARNOUX** itself the hills once more close in on the Durance, blocking off St-Auban's plain from view. Here, the river takes on a smoother and more majestic prospect as a seven-kilometre-long artificial lake ending at the barrage just south of Château-Arnoux. An imposing Renaissance **castle** (group tours only; ask at the tourist office), which now serves as the *mairie*, dominates the centre of the town. With two round towers at the back, two square ones at the front and a hexagonal tower in the middle, this is a mighty building. The tower staircase is carved from one block of stone, all 84 steps of it. The roofs are covered in tiles of different colours, with gargoyles glaring from below the eaves. If unable to visit the castle, you can still take a wander in its **park**, which has the best and most diverse collection of trees in Haute-Provence: Chinese mulberries, bananas, Judas trees and ebony, as well as native species.

Château-Arnoux practicalities

The **tourist office** is at Ferme Font Robert (Mon–Fri 9am–noon & 2–6pm; ☎04.92.64.02.64), signed off the N85 heading north out of the Vieille Ville.

Hotels here range from the de luxe *La Bonne Étape* (☎04.92.64.00.09; ⑧) to *La Taverne Jarlandine* (☎04.92.64.04.49; ②), an old-fashioned cheapie in the centre of the village. Rooms overlooking the Château-Arnoux lake at the *Hôtel du Lac*, 12 allées des Erables (☎04.92.64.04.32; ③), are very pleasant and not exorbitantly priced.

Château-Arnoux is a **centre of gourmandise**: *La Bonne Étape*, on chemin du Lac (☎04.92.64.00.09, fax 04.92.64.37.36; menus from 200F; à la carte from 300F; closed Mon out of season & Sun eve), is one of the best **restaurants** in Provence. It's expensive – though less so than its handful of coastal rivals – needs booking in advance and has the sort of château decor that recommends (though never requires) smart dress. Pierre Gleize, the co-owner with his son Jany, belongs to the exclusive band of master chefs of France. A dream of a meal is assured, and one that celebrates the produce of the region without any trendy foreign influences. If you do treat yourself, take a look at the collection of *santons* in the restaurant, made by Liliane Guiomar, one of the greatest living practitioners of this Provençal art. It includes the easily recognizable figure of Monsieur Gleize senior dangling a hefty salmon.

The place for a low-cost meal is the excellent *Casa Mia* pizzeria on av Général-de-Gaulle. For **snacks** and ice creams there's the *Tchin-Tchin* bar on the central place

Camille-Reymond, where the clientele is young and the music loud. Or there's *Le Stendhal* in the Centre Culturel des Lauzières on av Jean-Moulin, the main road coming in from the south, where you'll also find a **cinema** and **exhibition space**.

Sisteron and around

The last Provençal stretch of the Route Napoléon (see p.310), runs from Château-Arnoux to **SISTERON**. If you can choose which road you take, follow Napoléon's footsteps via the D4 on the left bank of the Durance. The first sight of Sisteron reveals its strategic significance as the major mountain gateway of Provence. The site, which has been fortified since ancient times, was half-destroyed by the Anglo-American bombardment of 1944, but its **citadel** still stands as a fearsome sentinel over the city and the solitary bridge across the river.

Sisteron gave Napoléon something of a headache. Its mayor and the majority of its population were royalist, and given the fortifications and geography of the town, it was impossible for him to pass undetected. However, luck was still with the Corsican in those days, as the military commander of the *département* was a sympathizer and removed all ammunition from Sisteron's arsenal. Contemporary accounts say Napoléon sat nonchalantly on the bridge, contemplating the citadel above and the tumultous waters below, while his men reassembled and the town's notables, ordered to keep their pistols under wraps, looked on impotently. Eventually Napoléon entered the city, took some refreshment at a tavern and received a tricolour from a courageous peasant woman before rejoining his band and taking leave of Provence.

Sisteron today feels a bit grey and abandoned. The promise of prosperity that builders of new roads always hold out has yet again proved false; fewer people stop here now; shops and restaurants have closed; the old quarter has become even more run down. One advantage – for the visitor, at least – of this downturn in the town's fortunes is the hotel prices, which are some of the cheapest in Provence.

Arrival, information and accommodation

From Sisteron's **gare SNCF** turn right and head along av de la Libération until you reach place de la République. Here you'll find the **gare routière**, post office and **tourist office** (July & Aug Mon–Sat 9am–7pm, Sun 10am–noon & 2–5pm; rest of year Mon–Sat 9am–noon & 2–5pm; ☎04.92.61.12.03 or 04.92.61.36.50), which can provide details of good walks and advise on **bike rental**. If you prefer a **horse** for transport, make enquiries at the Écuries Val de Durance (☎04.92.62.53.09 or 06.12.58.19.05) at Peipin, on the road back to Château-Arnoux.

For pleasant and comfortable **rooms**, try the cheerful *Select'Hôtel* on place de la République (☎04.92.61.12.50; ①) or *Les Andrônes* (☎04.92.61.01.68; ①), on av Jean-Moulin just up from place de la République. *La Citadelle*, overlooking the river at the end of rue Saunerie (☎04.92.61.13.52; ③); the *Tivoli*, 21 place du Tivoli (☎04.92.61.15.16, fax 04.92.61.21.72; ③), and the genteel and old-fashioned three-star *Grand Hôtel du Cours*, allée de Verdon (☎04.92.61.04.51, fax 04.92.61.41.73; ④), are all exceptionally good value too. The four-star **campsite**, *Les Prés-Hauts* (☎04.92.61.19.69; closed Nov–Feb), is over the river and 3km along the D951 to the left. Equipped with a pool, it also organizes horse-rides, walks and a variety of sports including hang-gliding.

The Town

To visit the **citadel** (July & Aug daily 9am–6pm; mid-March to June & Sept to mid-Nov 9am–5pm; 22F) can easily take up half a day. There are no guides, just tape-recordings

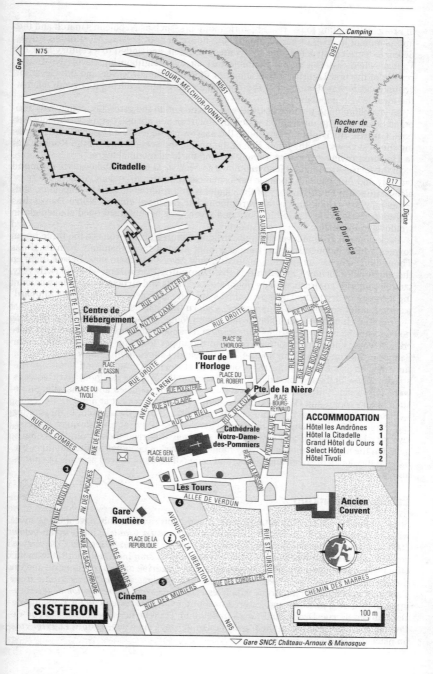

SISTERON

Camping

N75
Gap

N551

Cours Melchior-Donnet

D951

Rocher de la Baume

Citadelle

Rue Saunerie

River Durance

D17
D4
Digne

Montée de la Citadelle

Rue des Poteries

Rue Notre-Dame

Rue Droite

Rue Merchie

Rue de Font-Chaude

Rue Grand-Couven

Rue Chapuze

Rue Poterne

Rue Bourg-Reynaud

Rue Basse-des-Remparts

Centre de Hébergement

Rue de la Coste

Tour de l'Horloge

Place de l'Horloge

Place R. Cassin

Place du Tivoli

Rue Droite

Avenue P. Arène

Rue Pousterie

Place du Dr. Robert

Pte. de la Nière

Place Bourg-Reynaud

Rue des Combes

Rue de Provence

Rue Ste-Claire

Rue de Rieu

Rue Deleuze

Rue Porte Sauve

Rue Saunerie

Cathédrale Notre-Dame-des-Pommiers

Rue de la Mission

Rue Chapuze

Place Gen. de Gaulle

ACCOMMODATION

Hôtel les Andrônes   3
Hôtel la Citadelle   1
Grand Hôtel du Cours   4
Select Hôtel   5
Hôtel Tivoli   2

Les Tours

Allée de Verdun

Ancien Couvent

Gare Routière

Avenue Moulin

Av. des Arcades

Avenue Alsace-Lorraine

Rue des Arcades

Place de la République

Avenue de la Libération

Rue Ste-Ursule

N

Rue des Muriers

Cinéma

Rue des Cordeliers

Chemin des Marres

N85

0   100 m

Gare SNCF, Château-Arnoux & Manosque

in French attempting to re-create historic moments, such as Napoléon's march and the imprisonment in 1639 of Jan Kazimierz, the future king of Poland. Most of the extant defences were constructed after the Wars of Religion, and added to a century later by Vauban when Sisteron was a front-line fort against neighbouring Savoy. No traces remain of the first Ligurian fortification nor of its Roman successor, and the eleventh-century castle was destroyed in the mid-thirteenth century during a pogrom against the local Jewish population.

As you climb up to the fortress, there seems no end to the gateways, courtyards and other defences. The outcrop on which the fortress sits abruptly stops at the lookout post, **Guérite du Diable**, 500m above the narrow passage of the Durance, and affording the best views. On the other side of the ravine, the vertical folds of the **Rocher de la Baume** provide a favourite training ground for local mountaineers.

In the fortress grounds, a **festival** known as *Nuits de la Citadelle* takes place throughout July and August, with open-air performances of music, drama and dance. There is also a **museum** on the history of the citadel with a room dedicated to Napoléon, and temporary art exhibitions in the vertiginous late medieval chapel, **Notre-Dame-du-Château**, restored to its Gothic glory and given very beautiful subdued stained-glass windows in the 1970s.

Back down at ground level the most striking features of Sisteron are the three huge **towers** which belonged to the ramparts built around the expanding town in 1370. Though one still has its spiralling staircase, only ravens use them now. Beside them is the much older former **Cathédrale Notre-Dame-des-Pommiers**, whose strictly rectangular interior contrasts with its riot of stepped roofs and an octagonal gallery adjoining a square belfry topped by a pyramidal spire. The altarpiece incorporates a Mignard painting; other seventeenth-century works adorn the chapels.

From the church you can follow a signposted route through the lower town. The tall houses enclose narrow passages with steps and ramps that interconnect through vaulted archways, known here as **andrônes**. In the upper town, on the other side of rue Saunerie and rue Droite, the houses, like the citadel above them, follow the curves of the rock. In some places the third or fourth storeys become ground floors on the streets above. In the troubled days of 1568 (during the Wars of Religion) sixty lanterns were put in place to light the alleyways and deter conspiracies and plots; there's no such luxury today, and Old Sisteron can take on a sinister aspect at night.

Place de l'Horloge, at the other end of rue Deleuze from the church, is the site for the Wednesday and Saturday **market**, where stalls of sweet and savoury *fougasse*, lavender honey, nougat and almond-paste *calissons* that rival those from Aix congregate. On the second Saturday of every month the market becomes a **fair**, and there are likely to be flocks of sheep and lambs, and cages of pigeons as well as stalls of clothes and bric-à-brac.

Eating and drinking

Sisteron has no outstanding **restaurants**, though you can certainly have a filling meal without paying over the odds. Of the hotel-restaurants *La Citadelle* has a menu below 100F and a terrace above the river where you can eat; the *Grand Hôtel du Cour* serves copious meals with the renowned *gigot d'agneau de Sisteron* included on a 120F menu. Otherwise you'll find **crêperies**, **brasseries** and **pizzerias** along rue Saunerie and on the squares around the clock tower. The best nougat and *calissons* come from Canteperdrix on place Paul-Arène which also runs *Le Grand Salon*, a *salon de thé* serving salads as well as cakes and ice creams. For anchovy *fougasse* head for Boulangerie Bernaudon, 37 rue Droite, and for *charcuterie* to Traiteur des Gourmets, 136 rue de Provence. *Le Mondial* **bar** at the top of rue Droite stays open late, as does *Le Primerose* on place de l'Horloge.

Vilhosc and Vaumeilh

If you're staying in Sisteron for several days there are some worthwhile expeditions into the wilds. To the east along the D17 you come to **VILHOSC** whose priory has an eleventh-century crypt hidden in its walls; a few kilometres further on is the graceful fourteenth-century **Pont de la Reine Jeanne**, which crosses the River Vançon. The roads end here, but the long-distance walkers' route, the GR6, leads onwards and upwards, past villages that are almost all abandoned and in ruins.

Ten kilometres to the north of Sisteron, through Valernes off the D951 is the village of **VAUMEILH**, where the Aérodrome de Vaumeilh (☎04.92.62.17.45) can arrange for you to go flying, either in a **glider** or **microlight**. You could also **stay** at *Le Plan* (☎04.92.62.17.45; ①), the aerodrome's hotel, which also offers camping facilities.

travel details

Trains

Draguignan to: Les Arcs (frequent; 5min).

Manosque to: Aix (5 daily; 40min); Château-Arnoux (5 daily; 25min); La Brillane (4 daily; 10min); Marseille (5 daily; 1hr 15min); Sisteron (5 daily; 40min).

Buses

Aups to: Aiguines (1 daily; 1hr 10min); Brignoles (2 daily; 1hr 20min); Cotignac (2 daily; 20min); Draguignan (1–2 daily; 1hr–1hr 20min); Salernes (1 weekly; 10min); Sillans (1–2 daily; 10min); Tourtour (1–2 daily; 20min).

Banon to: Aix (1 daily; 2hr 10min); Marseille (1 daily; 2hr 40min); Simiane (1 daily; 10min).

Draguignan to: Aix (2 daily; 2hr 30min); Aups (1 daily; 1hr–1hr 20min); Bargemon (3 daily; 45min); Barjols (1 daily; 1hr 40min); Brignoles (2 daily; 1hr); Callas (3 daily; 40min); Entrecasteaux (2 weekly; 40min); Fayence (3 daily: 1hr 40min); Grasse (2 daily; 2hr); Les Arcs (frequent; 20min); Lorgues (4 daily; 15min); Nice (3 weekly; 1hr 30min); St-Raphaël (10 daily; 1hr 15min–1hr 30min); Salernes (3 daily; 1 hr); Seillans (3 daily;

1hr 20min); Toulon (4 daily; 2hr 10min); Tourtour (1 daily; 1hr); Villecroze (1 daily; 1hr).

Fayence to: Draguignan (3 daily; 1hr 30min); Grasse (3 daily; 1hr); St Raphaël (2 daily; 1hr 20min); Seillans (3 daily; 10min).

Forcalquier to: Apt (2 daily; 1hr); Avignon (2 daily; 2hr 10min); Château-Arnoux (2 daily; 45min); Digne (2 daily; 1hr 10min); La Brillane (2 daily; 10min); Lurs (2 daily; 15min); Mane (2 daily; 5min); Peyruis (2 daily; 30min); St-Auban (2 daily; 40min); St Michel l'Observatoire (2 daily; 10min).

Manosque to: Aix (10 daily; 40min–1hr); Château-Arnoux (3 daily; 45min); Digne (4 daily; 45min–1hr); Marseille (10 daily; 1hr–1hr 30min); Riez (1 daily; 1hr 15min); St-Auban (3 daily; 40min); Sisteron (4 daily; 1hr).

Riez to: Barjols (1 daily; 45min); Digne (1 daily; 1hr 15min); Manosque (1 daily; 1hr 15min); Moustiers-Ste-Marie (1 daily; 30min).

Sisteron to: Aix (5 daily; 1hr 10min–2hr); Château-Arnoux (9 daily; 15–30min); Château-Arnoux – St Auban gare SNCF (2 daily; 10min); Digne (1 daily; 45min); Lurs (3 daily; 40min); Manosque (4 daily; 1hr); Marseille (4 daily; 1hr 30min–1hr 45min); Nice (1 daily; 3hr 45min); Peipin (2 daily; 15min).

CHAPTER SIX

THE RIVIERA: CANNES TO MENTON

The seventy-kilometre stretch of the coast between Cannes and the Italian border known as the **Riviera** was once an inhospitable shore with few natural harbours, its tiny local communities preferring to cluster around feudal castles high above the sea. It is now an almost uninterrupted promenade, lined by palms and mega-buck hotels, with speeding sports cars on the corniche roads and yachts like minor ocean liners moored at each resort. The sea is speckled with boats, boards, bikes and skis; the beaches – many of them shingle or made from imported sand – with a gaudy pattern of parasols and beds. The occasional breaks in the garish, grotesque and inter-mittently gorgeous facades overlooking the Mediterranean are filled by formal parks or gardens, and, where vertical contours limit construction, roads and rail lines have been cut on the water's edge.

The Riviera's largest city, **Nice**, became fashionable as a winter resort in the eigh-teenth century. The fishing village of **Cannes** was discovered in the 1830s by a retired British chancellor who couldn't get to Nice because of a cholera epidemic. Up until World War I, aristocrats and royals from all ends of Europe came here to build their Riviera mansions, and artists like **Renoir** sought warm retreats here while the local population continued to farm and fish. The inter-war years saw the advent of more artists – **Picasso, Matisse, Dufy, Bonnard, Miró** – and the beginnings of a switch from winter to summer as the favoured season.

By the 1950s **mass summer tourism** started to take off and the real transformation began. It became far more profitable to service the new influx of visitors than to make a living from the land or sea. Property speculation and despoiling the environment went hand in hand – only in the 1970s were any serious controls implemented, by which time no wild Riviera coast was left.

Attractions, however, still remain, most notably in the legacies of the **artists** who stayed here: Picasso in **Antibes** and **Vallauris**; Léger in **Biot**; Matisse in **Nice** and **Vence**; Renoir in **Cagnes-sur-Mer**; Cocteau in **Villefranche** and **Menton**; Chagall in

ACCOMMODATION PRICE CATEGORIES

Throughout this guide, all hotels and guesthouses have been priced on a scale of ①–⑧, indicating the lowest price you could expect to pay for a double room in high season. What you get for your money varies enormously between establishments, but in the lower-priced hotels you should expect to pay considerably more for en-suite facilities. If you are staying anywhere for more than three days it's often possible to negotiate a lower price, particularly out of season.

① Under 160F	③ 220–300F	⑤ 400–500F	⑦ 600–700F
② 160–220F	④ 300–400F	⑥ 500–600F	⑧ Over 700F

Nice; and all of them in **St-Paul-de-Vence** and **Haut-de-Cagnes**. The relatively unspoilt villages in the Nice hinterland, too, guard superb artworks from the medieval School of Nice in their churches and chapels. There are the thrills of the **corniches** running across the mountains between Nice and Menton; the good times to be had in Vieux Nice; and the vicarious pleasures of **Cannes** and the independent principality of **Monaco**. This region also has some of the world's best **restaurants**, catering for some of the world's most loaded clientele.

Speedy and inexpensive **train connections** make it easy to visit all the coastal towns and villages without committing yourself to staying overnight.

Cannes and around

Movies and their stars are what normally bring the name of **CANNES** to people's lips: this year's winner of the Palme d'Or award; the latest producers' takeover; the youngest, richest director; or the most photographed star. Cannes might be more than its film festival, but it's still a grotesquely over-hyped urban blight on this once exquisite coast, a contrast sublimely reinforced by the **Îles de Lérins**, a short boat-ride offshore.

The film industry, and all manner of business junketing, represent Cannes' main source of income in an ever-multiplying calendar of festivals, conferences, tournaments and trade shows. The main venue for all the big events is the **Palais des Festivals**, an orange concrete mega-bunker on the prime seaside spot between the Vieux Port and La Croisette, the seafront promenade and the main focus of Cannes life.

Arrival, information and city transport

The central **gare SNCF** is on rue Jean-Jaurès. There are two **gare routières**: the one right next to the train station serves inland towns such as Grasse; and the one on place B-Cornut Gentille overlooking the Vieux Port is for destinations along the coast. The central axis of Cannes is **rue d'Antibes**, halfway between rue Jean-Jaurès and La Croisette, becoming rue Félix-Faure behind the Vieux Port. With just five blocks between rue Jean-Jaurès and the seafront, central Cannes is not particularly big, though it manages to look daunting. **Le Suquet**, the hill overlooking the modern town from the west, is the heart of Old Cannes. **Urban buses** run from outside the *mairie*; you can buy individual **tickets** for 7.50F, a *carnet* of ten for 49F and a weekly pass, the *Carte Palm'Hebdo*, for 54F. A useful service is the **minibus shuttle** or the #8 bus along the seafront from place Frédéric-Mistral, west of Le Suquet, to Palm Beach Casino on Pointe Croisette, at the other end of the bay. If you prefer to cycle, **bikes** can be rented from Cannes Locations, 5 rue Allieis (☎04.93.39.46.15); FRL, 14 rue Clemenceau (☎04.93.39.33.60); or Holiday Bikes, 16 rue du 14 Juillet (☎04.97.06.30.30).

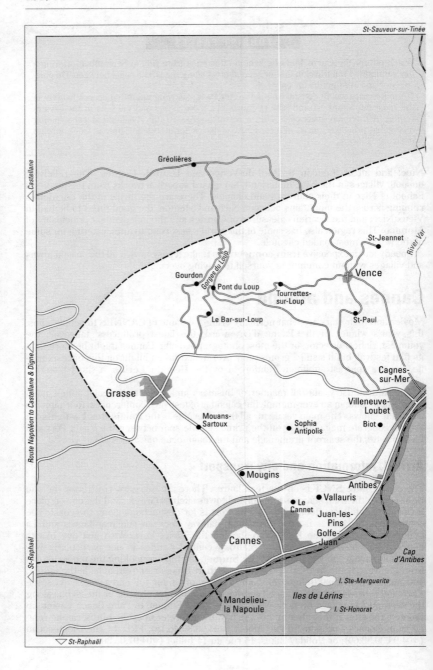

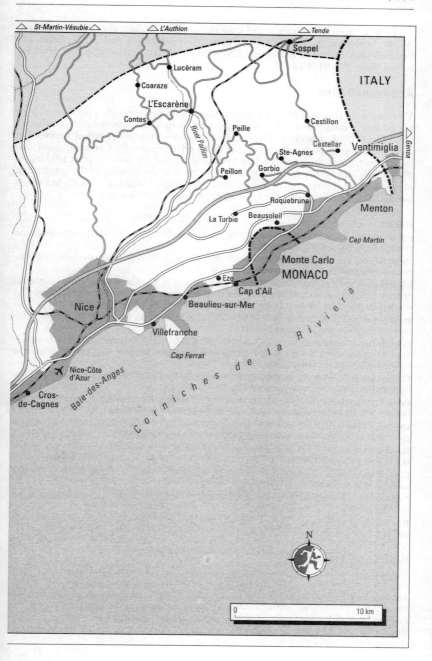

There are **tourist offices** at the train station (July & Aug Mon–Fri 9am–1pm & 3–7pm; Sept–June 9am–12.30pm & 2–6pm; ☎04.93.99.19.77) and in the Palais des Festivals (July & Aug daily 9am–8pm; Sept Mon–Sat 9am–7pm; rest of year Mon–Sat 9am–6.30pm; ☎04.93.39.24.53).

Accommodation

There's a wide choice of **hotels** in central Cannes, and you shouldn't have much trouble finding somewhere to stay, whatever your budget; for the cheaper options it's important to book in advance. The tourist offices have a free **reservation service** but can't guarantee rooms for late arrivals or at the price you specify. **Camping** opportunities are not good: the sites are well over capacity and far from central; pitching in Mandelieu, 7km west, is likely to be easier and cheaper. As sleeping on the beach is out of the question, it is not a good idea for anyone on a tight budget to get stuck in Cannes late at night, especially after public transport services have stopped.

Hotels

Alnea, 20 rue Jean-de-Riouffe (☎04.93.39.39.90, fax 04.92.98.07.05). Moderately priced, but with service and style that puts it in a class above. ⑤.

Beau Séjour, 5 rue des Fauvettes (☎04.93.39.63.00, fax 04.92.98.64.66). Just to the northwest of Le Suquet, with good facilities and a quiet location. ⑤.

Bleu Rivage, 61 La Croisette (☎04.93.94.24.25, fax 04.93.43.74.92). A seafront hotel in a nineteenth-century building with its own stretch of beach, neighbouring all the de luxe establishments but much more affordable. ⑤.

Bourgogne, 11 rue du 24 Août (☎04.93.38.36.73, fax 04.92.99.28.41). No-frills place, but one of the cheapest and very central. Closed Dec. ④.

Carlton Intercontinental, 58 La Croisette (☎04.93.06.40.06, fax 04.93.06.40.25). This is the palace-hotel where you stay if you're a Hollywood big-timer or if you've just won the lottery. Rooms at the back in low season start from 1220F. ⑧.

Chanteclair, 12 rue Forville (☎ & fax 04.93.39.68.88). By the Vieille Ville and a cut above the other budget places, with quiet rooms and no TVs. ③.

Cristal, 13 rond-point Duboys-d'Angers (☎04.93.39.45.45, fax 04.93.38.64.66). Just off La Croisette but with palatial decor. Panoramic restaurant, bar and pool on the sixth floor. ⑧.

Cybelle, 14 rue du 24 Août (☎04.93.38.31.33, fax 04.93.38.43.47). Small place, just ten rooms in all; good-value for the price, and well known for its excellent restaurant. ②.

Hôtel le Florian, 8 rue du Commandant-André (☎04.93.39.24.82, fax 04.92.99.18.30). Friendly owners, central and reasonable. ④.

Little Palace, 18 rue du 24 Août (☎04.92.98.18.18, fax 04.93.68.65.73). Central location and well soundproofed rooms. ④.

National, 8 rue Maréchal-Joffre (☎04.93.39.91.92, fax 04.92.98.44.06). Clean, adequate, a bit depressing but close to the station. ③.

Ruc Hôtel, 15 bd de Strasbourg (☎04.92.98.33.60, fax 04.92.39.54.18). Away from the central hub-bub to the northeast of town. Pool, tennis court and elegant old furnishings. ⑤.

Hostels and campsites

HI youth hostel, 35 av de Vallauris (☎ & fax 04.93.99.26.79). Ten minutes' walk from the train station; airy rooms for four to six people, with its own garden and good kitchen facilities. Curfew 1am.

Auberge Le Chalit, 27 av Galliéni (☎ & fax 04.93.99.22.11). Five minutes' walk from the train station; at 90F, more expensive than the youth hostel, and it's far more cramped, but there's no curfew.

Camping Bellevue, 67 av Maurice-Chevalier (☎04.93.47.28.97, fax 04.93.48.66.25). Three-star site 3km northwest of the centre in the suburb of Ranguin; bus #10 from La Bocca (direction Cimetière Annexe Abadie, stop Le Plateau). Closed Oct–March.

Le Grand Saule, 24 bd Jean-Moulin (☎04.93.90.55.10, fax 04.93.47.24.55). Three-star site 2km out of town, off the D9 towards Pégomas; bus #9 from the gare SNCF (direction Lamartine, stop Le Grande Saule). Closed mid-Oct to March.

Le Ranch Camping, chemin St-Joseph l'Aubarède (☎04.93.46.00.11, fax 04.93.46.44.30). Three-star site 2km out and very close to the highway; bus #1 from the *mairie* (direction Les Pins Parasols, stop Le Ranch). Closed Nov–March.

The Town

Though the centre of Cannes is neatly defined by the loop of the rail line tunnelled beneath the expressway and the sea, the town's urban sprawl stretches west to **Mandelieu-La-Napoule**, north to **Mougins** and **Mouans-Sartoux** more or less to **Grasse**, and east to **Vallauris** and **Juan-les-Pins**. It incorporates the erstwhile village of **Le Cannet** on the heights just below the highway, a good place to escape to if you find yourself staying longer than a day. If you're just popping into Cannes for a quick look, the seafront **La Croisette** is the bit to experience. An afternoon's visit could take in **Le Suquet**, the old town to the west of the Vieux Port. The **Îles de Lérins** should definitely be seen if you can spare the time.

The seafront

You'll find free **beaches** to the west of Le Suquet, along the Plages du Midi and at both extremities of Les Plages de la Croisette. Cannes' most famous boulevard, **La Croisette**, sweeps along the seafront; in high season, the fine sand **beach** below it, cleaned and raked overnight, looks like an industrial production line for parasols with neat rows extending the length of the shore, changing colour with each change of concession. It is possible to find your way down to the main sections of the beach without paying, but not easy. The stretch of beach owned by the de luxe palace-hotels on La Croisette, the *Majestic*, the *Martinez*, the *Carlton Intercontinental* and the *Noga Hilton*,

---

THE FILM FESTIVAL

Each May sees the **Festival International du Film** at Cannes. This most famous of all movie media events was first conceived when the major festival was based at Venice and under Mussolini's influence. Since only pro-fascist films had any chance of winning prizes, an alternative competition was planned for 1939 in Cannes. World War II dictated otherwise and it was not until 1946 that the first Cannes festival took place.

Winning the top prize, the **Palm d'Or**, can't compete with Oscars for box-office effect, but within the movie world you can't do better. Some years it seems as if the big names are all too busy talking finance in LA to come to Cannes; the next they are all begging for the accolades. Even if the Hollywood moguls keep their new blockbusters under wraps, they still send minions to wheel and deal.

There are over thirty thousand film professionals, journalists and hangers-on who get accreditation for the festival. Though most tickets are pre-allocated for the media, ten percent of the **tickets** to the official selections are reserved for local people – they elect the *Prix Populaire*. The **Palais des Festivals** sells tickets for some screenings one week in advance, and hands out a select number of **passes** to those considered to be true cineastes (a student card for an internationally recognized film school is helpful), plus free **programmes** to anyone who asks for them.

Cultivating contacts reaches fever pitch as the festival progresses and casual visitors are left well excluded. However, not all the new films being shown are official entries to the festival, nor are all screened within the heavily guarded Palais des Festivals. Every cinema and conference hall in town is a venue and at some of these you can buy tickets, but don't expect to do so on the day.

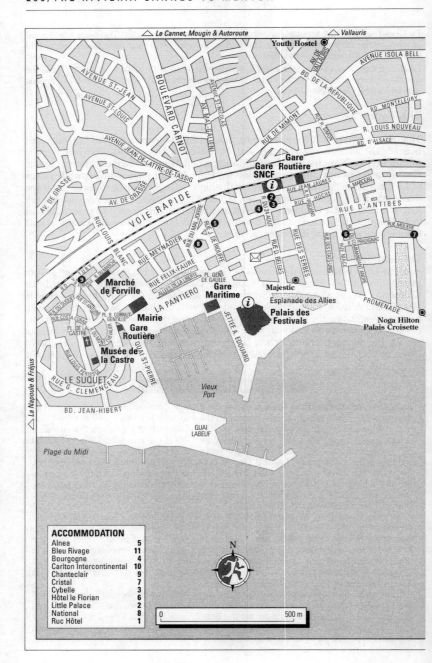

△ *Le Cannet, Mougin & Autoroute* △ *Vallauris*

Youth Hostel

AV. DE VALLAURIS
BD. DE LA RÉPUBLIQUE
AVENUE ISOLA BELL
AVENUE ST-JEAN
AVENUE ST-LOUIS
BOULEVARD CARNOT
AVENUE ST-NICOLAS
AV. MALGUEN
RUE DE MIMONT
RUE H. SIMON
BD. MONTFLEURY
R. LOUIS NOUVEAU
BD. D'ALSACE
AVENUE JEAN-DE-LATTRE-DE-TASSIG
AV. DE GRASSE
AV. DE GRASSE
Gare Routière
Gare SNCF
VOIE RAPIDE
RUE JEAN JAURÈS
RUE HOCHE
RUE D'ANTIBES
R. MARCEAU
RUE MOLIÈRE
RUE LOUIS BLANC
RUE DU MALJOFFRE
RUE DE ROUFFE
R. DU 24 AOÛT
RUE EMILE NEGRIN
RUE DES SERBES
RUE DES ETATS-UNIS
RUE COMMANDANT ANDRE
RUE DU COMMANDANT PRADIGNAC
RUE MACE
RUE MEYNADIER
RUE FELIX-FAURE
ALLÉES DE LA LIBERTÉ
Marché de Forville
PL. GEN. DE GAULLE
Gare Maritime
Majestic
Esplanade des Allies
PROMENADE
Palais des Festivals
Noga Hilton Palais Croisette
BD. VICTOR HUGO
BD. FRANCE DU MARCHÉ
RUE STANISLAS
RUE DU SUQUET
RUE COSTA CORSA
PL. B. CORNUT GENTILLE
Mairie
Gare Routière
LA PANTIERO
PL. DE LA CASTRE
Musée de la Castre
RUE LOUIS PERISSOL
RUE ST-PIERRE
QUAI ST-PIERRE
LE SUQUET
RUE G. CLEMENCEAU
QUAI LABEUF
BD. JEAN-HIBERT
JETTÉE A. EDOUARD
Vieux Port
Plage du Midi

△ *La Napoule & Fréjus*

ACCOMMODATION

Alnea	5
Bleu Rivage	11
Bourgogne	4
Carlton Intercontinental	10
Chanteclair	9
Cristal	7
Cybelle	3
Hôtel le Florian	6
Little Palace	2
National	8
Ruc Hôtel	1

N

0   500 m

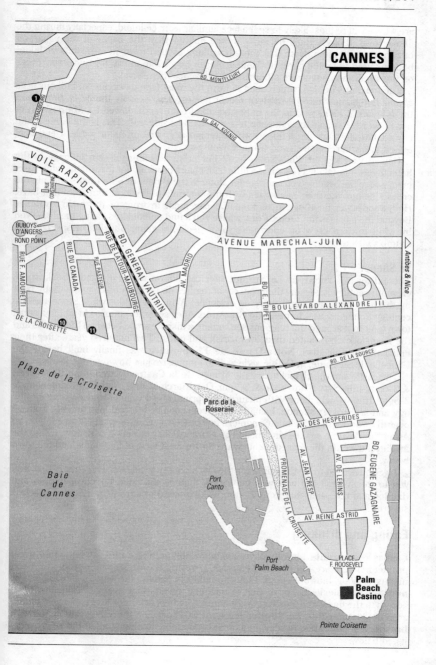

CANNES

are where you're most likely to spot a face familiar from celluloid, especially during the film festival, though you'll be lucky to see further than the backs of the paparazzi buzzing around them. Note that though walking around town in swimsuits or bikini bottoms used to be the norm in Cannes, there's now a fine of 75F for "indecent" dress on the streets and anywhere other than the beaches themselves.

The buildings behind, which used to form the most famous skyline of bulbous *belle époque* hotels, now include modern monstrosities, most notably the *Noga Hilton* and the *Hôtel de la Reine* next to the rather beautiful but overshadowed **La Malmaison** at no. 47, which has an excellent palm tree mural on its side wall. This is the home of the city's cultural affairs department, where temporary exhibitions of modern and contemporary art are often staged (Mon & Wed–Sun; 10F).

Having watched the Rolls-Royces and Ferraris unloading pig-skin luggage in the hotel foyers – or taken a rest on the little blue chairs provided for free on the wide pavement above the beach – you can wander along to the **Palais des Festivals** and join the crowds comparing their hand-sizes with the imprints of those of film stars that have, Hollywood-style, been set in tiles on the pavement in front of the main entrance. Beyond the palais is the **Vieux Port**, where you'll find millionaires eating meals served by white-frocked crew on enormous yacht decks, feigning oblivion of spectators a crumb's flick away.

Le Suquet

The old town is known as **Le Suquet** after the hill on which it stands. Back in the eleventh century it became the property of the Îles de Lérins monks, and a castle built by the *abbé* in 1088, is still there as evidence. Alongside is the white stone twelfth-century Romanesque **Chapelle de Ste-Anne**. After several centuries in which a small town took root around the religious settlement, a dispute arose between the monks and the townsfolk who wanted their own parish and priest. Two hundred years after their initial demand in 1648, **Notre-Dame de l'Espérance** was finally built beside the Chapelle de Ste-Anne, in Gothic style as if to emphasize just how overdue it was.

The castle and the chapel house the **Musée de la Castre** (March–June 10am–noon & 2–6pm; July–Sept 10am–noon & 3–7pm; Oct–March Mon & Wed–Sun 10am–noon & 2–5pm; 10F), which, along with pictures and prints of old Cannes and a strong ethnology and archeology section, has a brilliant collection of musical instruments from all over the world. These include Congolese bell bracelets, an Ethiopian ten-string lyre, an Asian "lute" with a snake-skin box and an extraordinary selection of drums. Climb the medieval tower in the museum courtyard for the best view of Le Suquet and the town below.

Le Suquet used to be the home for the city's poorer residents. The streets that lead you to the summit are now well gentrified, though still good for cheaper **eats** and **drinks**, and the panorama from the top looking eastwards over the 12km of beach is superb.

Eating and drinking

Cannes **restaurants** tend to stay open very late; getting a meal at 4am is no great problem. There are hundreds of eateries, covering the whole range from 75F fixed menus to 500F blowouts, and, though quality is patchy, the vigour of the Forville **market**, two blocks north of the Vieux Port, means that every chef in town has access to the finest and freshest ingredients. The best areas for less expensive dining are **rue Meynardier**, **Le Suquet** and **quai St-Pierre** on the Vieux Port, lined with **brasseries** and **cafés**. Reserving a table is advisable at almost all of the restaurants listed below.

Playing boules

St Tropez

Villefranche-sur-Mer

In the Vieille Ville, Nice

The seafront, Cannes

Santons

The promenade des Anglais, Nice

Vieux Port, Marseilles

Lavender fields, near Valensole

Grand Canyon du Verdon

Parc National du Mercantour

Port de Monaco

Èze

Restaurants

Au Bec Fin, *Hôtel Cybele*, 12 rue du 24 Août (☎04.93.38.35.86). Traditional cooking with an excellent choice of plats du jour and generous portions. Menus around 100F. Closed Sat & Sun evening.

Le Bouchon d'Objectif, 10 rue de Constantine (☎04.93.99.21.76). An excellent local bistro serving monkfish terrine, duck à l'orange and other staple dishes with admirable simplicity. Menus from 88F and very generous helpings on the 135F menu. Closed Sun & mid-Nov to mid-Dec.

La Brouette de Chez Grand-Mère, 9 rue d'Oran (☎04.93.39.12.10). A single menu (around 200F) that includes an aperitif and as much wine as you can drink, with filling dishes such as a five-meat stew, quails in grapes, or Bresse chicken steamed in tarragon for the main course. Fun and good value. Closed midday, Sun & Nov to mid-Dec.

La Croisette, 15 rue du Commandant-André (☎04.92.48.62.82). Grilled fish is the speciality here, cooked to perfection. If the supplements on some of the fish dishes astound you, take a look at the Forville market to see just how few fish are caught; around 160F. Closed Sun out of season.

La Grande Brasserie, 81 rue d'Antibes (☎04.93.39.06.26). A good standby for meals and snacks, including gorgeous puddings in classic Art Nouveau brasserie surroundings. Menus from around 100F, with a supplement for eating on the terrace. Closed Sun.

Le Lion d'Or, 45 bd de la République (☎04.93.38.56.57). On the north side of the rail tracks with no pretensions to gourmandise but edible and filling home-made food all the same. Menus from 70F. Closed Sat.

Lou Souléou, 16 bd Jean-Hibert (☎04.93.39.85.55). A fish specialist serving a good range of seafood on very reasonably priced menus in view of the sea west of Le Suquet. Menus from 115F. Closed Mon lunchtime & Nov.

La Mère-Besson, 13 rue des Frères-Pradignac (☎04.93.39.59.24). Each day has a different speciality: *estouffade*, *aïoli* and *lottes niçoises* (tiny fried monkfish) among them. Menus from 90F. Closed Mon & Sat midday, plus all Sun.

Montagard, 6 rue Mal-Joffre (☎04.93.39.98.38). Excellent vegetarian and fish restaurant with menus from 85F. Closed Sun & Mon lunchtime.

La Palme d'Or, *Hôtel Martinez*, 73 La Croisette (☎04.92.98.74.14). Cannes' temple of taste, where you'd celebrate a film festival prize with some of the most exquisite and original food this coast has to offer. Weekday midday menu around 300F, à la carte over 500F; wine included. Closed Mon, Tues & mid-Nov to mid-Dec.

La Pizza, 3 quai St-Pierre (☎04.93.39.22.56). The major pizzeria of the Vieux Port. Menus from 120F, but slices of pizza also available – the seafood one is excellent. Open till 3am in summer.

Nightlife

As you'd expect, Cannes abounds with exclusive **clubs**. The clientele that step off their yachts or out of a festival prize-giving disappear behind closed doors: the more private and unmarked a club is, the more it's raking in. The late-night restaurants can be the most congenial after-dark venues, but there are **bars** and **clubs** where you can get through the evening and still have change from 300F. If you are determined to lose money in Cannes, choose from **casinos** at the Palais des Festivals, and the *Carlton Intercontinental* and the *Noga Hilton* hotels.

Blue Bar, 42 La Croisette. Recently reopened; expensive and fashionable place to be seen in.

La Brasserie des Artistes, 48 bd de la République. Disco for young vanities.

Le Blitz, 22 rue Macé. Disco and live pub music with very reasonable rates. Closed Mon & Tues out of season.

Le Whisky à Go-go, 115 av des Lérins. The disco where everyone beneath the jet set goes to be seen.

Roxburg Salon, 36 bd de Lorraine. Expensive late-night bar for the designer crowd.

Le Zanzi-Bar, 85 rue Félix-Faure. An old favourite with Cannois gays; drinks are cheaper before 10pm but the ambience gets better later. Open 6pm–6am.

Listings

Airlines Air France, 2 pl du Général-de-Gaulle (☎04.93.39.39.14 or 08.02.80.28.02).

Airport Cannes-Mandelieu (☎04.93.90.40.40).

Banks Most banks on rue d'Antibes have cash dispensers.

Boat terminal Gare maritime, jetée Albert-Edouard (☎04.93.39.11.82).

Bookshop Librairie Anglaise, 11 rue Bivouac-Napoléon (☎04.93.99.40.08), sells new and some second-hand English-language books.

Bus terminals For Grasse, Mougins and Vallauris you need the station by the gare SNCF; for Juan-les-Pins, Antibes, Nice, La Napoule and St-Raphaël, buses leave from the hôtel de ville.

Car rental Avis, 68 La Croisette (☎04.93.94.15.86) and at the gare (☎04.93.38.38.93); Budget, 160 rue d'Antibes (☎04.93.99.44.04); City Loc, 50 bd Croisette (04.93.38.17.17); Europcar, 3 rue du Commandant-Vidal (☎04.93.39.75.20 or 08.01.01.00.00).

Currency exchange Office Provençal, 17 av Maréchal-Foch.

Emergencies ☎18 or ☎15; SOS médecins (☎04.93.38.39.38); Hôpital des Broussailles, 13 av des Broussailles (☎04.93.69.70.00).

Parking Cheap overnight parking between 8pm and 8am beneath the Palais des Festivals and gare SNCF.

Pharmacy Call ☎04.93.68.33.33 for the address of a 24hr pharmacy.

Police Commissariat Central de Police, 15 av de Grasse (☎04.93.39.10.78).

Post office 22 rue Bivouac-Napoléon, Cannes 06400.

Taxis At the gare SNCF (☎04.93.38.30.79), on La Croisette (☎04.93.38.09.76, 04.93.99.52.10 or 04.93.94.13.39), at Pointe Croisette (☎04.93.43.41.44), and at the hôtel de ville (☎04.93.39.60.80).

Îles de Lérins

The **Îles de Lérins** would be lovely anywhere, but at only a fifteen-minute ferry-ride from Cannes, they're a haven away from the madness of the modern city. Known as Lerina or Lero in ancient times, the two islands have a long historical pedigree, and today appear to have little to do with the modern world.

Getting to the islands

Boats leave from the Vieux Port (summer 9 daily; winter 5 daily), with the last boats back leaving St-Honorat at 4.45 or 5.45pm, and Ste-Marguerite at 5 or 6pm, depending on the season. Trans Côte d'Azur, quai Laubeuf (☎04.92.98.71.30), has services to both islands, stopping first at Ste-Marguerite, with less regular connections on from there to St-Honorat (circuit of two islands 60F; Ste-Marguerite only, 40F; St-Honorat only, 45F). You can also reach the islands from **La Napoule** (☎04.92.97.77.77) and **Golfe-Juan** (quai St-Pierre ☎04.93.63.45.94), between Cannes and Juan-les-Pins.

Taking a **picnic** is a good idea: as the handful of restaurants and snack outlets on the islands have a captive market they tend to be over-expensive.

Ste-Marguerite

Of the two islands, **STE-MARGUERITE** is by far the most touristy and has a completely different set-up to its more peaceful, less commercial neighbour. It still has beautiful parts, though, and is large enough for vistors to find seclusion if they're prepared to get away from the crowded restaurants and snack-bars of the port by following some of the paths through woods of Aleppo pines and evergreen oaks that are so thick they cast a sepulchral gloom. The **Chemin de la Chasse** from the harbour crosses to the southern shore where an arc of rocky inlets provides good bathing points. The **Chemin de la Ceinture** follows the island's edge for about 3km till it reaches the battery on the eastern headland. Returning via the northern shore provides you with views back to Cannes.

The dominating structure and crowd-puller of the island is the **Fort Ste-Marguerite** (April–June Mon & Wed–Sun 10.30am–noon & 2pm–5.30pm; July–Sept Mon & Wed–Sun 10.30am–noon & 2pm–6.30pm; rest of year Mon & Wed–Sun 10.30am–noon & 2–4.30pm; 10F), a Richelieu commission which failed to prevent the Spanish occupying both Lérins islands between 1635 and 1637. Later, Vauban rounded it off, presumably for Louis XIV's glory, since the strategic value of greatly enlarging a fort facing the mainland without upgrading the one facing the sea is pretty minimal. The main interest in the Fort Ste-Marguerite today is the identification of one cell as having held the **Man in the Iron Mask**, a mythical character given credence by Alexandre Dumas – author of *The Three Musketeers* and *The Count of Monte Cristo* – and by Hollywood. Other cells undoubtedly held the prisoners attributed to them, mostly Huguenots held for refusing to submit to Louis XIV's vicious suppression of Protestantism. Also housed in the fort is a small **aquarium** hosting local marine life and the **Musée de la Mer** (times and entry as for fort), containing mostly Roman local finds, and including remnants of a tenth-century Arab ship.

There's free access to the grassy ramparts of this vast construction, where you're likely to find French tourists, having done their sightseeing, relaxing with guitars and playing games of *boules* and even cricket.

St-Honorat

ST-HONORAT, the smaller southern island, has been owned by monks almost continuously since its namesake and patron founded a monastery here in 410 AD. Honoratus, a Roman noble turned good, is said to have chosen the isle of Lerina because of its reputation for being haunted, full of snakes and scorpions, and lacking any fresh water. Quickly divining a spring and gradually exterminating all the vipers, the saint and his two companions found themselves with precisely the peace and isolation they sought. In time, visitors started to increase in frequency and numbers; the monastic order was established to structure a growing community. By the end of Honoratus's life the Lérins monks had monasteries all over France, held bishoprics in cities such as Arles and Lyon, and were renowned throughout the Catholic world for their contributions to theology. Saint Patrick was one of the products of the Lérins bishops' seminary, training here for seven years before setting out for Ireland.

The present **abbey** buildings are mostly nineteenth-century, though some vestiges of the medieval and earlier constructions remain in the church and within the cloisters. Visiting the austere church is free, but there is an entrance charge for the monastery between June and September (no bikinis or beach gear; 10am–12.30pm & 2.30–5pm; 15F). Nowadays, 28 Cistercian monks live and work here, tending an apiary and a vineyard that produces a sought-after white wine, as well as making liqueurs, all of which are on sale in the abbey's shop. Behind this complex of buildings, on the sea's edge, stands an eleventh-century **fortress**, a monastic bolthole that was connected to the original abbey by a tunnel, and used to guard against the threat of invaders, especially the Saracens. Of all the protective forts built along this coast, this is the only one that looks as if it might still serve its original function. If there is anywhere in Provence that can give a ghostly sense of the Dark and Middle Ages, it is here.

The other buildings on St-Honorat are the churches and chapels that served as retreats. **St-Pierre**, beside the modern monastery, **La Trinité**, on the eastern end of the island, and **St-Sauveur**, west of the harbour, are more or less unchanged. By **St-Cabrais**, on the eastern shore, is a furnace with a chute for making cannonballs, evidence that the monks were not without worldly defensive skills.

Today, the main attractions of this island are peace and silence within the sound of pine leaves stirring and the sea mapping out its minuscule tide. In complete contrast to

Ste-Marguerite, there is only one small restaurant (by the landing stage), and there are no cars or hotels: just the cultivated vines, lavender, herbs and olive trees mingled with wild poppies and daisies; and pine and eucalyptus trees shading the paths beside the white rock shore and mixing with the scent of rosemary, thyme and wild honeysuckle.

Le Cannet

The upper part of **Le Cannet** along rue St-Sauveur has the charm of a medieval village, far removed from the city of Cannes just 3km away and spread below you as viewed from the *terrasse* of **place Bellevue**. Circled by seven hills, the land originally belonged to the Îles de Lérins monks who summoned 140 families from Genoa to come to cultivate the orange trees. These original "Le Cannois" are commemorated by the mural of portraits and orange trees on place Bellevue. If you approach the *place* from the south you'll pass the tiny fifteenth-century **Chapelle de St-Sauveur** (Mon–Fri 9am–noon & 2–5pm, Sat & Sun 10am–12.30pm & 3–6pm; free; key from *mairie* annexe at no. 74), exuberantly decorated by the contemporary artist Tobiasse and, further up at no. 190 rue St-Sauveur, a mural by Peynet of a bride, bridegroom and cherubs floating away to wedded bliss.

Below place Bellevue, on bd Sadi-Carnot, is the stridently Côte d'Azurian *belle époque* **Hôtel de Ville**, with more fancy turn-of-the-century villas down rue Cavasse opposite, which leads to an open-air theatre and a children's library, decorated with yet more murals. To the east is another ancient little chapel, the **Espace Bonnard**, named after the painter who spent his last years here, which hosts temporary art exhibitions (July–Sept 3–7pm; rest of year 2–6pm; free). Le Cannet's streets are wonderfully sleepy and relaxed, particularly between rue de Cannes, with its proud medieval tower, and the old **quartier Ste-Catherine** over to the west around the sixteenth-century **Église Ste-Catherine** and **Chapelle St-Bernardin**, and, though it may not feel exclusive, this is an understandably desirable part of the Cannes conglomeration to live in.

Practicalities

Le Cannet is easily reached from the centre of Cannes on **bus** #4 from the gare SNCF or bus #5 from the *mairie*, both of which will drop you off at the muralled Hôtel de Ville or place Leclerc stops. There's a **tourist office** annexe on bd Carnot just above the start of rue St-Sauveur (Mon–Fri 10am–noon), much more accessible than the main office south of the centre on place de Benidorm (summer daily 9.30am–12.30pm & 1.30–6.30pm; winter Mon–Sat 9am–noon & 2–6pm; ☎04.93.45.28.06).

For eating, Le Cannet has an excellent Caribbean **restaurant**, *Le Pezou*, 346 rue St-Sauveur (☎04.93.69.32.50; closed Wed & Sun eve out of season), with menus from 80F. For something lighter, there's a *pâtisserie-salon-de-thé*, *Le Tivoli* at 25 bd Carnot.

Vallauris

It was during 1946, while he was installed in the castle at Antibes, that Picasso met some of the few remaining potters of **VALLAURIS**. The town's association with this craft goes back to Roman times, but it was in the early sixteenth century, after the Plague had decimated the population, that **pottery** became its major industry. The bishop of Grasse rebuilt the village from its infested ruins and settled Genoese potters to exploit the clay soil and the fuel from the surrounding forests. By the end of World War II, however, aluminium was the cheap and easy material for pots and plates, and redundancy was setting in.

Picasso was invited to Vallauris by the owner of a ceramics studio, Georges Ramié. The mega-man of twentieth-century art, who turned his hand to every visual medium, got hooked on clay and spent the next two years working at Ramié's **Madoura**

workshop. The result, apart from adding pages to the catalogue of the Picasso *oeuvre*, was a rekindling of the age-old industry of this little town in the hills above Golfe-Juan. Today the main street, av Georges-Clemenceau, sells nothing but pottery, much of it the garishly glazed bowls and figurines that could feature in souvenir shops anywhere. The Madoura pottery is on av des Anciens Combattants d'AFN, to the right as you come down av Clemenceau, and still has sole rights on reproducing Picasso's designs, for sale, at a price, in the shop (Mon–Fri 10am–12.30pm & 2.30–7pm).

A bronze **Man with a Sheep**, Picasso's gift to the town, stands in the main square and marketplace, place de la Libération, beside the church and castle. The municipality had some misgivings about the sculpture but decided that the possible affront to their conservative tastes was outweighed by the benefits to tourism of Picasso's international reputation. In the end they need not have worried; the statue looks quite simply like a shepherd boy and sheep.

The local authorities then offered Picasso the task of decorating the early medieval deconsecrated **chapel** in the castle courtyard (Mon & Wed–Sun: July & Aug 10am–12.30pm & 2–6.30pm; rest of year 10am–noon & 2–5pm; 13F), which he finally did in 1952. The space is tiny and, with the painted panels covering the vault, has the architectural simplicity of an air-raid shelter. Picasso's subject is *War and Peace*. At first glance it's easy to be unimpressed (as many critics still are) – it looks mucky and slap-dash with paint runs on the unyielding plywood surfaces. Stay a while, however, and the passion of this violently drawn pacifism slowly emerges. On the War panel a music score is trampled by hooves and about to be engulfed in flames; a fighter's lance tenuously holds the scales of justice and a shield bears the outline of a dove; while from a deathly chariot skeletons escape. Peace is represented by Pegasus; people dancing and suckling babies; trees bearing fruit; owls; books – and the freedom of the spirit to mix up images and concepts with innocent mischief.

The **ticket** for the chapel also gives admission to the **Musée de Céramique/Musée Magnelli** (same hours) in the castle, which for some years has exhibited many of the ceramics Picasso made at the Madoura, in addition to several Pre-Columbian pieces and a collection of paintings by Alberto Magnelli.

Buses from Cannes and Golfe-Juan gare SNCF arrive at the castle on place de la Libération. The **tourist office** is at the bottom of av Clemenceau on place du 8 mai 1945 (Mon–Sat: July & Aug 9am–noon & 2–6pm; rest of year 9am–noon & 2–5pm; ☎04.93.63.82.58). You can **eat** for very little at *La Grupi*, 47 av Clemenceau, and very well at *La Gousse d'Ail*, 11 av de Grasse (☎04.93.64.10.71; menus from 105F; closed Tues, & Wed evening out of season).

Mougins and around

Those who live in **MOUGINS** are not going to let any quick-buck entrepreneur come and sully their exquisitely tasteful setting. House painters, tile-makers, French polishers, orchid specialists, other skilled artisans, and even the new expressway passing in close proximity, yes, but not fast-food merchants or souvenir vendors. They occasionally have to suffer the embarrassment of press interest in some of the residents of the luxurious villas that surround the village – the exiled dictator of Haiti, Baby Doc, for example, who finally fled his creditors after running up astronomical phone, jewellery and nightclub bills. But on the whole, people with homes here can be relied upon to be connoisseurs of discretion and good taste.

There's an excellent **photography museum** (July & Aug daily 2–11pm; Sept, Oct & Dec–June Mon & Wed–Sun 1–6pm; 5F), just beyond the Porte Sarrasin, with changing exhibitions every two months. It has its own small collection, among which are pictures of Jacques Lartigue (who lived in the neighbouring village of Opio) and rather too many portraits of Picasso. The old wash house, **La Lavoir** (March–Oct), at the top end of the village on av Charles-Mallet, forms another exhibition space for the visual arts, its wide basin of water playing reflecting games with the images and the light, and the **Musée Municipal** (July & Aug daily 10am–noon & 2–6pm; Sept–Oct & Dec–June Mon–Fri 10am–noon & 2–6pm; free) on place de la Mairie holds very classy exhibitions of art and design.

Between Mougins and Cannes, just by the D3's slip road onto the highway, is a museum that will delight even those who don't share the passion of its subject, the **Musée de l'Automobiliste** (daily: April–Sept 10am–7pm; Oct–March 10am–6pm; 40F). No expense has been spared on this indulgent dedication to the motorcar and its two-wheeled relations. Sculptures made of shiny tangled exhaust pipes line the pathway to the hangar-like exhibition space. There are glamour cars, including a 1933 Hispano-Suiza; toy cars; German army vehicles; record-breaking racing cars; a simulation of the traffic control room for the Nice–Menton *autoroute*; bizarre prototypes; and films of classic races.

Practicalities

The frequent Cannes–Grasse **buses** all stop at Mougins. If price is no object then you should **stay** at *Les Muscadins*, 18 bd Courteline (☎04.92.28.28.28, fax 04.92.92.88.23; ⑨; closed Nov & Dec), the last word in relaxed luxury; alternatively there's the less extravagant *Les Liserons de Mougins*, 608 av St-Martin (☎04.93.75.50.31, fax 04.93.75.56.13; ④).

Mougins has some very fine **restaurants**, none of them cheap. The best is *Les Muscadins* (☎04.92.28.28.28; midday weekday menu under 120F, otherwise from 175F; closed Tues out of season) which needs booking well in advance. Less grand is the congenial *Bistrot de Mougins* on place du Village (☎04.93.75.78.34; menus from 125F; closed Wed) serving Provençal specialities, and the *Brasserie de la Méditerranée*, place de la Mairie (☎04.93.90.03.47), where there are menus from128F. *Le Feu Follet*, on place de la Mairie (☎04.93.90.15.78; menus from 128F; closed Mon), and *L'Estaminet des Remparts*, 24 rue Honoré-Henri (☎04.93.90.05.36; menus from 110F; closed Mon eve & Tues), are both dependable with pleasant atmospheres.

Mouans-Sartoux

The built-up areas along the Cannes–Grasse road are such that it's easy to miss **MOUANS-SARTOUX** altogether. The old village lies to the west of the main road and is designed on a grid pattern, with the residential streets running north to south and the commercial streets east to a high wall at the west end, all to protect the good citizens from the Mistral wind.

The **Centre Culturel** has one of the biggest collections of literature in the Provençal language, but the main focus for a visit is the **château**, rebuilt to its medieval design in the nineteenth century. The château is one of twenty provincial venues in France chosen by the Socialist former minister for culture, Jack Lang, to be a centre for modern and contemporary art. Since the municipality already had a collection of Concrete art, it was decided to concentrate on this rationalist form of art defined by Théo Van Doesburg as "concrete rather than abstract because nothing is more real than a line, a colour or a surface". **L'Espace de l'Art Concret** (Mon & Wed–Sun: June–Sept 11am–7pm; rest of year 11am–6pm; 15F), the name of the château's beautiful space of white galleries, stages three exhibitions a year. The staff are very keen to welcome visitors and to help them appreciate the art on show: you can get a personal guided tour just by asking.

Grasse

GRASSE, with its medieval heart, its site with an uninterrupted view of the sea, and its location amongst two hundred acres of scented flowers, has been capital of the **perfume industry** for over two hundred years. Making perfume is usually presented as a mysterious process, an alchemy, turning the soul of the flower into a liquid of luxury and desire. The reality, including traditional methods of *macération* – mixing the blossoms with heated animal fat – and *enfleurage* – placing the flowers on cold fat, then washing the result with alcohol and finally distilling it into the ultimately refined essence – are far more vividly described in Patrick Süskind's novel *Perfume*, set in the city, than in the perfume factories in Grasse. Since the 1920s synthetic ingredients have been added to the perfumeries' repertoire but locally grown jasmine and roses are still used, with the industry preferring to keep quiet about modern innovations and techniques.

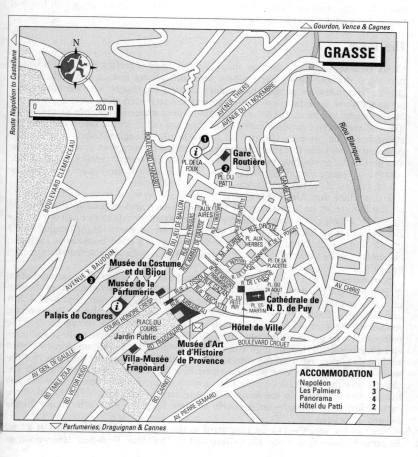

Arrival, information and accommodation

Grasse's **gare routière** is to the north of the Vieille Ville at the Notre-Dames-des-Fleurs car park. Turning left out of the compound and heading downhill on av Thiers, you'll pass an annexe of the tourist office immediately on your right, where av Thiers becomes bd du Jeu de Ballon. You'll find the old casino three minutes' walk further down on cours Honoré-Cresp, now converted into a Palais des Congrès, which houses the main **tourist office** (July to mid-Sept Mon–Sat 9am–5pm, Sun 9am–12.30pm & 1.30–6pm; rest of year Mon–Sat 9am–12.30pm & 4.30–6pm; ☎04.93.36.66.66).

Of the **hotels**, the best budget options are the *Napoléon*, 6 av Thiers (☎ & fax 04.93.36.05.87; ②), right next to the gare routière but rather spartan; and *Les Palmiers*, 17 av Y-Baudoin (☎04.93.36.07.24; ②), which has a pleasant garden with good views of the surrounding countryside and down to the coast. Slightly more expensive is the *Panorama* on place du Cours (☎04.93.36.80.80, fax 04.93.36.92.04; ④), which offers rooms with a view and all mod cons. Even more comfortable, if less well located, is the *Hôtel du Patti*, place du Patti (☎04.93.36.01.00, fax 04.93.36.36.40; ⑤), which has two rooms designed for wheelchair users.

The Town

Vieux Grasse, despite its touristy shops and full range of restaurants, is surprisingly humble, a working-class enclave where lines of washing festoon the high, narrow streets. The mansions of sixteenth-century tanning merchants, seventeenth-century perfumed-glove manufacturers and eighteenth-century *parfumiers* have been turned into museums and municipal offices or divided into apartments. The inhabitants say it's like a village where everyone knows each other, and out of season that is certainly the atmosphere that prevails. The rich all live in nearby Mougins, Cabris and the surrounding countryside that gets progressively less rural every year. Even when Grasse was part of the aristocratic tourist boom of the late nineteenth century, the desirable addresses, Queen Victoria's among them, were all east of the Vieille Ville, but the movement out of the city has increased over the last decade.

Today, **place aux Aires**, at the top of the Vieille Ville, is the main meeting point for all and the venue, each morning, for the **daily flower and vegetable market**. It is ringed by arcades of different heights with an elegant wrought-iron balcony on the Hôtel Isnard at no. 33, and at one time was the exclusive preserve of the tanning industry. On the rue de l'Oratoire just below the square is a good **bookshop**, La Route Napoléon, run by the gently eccentric Monsieur Lazou, with some second-hand tomes in English.

Spiritual power was concentrated at the opposite end of Vieux Grasse, around place du Petit-Puy and place du 24 Août, one of the most dark and deserted quarters of nighttime Grasse today. The **cathedral** (Mon–Sat 8–11.30am & 2.30–6pm, Sun 8–11.30am) and **Bishop's Palace**, between the two squares, were built in the twelfth century, replacing a 200-year-old fortress of which part of a tower remains, incorporated in the palace that now serves as the hôtel de ville. The cathedral, despite endless additions and alterations, still has its high gaunt nave in which the starkly unadorned ribbed vaulting is supported from the side walls. Its astonishing, weighty columns and the walls surrounding the altar were fractured in a fierce fire that blazed through the church after the Revolution, giving the masonry an incredible, organic, cave-like feel that is most arresting. In the south aisle hang various paintings, a Fragonard, three early Rubens and, best by far, a poorly lit triptych by the sixteenth-century Niçois painter Louis Bréa.

You can see more works by Fragonard in the **Villa-Musée Fragonard** at 23 bd Fragonard (June–Sept daily 10am–7pm; Oct & Dec–May Wed–Sun 10am–noon &

THE PERFUME FACTORIES

There are thirty major **parfumeries** in and around Grasse, most of them producing the different essences-plus-formulas which are then sold to Dior, Lancôme, Estée Lauder and the like, who make up their own brand-name perfumes. One litre of pure rose essence can cost as much as 125,000F, and to extract a litre of pure jasmine essence, it takes almost a tonne of jasmine flowers. Perfume contains twenty percent essence (eau de toilette and eau de Cologne considerably less) and the bottles are extremely small. The major cost to this multi-billion-pound business is marketing, with over £10 million a year spent on advertising alone. The grand Parisian couturiers, whose clothes, on strictly cost-accounting grounds, serve simply to promote the perfume, go to inordinate lengths to sell their latest fragrance. As you might imagine, however, the rates paid to those who pick the raw materials, mostly in the Third World, are notoriously low.

A good place to get an overview, and a fairly close-up look at the production, is the **Parfumerie Fragonard** (summer daily 9am–6.30pm; winter Mon–Sat 9am–12.30pm & 2–6pm; free), actually two venues, one in the centre of town at 20 bd Fragonard and the other 3km towards Cannes at Les Quatre Chemins. The first shows traditional methods of extracting essence and has a collection of antique cosmetics bottles and bejewelled flagons. The one outside town is more informative and at least admits to modernization of the processes. A map of the world shows the origins of all the various and strange ingredients: resins, roots, moss, beans and bark join civet (extract of a wild cat's genitals) and ambergris (intestinal goo from whales), bits of beaver and musk from Tibetan goats in the array of scents the "nose" – as the creator of the perfume's formula is known – has to play with. A professional "nose" (of which there are no more than twenty in the world) can recognize up to three thousand different scents.

Other parfumeries to tour include Galimard, 73 rte de Cannes (daily: summer 9am–6.30pm; winter 9am–12.30pm & 2–6pm; free), and Molinard at 60 bd Victor-Hugo (summer daily 9am–6.30pm; winter Mon–Sat 9am–12.30pm & 2–6pm; free). All have shops and give frequent tours in French and English, as well as offering you the chance to create your own personal fragrance.

2–5pm; 10F). The painter was the son of an early and not very successful Grassois perfumed-glove maker and came back to this villa after the Revolution, when his work was no longer finding favour with the new ideologies of the time. During the last week of May a **rose exhibition** is held in the gardens and reception rooms of the Villa Fragonard, with tens of thousands of flowers displayed.

Another museum to quickly flit through is the **Musée d'Art et d'Histoire de Provence**, 2 rue Mirabeau (June–Sept daily 10am–7pm; Oct & Dec–May Wed–Sun 10am–noon & 2–5pm; 20F), set in a luxurious town house commissioned by Mirabeau's sister for her social entertainment duties. As well as all the gorgeous fittings and the original eighteenth-century kitchen, the historical collection adds a nice eclectic touch. It includes wonderful eighteenth- to nineteenth-century faïence from Apt and Le Castellet, Mirabeau's death mask, a tin bidet, six prehistoric bronze leg bracelets; costumes, *santons* and oil presses. There is an opulent eighteenth-century Turkish bed, a collection of brutal, leaden-faced portraits of the seventeenth-century Provençal nobility, and a tremendous sunset painted by René Seyssaud a century ago, whose cracked surface augments the movement of a hazy evening sky near the Étang de Berre.

Also in this part of town is the small **Musée Provençal du Costume et du Bijou**, 2 rue Jean Ossola (June–Oct 10am–1pm & 2–6.30pm; free) with displays of the region's traditional dress and jewellery, and the **Musée International de la Parfumerie**, 8 place du Cours (June–Sept daily 10am–7pm; Oct & Jan–May Wed–Sun 10am–noon & 2–5pm; 25F), whose displays are fascinating and fun, even if you're not an enthusiast of the perfume industry. There are lots of perfume bottles dating from the ancient Greeks to the present via Marie-Antoinette. There's also a greenhouse full of roses, jasmine, vanilla and other prized plants, and you can take a test on recognizing perfumes.

If you're around on a Friday, more relaxed flower-smelling can be done at the **Jardin de la Villa de Noailles**, 59 av Guy-de-Maupassant (Fri 10.30am–2.30pm; ☎04.93.36.07.77; 50F) to the west of the town centre: take rue Jeanne-Jugan off av Gal-de-Gaulle, then left down Chemin Noailles, and left again. Camelias, magnolias and peonies are the star attractions here.

Eating and drinking

Bars and **restaurants** in the Vieille Ville are good value. The *Crêperie Bretonne* (closed Sun), *La Galerie Gourmand* and *Casablanca*, all on rue Fabreries, are good stand-bys and you'll find many more menus to choose from on rue de la Fontette – try *Pierre Baltus* at no. 15 (☎04.93.36.32.90; menus from around 100F; closed Wed eve, Sat lunchtime & mid-Feb to early March). At the *Maison Venturini*, 1 rue Marcel-Journet (closed Sun & Mon), you can buy fabulous sweet *fougassettes*, flavoured with the Grasse speciality of orange blossom. Tasty pizzas and *socca* (chickpea pancakes) won't break the bank at the relaxed *La Socca*, 17 rue Paul-Goby (☎04.93.36.18.48), and the modern *Brasserie de l'Évêché* (☎04.93.36.40.12), on the place de l'Évêché, serves up good mid-day menus from about 70F.

The **bars** on place aux Aires give the most opportunity for encounters with the locals; the *Bar-Tabac L'Ariel* is a good place to start.

Around Grasse

The countryside around Grasse is pleasant for a day or two's stay, especially if you have a car. To the north is the **Plateau de Calern**, almost deserted save for the British archeologists who arrive every September to map the changing patterns of land use and ownership by the commune of **Cipières**. Running northwest is the **Route Napoléon** and to the northeast, the gorges of the **Loup River** pass the cliff-hanging stronghold of **Gourdon** and the mortality reminders of **Le-Bar-sur-Loup**. To the west, towards the Upper Var, there are good dinners to be had at **Cabris** and musical caves to witness at **St-Cézaire**.

The Route Napoléon: St-Vallier-de-Thiey

The road north from Grasse is the **Route Napoléon**, the path taken by the emperor in March 1815 after his escape from Elba, in pursuit of the most audacious recapture of power in French history. In typically French fashion the road was built in the 1930s specifically to commemorate their greatest leader's journey.

Inevitably the route does not follow the imperial boot tracks precisely, going miles off course in some places, but it serves a useful communications purpose. After several kilometres of zigzagging bends you get fantastic views back to Grasse, its basin and the coast. At the first village, **ST-VALLIER-DE-THIEY**, 12km from Grasse, you'll find three **campsites**, including the three-star *Parc des Arboins* (☎04.93.42.63.89, fax 04.93.09.61.54) on the rte Napoléon, plus Napoleonic souvenirs, and prehistoric ones in the form of dolmens and tumuli. The **tourist office** on place du Tour (Mon–Fri 9am–noon & 2.30–5.30pm, Sat 10am–noon; ☎04.93.42.78.00) has walking maps for these sites and the true path taken by Napoléon. The place to **eat** and **stay** is *Le Préjoly* at place Rougière (☎04.93.42.60.86, fax 04.93.42.67.80; menus from around 100F; ④; closed Dec & Jan).

Beyond St-Vallier, the Route Napoléon heads, almost uninterrupted by settlement, towards Castellane (see p.371). Wayside stalls sell honey and perfume; each little hamlet has a petrol station and hotel-restaurant, and every so often you see a commemorative plaque carved with Napoléon's winged eagle.

Cabris

CABRIS, just 6km southwest of Grasse, has all the trappings of a picture-postcard village: a ruined château providing panoramas from the Lac de St-Cassien to the Îles de Lérins, sometimes even Corsica, and arty residents who no longer find it fashionable to live in Grasse. If you want to **stay**, try the chambre d'hôtes at *L'Écurie du Château* (☎04.93.60.56.19; ④) in the courtyard of the old château on place Mirabeau, which offers large tasteful rooms decorated with watercolours and has wonderful views. The warm and welcoming *Le Petit Prince* **restaurant** at 15 rue Frédéric-Mistral (☎04.93.60.51.40; closed Tues evening & Wed out of season), overlooking the park lined with chestnut trees, is a treat, with a weekday menu of around 100F. The puddings are gorgeous, as is the smoked salmon *mille feuilles* and the wild mushroom dishes.

The Grottes des Audides and Grottes de St-Cézaire

At the **Grottes des Audides**, on the road from Cabris to St-Vallier (July & Aug daily 10–11am & 2–5pm; Sept, Oct & mid-Feb to June Wed–Sun 2–5pm; Nov to mid-Feb phone for information; ☎04.93.42.64.15; 25F for caves, 20F for prehistoric park), you descend 60m into caves that were neolithic dwellings. Scenes of prehistoric life have been re-created including stone tools found in the caves.

Just outside St-Cézaire-sur-Siagne (signed off the Cabris road) are the **Grottes de St-Cézaire** (tours: July & Aug daily 10.30am–6.30pm; June & Sept daily 10.30am–noon & 2.30–6pm; mid-Feb to May & Oct daily 2.30–5pm; Nov to mid-Feb Sun 2.30–4.30pm; 27F). The visit to the **caves** does not involve a very deep descent, and visually it is not a great treat because of the uniform rust-red colour of all the natural sculptures. What is special is the aural experience of the stalagmites and stalactites with the most iron in them; the guide plays them like a xylophone, with an eerie resonance in this most irregular of acoustic chambers.

West from Grasse towards Draguignan, along the D2562, there's a great **lunch** stop, *Le Pont de la Siagne* (☎04.93.66.10.36; closed Tues), about ten kilometres out of town, where the 120F menu is an enormous feast in the best French tradition, served with a minimum of pomp but with considerable respect and designed to be eaten leisurely over a couple of hours.

Along the Gorges de Loup

From Grasse the main approach to the Gorges de Loup is via **LE-BAR-SUR-LOUP**. The little **Église de St-Jacques** contains an altarpiece attributed to the Niçois painter, Louis Bréa, and a fifteenth-century *Danse Macabre* painted on a wooden panel at the west end of the nave. The latter is a tiny but detailed illustration of courtly dancers being picked off by Death's arrows, their souls gathered up by devils, failing Saint Michael's test of blessedness and being thrown into the teethed and tongued mouth of hell. Alongside is a poem, in Provençal, warning of mortality and of the heavy risk involved in committing sins as grievous as dancing.

From here, you can follow the **gorges road**, through dark, narrow twists of rock beneath cliffs that look as if they might tumble at any minute, through the sounds of furiously churning water, to corners that appear to have no way out. Alternatively, you could miss out Le-Bar-sur-Loup and take the D3 from **Châteauneuf-Grasse** up along the northern balcony of the gorges to Gourdon.

Gourdon

Like every *village perché* in striking distance of the coast, **GOURDON**, on the edge of the Gorges de Loup, has turned itself into an unofficial theme park. The air is permeated with perfume even more so than in Grasse, and is fatally infected with the related commerce. Only the iron-willed can leave without having bought soap, scented oil, crystal glass or an olive-wood figurine.

The village's **château** (June–Sept daily 11am–1pm & 2–7pm; rest of year Mon & Wed–Sun 2–6pm; 25F) is the one escape, an immaculately restored private residence containing a historical museum and a collection of naive paintings. The first houses the better art: a self-portrait by Rembrandt (not always on show), a glowing *Descent from the Cross* by Rubens and other religious paintings of the early sixteenth century, as well as Saracen helmets made in Damascus, a writing desk used by Marie-Antoinette and letters signed by Henri IV. After this miscellany, the naive art seems very one-track-minded. In fact the owner of the château has an immense art collection, but for insurance purposes exhibits only the cheapest ones permanently. You're allowed out to the terraced garden from where you can enjoy the view, but not the swimming pool and tennis courts added to the formal pattern.

Antibes, Cap d'Antibes and Juan-les-Pins

Antibes, or rather its promontory the **Cap d'Antibes**, is one of the select places on the Côte d'Azur where the really rich and the very successful still live, or at least have residences. However, even in this world the recession has taken its toll. Recently, a château on the Cap whose past residents include the duke of Windsor, Onassis and Niarchos had to drop its price from $50 million to a mere $27 million. Graham Greene lived out the last years of his life here in a small apartment. Shortly before his death he revealed the simple reason for his choice: to be near the woman he loved. But for the rest it's not so obvious why this area should be so desirable. It is as built up as the rest of the Riviera, with no open countryside separating Golfe Juan, **Juan-les-Pins** and **Antibes**, nor is Antibes spared the high-rise apartments scorned by the old Côte aristocrats for allowing ordinary tourists a taste of this coast. The southern end of the Cap, however, still has its woods of pine, in which the most exclusive mansions hide, and with yacht or helicopter access, one could no doubt pretend that little had changed in the last forty years.

For visitors, the Cap offers walks and intermittent access to the wonderful rocky shore as well as one garden that isn't private, the **Jardin Thuret**. Antibes is animated by street upon street of bars and restaurants, has one of the finest **markets** on the coast, and a superb **Picasso collection** in its ancient seafront castle. Juan-les-Pins is pretty low on glamour these days, though there's any number of nightclubs, discos and hotels. But its **jazz festival** is still a treat and the beach more attractive than the one at Antibes.

Antibes

Very little of the medieval centre **ANTIBES** is left thanks to border squabbles from the fifteenth century to the Revolution when Antibes belonged to France and Nice to Savoy. Yachts and fishing boats moor in a harbour designed by sixteenth- and seventeenth-century military architects to be under the dependable protection of the vast **Fort Carré**, enlarged by Vauban to an impregnable eight-pointed star of bastions. This is the dominant landmark of Antibes if you approach from Nice and Cagnes. Seventeenth-century ramparts still separate the port from the Vieille Ville whose focus is the solidly rectangular medieval masses of the **Château Grimaldi** and the belfry of the former **cathedral** rising above the sea wall.

Arrival, information and accommodation
The Vieille Ville fits in the triangle formed by the coast, the ramparts along bd de l'Aiguillon, and av Robert-Soleau and bd Albert-1er, with the gare SNCF at the apex, a

block back from the head of the port at the junction of av Robert-Soleau and rte du Bord-de-la-Mer. Turn right out of the station from where it's a short walk along av R-Soleau until you reach the spacious place du Général-de-Gaulle which has the **tourist office** at no. 11 (July & Aug Mon–Sat 8.30am–7.30pm, Sun 10am–1pm; rest of year Mon–Fri 9am–12.30pm & 2–6.30pm, Sat 9am–noon & 2–6pm; ☎04.92.90.53.00). The **gare routière** is just off the southeast corner of place du Gal-de-Gaulle on the adjoining place Guynemer with frequent buses (not Sun) to and from the gare SNCF, a five-minute walk away. Bus #2A goes to Cap d'Antibes; bus #1A and #3A to Juan-les-Pins, and #10A to Biot. **Bikes** can be rented from Midi Location Service, Galerie du Port, rue Lacan (☎04.93.34.48.00), and Holiday Bikes, 122 bd Wilson (☎04.93.67.66.94).

From the gare routière, rue de la République leads down through place des Martyrs into the heart of Vieux Antibes around **place Nationale**, which in turn is linked by rue Sade to the **cours Masséna**, the limit of the original Greek settlement and the daily **market-place**. The castle and cathedral lie between cours Masséna and the sea.

Though cheap **hotels** are thin on the ground, there are plenty of rooms to be had in and around Antibes and a **youth hostel** on the Cap. Booking in advance for the summer is recommended. All of Antibes' **campsites** are a few kilometres north of the city in the quartier de la Brague (bus #10a or one train stop to Gare de Biot).

HOTELS

Brasserie Nouvelle, 1 av Niquet (☎04.93.34.10.07). Close to the gare routière, with just five rooms. ②.

La Gardiole, 74 chemin de la Garoupe (☎04.93.61.35.03, fax 04.93.67.61.87). Lovely location on a lane in Cap d'Antibes; friendly, quiet and with a terrace overlooking the garden on which to dine. Closed Nov–March. ⑦.

Hôtel du Levant, 50 chemin de la Plage (☎04.92.93.72.99). On Cap d'Antibes, backed by woods and overlooking the sea. Closed Nov to mid-April. ⑧.

Mas Djoliba, 29 av de Provence (☎04.93.34.02.48, fax 04.93.34.05.81). Between the Vieille Ville and the main beach, with a large garden; very pleasant. Closed Nov–Jan. ⑤.

Le Nouvel Hôtel, 1 av du 24 août (☎04.93.34.44.07, fax 04.93.34.44.08). Not a bad location close to the gare routière and the rooms at the top have good views. ③.

Le Ponteil, 11 impasse Jean-Mensier (☎04.93.34.67.92, fax 04.93.34.49.47). Quiet location at the end of a cul-de-sac close to the sea. ④.

Auberge Provençale, 61 pl Nationale (☎04.93.34.13.24, fax 04.93.34.89.88). Right in the centre of Vieux Antibes and with only seven rooms, so book in advance. ⑥.

Le Relais du Postillon, 8 rue Championnet (☎04.93.34.20.77, fax 04.93.34.61.24). Centrally located near the bus station, with comfortable rooms above a high-quality restaurant. ③.

HOSTEL AND CAMPSITES

Relais International de la Jeunesse, bd de la Garoupe, Cap d'Antibes (☎04.93.61.34.40, fax 04.93.34.89.88). Youth hostel which needs booking well in advance. Take bus #2a from gare routière to La Bouée and head north along bd de la Garoupe to junction with av de l'Antiquité. Closed 10am–5.30pm; midnight curfew. Closed Oct–May.

Logis de la Brague, 1221 rte de Nice (☎04.93.33.54.72). Three-star campsite, the closest to Biot's station. Closed Oct–April.

Idéal-Camping, 991 rte de Nice (☎04.93.74.27.07). Two-star site south of Biot's station; and close to the sea. Closed mid-Oct to March.

The Town

The most atmospheric and uncrowded approach to the castle and cathedral is from the south through the distinctive **quartier du Safranier**. The place du Safranier and the little residential streets off rue de la Tourraque and rue de l'Esperon, including rue de Lavoir with its old public **wash house**, have a very appealing villagey atmosphere, and commerce is minimal. By turning right on rue de l'Orme – rather than continuing straight into cours Masséna – and left on rue du Bateau, you'll find yourself on place Marie-Jol, in front of the **Château Grimaldi**, rebuilt in the sixteenth century but still with its twelfth-century Romanesque tower.

In 1946 Picasso had returned from Paris and was living with Françoise Gilot in an apartment in Juan-les-Pins which had very little space for him to work. He met the director of the museum who suggested he use the château as a studio. Several extremely prolific months followed before he moved to Vallauris, leaving all his Antibes output to what is now the **Musée Picasso** (Tues–Sun: June–Sept 10am–6pm; Oct–May 10am–noon & 2–6pm; 30F). Although Picasso donated other works later on, the bulk of the collection belongs to this one period. At this time, the artist was involved in one of his better love relationships; his friend Matisse was just up the road in Vence; the war was over; and the 1950s had not yet arrived to change the Côte d'Azur for ever. There's an uncomplicated exuberance in the numerous still-lifes of sea urchins, the goats and fauns in Cubist non-disguise, and the wonderful *Ulysses and the Sirens*, a great round head against a mast around which the ship, sea and sirens swirl. The materials reveal postwar shortages – odd bits of wood and board instead of canvas, and boat paint rather than oils. Picasso is also the subject here of other painters and photographers, including André Villers, Brassai, Man Ray and Bill Brandt. The photo of him holding a sunshade for Françoise Gilot catches the happiness of this period in the artist's life.

By contrast, on the second floor, in Picasso's old studio, the anguished works of Nicolas de Staël, who eventually killed himself, are displayed. He stayed in Antibes for a few months from 1954 to 1955, painting the sea, gulls and boats with great washes of grey. A disturbing red dominates *The Grand Concert* and purple the *Still Life with Candlestick*. Works by other great twentieth-century artists are included in the museum's **modern art** collection, with thirteen special commissions for the tenth anniversary of Picasso's death. The terrace overlooking the sea is adorned by Germaine Richier sculptures along with works by Miró, César and others, and a violin homage to Picasso by Arman. The combination of the terrace, the beautifully cool, light space of the galleries with their hexagonal terracotta floor tiles, and the windows over the sea makes this an exceptional setting for the superb work within it.

Alongside the castle is the **cathedral**, built on the site of an ancient temple. The choir and apse survive from the Romanesque building that served the city in the Middle Ages while the nave and stunning ochre facade are Baroque. Inside, in the south transept, is a sumptious altarpiece by Louis Bréa surrounded by immaculate panels of tiny detailed scenes.

One block inland, the **covered market** on cours Masséna overflows with Provençal goodies including a particularly good line in differently prepared olives, and a profusion of cut **flowers**, the traditional and still flourishing Antibes business (June–Aug daily 6am–1pm; rest of year Tues–Sun 6am–1pm). On Friday and Sunday (plus Easter–Sept Tues & Thurs) a **craft market** takes over in the afternoon from about 3pm. When the stalls are all packed up, café tables take their place.

There's a museum of local history and traditions in a medieval tower at the southern end of cours Masséna, the **Musée de la Tour** (Wed, Thurs & Sat afternoons; 10F). Though it's not wildly interesting it does have the first ever water skis, invented in Juan-les-Pins in the 1930s.

Further south, beyond the quartier du Safranier, where the coast ramparts end, the Bastion St-André houses the **Musée d'Histoire et d'Archéologie** (Tues–Sun 10am–noon & 2–6pm; closed Nov; 10F), which gathers together the Greek, Roman, medieval and later finds of the region. Modern art is Antibes' strength: there's a **gallery of contemporary art** with temporary exhibitions at 24 promenade Amiral-de-Grasse, alongside the archeological museum. Of the town's **commercial galleries**, Albert-1er at 7 bd Albert-1er, Pams at 25 cours Masséna, Fersen at 27 rue de Fersen, and Galerie Domus, at 3 rue Thuret, offer a varied and sometimes outstanding selection of current work.

Another Antibes artist is honoured in the town with his own museum. The **Musée Peynet** on place Nationale (Tues–Sun: mid-June to mid-Sept 10am–6pm; rest of year 10am–noon & 2–6pm; 20F), pays homage to the cartoonist whose most famous creation was the 1940s series of "the lovers", a truly old-fashioned conception of romance which, if you're not careful, may even induce nostalgia.

Eating and drinking

Place Nationale and cours Masséna are lined with **cafés**; rue James-Close has nothing but **restaurants** and rue Thuret and its side streets also offer numerous menus to browse through. If you've missed the market, you'll find excellent **food shops** on rue du Sade, including the Charcuterie Lorraine at no. 15.

Auberge Provençale, 61 pl Nationale (☎04.93.34.13.24). Fish grills and seafood served in the covered garden of this welcoming hotel; menus from 145F. Closed Mon, Tues midday & Jan.

Restaurant de Bacon, bd de Bacon, Cap d'Antibes (☎04.93.61.50.02). The best restaurant in the region, overlooking Vieux Antibes and serving fabulous fish soups and stews, including a superb bouillabaisse. Menus at 250F and 500F. Closed Mon & Nov–Jan.

L'Eléphant Bleu, 28 bd de l'Aguillon (☎04.93.34.28.80). Thai and Vietnamese specialities with good vegetarian dishes. Midday menu at 75F, otherwise from 105F.

La Famiglia, 34 av Thiers (☎04.93.34.60.82). A cheap, family-run outfit serving good pizzas and pasta. Closed Wed.

Il Giardino, 21 rue Thuret. Great pizzas though you may have a long wait to be served.

La Marmite, 20 rue James-Close (☎04.93.34.56.79). One of the best on this street; around 120F. Closed Mon out of season & mid-Nov to mid-Dec.

Le Marquis, 4 rue Sade (☎04.93.34.23.00). Traditional Provençal food in a charming setting; mid-day weekday menu under 100F, otherwise from 130F. Closed Mon & Tues midday.

Chez Olive, 2 bd Maréchal-Leclerc (☎04.93.34.42.32). Provençal specialities, with midday menu at under 90F, otherwise around 160F. Closed Sun eve, Mon & mid-Dec to mid-Jan.

L'Oursin, 16 rue de la République (☎04.93.34.13.46). Superb fish and traditional seafood, with menus starting at 100F. Closed Mon & Sun eve.

Café Pimms, cnr of rue de la République and pl Guynemer. Brasserie with carousel decor and friendly atmosphere. Closed Sun.

Chez les Poissonniers, 16 cours Masséna (☎04.93.34.23.10). Another fantastic seafood restaurant, with fine à la carte menu. Closed Mon & first two weeks of both Jan & June.

Café de la Porte du Port, bd de l'Aiguillon by the archway through the ramparts. One of many lively cafés in the rampart arcades.

Le Romantic, 5 rue Rostan (☎04.93.34.59.39). Charming, small restaurant with an excellent 125F menu on which the grilled sardines are delicious. Closed Wed midday & Tues.

Taverne da Cito, in the covered market, at 23 cours Masséna. Café with a wide selection of beers; *moules marinières*, *frites* and beer for 65F. Open 3pm–midnight.

Les Vieux Murs, near the castle at av Amiral-de-Grasse (☎04.93.34.06.73). Very classy food such as oysters cooked in champagne and a perfect setting on the ramparts. Menu 200F, à la carte from 300F. Closed Mon & Oct–March.

Nightlife

Many **cafés** and **bars** stay open late, but if you want to **dance**, you'd be better off in Juan-les-Pins (see below). Most nightclubs charge an initial 100F entrance with a "complimentary" first drink. The most frequented **nightclub** is *La Siesta*, between Antibes and La Brague on the route du Bord-de-la-Mer. There are seven dance floors with a choice of night-time sky for ceilings and drinks from 80F a go. At *Sommersby*, a Tex-Mex brasserie at 1 av Maizière next to the Bastion St-André, you can drink beer, watch cable TV, play billiards, and listen to fairly mainstream live rock on Friday and Saturday nights (open till 2am).

Cap d'Antibes

Plage de la Salis, the longest Antibes beach, runs along the eastern neck of **Cap d'Antibes** and is free to anyone who wants to sunbathe on the sand. It's an amazing rarity on the Riviera, with no artificial landscaping and without the rows of big hotels owning mattress exploitation rights. The success of Juan-les-Pins spared this side of the Cap from wild development in the days before all coastal promontories became protected by more stringent planning laws.

A second beach, **Plage de la Garoupe**, equally public and untrammelled, is along bd de la Garoupe before the promontory of Cap Gros. From here a **footpath** follows the shore for quite some way but private property prevents it joining up with chemin des Douaniers. To reach the most southern point, the Pointe de l'Îlette, you have to take chemin de la Mosquée from av J-F-Kennedy, passing the superstars' favourite hang-out, the *Hôtel du Cap*. At the end of av J-F-Kennedy is one of the very few public buildings on the Cap, the **Musée Naval et Napoléonien** (Mon–Fri 9.30am–noon & 2.15–6pm, Sat 9.30am–noon; closed Oct; 20F), documenting the general's great return from Elba (see under "Juan-les-Pins") along with the usual Bonaparte paraphernalia of hats, cockades, and signed commands; and presents models of seventeenth- and eighteenth-century ships. It also allows you views over the woods of the southern Cap, all parcelled up into large private domains.

Another public building is the **Église de la Garoupe**, at the top of chemin du Calvaire above the southern end of plage de la Salis (10am–noon & 2.30–5pm), which is full of ex-votos for deliverances from accidents that range from battles with the Saracens to collisions with speeding Citroëns. It also contains a Russian Byzantine medieval icon and a painting on silk, both spoils from the Crimean War. Next to the church is a viewing platform and an immensely powerful lighthouse whose beam is visible 70km out to sea.

In the middle of the Cap, on bd du Cap between chemins du Tamisier and G-Raymond, is the **Jardin Thuret** (Mon–Fri 8.30am–noon & 2.30–5.30pm; free), established in the mid-nineteenth century by a famous botanist and now belonging to INRA, a national research institute which, amongst other things, tests out and acclimatizes subtropical trees and shrubs in order to diversify the Mediterranean plants of France. You can wander around freely; don't expect anything other than Latin names on the labels, but whether you're a botanist, forester or complete amateur, you are sure to be surprised by some of the trees and shrubs growing here.

Walking or **cycling** between the Jardin Thuret and the Musée Naval, along the western side of the Cap along bd du Maréchal-Juin, is very pleasant, with rocks and jetties, little sand beaches, high walls around gardens on the inland side of the road, and the tiny **Port de l'Olivette** near the Musée Naval full of small, unflashy boats.

Juan-les-Pins

JUAN-LES-PINS, just 1.5km west of Antibes, is another of those overloaded Côte d'Azur names. It's the legendary summer night-time playground for the most expensively outfitted and consistently photographed celebrities who retreat at dawn, like supernatural creatures, to their well-screened cages on Cap d'Antibes.

Arrival, information and accommodation

Walking from the **gare SNCF** on av de l'Esterel down av Dr-Fabre and rue des Postes you reach the carrefour de Nouvelle Orléans, beyond which is La Pinède; by bus from

Antibes the most central stops are Pin Doré and Palais des Congrès. The **tourist office** is at 51 bd Guillaumont on the seafront at the western end of the town (July & Aug Mon–Sat 8.30am–7.30pm, Sun 10am–1pm; rest of year Mon–Fri 9am–12.30pm & 2–6.30pm, Sat 9am–noon & 2–6pm, Sun 10am–noon; ☎04.92.90.53.05).

If you haven't already booked a **hotel** the two streets to try are av Gallet between av de l'Esterel and the seafront, and av Alexandre III which crosses it. *Hôtel de la Pinède*, 7 av Georges-Gallice (☎04.93.61.03.95; ③; closed Dec–Feb), has some cheap rooms and is right in the centre; the *Parisiana*, 16 av de l'Esterel (☎04.93.61.27.03, fax 04.93.67.97.21; ③), is close to the station. For more than just the basics, try *Pré-Catelan* on the corner of av des Palmiers and av des Lauriers (☎04.93.61.05.11, fax 04.93.67.83.11; ⑤; closed mid-Nov to Jan), or the very upmarket and beautiful *Hôtel du Parc*, corner of av Maupassant and av Gallet (☎04.93.61.61.00, fax 04.93.67.92.42; ⑧; closed Nov–March).

The Town

Beyond the image, Juan-les-Pins has very little in the way of history. Unlike St-Tropez it was not a fishing village, just a pine grove by the sea, which tried to become fashionable in the late nineteenth century with the help of one of Queen Victoria's sons. It had a casino built in 1908, but took off only in the late 1920s as the original summer resort of the Côte d'Azur. Revealing swimsuits, as opposed to swimming "dresses", were reputedly first worn here in the 1930s; its trail-blazing style and attraction for global aristocrats and royals, fashionable writers and dancers, and the star creations of the film world continued unabated through the 1950s and 1960s. Now, like so much of the Côte, it's so overcrowded and overbuilt that it's impossible to see what all the fuss is about – or to imagine it as a pine forest. But its **jazz festival** is the best in the region.

The main venue for the jazz festival, and what's left of the pine forest, is the **Jardin de La Pinède** (known simply as La Pinède) and **Square Gould** above the beach by the casino and divided by bd Edouard-Baudon. The pines are very old and very beautiful but a wood it most certainly is not. This urban park and the 2km of sheltered sand beach are all that Juan-les-Pins has to offer for free, apart from the dizzying array of architectural styles along its streets.

Eating and drinking

La Terrasse overlooking La Pinède on av Gallice (☎04.93.61.20.37) is one of the star **restaurants** on this coast, and needs booking several weeks in advance. It will set you back at least 275F at midday, 420F at other times; but the original 1930s decor, the exquisite fish and seafood dishes, mouthwatering desserts and the high culinary art of the whole meal, may make the expense worthwhile. That apart, Juan-les-Pins is not blessed with dependable restaurants, so take pot luck from the countless menus on offer on the boulevards around La Pinède. You can get brasserie food, crêpes, pizzas and similar snacks from street stalls till the early hours, and many shops and bars also keep going in summer till 3 or 4am.

Nightlife

The fads and reputations of the different **discos** in Juan-les-Pins change by the month (and all the starry *boîtes* are members-only). In general, however, opening hours are 11pm to dawn and you can count on paying at least 100F for entrance plus your first drink. Some to try are: *Joy's Club*, 142 bd Président-Wilson; *Les Pêcheurs* at Port Gallice and *Voom-Voom*, 1 bd de la Pinède.

Le Pam-Pam, 137 bd Wilson, is the most popular music venue with live Brazilian **bands** (cocktails from 60F), but go early to get a seat. *Le Festival* opposite at 146 bd Wilson also offers Latin American sounds but lacks the cachet of *Le Pam-Pam*. In the basement of the *Beachôtel* on av Alexandre III there's a piano-bar, *Le Madison*, with jazz bands several nights a week; or you can listen to small jazz combos or soloists in the much less flashy *Le Jazzman*, on 5 bd de la Pinède.

The Côte d'Azur Festival International de Jazz

The best jazz event on the Côte d'Azur, the **Festival International de Jazz**, takes place during the **last two weeks of July** in the open air of La Pinède and Square Gould. Recent perfomers include B.B. King, Chuck Berry, Keith Jarrett, Didier Lockwood, the Newport Jazz Festival All Stars, George Benson, Wynton Marsalis and Sonny Rollins. The music is always chosen with serious concern for every kind of jazz, both contemporary and traditional, rather than commercial popularity. Programme details and **tickets** (120–200F) are available from the Maison de Tourisme at 11 place de Gaulle, Antibes (☎04.92.90.53.00) and 51 bd Guillaumont, Juan-les-Pins (☎04.92.90.53.05); tickets can also be bought from FNAC and Virgin shops.

Biot and Sophia-Antipolis

Twenty years ago, the area inland from Antibes above the *autoroute* was still the more-or-less untouched Forêt de la Brague, stretching from Mougins in the west to Biot in the east. Now transnational companies have offices and laboratories linked by wide roads cut through the forest, notably at **Sophia-Antipolis**, a futuristic industrial park. Nearby **Biot**, meanwhile, has become one of the most visited places on the Côte, for its *village perché* charm, its glassworks and its monumental museum to Fernand Léger.

Biot

The village of **BIOT**, above the coast 8km north of Antibes, is extremely beautiful and oozes with art – architectural, sculpted, ceramic, jewelled, painted and culinary. It's inevitably packed out in high season but it's not a place to miss if you can help it.

Arrival, information and accommodation

The **gare SNCF** for Biot is by the sea at La Brague. It's a four-kilometre walk along a dangerous main road to the village, so it's far better to catch one of the Antibes buses

---

THE ROUTE NAPOLÉON

The pines and silver sand between Juan-les-Pins and Cannes, now **Golfe-Juan,** witnessed Napoléon's famous return from exile in 1815. The emperor knew the bay well, having been in command of the Mediterranean defences as a general in 1794 with Antibes' Fort Carré as his base. This time, however, his emissaries to Cannes and Antibes were taken prisoner upon landing, though the local men in charge decided not to capture him. The lack of enthusiasm for his return was enough to persuade the ever-brilliant tactician to head north, bypassing Grasse, and take the most isolated snowbound mule paths up to Sisteron and onwards – the path commemorated by the modern **Route Napoléon**. By March 6 he was in Dauphiné. On March 19 he was back in the Tuileries Palace in the capital. One hundred days later he lost the battle of Waterloo and was finally and absolutely incarcerated on St Helena.

An anecdote relates that on the day of landing at Golfe-Juan, Napoléon's men accidentally held up the prince of Monaco's coach travelling east along the coast. The Revolution incorporated Monaco into France but the restored Louis XVIII had just granted back the principality. When the prince told the former emperor that he was off to reclaim his throne, Napoléon replied that they were in the same business and waved him on his way.

For **continuations of the Route Napoléon**, see "Grasse", "Sisteron" and "Castellane".

(10 daily to Biot). From the bus stop in the village head up Chemin Neuf and you'll find rue St-Sébastien, the main street, running off to your right. The **tourist office** (Mon–Fri 9am–noon & 2–6pm, Sat & Sun 2–6pm; ☎04.93.65.05.85) is on place de la Chapelle at the far end of rue St-Sébastien, and can provide copious lists of art galleries, should you need them.

There's not a lot of **accommodation** in Biot. If you book well in advance you could stay at the very reasonable *Hôtel des Arcades*, 16 place des Arcades (☎04.93.65.01.04, fax 04.93.65.01.05; ③), with huge rooms and full of old-fashioned charm in the medieval centre of the village. There are plenty of **campsites** in the vicinity – the best are the two-star *Le Mistral* on rte de la Mer (☎04.93.65.61.48); the two-star *Typhas*, 144 chemin de la Romaine (☎04.93.65.10.07); and the three-star *L'Eden*, chemin du Val-de-Pôme (☎04.93.65.63.70; closed Oct–March), a couple of hundred metres from the Léger Museum.

The village

The painter Fernand Léger lived in Biot for a few years at the end of his life. A stunning collection of his intensely life-affirming works can be seen at the purpose-built **Musée Fernand Léger**, just southeast of the village on the chemin du Val-de-Pôme, a thirty minute walk from the gare SNCF (Mon & Wed–Sun: July–Sept 11am–6pm; rest of year 10am–noon & 2–5pm; 38F, 28F on Sun). It was the experience of fighting alongside "the entire French populace . . . miners, labourers, artisans who worked in wood or metal", and the sight of "the breechplate of a 75-mm cannon lying in the open sun, the magic of the light on the polished metal" in World War I that turned Léger away from the abstraction of Parisian painters. Not that he favoured realism, but, as he put it, he wanted his paintings to share the toughness and directness of the working class and have a popular appeal. He was vocal on the politics of culture, arguing for museums to be open after working hours; for public spaces to be adorned with art in the way of "incidental background", on which he collaborated often with Le Corbusier; and for making all the arts more accessible to working people.

Few painters have had such consistency and power in their use of space and colour and the ability to change the relations between objects or figures without ever descending to surrealism. Without any realism in the form and facial expressions, the people in such paintings as *Four Bicycle Riders* or the various *Construction Workers* are forcefully present as they engage in their work or leisure, and are visually on an equal footing with the objects. Of the *Construction Workers*, Léger describes seeing a factory being built and men like fleas balancing on the steel beams: "this is what I wanted to depict: the contrast between man and his creations, between the worker and this whole architecture of metal". *Mona Lisa with Keys* speaks of his deep concern about the relationship between works of art and ordinary people.

Léger's art has the capacity for instant pleasure – the pattern of the shapes, the colour, particularly in his ceramic works – though he can also draw it back to harsh horror as with *Stalingrad*. It's instructive to compare Léger's life and work with that of Picasso, his fellow pioneer of **Cubism** and long-time comrade in the Communist Party. While Legér's commitment to collective working-class life never wavered, Picasso waved at it only when he needed it. Picasso wanted to embrace the whole world and be embraced in return. He chose a complex, dominating and sometimes perverted persona through which to do it, while Léger stuck within the reality of himself and the world, an outlook captured by Alexander Calder's wire sculpture portrait of Léger in the museum.

It was the **potteries** that first brought Léger to Biot, where one of his old pupils had set up shop to produce ceramics of his master's designs. After Léger's death five years later in 1956, the Biot **glassworks** were established. Today, you can watch the glass-blowers at work, visit an Eco-musée du Verre, and see some extraordinary and extravagant glass creations in the Galerie Internationale du Verre in the **Verrerie de Biot** on chemin des

Combes, the third turning off the D4 after the Léger museum (June–Sept Mon–Sat 8am–7pm, Sun 10am–1pm & 3–7pm; rest of the year Mon–Sat 8am–6pm, Sun 10.30am–1pm & 2.30–6.30pm; free). Particularly famous is the beautiful hand-blown **bubble glass** (*verre bullé*). There are several other glass-makers in the same area, all keen for you to visit and buy their products.

If **children** are getting bored with street wandering and window gazing there are a number of attractions – all expensive – back on the main sea road. They include the performing dolphins of Marineland (adults 165F, children 117F), the water toboggans, chutes and slides of the neighbouring Aquasplash and a funfair, Antibesland.

Eating and drinking

Among the **restaurants**, the one in the *Hôtel des Arcades* (closed Sun evening & Mon; 160F menu) is a very appealing combination of café, art gallery and resto with traditional Provençal cooking. *L'Auberge du Jarrier*, 30 passage de la Bourgade (☎04.93.65.11.68; menus from 240F; closed Tues & Wed lunchtime, plus Mon eve & Tues out of season), serves up Biot's best dinners.

Sophia-Antipolis

If Cap d'Antibes symbolizes the old wealth of land and business, then **SOPHIA-ANTIPOLIS** represents the diverse multi-billion dollar power of current multinationals. When labour and production can be shifted round the world, why not have your communications centre, your researchers and most skilled technicians, or just your most sophisticated inorganic intelligence, in the planet's most desirable corner, the hills above Antibes?

IBM, Wellcome, Toyota, Dow Chemicals and Air France are just a few of the hundreds of companies who have set up operations just west of Biot in this **industrial park** with a difference. A large expanse of forest has been cut by wide, smooth roads named after ancient greats in science, music and literature. Behind them lurk heavily fenced buildings that make the promenade hotels look like cottages. In the ground, miles of fibre-optic cable whizz moving images and electronic money back and forth. They say that productivity goes up in this environment. What's certain is that business income now outstrips tourism in the Côte d'Azur.

The park is expanding towards **Valbonne** and a rail line from Nice airport is being built. In the meantime, the only way to see it is with your own transport (signed off the D4 from Biot or from the Antibes highway exit). You can only admire the exterior shapes and facades of the extravagant buildings, some of which are spectacular.

Villeneuve-Loubet and Cagnes

Villeneuve-Loubet and **Cagnes** flash past on the speedy train and road connections between the conurbations of Cannes, Antibes and Nice. Glimpses in transit suggest these places are the direst consequence of late-twentieth-century coastal planning consents, but the seaside extensions have little to do with Cagnes and Villeneuve-Loubet proper. Both are worth a look: Villeneuve for its castle from the Middle Ages and place in culinary history; Cagnes for its wonderfully preserved medieval quarter and its artistic connections, with Renoir in particular.

Villeneuve-Loubet

Villeneuve-Loubet-Plage is dominated by a gigantic marina, constructed in the 1970s to a design by André Minangoy with petrified sails topped by vicious points, inescapably visible from Cap d'Antibes to Cap Ferrat. When the French government started to mind about the despoliation of the Côte d'Azur, apartments in this marina were changing hands for far too much for it to be knocked down. So there it stays, snubbing its nose at all the older artistry of this coast.

On the other side of the main road and highway, following the last stretch of the Loup River, you reach the tiny, quiet village of **VILLENEUVE-LOUBET** itself, grouped around its undamaged twelfth-century castle. The borders of the river are park and pastures and a stopover point for migrating birds.

The castle here, which was once François I's residence, is not open to the public, but you can visit the **Musée de l'Art Culinaire**, 3 rue Escoffier (Tues–Sun: summer 2–7pm; winter 2–6pm; closed Nov; 10F), in the house where a king of culinary arts was born in 1846. The son of a blacksmith, **Auguste Escoffier** began his career in restaurants aged thirteen, skivvying for his uncle in Nice. By the end of the century he had reached the top in a business the French value as much as design or art. In London he was the *Savoy*'s first head chef, then the *Carlton*'s, and had fed almost every European head of state. *Pêche melba* was his most famous and lasting creation, but his significance for the history of indulgent and expensive eating was in breaking with the tradition of health-hazard richness and quantity. He also showed concern for those who would never be his clients, publishing a pamphlet in 1910 proposing a system of social security to eliminate starvation and poverty.

It must be said that the Musée de l'Art Culinaire is of limited appeal – for a start there's nothing to eat. But there are videos of great chefs demonstrating recipes; extraordinary models made of sugar and flour and a portrait in chocolate; photographs of chefs and famous clients; menus, letters and bills; and the original kitchen of the house.

Cagnes

The various parts of **CAGNES** are somewhat confusing: the nondescript coastal district is known as **Cros-de-Cagnes**; **Cagnes-sur-Mer** is inland, above the *autoroute*, and constitutes the town centre; while **Haut-de-Cagnes**, the original medieval village, overlooks the town from the northwest heights. Cros-de-Cagnes has plenty of beach, and for horse fanatics there's racing from December to March and trotting in July and August at the Hippodrome on the seafront to the west of the resort. Cagnes-sur-Mer, pleasant enough as a bustling town, is only really notable for Renoir's house. Haut-de-Cagnes, however, has a stunning **castle** containing the fabulous **Donation Suzy Solidor** (see p.315) and a changing array of contemporary art.

Arrival and information

The **gare SNCF Cagnes-sur-Mer**, one stop from the gare SNCF Cros-de-Cagnes, is southwest of the centre alongside the *autoroute*. You need to turn right on the northern side of the *autoroute* along av de la Gare to reach the town centre. If you want to rent an ordinary **bike**, take the second right, rue Pasqualini, where you'll find Cycles et Cyclomoteurs Marcel at no. 5 (☎04.93.20.64.07) or the fifth right into rue du Logis where Location 2 Roux at no. 3 rents scooters and mountain bikes. The sixth turning on your right, rue des Palmiers, leads to the welcoming **tourist office** at 6 bd Maréchal-Juin (June to Sept Mon–Sat 9am–12.45pm & 3–7pm; rest of year Mon–Sat 8.30am–12.15pm & 2–6pm; ☎04.93.20.61.64).

Bd Maréchal-Juin, which becomes av de l'Hôtel-des-Postes and then av Mistral, is the main street, running parallel to av de la Gare, which becomes av Renoir. The central place de Gaulle lies between the two, and at the top, where av Renoir veers eastwards, place Bourdet is where you'll be dropped if you're arriving from Cannes or Nice by **bus**. From here bus #2 runs to the gare SNCF; bus #1 to Cros de Cagnes and the seafront; bus #4 to the Renoir museum; and bus #3 to Haut-de-Cagnes, a steep ascent along rue Général-Bérenger, which forks left at the end of av de la Gare and turns into montée de la Bourgade.

Accommodation

Cros-de-Cagnes has the greatest choice of **hotels**; two of the most economical are *La Caravelle*, 42 bd de la Plage (☎04.93.20.10.09; ①) on the seafront, and *Le Saratoga*, 111 av de Nice (☎04.93.31.05.70; ②) on the busy N7. If you have the budget, try the ultra-luxurious *Le Cagnard*, rue Sous Barri in Haut-de-Cagnes (☎04.93.20.73.21, fax 04.93.22.06.39; ⑨), the ancient guard room for the castle to which twentieth-century comforts have been added without touching the authentic medieval architecture and decor. Alternatively there are seven rooms at the less exciting but well-situated *Le Grimaldi*, 6 place du Château (☎04.93.20.60.24, fax 04.92.02.19.47; ③).

Campsites are not marvellous, though there are plenty of them. The four-star *Panoramer*, chemin des Gros-Buaux (☎04.93.31.16.15; closed Nov–March), about 1km northeast of Cagnes-sur-Mer, is expensive but well equipped. Less expensive are the two-star *La Rivière* at 168 chemin des Salles, 4km north of the town (☎04.93.20.62.27), and the two-star *Le Todos*, a similar distance out at 159 Vallon des Vaux (☎04.93.31.20.05; closed Nov–Jan).

Renoir's house

Les Collettes, the house that **Renoir** had built in 1908 and where he spent the last twelve years of his life, is now a memorial museum, the **Musée Renoir**, chemin des Collettes (Mon & Wed–Sun: May–Sept 10.30am–12.30pm & 1.30–6pm; Oct & late-Nov to April 10am–noon & 2–5pm; closed first 3 weeks of Nov; 20F), which you are free to wander around. You can also explore the olive and rare orange groves that surround it (same times as the museum). Renoir was captivated by the olive trees and by the difficulties of rendering "a tree full of colours"; remarking on how a gust of wind would change the tree's tonality, he said, "The colour isn't on the leaves, but in the spaces between them." One of the two studios in the house, north-facing to catch the late afternoon light, is arranged as if Renoir had just popped out. Despite the rheumatoid arthritis that had forced him to seek out a warmer climate than Paris, he painted every day at Les Collettes, strapping the brush to his hand when moving his fingers became too painful. There are portraits of him here by his closest friends: a painting by Albert André, *À Renoir Peignant*, showing the ageing artist hunching over his canvas; a bust by Aristide Maillol; and a crayon sketch by Richard Guido. Bonnard and Dufy were also visitors to Les Collettes and there are works of theirs here, including Dufy's *Homage to Renoir*, transposing a detail of *Moulin de la Galette*. Renoir himself is represented by several sculptures including two bronzes – *La Maternité* and a medallion of his son Coco – some beautiful, tiny watercolours in the studio, and ten paintings from his Cagnes period (the greatest, the final version of *Les Grandes Baigneuses*, hangs in the Louvre).

To **get to Les Collettes**, take bus #5 from place Bourdet or, on foot, follow av Renoir eastwards and turn left up passage Renoir; coming by bus from Antibes or Nice get off at Béat-Les Collettes.

Haut-de-Cagnes

HAUT-DE-CAGNES, a favourite haunt of successes in the contemporary art world, as well as those of decades past, lives up to everything dreamed of in a Riviera hilltop village: no architectural excrescences to spoil the perfection of tiers of tiny streets hanging on the rock, where the light shifts from brilliant sunshine to darkest shadow at every turn. Even the flowers spilling over earthenware pots or climbing the soft stone walls never seem to die or show the slightest defect.

The ancient village backs up to a crenellated feudal **château**, which houses the **Musée Méditerranéen d'Art Moderne**, the **Musée de l'Olivier** and the **Donation Suzy Solidor** (all: June–Sept daily 10am–noon & 2.30–6.30pm; Oct & mid-Nov to May Mon & Wed–Sun 10am–noon & 2–5pm; 20F). The castle's Renaissance interior is itself a masterpiece, with tiers of arcaded galleries, vast frescoed ceilings, stuccoed reliefs of historical scenes and gorgeously ornamented chambers and chapels. The **Donation Suzy Solidor** consists of wonderfully diverse portraits of the cabaret star, whose career in Paris and on the Côte spanned the 1920s to the 1970s; almost all the great painters of the period are represented. Suzy Solidor was quite a character: extremely talented, totally independent and immensely sexy. She declared herself a lesbian years before the word, let alone the preference, was remotely acceptable, and, incidentally, was the inspiration for the music-hall song "If you knew Suzy, like I know Suzy". The qualities that most endeared her to each artist, or the fantasies she provoked, are clearly revealed in every one of the canvases, giving a fascinating insight into the art of portraiture as well as a multi-faceted image of the woman. The stylistic signatures are apparent too: Dufy, Cocteau, Laurençin, Foujita, Friesz, Van Dongen and Kisling, among others.

Downstairs is a reconstruction of an olive mill and exhibitions concerning the importance of the olive to the region; whilst upstairs plays hosts to temporary exhibitions of modern art and, from the end of November to January, the *Festival International de la Peinture*. The latter is the big event of the year, with entries from forty-odd countries, representing highly disparate strands in painting. The selection is made by an august body, similar to Britain's Royal Academy.

Eating and drinking

Cagnes' best eating places are in Haut-de-Cagnes and Cros-de-Cagnes, and for café lounging, place du Château or place Grimaldi, to either side of the castle, are the obvious spots.

In Haut-de-Cagnes, montée de la Bourgade is the main **restaurant** street: *Restaurant des Peintres* at no. 71 (☎04.93.20.83.08; from 200F; closed Wed) has an excellent reputation; *Le Clap*, just off the street at 4 rue Hippolyte-Guis (☎04.92.02.06.28; one menu at 95F; closed Wed) serves very reasonably priced specialities from southwest France. *Le Cagnard* hotel has a predictably smart restaurant (☎04.93.20.73.21; menus from 300F; closed Nov–Easter) or there's *Josy-Jo*, 8 place Planastel (☎04.93.20.68.76; from 330F; closed Sat midday & Sun, first half of Aug & second half of Nov), with Provençal delicacies served in the space that served as Soutine's workshop in the inter-war years.

In Cros-de-Cagnes, a couple of places serve good seafood: *La Neptune* on rte du Bord de Mer (☎04.93.20.10.59; menus from 100F), and *La Villa du Cros* (☎04.93.07.57.83; menus from 90F; closed Sun & Mon evening out of season), on the port.

Nightlife

Haut-de-Cagnes is the centre of the town's **nightlife**. On place du Château is the famous (and expensive) *Jimmy's* restaurant and members-only piano-bar, where – if you can manage to get in – you can relax luxuriously amongst the *habitués*; the *terrasse* café-bar is open to everyone in the afternoon. *Le Vertigo*, on the opposite corner of the square, is a very reasonably priced **disco** but without much charm; *Le Quatre*, nearby, is a bit more expensive and much more lively (open from midnight). Haut-de-Cagnes also has a crowded calendar of cultural events, including free **jazz concerts** on place du Château in mid-July and a bizarre **square boules** competition on montée de la Bourgade at the beginning of August. The annual Fête de la Musique on June 21 is a fun, informal night of eclectic modern music and jazz where bands take over the town to entertain the crowds.

St-Paul-de-Vence

Further into the hills, halfway between Villeneuve-Loubet or Cagnes and Vence, lies the fortified village of **ST-PAUL-DE-VENCE**, home to the remarkable **Fondation Maeght** (daily: July–Sept 10am–7pm; rest of year 10am–12.30pm & 2.30–6pm; 40F, 50F during exhibitions), the artistic centre that most fully represents the link between the Côte d'Azur and modern European art. The foundation was created in the 1950s by Aimé and Marguerite Maeght, art collectors and dealers who knew all the great artists who worked in Provence. They commissioned the Spanish architect José Luis Sert, along with a number of the painters, sculptors, potters and designers who were on their books for the decoration. Both structure and ornamentation were conceived as a single project with the aim of creating a museum in which the concepts of entrance, exit and *sense de la visite* would not apply. It worked.

Once through the gates, any idea of dutifully checking off a catalogue of priceless museum pieces crumbles. Giacometti's *Cat* is sometimes stalking along the edge of the grass; Miró's *Egg* smiles above a pond and his totemed *Fork* is outlined against the sky. It's hard not be bewitched by the Calder mobile swinging over watery tiles, by Léger's flowers, birds and a bench on a sun-lit rough stone wall, by Zadkine's and Arp's metallic forms hovering between the pine trunks, or by the clanking tubular fountain by Pol Bury. And all this is just a portion of the garden.

The building itself is a superb piece of architecture: multi-levelled and flooded with daylight, with galleries opening on to terraces and courtyards, blurring the boundaries between inside and outside. The collection it houses – sculpture, ceramics, paintings and graphic art by Braque, Miro, Chagall, Léger, Kandinsky, Dubuffet, Bonnard, Dérain and Matisse, along with more recent artists and the young up-and-comings – is impressive. Not all the works are exhibited at any one time, however, and during the summer, when the main annual exhibition is mounted, the only ones on show are those that make up the decoration of the building.

There are several major **exhibitions** every year, from retrospectives to shows on contemporary themes, along with workshops by musicians or writers with strong links to the visual arts, concerts, theatre and dance, and films screened daily throughout the summer until mid-October.

The Nice–Vence **bus** that stops at place de Gaulle in Cagnes-sur-Mer has two stops in St-Paul; the Fondation, about one kilometre from the village itself, is signed from the second. By **car or bike**, follow the signs just before you reach the village, off the D7 from La-Colle-sur-Loup or the D2 from Villeneuve.

Vence and around

Set 10km back from the sea, and with abundant water and the sheltering Pre-Alpes behind, **VENCE** has always been a city of significance. Its Ligurian inhabitants, the Nerusii, put up stiff opposition to Augustus Caesar, but to no avail; Roman funeral inscriptions and votive offerings from the period remain embedded in the fabric of the old cathedral. In the Dark Ages of Visigoth and Ostrogoth invasions, the bishop of Vence, **Saint Véran** from the St-Honorat seminary, was as effective in organizing the defence of the city as in rebuilding its moral fabric. When he died in 481 he was canonized by popular request – in those days the democratic principle of *vox populi vox Dei* (the voice of the people is the voice of God) operated. But the people of Vence had no spiritual or temporal power to call on to save them from the Saracens who razed both the town and St-Véran's cathedral to the ground.

In the twelfth century the second patron saint of Vence, St-Lambert, took up residence at the same time as the baron **Romée de Villeneuve**, chief minister of Raymond Béranger IV, count of Provence. It was Villeneuve who arranged the powerful marriages of Béranger's four daughters, as part of his strategic scheming (see p.274). From then on, until the Revolution, Vence was plagued by rivalry between its barons and its bishops.

In the 1920s Vence became yet another haven for **painters and writers**, for André Gide, Paul Valéry, Soutine, Dufy and D.H. Lawrence (who died here, in 1930). Near the end of World War II **Matisse** moved to Vence to escape the Allied bombing of the coast and his legacy is the town's most famous building, the **Chapelle du Rosaire**, built under his design and direction. **Vieux Vence** too has its charms, with its ancient houses, gateways, fountains and chapels as well as the **St-Véran Cathedral**.

In late July or early August the open-air **Latin and World music festival** takes place. The festival attracts a high calibre of bands and its reputation is growing fast.

Arrival and information

From Cagnes-sur-Mer there are two **roads into Vence**. One enters the town as av Maréchal-Leclerc, leading straight up to the eastern end of the old walled city. The other, along with the roads from Grasse, St-Paul and the north, arrives at place du Maréchal-Juin and the two main avenues of the modern town, av de la Résistance and av des Poilus/Henri-Isnard. Coming by bus you'll be dropped at the **gare routière** on place du Grand-Jardin, next door to place du Frêne and the western gateway of Vieux Vence. On place du Grand-Jardin you'll find the **tourist office** (Mon–Sat 9am–noon & 2–6.30pm; ☎04.93.58.06.38) and Vence Motocycles for **bike rental**.

Accommodation

Vence has a good choice of **places to stay**, though as ever it would be as well to book ahead in the summer.

Hotels

Hôtel des Alpes, 2 av Général-Leclerc (☎04.93.58.13.30). On the eastern edge of Vieux Vence, rather down-at-heel, but friendly and the most economical option. Closed Nov; reception closed Sat pm and Sun. ①.

La Closerie des Genêts, 4 impasse Maurel, off av M-Maurel to the south of Vieux Vence (☎04.93.58.33.25, fax 04.93.58.78.50). Pleasant, peaceful rooms and very welcoming, with a fine restaurant and garden. Closed Sun eve. ③.

Diana, av des Poilus (☎04.93.58.28.56, fax 04.93.24.64.06). Modern building in a quiet location. ⑤.

La Provence, 9 av Marcellin-Maurel (☎04.93.58.04.21, fax 04.93.58.35.62). Decent value for the price, with a lovely garden. Closed mid-Jan to mid-Feb. ③.

La Roseraie, 14 av H-Giraud (☎04.93.58.02.20, fax 04.93.58.99.31). Classic, rich Provençal homestead with ancient cedars and magnolias overhanging the terrace on the road to the Col de Vence northwest of town. Charming reception and lovely pool in the garden. ⑤.

Auberge des Seigneurs, pl du Frêne (☎04.93.58.04.24). Just within Vieux Vence with rooms named after the painters who lodged there; the food is excellent. ④.

La Victoire, pl du Grand-Jardin (☎04.93.58.61.30, fax 04.93.58.74.68). Noisy but very central. ②.

Campsite

La Bergerie, rte de la Sine (☎04.93.58.09.36). Three-star site 3km west off the road to Tourrettes-sur-Loup. Closed mid-Oct to mid-March.

The Town

Vieux Vence has its fair share of chic boutiques and arty restaurants, but it also has an everyday feel about it with ordinary people going about their business, seeking out the best market deals, stopping for a chat and a *petit verre* at run-of-the-mill cafés. The **castle** and the **cathedral** are the two dominant buildings in this part of town; while **Matisse's chapel** (with its very limited opening hours) and the **Centre d'Art Vaa** both provide a welcome diversion in the modern town.

Vieux Vence

The 450-year-old ash tree that gives its name to **place du Frêne** stands in front of Vence's castle, the **Château de Villeneuve** (June to mid-Oct daily 10am–6pm; rest of year Tues–Sun 10am–12.30pm & 2–6pm; 25F), built just outside the city walls in a calm period of fifteenth-century expansion. It was rebuilt in the seventeenth century and renovated in 1992 to become a beautiful temporary exhibition space for the works of artists like Matisse, Dufy, Dubuffet and Chagall – all associated with the town – along with other modern and contemporary art.

The **Porte du Peyra** and its sheltering tower that adjoins the castle have remained more or less untouched from the twelfth century and provide the best entry into Vieux Vence. **Place du Peyra**, within the medieval walls, has the town's oldest fountain. The narrow, cobbled **rue du Marché** off to the right is a wonderfully busy street of tiny and delectable food shops, all with stalls; it is said to be one of the most expensive streets in France for food. Behind rue du Marché you'll find **place Clemenceau**, which centres on the cathedral and hosts the main Tuesday and Friday **market**, spilling into place Surian.

The **St-Véran Cathedral** is a tenth- and eleventh-century replacement for the church St-Véran presided over in the fifth century, which in turn was built on the ruins of a Roman temple to Mars and Cybele. Like so many of the oldest Provençal churches, it is basically square in shape, with an austere exterior which gives the appearance of monastic exclusion. Over the centuries bits have been demolished and other bits added, leaving none of the clear lines of Romanesque architecture. But with each project, including the initial construction, fragments of the Merovingian and Carolingian predecessor and Roman Vence were incorporated. In the chapel beneath the belfry two reliefs from the old church show birds, grapes and an eagle. More stone birds, flowers, swirls of leaves and interlocking lines are embedded in the walls and pillars throughout the church. Roman inscriptions from an aqueduct adorn the porch and more have found their way into the walls of the southwestern tower. The purported **tomb of St-Véran**, in the southern chapel nearest the altar, is a pre-Christian sarcophagus. St-Véran and his fellow patron saint of Vence, St-Lambert, survive in reliquary form in the neighbouring chapel. Of later adornments there are some superb, irreverent Gothic carved **choir stalls** that are housed alongside some powerfully human, if crude, polychrome wooden statues of the calvary, up above the western end of the nave (exhibited July to mid-Sept Mon–Fri & Sun 10.15am–12.30pm & 3.15–6.30pm). In the baptistry, a **Chagall mosaic** depicts the infant Moses being saved from the Nile by the Pharaoh's daughter. Church-as-museum devotees can have a field day examining all the treasures, but those who go for a sense of awesome space will probably be disappointed.

On the east side of the cathedral is **place Godeau**, almost totally medieval save for the column in the fountain that was given to the city, along with its twin on place du Grand-Jardin, by the Republic of Marseille some time in the third century. Rue St-Lambert and rue de l'Hôtel-de-Ville lead from place Godeau down to the original eastern gate, the **Porte du Signadour**, with another fifteenth-century fountain just outside on place Antony-Mars celebrating the town's expansion. In the thirteenth century the only other gate was the Portail Levis on the opposite corner of the city to Porte du Signadour.

The fountain on **place Vieille**, between the Portail Levis and the cathedral, was redesigned in 1572, this time to celebrate the town getting the better of both its feudal and spiritual lords. The town's bishop had been condemned as a heretic for his dablings with Protestantism. The people of Vence kicked him out not because of his the new religion but because he'd sold his seigneurial rights to Baron Villeneuve, who now had exclusive jurisdiction over them. Using the courts both of Rome and of Provence, the town acquired the illegally transferred rights itself. What is more, when the baron laid siege to Vence with Protestant troops in 1592, the town held out. The townspeople didn't like it when Rome sent a new envoy the same year, accepting him only after he had won the approval of the new king in 1594.

Matisse's Chapelle du Rosaire

Henri Matisse was never a Christian believer, though some have tried to explain the **Chapelle du Rosaire** at 466 av Henri-Matisse, the road to St-Jeannet from the Carrefour Jean-Moulin at the top of av des Poilus (Tues & Thurs 10–11.30am & 2.30–5.30pm; Sunday Mass 10am; closed Nov; additional openings during school holidays, check with tourist office), as a late-life conversion. "My only religion is the love of the work to be created, the love of creation, and great sincerity," he said in 1952, when he five-year project was completed.

A serious illness in 1941 had left Matisse an invalid. In August 1943, during his convalescence in Vence, where he was nursed by the Dominican sisters who were to involve him in the design of the chapel, he wrote to Louis Aragon: "I am an elephant, feeling, in my present frame of mind, that I am master of my fate, and capable of thinking that nothing matters for me except the conclusion of all these years of work, for which I feel myself so well equipped."

The artist moved back to his huge rooms in Nice in 1949 in order to work on the designs using the same scale as the chapel. There is a photograph of him in bed drawing studies for the figure of St-Dominic on the wall with a paintbrush tied to a long bamboo stick. It's not clear how much this bamboo technique was a practical solution to his frailty, and how much a solution to an artistic problem. According to some critics, Matisse wanted to pare down his art to the basic essentials of human communication, and to do this he needed to remove his own stylistic signature from the lines.

The drawings on the chapel walls – black outline figures on white tiles – succeed in this to the extent that many people are bitterly disappointed, not finding the "Matisse" they expect. The east wall is the most shocking; it shows the Stations of the Cross, each one numbered and scrawled as if it were an angry doodle on a pad. Matisse described the ceramic murals as "the visual equivalent of an open book where the white pages carry the signs explaining the musical part composed by the stained-glass windows". The full-length windows in the west and south walls are the aspect of the chapel most likely to live up to expectations. They are the only source of colour in the chapel, changing with the day's light through opaque yellow, transparent green and watery blue, and playing across the black and white murals, floor and ceiling.

Every part of the chapel is to Matisse's design (with some architectural input from Auguste Pérret): the high cross with oriental leanings on the roof; the brightly coloured silk vestments (still worn by the priest at Mass), chasubles, crucifix and candelabra; the layout of the chapel; the decoration on the floors, steps and roof. It is a total work and one with which Matisse was content. It was his "ultimate goal, the culmination of an intense, sincere and difficult endeavour".

The Centre d'Art VAAS and the Galerie Beaubourg

The **Centre d'Art VAAS**, 14 traverse des Moulins, just north of Vieux Vence (April–Sept Tues–Sat 9.30am–noon & 2.30–6pm; rest of year by appointment only, call ☎04.93.58.29.42 or fax 04.93.58.30.83; free), takes its name from the first letters of the

Latin words for truth, love, art and spirituality. You walk through a garden of sculptures into what was, from 1955 to 1970, Jean Dubuffet's studio. As well as a gallery of figurative art belonging to its founder, Marion Duteurtre, this is a space for artists to meet and work and for amateurs to learn techniques from practising artists.

Yet more art, this time by the likes of César, Klein, Arman, Ben, Tinguely and Warhol, are shown in temporary exhibitions at the **Galerie Beaubourg** in the Château Notre-Dame des Fleurs, halfway along the road from Vence to Tourrettes-sur-Loup (April–Sept Mon–Sat 11am–7pm; Oct–March Tues–Sat 11am–5.30pm; 30F).

Eating and drinking

You'll find plenty of **cafés** in the squares of Vieux Vence. *La Clemenceau* on place Clemenceau is well located, but you might find *Henri's Bar* on place de Peyra more congenial. *La Régence* on place du Grand-Jardin serves excellent coffee to sip beneath its stylish parasols. Rue du Marché is the place for **picnic** food; *Au Poivre d'Âne* at no. 12 specializes in **cheeses** and serves cheese dishes at the back.

Restaurants

Château Saint-Martin, rte de Coursegoules (☎04.93.58.02.02). Housed in a Templars' castle perching on a rock and complete with stunning views, this is the most extravagant and beautiful place to eat. Classic French food served with due pomp and ceremony. Weekday midday menu 300F, otherwise from 430F. Closed Wed out of season & Nov–March.

La Closerie des Genîts 4 impasse Maurel, off av M-Maurel to the south of Vieux Vence (☎04.93.58.33.25, fax 04.93.58.78.50). This hotel's restaurant is cosy, very welcoming and serves excellent food. Menus from 130F, from 95F for residents; closed Sun eve.

La Farigoule, 15 av Henri-Isnard (☎04.93.58.01.27). Not always brilliant food but a great atmosphere. Menus from 115F. Closed Fri.

Maximin Restaurant, 689 chemin de la Gaude (☎04.93.58.90.75). Gourmet cuisine from one of France's fabled chefs, Jacques Maximin, with menus starting from 250F, and rising steeply in price and indulgence.

Le Pêcheur du Soleil, 1 pl Godeau (☎04.93.58.32.56). An astounding choice of pizzas. Around 80F. Closed Fri lunchtime.

La Vieille Douve, 10 av Henri-Isnard (☎04.93.58.10.02). Lovely *terrasse* with a view of the zigzagging blue roof of the Chapelle du Rosaire. Menu 100F. Closed Thurs.

La Gaude and Tourrettes-sur-Loup

LA GAUDE, 3km due east of Vence but accessible by road only via St-Jeannet to the north, is a pleasant *village perché*. You can **stay** at the *Trois Mousquetaires* just outside the village on rte de St-Laurent (☎04.93.24.40.60, fax 04.92.11.07.99; ③) and **eat** delicious pasta at *La Romane*. The local **wine** is very good, though not easy to find; unfortunately there are only four or five vineyards, and they tend to produce wine for friends and family only.

TOURRETTES-SUR-LOUP, 6km west of Vence, is an artisans' paradise. The three towers from which the village derives it name plus the rose-stone houses which cling to the high escarpment, almost all date from the fifteenth century; the best views can be had from just above the town from the curious rock-shelf known as Les Loves. The Grande-Rue is lined with *ateliers* for sculpture, jewellery, weaving, pottery, olive-wood carvings, papier-mâché puppets, cushions, decorated doors and dressers, murals and a hundred other desirable and incredibly expensive designer household items.

The town is famous for its **violet festival**, held on the first Sunday after the harvest around early March, when floats are decorated with thousands of these blooms. Violets, which thrive in the mild microclimate, are grown here in vast quantities for the perfume trade as well as for subsidiary cottage industries such as old-fashioned candied violets.

Tourrettes' **tourist office** is at 2 rte de Vence (Mon–Sat 10am–1pm & 3–7pm; ☎04.93.24.18.93). If you are looking for somewhere to stay, a reasonable **hotel** to try is *La Grive Dorée*, 11 rte de Grasse (☎04.93.59.30.05, fax 04.93.59.28.66; ③) on the edge of the village. Local **campsites** include the three-star *La Camassade*, 523 rte de Pie Lombard (☎ & fax 04.93.59.31.54), about 3km along the road to Pont du Loup and, further on, the three-star *Les Rives du Loup*, rte de la Colle (☎ & fax 04.93.24.15.65; closed mid-Oct to March). For somewhere to **eat** that won't break the bank, try *Le Médiéval* at 6 Grande Rue (☎04.93.59.31.63; menu around 90F; closed Wed eve & Thurs), or *Le Petit Manoir* at 21 Grande Rue (☎04.93.24.19.19; weekday menu around 100F, otherwise from 150F; closed Sun eve & Wed).

Nice

The capital of the Riviera and fifth-largest town in France, **NICE** lives off its glittering reputation. In the eighteenth century Russian and English aristocrats built their mansions here. Today, as well as the annual influx of tourists, a high proportion of the city's population is made up of *rentiers* and retired people of all nationalities; their dividends and pensions all contributing to the city's startlingly high ratio of per capita income to economic activity.

Politics here is decidedly right-wing, with a monopoly of municipal power being held for decades by a dynasty, whose corruption was finally exposed in 1990 when Mayor Jacques Médecin fled to Uruguay; he was later extradited and jailed. Despite some 400 million francs of taxpayers' money having disappeared, public opinion remained in his favour. From his Grenoble prison cell, Médecin, who had twinned Nice with Cape Town during the height of South Africa's apartheid regime, backed Jacques Peyrat, the former *Front National* member and close friend of Jean-Marie Le Pen, in the 1995 local elections. Peyrat won with ease.

Though it has all the usual drawbacks of the Côte resorts, Nice manages to be delightful. The sun and the sea and the laid-back, affable Niçois cover a multitude of sins. A thousand sprinklers keep the grass lush in the numerous green spaces of the city as temperatures soar into the thirties. Fountains ease the harshness of new prestige developments and every park is full of flowers. Along the famous seafront the frayed but sturdy palms survive against all odds the fumes of speeding cars. On summer nights the old town buzzes with contented crowds. It's very hard not to love Nice.

Recent architectural aberrations apart, the city has retained its historical styles almost intact: the medieval rabbit warren of **Vieux Nice**, the Italianate facades of **modern Nice** and the rich exuberance of **fin-de-siècle residences** dating from when the city was Europe's most fashionable winter retreat. It has also retained mementoes from its ancient past, when the Romans ruled the region from here, and earlier still, when the Greeks founded the city. Nice's **museums** are a treat for art lovers with the **Musée Matisse**, the **Musée d'Art Moderne**, the **Musée des Beaux-Arts**, **Musée Dufy**, Chagall's **Message Biblique** and the numerous private and municipal art galleries with their changing exhibitions. A great many of the artists represented by these collections have a direct connection to the city.

Arrival, information and city transport

From terminal 1 at the **airport**, several buses run to the city: one to the junction of av Gustav V and the promenade des Anglais, and on to the gare routière (every 20min; 22F); two other services connect with the SNCF gare – a fast shuttle (15min; 26F) and

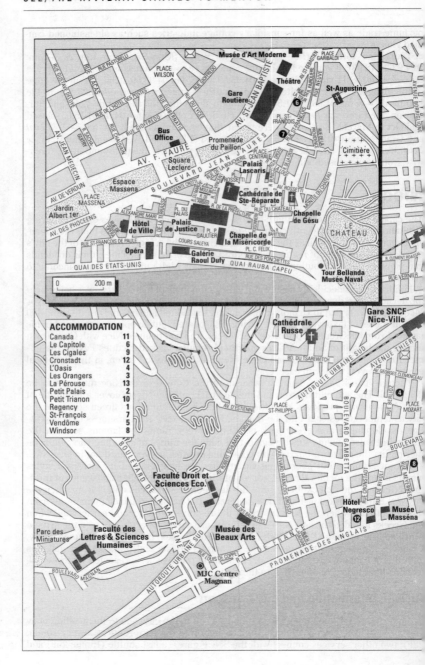

ACCOMMODATION
Canada	11
Le Capitole	6
Les Cigales	9
Cronstadt	12
L'Oasis	4
Les Orangers	3
La Pérouse	13
Petit Palais	2
Petit Trianon	10
Regency	1
St-François	7
Vendôme	5
Windsor	8

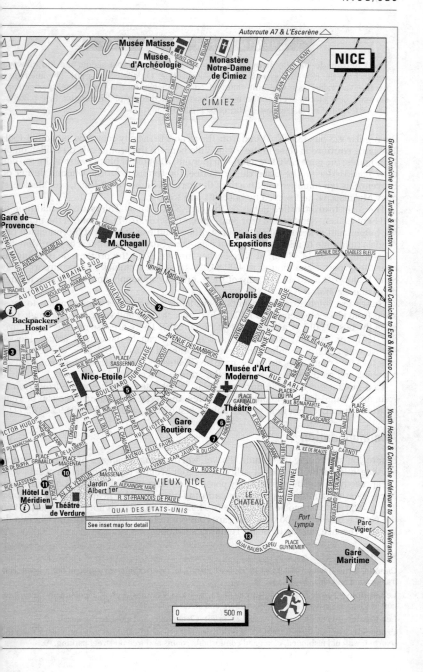

Autoroute A7 & L'Escarène △

NICE

Musée Matisse

Musée
d'Archéologie

Monastère
Notre-Dame
de Cimiez

CIMIEZ

Gare de
Provence

Musée
M. Chagall

Palais des
Expositions

AVENUE DES DIABLES BLEUS ▷

Tunnel Mariaux

Acropolis

Backpackers'
Hostel

Nice-Etoile

Musée d'Art
Moderne

Gare
Routière

Théâtre

VICTOR HUGO

Hôtel Le
Méridien

Théâtre
de Verdure

Jardin
Albert 1er

VIEUX NICE

LE
CHATEAU

Port
Lympia

Parc
Vigier

Gare
Maritime

See inset map for detail

QUAI DES ETATS-UNIS

Grand Corniche to La Turbie & Menton ▷

Moyenne Corniche to Eze & Monaco ▷

Youth Hostel & Corniche Inférieure to ▷ Villefranche

N

0   500 m

CHEMIN DE FER DE PROVENCE

The **Chemin de Fer de Provence** runs one of France's most scenic and fun railway routes from the new station on Nice's rue Alfred-Binet (4 daily; 3hr 15min). The line runs up the Var valley into the hinterland of Nice, and climbs through some spectacular scenery, past places such as the tremendous fortified town of **Entrevaux** (see p.368), before terminating at **Digne-les-Bains** (see p.373).

the regular #23 bus (8.50F). A **taxi** from the airport to the city centre costs around 150F. The **gare routière** is close to the Vieille Ville beneath the promenade du Paillon on bd Jean-Jaurès; the **gare SNCF** is a little further out, a couple of blocks west of the top end of av Jean-Médecin. The **Gare de Provence**, the terminus for the Chemin de Fer de Provence, is ten minutes' walk north of the gare SNCF on rue A-Binet, one block east of av Malaussena, and served by buses #4 and #5.

The main **tourist office** is beside the gare SNCF on av Thiers (daily: mid-June to mid-Sept 7.30am–8pm; rest of year 8am–7pm; ☎04.93.87.07.07). It's one of the most useful, helpful and generous of Côte tourist offices and has annexes at 5 promenade des Anglais (mid-June to mid-Sept Mon–Sat 8am–8pm, Sun 9am–1pm; rest of year Mon–Sat 9am–6pm; ☎04.92.14.48.00); at Nice-Ferber further along the promenade des Anglais near the airport (same hours; ☎04.93.83.32.64); and at terminal 1 of the airport (daily 8am–10pm; ☎04.93.21.44.11). Any of these offices can supply you with a free listings magazine, *Le Mois à Nice*.

Buses are frequent and run until about 9pm, with four services running to most areas from place Masséna until 1.10am. Fares are flat rate and you can buy a single ticket on the bus (8.50F) or a *carnet* of ten tickets (68F). There are also one-day (22F), five-day (85F) or weekly passes (110F), all of which can be bought at *tabacs*, kiosks, newsagents and from Sunbus, the transport office at 10 av Félix-Faure, where you can pick up a free route map. From the gare SNCF buses #12 and #15 will take you to place Masséna and on the short distance to the Sunbus office (stop Félix-Faure).

Taxi fares are reasonable during the day; night rates, which operate from 7pm to 7am, are around 10F per kilometre. **Bicycles**, **mopeds** and **motorbikes** can be rented from Nicea Location Rent at 9 av Thiers, just by the gare SNCF (☎04.93.82.42.71).

Accommodation

Before you start doing the rounds, it's well worth taking advantage of the **reservation service** offered by the tourist office. The area around the train station teems with cheap, seedy hotels, but it's perfectly possible to find reasonably priced rooms in Vieux Nice, even in summer. Options for **camping** are poor: the nearest site is *Camping Terry*, 768 rte de Grenoble St-Isodore (☎04.93.08.11.58), 6.5km north of the airport on the N202 – take bus #700 from the gare routière to La Manda stop, or the Chemin de Fer de Provence railway to Bellet-Tennis des Combes.

Hotels

Canada, 8 rue Halévy (☎04.93.87.98.94, fax 04.93.87.17.12). Nothing very special but a good, central location and close to the sea. ④.

Le Capitole, 4 rue de la Tour (☎04.93.80.08.15, fax 04.93.85.10.58). A good, if potentially noisy, location in Vieux Nice with a warm atmosphere and small rooms. ④.

Les Cigales, 16 rue Dalpozzo (☎04.93.88.33.75). Clean, quiet and close to the beach. ②.

Cronstadt, 3 rue Cronstadt (☎04.93.82.00.30, fax 04.93.16.87.40). Hidden away one block from the seafront, with old-fashioned, clean and comfortable rooms and free on-street parking. ④.

L'Oasis, 23 rue Gounod (☎04.93.88.12.29, fax 04.93.16.14.40). In a quiet part of town, not far from the station. Small rooms, but comfortable. ⑤.

Les Orangers, 10 bis av Durante (☎04.93.87.51.41, fax 04.93.82.57.82). A good budget option, particularly popular with American students. Closed Nov. ②.

La Pérouse, 11 quai Rauba-Capeu (☎04.93.62.34.63, fax 04.93.62.59.41). A wonderful location at the foot of Le Château with views across the bay. Very comfortable and spacious. ⑦.

Petit Palais, 10 av Émile-Bieckert (☎04.93.62.19.11, fax 04.93.62.53.60). Turn-of-the-century mansion on the heights of Cimiez. Quiet and very comfortable. ⑤.

Petit Trianon, 11 rue Paradis (☎04.93.87.50.46). A fairly basic, friendly hotel close to place Masséna and the Vieille Ville. ②.

Regency, 2 rue St-Siagre (☎04.93.62.17.44, fax 04.93.92.23.26). Good-value, self-contained studio apartments for up to four people run by a friendly, helpful manager. Near station, but quiet. ②.

St-François, 3 rue St-François (☎04.93.85.88.69). On a busy pedestrian thoroughfare in the Vieille Ville, above a restaurant hosting live jazz on Fri nights. Close to the gare routière, and an ideal base if you're not bothered by the noise or the rather depressing, basic amenities. ②.

Vendôme, 26 rue Pastorelli (☎04.93.62.00.77, fax 04.93.13.40.78). A very handsome building. Excellent service. ⑦.

Windsor, 11 rue Dalpozzo (☎04.93.88.59.35, fax 04.93.88.94.57). Where the stars of Truffaut's *Day for Night* were filmed having their off-set hysterics. Chinoiserie in the foyer and a swimming pool in the verdant courtyard at the back. ⑥.

Hostels

Backpacker's Hotel, 32 rue Pertinax (☎04.93.80.30.72). Close to station, with kitchen facilities and no curfew.

Clairvallon Relais International de la Jeunesse, 26 av Scudéri (☎04.93.81.27.63, fax 04.93.53.35.88). Slightly cheaper than the youth hostel but 10km north of the centre and with a 10.30pm curfew. Location apart, it's pleasantly informal and has a pool; take bus #15 or #25 (stop Scudéri). Reception closes 6pm.

HI youth hostel, rte Forestière du Mont-Alban (☎04.93.89.23.64). Four kilometres out of town and not a lot cheaper than sharing a hotel room. Take bus #14 from pl Masséna (direction pl du Mont-Boron, stop L'Auberge); the last bus from the centre leaves at 7.30pm. Curfew 11.30pm. Reception 7–10am & 5–11pm.

MJC Magnan, 31 rue Louis-de-Coppet (☎04.93.86.28.75, fax 04.93.44.93.22). This is the least expensive of the hostel options: not too far from the centre and close to the beach. Take bus #3, #9, #10, #12, #22 or #23 (stop Magnan). Closed mid-Sept to mid-June.

The City

It doesn't take long to get a feel for the layout of **Nice**. Shadowed by mountains that curve down to the Mediterranean east of its port, it still breaks up more or less into old and new. Vieux Nice groups beneath the hill of **Le Château**, its limits signalled by boulevard Jean-Jaurès, built along the course of the **River Paillon**. Along the seafront, the celebrated **promenade des Anglais** runs for 5km until forced to curve inland by

---

MUSEUM CHARGES

Up until the end of 1995 most of Nice's museums had free **admission**. The decision, made in 1996, to charge for entry reflected the city's financial troubles since Médecin's embezzling reign. New rates are approximately 25F per museum, with free entrance on the first Sunday of each month, but it makes much better sense to purchase the 40F **seven-day pass**, which is valid for all the city's museums, with the exception of the Musée Chagall.

the runways of the airport. The central square, **place Masséna**, is at the bottom of the modern city's main street, **avenue Jean-Médecin**, while off to the north is the exclusive hillside suburb of **Cimiez**.

Le Château

For initial orientation, with brilliant sea and city views, fresh air, a cooling waterfall and the scent of Mediterranean vegetation, the best place to head for is the park of **Le Château** (daily: June–Aug 9am–8pm; April, May & Sept 9am–7pm; rest of year 10am–5.30pm). There's no château; the city's fortress was destroyed by the French in the early eighteenth century when Nice belonged to Savoy. But this is where Nice began as the ancient Greek city of Nikea: hence the mosaics and stone vases in mock Grecian style. Excavations have revealed Greek and Roman levels beneath the foundations of the city's first, eleventh-century cathedral on the eastern side of the summit. Rather than ruin-spotting, however, the real pleasure here lies in looking down on the scrambled rooftops and gleaming mosaic tiles of Vieux Nice, on the yachts and fishing boats in the port on the eastern side, along the sweep of the promenade des Anglais, and of course at the sea itself in the smooth arc of the Bay of Angels between Antibes and the rock on which you stand. At the top of the hill a viewing platform points out the direction of St Petersburg among other places. In the cemetery to the north of the park are buried the two great Niçois revolutionaries, Giuseppe Garibaldi and Léon Gambetta.

To reach the park, you can either take the lift by the **Tour Bellanda**, at the eastern end of quai des États-Unis – which also houses a small **naval museum** (Wed–Sun 10am–noon & 2–5pm; 15F) – or climb the steps from rue de la Providence or rue du Château in Vieux Nice.

Vieux Nice

Only a handful of years ago, any ex-pat or police officer would tell you that **Vieux Nice** was a dangerous place, brimming with drug-pushers, "dark-skinned" muggers and car thieves. That was always a gross exaggeration, but it still reveals how much the *quartier* has changed of late. In the early 1980s, a process of gentrification started with the renovation of low-rent apartments. Rents then went up and the first batch of old residents were moved out to high-rise hutches on the city's perimeter. Then the town hall moved in on the private sector, giving itself first option on any property for sale, on the grounds that it could then ensure renovation. In practice, what it ensured was more money for the municipal – or more particularly Médecin's – coffers, higher prices and a selection process of would-be buyers. The Arab, Chinese and other ethnic communities are now almost entirely absent from Vieux Nice. A few of the old residents still remain, however; co-existing with the glitzier places are little hardware stores selling brooms and bottled gas, clothes lines are strewn high across the streets and tiny cafés are packed with blue-overalled men.

The streets of Vieux Nice are too narrow for buses and, though the natives insist on driving round and round looking for parking space, it's an area made for walking. The central square is **place Rossetti** where the soft-coloured Baroque **Cathédrale de St-Réparate** (daily 8am–7pm) just manages to be visible from the eight narrow streets which meet here. There are cafés to relax in, with the choice of sun or shade, and a magical ice-cream parlour, *Fenocchio*, with an extraordinary choice of flavours. Head to the neighbouring **place du Palais de Justice** on a Saturday, and you'll be able to browse through a jumble of old paintings, books and postcards.

The real magnet of Vieux Nice is the **cours Saleya** and adjacent places Pierre-Gautier and Charles-Félix. These wide-open, sun-lit spaces, lined with grandiloquent municipal buildings and Italianate chapels, are the site of the city's main **market** (Tues–Sun 6am–1pm), where there are gorgeous displays of fruit, vegetables, cheeses and sausages – along with cut flowers and potted roses, mimosa and other scented plants till 5.30pm. On Monday the stalls sell bric-à-brac and secondhand clothes. On summer nights café and restaurant tables fill the *cours*.

A collection of exotic shells is displayed in the **Galerie de Malacologie** at 2 cours Salaya (Tues–Sat 10.30am–1pm & 2–6pm). Equally alluring is the display of different flavoured olive oils, soaps, dried fruit and flowers at Aux Allées de la Côte d'Azur, 1 rue St-François-de-Paule. Further up the street, which runs west from the *cours*, is the suitably grand *belle époque* **Opéra**. While on the north side of Vieux Nice, the narrow **rue du Marché** and its continuations – rue de la Boucherie, rue du Collet, rue St-François-de-Paule and rue Pairolière – have the atmosphere of a covered market, lined with food stores and invitingly laid out clothes, with special offers and sales year-round. The diminutive **fish market** is in place St-François (Tues–Sun 6am–1pm), its odours persisting till late at night when all the old streets are hosed down with enough water to go paddling.

The light and joyous art of Raoul Dufy can be seen at the **Musée Dufy/Galerie des Ponchettes** between cours Saleya and the sea at 77 quai des États-Unis (Tues–Sat 10am–noon & 2–6pm, Sun 2–6pm; 15F, or 25F combined ticket with Musée Mossa). Temporary exhibitions, changing every three months, display the town's considerable collection of Dufy's works, many of which were painted in Nice. Nearby, at 59 quai des États-Unis, is the less appealing collection of the **Musée Alexis et Gustav Adolf Mossa** (Tues–Sat 10am–noon & 2–6pm, Sun 2–6pm; 15F, or 25F with Musée Dufy), both figures of the Nice establishment. Alexis initiated the Carnival and painted it in vapid watercolours; his son Gustav, who died in 1971, produced lurid symbolist paintings that reek of misogyny.

If you want to feast your eyes on Baroque splendour, pop into the **chapels** and **churches** of Vieux Nice: La Chapelle de la Miséricorde on cours Saleya (open for Sunday Mass 10.30am and by contacting the Palais Lascaris); L'Église du Gesú on rue Droite (9am–6pm); or L'Église St-Augustine on place St-Augustine (open for Mass Sat 4pm & Sun 9am), which contains a fine *Pietà* by Louis Bréa. For contemporary graphic and photographic art some of the best **art galleries** in Vieux Nice include Espace Sainte Réparate, 4 rue St-Réparate (Tues–Sat 10.30am–1pm & 2–6pm; free), a municipal gallery that loans out works to schools and institutions; Galerie Municipale Renoir, 8 rue de la Loge on the corner of rue Droite (same hours; free); and, diagonally opposite at 14 rue Droite, the Galerie du Château/Espace Photographique Quinto Albicocco (same hours; free).

Also on rue Droite, at no. 15, is the **Palais Lascaris** (Tues–Sun 10am–noon & 2–6pm; closed Nov; 25F), an extravagantly decorated, seventeenth-century palace built by a family whose arms, engraved on the ceiling of the entrance hall, bear the motto "Not even lightning strikes us". It's all very noble, with frescoes, tapestries and chandeliers, along with a collection of porcelain vases from an eighteenth-century pharmacy.

Place Masséna and the course of the Paillon

The stately, red-ochre **place Masséna** is the hub of the new town, built in 1835 across the path of the River Paillon, with good views north past fountains and palm trees to the mountains. A balustraded terrace and steps on the south of the square lead to Vieux Nice; the new town lies to the north. It's a pretty and spacious expanse, without being very significant – the only thing of interest here are the sundry ice-cream vendors who shelter their goods under the arcades during summer. To the west, the **Jardins Albert-1er** lead down to the promenade des Anglais, where the Théâtre de Verdure hosts concerts and theatre.

The covered course of the Paillon to the north of place Masséna has provided the sites for the city's more recent municipal prestige projects. At their worst, up beyond traverse Barla, they take the form of giant packing crates for high-tech goods, in the multi-media, mega-buck conference centre called the **Acropolis**. Though theoretically it is a public building, with exhibition space, a cinema and bowling alley (11am–2am), international business often limits casual entry.

Downstream from the Acropolis is the vast, futuristic 1980s monument to the ambitions of the city's former leader, composed of four towers clad with streaky marble and linked by glass-panelled steel girders. The **Musée d'Art Moderne et d'Art Contemporain** or MAMAC (Mon & Wed–Sun 10am–6pm; 25F) has a rotating exhibition of its collection of the avant-garde French and American movements of the 1960s to the present. **Pop Art** highlights include Lichtenstein cartoons and Warhol's Campbell's soup tin, while the **French New Realists** are represented in Arman's *The Birds II* – a flock of flying wrenches – and Yves Klein's two massive sculptures, *Wall of Fire* and *Garden of Eden*, along with works by other members of the school, including César, Spoerri, Christo, Jean Tinguely. The **Supports-Surfaces** group, led by Alocco, Bioulès and Viallat, take paintings themselves as objects, concentrating on the frame, the texture of the canvas, and so on, and there are also sections on the **Fluxus International** artists like Ben, who were into "Happenings", street life and graffiti. The collection also includes American Abstractionists and Minimalists, and the 1980s return to figurative art. It's a very masculine collection, and leaves you feeling sometimes that the works are little more than sterile by-products of the various intellectual theories upheld by the different schools, but it's good fun nonetheless, with huge, light galleries that are hardly ever crowded.

The modern city centre

Running north from place Masséna, **avenue Jean-Médecin** is the city's main **shopping** street, named after a former mayor, the father of corrupt mayor Jacques Médecin. The late nineteenth-century architecture and trees don't distinguish it from any other big French city high street; the cafés are not particularly inviting; the cinemas show predictable blockbusters; street stalls sell overpriced bags and costume jewellery; and the traffic fumes have no escape. The Nice-Étoile shopping complex between rue Biscarra and bd Dubouchage has all the mainstream chains, and you'll find other big department stores along the street.

Couturier shops are concentrated west of place Masséna on rue du Paradis and av de Suède. Both streets lead to the pedestrianized **rue Masséna** and the end of **rue de France** where tourists congregate. It's filled with hotels, bars, restaurants, ice-cream and fast-food outlets, with no regard for quality or style. Skirting this, the chief interest in the modern town is in the older architecture: eighteenth- and nineteenth-century Italian Baroque and Neoclassical, florid *belle époque*, and unclassifiable exotic aristo-fantasy. The trophy for the most gilded, exotic and elaborate edifice must go to the early twentieth-century **Russian Orthodox Cathedral**, beyond the train station, at the end of av Nicolas II, off bd Tsaréwitch (summer 9am–noon & 2.30–6pm; winter 9.30am–noon & 2.30–5pm; closed Sun morning; 15F), reached by bus #14 or #17 (stop Tsaréwitch).

The promenade des Anglais

The point where the Paillon flows into the sea marks the beginning of the famous palm-fringed **promenade des Anglais**, which began as a coastal path created by nineteenth-century English residents for their afternoon's sea-breeze stroll. Today it's the city's unofficial high-speed racetrack, bordered by some of the most fanciful architecture on the Côte d'Azur.

Past the first promenade building, the glittery Casino Ruhl, is the 1930s Art Deco facade of the **Palais de la Méditerranée**, all that remains of the original municipal casino, closed due to intrigue and corruption, and finally demolished. A commercial centre is being constructed behind the old facade. Nearby, at 2 rue Congrès, the art gallery Ferraro has a permanent collection of New Realists – Ben, César, Arman and Yves Klein.

The most celebrated of all the promenade buildings is the opulent **Negresco Hotel** at no. 37, filling up the block between rues de Rivoli and Cronstadt, built in 1906, and one of the great surviving European palace-hotels, where self-made millionaires rubbed shoulders with royalty. During the day you could try to wander in past the flunkies in ludicrous operatic dress to take a look at the Salon Louis XIV and the Salon Royale, but unless you are deemed to be wearing *tenue correcte*, you will be stopped; the dress-code is stricter still in the evening. The Salon Louis XIV, on the left of the foyer, has a seventeenth-century painted oak ceiling and mammoth fireplace plus royal portraits that have all come from various French châteaux. The Salon Royale in the centre of the hotel is a vast colonnaded oval room with a dome built by Gustav Eiffel's workshops. The stucco and cornices are decorated with 24-carat gold leaf, the carpet is the largest ever made by the Savonnerie factory and the bill for it accounted for a tenth of the total cost of the hotel. The chandelier is one of a pair commissioned from Baccarrat by Tsar Nicholas II – the other hangs in the Kremlin. You can also take a peep at *La Rotonde*, the smaller of the hotel's two restaurants, all done up as a childhood fantasy with carousel horses, cupids and puppets beneath a chandelier of grapes and a ceiling of circus scenes. Also within the hotel, with an entrance on rue de Rivoli, is the Gye Jacquot art gallery, which specializes in Impressionists and Post-Impressionists. You don't have to be a potential buyer to have a look.

Just before the Negresco, with its entrance at 65 rue de France, is the **Musée Masséna** (April–Sept Tues–Sun 10am–noon & 2–6pm; Oct–March closes 5pm), a rather lacklustre historical museum, with sections on Garibaldi, who fought against oppression in Italy, France, Brazil and Uruguay; the 1860 plebiscite in 1860 on Nice becoming part of France; plus the usual Napoleana – busts, drawings and paintings – and medieval artworks and bits and pieces from just about every other era.

A kilometre or so down the promenade and a couple of blocks inland at 33 av des Baumettes, in a house built by a Ukrainian princess in 1878, is the **Musée des Beaux-Arts** (Tues–Sun 10am–noon & 2–6pm; 25F) reached by bus #38 (stop Chéret). It has rather too many whimsical canvases by Jules Chéret, who died in Nice in 1932, a great many *belle époque* paintings, a room dedicated to Van Loos, plus modern works such as a bust of Victor Hugo by Rodin and some very amusing Van Dongens, including the *Archangel's Tango*. Works by Monet, Sisley and Degas also grace the walls.

The **Musée International d'Art Naïf Anatole Jakovsky** is behind the promenade and the expressway a further kilometre west in the Château Ste-Hélène, av Val-Marie (Mon & Wed–Sun 10am–noon & 2–6pm; 25F), reached by bus #9, #10 or #12 (stop Fabron), then bus #34 (stop Art Naïf). The six hundred examples of the genre here from the eighteenth century to the present day include works by Vivin, Rimbert, Bauchant and the Yugoslavian masters of the art, Yvan, Generaliã and Laakoviã.

Not far from here, halfway between the city and the airport on bd Impératrice-Eugénie is the **Musée des Trains Miniatures**, which consists of model train sets with all the scenery and rolling stock from steam to TGV (daily 9.30am–5.30pm; 30F; bus #22). Right out by the airport is a vast tourist attraction, the **Phoenix Parc Floral de Nice**, 405 promenade des Anglais (Tues–Sun: April–Sept 9am–7pm; Oct–March 9am–5pm; closed Jan; 45F; exit St-Augustin from the highway or bus #9, #10 or #23 from Nice). It's a cross between botanical gardens, bird and insect zoo, and theme park: a curious jumble of automated dinosaurs and mock Maya temples, alpine streams, ginkgo trees, butterflies and cockatoos. The greenhouse full of fluttering butterflies is the star attraction.

The beaches and the port

Though mostly public and with showers provided, the **beach** below the promenade des Anglais is all pebbles, not particularly clean and riddled with broken glass. You're better off heading for the small, secluded **Plage de Païola**, on the west side of Le

Château, below the sea wall of the port with big blocks of concrete to sunbathe on and a little café for drinks and ice creams. But the best, and cleanest, place to swim, if you don't mind rocks, is the string of coves beyond the port that starts with the **Plage de la Réserve** opposite Parc Vigier (bus #32 or #3). From the water you can look up at the nineteenth-century fantasy palaces built onto the steep slopes of the Cap du Nice.

The **port**, flanked by gorgeous red-ochre eighteenth-century buildings and headed by the Neoclassical Notre-Dame du Port, is full of bulbous yachts but has little quay-side life despite the restaurants along quai Lunel.

Cimiez

Nice's northern suburb, **Cimiez**, has always been a posh place. Its principal streets, av des Arènes-de-Cimiez and bd de Cimiez, rise between plush, high-walled villas to what was the social centre of the town's elite some 1700 years ago, when the city was capital of the Roman province of Alpes-Maritimes. Part of a small amphitheatre still stands, and excavations of the Roman baths have revealed enough detail to distinguish the sumptuous and elaborate facilities for the top tax official and his cronies from the plainer public baths and a separate complex for women. The **archeological site** is overlooked by the impressive, modern **Musée d'Archéologie**, on rue Monte-Croce, which displays all the finds and illustrates the city's history up to the Middle Ages (Tues–Sun: April–Sept 10am–noon & 2–6pm, Oct–March 10am–1pm & 2–5pm; 25F); take bus #15, #17, #20 or #22 to the Les Arènes stop.

The seventeenth-century villa between the excavations and the amphitheatre is the **Musée Matisse**, 164 av des Arènes (Mon & Wed–Sun: April–Sept 10am–6pm; Oct–March 10am–5pm; 25F). Matisse spent his winters in Nice from 1916 onwards, staying in hotels on the promenade – from where he painted *Storm over Nice* – and then from 1921 to 1938 renting an apartment overlooking place Charles-Félix. It was in Nice that he painted his most sensual, colour-flooded canvases featuring models as oriental odalisques posed against exotic draperies. In 1942, when he was installed with his tropical birds and plants in the *Régina* palace-hotel in Cimiez, he said that if he had gone on painting in the north "there would have been cloudiness, greys, colours shading off into the distance". As well as the Mediterranean light, Matisse loved the cosmopolitan aspect of Nice, the rococo salons of the hotels, the times he spent rowing at the Club Nautique, the Carnival, and the presence of fellow artists Renoir, Bonnard and Picasso in neighbouring towns. He returned to the *Régina* from his stay in Vence in 1949, having developed his solution to the problem of "drawing in colour" by cutting out shapes and putting them together as collages or stencils. Almost all his last works in Nice were these cut-out compositions, with an artistry of line showing how he could wield a pair of scissors with just as much strength and delicacy as a paintbrush. He died in Cimiez in November 1954, aged 85.

The museum's collection includes work from every period, a great number of drawings and an almost complete set of his bronze sculptures. There are sketches for one of the *Dance* murals; models for the Vence chapel plus the priests' robes he designed; book illustrations including those for a 1935 edition of Joyce's *Ulysses*; and excellent examples of his cut-out technique, of which the most delightful are *The Bees* and *The Creole Dancer*. Among the paintings are the 1905 portrait of Madame Matisse; *Storm over Nice* (1919–20) which seems to get wetter and darker the further you step back from it; *Odalisque Casquette Rouge* from the place Charles-Félix years; the 1947 *Still Life with Pomegranates*; and one of his two earliest attempts at oil painting, *Still Life with Books* painted in 1890.

The Roman remains and the Musée Matisse back onto an old **olive grove**, one of the best open spaces in Nice and venue for the July **jazz festival** (see p.334). At its eastern end on place du Monastère is the **Monastère Notre-Dame de Cimiez** (church daily 8am–12.30pm & 3–7pm), with a pink flamboyant Gothic facade of nineteenth-century origin topping a much older and plainer porch. Inside there's more gaudiness, reflecting the rich benefactors the Franciscan order had access to, but also three masterpieces of medieval art: a *Pietà* and *Crucifixion* by Louis Bréa and a *Deposition* by Antoine Bréa. Adjoining the church is **Musée Franciscain** (Mon–Sat 10am–noon & 3–6pm; free), which paints a picture of the mendicant friars and relates some of the gruesome fates that befell early martyrs in the course of their evangelical missions. The sixteenth-century **monastic buildings** (guided tours Mon–Fri 10.30am, 3.30pm & 4.30pm) include two cloisters, the sacristy and the oratory, which has extraordinary murals above the heavy wood panelling full of alchemical symbols. You can see a copy of a 1687 engraving of Nice viewed from the monastery **garden** (to which there's public access), showing the walled city with its fortress and fields leading up from the River Paillon to Cimiez. To the north of the monastery is the **cemetery** where Matisse and Raoul Dufy are buried.

At the foot of Cimiez hill, just off bd Cimiez on av du Docteur-Menard, **Chagall's Biblical Message** is housed in a perfect custom-built museum (Mon & Wed–Sun: July–Sept 10am–6pm; rest of year 10am–5pm; 30F, 38F during the summer exhibition; bus #15, stop Musée Chagall) opened by the artist in 1972. The rooms are light, white and cool, with windows allowing you to see the greenery of the garden beyond the indescribable pinky red shades of the *Song of Songs* canvases. The seventeen paintings are all based on the Old Testament and are complemented by etchings and engravings. To the building itself, Chagall contributed a mosaic, the painted harpsichord and the *Creation of the World* stained-glass windows in the auditorium.

The Villa Arson

The **Villa Arson**, 20 av Stephen-Liégeard (July–Sept daily 1–7pm; rest of year Tues–Sun 1–6pm; free; bus #36 stop Arts Décoratifs), lies in the district of St-Barthélemy, also in the north of the city but much further west than Cimiez. It is an unlikely mix of seventeenth-century mansion surrounded by Sixties concrete construction and houses a national school for the plastic arts and an international centre for the teaching of contemporary art. Along with several exhibitions a year and displays of work by pupils, the school has fantastic views over the city to the sea, a pleasant garden to lounge about in, a cafeteria, bookshop and a very friendly, unelitist atmosphere.

Two blocks to the east of the Villa Arson, at 59 av St-Barthélemy, the **Prieuré du Vieux Logis** (Wed, Thurs, Sat & first Sun of month 3–5pm; free; bus #5, stop Gorbella) contains a collection of fourteenth- to sixteenth-century furniture, household objects and works of art in a sixteenth-century farm, turned into a priory by a Dominican father in the 1930s.

Eating and drinking

Nice is a great place for **food**, whether you're picnicking on market fare, snacking on **Niçois specialities** like *pan bagnat* (a bun stuffed with tuna, salad and olive oil), *salade niçoise*, *pissaladière* (onion tart with anchovies) or *socca* (a chickpea flour pancake), or dining in the palace hotels. The **Italian** influence is strong in all restaurants, with pasta on every menu; **seafood** and **fish** are also staples, with good *bourride* (fish soup), *estocaficada* (stockfish and tomato stew), and all manner of sea-fish grilled with fennel or Provençal herbs. The local Bellet wines from the hills behind the city provide the perfect light accompaniment. For **snacks**, many of the cafés sell sandwiches with typically Provençal fillings such as fresh basil, olive oil, goats' cheese and *mesclum*, the unique green-salad mix of the region. If you want to buy the best **bread** or croissants in town, seek out Espuno André, at 22 rue Vernier in the old town (closed Sun afternoon & Mon). For **wines** at very decent prices there's the Caves Caprioglio, 16 rue de la Préfecture.

Most areas of Nice have excellent **restaurants**. Vieux Nice has a dozen on every street catering for a wide variety of budgets; the port quaysides have excellent, though very pricey, fish restaurants, and the streets behind are very good for low-budget meals. From June till September it's wise to **reserve** tables, or turn up before 8pm, especially in Vieux Nice.

Restaurants

L'Âne Rouge, 7 quai des Deux-Emmanuel (☎04.93.89.49.63). Lobster is the speciality of this portside gourmet's palace – grilled, baked or stuffed into little cabbages. Sea bass on a bed of fresh asparagus, turbot with salmon eggs, and the creamiest *bourride* are some of the other delights. Classic, classy and very expensive. Menus from 400F. Closed Wed & most of Jan.

L'Antre d'Or, 19 av Audiffret. Good, affordable Chinese and Vietnamese food. Closed Wed, & Thurs midday.

L'Arbalète, 8 rue Jules-Gilly (☎04.93.80.58.28). Family-run, cosy and low-priced pizzeria. Menu from 80F.

L'Avion Bleu, 10 rue Alphonse Karr (☎04.93.87.77.47). Theme nights for would-be jet-setters, with decor inspired by the early days of aviation. Good grilled meat and fish. Weekday lunch menu 70F, otherwise from 100F. Open till midnight; last orders 11pm.

Le Bateleur, 12–14 cours Saleya (☎04.93.85.77.15). Generous and delicious pizzas for under 50F, plus live bands of dubious talent. Open till 2.30am.

Chantecler and La Rotonde, *Hôtel Negresco*, 37 promenade des Anglais (☎04.93.16.64.00). The *Chantecler* is the best restaurant in Nice and well over 400F à la carte, but chef Dominique Le Stanc provides a lunchtime menu, including wine and coffee, for 250F, which will give you a good idea of how sublime Niçois food is at its best. At *La Rotonde* you can taste less fancy but still mouthwatering dishes on the 100F lunchtime menu, with à la carte at around 250F. Closed mid-Nov to mid-Dec.

Chez Flo, 4 rue Sacha-Guitry (☎04.93.13.38.38). Huge brasserie behind the Galeries Lafayette, serving *choucroute*, *confit de canard*, seafood and great *crème brûlée*. Around 200F, also 95F menu after 10pm including wine. Last orders 12.30am.

Chez René Socca, 2 rue Miralhéti, off rue Pairolière (☎04.93.92.05.73). The cheapest meal in town: you can buy helpings of *socca*, *pissaladière*, stuffed peppers, pasta or calamares at the counter and eat with your fingers on stools ranged haphazardly across the street; the bar opposite serves the drinks. Closed Mon & Nov.

Le Comptoir, 20 rue St-François-de-Paule (☎04.93.92.08.80). Very chic 1930s-style brasserie by the Opéra. Superb sea bass in salt crust. Menu from 120F; à la carte from 250F. Evenings only until 1am, closed Sun.

Don Camillo, 5 rue des Ponchettes (☎04.93.85.67.95). A strong Italian influence, and ingredients straight from the cours Saleya market. Menus from 200F. Closed Sun.

Dounia-Zed, 7 rue Assalit (☎04.93.80.40.91). Excellent couscous and a warm welcome. Very good quality for the price. Around 110F.

L'Estrilla, 13 rue de l'Abbaye (☎04.93.62.62.00). Reservations essential in summer for this popular restaurant that serves superb *petites fritures* and paella in huge earthenware pots. Around 100F before 8pm, otherwise around 150F. Closed Mon midday & Sun.

Du Gesú, 1 place du Jésus (☎04.93.62.26.46). Extremely popular restaurant with a great atmosphere, serving no-nonsense Niçois/Provençal food, including good *daube* and pizzas. In an attractive church square in the heart of Vieux Nice. Closed Sun.

La Grange, 7 rue Bonaparte (☎04.93.89.81.83). Good-value and well-prepared food in a congenial atmosphere. Around 100F. Closed Sun.

Grigi Panini, 5 rue St-Réparate. Hot Italian sandwiches known as *panini* from the counter, plus plats du jour.

La Mérenda, 4 rue de la Terrasse. The menu scribbled up on a blackboard usually includes courgette fritters, fresh pasta with pistou, *trulle* (a Niçois black pudding) and gorgeous chocolate mousse. A la carte only, from 180F. Closed Mon, Sat, Sun, Feb & Aug.

Nissa La Bella, 6 rue Ste-Réparate (☎04.93.62.10.20). *Socca*, pizzas and other Niçois specialities. From 80F. Closed Wed & Sun lunchtime.

La Noisetine, cours Saleya, near rue Gassin. One of the cheapest places to eat on the cours Saleya, with generous and tasty crêpes, huge salads, nice desserts and fresh fruit juices. Open till midnight.

Prum-Bayon, 8 rue Dr-Pierre-Richelmi (☎04.93.26.69.80). Excellent Cambodian, Chinese and Thai food. Around 120F.

Socca d'Or, 45 rue Bonaparte (☎04.93.56.52.93). A few blocks back from the port. Closed Mon & Tues.

Le Table de Chine, 57 quai des États-Unis (☎04.93.80.94.70). Chinese cuisine amid stunning decor including aquariums in the floor, plus views of the sea. From 150F.

Virginie, 2 pl A-Blanqui (☎04.93.55.10.07). Excellent *plateau des fruits de mer*. From 80F.

Cafés and bars

Bar des Oiseaux, 9 rue St-Vincent. Named for the birds that fly down from their nests in the loft and the pet parrot and screeching myna bird that perch by the door. Serves delicious baguette sandwiches. Erratic opening hours, sometimes closed all afternoon; live jazz some evenings.

Caves Ricord, 2 rue Neuve. Old-fashioned wine bar with faded, peeling posters. A wide selection of wine by the glass, plus pizzas and other snacks. Open till 7pm.

Grand Café de Lyon, corner of avs Jean-Médecin and Maréchal-Foch. One of the more attractive big *terrasse* cafés on the main street.

Pauline Tapas, 14 rue Emma-Tiranty. Bar-resto with music, cocktails and a pleasant, easy-going atmosphere. Open till 2am. Closed Sun.

Les Ponchettes and La Civette du Cours, cours Saleya. At Le Château end of the marketplace, neighbouring cafés with cane seats fanning out a good 50m from the doors. Open late in summer.

Nightlife

Pubs have long been a very popular element of the Nice nightlife, particularly with the young. For the older, more staid and affluent generation, the luxury **hotel bars** with their jazzy singers and piano accompaniment have held sway for decades, and so they should as an essential ingredient of Riviera nightlife. There are plenty of **discos**, too, and, particularly in Vieux Nice, a wide choice of venues for drinking and dancing, though the music tends not to be very novel. As for the **clubs**, bouncers judging your wallet or exclusive membership lists are the rule.

B52, 8 Descente Crotti. Small dance floor, young clientele and good value. Daily 10.30pm–4am, free entry until 1am.

Le Baby Doll, 227 bd de la Madeleine. Lesbian disco. Daily from 10pm.

Le Baccara, *Hôtel Méridien*, 1 promenade des Anglais. Be-bop, blues, rock'n'roll or old French *chansons* sung to piano accompaniment. Very stylish. Music 11pm–1pm.

Factory, 26 quai Lunel. Bar and mainstream disco; no entry charge and low-priced drinks. Closed Tues.

Le Blue Boy, 9 rue Jean-Baptiste-Spinétta, off bd François-Grosso. Nice's best gay venue. Lesbians and heteros are welcome. There are two bars, two dance floors, DJs who know what's what, and a floorshow every Wed night. Entrance charge on Wed and weekends.

Blue Whales, 1 rue Mascoïnat (☎04.93.85.00.57). Intimate venue with friendly atmosphere, and live music after 10pm ranging from Latin to rock. Open till 2.30am.

Chez Wayne, 15 rue de la Préfecture. Popular bar on the edge of Vieux Nice run by an ex-pat who shares the French penchant for good old rock'n'roll. Live bands, of greatly varying quality, Fri & Sat nights. Open daily.

Havanita, 2 place Vieille. Latin and African salsa bar open till 3am. Pricey drinks.

L'Iguane, 5 quai des Deux-Emmanuel. Very stylish night bar with dance floor. Open till 6am.

Pub Oxford, 4 rue Mascoïnat. English-style pub (in theory); excellent range of beers; live music every evening from 9.30pm; closes 2.30am.

Le Salon, 2 rue Bréa. A fashionable late-night bar in Vieux Nice.

Scarlet O'Hara, 22 rue Droite. Tiny Irish folk bar on the corner of rue Rosetti. Closed Mon & first 2 weeks of July.

Subway, 19 rue Droite. Reggae, soul and rock; reasonably priced. Closed Sun & Mon.

Le Zoom, 6 cours Saleya. Tapas bar with live soul and acid jazz Thurs–Sat; reasonable prices. Open from 6pm.

Entertainment and festivals

Of Nice's many **festivals** – which begin with the Mardi Gras **Carnival** in February – probably the most interesting is the **Festival de Jazz**, staged in the second week of July in the amphitheatre and gardens of Cimiez (for details, call ☎04.93.87.19.18, or fax the main tourist office in May or June).

Nice's **opera**, Opéra de Nice, 4–6 rue St-François-de-Paule (☎04.92.17.40.40), and **theatre**, Théâtre de Nice, promenade des Arts (☎04.93.80.52.60), have no special reputation; of the small independent theatres, Théâtre de la Cité, 3 rue Paganini (☎04.93.16.82.69), stages the most exciting shows. The best **cinema** is Le Nouveau Mercury, 16 place Garibaldi (☎08.36.68.81.06). It shows subtitled films in the original language, as do the UGC Variétés, 7 bd Victor-Hugo (☎04.93.87.74.97); and the UGC Rialto, 4 rue de Rivoli (☎04.93.88.08.41) on occasion.

Other than looking through the **listing mag** *Le Mois à Nice*, the best place to find out about concerts, plays, films and so on is FNAC in the Nice-Étoile shopping complex on av Jean-Médecin, where you can also buy **tickets** for most events.

The biggest sporting event is the **Triathlon de Nice** in late September when competitors from all round the world swim 4km in the Baie des Anges, cycle 120km in the hills behind the city and run 30km ending up along the promenade des Anglais.

Listings

Airlines Air France ☎08.02.80.28.02; British Airways ☎08.02.80.29.02; Debonair ☎08.00.90.16.16; Delta ☎08.00.35.40.80; EasyJet ☎04.93.21.48.33; Virgin Express ☎08.00.52.85.28.

Airport information ☎04.93.21.30.30.

Boat trips Trans Côte d'Azur, quai Lunel (☎04.92.00.42.30), runs summer trips to Îles de Lérins, Cannes, Monaco, St-Tropez, Villefranche and Cap Ferrat.

Bookshop English-language books are available from The Cat's Whiskers, 26 rue Lamartine (☎04.93.80.02.66)..

Car breakdown Dépannage Côte d'Azur Transport 24hr service ☎04.93.29.87.87.

Car parks Acropolis; rue Rossini; promenade du Paillon; gare SNCF; pl Masséna; pl de la Préfecture; cours Saleya.

Car rental Most firms have offices at the airport. Try also: ADA, 24 av Clemenceau (☎04.93.82.27.00); Avis, 2 av Phocéens (☎04.93.80.63.52); Budget, quai Papacino (☎04.93.56.45.50); Europcar, 89 rue de France (☎04.93.88.64.04); Hertz, 12 av de Suède (☎04.93.87.11.87).

Consulate Canada, 64 av Jean-Médecin (☎04.93.92.93.22); Italy, 72 bd Gambetta (☎04.93.88.79.86); Britain, 8 rue Alphonse-Karr (☎04.93.82.32.04); USA, 31 rue Maréchal-Joffre (☎04.93.88.89.55).

Currency exchange American Express, 11 promenade des Anglais; Change Halévy, 1 rue Halévy; Change d'Or Charrière, 10 rue de France.

Disabled access Transport for people with reduced mobility ☎04.93.86.39.87 or 04.93.96.09.99.

Emergencies ☎15 or 04.93.92.55.55; SOS Médecins (☎04.93.85.01.01); Nice Médecins (☎04.93.52.42.42); Hôpital St-Roch, 5 rue Pierre-Dévoluy (☎04.92.03.33.75).

Ferries to Corsica SNCM gare maritime, quai du Commerce (☎04.93.13.66.66); Corsica Ferries (☎04.92.00.42.93).

Laundry Taxi-Lav, 24 av St-Augustine; France Lav, 2 rue Provana de Leyni; Lavomatique, 11 rue du Pont-Vieux.

Lost property 10 cours Saleya (☎04.93.80.65.50). SOS Voyageurs for help with lost or stolen luggage at gare SNCF (Mon–Fri only; ☎04.93.16.02.61).

Pharmacy 7 rue Masséna (☎04.93.87.78.94), open daily 7.30pm–8am; 66 av J-Médecin (☎04.93.62.54.44).

Police Commissariat Central de Police, 1 av Maréchal-Foch (☎04.92.17.22.22).

Post office PTT, pl Wilson, 06000 Nice.

Taxis ☎04.93.80.70.70 or 04.93.13.78.78.

Trains General information and reservations ☎08.36.35.35.35; information on the Chemin de Fer de Provence, 4 bis rue Alfred-Binet (☎04.93.82.10.17).

Youth information Centre Information Jeunesse, 19 rue Gioffredo (☎04.93.80.93.93).

Niçois villages

The **foothills of the Alps** come down to the northern outskirts of Nice, and right down to the sea on the eastern side of the city: a majestic barrier, snowcapped for much of the year, beyond which crest after crest edges higher while the valleys get steeper and livelihoods more precarious. From the sea, the wide course of the Var to the west appears to be the only passage northwards. But the hidden river of Nice, the **Paillon**, cuts its way southwestwards through the mountains, its course connecting small communities since the Middle Ages, which still live in the defensive architecture of the period. The **Nice–Turin railway line** follows the Paillon for part of its way – one of the many spectacular train journeys of this region. If you have your own transport this is hard, hairpin-bend country where the views are a serious distraction. **Buses** from Nice to its villages are infrequent.

With their proximity to the metropolis, the perched villages of **Peillon**, **Peille**, **Lucéram**, **L'Escarène**, **Coaraze** and **Contes** are no longer entirely peasant communities, though the social make-up remains a mix. You may well hear Provençal spoken here and the **traditional festivals** are still communal affairs, even when the participants include the well-off Niçois escaping from the coastal heat. The links between the city and its hinterland are strong: the villagers still live off the land and sell their olives and olive oil, goats' cheese or vegetables and herbs in the city's markets; many city dwellers' parents or grandparents still have homes within the mountains and for every Niçois this wild and underpopulated countryside is the natural remedy for city stress.

Peillon

For the first 10km or so along the River Paillon, after you leave the last of Nice, the valley is marred by quarries, supplying the city's constant demand for building materials. However, once you reach Peillon's nearest gare SNCF at Ste-Thècle, the road begins to climb, looping for 5km through olive groves, pine forest and brilliant pink and yellow broom before you reach the gates of **PEILLON**'s medieval enclave. By bus from Nice, the closest you can get is the Les Moulins stop, from where it is a 3.5-kilometre uphill walk.

Peillon is beautifully maintained, right up to the lovely place de l'Église at the top. There is very little commerce, save for the gallery of Gabriel Mariani's bronze and wood sculptures in Le Vieux Logis, and very little life during the week – most of the residents commute to their jobs in Nice. Just outside the village stands the **Chapelle des Pénitents Blancs**, decorated with violent fifteenth-century frescoes similar to those by Jean Canavesio at La Brigue (see p.393). You can peer through the grille across the chapel door, but getting a closer look is more complicated, as you must try to link up with a pre-arranged group (try phoning the *mairie* on the off-chance; ☎04.93.79.91.04). From the chapel a path heads off across the hillside northwards to Peille. It's a two-hour walk along what was once a **Roman road**, and a more direct route than going via the valley.

Peillon has an extremely glamorous **hotel-restaurant**, *Auberge de la Madone* (☎04.93.79.91.17, fax 04.93.79.99.36; booking essential; closed late Oct to mid-Dec & middle 2 weeks of Jan; ⑤), with balconies overlooking the valley. If you're on a tighter budget, try *Le Pourtail*, under the same management, across the street (②–④), or there's a two-star **campsite**, *La Laune*, at the *Moulins de Peillon*, chemin des Prés (☎04.93.79.91.61; closed Nov–April). The **restaurant** at the *Auberge de la Madone* (closed Wed) is excellent, offering a *menu peillonnais* of local quails, hare and fresh goats' cheese salad flavoured with herbs from the garden (200F, also 130F menu).

Peille

PEILLE lies at the end of 6.5km of hair-pin bends from its gare SNCF in the valley below. The atmosphere here is very different to that in Peillon. It was excommunicated several times for refusing to pay its bishop's tithes, and the republicanism of the small town was later manifested by the domed thirteenth-century Chapelle de St-Sébastien being turned into the **Hôtel de Ville**, and the Chapelle des Pénitents Noirs into a communal **oil press**. Peille claims to be the birthplace of the Roman emperor Pertinax who was assassinated within thirteen weeks of his election on account of his egalitarian and democratic tendencies.

In the Romanesque **church** at the eastern end of the village you can see a painting of the village in medieval times, the count of Provence's castle – in ruins now – standing guard above the ravine. This and the other fourteenth- and sixteenth-century adornments will be shown to you by someone from the hospice next door to the church – you cannot visit unaccompanied. The main square, **place A. Laugier**, is graced with a Gothic fountain and two half-arches supporting a Romanesque pillar; on rue St-Sébastien the former salt tax office, the **Hôtel de la Gabelle**, still stands; on place de Colle the medieval **court house** bears a plaque recalling Peille's transfer of its rights over Monaco to Genoa. The only thing detracting from the beauty of the village is the view to the southwest, marred by the cement-quarrying around La Grave, its suburb down in the valley by the rail line. You can, however, take labyrinthine winding routes to La Turbie, Ste-Agnes or L'Escarène from the village, on which precipitous panoramas are assured.

Regular **buses** make the connection between Peille's **gare SNCF** and the village. If you want to **stay** you'll need to have booked in advance at Peille's one **hotel-restaurant**, *Le Belvédère* (☎04.93.79.90.45; ③; closed Dec) at the western entrance to the village. *Restaurant Cauvin/Chez Nana* on place Carnot (☎04.93.79.90.41; menu at 100F) does a great Sunday lunch with real Provençal cooking and a generous choice of hors d'oeuvres; or you can snack at *Le Serre* and *L'Absynthe* (closed Tues) **bars** at the end of rue Centrale, where menus cost 80F.

L'Escarène

At **L'ESCARÈNE** the rail line leaves the Paillon and heads northeast to **Sospel**. In the days before rail travel, this was an important staging post on the road from Nice to Turin, when drivers would rig up new horses to take on the thousand-metre Braus pass, which the rail line now tunnels under. The village's single-arched bridge (rebuilt after its destruction in World War II) was the crucial river crossing, yet the people who first lived beside it obviously mistrusted all travellers; their houses had no windows overlooking the river, nor any doors, and access was by retractable ladders.

If you want to stop off for the day – there's nowhere to stay – head for the beautiful **place de l'Église** surrounded by pale yellow, green and ochre houses; opposite the great Baroque church is the *Café de l'Union* bar.

Upstream to Lucéram

Following the Paillon upstream for 6km from L'Escarène, you pass the fifteenth-century **Chapelle de St-Grat** with frescoes by Jean Beleison, a colleague of Louis Bréa. Just 1km distant, **Lucéram** clings to the side of the valley, the walls of its interlocking houses showing the erosion of their age. Above the houses, the belfry of **Ste-Marguerite** rises in defiance, its cupola glittering with polychrome Niçois tiles. Within are some of the best late-medieval artworks in the Comté de Nice, though several have been removed and taken to the Musée Masséna in the city.

All these works belong to the School of Nice and both the Retable de Ste-Marguerite, framed by a tasteless Baroque baldaquin, and the painting of Saints Peter and Paul, with its cliff-hanging castle in the distance, are attributed to Louis Bréa. There are more local landscapes in the Retable de St-Antoine, painted on flamboyant Gothic panelling, with generous additions of gold, and said to be by Jean Canavesio. Popular art is present in a thirteenth-century plaster *Pietà*, probably by a local craftsman, to the left of the choir, and the black and red processional lanterns kept in the choir.

To have the works illuminated you need to apply to the presbytery to the right of the church. The priest can also give you the keys to the **Chapelle St-Grat** and the **Chapelle de Notre-Dame de Bon Coeur**, 2km northwest of the village off the road to the St-Roch pass. The walls and ceilings in this chapel are also painted by Jean Beleison.

The village of **LUCÉRAM** itself has the friendliness of a still-peasant community, full of well-fed cats and mangy dogs. The communal oil press remains in service and at the start of the olive season in October the villagers dip their traditional *brissaudo* – toasted garlic bread – in the virgin oil. At Christmas the shepherds bring their flocks into the church and after Mass make their offerings of dried figs and bread.

Like L'Escarène, Lucéram has no hotels but you can get an excellent huge plat du jour for under 50F at *Le Pin* (open daily), perched above the main road opposite the steps leading up past the pink *mairie* into the medieval village.

Coaraze

COARAZE overlooks the valley of the Paillon de Contes, a tributary running west of the main Paillon. From Lucéram and the pass of St-Roch the road hangs over near-vertical descents, turning corners onto great open views of these beautiful but inhospitable mountains.

The population of Coaraze is less than five hundred, though this is one of the more chic Niçois villages, with many an artist and designer in residence. The facades of the post office and *mairie*, and place Félix-Giordan near the top of the village are decorated with **sundials** signed by various artists including Cocteau and Ponce de Léon. The latter decorated the **Chapelle Notre-Dame du Gressier** just north of the village in 1962, known now as the Chapelle Bleu from the single colour he used in the frescoes. Place Félix-Giordan also has a **lizard mosaic** and a Provençal poem engraved in stone. The church, destroyed and rebuilt three times, is famous for the number of angels in its interior decoration, 118 in all.

Unlike the other Niçois villages, Coaraze has a **tourist office** – volunteer-run – on place A-Mari below the village (no fixed hours; ☎04.93.79.37.47), which has the key to the church and chapel. There's also an excellent **hotel-restaurant**, the *Auberge du Soleil* (☎04.93.79.08.11, fax 04.93.79.37.79; ④; closed mid-Nov to mid-March), with wonderful views from the rooms and the dining terrace. Access is on foot only, but you won't be expected to drag your cases up yourself.

Contes

The story always told about **CONTES**, 9km downstream from Coaraze, is of its **caterpillar plague** in 1508, which was so bad the bishop of Nice had to be called in to exorcise the leaf-eating army. With the full weight of ecclesiastical law the caterpillars were sentenced to exile on the slopes of Mont Macaron on the other side of the valley. A procession to the mountain was organized with all the villagers plus saintly relics, holy oil and so forth, and lo and behold, every last caterpillar joined the ranks and never bothered Contes again.

Contes has spread down the valley from its old village, and is quite a major town for these parts with a population of over four thousand. The **tourist office** is on place A-Olivier in the modern town (Mon–Sat 2–6pm); buses #300 and #302 leave from the square for Haute Contes. There are **places to stay** in the modern town: *Le Chaudron*, bd Raiberti (☎04.93.79.11.00; ③; closed Sun eve), and *Le Relais de la Vallée* next door (☎04.93.79.01.03; ②), both on the main Nice road and not much to write home about.

Châteauneuf-de-Contes

Across the river from Contes a road winds up the mountainside to **CHÂTEAUNEUF-DE-CONTES**, a hilltop gathering of houses around an eleventh-century Romanesque church. About 2km further on a path to the left leads to a more recent but **ruined village**, also called Châteauneuf-de-Contes, which was last inhabited before World War I. That this village was abandoned gradually is evident from the varying degrees of building decay and vegetation growth. Ivy-clad towers and crumbling walls rise up among once-cultivated fig trees and rose bushes, and insects buzz in the silence and butterflies flit about the wild flowers that have replaced the gardens. The crescent of walled terraces where the people grew their vegetables is still clearly defined. The passing of time rather than some cataclysm saw its decline – there are no ghosts, nor even a whiff of eeriness; just immense, unthreatening horizons on either side.

Apart from the odd railings around the most insecure bits of masonry, there are no gates or fences and you can wander around at any time of the day or night. On the Monday of Pentecost the inhabitants of the surviving village make a pilgrimage to the ruins which finishes with a communal meal.

The corniches

Three **corniche roads** run east from Nice to the independent principality of Monaco and on to Menton, the last town of the French Riviera. Napoléon built the **Grande Corniche** on the route of the Romans' Via Julia Augusta. The **Moyenne Corniche** dates from the first quarter of the twentieth century, when aristocratic tourism on the Riviera was already causing congestion on the coastal road, the **Corniche Inférieure**. The upper two are popular locations for shooting car commercials, and films where people are killed driving along them. They are, indeed, dangerous roads: Grace Kelly, princess of Monaco, died here when she took a bend too fast on the Moyenne Corniche.

Buses take all three routes; the **train** follows the lower corniche; and all three are superb means of seeing the most mountainous stretch of the Côte d'Azur. For the long-distance panoramas you follow the Grande Corniche, for precipitous views the Moyenne Corniche, and for close-up encounters with the architectural riot of the continuous coastal resort, take the Corniche Inférieure. There's also a hydrofoil service between Nice and Monaco which takes thirty minutes and costs around 100F return (☎04.92.16.15.15).

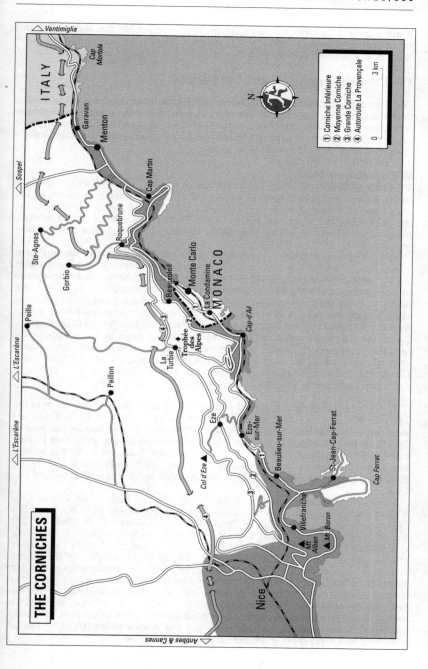

THE CORNICHES

① Corniche Inférieure
② Moyenne Corniche
③ Grande Corniche
④ Autoroute La Provençale

0   3 km

N

Staying along the corniches, anywhere between Nice and Menton, is expensive and impractical if you haven't booked well in advance. On a limited budget it makes more sense to base yourself in Menton or Nice and treat the corniches as pleasure-rides.

The Corniche Inférieure and Cap Ferrat

The characteristic **Côte d'Azur mansions** that represent the unrestrained and stylistically incompatible fantasies of the original owners parade along the **Corniche Inférieure**. Others lurk screened from view on the promontory of **Cap Ferrat**, their gardens full of man-eating cacti and piranha ponds if the plethora of *"Défense d'entrer – Danger de Mort"* signs are anything to go by.

Villefranche-sur-Mer

VILLEFRANCHE-SUR-MER, the resort closest to Nice, has been spared architectural eyesores only to be marred by lurking US and French warships attracted by the deep waters of the bay. However, as long as your visit doesn't coincide with shore leave, the old town on the waterfront, with its active fleet of fishing boats and its covered, medieval **rue Obscure** running beneath the houses, is a tranquil place to while away an afternoon.

The tiny fishing harbour is overlooked by the medieval **Chapelle de St-Pierre** (Tues–Sun: spring 9.30am–noon & 3–7pm; summer 10am–noon & 4–8.30pm; winter 9.30am–noon & 2–6pm; closed mid-Nov to mid-Dec; 12F), decorated by **Jean Cocteau** in 1957 in shades he described as "ghosts of colours". In the guide to the chapel written by Cocteau, the artist invites travellers to enter without any aesthetic preconceptions. The ghostly colours fill drawings in strong and simple lines, portraying scenes from the life of St Peter and homages to the women of Villefranche and to the Gypsies. Above the altar Peter walks on water supported by an angel to the outrage of the and the amusement of Christ. The fishermen's eyes are drawn as fishes; the ceramic eyes on either side of the door are the flames of the apocalypse and the altar candelabras of night-time fishing forks rise above single eyes. On June 29 each year the local fishermen celebrate the feast day of St Peter and St Paul with a Mass, the only time the chapel is used.

To the west of the fishing port, the massive **Citadelle de St-Elme** shelters the hôtel de ville, an open-air cinema and theatre, a conference centre and two **art museums** (Mon & Wed–Sat: July & Aug 10am–noon & 3–7pm, Sun 3–7pm; June & Sept 9am–noon & 3–6pm; Oct & Dec–May 10am–noon & 2–5pm; free). One is dedicated to the voluptuous works of Villefranche sculptor **Volti**, whose bronze woman lies in the fountain outside the citadel gates; the other, dedicated to the couple **Henri Goetz** and **Christine Boumeester**, contains two works by Picasso and one by Miró.

Villefranche's **tourist office** is in the Jardins François-Binon (July & Aug daily 8.45am–7pm; rest of year Mon–Sat 8.30am–noon & 2–7pm; ☎04.93.01.73.68), just below the corniche as it changes from bd Princesse-Grace-de-Monaco to av Albert-1er. For **hotels** in the area, a good-value, low-budget possibility is *Pension Patricia*, on chemin des Pépinières, Pont St-Jean (☎04.93.01.06.70; ③; closed mid-Nov to Dec). *Hôtel Welcome*, 1 quai Amiral-Courbet (☎04.93.76.27.62, fax 04.93.76.27.66; ⑧), the former convent where Cocteau used to stay, is in a prime position overlooking the port and is highly recommended. *La Résidence Carlton*, 9 bis av Albert-1er in the neighbouring town of Beaulieu (☎04.93.01.06.02; ⑦), has pretty rooms with balconies, 200m from the sea. Of the fresh-fish **restaurants** on quai Amiral-Courbet, *Le Saint-Pierre* (☎04.93.76.27.27; menus from 150F) is the most desirable; also on the port, *Le Nautic* (☎04.93.01.94.45; closed Sun eve & Mon) and *Lou Roucas* (☎04.93.01.90.12; menus from 95F; closed Tues) are good, and rather more affordable.

Cap Ferrat

Closing off Villefranche's bay to the east is **Cap Ferrat**, the Côte d'Azur's most desirable address. Its one town, **ST-JEAN-CAP-FERRAT**, is a typical Riviera hideout for the wealthy: old houses overlooking modern yachts in a fishing port turned millionaires' resort. The not-too-frequent #111 **bus** service does the circuit of the promontory.

The St-Jean **tourist office** is at 59 av Dénis-Séméria (July & Aug Mon–Sat 8.30am–noon & 1–6.30pm, Sun 9am–noon & 1–5.30pm; rest of year Mon–Fri 8.30am–noon & 1.30–5.30pm; ☎04.93.76.08.90). The cheapest **hotel** option is *La Frégate*, av Dénis-Séméria (☎04.93.76.04.51, fax 04.93.76.14.93; ③). For rooms with good views of the sea try *La Bastide*, 3 av Albert-1er (☎04.93.76.06.78, fax 04.93.76.19.10; ③), or *La Costière*, av Albert-1er (☎04.93.76.03.89; ④), with its own garden. *Brise Marine*, 58 av J-Mermoz (☎04.93.76.04.36, fax 04.93.76.11.49; ⑦; closed Nov–Jan) has spacious rooms 100m from the sea, while the pleasant *Clair Logis*, 12 av Centrale (☎04.93.76.04.57; ⑤), boasts a lovely large garden and balconies to each room. The best **dinners** to be had are both on the pleasure port: *Le Sloop* (closed Wed out of season; ☎04.93.01.48.63; 155F menu) serves prime fish in delicate and original flavours; and the hotel *La Voile d'Or* (☎04.93.01.13.13; menus from 250F; closed Nov to mid-March; rooms ⑧) which provides very sophisticated and imaginative Mediterranean cuisine; the welcome and comfort at both are exceptional, too. For plats du jour, salads and pasta for less than 80F, head for *Le Pirate*, also on the port (☎04.93.76.12.97).

East of St-Jean's new port you can follow av Jean-Mermoz then a **coastal path** out along the little peninsula, past the Plage Paloma to **Pointe Hospice**, where a nineteenth-century chapel cowers behind a twelve-metre-high turn-of-the-century metal Virgin and Child. From av Claude-Vignon back in St-Jean another coastal path runs right round to chemin du Roy on the opposite side of the peninsula. At the southernmost point of the Cap you can climb a **lighthouse** (9.30am–noon & 3–4pm) for an overview of what you cannot reach – most of Cap Ferrat. Two exceptions to the formidable restrictions of passage are the **zoo** at the northern end of bd Général-de-Gaulle (July & Aug 9.30am–7pm; rest of year closes 5.30pm; 55F), in the park of King Léopold of Belgium's old residence, and the Villa Ephrussi on the road from the mainland.

The **Villa Ephrussi** (July & Aug daily 10am–7pm; mid-Feb to June, Sept & Oct daily 10am–6pm; Nov to mid-Feb Mon–Fri 2–6pm, Sat & Sun 10am–6pm; last entry 30min before closing; 46F) was built in 1912 for Baroness Ephrussi née Rothschild, a woman of unlimited wealth and highly eclectic tastes. The result is a wonderful profusion of decorative art, paintings, sculpture and artefacts ranging from the fourteenth to the nineteenth century and from European to Far Eastern origin. Among the highlights are a fifteenth-century d'Enghien tapestry of fabled hunting scenes; paintings by Carpaccio and other works of the Venetian Renaissance; Dresden porcelain; Ming vases; Mandarin robes; and canvases by Monet, Sisley and Renoir. Visits to the villa are unguided, giving you time to make your own selection of favourites. In order to make the **gardens** the baroness had a hill removed to level out the space in front and then had tons of earth brought back in order that her formal French design could grow above the rock. She named the house after an ocean liner, the *Île de France*, and had her 35 gardeners wear sailors' costumes. They tended Spanish, English, Japanese and Florentine gardens all on a grand scale with attendant statuary and pools. One part of the park, the eastern slope, remained wild Provençal growth, because funds did eventually run out. In 1915 the baroness divorced and moved to Monaco, after just three years in her extraordinary creation.

Beaulieu

To the eastern side of the Cap Ferrat peninsula, overlooking the pretty Baie des Fourmis and accessible by foot from St-Jean along the promenade Maurice-Rouvier, is **BEAULIEU**, sheltered by a ring of hills that ensure its temperatures are amongst the highest on the Côte. The most interesting thing in town is undoubtedly the **Villa Kerylos** (July & Aug daily 10.30am–7pm; mid-Feb to June & Sept to mid-Nov daily 10.30am–6pm; mid-Dec to mid-Feb Mon–Fri 2–6pm, Sat & Sun 10.30am–6pm; closed mid-Nov to mid-Dec; 40F), a near perfect reproduction of an ancient Greek villa, just east of the casino on av Gustave-Eiffel. The only concessions made by Théodore Reinach, the archeologist who had it built, were glass in the windows, a concealed piano, and a minimum of early twentieth-century conveniences. He lived here for twenty years, eating, dressing and behaving as an Athenian citizen, taking baths with his male friends and assigning separate suites to women. However perverse the concept, it's a visual knockout, with faithfully reproduced frescoes, ivory and bronze copies of mosaics and vases, authentic antiquities and lavish use of marble and alabaster.

The **tourist office** (July & Aug daily 9am–12.30pm & 2–7pm; rest of year Mon–Sat 9am–12.15pm & 2–6pm; ☎04.93.01.02.21) is next to the **gare SNCF**, five minutes' walk from Villa Kerylos. For those tempted to **stay** overnight, two economical options worth trying are the family-run *Hôtel Riviera*, at 6 rue Paul-Doumer right in the centre near the sea (☎04.93.01.04.92, fax 04.93.01.19.31; ③), and *Select*, 1 place Gén-de-Gaulle (☎04.93.01.05.42, fax 04.93.01.34.30; ③), which is basic but clean and comfortable, and excellent value for this part of the world. For **food**, there's *La Réserve* at 5 bd du Général-Leclerc (☎04.93.01.00.01; midday menu 310F; closed Nov–March), which features the grand old dishes of French cuisine; and the more affordable *Le Maxilien*, 43 bd Marinoni (☎04.93.01.47.70; menus from 155F; closed Oct to mid-April).

Èze-sur-Mer and Cap d'Ail

The next stop on the train is **ÈZE-SUR-MER**, the seaside extension of **Èze** village on the Moyenne Corniche (see p.343), with a narrow shingle beach and less pretensions than its western neighbours.

There's a small **tourist office** (July & Aug Mon–Sat 9.30am–1.15pm & 2.15–6.30pm) by the train station and a shuttle bus up to Èze village every hour (20F). For reasonable **accommodation**, try *Mimosas Cottage*, av de la Liberté (☎04.93.01.54.82, fax 04.93.01.57.67; ③; closed mid-Nov to mid-Dec), on the corniche, but not quite as charming as the name suggests.

CAP D'AIL feels equally informal though it suffers from the noise and congestion of the lower and middle corniches running closely parallel. Having said that, its tiny eastern promontory has for years maintained one of the few open public spaces left on the Riviera, around M Jeannot's little cabin **bar-restaurant** on Cap Fleuri, which serves its faithful customers who come down here to fish, play *boules* or just look out to sea. A short coastal path leads from here to **Monaco**.

The Moyenne Corniche

The first views from the **Moyenne Corniche** are back over Nice as you grind up Mont Alban, which, with its seaward extension, Mont Boron, separates Nice from Villefranche. Two forts command these heights: **Fort Boron** which is still in naval service, and **Fort Alban**, as endearing a piece of military architecture as is possible to imagine – though now overgrown, it still remains in one piece, with its four tiny turrets glimmering in glazed Niçois tiles. The fort was continually taken by the enemies of Villefranche, who could then make St-Elme (see p.340) surrender in seconds. You can wander freely around the fort and see why Villefranche's citadel, so unassailable from the sea, was so vulnerable from above. To reach it you turn sharp right off the corniche along rte Forestière before you reach the Villefranche pass. The #14 bus from Nice stops at Chemin du Fort from which the fort is signed.

Once through the pass, the cliff-hanging car-chase stretch of the Moyenne Corniche begins, with great views, sudden tunnels and little habitation.

Èze

ÈZE is unmistakable long before you arrive, its streets wound around a cone of rock below the corniche, whose summit is 470m above the sea. From a distance the village has the monumental medieval unity of Mont St-Michel and is a dramatic sight to behold, but seen up close, its secular nature exerts itself. Of the *villages perchés* in Provence, only St-Paul-de-Vence can compete with Èze for having so many antique dealers, pseudo artisans and other caterers to the touristic rich. It takes a mental feat to recall that the labyrinth of tiny vaulted passages and stairways was designed not for charm but from fear of attack.

The ultimate defence, the castle, no longer exists, but the cacti **Jardin Exotique** (July & Aug daily 9am–8pm; March–June, Sept & Oct daily 9am–6.30pm; Nov–Feb daily 9am–noon & 2–5.30pm; 15F) which replaces it offers fantastic views from the ruins and a respite from the commerce below. Also worth visiting for atmosphere alone is the **Chapelle des Pénitents Blancs** on place du Planet, where the crucifix, of thirteenth-century Catalan origin, has Christ smiling down from the cross.

From place du Centenaire, just outside the old village, you can reach the shore through open countryside, via the **sentier Frédéric-Nietzsche**. The philosopher Nietzsche is said to have conceived part of *Thus Spoke Zarathustra* on this path. You arrive at the Corniche Inférieure at the eastern limit of **Èze-sur-Mer**.

Èze's **tourist office**, on place du Gal-de-Gaulle by the first car park you come to (July & Aug daily 9am–7pm; rest of year Mon–Sat 9am–6pm; ☎04.93.41.26.00), can supply a map of the many footpaths through the hills linking the three corniches.

For **rooms** with a sea view, the *Auberge des Deux Corniches* on the D46, 1km from the village (☎04.93.41.19.54; ④; closed Nov), is worth checking out. *Hôtel le Belèze*, place de la Colette on the Moyenne Corniche (☎04.93.41.19.09, fax 04.93.26.27.84; ③), is a bit noisy but reasonable for the price.

Èze's top **restaurants** are in this tiny village's two four-star luxury **hotels**: *Château Eza* (☎04.93.41.12.24, fax 04.93.41.16.64; menus from 250F; rooms from 2000F; closed Nov–March), where a fortune can be spent on ravioli stuffed with white truffle or *langoustine*, and the *Château de la Chèvre d'Or* (☎04.92.10.66.66, fax 04.93.41.06.72; rooms from 1700F; closed mid-Nov to March), where even the lunch menu will set you back a cool 360F. More affordably is *La Taverne*, rue du Barri (also known as *Le Grill du Château*; ☎04.93.41.00.17; main courses around 120F; closed Wed), serving grills and pizzas; the *Au Nid d'Aigle*, at the very top of the village (☎04.93.41.19.08; menus from 130F; closed Wed); and the *Crêperie Le Cactus*, as you enter the village (☎04.93.41.19.02; menus from 95F).

The Grande Corniche

At every other turn on the **Grande Corniche** you're invited to park your car and enjoy a *belvédère*, and at certain points, such as **Col d'Èze**, you can turn off upwards for even higher views. For drivers the main danger, apart from being tempted by the views, is the switches between dazzling light and darkness as you go in and out of the tunnels.

Col d'Èze

The upper part of Èze is backed by the **Parc Forestier de la Grande Corniche**, a wonderful oak forest covering the high slopes and plateaux of this coastal range. Paths are well signed, and there are picnic and games areas and orientation tables – in fact it's rather over-managed, but at least it isn't built on. If you take a left (coming from Nice) to cross the col and keep following rte de la Revère, you come, after 1.5km or so, to an observatory, **Astrorama** (April–June & Sept Tues, Fri & Sat 6.30–11pm; July & Aug Mon–Sat 6.30–11pm; Oct–March Tues & Fri 5.30–10pm; 40F; concessions 20F) where you can look at the evening and night sky through telescopes.

For somewhere **to stay**, try the *Hôtel L'Hermitage*, on the corniche (☎04.93.41.00.68, fax 04.93.41.21.11; ③; closed mid-Dec to mid-Jan), which has magnificent views, passable meals and a **restaurant** (closed from mid-Oct to mid-Feb).

La Turbie

After eighteen stunning kilometres from Nice, you reach **LA TURBIE** and the **Trophée des Alpes**, a sixth-century monument to the power of Rome and the total subjugation of the local peoples. Originally a statue of Augustus Caesar stood on the 45-metre plinth which was inscribed with the names of 45 vanquished tribes and an equally long list of the emperor's virtues. In the fifth century the descendants of the suppressed were worshipping the monument, to the horror of St Honorat who did his best to have the graven image destroyed. However, it took several centuries of barbarian invasions, quarrying, and incorporation into military structures before the trophy was finally reduced to rubble in the early eighteenth century by Louis XIV's engineers, who blew the fortress up to prevent it being used by the king's enemies. Its painstaking reconstruction was undertaken in the 1930s, and it now stands, statueless, at 35m.

Viewed from a distance along the Grande Corniche, however, the *Trophée* can still hold its own as an imperial monument. If you want to take a closer look and see a model of the original, you'll have to buy a ticket for the fenced-off plinth and its little **museum** (April–June daily 9.30am–6pm; July to mid-Sept daily 9.30am–7pm; rest of year Tues–Sun 10am–5pm; 25F). Regrettably, you are not allowed to climb up to the viewing platform and enjoy the spectacular view, for fear of potential suicides.

In the town, just west of the *Trophée*, the eighteenth-century **Église de St-Michel-Archange** is a Baroque concoction of marble, onyx, agate and oil paint, with pink the overriding colour, and, among the paintings, a superb *St Mark writing the Gospel* attributed to Veronese. The rest of the town is less colourful, with rough-hewn stone houses, most of them medieval, lining rue Comte-de-Cessole, the main street which was part of the Via Julia leading to the *Trophée*.

If you're thinking of **staying** here, try *Hôtel Le Napoléon*, 7 av de la Victoire (☎04.93.41.00.54, fax 04.93.41.28.93; ④; closed Tues out of season), set in an attractive building, with views onto the *Trophée* and very good **food**; or the less expensive *Cosmopolite*, 4 rue de la Turbie (☎04.93.30.16.95; ③), near where the buses from Peille, Nice and Monaco stop.

Roquebrune Cap Martin

As the corniche descends towards Cap Martin, it passes the eleventh-century castle of **ROQUEBRUNE** and its fifteenth-century village nestling round the base of the rock. The **castle** (Feb–May Mon–Thurs, Sat & Sun 10am–12.30pm & 2–6pm; June–Sept daily 10am–12.30pm & 3–7.30pm; rest of year Mon–Thurs, Sat & Sun 10am–12.30pm & 2–5pm; 20F) might well have become yet another Côte-side architectural aberration, thanks to its English owner in the 1920s. He was prevented from continuing his "restorations" after a press campaign brought public attention to the mock-medieval tower by the gateway, now known as the *tour anglaise*. The local authority has since made great efforts to kit the castle out in an authentic medieval fashion, and one of the best, if perhaps not most authentic, ideas has been to create an **open-air theatre** for the concerts and dance performances held here in July and August, with a most spectacular natural backdrop down the precipitous slopes to Monaco and the coast.

The village itself is a real maze of passages and stairways that eventually lead either to one of the six castle gates or to dead ends. If you find yourself on rue de la Fontaine you can leave the village by the Porte de Menton and find, on the hillside about 200m beyond the gate, an incredible spreading **olive tree** that was perhaps one hundred years old when the count of Ventimiglia first built a fortress on Roquebrune's spur in 870 AD.

Southeast of the old village, just below the joined middle and lower corniches and the station, is the peninsula of **Cap Martin**, with a **coastal path**, giving you access to a wonderful shoreline of white rocks and wind-bent pines. The path is named after **Le Corbusier**, who spent several summers in Roquebrune and died, tragically, by drowning off Cap Martin in 1965. His grave – a work of art designed by himself – is in the cemetery (square J near the flagpole), high above the old village on promenade 1er DFL, and his beach house (visits arranged through the tourist office; Tues am only) is on the shore just east of Plage du Buse, the beach just below the station.

Roquebrune Cap Martin's main **beach** is the Plage de Carnolès, a great long stretch of east-facing sand running northeast from Cap Martin. Close by the tourist office, at the junction of the Via Aurelian and Via Julia, is a remnant from the Roman station. Known as the **Tombeau de Lumone**, it comprises three arches of a first-century BC mausoleum, with traces of frescoes still visible under the vaulting.

PRACTICALITIES

To get to Roquebrune's Vieux Village from the **gare SNCF**, a forty-minute walk uphill, turn east and then right up av de la Côte d'Azur, then first left up escalier Corinthille, across the Grande Corniche and up escalier Chanoine JB Grana. Between the station and the beach, on the main road av Paul-Doumer you'll find the **tourist office** near the *mairie* at no. 20 (July & Aug daily 9am–6pm; rest of year Mon–Fri 9am–noon & 2–5.30pm; ☎04.93.35.62.87).

Hotels to try on the coast in Roquebrune are *Westminster*, 14 av Louis-Laurens (☎04.93.35.00.68, fax 04.93.28.88.50; ⑤), close to the sea, west of the station, and *Reine d'Azur*, 29 promenade du Cap (☎04.93.35.76.84, fax 04.93.28.02.91; ④), overlooking the Plage de Carnolès. In the old village itself, try *Les Deux Frères*, place des Deux-Frères (☎04.93.28.99.00, fax 04.93.28.99.10; ⑤); rooms #1 or #2 here have awesome views, so it's well worth trying to book these in advance.

Good **restaurants** in Roquebrune involve hefty bills that aren't always justified. Places to try include *La Dame Jeanne*, 1 chemin Ste-Lucie (☎04.93.35.10.20; menus from 120F; closed Sun eve out of season); *Au Grand Inquisiteur*, 18 rue du Château (☎04.93.35.05.37; good menu at 140F; closed Mon & Tues lunchtime); or the **bar** *La Grotte* on place des Deux-Frères (closed Wed out of season), which serves generous plats du jour for around 60F. A gourmet treat is the panoramic **restaurant** *Le Vistaero*, on the Grande Corniche (☎04.92.10.40.20), with a brilliant lunchtime menu for 190F (closed Sun & mid-Jan to Feb).

Monaco

Though you may miss the signs telling you that you've entered **MONACO** it will be instantly clear from the dramatic switch to especially pristine streets and buildings. This tiny independent principality, no bigger than London's Hyde Park, has been in the Grimaldi family's hands since the fourteenth century – save for the two decades following the French Revolution – and, legally, Monaco would again become part of France were the royal line to die out. For the last hundred years the principality has lived off gambling and catering for the desires of the idle international rich. While still carrying out these functions it has also become one of the most rampant property speculation sites in the world, a sort of Manhattan-on-sea.

Finding out about the workings of the regime is not easy, but it is certainly true that **Prince Rainier** is the one constitutionally autocratic ruler left in Europe. There is a parliament, but it is of limited function and elected only by Monégasque nationals, about sixteen percent of the population. A copy of every French law is automatically sent to it, reworded and put to the prince. If he likes the law it is passed; if not, it isn't.

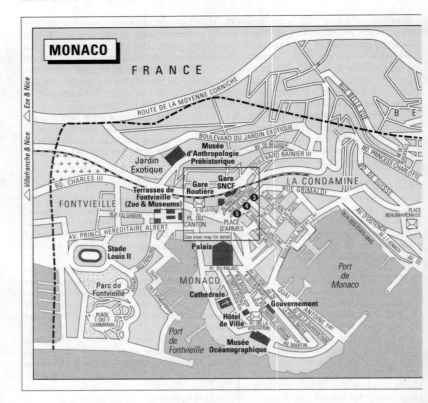

The only other power is the Société des Bains de Mer (SBM), which owns the casino, the opera house, four of the grandest hotels, a handful of the most expensive cafés, restaurants, nightclubs and sports clubs, and large chunks of land including the Monte Carlo beach. The principality is the major shareholder and the director is usually a former minister, in other words someone very close to Rainier.

There is no real opposition to the ruling family. What the citizens and residents like so much is that, despite living in the most densely populated country in the world, they pay no income tax and their riches are protected by rigorous security forces. There are more police per square metre than in any other country in the world, and probably more closed-circuit television cameras too. Unlike France, where hotel registration forms are a widely ignored formality, here they are strictly enforced, collected nightly and filed. Such efficient surveillance can have its embarrassments for the state, as in the case of an Italian wanted for his involvement in the Ambriosi affair who was extradited even though his actual crime was the Monégasque way of life – tax evasion. Should you feel tempted to take up residence, $1 million is about the minimum you need for a very small apartment.

One time to avoid Monaco – unless you're a motor-racing enthusiast – is the second week in May, when racing cars burn around the port and casino for the **Formula 1 Monaco Grand Prix**. Every space in sight of the circuit is inaccessible without a ticket, making casual sightseeing out of the question.

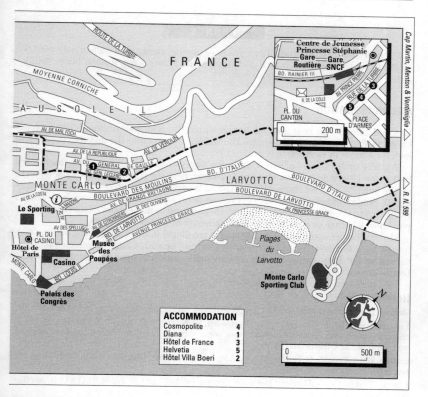

Arrival and information

The three-kilometre-long state consists of the old town of **Monaco-Ville** around the palace on the high promontory, with the new suburb and marina of **Fontvieille** built on land claimed from the sea in its western shadow. **La Condamine** is the old port quarter on the other side of the rock; **Larvotto**, the bathing resort with artificial beaches of imported sand, reaches to the eastern border; and **Monte Carlo** is in the middle. French **Beausoleil**, across the border to the north, is a bit of a dormitory town, with many of its residents working in Monaco.

The **gare SNCF** is on av Prince-Pierre in La Condamine, a short walk from the main **gare routière** on place d'Armes. Buses following the middle and lower corniches stop here; other routes have a variety of stations; all stop in Monte Carlo. There's an annex of the **tourist office** at the gare SNCF (June–Sept 8am–7pm), but the main office is at 2a bd des Moulins near the casino (Mon–Sat 9am–7pm, Sun 10am–noon; ☎92.16.61.16); catch local bus #4 from the train station (Casino-Tourisme stop). **Buses** run from 7am to 9pm; tickets are a flat rate near the station. **Bikes** can be rented from Auto-Moto-Garage, 7 rue de Millo (☎93.50.10.80), just off the place d'Armes. One very useful public service are the incredibly clean and efficient **free lifts** linking lower and higher streets (marked on the tourist office's map). As for the **practicalities of statehood**, there are no border formalities and French currency is valid.

PHONES

If **phoning** into Monaco from France you must use the international dialling code ☎00377 (instead of the ☎04 French area prefix); calls into France from Monaco begin ☎0033, dropping the first zero of the local code.

Accommodation

La Condamine is the best area for **hotels** within the principality, though don't expect bargains. For something a little more affordable, you can cross the invisible border and look for a room in Beausoleil.

If you're under 26 and arrive early in the day, you may be able to get a **dormitory bed** at the *Centre de Jeunesse Princess Stéphanie*, near the station at 24 av Prince-Pierre on the junction with bd Rainier III (☎93.50.83.20, fax 93.25.29.82; 7–10am & noon–midnight). Students under 31 can also get rooms here, and as staff rarely check for ID, it's worth trying even if you're not a student. Be prepared to hang about all morning before you know whether one of the forty beds (seventy in summer) is yours.

Monaco has no **campsite** and **caravans** are illegal in the state (as are bathing costumes, bare feet and chests once you step off the beach). Camping vehicles must be parked at the Parking des Écoles in Fontvieille which is open only during the day (8am–8pm).

Hotels

Balmoral, 12 av Costa (☎93.50.62.37, fax 93.15.08.69). An elegant old building in Monte Carlo. ⑦.

Villa Boeri, 29 bd du Général-Leclerc, Beausoleil, France (☎04.93.78.38.10, fax 04.93.41.90.95). A cheapish option with reasonably sized rooms, some with sea views, and only a couple of minutes' walk from Monte Carlo centre. ③.

Cosmopolite, 4 rue de la Turbie (☎93.30.16.95, fax 93.30.23.05). Characterless but very clean and respectable; near the station. ③.

Diana, 17 bd du Général-Leclerc, Beausoleil, France (☎04.93.78.47.58, fax 04.93.41.88.94). Another fairly characterless hotel, but inexpensive and right by Monte Carlo centre. ④.

Hôtel de France, 6 rue de la Turbie (☎93.30.24.64, fax 92.16.13.34). Cheerful rooms and good value for the principality. ④.

Helvetia, entrances at 1 rue Grimaldi and rue de la Turbie (☎93.30.21.71, fax 92.16.70.51). A reasonable option. Clean and comfortable, but fairly basic. ⑥.

Monte Carlo

The **Casino** of **Monte Carlo** is one place not to be missed on a trip to Monaco. Entrance is restricted to those over 21 and you may have to show your passport; dress code is strict, with shorts and T-shirts frowned upon, and skirts, jackets, ties and so forth more or less obligatory for the more interesting sections. Any coats or large bags must be left in the cloakroom, which charges a hefty fee.

In the first gambling hall, the Salons Européens (open from noon; 50F), slot machines surround the American roulette and blackjack tables, the managers are Vegas-trained, the lights low and the air oppressively smoky. Above this slice of Nevada, however, the decor is turn-of-the-century Rococo extravagance, while in the adjoining Pink Salon Bar, female nudes smoking cigarettes adorn the ceiling.

The heart of the place are the Salons Privés (open from 4.15pm), through the Salles Touzet. You must look like a gambler, not a tourist (no cameras), to get in, and hand over 100F at the door. More richly decorated than the Salons Européens and much bigger, the atmosphere in here in the early afternoon or out of season is that of a cathedral. No clinking coins, just quiet-voiced croupiers and sliding chips. Elderly gamblers pace silently, fingering 500F notes (the maximum un-negotiated stake is 500,000F), closed-circuit TV cameras above the chandeliers watch the gamblers watching the tables, and no one drinks. On midsummer evenings the place is packed out and the vice loses its sacred and exclusive touch.

Charles Garnier, the nineteenth-century architect of the Paris Opera, designed both the casino and the neighbouring **Opera House** which is open to ticket holders only during the January to March season. Its typically Baroque interior is an excess of gold and marble with statues of pretty Grecian boys, frescoed classical scenes and figures waving palm leaves.

From the terraces behind the casino you can look down onto the **Centre de Congrès Auditorium** which juts out over the sea and has a blazingly coloured hexagonal roof designed by Vasarely.

Around place du Casino are more **casinos** and the city's **hôtels-palais** and **grands cafés**, all owned by the SBM monopoly. The *American Bar* of the *Hôtel de Paris* is, according to its own publicity, the place where "the world's most elite society" meets. As long as you dress up and are prepared to be outraged (in English) if asked why you haven't ordered a 200F drink, you can entertain yourself, free of charge, watching the wealthy enjoy themselves against the background of *belle époque* decadence.

People here really do live up to their stereotypes. You may not catch sight of Caroline and Stéphanie, but you can be sure of a brilliant fashion parade of clothes and jewels, cars and luggage. You can even see how much they cost, if you're interested, in the shops and showrooms along bd des Moulins.

For an alternative to people-watching, head for the **Musée National** at 17 av Princesse-Grace (Easter–Sept daily 10am–6.30pm; Oct–Easter daily 10am–12.15pm & 2.30–6.30pm; 26F). Dedicated to the history of **dolls and automata** from eighteenth-century models to the latest Barbie dolls, it's much better than sceptics might think. Some of the doll's house scenes and the creepy automata are quite surreal and fun.

Monaco-Ville

After the casino, the amusements of **Monaco-Ville**, where every other shop sells Prince Rainier mugs and assorted junk, are less rewarding. You can trail gasping round the state apartments of the **Palace** (June–Sept daily 9.30am–6.30pm; Oct daily 10am–5pm; 30F); look at waxwork princes in **L'Historial des Princes de Monaco**, 27 rue Basse (daily: April–Sept 9.30am–6pm; Oct–March 11am–4pm; 26F); or traipse around the tombs of the former princes and Princess Grace in the Neo-Romanesque-Byzantine **cathedral**.

One place that rises above the general level of dull sycophancy is to be found on the place de la Visitation: the **Musée de la Chapelle de la Visitation** (Tues–Sun 10am–4pm; 20F), displaying part of the religious art collection of Barbara Piasecka Johnson (an heir to the Johnson & Johnson fortune). This small but exquisite collection includes works by Zurbarán, Rivera, Rubens, and even an extremely rare, early religious work by Vermeer, *St Praxedis*.

One of Monaco's best, though pricey, sites to visit is the **aquarium** in the basement of the **Musée Océanographique**, av St-Martin (July & Aug 9am–8pm; April–May & June–Sept 9am–7pm; March & Oct 9.30am–7pm; Nov–Feb 10am–6pm; 60F), where delicate leafy seadragons, living nautiluses and hideous anglerfish are just some of the bizarre and colourful creatures you will witness. This is also an institute for serious scientific research, and it is proud of the fact that it has succeeded in keeping living corals in the aquariums, something reputedly unique in the world. Films by the famous underwater explorer Jacques Cousteau, who for many years was the director of the institute, are screened in the museum's conference hall. Upstairs, the museum itself details the whale-hunting adventures of the institute's founder, Prince Albert I, who devoted a considerable part of his fortune to his passion of oceanography. It has a collection of finely crafted mother-of-pearl and other items taken from the sea and prized by man in the different areas of the world; early bathyscaphs for discovering the secrets of the depths; and some magnificent views out to sea from the upper floors.

Bus #1 or #2 will take you to Monaco-Ville; **by car** head for the Parking du Chemin des Pêcheurs from where there's a lift up to av St-Martin by the Musée Océanographique. Only Monégasque- and Alpes Maritimes-registered cars are allowed in Monaco-Ville itself.

Fontvieille, the Jardin Exotique and La Condamine

Below the rock of Monaco-Ville by the Port de Fontvieille a whole new complex, the **Terrasses de Fontvieille** (bus #5), has been built to house more museums. These include the prince's collection of private cars, everything from Cadillacs and Rollers to Trabants, Morris Minors and US jeeps (daily 10am–6pm; closed Nov; 30F); a **Musée Naval** (daily 10am–6pm; 25F) containing His Serene Highness's toy ships; a **zoo** (June–Sept 9am–noon & 2–7pm; Oct–May 10am–noon & 2–5pm; 20F); and a museum of stamps and coins, the **Musée des Timbres et des Monnaies** (daily 10am–5pm; 20F). Below all these, a very discreet McDonald's forgoes its normal red and yellow colours in favour of racing green awnings and parasols. Also in Port de Fontvieille, there's a **bric-à-brac market** every Saturday (9.30am–5.30pm).

Surrounded by car parks (spotlessly clean and with a range of cars almost as impressive as the prince's collection) the **Parc de Fontvieille** and Princess Grace's **rose garden** on the west side of the port are rather more rewarding than the museums. The prime garden in Monaco, however, is the **Jardin Exotique**, full of bizarre cacti emerging from the hillside high above Fontvieille on bd du Jardin Exotique (mid-May to mid-Sept 9am–7pm; rest of year 9am–6pm; 39F; bus #2). Admission also includes entry to the **Musée d'Anthropologie Préhistorique**, tracing the history of the human race from Neanderthal man to Grimaldi prince, and the **Grotte de l'Observatoire**, prehistoric caves with illuminated stalagmites and stalactites.

The yachts in the **Port de Monaco** in **La Condamine** are, as you might expect, gigantic. If the idea of getting on one and sailing out of the harbour gives you a buzz, try one of the mini **cruises** on the *Monte-Carlo* catamaran, quai des Etats-Unis, which has a glass hull for underwater viewing (☎92.16.15.15; around 70F). The other thing worth taking advantage of by the port is the tremendous Olympic-size, saltwater **swimming pool** with high-dive boards.

Eating and drinking

La Condamine and Monaco-Ville are replete with **restaurants**, **brasseries** and **cafés** but good food and reasonable prices rarely coincide. The best-value cuisine is Italian, and it's really not worth going upmarket in Monaco unless you're prepared to hit 900F-a-head bills, in which case you dine in the *belle époque* glory of the *Louis XV* in the *Hôtel de Paris*. As for **food shopping**, you can buy caviar, champagne and smoked salmon without any problem on and around av St-Charles, but finding *boulangeries* can be difficult. There are **markets** at place d'Armes and bd de France every morning but they're minimal affairs; you'd be better off heading to rue du Marché in Beausoleil.

Restaurants

Castelroc, pl du Palais (☎93.30.36.68). A crowded but convenient place if you've been doing the palace tours; menus from 120F; midday only. Closed Sat, Dec & Jan.

La Cigale, 18 rue de Millo (π93.30.16.14). Between the station and the Port de Monaco; decent menu at 75F. Closed Sat, Sun & Aug.

L'Orangeraie, 42 quai des Sanbarbani, Fontvieille (π92.05.67.37). Excellent value for this part of the world with good seafood, and a menu at 135F. Last orders at 10pm.

Le Pinocchio, 30 rue Comte F-Gastaldi (π93.30.96.20). Dependable Italian in Monaco-Ville; menus from 200F. Open till midnight in summer. Closed Wed out of season & Dec to mid-Jan.

Polpetta, 2 rue Paradis (π93.50.67.84). Attractive terrace and vaulted dining hall in Monte Carlo; Italian food; menu at 150F. Closed Tues, Sat midday & late-Oct to Feb.

Pulcinella, 17 rue du Portier (π93.30.73.61). Traditional Italian cooking in Monte Carlo; menu at 150F.

Nightlife, entertainment and festivals

There are better places to throw away money on **nightlife** than Monaco, and the top discotheques like, *Jimmy'z* by the Monte-Carlo Sporting Club, are not going to let you in unless you're dripping with real jewels. American- or British-style **bars** and pubs abound and your best bet is the large, informal bar on the quai Antoine-1er, *Stars 'N' Bars*: packed out on Fridays and Saturdays, with a lively club upstairs where drinks will cost you 60F. Otherwise you might like to try out *McCarthy's*, 7 rue du Portier, for Guinness and occasional live music; or *Chérie's Café*, near Monte Carlo's Casino, at 9 av des Spélugues, which serves food throughout the night and has regular live bands.

By contrast, the **opera season** (Jan–March) is pretty exceptional, the SBM being able to book up star companies and performers before Milan, Paris or New York gets hold of them. The programme of **theatre**, **ballet** and **concerts** throughout the year is also impressive, with the **Printemps des Arts de Monte Carlo** in April and May seeing performances by famous classical and contemporary dance troupes from all over the world. The main booking office for ballet, opera and concerts is the casino foyer, place du Casino, Monte-Carlo (Tues–Sun 10am–12.30pm & 2–5pm; π92.16.22.99); for theatre, book at the Théâtre Princesse Grace, 12 av de l'Ostende, Monte-Carlo (Mon–Sat 10am–12.30pm & 3–6.30pm; π93.25.32.27).

Monaco's **festival calendar** is spectacular, especially the **International fireworks Festival** at the end of July and the beginning of August at the Port de Monaco, though these can be witnessed from Cap d'Ail or Cap Martin. Mid- to late-January sees vast trailers entering Monaco for the **International Circus Festival** at the Espace Fontvieille, a rare chance to witness the world's best in this underrated performance art (details on π92.05.23.45). **Holidays** in Monaco are the same as in France, with the addition of January 27 (*Fête de Ste-Dévote*) and November 19 (*Fête Nationale Monégasque*).

The **Monte-Carlo Automobile Rally** takes place at the end of January and the **Formula 1 Grand Prix** in mid-May. Every space in sight of the circuit, which runs round the port and the casino, is inaccessible without a ticket (π93.15.26.00). Monaco also has a first-division **football team**, AS Monaco, whose home ground is the enormous Stade Louis II in Fontvieille, 2 av du Prince-Héréditaire-Albert (π92.05.40.00; tickets from as little as 35F).

Listings

Banks Most banks have a branch in Monaco, and congregate on bd des Moulins, av de Monte-Carlo and av de la Costa; opening hours are Mon–Fri 9am–noon & 2–4.30pm.

Bookshop Scruples, 9 rue Princesse-Caroline (π93.50.43.52), sells English-language books.

Consulates Britain, 33 bd Princesse-Charlotte (π93.50.99.66); Denmark, 74 bd d'Italie (π93.50.02.03); Ireland, 1 pl Ste-Dévote (π93.15.70.00); Norway, Palais Héraclès, 17 bd Albert-1er (π93.50.91.01); Sweden, 7 av de Grande-Bretagne (π93.50.75.60).

Currency exchange Crédit Foncier de Monaco, 11 bd Albert-1er, has a 24hr automatic currency exchange machine; change offices can be found at the station and the parking des Pêcheurs.
Emergencies ☎18 or 93.30.19.45; Centre Hospitalier Princesse Grace, av Pasteur (☎97.98.97.69).
Pharmacy Call ☎141, or 93.25.33.25 from public phones.
Police and Lost property 3 rue Louis Notari (☎93.15.30.15).
Post office PTT Palais de la Scala, Place Beaumarchais (Mon–Fri 8am–7pm & Sat 8am–noon).
Taxis ☎93.15.01.01 or 93.50.56.28.

Menton

Of all the Riviera resorts **MENTON**, the warmest and the most Italianate, is the one that most retains an atmosphere of aristocratic tourism. Today it is even more of a rich retirement haven than Nice, and it's precisely that genteel, slow promenading pace of the town that makes it easy to imagine the presence of arch duchesses, grand dukes, tsars and other autocrats, as well as sick artists such as Guy de Maupassant and Katherine Mansfield. Menton does not go in for the ostentatious wealth of Monaco nor the creative cachet of Cannes or some of the hilltop towns. What it chiefly glories in is its climate and its all-year-round lemon crops. Ringed by protective mountains, hardly a whisper of wind disturbs the sun-trap of the city. Winter is when you notice the difference most, with Menton several vital degrees warmer than St-Tropez or St-Raphaël.

The town's history, like that of Monaco, almost took an independent path. In the revolutionary days of 1848, Menton and Roquebrune, both at the time under Monaco's jurisdiction, declared themselves an independent republic under the protection of Sardinia. When the prince of Monaco came to Menton in the hope that his regal figure would sway the people he had to be rescued by the police from a furious crowd and locked up overnight for his own protection. Eventually, following an 1860 vote by Roquebrune and Menton to remain in France, Grimaldi agreed to the sale of the towns to the French state for four million francs.

Arrival and information

Roquebrune and Cap Martin merge into Menton along the three-kilometre shore of the **Baie du Soleil**. The modern town is arranged around three main streets parallel to the promenade du Soleil. The **gare SNCF** is on the top one, bd Albert-1er, from where it's a short walk east to the **gare routière** at the head of the north–south avenues de Verdun and Boyer. The **tourist office** is at 8 av Boyer (July & Aug Mon–Sat 8.30am–7pm, Sun 10am–noon; rest of year Mon–Fri 8.30am–12.30pm & 1.30–6pm, Sat 9am–noon & 2–6pm; ☎04.93.57.57.00); it's in the Palais de l'Europe, a former casino which now hosts various cultural activities, annual contemporary art exhibitions and an international art *biennale*. The Vieille Ville lies further east, above the old port and the start of the Baie de Garavan. The district of Garavan, further east again, is the most exclusive residential area and overlooks the modern marina.

Accommodation

Accommodation, though good value, is difficult to find. Menton is as popular as the other major resorts, so in summer you should definitely book ahead. The tourist office won't make reservations for you, though they will tell you where rooms are still available.

Hotels

L'Aiglon, 7 av de la Madone (☎04.93.57.55.55, fax 04.93.35.92.39). Spacious rooms in a nineteenth-century residence surrounded by a large garden. ⑤.

Auberge Provençale, 11 rue Trenca (☎04.93.35.77.29, fax 04.93.28.88.88). Centrally located and reasonable enough. ⑥.

Beauregard, 10 rue Albert-1er (☎04.93.28.63.63, fax 04.93.28.63.79). Traditionally furnished rooms and a relaxed atmosphere. Closed Oct–Dec. ③.

Belgique, 1 av de la Gare (☎04.93.35.72.66, fax 04.93.41.44.77). A bit mundane but clean, friendly and conveniently close to the station. Closed Dec. ③.

Chambord, 6 av Boyer (☎04.93.35.94.19, fax 04.93.41.30.55). Large rooms and well located. ⑤.

Napoléon, 29 porte de France, Garavan (☎04.93.35.89.50, fax 04.93.35.49.22). Wonderful views from the rooms. ⑤.

Terminus, pl de la Gare (☎04.92.10.49.80, fax 04.92.10.49.81). Basic and inexpensive, right by the station.③.

Viking, 2 av Gal-de-Gaulle (☎04.93.57.95.85, fax 04.93.35.89.57). No beauty but with comfortable rooms and a good seafront location. ⑤.

Hostel, chambre d'hôtes and campsite

HI youth hostel, plateau St-Michel (☎04.93.35.93.14, fax 04.93.35.93.07). This well-run hostel is up a gruelling flight of steps (signposted Camping St-Michel) from the northern side of the railway to the east fo the station, or take bus #6 from the gare routière (direction Ciappes de Castellar, stop Camping St-Michel). Good food and views; no advance booking or HI card necessary; 11pm curfew. Reception closed 10am–5pm.

Chambre d'hôtes, M. Paul Gazzano, 151 rte de Castellar (☎04.93.57.39.73). Two kilometres from Menton, a delightful house with a terrace looking down over the wooded slopes to the sea. ③.

Camping St-Michel, plateau St-Michel (☎ & fax 04.93.35.81.23). Reasonably priced campsite in the hills above the town, with plenty of shade and good views out to sea; follow directions for HI youth hostel. Closed Dec–Feb.

The Town

Menton's greatest attraction is not its seafront or pebble beach, but the fabulous facade of the **Vieille Ville** around the parvis St-Michel; and the works of **Jean Cocteau** – in particular his decoration of the registry office – and the **gardens** in Garavan.

The modern town

The **Salle des Mariages**, or registry office, in the hôtel de ville on place Ardoiono was decorated in inimitable style by **Jean Cocteau** (1889–1963) and can be visited without matrimonial intentions by asking the receptionist by the main door (Mon–Fri 8.30am–12.30pm & 1.30–5pm; 10F). On the wall above the officials' desk a couple face each other, with strange topological connections between the sun, her headdress and his fisherman's cap. The *Saracen Wedding Party* on the right-hand wall reveals a disapproving mother of the bride, spurned girlfriend of the groom and her armed vengeful brother amongst the cheerful guests. On the left wall is the story of *Orpheus and Eurydice* at the doomed moment when Orpheus has just looked back. Meanwhile on the ceiling are *Poetry rides Pegasus*, tattered *Science juggles with the Planets* and *Love*, open-eyed, waiting with bow and arrow at the ready. Just to add to the confusion the carpet is mock panther-skin.

The **Musée de Préhistoire Régionale**, at the top of rue Lorédan-Larchey close to the hôtel de ville (Mon & Wed–Sun 10am–noon & 2–6pm; free), is one of the best on the subject. There are good videos to watch, life-size re-created scenes of early human life, and the famous 27,000-year-old skull of "Menton Man" found in a cave near the town, encrusted with shells and teeth from his head gear.

Close to the museum are the pretty **market halls** of place du Marché off quai de Monléon where food and flowers are sold every morning. Behind place du Marché is

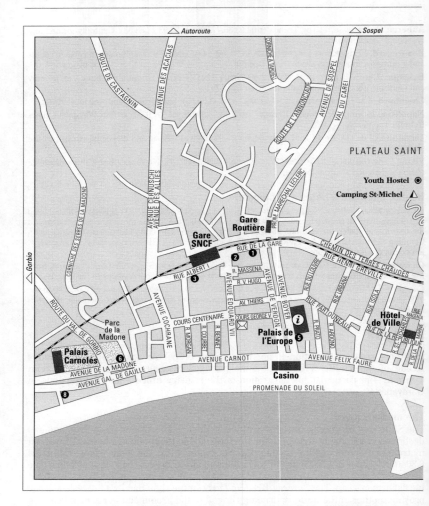

the attractive place aux Herbes with a bric-à-brac market every Friday morning, and the pedestrianized rue St-Michel, lined with cafés and restaurants and citrus trees, linking the old and modern towns.

There are other works by Cocteau in the **Musée Jean Cocteau** (Mon & Wed–Sun 10am–noon & 2–6pm; 20F) which he set up himself in the most diverting building on the front, a seventeenth-century bastion with tiled turrets on quai Bonaparte below the Vieille Ville. The building is decorated with pebble mosaics conceived by Cocteau and contains more Mentonaise lovers in the *Inamorati* series, a collection of delightful *Animaux Fantastiques* and the powerful tapestry of *Judith and Holopherne* simultaneously telling the sequence of seduction, assassination and escape. The walls are also hung with photographs, poems, a portrait by his friend Picasso and ceramics.

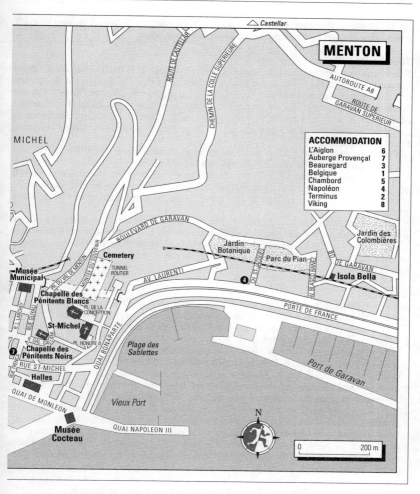

△ Castellar

MENTON

ROUTE DE CASTELLAR

CHEMIN DE LA COLLE SUPÉRIEURE

AUTOROUTE A8

ROUTE DE GARAVAN SUPÉRIEUR

MICHEL

BOULEVARD DE GARAVAN

ACCOMMODATION

L'Aiglon	6
Auberge Provençal	7
Beauregard	3
Belgique	1
Chambord	5
Napoléon	4
Terminus	2
Viking	8

Jardin des Colombières

Jardin Botanique

Parc du Pian

Cemetery

MONTÉE DU SOUVENIR

PL. DUVAL DE MENTON

Musée Municipal

TUNNEL ROUTIER

AV. LAURENTI

CH. ST. JACQUES

AV. BLASCO IBAÑEZ

BD DE GARAVAN

Isola Bella

④

Chapelle des Pénitents Blancs

PL. DE LA CONCEPTION

PORTE DE FRANCE

R. LLABORDI

RUE GAL. GAS

St-Michel

PL. HONORE II

QUAI BUONAPARTE

Plage des Sablettes

Chapelle des Pénitents Noirs

⑦

RUE ST-MICHEL

RUE ST-MICHEL

Port de Garavan

Halles

QUAI DE MONLEON

Vieux Port

Musée Cocteau

QUAI NAPOLEON III

N

0   200 m

At the far western end of the modern town, on av de la Madone, an impressive collection of paintings from the Middle Ages to the twentieth century can be seen in the sumptuous **Palais Carnolès** (Mon & Wed–Sun 10am–noon & 2–6pm; free; bus #3 or #7 to Madone Parc), the old summer residence of the princes of Monaco. Of the early works, the *Madonna and Child with St Francis* by Louis Bréa is exceptional; there are excellent Dutch and Venetian portraits; and an anonymous sixteenth-century École Français canvas of a woman holding a scale. The small modern and contemporary collection includes a wonderful Suzanne Valadon and works by Graham Sutherland, who spent some of his last years in Menton. The downstairs of the building is given over to temporary exhibitions and there's a **jardin des sculptures** in the adjoining lime, lemon and orange grove. Due north of here, at 74 Route du Val de Gorbio, is **La Serre**

de la Madone (summer 10am–6pm; winter 10am–4pm), a botanical garden of great tranquillity created by an Englishman in the interwar years.

The Vieille Ville

Where the *quai* bends round the western end of the Baie de Garavan from the Cocteau museum, a long flight of black and white pebbled steps leads to the **parvis St-Michel** and the perfect pink and yellow proportions of the **Église St-Michel** (Mon–Fri & Sat 10am–noon & 3–5pm). The interior of the church is a stupendous Italian Baroque riot of decoration, with an impressive vast organ casing, a sixteenth-century altarpiece in the choir by Antonio Manchello and a host of paintings, sculptures, gilded columns, stucco and frescoes.

From the church, take a few more steps up to another square and the apricot and white marbled **Chapelle des Pénitents Blancs** (Mon–Sat 3–5pm), home to a collection of processional lanterns and with a fine trompe-l'oeil over the altar. All this, as well as the pastel campaniles and disappearing stairways between long lived-in houses, are a sure sign that you've arrived at the most Italianate and beautiful of the Riviera's Vieilles Villes.

From here, head north, or uphill. At the top you'll reach the **Cimetière du Vieux Château** which is low on gloom and high on views, with cream-coloured mid-nine-teenth-century sculpted stone and diverse foreign names ranging from Russian princes to William Webb-Ellis, credited, in language redolent of public schools, with the invention of rugby.

Garavan

If it's cool enough to be walking outside, the public **parks** up in the hills and the **gardens** of **Garavan**'s once elegant villas make a change from shingle beaches. From the Vieux Cimetière you can walk or take bus #8 along bd de Garavan past houses hidden in their large, exuberant gardens.

The first public garden you come to is the **Jardin Botanique** (Mon & Wed–Sun: June–Sept 10am–12.30pm & 3–6pm; Oct–May 10am–12.30pm & 2–5pm; 20F) which surrounds the Villa Val Rahmeh. Though there's a good variety of plants it's not brilliantly maintained and you can get the same views for free from the **Parc du Pian**, an olive grove reached from the boulevard just past the Jardin Exotique. Further on, down av Blasco-Ibañez and north up rue Webb-Ellis and chemin Wallaya, is the **Isola Bella** where Katherine Mansfield stayed. Above here, up rte des Colombières from bd de Garavan, are the **Jardins Les Colombières** (temporarily, possibly permanently, closed; check at tourist office for latest status; bus #8, direction bd de Garavan, stop Colombières) which used to be the best of all the Garavan gardens. Designed by the artist Ferdinand Bac, they lead you through every Mediterranean style of garden. There are staircases screened by cypresses; balustrades to lean against for the soaring views through pines and olive trees out to sea; fountains, statues and a frescoed swimming pool.

Eating, drinking and entertainment

Menton has few exceptional **restaurants** so most people usually cross into Italy for a blow-out meal. If you're not that bothered what you eat as long as it's cheap, the pedestrianized rue St-Michel is promising ground. There are plenty of snack bars among the burger houses, as well as outlets for omelettes or steak and chips and occasionally interesting plats du jour. For a proper restaurant meal in very elegant surroundings, there's *La Veranda* in *Hôtel Les Ambassadeurs*, 2 rue du Louvre (☎04.93.28.75.75; closed Sun eve), with an evening bistro menu for 160F. There are also two excellent Moroccan restaurants, both with menus for around 200F: *Le Darkoum*, 23 rue St-Michel (☎04.93.35.44.88), and *La Mamounia*, 51 porte de France, Garavan (☎04.93.57.95.39).

As well as the covered market there's great fruit and veg and other foodstuffs at the **marché du Carei** on promenade du Mal-Leclerc. Good bread and *fougasse* can be bought from the Midi Boulangerie on rue St-Michel.

In August the pebbled mosaic of the Grimaldi arms on the parvis St-Michel is covered by chairs, music stands, pianos and harps for the **Festival de Musique de Chambre**. The nightly concerts are superb and can be listened to from the quaysides without buying a ticket. If you want a proper seat make a reservation at the tourist office.

More bizarrely, the town's **lemons** are celebrated in the citrus fruit extravaganza every February. Have no illusions, however, about cheap local produce: a *citron pressé* served in a Menton bar still costs twice as much as an imported Belgian beer.

Around Menton

In the hills above Menton and Roquebrune are the tiny villages of **Gorbio** and **Ste-Agnes**, and on the road to Sospel, **Castellar** and **Castillon**. All give god's-eye views over steep, forested slopes to the sea.

Ste-Agnes

Ten kilometres northwest of Menton and 800m above sea level is **STE-AGNES**, the place which claims to be the highest coastal village in Europe, milling with crystal engravers, painters, herbalists, jewellers and leather workers. Perched at the foot of a cliff, it commands breathtaking views, especially from the ancient Saracen fortress currently being restored, at the top of the crag above. The Saracens had an impeccable eye for choosing defensive positions: such is the site's commanding vantage point that another important **fort** was built into the mountain top a millennium later, this time as part of the Maginot defences of the 1930s (guided tours daily 3pm & 5.30pm).

The village is also an excellent starting point for **walks**, and the syndicat d'initiative, in the Espace de Culture at the entrance to the village, will provide you with a free list of suggested hikes (in French only). One popular route, offering the best chance of glimpsing Corsica, is up the **Pic/Cime de Baudon** (1hr 45min to the summit at 1264m), with possibilities of continuing on to Gorbio or Peille.

Two hospitable places to stay in the village are the **hotel-restaurant** *Saint Yves* (☎04.93.35.91.45, fax 04.93.35.65.85; ②), with some good views; and *La Vieille Auberge* (☎04.93.35.92.02; ②), entered from the approach road into the village (the entrance from the village side is often locked), where they also serve an enormous, filling five-course meal for only 70F. The best-quality **food** is served in *Le Logis Sarrasin* (☎04.93.35.86.89; closed Mon), where they prepare a fine *tarte Agnésoise*, made with courgette flowers; while *Le Righi*, around the Maginot fort (☎04.92.10.90.88; menus from 110F; closed Wed), has the best views. **Bus #902** runs from Menton to Ste-Agnes (3 daily; 30min).

Gorbio

GORBIO, to the southwest of Ste-Agnes, is an exquisite hilltop village with very few arts and crafts boutiques or other tourist fodder, lending it a tranquil atmosphere that's rare for so scenic a place. Though the two villages are only 2km apart as the crow flies, the roads between them meet approximately 8km away, below the *autoroute*. Walkers can take a more direct route (45-minute walk): the road from Ste-Agnes drops downhill, and then crosses the path to Gorbio at L'Auribel bus stop, on a sharp hairpin bend after about 2km. You can also get to the village directly from Menton; bus #901 makes the climb five times daily from the gare routière in thirty minutes.

On the Thursday after Corpus Christi in June, the annual rite of the **Procession des Limaces** takes place, when the streets are illuminated by tiny lamps of snail-shells filled with olive oil – a custom dating back to medieval times and occurring in villages throughout this area (check with the tourist office in Menton for exact dates).

If you can, time a trip so that you can **eat** at the *Auberge du Village* at 8 rue Gambetta (☎04.93.35.87.83; from 100F; closed Mon); after feasting on vegetable fritters, seafood salad, ravioli and courgette flowers you can sit on the benches of place de la République at the entrance to the mottled grey medieval quarter, watching kids play and soaking up the sun and the view.

Castillon and Castellar

A railway used to run along the Carei valley from Menton up to Sospel. Though the tracks and tunnels are still there, it's been closed for over forty years and there are currently no plans to revive it, which is a great pity as this valley offers one of the best roller-coasting descents to the sea. The villages are few and far between and much of the valley is thickly forested. The Sospel bus (#910) from Menton passes through **Castillon** (3 daily; 25min); for **Castellar** there's a local bus (#903; 5 daily; 25min).

To the east of the Carei valley, and closer to Menton, **CASTELLAR** marks the point where the pines start to take over from the lemon groves and the sea is all-visible. It is another old *village perché*, but not overrun by tourist commerce. It's also good for **walks**, with several paths radiating out into the hills around it as well as the GR52 from Gorbio and Ste-Agnes, which turns north along the Italian border to Sospel. Details of paths, plus **rooms** and **food** can be had from the *Hôtel des Alpes*, place Georges-Clemenceau (☎04.93.35.82.83, fax 04.93.28.24.25; ③), and you can sip a coffee or beer on the edge of the rock spur at *La Renaissance bar-tabac*. For those wanting a more isolated and interesting place to stay, there is a **campsite** at *La Ferme St-Bernard* (☎04.93.28.28.31), commanding fantastic views from high up a mountain slope to the north of the village. If you phone in advance, the owner will pick you up in his 4WD vehicle and take you to the site. Organic produce is cooked up for 130F a meal.

CASTILLON, a few kilometres south of Sospel, has twice been destroyed and rebuilt, by an earthquake in 1887 and by bombing in 1944. The current village, a short way down from Vieux Castillon, dates from the 1950s with **Les Arcades des Serres**, a terrace of artists' and crafts workers' studios added in the 1980s. Its status as an artists' village – the turning from the main road is marked by a dazzling ceramic – is not based on the normal Riviera riches market; the studios and galleries are provided at low rents in a genuine attempt to help local practitioners; and the works you see are very original and of a high standard. The **restaurant-salon de thé St-Julien** (☎04.93.04.19.10) has menus from 120F; *La Bergerie* **hotel-restaurant** (☎04.93.04.00.39; ④; closed Oct–Dec), on the southern edge of the village, has great views and pleasant rooms.

travel details

Trains

Cannes to: Antibes (10–15min); Biot (15min); Cagnes-sur-Mer (25min); Cros-de-Cagnes (30min); Golfe Juan-Vallauris (5min); Juan-les-Pins (10min); Marseille (1hr 5min); Nice (30–40min); St-Raphaël (25–35min); Villeneuve-Loubet-Plage (20min).

Nice to: Annot (4 daily; 1hr 45min); Beaulieu (15min); Breil-sur-Roya (4 daily; 1hr); Cap d'Ail (25min); Cap Martin-Roquebrune (40min); Digne (4 daily; 3hr 10min); Entrevaux (4 daily; 1hr 30min); L'Escarène (4 daily; 35–45min); Èze-sur-Mer (20min); Marseille (2hr 45min–3hr 15min); Menton (25–35min); Monaco (25min); Peille (4 daily; 30min); Peillon (2 daily; 25min); Puget-Théniers (4 daily; 1hr 20min); St-Raphaël (1hr–1hr 20min); Sospel (4 daily; 50min); Tende (2 daily; 2hr); Touët-sur-Var (4 daily; 1hr 10min); Villars-sur-Var (4 daily; 1hr); Villefranche (10min).

Buses

Cannes to: Aéroport Nice-Côte-d'Azur (12 daily; 45min); Golfe-Juan (frequent; 15min); Grasse (frequent; 45min); Mouans-Sartoux (frequent; 25min); Mougins (frequent; 20min); St-Raphaël (3–7 daily; 1hr 10min); Vallauris (frequent; 15min).

Grasse to: Le-Bar-sur-Loup (9 daily; 15–20min); Cabris (5 daily; 15min); Castellane (1 daily; 1hr 10min); Digne (1 daily; 2hr 20min); Draguignan (2 daily; 2hr 40min); Grenoble (1 daily; 6hr 10min); Mouans-Sartoux (frequent; 20min); Mougins (frequent; 25min); Nice (frequent; 1hr–1hr 15min); St-Cézaire (5 daily; 35min); St-Vallier (6 daily; 15min); Tourettes-sur-Loup (3 daily; 40min); Vence (3 daily; 50min).

Menton to: Nice (14 daily; 50min); Sospel (3 daily; 35–55min).

Monaco to: Èze Village (7 daily; 35min); Menton (frequent; 25min); Nice (frequent; 30–40min); La Turbie (5 daily; 30min).

Nice to: Aix (3 daily; 2hr 20min–4hr 30min); Beaulieu (14 daily; 20min); Cagnes-sur-Mer (frequent; 25–50min); Cap d'Ail (14 daily; 30min); Châteauneuf-de-Contes (2 daily; 1hr 10min); Coaraze (2 daily; 1hr); La Colle-sur-Loup (frequent; 35min); Contes (frequent; 30–40min); Cros-de-Cagnes (frequent; 20–35min); Digne (1 daily; 3hr–3hr 30min); Draguignan (3 weekly; 1hr 15min); L'Escarène (6 daily; 45min–1hr); Èze-sur-Mer (14 daily; 20min); Èze-Village (3 daily; 20min); Geneva (1 daily; 10hr 15min); Grasse (frequent; 1hr–1hr 15min); Grenoble (1 daily; 7hr 15min); Lucéram (4 daily; 45min–1hr); Marseille (4 daily; 2hr 45min–4hr 5min); Menton (14 daily; 1hr 15min); Monaco (14 daily; 30–40min); Peille (3 daily; 1hr); Roquebrune (14 daily; 40min–1hr); St-Paul (frequent; 45min); Sisteron (1 daily; 3hr 45min–4hr 10min); Toulon (2 daily; 2hr 30min); La Turbie (4 daily; 40min); Vence (frequent; 1hr); Villefranche (14 daily; 10min).

Ferries

Nice to: Corsica (April–Sept daily; Oct–May 3 weekly; 2hr 30min–11hr 30min).

Flights

Nice to: Amsterdam (2 daily; 2hr); Birmingham (2 weekly; 2hr); Dijon (1 weekly; 1hr 20min); Dublin (1 weekly; 2hr 30min); East Midlands (2 weekly; 2hr); Lille (1 daily; 1hr 30min); London (9–10 daily; 2hr); Lyon (4 daily; 50min); Manchester (1 weekly; 2hr 10min); Marseille (1 daily; 45min); New York (4 daily; 9hr); Ottawa (2 weekly; 8hr 30min); Paris (frequent; 1hr 20min); Rome (2 daily; 2hr); Strasbourg (3 daily; 1hr 10min); Toulouse (2–4 daily; 1hr).

CHAPTER SEVEN

HAUTE PROVENCE

The mountainous northeastern corner of Provence, **Haute Provence**, is a different world from season to season. In **spring** the fruit trees in the narrow valleys blossom, and melting waters swell the Verdon, the Vésubie, the Var, the Tinée and the Roya, sometimes flooding villages and carrying whole streets away. In the foothills, the groves of chestnut and olive trees bear fruit in **summer** and **autumn**, while higher up the pine forests are edged with wild raspberries and bilberries, and the moors and grassy slopes with white and gold alpine flowers. Above the line where vegetation ceases there are rocks with eagles' nests and snowcaps that never melt.

In **winter** the sheep and shepherds retreat to warmer pastures, leaving the snowy heights to antlered mouflons and chamois, and the perfectly camouflaged ermine. The villages where the shepherds came to summer markets are battened down for the long cold haul, while modern conglomerations of Swiss-style chalet houses, sports shops and discotheques come to life around the ski lifts. From November to April many of the mountain passes are closed, cutting off the dreamy northern town of **Barcelonnette** from its lower neighbours.

This is not an easy place to live. Abandoned farms and overgrown terraced slopes bear witness to the declining viability of mountain agriculture. But the **ski resorts** bring in money and summer brings the dedicated **trekkers**, naturalists and **climbers**. One area, covering 75km from east to west, protected as the **Parc National du Mercantour**, has no permanent inhabitants at all. It's crossed by numerous paths, with refuge huts providing basic food and bedding for trekkers.

For centuries the border between Provence and Savoy ran through this part of France, a political divide embodied by the impressive fortifications of Entrevaux and **Colmars**, the principal town of the Haut Verdon. To this day most of the region is not considered to be part of Provence. The French refer to it by the geographical term, the **Alpes-Maritimes**, which is also the name of the *département* that stretches from between the Haut Var and Verdon valleys and just above the source of the Tinée Valley to the Italian border, and includes the Riviera. Where Provence ends and the Alps begin is debatable, with the Tinée Valley usually cited as definitely belonging to the latter – the mountains here are pretty serious and the Italian influence becomes noticeable.

ACCOMMODATION PRICE CATEGORIES

Throughout this guide, all hotels and guesthouses have been priced on a scale of ①–⑧, indicating the lowest price you could expect to pay for a double room in high season. What you get for your money varies enormously between establishments, but in the lower-priced hotels you should expect to pay considerably more for en-suite facilities. If you are staying anywhere for more than three days it's often possible to negotiate a lower price, particularly out of season.

① Under 160F	③ 220–300F	⑤ 400–500F	⑦ 600–700F
② 160–220F	④ 300–400F	⑥ 500–600F	⑧ Over 700F

Running along the southern limit of the Alps is the **Nice–Digne rail line**, known as the Chemin de Fer de Provence, the only remaining segment of the region's turn-of-the-century narrow-gauge network. One of the great train rides of the country, it takes in the isolated Var towns of **Puget-Théniers** and **Entrevaux**, and ends at **Digne**, a low-key but intriguing regional capital that serves as the centre of the lavender industry. Away from the Nice–Digne line, transport is a problem save in the **Roya Valley**, over in the east, where the **Nice–Turin rail line** links the very Italianate towns of **Tende** and **Sospel**. **Buses** are infrequent and many of the best starting points for walks or the far-flung pilgrimage chapels are off the main roads. If you have your own transport, you'll face tough climbs and long stretches with no fuel supplies, but you'll be free to explore the most exhilaratingly beautiful corner of Provence.

Clues de Haute Provence

To the west of the River Var, north of Vence and the Route Napoléon in the Pre-Alpes de Grasse, lies the area known as the **Clues de Haute Provence**, *clues* being the word for the gorges cut through the limestone mountain ranges by their torrential rivers. This is an arid, sparsely populated region, its seclusion disturbed only by the winter influx of skiers from the coastal cities to the 1777-metre summit of the **Montagne du Cheiron**, and the car rallies along the Route des Crêtes, which follows the contours of the Montagne de Charamel and the Montagne St-Martin between the Cols de Bleine and Roquestéron.

Each claustrophobic and seemingly collapsible *clue* opens onto a wide and empty landscape of white and grey rocks with a tattered carpet of thick oak and pine forest. The horizons are always closed off by mountains, some erupting in a space of their own, others looking like coastal cliffs trailing the **Cheiron**, the **Charamel** or the 1664-metre-high **Montagne de Thorenc**. It's the sort of scenery that fantasy adventure games take place in, with wizards throwing laser-bolts from the mountains.

To appreciate it, though, you really need your own **transport**. Not all the passes are open during the winter – notices on the roads forewarn you of closures – and you should keep an eye on the fuel gauge, as garages are few and far between. Routes that go through the *clues* rather than over passes are manageable for cyclists: this is gorgeous, clean-air, long-freewheeling and panoramic terrain. There are plenty of footpaths, with the **GR4** as the main through-route for walkers from Gréolières to Aiglun across the Cheiron.

Accommodation isn't plentiful. What hotels there are tend to be very small, with a faithful clientele booking them up each year. Campsites are also thin on the ground, though there are a variety of gîtes scattered about. Even winter accommodation at **Gréolières** and **Gréolières-les-Neiges** is fairly minimal, as people tend to come up for a day's skiing or have their own weekend places. Most of the villages offer tourist information at the *mairie*. If you get stuck, the towns of Vence, Grasse, Puget-Théniers, Castellane or Nice are not far away.

Coursegoules and Gréolières

Coming from Vence you approach the *clues* via the Col de Vence, which brings you down to **Coursegoules**; from Grasse and the Loup Valley the road north leads to **Gréolières**, 11km west of Coursegoules.

Coursegoules

The bare white rocks that surround **COURSEGOULES** are not the most hospitable of sites for a working village, so it's no surprise that many of the smartly restored houses here are now used as second homes. The population has steadily declined to around

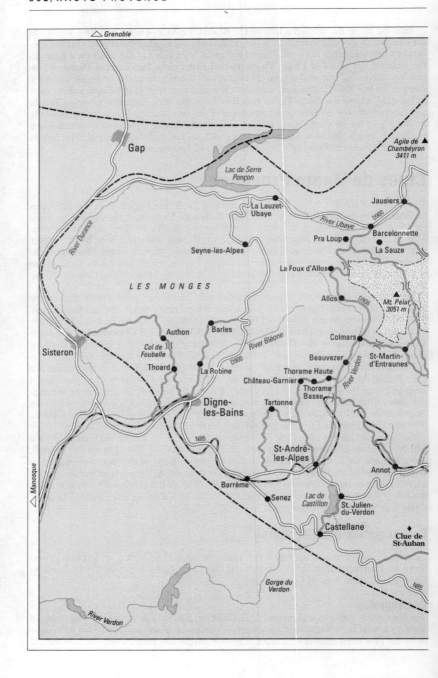

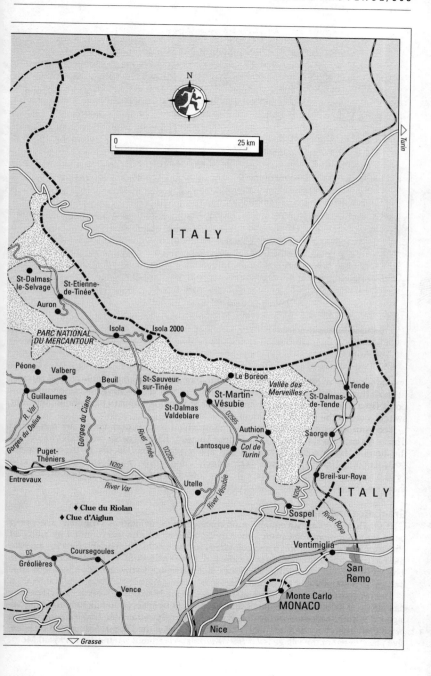

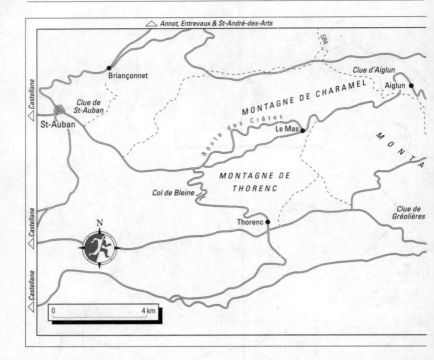

two hundred or so people who don't need to eke a living from the soil-scoured terrain. In the **church** the two obscure patron saints of the village have been honoured by Louis Bréa who painted them on each side of St John the Baptist (10am–noon; the light switches are to the left as you enter).

Accommodation possibilities here, all of which have superb views, are a chambre d'hôtes 400m from the village (M et Mme Durand, L'Hébergerie; ☎04.93.59.10.53; ②); the hotel *L'Auberge de l'Escaou* on the lovely place des Tilleuls in the old village (☎04.93.59.11.28; ③; closed Oct–May); and the *Saint-Antoine* **campsite** (☎04.93.59.12.36; closed Oct–March). The hotel has a perfectly good **restaurant** and there's a crêperie and small bistro in the village.

Gréolières and around

GRÉOLIÈRES seems an equally unpromising site for habitation. Originally a stopping point on the Roman road from Vence to Castellane, it's now surrounded by ruins, of Haut-Gréolières to the north and a fortress to the south. The parish church, opposite the fortress, has a Romanesque facade and a fifteenth-century retable of St Stephen. The village is liveliest during the winter, but passes as a summer resort as well after becoming a popular site for paragliding.

The **tourist office** (Mon–Fri 9am–noon & 2–6pm; ☎04.93.59.97.94) at 21 Grande-Rue has plenty of information on sports and activities in Gréolières and its neighbouring villages. For **hotel-restaurants** the only choice is the very reasonable *La Vieille Auberge* on place Pierre-Merle (☎04.93.59.95.07; ②) in the centre of the village. A good and inexpensive place to **eat** in the village is *La Barricade* pizzeria (menu around 100F; closed Mon).

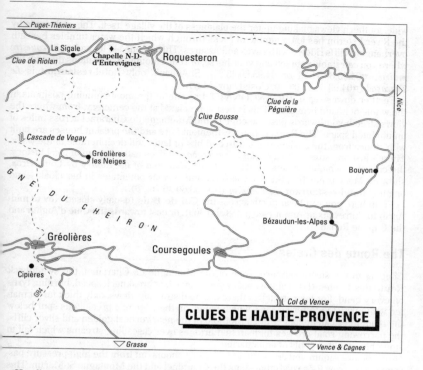

CLUES DE HAUTE-PROVENCE

Heading west around the mountains from Gréolières brings you through the Clue de Gréolières, carved by a tributary of the Loup, to the ski station **GRÉOLIÈRES-LES-NEIGES**, 18km by road from Gréolières. This is the closest **ski resort** to the Mediterranean and a centre for **cross-country skiing** (information on ☎04.93.59.70.57). Fourteen lifts ascend Mount Cheiron in winter, and in July and August a single chair lift operates for summer panoramas. There's just one **hotel**, the *Alpina* (☎04.93.59.70.19; ④; open Jan–March, July & Aug; rest of year by reservation only), which is more upmarket than the one in Gréolières, plus a handful of **cafés** and **restaurants**, most of which are open year round.

Thorenc, St-Auban and Briançonnet

THORENC, at the end off the D2 road, 13km west of Gréolières, is a popular paragliding and cross-country-skiing resort, created by English and Russians at the turn of the twentieth century, an origin reflected in the style of the older buildings. There's been a lot of new development and it's a lively place during both the winter and summer seasons. There are two very pleasant small **hotel-restaurants**: *Des Voyageurs*, 13 av du Belvédère (☎04.93.60.00.18; ③; closed mid-Nov to Jan), and *Les Mesiriers*, 24 av du Belvédère (☎04.93.60.00.23; ③; closed Tues).

To the north, the D5 crosses the Montagne de Thorenc by the Col de Bleine and then the D10 takes over for the ascent of Charamel, without a moment's pause in the looping climb. The D10 leads to Aiglun while the D5 takes the easier westward route to **ST-AUBAN** and its *clue*. St-Auban rests against the grassy slope of the mountainside, its wide southern views making up for the plainness of the village itself. The gash made by the River Esteron has left a jumble of rocks through which the water tumbles beneath overhanging cliffs riddled with caves and fissures. There's one ski lift and a *gîte equestre* where you can stable yourself and your horse, or rent a mount (reservations through the *mairie*; ☎04.93.60.41.23 or 04.93.60.43.20). St-Auban's only **hotel-restaurant** is *Le Tracastel* (☎04.93.60.43.06; ③; closed Nov–May).

Further downstream, **BRIANÇONNET** has one of the most stunning positions in the whole of inland Provence. This is best appreciated at the cemetery, from where the views stretch southwards past the edge of the Montagne de Charamel across miles of uninhabited space. The Romans had a settlement here and the present houses are built with stones from the ancient ruins with odd bits of Latin still decipherable in the walls. There's just one street with a *boulangerie*, a *tabac*, and a small museum of local history, the church – which contains a retable of *The Madonna of the Rosary* by Louis Bréa, showing Mary protecting the ecclesiastical and secular potentates in her cloak – and one tiny **hotel-restaurant**, *Le Chanan* (☎04.93.60.46.75; ②).

From here you can head north across the **Col de Buis** (usually closed Nov to mid-April) to Entrevaux or Annot (see p.368 and 369), or east towards the Clue d'Aiglun and the Clue de Riolan.

The Route des Crêtes

Clinging to the steep southern slope of the Montagne de Charamel, the switchback **Route des Crêtes** (D10) almost defies you to take it at breakneck speed, burning tyres on every bend. For long stretches there are no distracting views, only thick forest matted with mistletoe. After Le Mas, which hangs on the edge of a precipitous spur below the road, trees can no longer get a roothold in the near-vertical golden and silver cliffs; the narrowing road crosses high-arched bridges over cascading streams which fall to smoothly moulded pools of aquamarine.

Just before Aiglun you cross the Esteron as it shoots out from the high-pressure passage (too narrow for a road) that splits the Charamel and the Montagne St-Martin. This is the most formidable of all the *clues* and is impossible to explore. You can, however, follow the GR4 southwards from the D10, 1.5km west of the *clue*, to the **Vegay waterfall**, halfway between Aiglun and Gréolières-les-Neiges, where water destined for the Esteron plummets down a vertical cliff-face.

In the village of **AIGLUN** you can **stay**, if you're lucky, in one of the six rooms at the *Auberge de Calendal* (☎04.93.05.82.32; ②; closed Feb), which also manages dormitory-style accommodation in a *gîte communale* on the GR4. East from Aiglun the campanile and silvery olive groves of the ancient fortified village of La Sigale flicker into view.

Beyond La Sigale, midway to Roquesteron, the **Chapelle Notre-Dame d'Entrevignes** has preserved fragments of fifteenth-century frescoes including the unusual scene of Mary, ready to give birth, with Joseph expressing deep suspicion. To visit apply to La Sigale's *mairie* (Mon–Fri 2.30–5pm; ☎04.93.05.83.52) or to Mme Pellat (☎04.93.05.81.16).

ROQUESTERON, about 10km east of St-Aiglun, was divided for a hundred years by the France–Savoy border, which followed the course of the Esteron; it's now divided between the Alpes-Maritimes and the Alpes-de-Haute-Provence *départements*. There's one **hotel** here, the *Passeron* at 25 bd Salvago (☎04.93.05.91.01; ③). From Roquestéron you have the choice of following the D17 above the Esteron to the river's confluence with the Var, or taking the tangled D1, through passages of rock seamed in thin vertical bands to **BOUYON**, from where the D8 takes you back to Coursegoules. Both routes take you through a succession of eagle's-nest villages. At Bouyon you'll find an excellent **hotel-restaurant**, the *Catounière* in place de la Mairie (☎04.93.59.07.15; ②; closed Nov–Dec).

The Lower Var Valley

From Nice both the Chemin de Fer de Provence and the road stick closely to the left bank of the Var, which is wide, turbulent and not greatly scenic downstream of its confluence with the Esteron. Past the confluence with the Vésubie, a short way further north, you enter the **Défilé de Chaudan**, a long gorge between vertical cliffs through which the rail line and road have to tunnel. At the northern extremity of the gorge, the River Tinée comes rushing out of the **Gorges de la Mescla** to join the Var in a twisted, semi-subterranean junction of rock and water. From here the course of the Var runs almost due west for 40km, passing tiny medieval villages and the towns of **Puget-Théniers** and **Entrevaux**. The main road and the rail line then continue west along the River Vaïre to **Annot**.

Villars-sur-Var

VILLARS-SUR-VAR, 11km west of the Gorges de la Mescla, may have the northern-most vineyards of the Côtes de Provence *appellation*, but the quantity of wine produced is only just sufficient for local consumption, so you'll be lucky to get a glass of it in one of the two cafés.

The reason for stopping off here – apart from the charm of a *village perché* with stepped streets – is to see the **Église de St-Jean-Baptiste** and wander down the **allée des Grimaldi**. The carefully restored Baroque church is decorated with trompe-l'oeil frescoes and an eighteenth-century ex-votive painting to "Saint Patron de la Bonne Mort", thanking him for killing off only 66 residents in the previous year's plague. The main altar has a striking retable, with another on the left wall from the Nice School. A door to the right of the church leads into the allée des Grimaldi, a flowering alleyway formed by a trellis supported on stone columns. At the end you come to a platform with views over the Var Valley.

Touët-sur-Var and the Gorges du Cians

Crammed against a cliff 10km west of Villars-sur-Var, **TOUËT-SUR-VAR** also has a church that's rather special, though for a very different reason: it's built over a small torrent, visible through a grille in the floor of the nave. The village's highest houses look as if they are falling apart, but in fact the gaps between the beams are open galleries where the midday sun can reach the rows of drying figs.

For a **place to stay** try *Chez Paul*, on the road from Nice (☎04.93.05.71.03; ③; closed weekdays Oct–June). Touët has a very good **restaurant**, the *Auberge des Chasseurs*, also on the main road (☎04.93.05.71.11; menus from 110F; closed Tues), serving local fare which in autumn involves game and wild mushrooms. The specialities of the area are squash ravioli with nut sauce and *tartes des blettes* (Swiss chard tarts).

The River Cians joins the Var a short way west of Touët. The road along this tributary, the D28, leads to the ski resort of Beuil, passing first through the Gorges Inférieures du Cians, close to the confluence, and then the **Gorges du Cians** proper, a chaos of water tumbling over red schist rocks. This and the Gorges de Daluis to the west (see p.383) are a well-signed tourist routes, so be prepared for heavy traffic.

Puget-Théniers

After arriving by train at the small, dilapidated town of **PUGET-THÉNIERS**, the first monument you see is a statue of a powerful woman with her hands tied behind her back. It commemorates **Auguste Blanqui**, who was born here in 1805. Blanqui was one of the leaders of the Paris Commune of 1871, and spent forty years of his life in prison for – as the inscription states – "his fidelity to the sacred cause of workers' emancipation". There are few French revolutionaries for whom the description "heroic defender of the proletariat" is so true, and none who came from a more isolated and unindustrialized region.

Sculpted by Maillol and titled *L'Action Enchaînée*, the monument immediately stirred up controversy in the town. It was first placed behind the church, but the priest was not going to have processions passing by a naked woman. So it was moved to the vicinity of the World War I cenotaph, but the veterans objected. Its next home was the abattoir. Only after World War II, from which French Communism emerged with a fairly unblemished record of resistance, was the monument finally placed on the *cours* below the old town.

The **Vieille Ville**, on the right bank of the River Roudoule, is full of mangy cats and thirteenth-century houses, some bearing the symbols of their original owners' trades on the door lintels. Across the Roudoule, the town is dominated by the great semicircular apse of the Romanesque **church**, outreaching even the ancient cedar alongside it, and suggesting a fort or prison more than a religious building. It's not a pretty structure by any standards, but it contains a brilliantly realistic Flemish *Entombment*, painted in the 1500s and an expressive calvary sculpted in wood.

Practicalities

The **tourist office** (April to mid-Oct & Dec daily 9am–12.15pm & 3–7pm; rest of year Mon–Fri 9am–12.15pm & 2.30–6pm; ☎04.93.05.05.05) is on the main road by the gare Chemin de Fer de Provence and has information on walks, canoeing and the steam trains that run between Puget-Théniers and Annot.

The *Laugier* at 1 place A-Conil (☎04.93.05.01.00; ③) is the best place to **stay**; alternatively, try the *Alizé* (☎04.93.05.06.20; ③), which is by the busy N202, but has its own swimming pool. Puget's two-star municipal **campsite** is by the river (☎04.93.05.10.53; closed Oct–Feb).

On summer evenings the **cafés** and **restaurants** on place A-Cornil in the Vieille Ville and down along the Roudoule towards the Var manage to be livelier than you may expect from a small *haut-pays* town.

The **restaurant** in the *Laugier* hotel is your best bet in the centre of town, but your first choice for meals should be *Les Acacias* (☎04.93.05.05.25; closed Wed), 1km east of Puget-Théniers on the main road, with an excellent menu for around 120F plus a midday menu for around 90F (not Sun). Excellent old-fashioned *boulangeries*, *charcuteries* and *fromageries* can be found in the old quarter and, if you happen to be here at Pentecost, nearby La Croix-Sur-Redoule has a communal feast of bean soup cooked in a vast cauldron.

Entrevaux

Upstream from Puget-Théniers the valley widens, allowing space for pear, apple and cherry orchards. After 13km you reach **ENTREVAUX** whose striking feature is the fortification sealing the old town on the north bank of the river. Built on the site of a Roman settlement, this was once a key border town between France and Savoy.

The single-arched drawbridge across the Var – the only access – was fortified by Vauban, and it is Vauban's linking of the town with the ruined **Château** (access at any time; 10F) that gives the site its menacing character. Perched 135m above the river at the top of a steep spur, the château originally could be reached only by scrambling up the rock. By the seventeenth century this had become unacceptable, perhaps because soldiers leaving the garrison on their hands and knees did not do much for the army's image. Consequently, Vauban built the double-walled ramp, plus attendant bastions, that zigzags up the rock in ferocious determination.

The former **cathedral** (summer 9am–8pm; winter 9am–6pm), in the lower part of the old town, is well integrated into the military defences, with one wall forming part of the ramparts and its belfry a fortified tower. The interior, however, is all twirling Louis Quinze, with misericords, side altars and organ as overdecorated as they could possibly be. Just beyond the church, through the **Porte d'Italie**, you can escape from Baroque opulence and military might to wander along a path beside the river.

Practicalities

The **gare Chemin de Fer de Provence** is just downstream from the bridge on the south bank, and the **tourist office** (daily: May–Aug 9.30am–7pm; rest of year 9am–noon & 1.15–6pm; ☎04.93.05.46.73) is in the left-hand tower of the drawbridge; it organises guided tours of the town (May–Sept; 20F, 25F in medieval costume).

For places to stay, there's the rudimentary **hotel** *Hostellerie Vauban*, 4 place Moreau (☎04.93.05.42.40; ②; closed Dec), south of the river, and two **gîtes d'étapes**: the *Gîte des Moulins* (②) and the *Gîte de la Caserne* (①) – book through the tourist office.

For **food and drink** try the *Bar au Pont-Levis* opposite Vauban's bridge, where English-speaking tourists congregate, or head up to place Charles-Panier where you'll find *L'Échauguette* (☎04.93.05.46.89; menus from 70F), a restaurant specializing in trout, pasta and the local dry beef sausage (*secca de boeuf*), and *Le Planet* snack-bar, serving omelettes, *pan bagnat* and pizzas. The Lovera *charcuterie* (closed Mon) next door to *Le Planet* sells *secca de boeuf* if you want to try it as picnic food, though it's best seasoned with lemon and olive oil. On place du Marché there's an *épicerie* selling wonderful honey.

Annot

ANNOT is primarily a holiday centre for its climate, pure health-giving waters and clean air. The Vieille Ville, if not outstanding, does have some pretty arcades and a Renaissance clock tower on its church; the modern town is grouped around its *cours*, a large open space lined by plane trees to the south of the medieval quarter. It is an excellent base for walks, up past strange sandstone formations to rocky outcrops with names like *Chambre du Roi* (the King's Chamber) and *Dent du Diable* (the Devil's Tooth).

The **gare Chemin de Fer de Provence** is to the southeast of the town, at the end of av de la Gare, which leads to the main *cours*. The **tourist office** on place du Revely (Mon–Sat 10am–noon & 3–6pm, Sun 10am–noon; ☎04.92.83.23.03) has plenty of details on walks, rides, sports facilities, the steam train to Puget-Théniers, exhibitions and local festivities. It also rents **bikes**.

Accommodation is easy to come by, all of it reasonably priced. Of the **hotels**, budget options include the crumbling *La Cigale* to the north on bd St-Pierre (☎04.92.83.20.24; ①); and the *Beau Séjour*, by the entrance to the Vieille Ville on place du Revely (☎04.92.83.21.08; ①; closed Jan). The *Hôtel du Parc* on place du Germe (☎04.92.83.20.03; ③; closed Oct–April) is an old house on the western side of the *cours* with a large garden and a good restaurant (menus from 80F). The hotel on av de la Gare, *L'Avenue* (☎04.92.83.22.07; ③; closed Nov–March), has small cosy rooms and its **restaurant** is the best in town (menus from 85F). For **campers** there's a very pleasant two-star site, *La Ribière*, on the road to Fugeret (☎04.92.83.21.44; mid-Feb to mid-Nov) just north of the town.

St-André-les-Alpes, Castellane and the Route Napoléon

From Annot, the Chemin de Fer de Provence heads due north before tunnelling through to the Verdon Valley and **Thorame-Haute**'s station where you can take buses further north up the Verdon. The rail line turns south again with the next major stop at **St-André-les-Alpes**. St-André stands at the head of the **Lac de Castillon**, one of the Verdon's many artificial lakes, stretching a good 10km southwards to the Barrage de Castillon and the smaller Lac de Chaudanne from where the Verdon descends dramatically into **Castellane**, the second most significant town on the **Route Napoléon** after Grasse.

The main road along the Var Valley, the N202 from Entrevaux, skirts Annot and heads west to the Lac de Castillon at **St-Julien-du-Verdon**, then takes over from the D955 as the lakeside corniche up to St-André. The road and rail line run parallel again west from St-André along a beautiful stretch of rock, river and forest to meet the Route Napoléon at **Barrême**.

With good train and road access, plenty of accommodation and well-organized facilities for outdoor activities, particularly water and airborne sports, this is an easy corner of Haute Provence to explore. Castellane and St-Julien can feel a bit too subservient to entrepreneurial tourism, but traditional Provence is never far away, as the sight of sheep taking over the roads on their way to or from their summer pastures may well remind you.

St-André-les-Alpes

ST-ANDRÉ-LES-ALPES has a sleepy, old-fashioned feel to it with none of the tight, protective huddling of so many Provençal villages. Instead its streets and squares are open to the air, and to the magnificent views of the surrounding mountains and the lake. Accommodation and food are cheap; the only difficulty is choosing which of the beautiful routes out from St-André to explore.

The **gare Chemin de Fer de Provence** is in the centre of the village; the **tourist office** lies just to its south on place Marcel-Pastorelli (June–Aug Mon–Sat 8.30am–12.30pm & 1.30–7pm, Sun 10am–noon; rest of year 9am–noon & 2–5pm; ☎04.92.89.02.39), and is very helpful, offering information on the surrounding area, including St-Julien, Thorame and Moriez.

Of the seven **hotels** in and around St-André the *Lac et Fôret* on the road to St-Julien (☎04.92.89.07.38, fax 04.92.89.13.88; ③; closed Nov–Feb) has the best views over the lake; the *France* has budget rooms right in the centre of the village on place de l'Église (☎04.92.89.02.09; ②), where you'll also find the comfortable *Auberge du Parc* (☎04.92.89.00.03; ②), whose restaurant offers dependable meals from 80F. The two-star municipal **campsite**, *Les Iscles*, by the confluence of the Verdon and the Issole on the road to St-Julien (☎04.92.89.02.29; closed Oct–March) has good facilities. If you prefer a **gîte d'étape**, try the one in Moriez, the next stop on the Chemin de Fer de Provence or a five-minute drive west of St-André (☎04.92.89.13.20; closed mid-Nov to Feb). There's a good choice of **beers** at *Le Commerce* bar on place de l'Église.

Gliding and **hang-gliding** are popular here, taking place around Mont Chalvet to the west of the village, with short flights for the less experienced in the morning. It's very well organized and regulated to ensure maximum safety by the École de Vol Libre "Aerogliss" at the Base de Loisirs des Iscles to the south of the village (☎04.92.89.11.30; 400F for an initiation flight, including equipment rental). **Bikes** can be rented at Pro-Verdon Activités Nature on rue Basse (☎04.92.89.04.19); they also organize **walks**, and **rafting** and **canoeing** on the Lac de Castillon and the Gorges de Verdon.

North to Château-Garnier and Thorame

Following the River Issole north from St-André along the D2 brings you to **Château-Garnier** 15km north. This is a very pleasant route: the narrow road stays close to the banks most of the time, with well-signed footpaths leading off into the wooded hills; after 8km you can turn left towards Tartonne where there's a pleasant gîte d'étape with a good restaurant, *Les Robines* (c/o Mme Pascale Reybaud; ☎04.92.34.26.07; ②; menus from 60F), or keep going to La Bâtie where the valley opens out. Between La Bâtie and Château-Garnier, on the left along the footpath to Tartonne, is the twelfth-century **Chapelle St-Thomas**, decorated with medieval frescoes (the key is available from the first farm on the right after the turning).

The main reason to stop in **CHÂTEAU-GARNIER**, however, is to visit the serious and dedicated **honey** business Miellerie Chailan at the far end of the village on the left (Mon–Fri 8am–noon & 1.30–7pm, Sat 8am–noon & 2–5pm). Though only groups are given tours of the hives, you may see the gleaming machinery in action, and you can certainly buy superb honey with such flavours as rosemary, acacia, "thousand flowers", sunflower, pine and lavender, plus nougat, sweets, candles and medicinal derivatives.

From Château-Garnier the road veers east through **THORAME BASSE**, where the church has an unlikely train station-style clock on the spire and the *Café du Vallée* serves inexpensive plats du jour, then through wide open meadows to **THORAME HAUTE** where there's a **hotel-restaurant** *Au Bon Accueil* (☎04.92.83.90.79; ①), a *charcuterie* and a one-star municipal **campsite** *Fontchaude* (☎04.92.83.47.37), down by the river.

South along the Lac de Castillon

Depending on the water levels the **Lac de Castillon** can be a bit murky at the St-André end but you don't have to go far down the N202 to find places to **swim** and **rent boats**. The landscape gets more dramatic after the road crosses over the lake and the hills start to close in.

ST-JULIEN-DU-VERDON was a casualty of the creation of the lake. Today it's a tiny place with a two-star **campsite**, *Camping du Lac* (☎04.92.89.07.93; closed mid-Sept to mid-June), and a **hotel**, *Lou Pidanoux* (☎04.92.89.05.87; ②), but nothing to suggest that this was once Sanctus Julienetus, on the Roman road from Nice to Digne. Still, it's a pleasant, quiet spot if you just want to laze about by calm, clear water with a gorgeous backdrop of mountains.

The main road east from St-Julien leads to Annot, a fabulous ride through the dramatic *clues* of Vergons and Rouaine, and past the exquisite Romanesque chapel of Notre-Dame de Valvert. While off the Castellane road to the south there are more opportunities for bathing and boating; the gleam of gold up in the hills on the opposite bank that might catch your eye is the decoration of the Buddhist centre of Mandaron.

Castellane

Being the nearest town to the upper part of the Gorges du Verdon, some 17km away (see p.265), **CASTELLANE** has long been a major a tourist camp, claiming itself as the "gateway to the gorge" and entreating passers-by with the bizarre notion: "Napoléon stopped here; why not you?" Your reason for stopping is likely to be for the range of restaurants, hotels and cafés which in summer gives the town an animation rare in these parts. The place where Napoléon stopped to dine on March 3, 1815 is now the **Conservatoire des Arts et Traditions Populaires de Castellane et Moyen Verdon**, 34 rue Nationale, which has temporary exhibitions of variable interest.

The only distinguishing feature of the town is the abrupt and massive rock topped by a **chapel** dedicated, predictably enough, to Our Lady of the Rock. The path up to it begins behind the modern church set back at the head of place de l'Église from the central place Marcel-Sauvaire, and winds its way up past the Vieille Ville and the machicolated **Tour Pentagonal**, standing uselessly on the lower slopes. Twenty to thirty minutes should see you at the top, from where you cannot actually see the gorge, but you do get a pretty good view of the river disappearing into it and the mountains circling the town.

Practicalities

There are two **buses** a day in July and August into the Gorges du Verdon (1hr to La Maline) and one to the Lac de Castillon. The **tourist office** is at the top of rue Nationale (July & Aug Mon–Sat 9am–noon & 1.30–7pm, Sun 10am–12.30pm; rest of year Mon–Fri 9am–noon & 2–6pm; ☎04.92.83.61.14) and can provide a full list of hotels and campsites.

The best **hotel** deals in Castellane are the *Hostellerie du Roc*, place de l'Église (☎04.92.83.62.65; ③; closed Dec to mid-Jan); *Le Verdon*, bd de la République (☎04.92.83.62.02; ③); and the *Auberge Bon Accueil*, place Marcel-Sauvaire (☎04.92.83.62.01; ③; closed Oct–March). The *Nouvel Hôtel du Commerce* in place de l'Église (☎04.92.83.61.00; ④; menus from 120F; closed Nov–March) is the most upmarket, with questionable decor but wonderful **food** served in the garden. You can get cheap pasta dishes at *La Main à la Pâte* on rue de la Fontaine and there's a pleasant ice-cream bar at the end of the same street. Wednesday and Saturday are **market** days and there's a good wine shop between the tourist office and Aqua-Verdon (see below).

There are eleven **campsites** within 3km of the town. The closest is *Le Frédéric-Mistral* (☎04.92.83.62.27), by the river on the rte des Gorges du Verdon. Further on down the same road you'll see the caravans and bungalows of the *Camping Notre-Dame* (☎04.92.83.63.02; closed Nov–March), and 1.5km out of town the four-star *Camping du Verdon* (☎04.92.83.61.29; closed mid-Sept to mid-May) which offers **horse-rides**. In summer all the sites along this road are likely to be full. A good one to try that's further afield and away from the gorge is *La Colle* on the GR4 off the rte des Gorges (☎04.92.83.61.57; closed Nov–March).

For **canoeing** and **rafting** on Lac de Castillon and the Gorges de Verdon, Agence Aqua-Verdon at 9 rue Nationale (☎04.92.83.72.75) and École Française de Canoë-Kayak just down from the tourist office (☎04.92.83.75.74) are the places to get information. Aqua-Verdon also rents out **bikes**.

Along the Route Napoléon

North of Castellane the barren scrubby rocks lining the Route Napoléon need the evening light to turn them a more becoming pinkish hue. The town's landmark remains visible all the way up the zigzags to the **Col de Leque**. Here, in the night-time cold of over 1000m above sea level, you can find a bed at the **hotel-restaurant** *Les Peyrascas* (☎04.92.83.68.98; ③), assured of a sublime view to greet you in the morning.

From the Col de Leque the Route Napoléon traverses the **Clue de Taulanne**, then opens out onto a marvellous northward view of a circle of crests. To either side of the road lie some of the most obscure and empty quarters of Provence. The populations of villages such as **Blieux** and **Majastres**, on the slopes of the Mourre ridge to the west, have dwindled close to the point of desertion. Life here is rural poverty at its starkest, for all the seeming promise of the springtime or early summer land to the amateur's eye.

Back on the only significant road, the village of **SENEZ** speaks of the same decline, with its vast Romanesque ex-cathedral that could easily accommodate ten times the present number of residents. The episcopal see established here in the fourth century, one of the earliest in France, was throughout the centuries one of the poorest bishoprics in the country. The church is only open on Sunday, or else Mme Mestre, whose house is at the bottom of the village by the fountain, has the key and will let you in for 10F. There's a **gîte** on place du Coulet c/o Mme Guirao (☎04.92.34.24.99; 50F per person), should you wish to stay.

Digne-les-Bains and around

The capital of the Alpes-de-Haute-Provence *département*, **DIGNE-LES-BAINS**, is by far the largest town in northeastern Provence, with about 17,000 inhabitants. However, despite its status and superb position between the Durance Valley and the start of the real mountains, it can be a dispiriting place. This is partly due to its curative **baths**, visited by those afflicted with rheumatism and respiratory disorders, and partly due to the overdose of administrative offices in what is a very small city. Despite brand new architecture around the central place Gal-de-Gaulle, and some tasteful modern infill to the crumbling Vieille Ville, Digne is a dull place to explore.

It does, however, have a bursting calendar of festivals and celebrations of lavender cultivation (see p.377 for a full rundown), two interesting museums, a Tibetan foundation that has been visited by the Dalai Lama, and a geology reserve of some significance which encompasses a huge area surrounding the town. Every other year Digne runs a Symposium International de la Sculpture with the works exhibited throughout the town – the next one is in 1999. Digne also has an excellent choice of places to stay and eat, and, if you have your own transport, there are great trips to be made into the mountains.

To the north of Digne, the mountain range, which reaches its highest peak at Les Monges (2115m), forms a near impassable barrier between the valleys running down to Sisteron and the Durance in the west and those of the Bléone's tributaries in the east. There are footpaths, for serious walkers – which begin at Digne on the west bank of the Bléone north of the Grand Pont – and just one road loops south of Les Monges linking Digne and Sisteron via Thoard and Authon across the Col de Font-Belle. The D900a, which follows first the course of the Bléone, and then the Bès torrent, passes many of the protected sites of the **Réserve Naturelle Géologique de Haute Provence**, where shrubs, flowers and butterflies are now the sole visible wildlife.

Arrival, information and accommodation

From the Durance Valley the Route Napoléon enters Digne along the west bank of the Bléone, arriving at the rond-point du 4 Septembre, with the **gares SNCF** (☎08.36.35.35.35) and **Chemin de Fer de Provence** (☎04.92.31.01.58) just to the west, along av Paul-Sémard. Avenue de Verdon continues to Grand Pont, the main bridge, over which you reach the rond-point du 11 Novembre 1918, where you'll find the **tourist office** (July & Aug Mon–Sat 8.45am–12.30pm & 2–7pm, Sun 9am–noon & 3–7pm; Sept, Oct & May–June Mon–Sat 8.45am–noon & 2–6.30pm, Sun 9.30am–12.30pm; Nov–April Mon–Sat 8.45am–noon & 2–6pm, Sun 10am–noon; ☎04.92.31.42.73), the **gîtes de France** office and the **gare routière**. From the south the Route Napoléon comes in along the east bank of the river to the rond-point du 11 Novembre 1918. From the rond-point, the main street, boulevard Gassendi, leads up to place du Gal-de-Gaulle; and av Thiers, which becomes av du 8 mai 1945, leads further east towards the Établissement Thermal 3km from the centre. The **old town** lies between these two. **Bikes** can be rented from Gallardo, 8 cours des Arès (☎04.92.31.05.29), or Le Vallon des Sources, rte des Thermes (☎04.92.30.47.00).

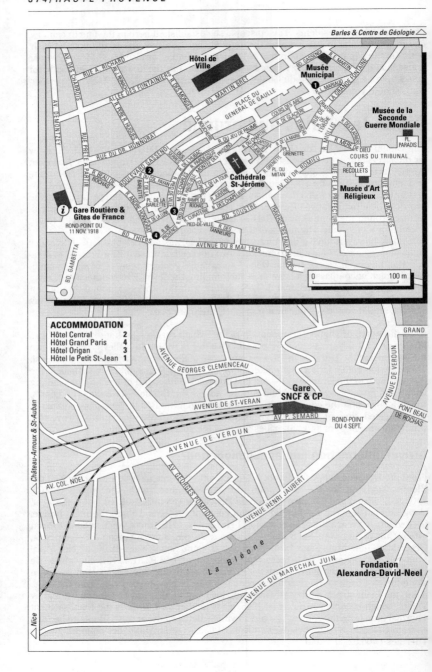

Barles & Centre de Géologie △

Hôtel de Ville

Musée Municipal ❶

Musée de la Seconde Guerre Mondiale

Musée d'Art Réligieux

AV. DES CHARROIS
RUE A. RICHARD
RUE J. BERNARD
ALLÉE DES FONTAINIERS
R. DES MONGES
R. PIERRE HUGUES
RUE DU DR. HONNORAT
AV. DEMONTZEY
R. PRÊLE LÉON
RUE PRÊLE À PARTIR
R. BEAU DE ROCHAS
R. ANDRÉ HONNORAT
BOULEVARD GASSENDI
BD. MARTIN BRET
PLACE DU GENERAL DE GAULLE
BD. GASSENDI
RUE MARTIN
RUE DE LA GRANDE FONTAINE
R. MARIAUD
RUE DORMOIE
RUE DE L'ÉGLISE
R. MOLLUS
RUE MERE DE DIEU
PL. PARADIS
COURS DU TRIBUNAL
PL. DES RECOLLETS
RUE DE LA PREFECTURE
RUE DES ARCHIVES

i Gare Routière & Gîtes de France
ROND-POINT DU 11 NOV. 1918

BD. GAMBETTA
BD. THIERS
BD. SOUSTRE
AVENUE DU 8 MAI 1945
TRAVERSE DES FAUX CHAUDS

Cathédrale St-Jérôme

❷
❸
❹

0   100 m

ACCOMMODATION

Hôtel Central	2
Hôtel Grand Paris	4
Hôtel Origan	3
Hôtel le Petit St-Jean	1

AVENUE GEORGES CLEMENCEAU

GRAND
AVENUE DE VERDUN

Gare SNCF & CP

AVENUE DE ST-VERAN
AV. P. SEMARD
ROND-POINT DU 4 SEPT.
PONT BEAU DE ROCHAS

△ Château-Arnoux & St-Auban

AV. COL. NOEL
AVENUE DE VERDUN
AV. GEORGES POMPIDOU
AVENUE HENRI JAUBERT

La Bléone

AVENUE DU MARECHAL JUIN

Fondation Alexandra-David-Neel

△ Nice

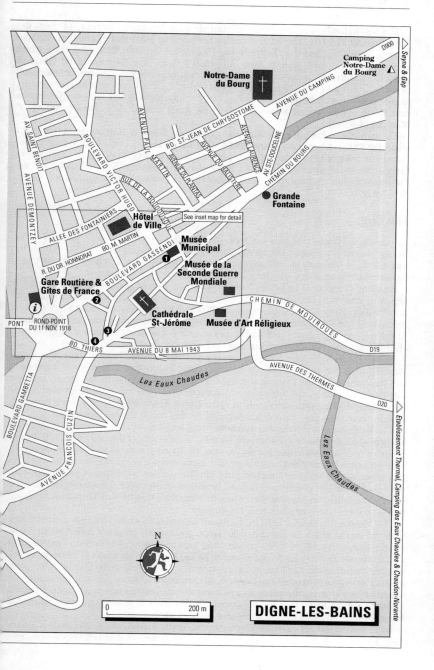

DIGNE-LES-BAINS

The best-value **hotels** are the simple but pleasant *Le Petit Saint-Jean,* 14 cours des Arès (☎04.92.31.30.04; ②), with a restaurant serving local and Spanish specialities (menus from 70F); and the *Origan*, 6 rue Pied-de-la-Ville (☎04.92.31.62.13; ②), which also serves good food (menus from 70F; closed Sun). The *Central*, 26 bd Gassendi (☎04.92.31.31.91; ③), is very comfortable and central; while for considerably more luxury, try *Le Grand Paris*, 19 bd Thiers (☎04.92.31.11.15; ⑤), in a seventeenth-century former convent with tastefully decorated large rooms and Digne's top gourmet restaurant (100F midday menu Mon–Sat, otherwise from around 200F; closed Sun eve & Mon out of season).

The two-star municipal **campsite** *Notre-Dame du Bourg* is 2km out from the centre along the D900 to Seynes-les-Alpes (☎04.92.31.04.87; closed Oct–March); take av Ste-Douceline left from the top of bd Gassendi and then turn right into av du Camping. Or there's the more pleasantly situated three-star *Camping des Eaux Chaudes*, rte des Thermes, 1.5km out towards the Établissement Thermal (☎04.92.32.31.04; closed Nov–March).

The City

Late medieval Digne had **two centres**: the area to the north around Notre-Dame du Bourg, where pre-Roman Digne developed; and the existing Haute Ville where the Cathédrale St-Jérôme was built as a small church at the end of the fifteenth century, to be successively enlarged as it took over the functions of Notre-Dame.

Standing in splendid isolation, **Notre-Dame du Bourg** (May–Oct daily 3–6pm) is typical of Provençal Romanesque, save for the vastness of its dimensions and the lightness of its yellowy stone. Built between 1200 and 1330, it contains fragments of early medallions and late medieval murals, the least faded illustrating the Last Judgement. Archeological digs have revealed a first-century construction and a fifth-century church from which a Merovingian altar and a mosaic floor remain.

In the Haute Ville, the fifteenth-century **Cathédrale St-Jérôme** (June–Oct Tues, Wed, Thurs & Sat 3–6pm) is in dire need of repair. The Gothic facade is still impressive and the features inside, in particular the Gothic stained-glass windows, clearly indicate that this was once an awesome place of worship. Work will no doubt be carried out on the cathedral, along with the streets of Vieux Digne which are gradually being restored, though there is no date currently scheduled for this much-needed restoration.

The Wednesday and Saturday **markets** bring animation to the otherwise rather clinically modernized **place Général-de-Gaulle**, to the north of the cathedral, with lots of lavender products, including honey, on sale. To the east, a statue of **Pierre Gassendi**, a seventeenth-century mathematician and astronomer, stands within the balustrades that separate the boulevard named after him from place Général-de-Gaulle. Gassendi used to dispute the precise location of the immortal soul with Descartes, but showed more materialism on his deathbed when he remarked that he would not now be dying had he not been so compliant with his doctors.

The **Musée Municipal** at 64 bd Gassendi (temporarily closed for restoration; check with the tourist office for latest details) has a particularly good art collection that covers the sixteenth century to the present, and includes numerous Provençal paintings of the nineteenth century and some stunning Italian and Flemish works. The museum celebrates the scientific tradition of the town with a fascinating collection of nineteenth-century scientific instruments, Gassendi mementoes of course, plus documentation on other natives of note, including an engineer who in 1880 designed a Channel tunnel. Another section illustrates life and society in the lower Alps through a reconstructed street with its goldsmith's, cobbler's and barber's shop.

Southeast of the old town, on place Paradis, is the **Musée de la Seconde Guerre Mondiale** (July & Aug Mon–Fri 2–6pm; May, June & Sept to mid-Oct Wed 2–5pm; rest of the year by appointment with Jacques Teyssier on ☎04.92.31.28.95; free). Digne was under Italian occupation from the end of 1942 to September 1943, when the Germans took over. The names of people in the photographs have had to be covered up in an effort to avoid the rows that still erupt here over who resisted and who did not. For a foreign visitor, however, this is a fascinating exposé of one town's experience of the war that left the people here, as throughout France, scarred by bitter divisions, even within the ranks of the Resistance.

The collection of reliquaries, chalices, robes and crucifixes on show at the **Musée d'Art Religieux** on nearby place des Récollets (June–Sept daily 10am–7pm; free) is less inspiring. The museum does, however, have videos on Romanesque architecture, Baroque altarpieces, and the Cathédrale St-Jérôme, which are quite interesting.

A very different world is conjured up in the **Fondation Alexandra-David-Neel** at 27 av Maréchal-Juin, the Nice road, south of the centre (guided tours daily: June–Oct 10.30am, 2pm, 3.30pm & 5pm; rest of year 10.30am, 2pm & 4pm; free; bus #3 stop Stade J. Rolland). A writer, musician, one-time anarchist, and traveller throughout Indo-China, Alexandra David Neel spent two months in Tibet's forbidden city of Lhasa in 1924, disguised as a beggar. She spent 25 years studying Tibetan philosophy, religion and culture, and died in Digne in 1969, aged 101, in the house – now the *Fondation* – she called Samten Dzong, her "fortress of meditation". The *Fondation* documents this remarkable woman's life and pays tribute to her favourite country; there are gorgeous silk hangings on the walls and a shop where you can buy current Tibetan products, all blessed by the Nobel-Prize-winning Dalai Lama, who has visited twice.

Eating, drinking and entertainment

The best **meals** to be had in Digne are at *Le Grand Paris* (☎04.92.31.11.15; menus from 100F) and the *Origan* (☎04.92.31.62.13; menus from 70F) hotels; or at *La Chauvinière*, 54 rue de l'Hubac (☎04.92.31.40.03; menus from around 100F, midday 70F; closed Mon & Sun eve). Or you could try the hotel *La Bourgogne's* restaurant, 3 av de Verdon (☎04.92.31.00.19; menus from 90F; closed Mon out of season), with specialities from Burgundy as well as Provence. Boulevard Gassendi has plenty of cafés and brasseries to choose from or try *Le Tampinet* café on place du Tampinet, opposite the tourist office, which is cheap and cheerful; or the *Happy Hours*, a lively brasserie at 43 bd Victor-Hugo, (☎04.92.31.23.37; closed Sun).

For evening **entertainment**, the Centre Culturel Pierre Gassendi, 45 av du 8 Mai 1945 (☎04.92.30.87.10), puts on shows, concerts and films. If you want to dance, head out towards Aiglun, 12km west from Digne along the N85 on rte de Marseille, where there are two **discos**, *La Boîte Fred* (☎04.92.34.75.89) and *Les Douze Chênes* (☎04.92.34.65.10).

The first weekend in August sees the **Corso de la Lavande**, a jamboree with parades of floats celebrating the lavender crop and its two key products, honey and perfume. The **Foire-Exposition de la Lavande** at the end of August and the beginning of September is more commercially minded but excellent for buying pots of goodies to take back home. July sees a **jazz** festival; in September the **Journées Tibétaines** celebrate all things Tibetan; and there are special **film** seasons in March, July, October and November.

The Réserve Naturelle Géologique de Haute Provence

Close to Digne, at the end of the road off to the left after the bridge across the Bléone, is the **Centre de Géologie** (April–Oct daily 9am–noon & 2–5.30pm, closing Fri 4.30pm; rest of the year Mon–Fri only; 25F; bus #2 stop Champourcin; 15-min walk from car park to Centre) which has extremely good videos, workshops and exhibitions on the

Réserve Naturelle Géologique de Haute Provence, the biggest protected geological area in Europe, covering an area of 150 square kilometres and stretching north from Digne to the Gorges du Verdon. The Réserve's sites include imprints and fossils of various Miocene creatures – crabs, oysters, ammonites, an ichthyosaurus – which record the time before the Alps had forced the sea southwards. The Centre de Géologie runs *jours de découverte* (discovery days) in July and August on Thursdays and Sundays, plus half days on Wednesday afternoons (days may change from year to year) where you go off with a guide to different sites in the Réserve (bookings at the tourist office; around 90F).

Just outside Digne, 3.5km north of the rond-point du 11 Novembre 1918 on the road to Barles, you can see, on the left of the road, a wall of ammonites, the fossils of shells whose creatures lived off these rocks 185 million years ago. Further on, the road forks left to **LA ROBINE**. From the car park near La Robine's school at the further end of the village, a path is signed with the logo of an ichthyosaurus. After a one-hour walk you'll come to the extraordinarily well-preserved fossilized skeleton of an ichthyosaurus, a 4.5-metre-long reptile that was swimming around these parts while dinosaurs lumbered about on land.

Along the Eaux Chaudes

The sulphurous water (29–49°C), whose health-giving properties have been known since antiquity, spouts out of the Falaise St-Pancrace just east of the town above av des Thermes; the stream called Eaux Chaudes, which runs alongside the avenue, however, is actually no warmer than any mountain stream. If you want to take a cure, the **Établissement Thermal** (☎04.92.32.32.92) will be only to happy to oblige, and if you're not sure what it entails there's a guided tour (March–Aug & Nov Thurs 2pm; bus #1, stop Thermes).

If you're more interested in stunning landscapes, the D20 along the Eaux Chaudes which meets the Route Napoléon at Chaudon-Norante is a great route to follow. Meadows contrast with the great wall of mountain to the north; acacia trees give way to larch forests as you climb to the Col du Corobin where the views open up to a vast expanse southwards. Near Digne you may notice women wearing floral scarves and long skirts of a distinctly un-Provençal style. They are likely to be Albanians, one of several foreign communities who have settled in this harsh and marginalized environment.

Massif les Monges and north to Seyne

North of Digne the mountains that reach their highest peak at Les Monges (2115m) form an impassable barrier, as far as roads go, between the valleys running down to Sisteron and the Durance and those of the Bléone's tributaries. There are footpaths, for serious walkers (which begin at Digne on the west bank of the Bléone north of the Grand Pont) and just one road loops south of Les Monges linking Digne and Sisteron via **Thoard** and **Authon** across the **Col de Font-Belle**. Fantastic forested paths lead off past vertical rocks from the pass.

The D900a, which follows first the course of the Bléone, and then the Bès torrent, before joining the main D900 and continuing north to **Seyne-les-Alpes**, passes many of the protected sites of the Réserve Naturelle Géologique de Haute Provence, where shrubs, flowers and butterflies are now the sole visible wildlife. After heavy rain the waters tear through the **Clues de Barles and Verdaches** like a boiling soup of mud in which it's hard to imagine fish finding sustenance.

Making any decent livelihood from the land here is difficult. A lot of "*marginaux*" (hippies or anyone into alternative lifestyles) manage to survive, making goats' cheese and doing seasonal work; the indigenous *paysans* are more likely to be opening gîtes and servicing the increasing numbers of city dwellers who come for trekking or skiing trips. But it's still very wild and deserted, with little accommodation other than gîtes and chambres d'hôtes; petrol stations are also few and far between.

Seyne-les-Alpes

SEYNE-LES-ALPES lies some 40km north of Digne. The town's main influx of visitors is in winter, when its three skiing stations, **St-Jean**, **Chabanon** and **Le Grand Puy**, are in operation. The rest of the year the Seyne is quieter, but still has plenty of accommodation on offer and scope for walking and riding into the mountains. It also has the only surviving horse fair in southeast France, held in October, and a mule breeder's competition at the beginning of August.

The **tourist office** is on Grande-Rue, the road past the church (Mon–Sat 9am–noon & 2.30–6pm, Sun 9am–noon; ☎04.92.35.11.00), and provides skiing, walking and horse-riding information. Also on Grande-Rue, you'll find *La Chaumière* **hotel-restaurant** (☎04.92.35.00.48; ②), and 1km from the town centre at Les Auches is *Au Vieux Tilleil* (☎04.92.35.00.04; ③), which has its own pool/skating rink. Below the town, on either side of the river, are two two-star **campsites**, *Les Prairies* (☎04.92.35.10.21; closed Oct–March) and *Camping de la Blanche* (☎04.92.35.02.55). The best place to **eat** is *Les Alisiers* (☎04.92.35.34.80; menus from 75F; closed Tues & Wed except during school holiday) on the D207 at the top of the old village.

Along the Ubaye to Barcelonnette

From the northern border of Provence at the Lac de Serre-Ponçon, the D900 follows the River Ubaye to **Barcelonnette**, a dramatic landscape of tiny, irregular fields backed by the jagged silhouettes of the mountains at the head of the valley, looking like something out of a vampire movie. There are **campsites** on the river bank in each village, and **canoe**, **raft** and **hydrospeed** bases at Le Lauzet-sur-Ubaye and Meolans-Revel. The Aérodrome de Barcelonnette-St-Pons is announced by a grounded aeroplane transformed into a restaurant.

Barcelonnette

Snow falls on **BARCELONNETTE** around Christmas and stays till Easter, yet, despite the proximity of several ski resorts, summer is the main tourist season. The town is immaculate, with cobbled streets, sunny squares and snowcapped mountains visible at the end of every avenue. A more ideal spot for doing nothing would be hard to find. The central square, **place Manuel**, has café tables from which to gaze at the blue sky and a white clock tower commemorating the centenary of the 1848 revolution. Some of the larger houses on av de la Libération have a strongly un-European appearance; their

---

SKIING

The tourist office in Barcelonnette has brochures for all the local **ski resorts**, which can also be contacted direct: Pra-Loup (☎04.92.84.10.04); Ste-Anne/La Condamine (☎04.92.84.32.88); Jausiers (☎04.92.81.21.45); Le Sauze/Super-Sauze (☎04.92.81.05.61); and Larche (☎04.92.84.32.97). During the skiing season a **free bus** does the rounds of the resorts from Barcelonnette. Pra-Loup's pistes link up with La Foux d'Allos (see overleaf under "The Haut-Verdon Valley").

Latin American style dates from the nineteenth century, when many of Barcelonnette's inhabitants emigrated to Mexico – being expert sheep farmers and wool merchants, several made their fortunes and returned home to build their dream houses. The Spanish association of the town's name, "Little Barcelona", is due to the town's foundation in the thirteenth century by Raimond Béranger IV, count of Provence, whose family came from the Catalan city.

One of the Mexican-style villas, *La Sapinière*, at 10 av de la Libération, houses the **Musée de la Vallée** (July & Aug daily 10am–noon & 3–7pm; school holidays and rest of the year daily 3–7pm; term time Wed, Thurs & Sat 3–6pm; 20F) which details the life and times of the people of the Ubaye Valley, the emigration to Mexico and the travels of a nineteenth-century explorer from the town. In summer, the ground floor becomes an information centre for the **Parc National du Mercantour** (mid-June to mid-Sept daily 10am–noon & 3–7pm; ☎04.92.81.21.31), a national reserve stretching from the mountain passes south of Barcelonnette almost to **Sospel** (see map p.384). They can provide maps, advise on walks and mountain refuges, and tell you about the fauna and flora of the area.

Practicalities

Barcelonnette is very small. **Buses** from Marseille or Gap arrive on place Aimé-Gassier, from where the main street, rue Manuel, leads up to place Manuel, beyond which is place F-Mistral where you'll find the **tourist office** (July & Aug daily 9am–8pm; May–June & Sept–Nov Mon–Sat 9am–noon & 2–6pm; Dec–April daily 9am–noon & 2–7pm; ☎04.92.81.04.71). **Bikes** can be rented from the Bureau des Loisirs, 1 rue Manuel (☎04.92.81.13.93), and **canoeing** and **rafting** trips can be organised through An Rafting, place Aimé-Gassier (☎04.92.81.23.00).

The best **place to stay** in the centre of town if you're on a low budget is the *Grand Hôtel*, overlooking place Manuel at no. 6 (June to mid-Oct & Jan to mid-May; ☎04.92.81.03.14; ②), an old-fashioned and comfortable place. Or there's the slightly more expensive *Cheval Blanc*, just down the road at 12 rue Grenette (☎04.92.81.00.19, fax 04.92.81.15.39; ③). The de luxe *Grande Épervière* at 18 rue des Trois-Freres-Arnaud (☎04.92.81.00.70, fax 04.92.81.29.50; ④), surrounded by its own park, is very good value, while *L'Azteca*, 3 rue François-Arnaud (☎04.92.81.46.36, fax 04.92.81.43.92; ⑤), in a Mexican-style house, is extremely pleasant with superb views of the mountains. There are two **campsites** on av Émile-Aubert, the D902 leading to the Col de la Cayolle: the closer, three-star *Camping Caravaneige du Plan* (☎04.92.81.08.11; closed mid-Sept to mid-May) is 500m out of town; the two-star *Le Tampico* (☎04.92.81.02.55) is 1km further out.

Beautifully prepared and delicious **food** is to be had at *La Mangeoire*, place des Quatre-Vents (☎04.92.81.01.61; menus from around 100F; closed Mon, Tues, last 2 weeks of May & Nov), in the rustic setting of an old sheep barn. *Le Troubadour* on place Frédéric-Mistral (☎04.92.81.24.24; menus from under 100F; closed Tues eve & Wed) serves more simple dishes, usually very good. Pizzas and lunchtime plats du jour

THE MOUNTAIN VALLEYS

From Barcelonnette there are four routes across the watershed of Mont Pelat, La Bonette, Chambeyron and their high gneiss and granite extensions. The Col d'Allos leads into the **Haut-Verdon** Valley; the Col de la Cayolle into the **Haut-Var** Valley; the road across the summit of La Bonette to the **Tinée** Valley; and the Col de Larche into Italy. All but the last are snowed up between November and April, and can sometimes be closed as late as June. Further east the **Vésubie** rises just below the Italian border; like the Tinée and the Verdon it runs into the Var.

are available for very little on the corner of place St-Pierre and rue Bellon (July & Aug only), and Tex-Mex snacks at *El Coco-Loco*, 2 rue Grenelle.

Wednesday and Saturday are the **market** days, where you'll find all manner of sweets, jams and alcohol made from locally picked bilberries, pâtés made from local birds – thrush, partridge, pheasant – and the favourite liqueurs of this part of the world, distilled from Alpine plants and nuts on place Aimé-Gassier and place St-Pierre.

The Haut-Verdon Valley

The most westerly route from Barcelonnette crosses the **Col d'Allos** at 2250m to join the River Verdon just a few kilometres from its source. A mountain refuge, *Col d'Allos* (☎04.92.83.89.28; closed Sept to mid-June), on the pass marks the junction with the GR56, which leads west to the Ubaye Valley and Seyne-les-Alpes, and east to the Col de Larche and the Tinée Valley. In late June pale wild pansies and deep blue gentians flower between patches of ice. The panorama is magnificent, though once you start backstitching your way down the side of the pass to the Verdon, the hideous vast hotels of **La Foux d'Allos** come into view.

La Foux d'Allos

If you're going to ski, **LA FOUX D'ALLOS** is probably the cheapest Provençal resort in which to do it. The lifts and *pistes* join up with Pra-Loup to the north and, for cross-country skiers, with Allos Le Seignus 7km to the south. The resort is also quite high (1800–2600m), so melting snow shouldn't be a problem.

La Foux d'Allos and its neighbours are also keen to promote themselves as summer resorts, with all kinds of activities on offer, from trapeze training to horse riding, archery, courses in wildlife photography, and water sports at the Parc de Loisirs in Le Seignus. The **tourist office** (June–Sept daily 8.30am–6.30pm; Dec–April Mon–Sat 8.30am–noon & 2–7pm, Sun 9am–noon & 3–7pm; May, Oct & Nov Mon–Sat 8.30am–noon & 2–6.30pm; ☎04.92.83.80.70) can provide details. The Parc du Mercantour also has an information point on rue de la Placette (July & Aug daily 10am–6pm; ☎04.92.83.04.18).

The best deal for a place to stay is in the **youth hostel**, *HI La Foux d'Allos* (☎04.92.83.81.08; closed Oct–Dec & May), which must be booked well in advance. Other options include the **hotels** *Le Sestrière* (☎04.92.83.81.70; ④; closed mid-April to mid-June & mid-Sept to mid-Dec) and *Le Toukal* (☎04.92.83.82.76; ④; closed May, June & mid-Sept to Nov) or the *Hameau de la Foux* **chalets** (☎04.92.83.82.26; from 2400F a week). For details of the ski-school, phone the École de Ski du Val d'Allos (☎04.92.83.00.65).

Allos and its lake

The medieval village of **ALLOS**, 8.5km south of La Foux d'Allos, was all but destroyed by fire in the eighteenth century; one tower of the ramparts half-survived and was turned into the current clock tower. The old livelihoods of tending sheep and weaving woollen sheets only just made it past the turn of the century when tourism began with the discovery of the **Lac d'Allos**, 14km east and 800m above Allos. Once skiing became an established pastime the agricultural days of Allos were numbered. But for all its *résidences secondaires*, it's not a bad place to spend a day or two.

The road to the lake stops some way short of its destination, leaving you with a thirty-minute walk to reach what was once the head of a glacier. If you want to walk the whole way from Allos, follow the path which starts by the church. Round and blue, reflecting the high amphitheatre half-circling it, the lake nourishes trout and char in its pure cold waters. Looking in the direction of the one-time glacier flow, you can just see the peak of **Mont Pelat**, the highest mountain in the Parc du Mercantour. Though there are always people dutifully reading the pedagogic noticeboards, there's no limit to the space in which to escape the crowds.

Practicalities

For information on paths, weather conditions and so forth, the Parc du Mercantour has a Maison du Parc at Allos on rue de la Placette (☎04.92.83.04.18), or there's the **tourist office** (June–Sept daily 8.30am–7pm; rest of year Mon–Sat 8.30am–noon & 2–6.30pm; ☎04.92.83.02.81) at the northen end of the old village. Note that the only **bank** in this stretch of the valley is the Crédit Agricole on the main road (Tues–Sat).

Hotels include the run-down but very cheap *Pascal* (☎04.92.83.00.04; ②) and *Les Gentianes* (☎04.92.83.03.50; ②), both in the old village, and the more upmarket but characterless *Plein Soleil* (☎04.92.83.02.16; ④) in Super-Allos, the modern extension northeast of the village. There's a very comfortable **chambre d'hôtes**, *La Ferme* (☎04.92.83.04.76; ②) and a **gîte d'étape**, the *Chalet Auberge L'Autapie* (☎04.92.83.06.31; ①). Walkers can also stay at the *Refuge du Lac d'Allos* on the lake itself (☎04.92.83.00.24; ②; closed Oct–June) for which booking well in advance is advisable.

The best **meal** to be had in Allos is at *Les Gentianes* hotel (menus at 75F and 110F). Upmarket picnic food can be bought from *La Ferme Gourmande* opposite the tourist office. A useful place to shop, for food and anything else you might need, is the Shopi supermarket on the main road (Mon–Sat 8.45am–12.15pm & 3.30–7pm).

Colmars-les-Alpes

The next town downstream from Allos is **COLMARS-LES-ALPES**, an extraordinarily well-preserved stronghold, whose name comes from a temple to Mars built by the Romans on the hill above the town. The sixteenth-century ramparts with their arrow slits and small square towers are complete; and though the two entrances, the Porte de France and Porte de Savoie, have been reduced to just gateways, the impression is still that this is a perfect historical model. The ramparts were constructed on the orders of François I of France to reinforce the defences that had existed since 1381 when Colmars became a border town between Provence and Savoy. When Savoy declared war on France in 1690, Vauban was called in to make the town even more secure. He designed the **Fort de Savoie** and the **Fort de France** at either end of the town.

Having passed through the Porte de France, the Porte de Savoie or the opening halfway between them – all adorned with climbing roses – you find yourself in an exquisite old and quiet Provençal town with cobbled streets and fountained squares. There's not a lot to do here except soak up atmosphere. The Fort de Savoie is open for guided tours in July and August (daily 10am; 20F; from the tourist office), when exhibitions of art or local traditions are set up beneath the magnificent larch-timbered ceilings. Or you can take a twenty-minute walk east of the town to the Lance waterfall.

The **tourist office** is by Porte de la Lance (July & Aug daily 8am–noon & 2–7pm; rest of the year Tues, Wed, Fri & Sat 8am–noon & 2–5pm, Thurs & Sun 8am–noon; ☎04.92.83.41.92). There are two **hotels**, *Le Vauban* (☎04.92.83.40.49; ②) and *Le Chamois* (☎04.92.83.43.29; ③; closed mid-Nov to mid-Dec); a **gîte d'étape**, the *Gassendi*, housed in a twelfth-century Templar hospice (☎04.92.83.42.25; ①); and a very scenic **campsite** *Le Bois Joly*, by the river (☎04.92.83.40.40; closed Oct–April). For **food** there's *Le Lézard* restaurant and *salon de thé* serving *raclette* on the corner of Grande-Rue and place Neuve; a *boulangerie*, *charcuterie* and wine shop on Grande-Rue; and the *Café Rétro* on place J-Girieud by the *mairie*.

Colmars is on the junction of the Verdon Valley road with the D78 which climbs up between the Frema and Encombrette mountains and descends to the Var Valley at St-Martin-d'Entraunes. Six kilometres along the road, signed left, is the **Ratery ski-station** (☎04.92.83.40.92), which rents out **bikes** and **ponies** in summer. You can trek from here over the Encombrette to the Lac d'Allos or east across the Col des Champs to the Var at Entraunes.

Beauvezer

If you're heading south towards Thorame, Annot or St-André (see pp.369–371), you can follow the D908 for 5km to **BEAUVEZER** – experienced cross-country skiers can take a looping route there through the Fôret de Monier and across the summit of the Laupon. The road sticks to the Verdon, a wide dramatic torrent in winter or spring, a wide messy track of scattered boulders and branches in summer. Beauvezer perches high above its right bank, a wonderful ancient village smelling of old timbers whose business used to be making linen. Beside the beautiful ochre church is one of the prettiest **hotel-restaurants** in Haute Provence, *Le Bellevue*, place de l'Église (☎04.92.83.51.60; ③).

The Haut-Var Valley

The route to the Haut-Var Valley from Barcelonnette first follows the River Bachelard through its gorge then east following its course between Mont Pelat to the south and the ridge of peaks to the north whose shapes have given them the names Pain de Sucre (Sugarloaf), Chapeau de Gendarme (Gendarme's Hat) and Chevalier (Horseman). At the *Bayasse* refuge (☎04.92.81.07.31), the main road turns south towards the **Col de la Cayolle**, while a track – and the GR56 – continues east towards La Bonette and the Tinée Valley.

The Var makes its appearance below the Col de la Cayolle and pours southwards through Entraunes and St-Martin-d'Entraunes to Guillaumes and on down through the **Gorges de Daluis** to Entrevaux. Its banks are punctuated with chapels built before and after disasters of avalanches, floods, landslides and devastating storms. Many are superbly decorated, like the Renaissance Chapelle de St-Sébastien, just north of Entraunes and the church at St-Martin-d'Entraunes, with its Bréa retable.

GUILLAUMES, the valley's minor metropolis and a favourite with cyclists in summer, is a traditional resting place for sheep on their way between the Haut-Var summer pastures and Nice. Though most flocks now travel by lorry, the old **sheep fairs** on September 16 and October 9 are still held in the village. Winter sees a migration in the opposite direction, as the residents of the Côte d'Azur flock to the ski resorts of Valberg and Beuil, to the east of Guillaumes, on the fabulous road that climbs over to the Tinée Valley.

The biggest **tourist office** in the area is in Valberg (daily 9am–noon & 2–6pm; ☎04.93.23.24.25), although Guillaume has a "chalet du tourisme" on the main road operating sporadic hours in season (☎04.93.05.57.76) and at other times you can call at the *mairie* for help (office hours; ☎04.93.05.50.13). For **accommodation** in Guillaumes, there's the *Les Chaudrons* hotel on the main road (☎04.93.05.50.01; ③) and *La Renaissance*, an old-fashioned establishment 100m up to your right just past the bridge as you look upstream (☎04.93.05.50.12; ②) with a restaurant serving a three-course meal for around 70F.

About 5km south of Guillaumes, the Var enters the dramatic red-rocked **Gorges de Daluis**. The Pont de la Mariée across the gorge is a popular spot for bungee-jumpers. It's also worth noting that the roads upstream have the better views while the downstream carriageway is in tunnels much of the way.

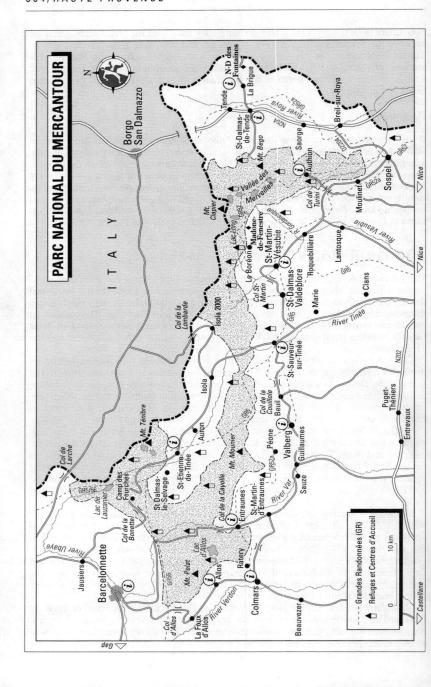

The Tinée Valley

The longest of the Var's tributaries, the Tinée rises just below the 2800-metre summit of **La Bonette**. The mountains on its left bank – under whose shadow **St-Étienne** and **Auron** nestle – rise up to the Italian border before the river's course turns south at **Isola** to cut a steep narrow valley before joining the Var 30km from the sea.

Across La Bonette

The road across **La Bonette**, claimed to be the highest stretch of tarmac in Europe, gives a feast of high-altitude views. The summit of the mountain, a ten-minute scrabble up scree from the road, is not particularly exciting, and is made more ugly by its military training camp. But the green and silent spaces of the approach, circled by barren peaks, are magical.

Before the hairpins begin for the southern descent, at Camp des Fourches, you can abandon your wheels and take the **GR5/56** north and parallel with the Italian border to the Col de Larche, then northwest towards Larche, where there's a gîte, (☎04.92.84.30.80). It's not exactly a stroll, but once you've climbed to the Col de la Cavale (after 5km or so) it's more or less downhill all the way, with the Ubayette torrent as your guide, and the **Lac de Lauzanier**, 5km on from the Col de la Cavale, a spot you may never want to leave.

A short way down from the Camp des Fourches is the *Gîte de Bousiéyas* (☎04.93.02.42.20; closed mid-Sept to May). About 5km on, a track on the left to the tiny hamlet of **Vens** leads to a footpath that follows the Vens torrent to the the Lacs de Vens and a refuge at 2380m (reservations through the Club Alpin Français in Nice ☎04.93.62.59.99; refuge closed mid-Sept to mid-June).

St-Étienne-de-Tinée, Auron and Isola

Continuing on the road, with the Tinée alongside, you descend to the small and isolated town of **ST-ÉTIENNE-DE-TINÉE** that comes to life only during its sheep fairs, held twice every summer, and the Fête de la Transhumance at the end of June. The **tourist office** at 1 rue des Communes-de-France (no fixed opening hours; ☎04.93.02.41.96), organizes tours of the town's chapels (20F), the museums of milk-making and traditional crafts and of the old school.

There are two **hotel-restaurants**: the *Regalivou*, bd d'Auron (☎04.93.02.49.00; ③), and *Des Amis*, 1 rue Val Gélé (☎93.02.40.30; ②).

On the west side of town, off bd d'Auron, a cable car ascends to the summit of La Pinatelle from where there are good walks – and skiing for the experienced – including a path to the **ski resort** of **AURON**. By road, Auron is 7km south of St-Étienne, on a dead-end spur from the main road. The resort also prides itself on its summer activities, which cover everything from hang-gliding and aerobics to tennis, pony rides and swimming. There are more cable cars, which operate in summer as well as winter, taking you further into the mountains for some serious high treks.

After the turning to Auron, there's nothing but the white quartz and white heather of the valley, with only the silvery sound of crickets competing with the river's roar. **ISOLA**, 14km south of St-Étienne, is a dying community. Only the needle-sharp belfry maintains an upright permanence, while groups of old men and women sit around and chat, suspicious cats sniff for food and the external murals on the chapels slowly fade. Nothing could be more dramatic a contrast to **ISOLA 2000**, the zappy ski resort just beyond the village.

St-Sauveur-sur-Tinée and downstream

Between Isola and **ST-SAUVEUR-SUR-TINÉE** the drop in altitude is marked by sweet chestnut trees taking over from the pines. St-Sauveur is dominated by its medieval needle belfry, which perches above the river in Mediterranean rather than Alpine fashion. The adornments of the Romanesque gargoyled church include a rather fine fifteenth-century retable behind the bloodied crucifix and a fifteenth-century statue of St Paul above the side door outside.

There's not a lot to do here other than sit in the sun above the river or head off along the GR52A, but it's an attractive place to stop. The centre of life is the *Café du Centre* and resto; the *boulangerie* on the corner of place de la Mairie sells basic provisions as well as scrumptious *tourtes de blettes* (closed Tues).

For **accommodation**, try the *Auberge de la Gare* at the southern end of the village (☎04.93.02.00.67; ①) or the *Relais d'Auron*, 18 av des Blavets (☎93.02.00.03; ③). The two-star municipal **campsite** is in quartier Les Plans (☎04.93.02.03.20; closed mid-Sept to mid-June).

The D30 towards Valberg and the Haut-Var Valley, a dramatically precipitous climb, starts from St-Sauveur. A few kilometres south of the village you can head east along the D2565 to Valdeblore and the Vésubie Valley.

Following the Tinée south leads you through the perched villages of Marie, Clans and La Tour, all of which have their charms as small mountain communities, with medieval decorations in their chapels and churches, and, at **MARIE**, a pleasant place for a meal, *Le Panoramique* (menus from 100F), with a few rooms as well (☎04.93.02.03.01; ②; closed Thurs).

The Vésubie and Bévéra valleys

The ancient town of **St-Martin-Vésubie** stands at the head of the **River Vésubie**, which is formed by two torrents, Le Boréon and La Madone de la Fenestre, descending from the north and east. The only through route to St-Martin comes from the Tinée Valley to the west, via **St-Dalmas-Valdeblore** with its ancient church. From St-Martin road and river head towards the Var, passing the flood-ridden *commune* of **Roquebillière**, the perched village of **Lantosque**, and the approach to the pilgrimage chapel of **Madonne d'Utelle**. An alternative southern route from the valley crosses east to the **Col de Turini** and down the **River Bévéra** towards Sospel.

St-Martin-Vésubie

ST-MARTIN-VÉSUBIE is at its busiest in July and August, though a few winter visitors pass through on their way to the ski resorts. In late spring and early autumn, the best times for quiet nights and long daytime walks, St-Martin is a perfect base for exploring the surrounding mountains. Even in the height of summer it's not jam-packed, and in winter, if you're not up to the cross-country skiing routes that pass through the town, you can still go for wonderful walks in snow-shoes.

The main artery of the old quarter, the **rue du Docteur-Cagnoli**, is a single-file cobbled street of Gothic houses with overhanging roofs and balconies, through which flows a channelled stream designed in the fifteenth century for sewage and now charged with rainwater or melting snow. Halfway down here, on the left as you descend, is the **Chapelle des Pénitents Blancs** decorated with eighteenth-century paintings. At the end of the street is St-Martin's **church**, with works attributed to Louis Bréa, a mirror on the high altar reflecting the stained-glass window above the door, and a venerated polychrome wooden statue of the Madonna that is taken up to the Chapelle de Madone de Fenestre (see below) at the beginning of July and brought back towards the end of September. Southeast of the church you can look down at the Madone de Fenestre torrent from place de la Frairie. In the opposite direction a narrow lane leads to the junction of rue Kellerman and the main road, beyond which is the old wash house and Le Vieux Moulin, the town's one **museum** (May–Oct Mon–Fri 2–6pm, Sat & Sun 3–6pm; Nov–April Sat & Sun 3–6pm; 20F), which illustrates the traditional way of life of the Vésubiens.

Heading back towards the main **place Félix-Fauré** along rue Kellerman, you'll pass the *Villa des Iris* at no. 8 which is the **Maison du Parc** with occasional wildlife exhibitions as well as information about the Parc du Mercantour (June–Sept daily 9am–12.30pm & 2–6pm; free). The **fountain** on allées de Verdun, the *cours* in front of place Félix-Fauré, has a placard detailing its mineral contents and citing the ministerial declaration of 1913 that the water has negative pathogenic germs.

Practicalities

You arrive in St-Martin on place Félix-Fauré to the west of the old town, along the allées de Verdun if you're coming from the Tinée Valley or av de la Gare from the south. The **gare routière** is on place de la Gare where av de la Gare loops south into av de Caqueray. The **tourist office** is on place Félix-Fauré (June–Aug daily 9am–12.30pm & 3–7pm; Sept–May Mon–Sat 10am–noon & 2.30–5.30pm, Sun 10am–noon; ☎04.93.03.21.28) along with the *mairie*, post office and a bank.

The tourist office has lists of gîtes and mountain refuges for St-Martin and the surounding area posted up outside, plus lists of walking guides and weather information. On rue du Dr-Cagnoli, just below place du Marché, you'll find the Bureau des Guides et Accompagnateurs de la Haute Vésubie (☎04.93.03.44.30) which organizes **walks** including winter expeditions with snow-shoe rental and can give advice for your own expeditions, and the Guides du Mercantour (☎04.93.03.31.32) which can arrange **canoeing**, **climbing**, **horse rides**, **walks** and **skiing**. Maps, compasses and the like can be purchased from Aux Milles Articles, 52 rue du Dr-Cagnoli.

Accommodation is plentiful. The least expensive of the town's five **hotels** is *Les Alpes* on place Félix-Fauré (☎04.93.03.21.06; ①); for more comfort there's *La Bonne Auberge*, a short way up the allées de Verdun (☎04.93.03.20.49; ③; closed mid-Nov to Jan) and nearby *La Châtaigneraie* (☎04.93.03.21.22; ⑤; closed Oct to May). The closest **campsite** is the two-star *Ferme St-Joseph* on the rte de Nice by the lower bridge over La Madone (☎04.93.03.20.14). Further down the same road, the two-star *Le Touron* camping (☎04.93.03.21.32) is rather overpriced; its gîte d'étape is better value. In the opposite direction out of town, on the rte de la Colmiane, there's the one-star *La Mério* (☎04.93.03.30.38; July & Aug only) and, to the southwest, on the rte de Venanson, the two-star *Le Champouns* (☎04.93.03.23.72), which also has apartments to let and dormitory accommodation.

For **meals**, *La Mavorine café-boulangerie* on place Félix-Fauré serves *bruschettas* for around 30F, plus ice creams, crêpes and cakes. The nicest **restaurant** is *La Trappa* on place du Marché (closed Mon in term-time) offering a pasta-based four-course meal for around 105F; the restaurant in *La Bonne Auberge* is also worth trying (menus from 100F).

Finally, there's an après-ski **disco**, *Le Piolet* (☎04.93.03.22.21) off rue du Dr-Cagnoli on the east slope of the old town.

Le Boréon and Madone de Fenestre

The main reason for heading to **LE BORÉON**, some 10km north of St-Martin and just within the borders of the Parc du Mercantour, is to eat trout, either caught yourself or by those who supply the clutch of **restaurants** and **hotels** at this small and impeccably scenic mountain retreat. During the fishing season, from mid-March to early

WILDLIFE OF THE MERCANTOUR

The least shy of the mammal inhabitants of these mountains is the **marmot**, a cream-coloured, badger-sized creature often to be seen sitting on its haunches in the sun. Chamois, mouflon and ibex are almost equally unwary of humans, even though it was not so long ago that they were hunted here. The male **ibex** is a wonderful, big, solid beast with curving, ribbed horns that grow to a metre long; the species very nearly became extinct, and it is one of the successes of the park that the population is now stable. Another species of goat, the **chamois**, is also on the increase. The male is recognizable by the shorter, grappling-hook horns and white beard. The **mouflon**, introduced to the Mercantour in the 1950s, is the ancestor of domestic sheep. Other animals that you might see include **stoats**, rare species of **hare**, and **foxes**, the most numerous predators since bears and lynxes became extinct in the region. The most problematic predator, however, is the **wolf**, once extinct, but stalking the region again since 1992, having crossed the border from Italy. With eight hundred sheep killed by wolves in 1997, sheep farmers are not happy, and the predators have been found killed despite their protected status.

The Mercantour is a perfect habitat for **eagles**, who have any number of crags on which to build their nests, and plenty to eat – including marmots. Pairs of **golden eagles** are now breeding, and a rare vulture, the **lammergeier**, has been successfully reintroduced to the region. Other birds of prey, **kestrels**, **falcons** and **buzzards**, wing their way down from the scree to the Alpine lawn and its torrents to swoop on lizards, mice and snakes. The **great spotted woodpecker** and the black and orange **hoopoe** are the most colourful inhabitants of the park. **Ptarmigan**, which turn snowy-white in winter, can sometimes be seen in June parading to their would-be mates on the higher slopes in the north. **Blackcocks**, known in French as *tétras-lyre* for their lyre-shaped white tails, burrow into the snow at night and fly out in a flurry of snowflakes when the sun rises.

The **flowers** of the Mercantour are an unmissable glory, with over two thousand species represented, about forty of which are unique to the region. The moment the snow melts, the lawn between the rocky crags and the treeline begins to dot with golds, pinks and blue. Rare species of **lily** and **orchid** grow here, as do the elusive **edelweiss** and the wild ancestors of various cultivated flowers – pansies, geraniums, tulips, gentian violets. Rarest of all is the **multi-flowering saxifrage** (*saxifraga florulenta*), a big spiky flower that looks as if it must be cultivated, though it would hardly be popular in suburban gardens since it flowers just once every ten years. Wild strawberries, raspberries and bilberries tempt you into the woods.

Camping, lighting fires, picking flowers, playing ghetto-blasters or doing anything that might disturb the delicate environment is strictly outlawed.

September, you can get a licence from the hotels here or from most of the bars in St-Martin. If fishing is not your passion, you can just sit down and order smoked trout or other local specialities such as crayfish, wild boar with *cèpes* mushrooms, and lamb. The two **hotel-restaurants** are *Le Boréon* (☎04.93.03.20.35; menus from 150F; ③; closed Nov–Feb) and *Le Cavalet* (☎04.93.03.21.46; menus from 120F; ③), with a **gîte** (☎04.93.03.27.27; ①; closed mid-Nov to mid-Feb) further up. Walks, from half-hour strolls to half-day treks, are signposted from the gîte.

The **Chapelle de Madone de Fenestre**, which lies to the east of Le Boréon and 12km northeast of St-Martin, stands above the treeline in a setting of barren rocks, also just within the borders of the Parc du Mercantour. Half a dozen gloomy, rough-hewn stone buildings, one of them housing a refuge and restaurant, surround the little nineteenth-century chapel in a thousand-year-old sanctuary, named for the hole in the rock above it through which you can see the sky. Floral murals and a bright blue ceiling add some welcome colour to this desolate little hamlet, but it's hardly worth coming all the way up here unless you intend to **trek onwards**. The GR52 passes by the sanctuary and leads eastwards to the Vallée des Merveilles (see p.393). This is not the shortest route but it's a very dramatic path that rarely descends below 2000m.

In summer there are regular **buses** three times a week from St-Martin to Le Boréon, and one, on Sunday, to Madone de Fenestre.

St-Dalmas-Valdeblore

West of St-Martin, along the D2565 to the Tinée Valley lies the Commune de Valdeblore which starts with La Colmiane ski resort, where you can take a chair lift for stunning views from the **Pic de Colmiane** (Christmas–March daily 9am–5pm; July & Sept Sat, Sun & hols 11am–6pm; Aug daily 11am–6pm; 20F). To the west are the medieval hamlets of La Bolline and La Roche, now suffering chalet rashes, and in the middle, the ancient village of **St-Dalmas**.

Built on the remains of a Roman outpost, **ST-DALMAS** lies on the strategic crossroads between the most accessible southern route across the lower Alps, linking Piedmont with Provence, and a north–south route through the mountain range linking Savoy with the sea. The importance of this fertile region is clear from the striking dimensions of the **Église Prieurale Bénédictine** (June–Sept 11am–6pm; rest of year by request only; call Jean Alcoy ☎04.93.02.82.29), whose construction possibly started as early as the tenth century. The extraordinary wonky columns and vaults in the **crypt** are thought to date from then. A gruesome tomb under glass in the floor of the church reveals a 900-year-old skeleton; more appealing are the fragments of fourteenth-century frescoes in the north chapel. The present structure is Romanesque, plain and fierce with its typically Alpine bell tower and rounded apsidal chapels on which eleventh-century Lombardian decoration is still visible. If your French is good it's worth getting a guided tour of the church from Jean Alcoy. M Alcoy may be found at the **museum** just up from the church (same hours as church; 20F) which, along with traditional agricultural tools and household items, has a working model train set.

Downstream to Madone d'Utelle

South from St-Martin on the other side of the valley, but approached by a circuitous route that heads north out of the town, is the little village of **VENANSON**, which declares itself, most appropriately, to be a "zone of silence". It has just the one **hotel-restaurant**, the *Bella-Vista* (☎04.93.03.25.11; ①), a chapel too dark to see its Baleison frescoes, and an excellent vantage point over St-Martin.

Back on the left bank you come to the scattered village of **ROQUEBILLIÈRE**, which since the Dark Ages has been rebuilt six times after catastrophic landslides and floods. The last major disaster was in 1926, with a less lethal upheaval in the 1980s. Apart from the archeological interest of the leftovers of superseded settlements and the beauty of the frequently rebuilt church, the new village on the right bank has a wonderful *boulangerie*, Chez Somiani (closed Sun pm) on the main street, av C-Moulinie.

The road along the **Gordolesque Valley** above old Roquebillière heads north for 16km with paths leading off eastwards towards the Vallée des Merveilles. Where the road ends you can continue upstream past waterfalls and high crags to Lac de la Fous where you meet the GR52 running west to Madone de la Fenestre and east to the northern end of the Vallée des Merveilles (see p.393). This triangle between the Mont Clapier on the Italian border (3045m), Mont Bego (2873m) to the east and Mont Neiglier (2785m) to the west is a fabulous area for walking, but not to be taken lightly. All the **mountain refuges** here belong to the Club Alpin Français and may well be unsympathetic if you turn up unannounced.

From the southern limit of Roquebillière, the D70 leaves the Vésubie Valley to head east through the chic resort of La-Bollène-Vésubie to the Col de Turini (see overleaf).

Staying with the Vésubie you reach **LANTOSQUE**, which, like Roquebillière, has had its share of earth tremors and was flooded badly in 1993. Yet it survives in picturesque if faded and partly crumbling form, a pyramid of winding, stepped streets full of nervous cats, with a wonderful café-brasserie, the *Bar des Tilleuls*, on the lower *place* serving copious and delicious plats du jour for around 50F. There is a swish **hotel** on the other side of the river here, the *Hostellerie de L'Ancienne Gendarmerie* (☎04.93.03.00.65; ⑤; closed Nov–Easter) with an excellent restaurant (menus from 170F).

A short way before the river starts to pick up speed through the gorge leading to the confluence with the Var, you can detour westwards and upwards to yet another far-flung **chapel**, dedicated to **La Madone d'Utelle**. It stands on a plateau above the village of Utelle, high enough to be visible from the sea at Nice. According to legend, two Portuguese sailors lost in a storm in about the year 850 navigated safely into port by a light they saw gleaming from Utelle. They erected the first chapel, rebuilt as it stands today in 1806. Pilgrimages still take place on Easter Monday, the Monday of Pentecost, August 15 and September 8, and are concluded with a communal feast on the grassy summit. If you can't partake of one of these meals, you'll still find reasonable fare in the village at *La Bellevue* **hotel-restaurant** (☎04.93.03.17.19; menus from 70F; ③; closed mid-Oct to May).

The Col de Turini and Bévéra Valley

At the **Col de Turini**, 15km east of Roquebillière, you know you're in a popular spot from the litter, tacky restaurants and snack bars. Four roads and two tracks meet at the pass, all giving access to the **Forêt de Turini**, which covers the area between the Vésubie and **Bévéra** valleys. Larches grow in the highest reaches of the forest, giving way further down to firs, spruce, beech, maples and sweet chestnuts.

The road north from the col to the small ski resort of **L'AUTHION** gives the strongest impression of limitless space, following the curved ridge between the two valleys and overlooking a hollow of pastures. There are plenty of walks to tempt you, but the sun, the flowers and the wild strawberries and raspberries are so pleasant you might just as well just pick any patch of grass and listen to the cow-bells. *Le Relais du Camp d'Argent* (closed May–June; ☎04.93.91.57.58; ③), is a pleasant place to stay, and offers inexpensive **meals**.

Between the Col de Turini and Sospel, to the south, there's one possible place to stop off for a coffee or a bite to eat by the banks of the Bévéra. **MOULINET** has all the charm of an ordinary Provençal village, a dusty square with *boules* being played beneath the plane trees, a couple of chairs slung outside the café, scented flowers in the gardens, no chalet-style architecture and an overriding sense of indolence.

Sospel and the Roya Valley

The most easterly valley of Provence, the **Roya**, is also the most accessible, being served by train lines from Nice, via **Sospel**, and from Ventimiglia in Italy which converge just south of **Breil-sur-Roya**. When Nice became part of France in 1860, the upper Roya Valley was kept by the newly appointed King Victor Emmanuel II of Italy to indulge his passion for hunting despite a plebiscite in which only one person in Tende and La Brigue voted for the Italian option. It was not until 1947 that the valley was finally incorporated into France. As you would expect from the result of the vote, everyone speaks French, though they do so with a distinctly Italian intonation.

Sospel

The road and rail line into the Roya Valley meet the road from St-Martin-Vésubie and Moulinet at **SOSPEL**, a dreamy Italianate town spanning the gentle River Bévéra. You may find it over-tranquil after the excitements of the high mountains or the flashy speed of the Côte d'Azur, but it can make a very pleasant break.

The main street, av Jean-Médecin, follows the river on its southern bank before crossing the most easterly of the three bridges to become bd de Verdun heading for the Roya Valley. The central bridge, the **Vieux Pont** with its tower between the two spans for collecting tolls, was built in the early eleventh century to link the town centre on the south bank with its suburb across the river.

The Vieux Pont is the linchpin of Sospel's townscape, a scene made yet more alluring by the balconied houses along the north bank which back on to the grimy rue de la République. The banks are lush with flowering shrubs and trees, and one house even has a trompe-l'oeil street facade. Viewed from the eastern end of av Jean-Médecin, with the hills to the west and the bridge tower reflected in the water, this scene would be hard to improve.

Yet there's another vista in the town that rivals the river scene. For maximum effect it's best approached down rue St-Pierre from the eastern place St-Pierre. The street, which is deeply shadowed and gloomy with equally uninviting alleyways running off it, suddenly opens onto **place St-Michel** and you have before you one of the most beautiful series of peaches-and-cream Baroque facades in all Provence. In front of you is the **Église St-Michel** with its separate austere Romanesque clock tower. To the left are the **Chapelle des Pénitents Gris** and the **Chapelle des Pénitents Rouges**, and to the right are the medieval arcades and trompe-l'oeil decoration of the **Palais Ricci**. St-Michel contains an altarpiece by François Bréa in which the background to the red and gold robes of the Madonna is a bewitching river landscape of mountains, monasteries and dark citadels. On the right-hand panel Saint Martha has the snarling *Tarasque* well under control on a lead.

The road behind the church, rue de l'Abbaye, which you can reach via the steps between the two chapels, leads up to an ivy-covered **castle ruin**, from which you get a good view of the town. Further up, along chemin de St-Roch, an even better view can be had from the **Fort St-Roch**, part of the ignominious inter-war Maginot line, which houses the **Musée de la Résistance** (June–Sept Tues–Sun 2–6pm; April, May & Oct Sat & Sun 2–6pm; 25F), illustrating the courageous local resistance movement during World War II. The French–Italian armistice followed ten days after the capitulation to the Germans in June 1940, but during the short period of heavy fighting on France's southeastern frontier, Sospel held out against the vastly superior Italian forces. Under Italian occupation the town hall continued to fly the French flag; when the Germans took over in 1943 life became much nastier. Only a few of the Jews who had taken refuge here managed to escape south to Monaco. After Menton was liberated in September 1944 the Allied force advanced north, carrying out airborne attacks on Sospel, but orders came to stay put within 5km of the town. The town was left to the mercy of the Germans, with American and Canadian artillery attacks adding to the casualties. At the end of October the Germans were forced to retreat, but not far enough, and the battle for Sospel continued until April 1945.

Practicalities

The **gare SNCF** is southeast of the town on av A-Borriglione, which becomes av des Martyrs-de-la-Résistance, before leading down to the park on place des Platanes opposite place St-Pierre. Sospel's **tourist office** is housed in the Vieux Pont (Easter–Sept daily 10am–noon & 2–6pm; Oct–Easter daily 10am–noon & 2–5pm; ☎04.93.04.18.44).

The *Auberge du Pont-Vieux*, 3 av J-Médecin (☎04.93.04.00.73; ②), is Sospel's cheapest **hotel**; the *Auberge Provençale*, on rte du Col de Castillon 1.5km uphill from the town (☎04.93.04.00.31; ④; closed mid-Nov to mid-Dec), offers much more comfort, with a pleasant garden and terrace from which to admire Sospel. The *Hôtel des*

Étrangers at 7 bd de Verdun (☎04.93.04.00.09; ④; closed Dec–Feb) has tacky decor but pleasant service, the use of a pool and **bikes** to rent. There are five **campsites** around the town, the closest of which is *Le Mas Fleuri* in quartier La Vasta (☎04.93.04.03.48), with its own pool, 2km along the D2566 to Moulinet following the river upstream.

There are various **eating places** along av J-Médecin including the *Bistrot Sospellois* which serves plats du jour for around 50F. At *L'Escargot d'Or*, 3 rue de Verdun (☎04.93.04.00.43; closed Fri out of season), just across the eastern bridge, you can eat for between 100F and 150F on a terrace above the river; the restaurant of the *Hôtel des Étrangers* next door is also good value (menus from 100F). A Thursday **market** is held on place des Platanes; on Sunday local produce is sold on place du Marché. You can find wines and Alpine liqueurs at the Caves Sospellois on av Jean-Médecin near the *Bistrot Sospellois*.

Breil-sur-Roya

By the time it reaches **BREIL-SUR-ROYA**, a few kilometres north of Sospel, the river has picked up enough volume to justify a barrage and to provide swift white water for canoeing. A town of modest industries – leather, olives and dairy products – Breil spreads back from both banks in an easy undefensive manner, with the old town on the eastern edge. A Renaissance chapel with a golden angel blowing a trumpet from its rooftop cross faces the river, while in the centre of the old town stands the **Église Santa-Maria-in-Albis**, a vast eighteenth-century edifice topped by a belfry with shiny multicoloured tiles and containing an impressive organ loft. On the road out towards Tende in a former SNCF depot, the **Ecomusée du Haut Pays** (temporarily closed for renovation; check with the tourist office for hours and price) presents interesting exhibitions on the history and wildlife of the Roya Valley set up in old railway carriages, including a section on hydro-power, a steam train, tramway and trolleybus.

Several good **walks** are signed from the village; if you just want a short stroll, follow the river downstream past the barrage and the wash houses, then fork upwards through an olive grove to a tiny chapel and an old Italian gatehouse. The path eventually leads up to the summit of the Arpette, which stands between Breil and the Italian border. Alternatively, if you want to battle with white water by **canoeing** up through the Gorges de Saorge, or paddle more gently through the village, the Base USBTP (☎04.93.04.46.66) north of the village on the right bank before you reach the gare SNCF is the place to go.

Of the two **hotels** in town, the *Castel du Roy*, chemin de l'Aigara, off the rte de Tende (☎04.93.04.43.66; ④; closed Dec–Feb), is the more luxurious and has a very good **restaurant** (menus from 110F; closed Tues out of season); the other, *Hôtel du Roya* on place Biancheri (☎04.93.04.48.10; ③), is more central, overlooking the barrage and has a decent restaurant (menus from 80F). The municipal two-star **campsite** (☎04.93.04.46.66) is by the river, just upstream from the village.

Saorge and Fontan

From the river, **SAORGE**, to the north of Breil, reveals an unaesthetic clutter of houses in grey and mismatched shades of red. Only the shimmering gold Niçois tiles on its church and chapel towers entice you to climb the 1.5km from the train station it shares with Fontan to the gateway into the village. But Saorge is much prettier at close quarters than from a distance: almost nothing is level, and vertical stairways turn into paths lined with bramble. There's just the one near-horizontal main street, and even that goes up and down flights of steps and through arches formed by the houses. At the end of the street a path leads across the cultivated terraces to **La Madone del Poggio**, an eleventh-century chapel guarded by an impossibly high belltower topped by an octagonal spire; the chapel is private property and can't be visited. Back in the village, there's a seventeenth-century **Franciscan convent** (April–Oct Mon & Wed–Sun 2–5pm; Nov–March Sat & Sun 2–5pm; 25F) with rustic murals around its cloisters; and the **Église St-Sauveur** (daily 10am–5pm), which has rich examples of ecclesiastical art.

    Chambre d'hôtes and **gîte** accommodation is available from M & Mme Chimène, quartier Bergeron (☎04.93.04.55.49; ①). For **food**, *Lou Pountin*, rue Revelli (closed Wed), serves delicious pizzas, ravioli and other pasta dishes for under 100F; and there's one *bar-tabac*, *Chez Gilou*.

    FONTAN, 2km upstream and with another shining Niçois-tiled belfry, has one **hotel** to fall back on; the *Terminus* (☎04.93.04.50.05; closed Dec; ③), overlooking the Roya at the north end of the village, with cheapish rooms and several reasonably priced menus to eat beneath a beautifully painted ceiling. At the hotels and at the **restaurant** *Les Platanes, chez Mario*, at the other end of the village, the main speciality is fresh trout from the river.

La Brigue and Notre-Dame-des-Fontaines

The very appealing village of **LA BRIGUE**, 8km northeast of Fontan, lies on an eastern tributary of the Roya, just south of Tende, surrounded by pastures and with the perennial snowcap of Mont Bego visible to the west. Its Romanesque church, the **Église St-Martin**, is full of medieval paintings, including several by Louis Bréa, most of them depicting hideous scenes of torture and death. But the church, and the octagonal seventeenth-century **Chapelle St-Michel** alongside it, pale into insignificance compared with the sanctuary of **Notre-Dame-des-Fontaines**, 4km east of the village.

    From the exterior this seems to be a plain, graceful place of retreat, but inside it's something more akin to an arcade of video nasties. Painted in the fifteenth century by Jean Baleison (the ones above the altar) and Jean Canavéso (all the rest), the sequence of restored **frescoes** contains 38 episodes. Each one, from Christ's flagellation, through the torment on the Cross to devils claiming their victims, and, ultimate gore, Judas's disembowelment, is full of violent movement and colour. The chapel is open daily in summer (9.30am–7pm) and in the winter you can let yourself in with a key obtained from the *mairie* or the *Auberge St-Martin* in La Brigue. There's no bus, but it's a very pleasant walk up the D43 for 2km, then turning right over the Pont du Coq, built, like the chapel, in the fifteenth century.

    If you want **to stay** in La Brigue, try the *Auberge St-Martin* (☎04.93.04.62.17; ②; closed Tues out of season & Dec–Feb) or the *Fleurs des Alpes* (☎04.93.04.61.05; ②; closed Wed out of season & Dec to mid–Feb), both on place St-Martin by the church and with **restaurants** serving very satisfying meals for under 100F. The more upmarket *Le Mirval* (☎04.93.04.63.71; ④; closed Nov–March), downstream from place St-Martin on rue Vincent-Ferrier, has rooms overlooking the Levenza stream.

The Vallée des Merveilles

The **Vallée des Merveilles** lies between two lakes over 2000m up on the western flank of Mount Bego. The first person to record his experience of this high valley of lakes and bare rock was a fifteenth-century traveller who had lost his way. He described it as "an infernal place with figures of the devil and thousands of demons scratched on the rocks". What his contemporary readers must have imagined to be delusions brought on by the terror of the place were no imaginings. The rocks of the valley are carved with thousands of images, of animals, tools, people working and mysterious symbols, dating from some time in the second millennium BC. More are to be found in the **Vallée de Fontanable** on the northern flank of Mont Bego, and west from the Vallée des Merveilles across the southern slopes of Mont des Merveilles. Very little is known about them and the instruments that fashioned them have never been found.

Over the centuries other travellers, shepherds and eventually tourists have added their own engravings to the collection. As a result explorations of the Vallée de Fontanable are restricted to one path unless accompanied by an official Mercantour guide with the same applying to the Mont des Merveilles area.

The easiest route to the Vallée des Merveilles is the ten-kilometre trek (6–8hr) that starts at *Les Mesces* refuge, about 8km west of St-Dalmas-de-Tende on the D91. The first part of the climb is through woods full of wild raspberries, mushrooms and bilberries, not all of it steeply uphill. Eventually you rise above the treeline and **Lac Long** comes into view. A few pines still manage to grow around the lake, and in spring the grass is full of flowers, but encircling you is a mountain wilderness. From the *Refuge des Merveilles* by the lake, you continue up through a fearsome valley where the rocks turn from black to green according to the light. From here to just beyond the **Lac des Merveilles** you can start searching for the engravings. For the Vallée de Fontanable the path starts 4.5km further up the D91 from the *Mesces* refuge, just before the Casterino information point.

The Bureau des Guides du Val des Merveilles, 18 rue de France in Tende, organizes **guided walks** (July & Aug daily; June & Sept Sun; 35F; (☎04.93.04.77.73), as does the Bureau des Guides in St-Martin-Vésubie (see above ☎04.93.03.44.30) and Destination Merveilles in St-Dalmas-de-Tende (☎04.93.16.08.72). These are all recommended: it's no fun being on your own when blue skies and sun suddenly turn into violent hailstorms and lightning, and it's perfectly possible to miss the engravings altogether.

Tende

TENDE, the highest town on the Roya, guards the access to the Col de Tende, which connects Provence with Piedmont but is now bypassed by a long road tunnel. Though not especially attractive, Tende is quite a busy place, with plenty of cheap accommodation, places to eat, bars to lounge around in and shops to browse through.

The town's old and gloomy rows of houses, built with green and purple schist, are blackened by fumes of heavy goods vehicles shunting beer and building materials between Italy and France. Above them rise the stridently cherry-coloured belfry of the **collegiate church**, the peachy-orange clock towers and belfries of various Renaissance **chapels**, and a twenty-metre needle of wall which is all that remains of a château destroyed by the French in the seventeenth century. An Italian-style terraced cemetery extends beyond the ruins. The **Musée des Merveilles** at the northern end of town on av du 16 Septembre 1947 (May to mid-Oct daily 10.30am–6.30pm; mid-Oct to April Mon & Wed–Sun 10.30am–5pm; 30F), details the geology, archeology and traditions of the areas where the engravings have been found. Scenes from the daily lives of Copper- and Bronze-Age man have been set up and reproductions of the rock designs are on display along with attempts to decipher the beliefs and myths that inspired them. Whether you've been to the Vallée des Merveilles or not, the museum is an invaluable insight into an intriguing subject.

The **Vieille Ville** is fun to wander through, looking at the symbols of old trades on the door lintels, the overhanging roofs and the balconies on every floor. On place de l'Église, the **Collégiale Notre-Dame de l'Assumption** is more a repository of the town's wealth than a place of contemplation, with Baroque excess throughout, though the Apostles wearing their halos like lids on the Renaissance porch and the lions supporting the two Doric columns are rather nice. The more interesting church is **St-Michel** at the other end of town near the station on place du Grande Marché. This former convent was entirely remodelled in the 1960s, when the chevet was replaced by a wall of glass looking onto the trees and shrubs of the former convent gardens. It's decorated with dream-inspired paintings of a semi-symbolist, semi-surrealist nature by a contemporary local artist, some dreadful, others striking an eerily appropriate note. Local folklore has it that a dragon lives under the tombstones.

Between the neighbouring square of place de la République and the old town, rue de France is a good street for browsing, with craft shops, art galleries and potteries.

Practicalities

The **gare SNCF** is set back from the top of the main street, av du 16 Septembre (becoming av Aimable-Gastaud and av Georges-Bidault as it runs southwards), at the end of av Vassalo. Turning right out of the station you'll see the **tourist office** at the back of the *mairie* on your left before you reach the avenue (Mon–Wed, Fri & Sat: May–Sept 9am–noon & 2–6pm; Oct–April 9am–noon & 1–5pm; ☎04.93.04.73.71). This central axis leads down left towards place de la République; the Vieille Ville is further down on your right to either side of the Roya's tributary.

Hotels in Tende are inexpensive: there's the *Miramonti* at 5–7 av Vassalo (☎04.93.04.61.82; ②), just by the station; the *Hôtel du Centre*, 12 place de la République (☎04.93.04.62.19; ②; closed Nov); and the more upmarket *Cheval Blanc*, 18 rue Maurice-Sassi (☎04.93.04.62.22; ③) just off the *place*. If you follow chemin Ste-Catherine, off rue St-Jean past the cathedral, you'll come to the edge of the town and the **gîte d'étape** *Les Carlines* (☎04.93.04.62.74; ①; closed Oct–March), which has gorgeous views down the valley. The one-star municipal **campsite** is 500m down a path to the left of the gare SNCF (☎04.93.04.76.08; June–Aug only).

Restaurants are to be found on av du 16 Septembre and rue de France: nothing very special but plenty of Italian dishes. *La Marguerita* pizzeria on av du 16 Septembre, with beams strung with dried herbs and garlic, and stuffed foxes on the walls, is the most popular.

travel details

Trains

Chemin de Fer de Provence (Nice–Digne)

Nice to: Annot (4–5 daily; 2hr); Barrême (4–5 daily; 2hr 50min); Digne (4–5 daily; 3hr 20min); Entrevaux (4–5 daily; 1hr 30min); Puget-Théniers (4–5 daily; 1hr 30min); St-André-des-Alpes (4–5 daily; 2hr 40min); Thorame-Gare (4–5 daily; 2hr 20min); Touët-sur-Var (4–5 daily; 1hr 10min); Villars-sur-Var (4–5 daily; 1hr).

From Digne a regular SNCF bus links the Chemin de Fer de Provence with the SNCF Marseille–Sisteron line at St-Auban–Château-Arnoux (30min).

From St André-les-Alpes an SNCF bus meets 2 trains daily for connections to: St-Julien (10min); Castellane (30min); La Garde (35min).

From Thorame-Gare an SNCF bus meets 3 trains daily for connections to: Beauvezer (20min); Colmars-les-Alpes (30min); Allos (45min); La Foux d'Allos (1hr 10min).

SNCF line

Nice to: Breil-sur-Roya (4–5 daily; 1hr 10min); La Brigue (4–5 daily; 1hr 50min); St-Dalmas-de-Tende (4–5 daily; 1hr 30min–1hr 45min); Saorge-Fontan (4–5 daily; 1hr 15min–1hr 40min); Sospel (4–5 daily; 50min); Tende (4–5 daily; 2hr 10min).

Buses

Barcelonette to: Digne (1 daily; 1hr 45min); Gap (3 daily; 1hr 20min); Marseille (2–3 daily; 4hr).

Digne to: Avignon (2 daily; 3hr 30min); Barcelonnette (1 daily; 2hr); Castellane (1 daily; 1hr 15min); Grenoble (1 daily; 4hr 30min); Manosque (5 daily; 45min–1hr); Marseille (4 daily; 2hr–2hr 40min); Nice (2 daily; 3hr 15min); Puget-Théniers (1 daily; 2hr); Pra-Loup (1 daily; 1hr 50min); St-André-les-Alpes (1 daily; 45min); Seyne-les-Alpes (1 daily; 40min); Sisteron (3 daily; 45min).

Gréolières to: Grasse (1 daily; 1hr).

Puget-Théniers to: Annot (1 daily; 20min); Barrême (1 daily; 1hr 30min); Digne (1 daily; 2hr); Entraunes (1 daily; 1hr 10min); Entrevaux (1 daily; 15min); St-André-les-Alpes (1 daily; 1hr); St-Martin-d'Entraunes (1 daily; 1hr).

St-André-les-Alpes to: Allos (1 daily in high season; 1hr); Barrême (1 daily; 15min); Castellane (2 daily; 30min); Digne (1 daily; 45min); La Foux d'Allos (3 daily; 1hr 30min); Nice (1 daily; 2hr); St-Julien (2 daily; 10min).

St-Étienne-de-Tinée to: Auron (2 daily; 15min); Isola (2 daily; 30min); La Tour (2 daily; 1hr 15min); Nice (2 daily; 2hr 10min); St-Sauveur-de-Tinée (2 daily; 40min).

St-Martin-Vésubie to: Lantosque (1–2 daily; 40min); Nice (1–2 daily; 1hr 40min); Roquebillière (1–2 daily; 20min); St-Dalmas (1–3 weekly; 10–20min).

Sospel to: Menton (3 daily; 50min); Moulinet (1 daily; 30min).

Thorame-Gare to: Allos (3 daily; 45min); Beauvezer (3 daily; 20min); Colmars-les-Alpes (3 daily; 30min); La Foux d'Allos (3 daily; 1hr 10min).

PART THREE

THE
CONTEXTS

THE HISTORICAL FRAMEWORK

FROM THE STONE AGE TO THE CELTO-LIGURIANS

Almost all the great discoveries of **Stone Age** life in France have been made in the southwest of the country. In Provence a few Paleolithic traces have been found at Nice and in Menton (the skull of "Grimaldi man", for example) but nothing to compare with the cave drawings of Lascaux. It's assumed, however, that the area, including large tracts now submerged under the sea, was equally populated.

The development of farming, characterizing the **Neolithic Era**, is thought to have been started in Provence around 6500 BC with the domestication of the indigenous wild sheep. Around 3000 BC the **Ligurians** came from the east, settling throughout southern France and cultivating the land for the first time. It is to these people that the carvings in the Vallée des Merveilles, the few megalithic standing stones, and the earliest *bories* belonged. It's also thought that certain Provençal word-endings in place-names and names of rivers and mountains, such as *-osc*, *-asc*, *-auni* and *-inc*, derive from the Ligurian dialects passed down through Greek and Latin.

At some later point the **Celts** from the north moved into western Provence, bringing with them bronze technology. The first known fortified

hilltop retreats, the *oppidi* (of which traces remain in the Maures, the Luberon, the upper Durance and the hills in the Rhône Valley), are attributed to this new ethnic mix, the **Celto-Ligurians**.

THE ANCIENT GREEKS DISCOVER PROVENCE

As the Celto-Ligurian civilization developed, so did its trading links with the other Mediterranean peoples. The name of the River Rhône may have been given by traders from the Greek island of Rhodes (in French the name can be made into an adjective, *Rhodien*). Etruscans, Phoeniecians, Corinthians and Ionians all had links with Provence. The eventual **Greek colonies** set up along the coast, starting with **Massalia** (Marseille) around 600 BC, were not the result of military conquest but of gradual economic integration. And while Massalia was a republic with great influence over its hinterland, it was not a base for wiping out the indigenous peoples. Prestige and wealth came from its port, and the city prided itself on its independence, which was to last well into the Middle Ages.

The Greeks introduced olives, figs, cherries, walnuts, cultivated vines and money. During the two hundred years following the foundation of Massalia, **colonies** were set up in La Ciotat, Almanarre (near Hyères), Bréganson, Cavalaire, St-Tropez (known as Athenopolis), Antibes, Nice and Monaco. Mastrabala at St-Blaize and Glanum by St-Rémy-de-Provence developed within Massalia's sphere of influence. The **Rhône** was the corridor for commercial expeditions, including journeys as far north as Cornwall to acquire tin. Away from the coast and the Rhône Valley, however, the Celto-Ligurian lifestyle was barely affected by the advantages of Hellenic life, continuing its harsher and more basic battle for survival.

ROMAN CONQUEST

Unlike the Greeks, the **Romans** were true imperialists, imposing their organization, language and laws by military subjugation on every corner of their empire. During the third century BC Roman expansion was concentrated on Spain, the power base of the Carthaginians – from where Hannibal had set off with his elephants to cross the Rhône somewhere above Orange and the Alps in order to attack the Romans in upper Italy. During this time Massalia nurtured good diplomatic relations with Rome which stood the city in good stead when Spain was conquered and the Romans decided to secure the land routes to Iberia.

This they achieved in a remarkably short time. From 125 to 118 BC, **Provincia** (the origin of the name Provence) became part of the Roman Empire. It encompassed the whole of the south of France from the Alps to the Pyrenees, stretching as far north as Vienna and Geneva, and with Narbonne as its capital.

While Massalia and other areas remained neutral or collaborated with the invaders, many Ligurian tribes fought to the death, most notably the Salyens, whose Oppidum d'Entremont was demolished and a victorious new city, Aquae Sextiae (Aix), built at its foot in 122 BC. Pax Romana was still a long way off, however. **Germanic Celts** moving down from the Baltic came into conflict with the ruling power, managing to decimate several Roman legions at Orange in 105 BC. A major campaign was undertaken to prevent the Barbarians from closing in on Italy. The northern invaders were defeated, as were local uprisings. Massalia exploited every situation to gain more territories and privileges; the rest of Provence knuckled under, suffering the various battles and the requisitions and taxes to pay for them. Finally from 58 to 51 BC all of Gaul was conquered by **Julius Caesar**.

It was then that Massalia finally blew its hitherto successful diplomatic strategy by supporting Pompey against Caesar, who then laid siege, defeated the city and confiscated all its territories which had stretched from the Rhône to Monaco. Unlike earlier emperors, Julius Caesar started to implant his own people in Provence (St-Raphaël was founded for his veterans). His successor Octavian followed the same policy. While the coastal areas duly latinized themselves, the **Ligurians** in the mountains, from Sisteron to the Roya Valley, refused to give up their identity without a fight. Fight they did, keeping Roman troops busy for ten years until their eventual defeat in 14 BC, which the Trophie des Alpes at La Turbie gloats over to this day.

This monument to Augustus Caesar was erected on the newly built **Via Aurelia**, which linked Rome with Arles, by way of Cimiez,

Antibes, Fréjus and Aix, more or less along the route of the present-day N7. The **Via Agrippa** went north from Arles, through Avignon and Orange. Only the rebellious mountainous area was heavily garrisoned. Western Provence, with Arles as its main town (Narbonne was still the capital of Provincia), dutifully served the imperial interests, providing oil, grain and, most importantly, ships for the superpower that ruled western Europe and the borders of the Mediterranean for five centuries.

Christianity appeared in Provence during the third century and spread fairly rapidly in the fourth when it became the official religion of the Roman Empire. The **Lérins Monastery** was founded around 410 AD and the **Abbey of St-Victor** in Marseille about six years later.

ROME FALLS: MORE INVASIONS

For a while in the early fifth century, when the Roman Empire was beginning to split apart, the invasions by the Germanic tribes bypassed Provence. But by the time the Western Roman Empire was finally done for in 476 AD Provence was under the domination of both the **Visigoths**, who had captured Arles and were terrorizing the lower Rhône valley, and the **Burgundians**, another Germanic tribe, who had moved in from the east. The new rulers confiscated land, took slaves and generally made life for the locals even more miserable than usual.

Over the next two hundred years **Goths** and **Franks** fought over and partitioned Provence; famine, disease and bloodshed diminished the population; lands that had been drained returned to swamp; intellectual life declined. Under the **Merovingian dynasty** in the eighth century Provence was, in theory, part of the **Frankish empire**. But a new world power had emerged – **Islam** – which had spread from the Middle East into North Africa and most of Spain. In 732 a Muslim army had reached as far as Tours before being defeated by the Franks at Poitiers. At this point the local ruler of Provence rebelled against the central authority, and called on the **Saracens** (Muslims) to assist. Armies of Franks, Saracens, Lombards (allies of the Franks) and locals rampaged through Provence, putting the Franks back in control.

Though the ports had trouble carrying on their lucrative trade while the Mediterranean was controlled by Saracens, agriculture developed under the Frankish **Carolingian dynasty**, particularly during the relatively peaceful years of **Charlemagne's rule**. But when, during the ninth century, Charlemagne's sons and then grandsons started squabbling over the inheritance, Provence once again became easy prey.

Normans took over the lower Rhône, and the **Saracens** returned, pillaging Marseille and destroying its abbey in 838, doing over Arles in 842, and attacking Marseille again in 848. For a century they maintained a base at Fraxinetum (La Garde-Freinet), from where they controlled the whole Massif des Maures.

The **hilltop villages** along the coast are commonly explained as the frightened response to the Saracens, though few date back this far. Well inland, people were just as prone to retreat to whatever defensive positions were available. In the cities this would be the strongest building (the Roman theatre at Orange, for example). The Rhône Valley villagers took refuge in the Luberon and the Massif de la Ste-Baume.

For all the terrors and bloodshed, the period was not without its evolution. The Saracens introduced basic medicine, the use of cork-bark, resin extraction from pines, flat roof tiles and the most traditional Provençal musical instrument, the tambourine.

THE COUNTS OF PROVENCE

The Saracens were expelled for good at the end of the tenth century by **Guillaume Le Libérateur**, count of Arles, who claimed Provence as his own feudal estate. After several centuries of anarchy a period of relative stability ensued. Forestry, fishing, irrigation, land reclamation, vine cultivation, bee-keeping, salt-panning, river transport and renewed learning (under the auspices of the Benedictine monasteries) began pulling Provence out of the Dark Ages.

Politically, Guillaume and his successors retained considerable independence from their overlords (first the kingdom of Burgundy then the Holy Roman Empire). In turn they tended to confine their influence to the area around Arles and Avignon, while local lords held sway throughout the rest of the countryside and the cities developed their own autonomy. The Rhône formed the border between France and the Holy Roman Empire but for much of the time this political division failed to cut the old

economic, cultural and linguistic links between the two sides of the river.

In the **twelfth century**, Provence passed to the counts of Toulouse and was then divided with the counts of Barcelona, while various fiefdoms – amongst them Forcalquier, Les Baux and Beuil on the eastern side of the Var – refused integration. Power was a bewildering, shifting pattern but sporadic armed conflicts apart (confined mainly to the lower Rhône Valley), the titleholder to Provence hardly affected the ordinary people who were bound in serfdom to their immediate seigneur.

As a consequence of the Crusades, **maritime commerce** flourished once again, as did trade along the Rhône, giving prominence to Avignon, Orange, Arles and, most of all, Marseille. In Nice, then under the control of the Genoese Republic, a new commercial town started to develop below the castle rock. The cities took on the organizational form of the Italian consulates, increasingly separating themselves from feudal power.

Troubadour poetry made its appearance in the langue d'oc language that was spoken from the Alps to the Pyrenees (and from which the **Provençal dialect** developed). Church construction looked back to the Romans for inspiration, producing the great Romanesque edifices of Montmajour, Sénanque, Silvacane, Thoronet and St-Trophime in Arles.

Raymond Béranger V, Catalan count of Provence in the early thirteenth century, took the unprecedented step of spending time in his domains. While fighting off the count of Toulouse and the Holy Roman Emperor, he made Aix his capital, founded Barcelonnette and travelled throughout the Alps and the coastal regions. Provence became, for the first time since the Romans, an organized mini-state with a more or less **unified feudal system** of law and administration.

THE ANGEVINS

After Béranger's death, Provence turned towards France, with the **house of Anjou** gaining control and holding it until the end of the fifteenth century. The borders changed: Nice, Barcelonnette and Puget-Théniers passed to Savoy in 1388 and remained separate from Provence until 1860. New extraneous powers claimed or bought territories within the country – the **popes at Avignon** (see p.67) and in the

Comtat Venaissin; the Prince of Nassau in Orange. Though armed conflicts, revolts and even civil war in 1388 chequered its medieval history, Provence was at least spared the devastations of the Hundred Years' War with England, which never touched the region.

By the end of this period the established trading routes from the Orient to Genoa and Marseille, and from Marseille to Flanders and London, were forming the basis of **early capitalism**, and spreading new techniques and learning. Though Marseille was not a great financial centre like Antwerp or Florence, its expanding population became ever more cosmopolitan. Away from the coast and the Rhône, however, feudal villages continued to live in isolation, unable to survive if a harvest failed. For a shepherd or forester in the mountains, life in Marseille or in the extravagant papal city of Avignon would have appeared to belong to another planet.

Provençal Jews exercised equal rights with Christians, owning land and practising a wide variety of professions in addition to finance and commerce. Though concentrated in the western towns, they were not always ghettoized. But the moment any kind of disaster struck, such as the Black Death in the mid-fourteenth century, latent hostility would violently manifest itself. **The Plague**, however, made no distinctions between Jew or Christian, rich or poor: around half the population died from the recurring epidemics.

In **cultural and intellectual life** the dominant centres were the **papal court at Avignon**, and later **King René of Anjou's court at Aix**. However, despite the area's key position between Italy and northern Europe, and the cosmopolitan influence of the popes, Angevin rulers and foreign trade, art and architecture remained surprisingly unmarked by the major movements of the time. The popes tended to employ foreign artists and it was not until the mid-fifteenth century that native art developed around the **Avignon School** – represented by such works as Nicolas Froment's *Le Buisson Ardent* and *La Couronnement de la Vierge* by Enguerrand Quarton. At the same time the **School of Nice** developed, more directly under Italian influence, represented by the frescoes of Canavesio and Baleison and the paintings of Louis and François Bréa. Avignon was the chief city of great **Gothic architecture**

– the Palais des Papes and many of the churches – but outside this city the only major examples of the new style were Tarascon's castle and the basilica of St-Maximin-de-la-Ste-Baume.

The **legends of the saints** fleeing Palestine and seeking refuge in Provence began to take root around this time, too, with pilgrimages to the various shrines bringing glimpses of the outside world to small towns and villages. It was at this time that the popes founded a **university in Avignon** (1303) which became famous for jurisprudence; Aix university was established a century later and in the mid-fourteenth century the first paper mills were in use. By King René's time, French was the official language of the court.

UNION WITH FRANCE

The short-lived Charles III of Provence, René's heir, bequeathed all his lands to **Louis XI of France**, a transfer of power that the *parlement* of Aix glossed over and approved in 1482. Within twelve months every top Provençal official had been sacked and replaced by a Frenchman; the castles at Toulon and Les Baux were razed to the ground; garrisons were placed in five major towns.

The *parlement* protested in vain, but after Louis XI's death a more careful approach was taken to this crucial border province. The **Act of Union**, ratified by *parlement* in 1486, declared Provence to be a separate entity within the kingdom of France, enshrining the rights to its own law courts, customs and privileges. In reality, the ever-centralizing power of the French state was systematically to erode these rights as it did with Brittany and the other once-autonomous provinces.

The **Jewish population** provided a convenient diversion for Provençal frustrations. Encouraged, if not instigated, by the Crown, there were massacres, expulsions and assaults in Marseille, Arles and Manosque in the last two decades of the fifteenth century. The royal directive was convert or leave – some, such as the parents of **Nostradamus**, converted, many fled to the Comtat. During the sixteenth century more expulsion threats and special taxes were the rule. In 1570 the Jews lost their papal protection in the Comtat.

Meanwhile Charles VIII, Louis XII and François I involved Provence in their **Italian Wars**. **Marseille** became a **military port** in

1488, and in 1496 **Toulon** was fortified and its first **shipyards** opened. While the rest of the province suffered troop movements and requisitions, Marseille and Toulon benefited from extra funds and unchecked piracy against the enemies of France. Genoese, Venetian and Spanish vessels were regularly towed into Marseille's port.

The war took a more serious turn in the 1520s after the French conquest of Milan. **Charles V**, the new Holy Roman Emperor, retaliated by sending a large army across the Var and into Aix. The French concern was to protect Marseille at all costs – the rest of the province was left to fend for itself. After the imperial forces had failed to take Marseille and retreated, the city was rewarded with the pomp and carnival of a royal wedding between François' second son, the future Henri II, and **Catherine de Medici**. The Château d'If was built to protect the roadstead.

Another round in the war soon commenced. Charles V took back Milan, the French invaded Savoy and occupied Nice. In 1536 an even bigger **imperial army invaded**, and again the French abandoned inland Provence to protect Marseille and the Rhône Valley. The people of **Le Muy** stopped the emperor for one day with fifty local heroes hanged for their pains. Elsewhere people fled to the forests, their towns and villages pillaged by the invaders. **Marseille** and **Arles** held out; French troops finally moved south down the Durance; dysentery and lack of sure supply lines weakened the imperial army. Twenty thousand Savoyards were dead or imprisoned by the time the imperial troops were safely back across the Var.

One effect of the Italian Wars was that Provence finally now identified itself with France, making it easier for the Crown to diminish the power of the États, impose greater numbers of French administrators, and, in 1539, decree that all administrative laws were to be translated from Latin into French, not Provençal.

LIFE IN THE EARLY SIXTEENTH CENTURY

Sixteenth-century Provence was ruled by two royal appointees – a governor and grand *sénéchal* (the chief administrator) – but the **feudal hierarchy** failed to achieve the same command over the structure of society as it did elsewhere in France. Few nobles lived on their estates and those that did were often poorer than the merchants and financiers of the major cities. In remoter areas people cultivated their absent seigneur's land as if it were their own; in other areas towns bought land off the feudal owners. It is estimated that nearly half the population had their own holdings. Advances in irrigation, such as **Craponne's canal through the Crau**, were carried out independently from the aristocracy.

While not self-sufficient in grain, Provence had surpluses of wine, fish and vermilion from the Camargue to export; **growing industries** in textiles, tanneries, soap and paper; and new foods, such as oranges, pepper, palm dates and sugar cane, introduced along the coast from across the Mediterranean. Olives provided the basic oil for food; orchards were being cultivated on a commercial scale; most families kept pigs and sheep; only vegetables were rare luxuries. People lived on their land, with the **old fortified villages** populated only in times of insecurity. Most small towns had weekly **markets**, and **festivals** celebrated the advance from survival being a non-stop struggle. Epidemics of the plague continued, however, and sanitation left a lot to be desired – a contemporary noted that even in Aix it "rained shit as often as it did in Arles or Marseille".

Free schools were set up by some of the larger towns, and secondary colleges established in Aix, Marseille, Arles and Avignon. **Nostradamus** (1503–1566) achieved renown throughout France – from the royal court down to his Salon and St-Rémy neighbours. His books had to be printed in Lyon, though, as there was as yet no market for printers in Provence.

Châteaux such as La Tour d'Aigue, Gordes and Lourmarin, with comfort playing an equal part to defence, were built at this time, as were the rich Marseille town houses of the Maison Diamentée and the Hôtel Cabre. The facade of St-Pierre in Avignon shows the Renaissance finally triumphing over Provence's artistic backwardness.

THE WARS OF RELIGION

Though the Italian Wars temporarily disrupted social and productive advances, they were nothing compared with the **Wars of Religion** that put all France in a state of **civil war** for most of the second half of the sixteenth century. The clash between the new reforming ideas of Luther and Calvin and the old Roman Catholic order was particularly violent in Provence. Avignon, as papal domain, was inevitably a rigid centre of Catholicism. The neighbouring principality of Orange allowed Huguenots to practise freely and form their own organizations. Haute Provence and the Luberon became centres for the new religion due to the influx of Dauphinois and Piedmontais settlers.

Incidents began to build up in the 1540s, culminating in the massacre of Luberon Protestants and the destruction of Mérindol (see p.139). In Avignon heretics were displayed in iron cages where they'd been slung to die; in Haute Provence churches were smashed by the reformers; while in Orange the Protestants pillaged the cathedral and took control of the city. The regent Catherine de Medici's **Edict of Tolerance** in 1562 only made matters worse. Marseille demanded and received an exemption; Aix promptly dispatched a Catholic contingent to massacre the Protestants of Tourves; Catherine's envoys prompted a massacre of Catholics at Barjols. The notorious Baron des Adrets, who had fought for the Catholics, now switched sides and carried out a series of terrifying attacks on Catholic towns and villages. The *parlement* chose to resign rather than ratify a new edict of tolerance in 1563, even though by this point Orange had been won back to the established Church, the garrison of Sisteron had been massacred for protecting the Protestants and the last armed group of reformers had fled north out of the province.

When Catherine de Medici and her son Charles XIV toured Provence in 1564, all seemed well. But within a few years fighting again broke out, with Sisteron once more under siege. In the mid-1570s trouble took a new turn with the rivalry between Henri III's governor and *sénéchal* adding to the hostile camps. This state of civil war was only terminated by another major outbreak of the **Plague** in **1580**.

With the Protestant **Henri de Navarre** (the future Henri IV) becoming heir to the throne in 1584, the *Guerres de Religion* hotted up even more. The pope excommunicated Henri; and the leaders of the French Catholics (the de Guises) formed the **European Catholic League**, seized Paris and drove out the king, Henri III. Provence found itself with two governors – the king's and the League's appointees; two capitals – Aix and Pertuis; and a split *parlement*. After Henri III's assassination, Catholic Aix called in the duke of Savoy whose troops trounced Henri de Navarre's supporters at Riez. At this point the main issue for the Provençaux was loyalty to the French Crown against invaders, rather than religion. Even the Aix *parlement* stopped short of giving Savoy the title to Provence, and after Marseille again withstood a siege, the duke gave up and went back home to Nice in 1592. For another year battles continued between the Leaguers and the Royalists, with Marseille refusing to recognize either authority. Finally Henri IV said his Mass; troops entered Marseille; and the war-damaged and impoverished Provence reverted back to **royal control**.

LOUIS XIII AND LOUIS XIV

The **consolidation of the French state** initiated by Louis XIII's minister **Richelieu** saw the whittling away of Provençal institutions and ideas of independence, coupled with ever-increasing tax demands plus enforced "free gifts" to the king. The power and prestige of the États and *parlement* were reduced by force, clever negotiation or playing off the different cities' rival interests.

Political power switched from governors and *sénéchals*, who were part of the feudal structure, to *intendants*, servants of the state with powers over every aspect of provincial life, including the military. The États, having refused to provide the royal purse with funds in 1629, were not convoked again. These changes, along with the failure of the aristocratic rebellions during Louis XIV's minority (the Frondes), and the increasing number of titles bought by the bourgeoisie, left the *noblesse d'épée* (the real aristos) disgruntled but impotent. The clergy (the First Estate) also lost a measure of their former power.

It was a time of **plague, famine,** further outbreaks of **religious strife and war**. To deal with opposition the Château d'If became a state prison. The **war with Spain**, for which Toulon's fortifications were upgraded and forts added to Giens and the Îles d'Hyères, increased taxation, decimated trade and cost lives. Marseille attempted to hold on to its ancient independence by setting up a rebel council in 1658. The royal response was swift. Troops were sent in, rebels were condemned to the rack or the galleys, a permanent garrison was established and the foundations laid for the Fort St-Nicolas to keep an eye on "*ce peuple violent et libertin*".

While the various upheavals and ever-multiplying tax burden caused untold misery, progress in production (including the faïence industry), education and social provision (mostly the work of the burgeoning Pénitents orders outside the Church establishment) carried on apace. The town houses of Aix, Marseille and Avignon, the Hospice de la Charité in Marseille, the Baroque additions to churches and chapels, all show the wealth accumulating, gained, as ever, by maritime commerce. But the greatest Provençal sculptor of the period, **Pierre Puget**, never received royal patronage and Provençal was still the language of all classes in society, though French for the first time was imposed on certain disciplines at Aix University.

As the reign of **Louis XIV**, the **Sun King**, became more grandiose and more aggressive, Provence, like all of France outside Versailles and Paris, was eclipsed. The **war with Holland** saw Orange and the valley of Barcelonnette annexed; Avignon and the papal Comtat swung steadily into the French orbit; attempts were made again to capture Nice. But for the Provençaux, the people of Orange, Avignon and the Comtat had always been their fellow countrymen and women, while Nice was a foreign city they had never wished to claim. Wars that involved the English navy blockading the ports were as unwelcome to the local bourgeois as they were to those who had to fight.

As the *ancien régime* slowly dug its own grave the rest of the country stagnated. The pattern for Provence of wars, invasions and trade blockades became entrenched. To add to the gloom, another outbreak of the **Plague** killed half the population of Marseille in **1720**. The extravagance of Louis XV's court, where the Grassois painter Fragonard found his patrons, had few echoes in Provence. Aix had its grandiose town planning, Avignon its mansions, Grasse its perfume industry, but elsewhere there was complete stagnation.

THE REVOLUTION

Conditions were ripe for revolution in Provence. The region had suffered a disastrous silk harvest and a sharp fall in the price of wine in 1787, and the severe winter of 1788–89 killed off most of the olive trees. Unemployment and starvation were rife and the hurtling rise in the price of bread provoked serious rioting in the spring of 1789. There was no lack of followers for bourgeois *députés* exasperated by incompetent administration and the constant drain on national resources that the court represented.

So in **July 1789**, while the Bastille was stormed in Paris, Provençal peasants pillaged their local châteaux and urban workers rioted against the mayors, egged on by the middle classes. There was only one casualty, at Aups. The following year **Marseillaise revolutionaries** seized the forts of St-Jean and St-Nicolas, with again just one lashing of violence when the crowd lynched St-Jean's commander. **Toulon** was equally fervent in its support for the new order, and at **Aix** one counter-revolutionary lawyer and two aristocrats were strung up on lamp posts. In the **papal lands**, where the crucial issue was reunion with France, Rome's representative was sent packing from Avignon and a revolutionary municipality installed.

Counter-revolutionaries regrouped in Carpentras and there were several bloody incidents, including the ice-house massacre. However, 1792 saw Marseille's staunchly Jacobin National Guard, the **Féderés**, demolish the counter-revolutionary forces in the Comtat and aristocratic Arles. Marseille's authorities declared that kingship was contrary to the principles of equality and national sovereignty. When the Legislative Assembly summoned all the Féderés to Paris to defend the capital and celebrate the third anniversary of the Bastille, five hundred Marseillais marched north singing Rouget de Lisle's **Hymn to the Army of the Rhine**. It was written for the troops at the front in the war declared in April with Germany and Austria. But for the Parisian *sans-culottes* it was a major hit, becoming the **Marseillaise**, France's national anthem. Even more so after the attack on the Tuileries palace that was swiftly followed by the dethronement of the king. According to the Swedish ambassador of the time, "Marseille's Féderés were the moving force behind everything in August 1792."

Provence had by now incorporated the papal states and was divided into **four départements**. Peasants were once again on the pillage, and still starving, while royalists and republicans fought it out in the towns. In 1793 the Var military commander was ordered to take Nice, a hotbed of émigré intrigue and part of the great European coalition out to exterminate the French Revolution. Twenty thousand people fled the city but no resistance was encountered. The Alpes-Maritimes *département* came into existence.

In the summer of the same year, political divisions between the various factions of the Convention and the growing fear of a dictatorship by the Parisian *sans-culottes* provoked the **provincial Federalist revolt**. The populace was fed up with conscription to the wars on every frontier, and a hankering after their old Provençal autonomy reasserted itself. Revolutionary cities found themselves fighting against government forces – a situation speedily exploited by the real **counter-revolutionaries**. In Toulon the entire fleet and the city's fortifications were handed over to the English. (In the battle to regain the city, the government's victory was secured by the young Napoléon.) Reprisals, in addition to the almost daily executions of the Terror, cost thousands of lives.

Much of Provence, however, had remained Jacobin, and so fell victim to the **White Terror of 1795** that followed the execution of Robespierre. The prisons of Marseille, Aix, Arles and Tarascon overflowed with people picked up on the street with no charge. Cannons were fired into the cells at point blank range and sulphur or lighted rags thrown through the bars. By the time the Revolution had given up all hopes of being revolutionary in terms of its 1789 manifesto, **anarchy reigned**. Provence was crawling with returned émigrés who had no trouble finding violent followers motivated by frustration, exhaustion and famine.

NAPOLÉON AND RESTORATION

Provence's experience of **Napoléon's reign** differed little from that of the rest of France, despite the emperor's close connection with the region (childhood at Nice; military career at Antibes and Toulon; then the escape from Elba). Order was restored and power became even more centralized, with préfets enlarging on the role of Louis XIV's *intendants*. The **concordat with the pope** re-establishing Catholicism as the state religion was widely welcomed, particularly since the new ecclesiastical authorities were not all the old First Estate, *ancien régime* representatives. However, secular power reverted to the old seigneurs in many places – the new mayor of Marseille, for example, was a marquise.

It was the **Napoleonic wars** that lost the emperor his Provençal support. Marseille's port was again blockaded; conscription and taxes for military campaigns were as detested as ever; the Alpes-Maritimes *département* became a theatre of war and in 1814 was handed over (with Savoy) to Sardinia. Monaco followed suit the following year, though with the Grimaldi dynasty reinstalled in their palace.

The **restoration of the Bourbons** after Waterloo unleashed another White Terror. Provence was again bitterly divided between royalists and republicans. Despite this split there was no major resistance to the **1830 revolution** which put Louis-Philippe, the "Citizen King" on the throne. The new regime represented liberalism – well tinged with anti-clericalism and a dislike of democracy – and was welcomed by the Provençal bourgeoisie. Despite the ardent Catholicism of the *paysans*, and the large numbers of émigrés that had returned under the Bourbons' amnesties, the attempt by the duchess of Berry to bring back the "legitimate" royalty (which had some initial success in western France) failed totally here.

1848 AND 1851

The first half of the nineteenth century saw the first major **industrialization** of France, and, overseas, the conquest of Algeria.

In Provence, Marseille was linked by rail with Paris and expanded its port to take steam ships; iron bridges over the Rhône and new roads were built; many towns demolished their ramparts to extend their main streets into the suburbs. By the 1840s the arsenal at Toulon was employing over three thousand workers.

This emerging proletariat was highly receptive to the visit by the socialist and feminist **Flora Tristan**, who was doing the rounds of France in 1844. A year later all the different trades in the arsenal went on strike. Throughout industrialized Provence – the Rhône Valley and the coast – workers overturned their traditional *compagnons* (guilds) to form more radical trade-union organizations. Things hardly changed, however, in inland Provence, as protectionist policies hampered the exchange of foodstuffs, and the new industries' demand for fuel eroded the forestry rights of the *paysans*. In 1847 the country (and most of Europe) was in severe economic crisis.

News of the **1848 revolution** arrived from Paris before the representatives of the new republic. Town halls, common lands and forests were instantly and peacefully reclaimed by the populace. In the elections that followed, very moderate republicans were returned, though they included three manual workers in Marseille, Toulon and Avignon. Two months later, however, the economic situation was deteriorating again and newly won improvements in working hours and wages were being clawed back by the employers. A demonstration in Marseille turned nasty and the **barricades** went up (see p.159).

Elsewhere, the most militant action was in Menton and Roquebrune, both under the rule of **Monaco**, where the people refused to pay the prince's high taxes on oil and fruit. Sardinian military assistance failed to quell the revolt and the two towns declared themselves independent republics. With his main source of income gone, the Grimaldi prince turned the focus of his state shrewdly towards tourism – already well established in Nice and Hyères – and opened the casino at Monte Carlo.

The 1848 revolution turned sour with the election of **Louis-Napoléon** as president in 1850. A law was introduced which in effect annulled the 1830 universal male suffrage by imposing a residency requirement. Laws against "secret societies" and "conspiracies" followed. Ordinary *paysans* discussing prices over a bottle of wine could be arrested; militants from Digne and Avignon were deported to Polynesia for belonging to a democratic party. Newly formed cooperatives were seen by the authorities as hotbeds of sedition. All this inevitably accelerated politicization of the *paysans*.

When Louis-Napoléon made himself emperor in the **coup d'état of 1851**, Provence, as many other regions of France, turned again to revolt. Initially there were insufficient forces in the small towns and villages to prevent the rebels taking control (which they did without any violence). In order to take the préfectures, villagers and townspeople, both male and female, organized themselves into disciplined "colonnes" which marched beneath the red flag. Digne was the only préfecture they held, though, and then for only two days. Reprisals were bloody – another White Terror in effect, with thousands of the rebels caught as they tried to flee into Savoy. Of all the insurgents in France shot, imprisoned or deported after this rebellion, one in five were from Provence.

THE SECOND EMPIRE

The **Second Empire** saw greater changes in everyday life than in any previous period. **Marseille** became the premier port of France with trade enormously expanded by the colonization of North and West Africa, Vietnam, and parts of China. The depopulation of inland Provence, which had been gradually increasing over the last century and a half, suddenly became a deluge of migration to the coast and Rhône Valley. While the railway was extended along the coast – encouraging the nascent Côte d'Azur tourism – communications inland were ignored.

At the end of the **war for Italian unification** in 1860, **Napoléon III** regained the Alpes-Maritimes as payment for his support of Italy against Austria. A plebiscite in Nice gave majority support for **reunion with France**. To the north, Tende and La Brigue voted almost unanimously for France but the result was ignored: the new king of Italy wished to keep his favourite game-hunting grounds. Menton and Roquebrune also voted for France. While making noises about rigged elections, Charles of Monaco agreed to sell the two towns – despite their independence – to France. The sum was considerably more than the fledgling gambling and tourism industry was as yet bringing in and saved the principality from bankruptcy. **Monaco's independence**, free from any foreign protector, was finally established.

One casualty of this dispersal of traditional Provence, combined with the spread of national primary education, was the Provençal language. This prompted the formation of the **Félibrige** in 1854, by a group of poets including Frédéric Mistral – a nostalgic, backward-looking and intellectual movement in defence of literary Provençal. There were other, more popularist, Provençal writers at the time, but they too were conservative, railing against gas lighting and any other modern innovation. The attempt to associate the language with some past golden age of ultra-Catholic primitivism only encouraged the association of progress with the French tongue – particularly for the Left.

By the end of the 1860s the **socialism** of the First International was gaining ground in the industrial cities, and in Marseille most of all. Opponents of the empire had the majority in the town hall, and in the plebiscite of 1870, in which the country as a whole gave Napoléon III their support, the Bouches-du-Rhône *département* was second only to Paris in the number of "nons". It was not surprising therefore that Marseille had its own commune (see p.163) when the Parisians took up arms against the right-wing republic established after the Prussians' defeat of France and the downfall of Napoléon III.

Honoré Daumier, the Marseillais caricaturist and fervent republican, was the great illustrator of both the 1851 and the 1871 events. In the middle of the century the **Marseille school of painting** developed under the influence of foreign travel and orientalism, attracting to the city such artists as Puvis de Chavannes and Félix Ziem. Provence's greatest native artist, **Cézanne**, though living in Paris from the 1860s to the 1880s, spent a few months of every year in his home town of Aix, or in Marseille and L'Estaque. He was sometimes accompanied by his childhood friend **Zola**, and by **Renoir** whom he introduced to this coast.

THIRD REPUBLIC: 1890–1914

Under the **Third Republic**, the division between inland Provence and the coast and Rhône Valley accentuated. Port activity at Marseille quadrupled with the opening of new trade routes along the Suez Canal and further colonial acquisitions in the Far East. Manufacturing began to play an equal role with commerce. The orchards of the Rhône Valley were planted on a massive scale, and light industries producing clothes, foodstuffs and paper developed in Aix and other cities to export to the North African colonies. Chemical works in Avignon produced the synthetics that spelt the rapid decline of the traditional industries of the small towns and villages of the interior – tanning, dyeing, silk and glass. Wine production, meanwhile, was devastated by phylloxera.

The one area of brilliance connected with the climate but not with commerce was art – painting in particular. Following on from Cézanne and Renoir, a younger generation of artists were discovering the Côte d'Azur. The Post-Impressionists and Fauvists flocked to St-Tropez in the wake of the ever-hospitable Paul Signac. Matisse, Dufy, Seurat, Dérain, van Dongen, Bonnard, Braque, Friesz, Marquet, Manguin, Camion, Vlaminck and Vuillard were all intoxicated by the Mediterranean light, the climate and the ease of living. The escape from the rigours of Paris released a massive creative energy and resulted in works that, in addition to their radical innovations, have more *joie de vivre* than any other period in French art. Renoir retired to Cagnes for health reasons in 1907; for Matisse, Dufy and Bonnard the Côte d'Azur became their permanent home; and Van Gogh, always a man apart, had a spell in Arles.

Ignoring these Bohemian characters, the **winter tourist season** on the coast was taking off. **Hyères** and **Cannes** had been "discovered" in the first half of the century (and Nice many years earlier). But increased ease of travel and the temporary restraint of simmering international tensions encouraged aristocratic mobility. The population of **Nice** trebled from 1861 to 1911; luxury trains ran from St Petersburg, Vienna and London; *belle époque* mansions and grand hotels rose along the Riviera seafronts; and gambling, particularly at Monte Carlo, won the patronage of the Prince of Wales, the Emperor Franz Joseph and scores of Russian grand-dukes.

The native working class meanwhile were forming the first French Socialist Party, which had its opening congress in Marseille in 1879. Support came not just from the city but from towns and villages that had fought in 1851. In 1881 Marseille elected the first socialist *député*. By 1892 the municipal councils of Marseille, Toulon, La Ciotat and other industrial towns were in the hands of socialists. In Aix, however, the old legitimist royalists (those favouring the return of the Bourbons) still held sway, managing to block the erection of a monument to Zola in 1911.

WORLD WAR I AND THE INTER-WAR YEARS

The battlefields of **World War I** may have seemed far away in northern France and Belgium, but conscription brought the people of Provence into the war. The socialists divided between pacifists and patriots, but when, in 1919, France took part in the attack on the Soviet Union, soldiers, sailors and workers joined forces in Toulon and Marseille to support the mutinies on French warships in the Black Sea. The struggle to have the mutineers freed continued well into 1920, the year in which the **French Communist Party** (PCF) was born; the party's adherents in Provence were again the heirs to the 1851 rebellion.

The casualties of the war led to severe depopulation in the already dwindling villages of inland Provence, some of which were actually deserted. **Land use** also changed dramatically, from mixed agriculture to a monocrop of vines in order to provide the army with its ration of one litre of wine per soldier per day. Quantity, thanks to the Provençal climate, rather than quality was the aim, leaving acres upon acres of totally unviable vineyards after demobilization. With the growth in tourism, it was easier to sell the land for construction rather than have it revert to its former use.

The **tourist industry** recovered fairly quickly from the war. The Front Populaire of 1936 introduced paid holidays, encouraging native visitors to the still unspoilt coast. International literati – Somerset Maugham, Katherine Mansfield, Scott and Zelda Fitzgerald, Colette, Anaïs Nin, Gertrude Stein – and a new wave of artists, Picasso and Cocteau amongst them, replaced the defunct grand-dukes, even if anachronistic titles still filled the palatial Riviera residences.

Marseille during the inter-war years saw the evolution of characteristics that have yet to be obliterated. The activities of the fascist Action Française led to deaths during a left-wing counter-demonstration in 1925. Modern-style **corruption** snaked its way through the town hall and the rackets of gangsters on the Chicago model moved in on the vice industries. Elections were rigged and even revolvers used at the ballot boxes.

The increasing popularity of the Communist Party in the city was due to its anti-corruption platform. After the failure of the Front Populaire (which the great majority of Provençaux had voted for, electing several Communist *députés*), there were constant pitched battles between the Left and Right in Marseille. In 1939 a state administrator was imposed by Paris with powers to obstruct the elected council.

WORLD WAR II

France and Britain declared **war on Germany** together on September 3, 1939. The French Maginot line, however, swiftly collapsed, and by June 1940 the Germans controlled Paris and all of northern France. On June 22, Marshall Pétain signed the **armistice with Hitler**, which divided France between the Occupied

Zone – the Atlantic coast and north of the Loire – and "unoccupied" Vichy France in the south. Menton and Sospel were occupied by the Italians, to whom the adjoining Roya Valley still belonged.

With the start of the British counter-offensive in 1942, **Vichy France** joined itself with the Allies and was immediately occupied by the Germans. The port of Toulon was overrun in November, with the French navy scuppering its fleet rather than letting it fall into German hands.

Resistance fighters and passive citizens suffered executions, deportations and the wholesale destruction of Le Panier quarter in Marseille (see p.159). The **Allied bombings** of 1944 caused high civilian casualties and considerable material damage, particularly to Avignon, Marseille and Toulon. The **liberation** of the two great port cities was aided by a general armed revolt by the people, but it was in the Italian sector – in Sospel and its neighbouring villages – that the fighting by the local populace was the most heroic.

MODERN PROVENCE

Before the Germans surrendered **Marseille** they made sure that the harbours were blown to bits. In the immediate **postwar years** the task of repairing the damage was compounded by a slump in international trade and passenger traffic. The nationalization of the Suez Canal was the next disaster to hit the city, spelling an end to its prime position on world trading routes. Company after company decamped to Paris leaving a growing problem of unemployment.

Marseille's solution was to orient its **port** and industry towards the Atlantic and the inland route of the Rhône. The **oil industries** that had developed in the 1920s around the Étang de Berre and Fos were extended. The mouth of the Rhône and the Golfe de Fos became a massive tanker terminal. **Iron and steel works** filled the spaces behind the new Port de Marseille that stretched for 50km beyond the Vieux Port. In the process, the city's population boomed. The urgent demand for housing was met by badly designed, low-cost, high-rise estates proliferating north and east from the congested city centre.

The depopulation of **inland Provence** was never halted, but considerably slowed by the massive **irrigation schemes** and development

THE ASSASSINATION OF YANN PIAT

On February 25, 1994, Hyères' UDF député, Yann Piat, was returning to the city by car when a motorcyclist drew alongside and opened fire, leaving Piat dead and her chauffeur badly injured. It was clearly a hit job and the immediate suspects were the members of the Hyères mafia.

Piat, originally a *Front National député* (and Jean-Marie Le Pen's goddaughter), had switched to the UDF (Union pour la Démocratie Française) because of her unhappiness with the extreme right-wing policies of her former party. Piat's real crusade was against drugs and corruption, especially since Hyères had become known as the Chicago of the Côte or "Hyères-les-Bombes" after a series of bomb attacks in the new marina where different racketeering gangs were battling for control. In her attempts to clean up the marina, it's believed that Piat discovered links between local politicians and the underworld.

Piat was also opposed to the endless spread of new developments but as a *député* had little influence over this area. A year before her assassination she commissioned an opinion poll which showed a very good chance of her becoming mayor. More intriguingly, a letter written in 1992, kept in a locked drawer in the Assemblée Nationale in Paris, was found after her assassination stating that in the event of her sudden death, five people should be questioned: Bernard Tapie, at the time Socialist *député* in Marseille; Maurice Arreckx, mayor of Toulon, member of the French senate and head of the Var regional council; two businessmen; and Jean-Louis Fargette, godfather of the Toulon underworld who had fled to Italy and had himself been assassinated a year before Piat died. Tapie, Arreckx and the businessmen were all ruled out as murder suspects though the investigation led to the revelations about Arreckx's corruption which put him behind bars until 1998.

The identity of those behind Piat's killing remains a mystery. The one witness whose testimony might have nailed not only the assassins but those who paid them has died in suspicious circumstances. Piat's daughter is battling to get the murder investigation speeded up. Many believe that it is not just the involvement of local politicians that is blocking the investigation but also someone high up in Paris.

of hydroelectric power which greatly increased the agricultural and industrial potential of regions impoverished earlier in the century. The isolated *mas* or farmhouses, positioned wherever there happened to be a spring, were left to ruin or linked up to the mains. Orchards, lavender fields and olive groves became larger, the competition for early fruit and vegetables fiercer, and the market for luxury foods greater. The rich **Rhône Valley** continued to export fruit, wine and vegetables, while the river was exploited for irrigation and power, both nuclear and hydroelectric, and made navigable for sizeable ships.

After Algeria won back its independence in 1962, hundreds of thousands of French settlers, the **pieds noirs**, returned to the mainland, bringing with them a virulent hatred of Arabic-speaking people. At the same time, the government encouraged immigration from its former colonies, North Africa in particular, with the promise of well-paid jobs, civil rights and social security, none of which was honoured. The resulting tensions, not just in Marseille but all along the coast, made perfect fodder for the **parties of the Right**. From being a bastion of socialism at the end of World War II, Provence gradually turned towards intolerance and reaction.

MUNICIPAL FIEFDOMS, CORRUPTION AND VICE

The activities of the local mafia, known as the **milieu**, with their invisible and inextricable ties to the town halls, have continued more or less unchecked since the 1920s. Not until the shocking assassination of the *député*, **Yann Piat**, in 1994 (see box) did the demand for a "clean hands" campaign really begin in earnest.

Drug trafficking became a major problem in Marseille in the early 1970s and is now prevalent all along the coast. Prostitution and protection rackets also flourish from Menton to Marseille, much of it controlled by the Cosonostra Italian mafia which has been spreading its tentacles westwards, taking advantage of the large numbers of Italians running businesses along the coast, the casinos and cash sales of high-priced properties for money-laundering, and the lack of specific anti-mafia laws in France.

As elsewhere in France, but particularly in Provence, **municipal fiefdoms** evolved

– particularly with the huge budgets and planning powers that came with increasing decentralization – offering opportunities for patronage, nepotism and corruption, along with the financial muscle that, until very recently, ensured incumbents a more-or-less permanent position.

In **Marseille**, the town hall was controlled by **Gaston Defferre** for 33 years until his death in 1986. As well as being mayor, he was a socialist *député* and minister, and owned the city's two politically opposed regional newspapers. Though people had their suspicions about underworld links with the town hall, no one pointed the finger at Defferre.

In 1995, **Bernard Tapie**, the most popular politician in Marseille and millionaire owner of the town's football team, was unable to run for mayor because he'd just been sentenced to a year in prison for **match-rigging** his football team in the French League. A flamboyant businessman, *député* and European Member of Parliament for the Bouche-du-Rhône *département*, Tapie had already been **disbarred from all public office** until 1999 due to bankruptcy. He has also been investigated for tax evasion, shady financial dealings and insulting the police.

Nice's police and judiciary were accused by Graham Greene in 1982 of protecting organized crime. Greene claimed he slept with a gun under his pillow after his *J'Accuse* was published (and banned in France) in which he detailed the corruption. The late **Jacques Médecin**, who succeeded his father as mayor of Nice in 1966, controlled just about every facet of public life until his downfall in 1990 for political fraud and tax evasion (see p.321) – only when Médecin fled to Uruguay were his mafioso connections finally discussed in public. But Médecin had so successfully identified his name with all the city's glamour that after his departure most Niçois gladly supported his sister Géneviève Assemat-Médecin. Those who didn't, backed his daughter, Martine Cantinchi-Médecin, who claimed Le Pen was the rightful heir. Finally extradited in 1994 Médecin served a very short prison term and was able to use his popularity to back the successful candidate in the 1995 municipal elections – one Jacques Peyrat, a close friend of Le Pen and former member of the *Front National*.

Toulon was another classic fiefdom, run for four decades by **Maurice Arreckx** and his clique of friends with their underworld connections until he was put away when financial scandals finally came to light. Investigators are still looking for a Swiss bank account where some of the money paid to Arreckx's campaign fund in return for a major construction contract may have been secreted. His successor, and former director of finances, tried in vain to win back the voters but merely ran up more debts and lost to the *Front National* in 1995. Arreckx was released from jail in September 1998.

In neighbouring **La-Seyne-sur-Mer** a planning officer who attempted to stop a corrupt planning deal was **murdered** in 1986. More recently a British project for a World Sea Centre that would have provided much needed jobs after the closure of the shipyards was disbanded after the British refused to pay protection money to the tune of £1 million.

François Léotard, the right-wing mayor of Fréjus, who held cabinet office (under Chirac in the late 1980s) and a seat in the Assemblée Nationale, was investigated for financial irregularities but the case eventually ran out of time and the charges were dropped. **Cannes' mayor, Michel Mouillot**, was disbarred from public office for five years and given a fifteen-month suspended sentence in 1989, then won his appeal and returned to the town hall only to be given an eighteen-month suspended sentence in 1996. **Pierre Rinaldi**, mayor of **Digne**, was investigated for fraud, **Jean-Pierre Lafond**, mayor of **La Ciotat**, for unwarranted interference, two successive mayors of **La Seyne** for corruption and abuse of patronage . . . and so the list goes on.

All these mayors were right-wingers; their exposure opened the way for the National Front gains in 1995, and for a return of the old industrial towns to their former favourites, the Communist Party.

THE RISE OF THE FRONT NATIONAL

The corruption, waste and general financial incompetence of right-wing municipal power has been one element in the rise of **Jean-Marie Le Pen's neo-fascist Front National** party. Another has been the significance of military bases to the region's economy. While the right-wing national government has made cuts in defence spending, Le Pen has trumpeted his ardent support for France retaining its maximum military capability. However, the most important factor has been the rampant racism of this area.

Cosmopolitan mixes of peoples have always been a feature of coastal Provence, and of Marseille in particular. But the experience of centuries has not bred tolerance. Algerians suffer the persecution meted out in the past to Jews, Armenians, Portuguese, Italians and other ethnic groups.

Jean-Marie Le Pen's *Front National* party developed its major power-base, after Paris, in **Marseille**, and in 1986 four FN *députés* were elected in the Bouches-du-Rhône *département*. They lost their seats when proportional representation was abandoned, but in 1989 the "respectable" parties of the right joined forces with the *Front National* in Grasse, Le Muy and elsewhere to oust Socialist and Communist mayors.

That the FN failed to win outright control of any councils then was due not to any great counterbalance to racism but rather to the similarity in policies of Gaullists such as Jacques Médecin of Nice, and because of the unassailable fortresses of municipal power.

In 1995, however, the *Front National* won **Toulon**, the ninth-largest city in France, plus **Orange** and **Marignane**. The main electoral promise was "Priority for the French", by which, of course, they meant the ethnically pure French. Despite the fact that giving priority to white citizens over black citizens is illegal, there have already been instances in Toulon of people of Algerian origin being overtaken in the housing queue. The town hall has also used municipal grants to promote their political preferences. So, for example, a book fair lost its subsidy when the organizers refused to include ten far-right authors, including a historian who denies the Holocaust took place. An AIDS charity has lost its grant along with many cultural organizations seen as threatening by Toulon's new masters. The former mayor's entertainment budget of 70 million francs is being used to quadruple the police force which may please some voters but not young French Algerians who are being stopped and searched far more frequently, accompanied by racist abuse. The Front's "clean" and "traditional" image has suffered a setback since the elections: the deputy mayor has been murdered and investigations into his death revealed that he frequented Toulon's gay clubs.

The **Front** had a **tumultuous year in 1998**. Firstly, **Jean-Marie Le Pen** found himself on the receiving end of **two court judgements**: one barring him from political office for two years for assaulting a political opponent; the other stripping him of his political immunity and thus allowing – in theory at least – for his prosecution in Germany over remarks he made there dismissing the importance of the Holocaust. The other setback came in the form of the triumphant multi-racial **World Cup** team, which was upheld by the nation's press as a symbol of the emergence of a confident, multicultural France. Players like the totemic Zidane, himself a Marsellais of Algerian descent, became heroes across France, and President Chirac was not slow to capitalize on the victory by awarding the whole team France's highest award, the Légion d'Honneur, in a highly-publicized ceremony. To top it all off, **internal feuding** split the party into two camps in December 1998. **Bruno Mégret**, Le Pen's deputy, attempted to seize leadership of the party only to be expelled by Le Pen along with several of Mégret's henchmen, Le Pen's daughter included. The ousted members had formed a new extreme-right breakaway party, the Front National Mouvement National, by the following January, headed by Mégret.

MASS TOURISM AND THE ENVIRONMENT

A crucial factor in Provence's postwar history has been the development of **mass tourism**. Beginning with the St-Tropez boom in the 1960s, the number of visitors to the Côte d'Azur has steadily grown beyond manageable – in any sane sense – proportions. By the mid-1970s the coast had become a nearly uninterrupted wall of concrete, hosting eight million visitors a year. Agricultural land, save for a few profitable vineyards, was transformed into campsites, hotels and holiday housing. **Property speculation** and construction became the dominant economic activities while the flaunting of planning laws and the ever-increasing threat to the **environment** – the area's prime asset – were ignored.

When **Brigitte Bardot** started to complain that her beloved **St-Tropez** was becoming a mire of human detritus, the media saw it as a sexy summer story. But when **ecologists** began warning that the main oxygenating seaweed in the Mediterranean was disappearing because of yacht anchors damaging the sea bed, new jetties and marinas modifying the currents, and dust from building sites clouding the water, no one was particularly interested. The loss of *Posidonia oceanica* is now affecting fish, and a toxic algae has appeared, spreading out from Monaco. According to some experts, nearly half of all current developments need to be demolished and a total embargo put on new developments, if the sea is to recover.

Short-term financial gain is still, of course, the overriding principle, so new marinas are still being built and new private villages and estates edge into supposedly protected areas such as the Esterel. A new resort, Antibes-les-Pins, is to be built alongside Juan-les-Pins. As for the pines themselves, fires are responsible for destroying great swathes of forest every year.

URBAN EXPANSION ON THE COAST

If sun-worshipping set the region's tone for the first three postwar decades, the 1980s saw different forces at work. While the encouragement of summer tourism exacted its toll, a new type of visitor and resident was being encouraged: the expense-account delegate to **business conferences** and the well-paid employee of **multinational firms**. Towns like Nice and Cannes led the way in attracting the former, while the business park of **Sophia-Antipolis** north of Antibes showed how easy it was to persuade firms to relocate their information technology operations to the beautiful Côte d'Azur hinterland. The result was a further erosion of Provençal identity and greater pressure on the environment. The Dutch, American, Parisian and Lyonnais employees of the high-tech industries needed more roads, more housing, more facilities. Sophia-Antipolis is to have not only its own new ring-road but a 25-kilometre métro line to Nice.

The business visitors, rather than countering the seasonal imbalance of tourism, made consumption and congestion a year-round factor. A black market even developed in game meat: venison and other game is shot with high-tech weaponry in areas such as the Clues de Haute Provence, and then sold to the promenade restaurants.

The rich Gulf Arabs decided Cannes and Monaco were the places to have palatial pied-à-terres. If hillsides needed shifting in order to get a better aspect for the gold and marble swimming pool then in came the heavy earthmoving equipment.

For the places that had always catered for flash extravagance, the last two decades have not seen a radical departure from what had gone before. In the big cities the distinctive Marseillaise and Niçois identities have recognizably remained, despite the dramatic changes in their economies. But elsewhere along the coast, and inland, continuities with the past have become ever harder to detect.

The money from business services and industry on the Riviera now outstrips the income from tourism. Economic growth is always visible while the recession hides in the back streets of Marseille and the villages of the interior that have never seduced the admen and the PR experts.

INLAND PROVENCE

Inland Provence has undergone a parallel transformation to the coast with second homes in the sun becoming a requisite for the high-salaried French from the 1960s onwards.

Though some villages were certainly saved from extinction by the new property buyers, all suffered from the out-of-season shutters syndrome. With the growth of ski resorts, however, the population of the Alpine valleys started to increase, reversing a centuries-old trend. The damage to trees, soil and habitats caused by the ski resorts has in part been offset by the creation of the **Parc National du Mercantour**, an enclave that has saved several Alpine animal and plant species.

In central Provence the Durance Valley alongside the new Marseille–Grenoble *autoroute* has become the latest corridor for sunrise industries. Meanwhile the *paysans* keeping goats and bees, a few vines and a vegetable plot are all of pensionable age. The cheeses and honey, the vegetables, olive oil and wine (unless it's A.O.C.) must compete with Spanish, Italian and Greek produce, from land that doesn't have the ludicrously high values of Provence. In order to exploit the consumption patterns of the 1990s the scale has to be larger than the traditional peasant plots, and there must be speedy access to the biggest markets.

TRANSPORT MANIA

Fast access to the Côte d'Azur has become the obsession of planners in Paris. The world's fastest train, the **TGV**, is having its special track **extended down the Rhône Valley to Marseille** and if current schedules are maintained, the TGV will reach St-Charles station by the year 2001. SNCF were determined that the journey time from Paris to Marseille had to be not a second over three hours, and planned the route accordingly. To their surprise protestors brought the entire region's rail services to a halt as they fought pitched battles with riot police. Amendments to the Rhône Valley route were made and the first section, to Valence, was completed on schedule. There were plans to extend the TGV route along the coast to Nice (at present it runs at low speeds on the existing lines), but opposition from environmental and residents' groups is well organized all along the proposed route and SNCF's financial problems have put all projects on hold.

A brand new *autoroute* is also planned: the **A8 bis** is to shadow the A8 along the most congested stretch from Fréjus to Monaco. In addition there'll be an expressway linking Cannes and Grasse with both the A8 and the A8 bis. Almost every local councillor is opposed to the route Paris has chosen; every sane person is opposed to the whole endeavour.

BOOKS

HISTORY

Most of the books listed below are in print and in paperback – those that are out of print (o/p) should be easy to track down in secondhand bookshops. Publishers are detailed in the form of British publisher/American publisher, where both exist; where the book is published by the same company in both countries, the name of the company appears just once. Where books are published in one country only, France, UK or US follows the publisher's name.

Édouard Baratier, *Histoire de la Provence* (Privat, Toulouse, France). Huge, well-illustrated tome by a group of French academics, which covers the province in about as much detail as anyone could conceivably desire.

Robin Briggs, *Early Modern France, 1550–1715* (Oxford UP). Readable account of the period in which the French state started to assert control over the whole country. Strong perspectives on the provinces, including coverage of the Marseille rebellion of 1658.

Alfred Cobban, *A History of Modern France* (3 vols: 1715–1799; 1799–1871; 1871–1962. Penguin, UK). Definitive account of three centuries of French political, social and economic life, from Louis XIV to mid-de Gaulle.

Margaret Crosland, *Sade's Wife* (Peter Owen, UK). Expert on Provence's most notorious resident examines how Renée-Pélagie de Montreuil coped with being married to the Marquis de Sade.

Colin Jones, *The French Revolution: A Companion* (Addison Wesley Longman, UK). Original quotes and documents, good pictures and an unusually clear explanation of events. Good background on Marseille's Fédérés and Mirabeau.

Emmanuel Le Roy Ladurie, *Montaillou* (Penguin, UK). Just outside the area but well worth reading, nevertheless, as the classic account of peasant life in a fourteenth-century Pyrenean village, reconstructed using the original court records of an anti-Cathar Inquisition.

John Noone, *The Man Behind the Iron Mask* (Sutton/St Martin). Fascinating enquiry into the mythical or otherwise prisoner of Ste-Marguerite fort on the Îles de Lérins, immortalized by Alexander Dumas.

Jean Tulard, *Napoléon: The Myth of the Saviour* (Routledge, UK). One of the classic French accounts of the rise and fall of the great man. Its interest is with the phenomenon rather than the personal life and characteristics of the man.

Simon Schama, *Citizens* (Penguin, UK). A fascinating, accessible treatment of the history of the Revolution, with a fast-moving narrative and a reappraisal of the customary view of a stagnant, unchanging nobility in the years preceding the uprising.

Theodore Zeldin, *France, 1845–1945* (2 vols, Clarendon/Oxford UP). Five thematic and very accessible volumes on all matters French over the last century.

SOCIETY AND POLITICS

John Ardagh, *France Today* (Penguin). Comprehensive, journalistic overview of the country from World War II up until 1987, covering food, film, education and holidays, as well as politics and economics.

Roland Barthes, *Mythologies* (Vintage, UK). Brilliant analyses of how the ideas, prejudices and contradictions of French thought and behaviour manifest themselves, in food, wine, travel guides and other cultural offerings.

Mary Blume, *Côte d'Azur: Inventing the French Riviera* (Thames & Hudson, UK). This attempt to analyse the myth only reconfirms it, mainly because the people Blume has interviewed have all at stake in maintaining the image of the Côte as cultured millionaires' dreamland. Great black and white photos.

Ann Tristan, *Au Front* (Gallimard, France). Compelling report by a Parisian journalist who infiltrated Le Pen's *Front National* in Marseille in 1987. Excellent on detail of the working-class milieu of Front sympathizers, but ultimately unconvincing in its attempt to explain the phenomenon.

Lawrence Wylie, *Village in the Vaucluse* (Harvard UP, US). Sociological study of Roussillon full of interesting insights into Provençal village life.

TRAVEL

John Flower and Charlie Waite, *Provence* (George Philip's, UK). Waite's gorgeous photographs encompass landscapes, architectural details, markets, and images obscure and familiar. Flower's text draws on over thirty years of residence and visits.

Peter Mayle, *A Year in Provence* (Penguin). A month-by-month account of the charms and frustrations of moving into an old French farmhouse in Provence; with entertaining accounts of everything from the local cuisine, tips for wooing fickle French contractors, handicapping goat races, and enduring winter's icy mistral.

Julian More, *More about France: A Sentimental Journey* (Cape, UK). Entertaining

tales of a lifetime's travel and sporadic residence, from the 1940s to the present, in the Côte d'Azur, Paris, Burgundy, Brittany, and the Midi.

ART AND ARTISTS

Good introductions to the modern artists associated with Provence are published by Thames and Hudson (UK/US), Clematis and Phaidon (UK) and Abrams (US). Bracken Books (UK) publishes a series "Artists by Themselves" – small, attractively produced books with extracts of letters and diaries to accompany the pictures – which includes Matisse, Picasso, Cézanne, Van Gogh and Renoir. More substantial editions of artists' own writings include *Matisse on Art* (Phaidon/NAL-Dutton), *Chagall: My Life* (Peter Owen/Humanities o/p), and *Cézanne by Himself: Drawings, Paintings, Writings* (Little/Brown).

Martin Bailey (ed), *Van Gogh: Letters from Provence* (Collins & Brown, UK). Attractively produced in full colour. Very dippable and very good value.

PROVENCE AND THE CÔTE D'AZUR IN LITERATURE

The Côte d'Azur has inspired many twentieth-century English, American and French writers, indulging in the highlife like Scott Fitzgerald, slumming it with the Bohemians like Anaïs Nin, or trying to regain their health like Katherine Mansfield. The two best-known Provençal writers of the twentieth century, Jean Giono and Maurice Pagnol, wrote about peasant life in inland Provence; many of their works have been turned into films. Nineteenth-century Provence features in Alexander Dumas' rip-roaring tale of revenge, *The Count of Monte Cristo*, and in some of Aix-born Émile Zola's novels, while the horrors of eighteenth-century Provence are brought to life in Victor Hugo's *Les Misérables*.

Below is a selective recommendation of literary works in which the region plays a significant role, including poetry – spanning the ages from Petrarch troubadour songs to Bonnefoy and Mistral – and a play by Anouilh set in Marseille.

Jean Anouilh *Point of Departure*
Yves Bonnefoy *In the Shadow's Light*
Anthony Bonner (ed) *Songs of the Troubadours*
Colette *Collected Stories*
Alphonse Daudet *Letters from My Windmill; Tartarin de Tarascon; and Tartarin of the Alps*
Alexandre Dumas (Père) *The Count of Monte Cristo*
Lawrence Durrell *The Avignon Quintet*
Scott Fitzgerald *Tender is the Night*
Jean Giono *To the Slaughterhouse; Two Riders of the Storm; Que ma Joie Demeure; Le Hussard sur le Toit; and La Femme du Boulanger*
Graham Greene *Loser Takes All*

Victor Hugo *Les Misérables*
Katherine Mansfield *Collected Short Stories*
Frédéric Mistral *Mirèio*
Anaïs Nin *Diaries*
Marcel Pagnol *Jean de Florette; Manon des Sources; The Time of Secrets; The Time of Love; Marius; and Fanny*
Francesco Petrarch *Songs and Sonnets*
Françoise Sagan *Bonjour Tristesse*
Patrick Süskind *Perfume*
Émile Zola *Fortune of the Rougons; Abbé Mouret's Transgression; and The Conquest of Plassans*

Françoise Gilot, *Matisse & Picasso: A Friendship in Art* (Bloomsbury, UK). A fascinating subject – two more different men in life and art would be hard to find.

D. and M. Johnson, *The Age of Illusion* (Thames & Hudson/Rizzoli, o/p). Links French art and politics in the inter-war years, featuring Provençal works by Le Corbusier, Chagall and Picasso.

Jacques Henri Lartigue, *Diary of a Century* (Penguin, UK). Book of pictures by a great photographer from the day he was given a camera in 1901 through to the 1970s. Contains wonderful scenes of aristocratic leisure and Côte d'Azur beaches.

Nicholas Watkins, *Matisse* (Phaidon, UK). A brilliant and accessible analysis of Matisse's use of colour with beautiful reproductions.

Barbara Ehrlich, *White Renoir: His Life, Art and Letters* (Abrams, US). A thorough and interesting work.

Sarah Whitfield, *Fauvism* (Thames & Hudson). Good introduction to a movement that encompassed Côte d'Azur and Riviera artists Matisse, Dufy and Van Dongen.

GARDENS AND FOOD

Robert Carrier, *Feasts of Provence* (Weidenfeld & Nicolson/Rivoli Bookstore). Yummy cookery book.

Timothy Shaw, *The World of Escoffier* (Zwemmer, UK). Biography of the famous chef who started his career on the Côte d'Azur.

GUIDES

Ely Boisson, *Mystères et Histoires des Calanques* (Editions Terradou, France). Anecdotes, stories and legends about the calanques, with practical descriptions of walks plus maps.

James Bromwich, *The Roman Remains of Southern France* (Routledge). The only comprehensive guide to the subject; detailed, well illustrated and approachable. In addition to accounts of well-known sites, it will lead you off the map to all sorts of discoveries.

Duijker, *Provence: A Wine Lover's Touring Guide* (Spectrum, UK). Useful Dutch guide.

W. Lippert, *Fleurs des Montagnes, Alpages et Forêts* (Miniguide Nathan Tout Terrain, France). Palm-sized colour guide to flowers, available from French bookshops in the trekking areas.

LANGUAGE

French can be a deceptively familiar language because of the number of words and structures it shares with English. Despite this it's far from easy, though the bare essentials are not difficult to master and can make all the difference. Even just saying *"Bonjour, Madame/Monsieur"* and then gesticulating will usually get you a smile and helpful service. People working in tourist offices, campsites, hotels and so on, almost always speak English and tend to use it if you're struggling to speak French – be grateful, not insulted.

On the **Côte d'Azur** you can get by without knowing a word of French, with menus printed in at least four languages, and half the people you meet fellow foreigners. In **Nice**, **Sisteron** and the **Roya Valley** a knowledge of **Italian** would provide a common language with many of the natives. But if you can hold your own in French -- however imperfectly -- speak away and your audience will warm to you.

PROVENÇAL AND ACCENTS

The one language you don't have to learn – unless you want to understand the meaning of street names – is **Provençal**. Itself a dialect of the *langue d'oc* (Occitan), it evolved into different dialects in Provence, so that the languages spoken in Nice, in the Alps, on the coast and in the Rhône Valley, though mutually comprehensible, were not precisely the same. In the mid-nineteenth century the *Félibrige* movement established a standard literary form in an attempt to revive the language. But by the time Frédéric Mistral won the Nobel Prize in 1904 for his poem *Mirèio*, Provençal had already been superseded by French in ordinary life.

Two hundred years ago everybody spoke Provençal whether they were counts, shipyard workers or peasants. Today you might, if you're lucky, hear it spoken by the older generation in some of the remoter villages. It just survives as a literary language: it can be studied at school and university and there are columns in Provençal in some newspapers. But unlike Breton or Occitan proper, it has never been the fuel of a separatist movement.

The French that people speak in Provence has, however, a very marked **accent**. It's much less nasal than northern French, words are not run together to quite the same extent, and there's a distinctive sound for the endings – *in*, *-en*, and for *vin*, and so on, that is more like *ung*.

A BRIEF GUIDE TO SPEAKING FRENCH

PRONUNCIATION

One easy rule to remember is that **consonants** at the ends of words are usually silent. *Pas plus tard* (not later) is thus pronounced "pa-plu-tarr". But when the following word begins with a vowel, you run the two together: *pas après* (not after) becomes "pazaprey".

Vowels are the hardest sounds to get right. Roughly:

a	as in h**a**t		*i*	as in mach**i**ne
e	as in g**e**t		*o*	as in h**o**t
é	between g**e**t and g**a**te		*o, au*	as in **o**ver
è	between g**e**t and g**u**t		*ou*	as in f**oo**d
eu	like the **u** in h**u**rt		*u*	as in a pursed-lip version of **u**se

More awkward are the **combinations** *in/im, en/em, an/am, on/om, un/um* at the ends of words, or followed by consonants other than n or m. Again, roughly:

in/im	like the **an** in **an**xious		*on/om*	like the **don** in **Don**caster said by someone with a heavy cold
an/am, en/em	like the **don** in **Don**caster when said with a nasal accent		*un/um*	like the **u** in **u**nderstand

Consonants are much as in English, except that: "*ch*" is always sh, "*c*" is s, "*h*" is silent, "*th*" is the same as t, "*ll*" is like the y in "yes", "*w*" is v, and "*r*" is growled (or rolled).

BASIC WORDS AND PHRASES

French nouns are divided into masculine and feminine. This causes difficulties with adjectives, whose endings have to change to suit the gender of the nouns they qualify. If you know some grammar, you will know what to do. If not, stick to the masculine form, which is the simplest – it's what we have done in this glossary.

today	*aujourd'hui*	that one	*celà*
yesterday	*hier*	open	*ouvert*
tomorrow	*demain*	closed	*fermé*
in the morning	*le matin*	big	*grand*
in the afternoon	*l'après-midi*	small	*petit*
in the evening	*le soir*	more	*plus*
now	*maintenant*	less	*moins*
later	*plus tard*	a little	*un peu*
at one o'clock	*à une heure*	a lot	*beaucoup*
at three o'clock	*à trois heures*	cheap	*bon marché*
at ten-thirty	*à dix heures et demie*	expensive	*cher*
at midday	*à midi*	good	*bon*
man	*un homme*	bad	*mauvais*
woman	*une femme*	hot	*chaud*
here	*ici*	cold	*froid*
there	*là*	with	*avec*
this one	*ceci*	without	*sans*

continued overleaf . . .

continued from previous page

TALKING TO PEOPLE

When addressing people you should always use *Monsieur* for a man, *Madame* for a woman, *Mademoiselle* for a girl. Plain *bonjour* by itself is not enough. This isn't as formal as it seems, and it has its uses when you've forgotten someone's name or want to attract someone's attention.

Excuse me	*Pardon*	please	*s'il vous plaît*
Do you speak English?	*Vous parlez anglais?*	thank you	*merci*
		hello	*bonjour*
How do you say it in French?	*Comment ça se dit en français?*	goodbye	*au revoir*
What's your name?	*Comment vous appelez-vous?*	good morning/ afternoon	*bonjour*
My name is . . .	*Je m'appelle . . .*	good evening	*bonsoir*
I'm English/	*Je suis anglais[e]/*	good night	*bonne nuit*
Irish/Scottish	*irlandais[e]/écossais[e]/*	How are you?	*Comment allez-vous?/ Ça va?*
Welsh/American/	*gallois[e]/américain[e]/*		
Australian/	*australien[ne]/*	Fine, thanks	*Très bien, merci*
Canadian/	*canadien[ne]/*	I don't know	*Je ne sais pas*
a New Zealander	*néo-zélandais[e]*	Let's go	*Allons-y*
yes	*oui*	See you tomorrow	*À demain*
no	*non*	See you soon	*À bientôt*
I understand	*Je comprends*	Sorry	*Pardon, Madame/Je m'excuse*
I don't understand	*Je ne comprends pas*		
Can you speak slower?	*S'il vous plaît, parlez moins vite*	Leave me alone (aggressive)	*Fichez-moi la paix!*
OK/agreed	*d'accord*	Please help me	*Aidez-moi, s'il vous plaît*

FINDING THE WAY

bus	*autobus/bus/car*	hitchhiking	*autostop*
bus station	*gare routière*	on foot	*à pied*
bus stop	*arrêt*	Where are you going?	*Vous allez où?*
car	*voiture*		
train/taxi/ferry	*train/taxi/ferry*	I'm going to . . .	*Je vais à . . .*
boat	*bâteau*	I want to get off at . . .	*Je voudrais descendre à . . .*
plane	*avion*		
train station	*gare (SNCF)*	the road to . . .	*la route pour . . .*
platform	*quai*	near	*près/pas loin*
What time does it leave?	*Il part à quelle heure?*	far	*loin*
		left	*à gauche*
What time does it arrive?	*Il arrive à quelle heure?*	right	*à droite*
		straight on	*tout droit*
a ticket to . . .	*un billet pour . . .*	on the other side of	*à l'autre côté de*
single ticket	*aller simple*	on the corner of	*à l'angle de*
return ticket	*aller retour*	next to	*à côté de*
validate your ticket	*compostez votre billet*	behind	*derrière*
		in front of	*devant*
valid for	*valable pour*	before	*avant*
ticket office	*vente de billets*	after	*après*
how many kilometres?	*combien de kilomètres?*	under	*sous*
		to cross	*traverser*
how many hours?	*combien d'heures?*	bridge	*pont*

QUESTIONS AND REQUESTS

The simplest way of asking a question is to start with *s'il vous plaît* (please), then name the thing you want in an interrogative tone of voice. For example:

| Where is there a bakery? | *S'il vous plaît, la boulangerie?* |
| Which way is it to the Eiffel Tower? | *S'il vous plaît, la route pour la tour Eiffel?* |

Similarly with requests:

| We'd like a room for two. | *S'il vous plaît, une chambre pour deux.* |
| Can I have a kilo of oranges? | *S'il vous plaît, un kilo d'oranges?* |

Question words

where?	*où?*	when?	*quand?*
how?	*comment?*	why?	*pourquoi?*
how many/how much?	*combien?*	at what time?	*à quelle heure?*
		what is/which is?	*quel est?*

ACCOMMODATION

a room for one/two people	*une chambre pour une/deux personnes*	do laundry	*faire la lessive*
a double bed	*un lit double*	sheets	*draps*
a room with a shower	*une chambre avec douche*	blankets	*couvertures*
		quiet	*calme*
a room with a bath	*une chambre avec salle de bain*	noisy	*bruyant*
		hot water	*eau chaude*
for one/two/three nights	*pour une/deux/trois nuits*	cold water	*eau froide*
		Is breakfast included?	*Est-ce que le petit déjeuner est compris?*
Can I see it?	*Je peux la voir?*	I would like breakfast	*Je voudrais prendre le petit déjeuner*
a room on the courtyard	*une chambre sur la cour*	I don't want breakfast	*Je ne veux pas de petit déjeuner*
a room over the street	*une chambre sur la rue*	Can we camp here?	*On peut camper ici?*
first floor	*premier étage*	campsite	*un camping/terrain de camping*
second floor	*deuxième étage*		
with a view	*avec vue*	tent	*une tente*
key	*clef*	tent space	*un emplacement*
to iron	*repasser*	youth hostel	*auberge de jeunesse*

CARS

service station	*garage*	put air in the tyres	*gonfler les pneus*
service	*service*	battery	*batterie*
to park the car	*garer la voiture*	the battery is dead	*la batterie est morte*
car park	*un parking*	plugs	*bougies*
no parking	*défense de stationner/ stationnement interdit*	to break down	*tomber en panne*
		gas can	*bidon*
gas station	*poste d'essence*	insurance	*assurance*
fuel	*essence*	green card	*carte verte*
(to) fill it up	*faire le plein*	traffic lights	*feux*
oil	*huile*	red light	*feu rouge*
air line	*ligne à air*	green light	*feu vert*

continued overleaf . . .

continued from previous page

HEALTH MATTERS

doctor	*médecin*	stomach ache	*mal à l'estomac*
I don't feel well	*Je ne me sens pas bien*	period	*règles*
medicines	*médicaments*	pain	*douleur*
prescription	*ordonnance*	it hurts	*ça fait mal*
I feel sick	*Je suis malade*	chemist	*pharmacie*
I have a headache	*J'ai mal à la tête*	hospital	*hôpital*

OTHER NEEDS

bakery	*boulangerie*	bank	*banque*
food shop	*alimentation*	money	*argent*
supermarket	*supermarché*	toilets	*toilettes*
to eat	*manger*	police	*police*
to drink	*boire*	telephone	*téléphone*
camping gas	*camping gaz*	cinema	*cinéma*
tobacconist	*tabac*	theatre	*théâtre*
stamps	*timbres*	to reserve/book	*réserver*

NUMBERS

1	*un*	11	*onze*	21	*vingt-et-un*	95	*quatre-vingt-quinze*
2	*deux*	12	*douze*	22	*vingt-deux*	100	*cent*
3	*trois*	13	*treize*	30	*trente*	101	*cent-et-un*
4	*quatre*	14	*quatorze*	40	*quarante*	200	*deux cents*
5	*cinq*	15	*quinze*	50	*cinquante*	300	*trois cents*
6	*six*	16	*seize*	60	*soixante*	500	*cinq cents*
7	*sept*	17	*dix-sept*	70	*soixante-dix*	1000	*mille*
8	*huit*	18	*dix-huit*	75	*soixante-quinze*	2000	*deux milles*
9	*neuf*	19	*dix-neuf*	80	*quatre-vingts*	5000	*cinq milles*
10	*dix*	20	*vingt*	90	*quatre-vingt-dix*	1,000,000	*un million*

DAYS AND DATES

January	*janvier*	November	*novembre*	August 1	*le premier août*
February	*février*	December	*décembre*	March 2	*le deux mars*
March	*mars*			July 14	*le quatorze juillet*
April	*avril*	Sunday	*dimanche*	November 23	*le vingt-trois novem-bre*
May	*mai*	Monday	*lundi*		
June	*juin*	Tuesday	*mardi*		
July	*juillet*	Wednesday	*mercredi*	1999	*dix-neuf-cent-quatre-vingt-dix-neuf*
August	*août*	Thursday	*jeudi*		
September	*septembre*	Friday	*vendredi*		
October	*octobre*	Saturday	*samedi*		

GLOSSARY

FRENCH TERMS

These are either terms you'll come across in the Guide, or come up against on signs, maps, etc while travelling around. For food items see Basics.

ABBAYE abbey

ARRONDISSEMENT district of a city

ASSEMBLÉE NATIONALE the French parliament

AUBERGE DE JEUNESSE (AJ) youth hostel

BASTIDE medieval military settlement, constructed on a grid plan

BEAUX-ARTS fine arts museum (and school)

BORIE dry stone wall, or building made with same

CALANQUE steep-sided inlet on coast, similar to Norwegian fjord, but not glacially formed

CAR bus

CFDT Socialist trade union

CGT Communist trade union

CHAMBRE D'HÔTE room for rent in private house

CHASSE, CHASSE GARDÉE hunting grounds

CHÂTEAU mansion, country house or castle

CHÂTEAU FORT castle

CHEMIN path

CIJ (Centre d'Informations Jeunesse) youth information centre

CODENE French CND

COL mountain pass

CONSIGNE luggage store

CÔTE coast

COURS combination of main square and main street

COUVENT convent, monastery

DEFENSE DE . . . It is forbidden to . . .

DÉGUSTATION tasting (wine or food)

DÉPARTEMENT county – more or less

DONJON castle keep

ÉGLISE church

EN PANNE out of order

ENTRÉE entrance

FAUBOURG suburb, often abbreviated to fbg in street names

FERME farm

FERMETURE closing period

FN (Front National) fascist party led by Jean-Marie Le Pen

FO Catholic trade union

FOUILLES archeological excavations

GARE station; **ROUTIÈRE** – bus station; **SNCF** – train station

GÎTE D'ÉTAPE basic hostel accommodation primarily for walkers

GOBELINS famous tapestry manufacturers, based in Paris; its most renowned period was in the reign of Louis XIV (seventeenth century)

GRANDE RANDONÉE (GR) long-distance footpath

HALLES covered market

HLM public housing development

HÔTEL a hotel, but also an aristocratic town house or mansion

HÔTEL DE VILLE town hall

JOURS FÉRIÉS public holidays

MAIRIE town hall

MARCHÉ market

PCF Communist Party of France

PLACE square

PORTE gateway

PRESQU'ÎLE peninsula

PS Socialist party

PTT post office

PUY peak or summit

QUARTIER district of a town

RELAIS ROUTIERS truckstop café-restaurants

REZ-DE-CHAUSSÉE (RC) ground floor

RN (Route Nationale) main road

RPR Gaullist party led by Jacques Chirac

SANTON ornamental figure used especially in Christmas cribs

SI (Syndicat d'Initiative) tourist information office; also known as OT, OTSI and maison du tourisme

SNCF French railways

SORTIE exit

TABAC bar or shop selling stamps, cigarettes, etc

TABLE D'HÔTE meal served in lodging at the family table

TOUR tower

TRANSHUMANCE Routes followed by shepherds for taking livestock to and from suitable grazing grounds

UDF centre-right party headed by Giscard d'Estaing

VAUBAN seventeenth-century military architect – his fortresses still stand all over France

VIEILLE VILLE old quarter of town

VIEUX PORT old port

VILLAGE PERCHÉ hilltop village

VOUSSOIR sculpted rings in arch over church door

ZONE BLEUE restricted parking zone

ZONE PIETONNÉ pedestrian precinct

ARCHITECTURAL TERMS

AMBULATORY covered passage around the outer edge of a choir of a church

APSE semicircular termination at the east end of a church

BAROQUE High Renaissance period of art and architecture, distinguished by extreme ornateness

CAROLINGIAN dynasty (and art, sculpture, etc) founded by Charlemagne, late eighth to early tenth century

CHEVET east end of church, consisting of apse and ambulatory, with or without radiating chapels

CLASSICAL architectural style incorporating Greek and Roman elements – pillars, domes, colonnades, etc – at its height in France in the seventeenth century and revived in the nineteenth century as **NEOCLASSICAL**

CLERESTORY upper storey of a church, incorporating the windows

FLAMBOYANT florid form of Gothic (see below)

FRESCO wall painting – durable through application to wet plaster

GALLO-ROMAN period of Roman occupation of Gaul (first to fourth century AD)

GOTHIC architectural style prevalent from the twelfth century to the sixteenth century, characterized by pointed arches and ribbed vaulting

MEROVINGIAN dynasty (and art, etc) ruling France and parts of Germany from the sixth to mid-eighth century

NARTHEX entrance hall of church

NAVE main body of a church

RENAISSANCE art-architectural style developed in fifteenth-century Italy and imported to France in the early sixteenth century by François I

RETABLE altarpiece

ROMANESQUE early medieval architecture distinguished by squat, rounded forms and naive sculpture

STUCCO plaster used to embellish ceilings, etc

TRANSEPT cross arms of a church

TYMPANUM sculpted panel above a church door

VOUSSOIR sculpted rings in arch over church door

INDEX

around the world

in twenty years

London Mini Guide ★ London Restaurants ★ Los Angeles ★ Madeira ★ Madrid ★ Malaysia, Singapore & Brunei ★ Mallorca ★ Malta & Gozo ★ Maui ★ Maya World ★ Melbourne ★ Menorca ★ Mexico ★ Miami & the Florida Keys ★ Montréal ★ Morocco ★ Moscow ★ Nepal ★ New England ★ New Orleans ★ New York City ★ New York Mini Guide ★ New York Restaurants ★ New Zealand ★ Norway ★ Pacific Northwest ★ Paris ★ Paris Mini Guide ★ Peru ★ Poland ★ Portugal ★ Prague ★ Provence & the Côte d'Azur ★ Pyrenees ★ The Rocky Mountains ★ Romania ★ Rome ★ San Francisco ★ San Francisco Restaurants ★ Sardinia ★ Scandinavia ★ Scotland ★ Scottish Highlands & Islands ★ Seattle ★ Sicily ★ Singapore ★ South Africa, Lesotho & Swaziland ★ South India ★ Southeast Asia ★ Southwest USA ★ Spain ★ St Lucia ★ St Petersburg ★ Sweden ★ Switzerland ★ Sydney ★ Syria ★ Tanzania ★ Tenerife and La Gomera ★ Thailand ★ Thailand's Beaches & Islands ★ Tokyo ★ Toronto ★ Travel Health ★ Trinidad & Tobago ★ Tunisia ★ Turkey ★ Tuscany & Umbria ★ USA ★ Vancouver ★ Venice & the Veneto ★ Vienna ★ Vietnam ★ Wales ★ Washington DC ★ West Africa ★ Women Travel ★ Yosemite ★ Zanzibar ★ Zimbabwe

also look out for our maps, phrasebooks, music guides and reference books